The Logic of the Latifundio

>→>→>→>×←←←←←←←←←←←←←←←←←←←←←←←

The Logic of the Latifundio

*The Large Estates of
Northwestern Costa Rica
Since the
Late Nineteenth Century*

Marc Edelman

>→>→>→>×←←←←←←←←←←←←←←←←←←←←←←←

Stanford University Press   Stanford, California   1992

Stanford University Press
Stanford, California
© 1992 by the Board of Trustees
of the Leland Stanford
Junior University
Printed in the
United States of America

CIP data appear at the end of the book

Published with the assistance of the
Frederick W. Hilles Publication Fund,
Yale University

A Debi y a Danielito

✦ Acknowledgments

My greatest debt is to the many people of different walks of life in Guanacaste who not only patiently tolerated my questions and explained their lives and work, but also invited me into their homes and offered me cool *refrescos* and *pinolillo* to drink, tamales and *gallo pinto* (rice and beans) to eat, and ripe *níspero* fruits and mangos for dessert. They are too many to mention here, but for frequent hospitality and much-valued friendship I am immensely grateful to Blanca Arce, Carmen Carballo, Marcos Ramírez, and Jack Wilson Pacheco (who would want me to mention that he is not related to other Wilsons mentioned in this study).

I first discussed many of the ideas in this book in working papers at the Instituto de Investigaciones Sociales of the Universidad de Costa Rica and at meetings of the Latin American Studies Association and the American Anthropological Association. I received many useful comments from participants in these fora, but I am particularly indebted to colleagues at the Instituto de Investigaciones Sociales who graciously offered suggestions on numerous occasions and who taught me much of whatever I was able to learn about Costa Rica and Central America. For friendship and support, I thank José Luis Vega, Manuel Solís, Jorge Rovira, Mario Fernández, Teresita Quirós, Otto Calvo, Rafael Bolaños, and the late Mario Flores. John Griffin, Lowell Gudmundson, Marvin Harris, Jacobo Schifter, Martha Soler, and Robert Wasserstrom also provided much useful advice in the early stages of research. Sidney Welcome served as a research assistant and became an esteemed friend and colleague. Jayne Hutchcroft also assisted with various aspects of the research and put me up in her house in San José more times than she likely cares to remember.

Many state and private organizations and several libraries in Costa Rica and the United States furnished documents and data and advice about how best to use them. The reader will find many of these institutions mentioned in citations to materials they provided. My inability to list here all the functionaries and employees who guided my work does not diminish my gratitude for their help. As I neared completion of the penultimate draft, I had the good fortune to attend a poetry reading and fiesta in Liberia, Guanacaste, where I met Roberto Cabrera, director of the newly founded Asociación Costarricense para el Estudio e Investigación de la Vertiente del Pacífico. His boundless enthusiasm for research on rural Guanacaste encouraged me much more than he probably realized.

The book itself has experienced various incarnations since the initial typewritten drafts, and many people read large and small pieces of it along the way. It has been much improved by the insightful comments of Philippe Bourgois, Lambros Comitas, Ross Hassig, Douglas Kincaid, Herbert Klein, María Lagos, Jeff Longhofer, Lynn Morgan, Martin Murphy, Joan Vincent, Robert G. Williams, and Eric Wolf. I am also most grateful for the generous support of the Inter-American Foundation, the Social Science Research Council, the Sigma Xi Scientific Research Society, the Institute for the Study of World Politics, the American Council of Learned Societies, and the Center for International and Area Studies and the Whitney-Griswold Faculty Research Fund, both of Yale University. Many thanks are also due Elizabeth Kyburg, who helped make the manuscript presentable. Plenum Publishing, Temple University Press, and Grove Weidenfeld kindly granted permission to use small portions of this work that appeared in *Human Ecology* (13, no. 2, 1985), in *Food and Evolution: Toward a Theory of Human Food Habits*, edited by Marvin Harris and Eric B. Ross (1987), and in *The Costa Rica Reader*, edited by Marc Edelman and Joanne Kenen (1989). I have also greatly appreciated working with Norris Pope and John Feneron of Stanford University Press and with Pat Castor, whose meticulous copy editing did much to improve my prose. Although all these individuals and organizations share responsibility for any merits this work may have, I alone am obviously responsible for its shortcomings.

While I was in Costa Rica my mother, Judith Edelman, tended to research-related and other chores that I was not able to handle from abroad and sent me frequent messages of encouragement. She and my father, Harold Edelman, have been a source of support throughout, and I hope that the completion of this project allays some of their concerns about what must have seemed like an interminable endeavor. Débora Soler Munczek, and later Danielito, endured a lot, and I am indeed grateful. I will always be most thankful, not so much for Debi's forbearance, but for the supportive prodding that helped me bring this work to a close.

M.E.

→ Contents

APPENDIXES

✦ Maps, Tables, and Figures

Figures

✦ Introduction: The Latin American Hacienda, Agrarian Capitalism, and Political Process

A traveler along the Pan-American Highway enters Costa Rica from the north through Guanacaste province, just a few kilometers from the Pacific Ocean, in an area of torrid lowland plains dotted with occasional trees and a few rolling hills. Barbed wire fences run parallel to the two-lane route for most of its length, marking the borders of properties and assuring that livestock stay out of the way of the intermittent traffic. The savannas—lush green during the rains and brown or yellow in the dry season—nurture scattered herds of cattle, and in a few spots with more abundant water, rice and sugarcane fields break the monotony of the flat landscape. This region of tropical prairies is, more than anything else, an immense pasture, covered with large expanses of grass and tangled brush, which give much of the land an almost abandoned look, as if its human inhabitants had tried to ensconce themselves and retreated in the face of the sweltering sun and the relentless secondary vegetation.

The scattering of cattle in distant pastures, the appearance of abandonment, and the chained, wrought iron gates securing the entrances of one or another important hacienda hint at a problem that has weighed heavily on much of rural Latin America—that of the *latifundio*, or large unproductive estate. But the evident underutilization of the land and the concentration of ownership also suggest a paradox that might become apparent to our traveler some seventy kilometers south of the border, at the provincial capital, Liberia. There trucks filled with fat bellowing steers line up at a modern slaughterhouse, shiny refrigerator trailers packed with beef pull onto the highway, headed for ocean ports, the giant silos of rice mills hover above the plains, and modern bank buildings adjoin the town plaza.

The abandonment of land so unmistakable in Liberia's rural hinterland is obviously not total, because nearby pastures and fields provide the raw material for this substantial agroindustrial infrastructure. More significant, though, is the disjunction between the ongoing dominance of the latifundio today and its insertion in what has been, by any standard, a modern, dynamic, export-oriented economy. How can stagnation exist at the farm level while the region is thoroughly integrated into national and foreign markets? Why, if lucrative alternatives to *latifundismo* appear to exist, does so much of the land remain unproductive thickets of scrub growth intermixed with enormous, almost empty grasslands?

Social scientists of widely varying orientations have come to remarkably similar conclusions about the latifundio's detrimental impact on Latin America's development and its supposed present demise in the face of economic modernization. Few students of large-estate systems consider contemporary latifundismo anything other than a vestige of an earlier age. Virtually all agree that large unproductive estates ought to have given way by now to modern capitalist farms. And those who acknowledge the continued existence of latifundismo profess bafflement about why it occurs. Remarkably, considering this consensus, an entire genre of research literature on what Norman Myers (1981) dubbed the "hamburger connection" reaches diametrically opposed conclusions. Concerned not specifically with large estates but with the deleterious environmental and social effects of cattle ranching in tropical America, numerous ecologists, anthropologists, and other social scientists have documented the spread in recent decades of extensive grazing economies. In effect, they establish that latifundismo is alive and well—indeed, expanding.

The antithetical conclusions of the large-estate and "hamburger connection" literatures about the raison d'être and destiny of the latifundio highlight several related problems, examined here in the context of a region where the concerns of both approaches converge. One problem involves defining the extent and fate of latifundismo. Are the backers of the demise thesis correct, or are the proponents of the "hamburger connection"? Clearly, deciding between the opposed conclusions of these two groups demands something beyond a single observer's sense impressions (or operational measures) of land underutilization and abandonment and a physical scale larger than the anthropologist's tiny, customary "square yard of turf" (Vincent 1977: 57).[1] It also involves examining the politics of land appropriation over time, the changing uses of that land, and transformations of the labor process. Only recently, as I indicate below, have anthropologists begun to consider in a central way the possibility that the development of large-estate systems might reflect eminently political and highly specific processes of appropriation of land and labor—and the result of contention and negotiation over the terms of appropriation.

Another, equally complex set of problems arising from an encounter between the large-estate and the "hamburger" literatures concerns what I have termed the "logic" (actually, the "logics") of the latifundio, past and present. What accounts for the persistence of such systems in different times and places? Here, the explanatory options range from environmental and economic versions of synchronic functionalism to "cultural lag," to the demand-based approaches of the dependency and "hamburger connection" schools. The situation becomes yet more complicated because contributors to both literatures, as I discuss in more detail shortly, have rarely questioned sufficiently—and have sometimes tended to reinforce—prevailing images of either the "precapitalist" past or the "modern" present and future. Coming up with historically grounded alternative explanations for latifundismo requires examining not only the changing relations that are shaping the use of land and labor, but also international markets and the state, especially the latter's roles as facilitator of development, mediator (or at times partisan) in social conflicts, provider of institutionalized income flows, and direct participant in the productive process.

Guanacastecan Latifundismo

This work focuses on a region—Guanacaste province, northwestern Costa Rica—where extensively operated haciendas or latifundios have long been dominant. A century ago Guanacaste was essentially an underpopulated, forested frontier zone with few roads, a minimal state presence, and limited economic significance—little more than a way station for fattening imported Nicaraguan steers for the central Costa Rican market. In subsequent years the region underwent a profound transformation, first through its increased integration into the national state and economy and later through Costa Rica's transformation from beef importer to exporter and the reorganization of many production processes along capitalist lines. Yet in spite of this penetration of world market forces and agrarian capitalism, key features of the traditional latifundio system, such as underutilization of land and extreme concentration of holdings, persist in the midst of a modern economy. However, it is not only that the "past" appears in the present, but the "present" in the past as well. Some elements usually considered to be defining characteristics of capitalism, such as the widespread use of wage labor, were found in Guanacaste even in the early nineteenth century, long before the advent of the technological and organizational changes that later permitted more intense processes of accumulation (see Chapter 3).

Squatters, as well as hacienda laborers, exercised remarkable power in Guanacaste until well into the twentieth century, limiting development of landlords' enterprises and forcing them to tolerate long-term peasant land occupations. Until the 1930s the balance of forces between landlords and the rural poor was such that laborers in need of cash routinely demanded and received wage advances as a condition of employment. Far from indicating that peasants always resist the "imposition" of wage labor, as some scholars have suggested, these superficially capitalist production relations were a sign of peasant strength. But these "free" labor relations were not part of a production system in which accumulation occurred through ever-increasing productivity based on new investment. Wealth derived instead largely from natural or quasi-natural products of the soil, such as timber or semiferal cattle.

By the 1930s the rural poor's bargaining position had deteriorated significantly, in part because the collapse of export-oriented sectors of the Costa Rican economy saturated the labor market and because state protectionism, intended to ameliorate the effects of the depression, increased the profitability of cattle haciendas. I argue below that struggles over state policies and the appropriation of land and labor ought to be central to an analysis of agrarian structure. But the Guanacastecan case would lead me to reject the notion—in effect a manifestation of the fashionable tendency to exalt "agency" at the expense of "structure"—that property or surplus-extraction relationships are somehow immune to "changes in demographic or commercial trends" (Brenner 1976: 31). Similarly, as I discuss in more detail in Chapter 8, the current fascination with the everyday resistance tactics of subordinate groups can only really transcend romanticism if it considers the alternatives available to the poor within the context of particular agrarian structures and state policies. This is especially important in a case of growing landlord hegemony, such as Guanacaste after 1950.

This recent landlord ascendancy remains anchored to latifundismo, albeit a modified variety inserted in a modern economy. In Guanacaste the traditional hacienda system has changed in two directions. On the one hand, technological developments and changes in the production process occurred, like those that diverse theoretical currents point to as part of the logical (and usually inevitable) denouement of traditional hacienda systems undergoing capitalist development or conversion into plantations. On the other hand, there has been a parallel process that is perhaps best characterized as one of continuing underinvestment or stagnation. Its most obvious manifestation is the extremely extensive land use that persists on many haciendas in spite of their integration into national and international markets. The two processes are not separate phenomena, nor are they merely the result of historical lags or uneven development. Rather, I argue that stagnation and the persistence of seemingly traditional haciendas are in large part the result of a conjunction of international market conditions and of regional and national political forces that permitted an influential landlord class to maintain itself in power and to shape policies in its favor. At the local level the modernization of large estates has often only been possible because more traditional, extensive production systems cushioned landowners against the risks involved in transforming traditional haciendas along capitalist lines. What the literature has often termed "haciendas" and "plantations" are not always contrasting enterprise types with opposing logics. They may be complementary economic strategies carried out by the same landlords on the same estates.

An approach to the transition to agrarian capitalism that stresses the growing predominance of wage labor and modern technology is clearly not sufficient for an understanding of the particularities of the Guanacastecan case such as those mentioned here. A view of the large estate that assumes a priori that landowners possess absolute power is likewise inadequate. Similarly inadequate is the preoccupation with defining enterprise types or modes of production that long dominated studies of large estates in cultural anthropology, neoclassical economics, dependency theory, and social history. My misgivings about these approaches should become clearer if we briefly examine some of the ways social scientists and historians have viewed the question of large landholdings. *Latifundio* and *hacienda* can, in broad terms, be considered synonymous, though it is important to remember that "latifundio" has negative connotations that "hacienda" does not have (although in peasant usage the two terms may be equally pejorative). In Latin America, to be a "latifundista" implies that the landlord has monopolized huge tracts of land and left much of it unproductive; to be an "hacendado" indicates nothing more than ownership of a large estate and is usually a mark of prestige.

Anthropologists and the Typologizing Impulse

In a seminal article on Latin American and Caribbean large estates, Eric Wolf and Sidney Mintz (1957) defined hacienda and plantation "types" distinguished by low versus high levels of capital investment, small- versus large-scale market orientations, and a preoccupation with status or consumption versus a concern with capital accumulation on the part of owners. Both haciendas and plantations were, Wolf and Mintz argued, "products of the expansion of the world economy . . . geared to the sale of surpluses produced into an outside market" (pp. 384–85).[2] They took pains to point out that the hacienda and plantation types were not polar opposites, nor were the two types necessarily inevitable "sequential stages in the development of modern agricultural organization" (p. 381). They did imply, however, that haciendas probably would eventually be supplanted by plantations, stating that "the two types do seem to represent responses to different levels of capital investment and market development, and the differences between them are—at least in large part—determined by differences in the kinds of market which they supply and the amounts of capital at their disposal" (p. 381).

Wolf and Mintz's 1957 distinction between hacienda and plantation has continued to serve as a point of departure for analyses of large landed estates in Latin America, because its heuristic usefulness and rich discussion of labor control, land use, capital, and markets still stimulate comparisons and discussion (Duncan and Rutledge 1977: 6–7; Grindle 1986: 30; Keith 1977; Sequiera 1985: 102–5). But while Wolf and Mintz's analysis was essentially ahistorical and directed at constructing a practical typology, it was permeated nonetheless by a strong appreciation for concrete particularities derived from studies in Puerto Rico, Mexico, and Jamaica. Though their article tended to treat "hacienda" and "plantation" types as entities that were relatively unchanging across time and space (Cardoso and Pérez 1979, 2: 46), it grew out of a larger project—*The People of Puerto Rico* (Mintz 1956; Steward 1956; Wolf 1956)—which virtually for the first time in

U.S. cultural anthropology linked community "subcultures" and histories to broader national and international processes and laid the basis for a conception of culture rooted in changing material conditions (Mintz 1978; Roseberry 1978; Wolf 1978).

Given that a fundamental historical sensitivity informed Wolf and Mintz's 1957 analysis, it is perhaps not surprising that the article on haciendas and plantations anticipated several specific aspects of large-estate social relations that only much later became subjects of inquiry. These included the basically instrumental nature of landowner paternalism and the possibility that employees' indebtedness to employers could reflect a seller's labor market rather than the subjugation of classical debt peonage (Wolf and Mintz 1957: 390, 399). Such subtleties were not always appreciated, however, by those who elevated the formal properties of the model to the status of unquestioned reality, attributing to one or another "type" an ever-larger number of supposedly universal characteristics and losing sight of the heterogenous forms on the ground.

Wolf and Mintz's article on haciendas and plantations was the most astute and serviceable of a number of classificatory efforts in the 1950s and 1960s by North American anthropologists concerned with agrarian systems and rural labor. Frequently, however, such works lacked the heuristic value of Wolf and Mintz's typology, relying instead on sweeping generalizations derived from empirical research at much lower levels of abstraction, such as one or a few studies of communities or individual large estates. The concern with typologies commonly gave rise as well to implicitly or explicitly deterministic notions about historical process. Typically, anthropologists in this period were preoccupied with correspondences between enterprise or cultural "types" and very broad geographical zones, such as all of "highland" or "lowland" America.

In 1955 the *American Anthropologist* published three influential essays that exemplified this trend. Wolf's article on "Types of Latin American Peasantries" suggested that "haciendas" were associated with "highland" peasantries living in corporate communities, while "plantations" were associated with "lowland" peasantries producing crops for market. Elman Service pursued a similar line of reasoning in his essay "Indian-European Relations in Colonial Latin America," which posited a division of the American continent into "Euro-," "Mestizo-," and "Indo-American" zones and which contended that plantations were a phenomenon of lowland regions where indigenous populations had been destroyed. Charles Wagley and Marvin Harris's article, "A Typology of Latin American Subcultures," like those by Wolf and by Service, argued for a distinction between highlands and lowlands, which in turn determined the presence of "subcultures," including haciendas and various kinds of lowland plantations. Nine years later, Harris's *Patterns of Race in the Americas* (1964), while shedding new light on the comparative study of ethnic relations, equated even more explicitly and deterministically "highlands" with haciendas and "lowlands" with plantations.

Curiously, Latin Americanist anthropologists in the 1950s and 1960s largely ignored the existence of lowland haciendas, which would have significantly confounded most of their elegant typologies. Such enterprises were (and are) found throughout the Pacific lowlands of southern Mexico and Central America and in much of lowland South America (Matos Mar 1976; Taussig 1977; Wasserstrom 1977). Usually they are livestock operations, though many also produce subsistence or cash crops, either in the landowner's enterprise or in those of peasant tenants or sharecroppers.

More important, however, than anthropologists' simple inattention to haciendas in zones not predicted by their bipolar typologies was what this neglect signified about their views of historical process. The highlands-haciendas / lowlands-plantations formula presupposed that enterprise types—with their associated class relations, ethnic configurations, "subcultures," and technologies—could be largely predicted or derived from geographical location, population density, or gross environmental features. Had anthropologists recognized that haciendas arose outside the zones predicted by geographic determinist models, they might have shifted their attention to the factors—cultural, political-economic, *and* demographic-geographical—that influenced the outcomes of these struggles over land and labor (and more broadly, over related development policies).

Economic Orthodoxies and the Latifundio

Neoclassical economists and economic anthropologists of the formalist school (Schneider 1974; Schultz 1964) have devoted considerable attention to peasant production, probably in part because of the similarities between the assumptions of perfect competition and conditions in smallholding areas. Few have attempted to apply the neoclassical paradigm to the study of large estates, where landownership concentration and monopsonistic control of labor constitute obvious "market imperfections." Some neoclassical economists are among those baffled by the problem of underutilized haciendas or latifundios. Theodore Schultz, for example, confessed bewilderment in his widely read book *Transforming Traditional Agriculture*: "Why many of the farmers who own and are responsible for the operation of very large farms, especially in some parts of South America, do not engage successfully in [the] search for modern agricultural factors is a puzzle" (p. 174). Schultz chose not to address this "puzzle."

Economist Shane Hunt (1975) sought to enhance Wolf and Mintz's hacienda-plantation model, using neoclassical tools. Rather like the geographical determinism of anthropologists in the 1950s and 1960s, however, Hunt's application of neoclassical orthodoxy to the problem of the Latin American large estate resulted in an economic determinism that obscured both historical process and on-the-ground diversity. Seeking to define the economic conditions in which haciendas and plantations could operate and those that would generate a transformation of the former into the latter, Hunt declared that the principal determinants of enterprise types were the degree of control over the labor force and the market price for the estate's products (p. 8), rather than the size of the market itself, as Wolf and Mintz had suggested. Haciendas, according to Hunt, were distinguished by "the total control exercised by the landlord over the labor force. Within wide limits, he can fix wages and tasks as he wishes, without diminishing the total labor force available in the hacienda-minifundio complex" (p. 13).

Marxian economists such as Alain de Janvry—who in *The Agrarian Question and Reformism in Latin America* (1981: 83) referred to the "serf . . . as a captive of the latifundio"—shared this belief about total landlord control over the labor force. For both kinds of orthodoxy, however, this certainty was but one of a number of instances in the discussion about enterprise types where characteristics of a model, once stated, became reified.[3] Hunt, in addition to universalizing aspects of hacienda and plantation social relations that may have been more idiosyncratic than he realized, tended to assume "market imperfections" to be given, rather than viewing them as outcomes of ongoing economic and political contention between large estates' owners, on the one hand, and their employees and nearby peasants, on the other. Ironically, given his harsh view of mainstream economics, de Janvry arrived at nearly identical conclusions, though without cloaking them in the neoclassical terminology of "market imperfections." The problem with this kind of interpretation is illustrated by Hunt's pronouncement that extensive land use on haciendas is best explained by "imperfections in the factors market, specifically the labor market" (p. 9). Such an assertion, rather than being a final conclusion, ought to be a first step in an examination of forces creating rigidities in the labor market. But this in turn is inseparable from the issues of peasants' access to land, their economic alternatives, and their historical experience of political struggle.

Hunt viewed the key cause of the transition from hacienda to plantation in similarly narrow, purely economic terms, as the result of increased profitability of estates brought about by the introduction of new technology or rising commodity prices.[4] This is certainly often the case. But, as Hunt also recognized, land for many hacendados is virtually "a free good," and they frequently invest little if any capital in their properties. This makes calculation of profits problematical (pp. 13, 19), a point which Hunt himself, and other students of Latin American and European large-estate systems as well, have not always sufficiently appreciated.

Orthodox defenders of neoclassical approaches are not the only economists who overlooked latifundistas' inability to calculate profits according to modern accounting conventions. De Janvry (1981), for example, ascribed to the hacendado a calculating mentality like that of any other capitalist, remarking that "the land of the latifundio is used extensively and consequently its opportunity cost is low" (p. 83), an assumption I question in Chapter 9. Witold Kula, a Marxian economic historian whose study of Eastern European large estates (1976) stimulated suggestive comparisons with Latin America (Kay 1980: 26, 117; Martínez Alier 1977b: 41–46), posited a similarly simple, economistic explanation for the equivalent in Poland of the hacienda-to-plantation transition. In the long term, he asserted, rising profit rates will inevitably "intersect" interest rates—considered a proxy for speculative rates of return—and lead to intensification of production (p. 180).

But hacendados who have not had to calculate profits as a proportion of returns to capital invested may not operate according to strict profitability criteria. If land for them is indeed a "free good"—or at least one attained at low cost in the distant past—the character and timing of the appropriation of the soil become critical variables in explaining their present economic behavior (and more generally, their vision of possible productive alternatives). Many landowners, in Guanacaste and elsewhere, do not regard as worthwhile the transformation of extensively exploited properties into intensively cultivated plantations, even where it would be technically and economically feasible. This raises another issue obscured by deterministic reasoning and fixed ideal types, that of *continuing* noneconomic influences on economic behavior and of other kinds of economic rationality beyond the narrow calculation of short-term returns to capital.

It is difficult, moreover, for the neoclassical approach, or for other approaches centered around the definition of abstract types, to explain a variety of phenomena commonly observed in the Latin American countryside, such as the different use of similar productive resources by neighboring landlords (or smallholders) or the purchase of lands at prices much higher than the income they may be expected to generate through production (Schejtman 1975: 489–91). These explanatory weaknesses do not result only from the narrow view of economic rationality as short-run maximization defined according to marginal criteria. The neoclassical approach also assumes an artificial separation of political power relations from economic behavior and tends to ignore or downplay the effects of risk, uncertainty, speculation, and the availability of other kinds of rent income, such as that obtained from the natural products of the land or low-cost production loans and mortgages. Since the state plays a major role in shaping these elements—as well as in influencing the extent of "market imperfections" through land, labor, and law enforcement policies—political processes at various levels figure significantly in the economic "solutions" sought by different individuals and groups.

More Monolithic Models

Like anthropologists and economists, historians too were bogged down for many years with a "traditional, monolithic model of the hacienda" (Van Young 1981: 3). Based to a large degree—though quite loosely—on François Chevalier's pioneering *Land and Society in Colonial Mexico* (1963 [1952]), this image of the hacienda emphasized institutional continuities with late-medieval Spain, such as owners' aristocratic pretensions, ostentatious patterns of consumption, and "peculiar" antiproductive mentality, their practice of binding labor to the estate through debt peonage, the fortresslike quality of the great houses, and the estates' self-sufficiency. Chevalier's pain-staking research actually revealed colonial Mexican haciendas to be extraordinarily varied across space and time in terms of size, production systems, labor relations, and virtually every other imaginable variable. But his vast scope, his highlighting of the great latifundios of the Mexican north, and his frequent generic references to "the hacienda," or even "the *classical* hacienda" (p. 278, emphasis added), lent themselves to interpretations of the great estate that were in fact little more than caricatures of his findings that served to feed existing stereotypes.

This tendency to generalize from one colonial reality to all of contemporary Latin America was epitomized by historical geographer Jacques Lambert, author of a text popular in the late 1960s and early 1970s. In *Latin America: Social Structure and Political Institutions* (1967 [1963]), Lambert wrote:

Nothing has had a more widespread and lasting effect on Latin America's social and political history than the large estate. In the rural areas, lands were divided into overly large estates where, after the abolition of forced labor, relationships of personal dependence persisted between the freed agricultural workers and their former masters. In Latin America the term *latifundios* is used to designate this antiquated form of land ownership, as opposed to other, newer forms of large estates whose function is more specifically economic. (p. 59)

Referring to latifundios as "quasi-feudal," "manorial" enterprises in which "serfs" or debt peons lived in "complete dependence" on their paternalistic "masters," Lambert asserted that the large estates were "an antiquated remnant of the colonial past in contemporary America . . . the essential feature . . . [of which] is that, even to this day, they live as much as they can outside the money economy" (pp. 67–68).

Lambert's conclusions about the hacienda's feudal labor relations, as well as its isolation, self-sufficiency, and dependence on unsubstantial local markets—but not strong distant ones—were echoed to varying degrees in a large number of general and monographic studies. Sometimes, as in Robert Keith's introduction to his anthology *Haciendas and Plantations in Latin American History* (1977), the model appeared basically in its entirety, embellished with novel, allegedly universal features ("there were no forests" in hacienda regions) and qualified with only an occasional caveat about the possibility that plantation and hacienda regions "tended to become blurred" in the long run (pp. 11, 19).[5] At other times, elements of the model entered historians' thinking in a more subtle but equally pernicious way. For example, Elisabeth Fonseca Corrales (a student of Chevalier's), in *Costa Rica colonial: la tierra y el hombre* (1983: 263–64), inferred from scanty evidence that peasant tenants were common on colonial Guanacastecan haciendas and that landlords "exercised power" over these renters, who supposedly paid cash to farm estate lands.[6]

Large Estates: Dependency and Mode of Production Approaches

The vision of the hacienda, and more generally of rural Latin America, as "feudal" generated acerbic reactions from dependency theorists in the 1960s and 1970s. The details of these polemics are not sufficiently arresting to warrant attention here (in any case, an overabundance of relevant literature is available for anyone who might still possess the stamina required to read it). Instead, I will briefly examine one prototypical example that illustrates the limitations of dependency approaches for an understanding of latifundismo and also their convergence in terms of fundamental notions of process with other ahistorical, universalizing currents of thought they claimed to oppose.

In distinguishing "feudalism" from "capitalism," dependency theory posited a fundamental antinomy like the hacienda-plantation distinction. But the "feudalism" category existed largely as a convenient straw man, the reality of which was denied in all cases under consideration. Its contraposition to "capitalism," conceived in such broad terms as to be virtually all-encompassing, had little heuristic value.

André Gunder Frank, a leading light of the dependency school, lambasted Marxists and liberals who labeled Brazilian agriculture "feudal" because it exhibited features supposedly not present in developed-country agricultures—for example, huge estates, extensive land use, a "non-rational mentality," and coerced forms of labor (1969, part 4). He argued that proponents of the feudalism thesis confused characteristics of the system with the system itself. "The crucial thing" about the feudal system, he wrote, "is that it is a *closed* system, or one only weakly linked with the world beyond" (p. 239, original emphasis). But latifundios in Brazil were, he convincingly showed, tied from the beginning to world markets. Even those that today appear isolated originated with European mercantile expansion. Moreover, "the reality of Brazilian agriculture is that the thousand and one variations and combinations of agricultural working relations are intermixed in all areas. Any number of forms of tenancy and hired labor may be found in the same region, the same farm, the same part of a single farm; and they exist almost entirely at the pleasure of the farm owner or manager" (p. 234).

Rather than integrating this apparent concern with specifics into an analysis, however, Frank allowed the complexity of the particularities itself to become a pretext for abandoning the search for explanations and for lumping all labor mobilization mechanisms in the same "capitalist" category. He went on to suggest that market forces and structures of land "monopolization" or ownership were the main determinants of production organization and production relations. Peasant tenants, sharecroppers, and subsistence agriculturalists were, he claimed, "shock absorbers" that cushioned commercial agriculture against cyclical declines.[7] Yet for all Frank's concern about the rural poor's struggle for survival and the huge inequities in the distribution of resources, he devoted little attention to the possibility that arrangements in agriculture may be the outcome of class conflicts and struggle—of political processes. The premise that particular relations of production, for example, were merely due to "the pleasure" of farm owners denied to all but the dominant groups any role as historical agents. Such an ahistorical view of the problem of large estates did not give any systematic methodological expression to the roles of political processes and class conflict in shaping agrarian production systems and land tenure patterns.

In one sense, dependency theory's view of the large estate marked a significant advance over previous approaches. By illustrating interconnections between processes of development and underdevelopment and by attacking "stage" theories of economic progress—whether Marxian or Rostowian—*dependentistas* questioned the supposition that present-day latifundismo was simply a vestige or an anachronism without any contemporary logic.[8] But most dependency theorists, like cultural anthropologists of the 1950s, assigned the market the key role as an agent of transformation. Consequently, they explained the stagnation of latifundio regions as a product of unlinking from the world economy (as in northeast Brazil after the decline of sugar) and the transformation from hacienda to plantation as the result of full-scale insertion in international economic circuits. As I suggest in Chapters 6 and 7, however, integration into the U.S. beef market has actually exacerbated traditional latifundista tendencies to underutilize productive land.

The sweeping generalizations of dependency theory stimulated a series of critiques that called for a return to the study of modes of production, usually conceived as distinct systems of forces and relations of production with corresponding ideological superstructures (Assadourian 1973; Laclau 1971; Long 1975; Semo 1973). The salutary effect of the early mode of production debate was the return of the focus of research to concrete labor processes and surplus-extraction relationships, which were reproduced or transformed under specific historical conditions. But here too a promising theoretical advance frequently foundered, either by adopting rigid structuralist schemata, such as those of the Althusserians (Althusser and Balibar 1970), which denied the role of human agency in history, or by positing such a large number of specific, "articulating" modes of production that the concept itself tended to lose much of its utility (Foster-Carter 1978; Palerm 1980).

Large Estates as Systems of Relations

The problem with many of the typologies in the literature—whether in cultural anthropology, neoclassical economics, dependency theory, or Marxism—is (as Wolf was later to remark in another context) that they "threaten to turn names into things" (Wolf 1982: 3). Certainly the most important advance of recent historical and anthropological analyses of Latin American large estates over earlier taxonomic approaches has been the movement away from static typologies toward a dynamic notion of process and an emphasis on changing relations rather than definitions of units (or modes) of production. This shift reflects not only a realization of the complexities and uniqueness of particular cases, but also an awareness that such a focus permits meaningful comparisons in a way that the construction of ideal types never did.

Some participants in this trend express occasional anxiety about what constitute sound axes of comparison and about the dangers of becoming mired in extreme particularism. Eric Van Young, for instance, comments that "it is probably easier to say what a hacienda was not than to say what it was" and "that the hacienda is hard to describe, but you know it when you see it" (1983: 14, 25). But this kind of tongue-in-cheek agnosticism reflects an increasingly widespread conviction that ultimately models and ideal types are most useful as heuristic devices rather than as ends in themselves and that the appropriate elements to abstract and compare in order to understand changing realities or underscore revealing contrasts may just as well be relations as things.

In the recent research that has contributed to breaking down monolithic models of large estates and providing a more realistic idea of the range of enterprise types, those works that focus on certain kinds of significant relations have been the most useful for comparative research. Cristóbal Kay (1974; 1977; 1980)—drawing on the work of Juan Martínez Alier (1975, 1977b), Rafael Baraona (1965), and others—suggests that hacienda systems are characterized by a dynamic conflict between landlord and peasant enterprises over the appropriation or control of agricultural resources and the labor force. He distinguishes four basic outcomes of this process: (1) "internal siege," when the peasant enterprises internal to the hacienda develop at the expense of the landlord economy; (2) "external siege," when the ascendance of the peasantry over the estate owner occurs through pressures, such as land invasions, brought to bear by external peasants; (3) "internal proletarianization," in which the growth of the landlord enterprise brings about the expropriation of peasant tenures within the estate; and (4) "external proletarianization," in which the expansion of the landlord enterprise produces the expropriation or sale of peasant enterprises outside the estate.

Similarly, a number of recent works have significantly clarified the relations of debt peonage and landownership itself. It is now abundantly clear that not all worker or peasant indebtedness to the landlord implied control by the latter over the former; indeed, in diverse contexts and times, indebtedness—worker demands for wage advances as a condition of employment—reflected the strength of local labor vis-à-vis its employers (Bauer 1979; Cross 1979; Knight 1986; Sabato 1989; Taylor 1972). Friedrich Katz's (1974) study of labor conditions on haciendas in Porfirian Mexico examined debt peonage, supposedly a universal element of the "classical" hacienda, and demonstrated that geographical differences in the content and strength of this institution—indeed its very existence or absence—could only be understood in relation to regional variations in labor supply and demand (both affected by myriad demographic, technological, and social factors), market characteristics, state construction of transport infrastructure and mobilization of corvée and slave workers, and—in the north—the presence of a national frontier. Katz's work established, importantly, that it was possible to inject a large and healthy dose of particularism into the analysis of large estates without abandoning the comparative concerns that lay behind earlier efforts to construct broad typologies.

If *peón-patrón* relations came to be seen in more dynamic, subtle terms, the link between owners and landed property also received greater critical scrutiny. Numerous studies (Kay 1980; Martínez Alier 1977a, 1977b; Orlove 1977) have now demonstrated definitively that simple juridical control of land did not always confer actual physical control or the ability to utilize or dispose of resources to which owners had title. These considerations are of special significance in the Guanacastecan case, where "inverted" debt peonage was common until the early 1930s, the majority of the rural population lived on lands to which someone else held title, and peasant land invasions continue to this day (see Chapters 3, 4, and 8 below).

But if historical research has provided a more nuanced view of Latin American large estates, the temporal and sometimes the spatial limitations of much of this literature have led certain important questions to be ignored. Implicitly or explicitly, both the majority of historical studies and the typologizing works discussed above assume that underutilized haciendas will meet their end with the development of capitalism in agriculture, a conclusion that, I argue, is not merited in the Guanacastecan case. This presumption of inevitable demise has stood in the way of understanding the continuities between "traditional" hacienda and plantation systems and the "modern" large estates that began to develop in many areas of Latin America in the past half century. In addition, as we shall see shortly, when such analyses of rural change are concerned largely with various kinds of gross indicators and international processes, they tend to give little emphasis to national- and local-level political factors that may play an important part in shaping regional systems of land use, land tenure, and production.

Disappearing Haciendas and the "Hamburger Connection"

The conviction that the latifundio "is in its death throes" (Lambert 1967: 91) is so widespread among researchers of diverse disciplines and orientations that to assert otherwise might seem quarrelsome or foolhardy. Yet in this regard even some of the most outstanding analysts of Latin American large estates appear to be wearing a kind of "modernization blinders" that color all realities with a tint of progress—the inverse, perhaps, of anthropologists' propensity for seeing "natural economy" at every turn. Magnus Mörner, for example, one of the most distinguished figures in the field of Latin American agrarian history, lamented the supposed "paradox" that the hacienda only began to attract the interest of researchers when it was already undergoing a gradual process of extinction. "The traditional system of large estates or haciendas," he wrote, "is now disappearing in country after country" (1973: 183). More recently, political scientist Merilee Grindle echoed Mörner in her book *State and Countryside: Development Policy and Agrarian Politics in Latin America* (1986), declaring that "in the period between 1940 and 1980, rural areas in Latin America were transformed. Traditional haciendas with stable resident labor forces gave way to large commercial farms using modern technology and wage labor" (p. 11).

The collapse of contemporary latifundismo—the "remnants" or "anachronisms" alluded to in so many studies of continental scope—has also been predicted in numerous case studies from different parts of Latin America, where it has sometimes been considered a concomitant of the proletarianization of the peasantry (Kay 1980: 111–12; Reyes 1978: 141; Rutledge 1987: 50). What to make, then, of the vast expanses of *tacotales* (secondary growth and brush) and the chained hacienda gates so ubiquitous in rural Guanacaste today? How might contemporary latifundismo be explained without resorting to such questionable principles as "cultural lag" or "vestigial structures" and without falling into an equally dubious synchronic functionalism that emphasizes solely the present-day "rationality" of rentier enterprises?

Ernest Feder's book *The Rape of the Peasantry* (1971), one of the most systematic examinations of contemporary land tenure problems in Latin America, expressed similar certainty about the ultimate fate of the unproductive hacienda or latifundio, but with some interesting qualifications. Traditionally, he noted, ownership of large blocks of land "is financially very lucrative. . . . But latifundismo is going to fall at some unforeseeable time in the future because it is poor business for the Latin American nations as a whole" (p. 261).

With large landowners under pressure primarily from technocrats, but also from reformers (often in conflict with each other), Feder pointed to the emergence of what he termed "technocratic latifundismo," or the conversion of underutilized haciendas into highly capitalized modern farms like those that the literature often refers to as plantations.[9]

To his credit, Feder foresaw the likelihood that, in contrast to the "technocratic" latifundios, "the remaining latifundio sector, in continuation of past trends, will not participate in the modernization process and will turn, as in the past, increasingly to extensive land uses in new and old farming areas such as cattle operations, as their soil becomes exhausted and yields decline" (p. 291).

At first glance Feder's critique of and prognosis for latifundismo appear not unlike those I develop in the present study of Guanacaste, Costa Rica. In particular, I share Feder's view that traditional haciendas are moving in two directions, which I describe as intensification and stagnation. Like the anthropological typologizing discussed above, however, Feder's analysis of the causes of continuing underinvestment or stagnation was basically ahistorical, culturalist, and ecological, ascribing the causes of this economically puzzling phenomenon to the traditionalist inertia that is part of the large landowners' mentality, to historical lags or survivals, or to soil exhaustion brought about by modern intensive agriculture. I argue, in Chapters 6 to 9, that the contemporary underutilized latifundios of northwestern Costa Rica are in many respects products of contemporary conditions, including the ways in which landowners have succeeded in influencing state policies for rural development and how the region is integrated in the world economy.

Parallel to this social scientific consensus about the demise of latifundismo, another body of research literature that emerged in the early 1970s arrived, surprisingly, at a diametrically opposed conclusion. A growing number of tropical ecologists, anthropologists, and other social scientists have linked developed-country demand for Latin American beef to a host of environmental and social ills, including forest destruction, decreased rainfall, soil erosion, replacement of food crops by pasture, "protein flight," rural unemployment, and concentration of land, credit, and other resources.[10] This "hamburger connection" (Myers 1981) literature, though not explicitly concerned with the problem of the large estate, pointed to the horizontal expansion of pastures that had long been virtually synonymous with latifundismo in much of Latin America as a major effect of extraregional demand for beef.

I have argued elsewhere (Edelman n.d.) that this genre of analysis, with its emphasis on external demand as the motor force of agrarian change, represents the last unself-conscious refuge of dependency theory in the social sciences (and one that, considering its origins in academic discourse, has had a surprisingly strong impact on popular thinking about environmental problems). Proponents of this approach have provided abundant evidence of the concentration of landownership and the low productivity associated with the spread of tropical ranching—in effect, of strengthened latifundios in Central America, the Amazon, and elsewhere. But because their concerns tended to be narrowly environmentalist rather than more broadly social or historical, champions of the "hamburger connection" thesis have never engaged those who predicted the imminent collapse of surviving latifundista "vestiges."

Extractive Economies and Rentier Enterprises

Several recent works have shed light on the seemingly paradoxical survival of underutilized latifundios in modern capitalist economies, using the concepts of ground rent (de Janvry 1981: 152–55) or extractive economies (Bunker 1985: 22–37). These discussions are particularly suggestive in the case of Guanacaste because in the early twentieth century a significant portion of hacienda income came from selling natural or quasi-natural resources such as timber and feral cattle. Promising prospects for speculative gains also motivated many real estate transactions (see Chapters 1 and 2). More recently, landlord political influence helped create a complex system of institutionalized flows of income that are at times only indirectly related to actual production (Chapters 6 and 9).

Much recent discussion of ground rent consists of overly abstract typologies, textual exegeses, or tortuous attempts to make sacred writ conform to observed realities (Flichman 1977; Moncayo 1976). Leaving aside such scholasticism (and eschewing any intention of basing an argument on "higher" authorities), we may still find it useful to paraphrase Marx's uncharacteristically straightforward definition of ground rent in *Capital* (1967, 3: 821). "Like the annually consumable fruits of a perennial tree," he said, ground rent was the portion of the annually created total product that a landlord may consume without exhausting the source of its reproduction, that is, the land. Ground rent, according to Marx, should be distinguished from the profit yielded by capital, since its essential condition is not an investment in forces of production, but rather the mere juridical possession of land. Although the price of ground rent may take the form of a payment from a capitalist or peasant tenant to the landlord, the concept does not necessarily imply such a separation between the legal owner of the land and the actual producer.

Private property in land and the low ratio of equipment to labor power in agriculture create conditions for what Marx termed "absolute rent," a category he distinguished from the "differential rent" accruing to owners of particularly fertile land (or other rich or well-located properties) (1967, 3: 760–62; Wolf 1983: 50–51). Since land, unlike capital and labor, is not physically mobile, owners may keep it out of production until they receive a rent. Initially, landlords also are able to produce commodities with less investment in machinery than investors in other sectors. Their average costs of production are thus likely to be lower than those of nonagricultural producers who receive similar market prices for their goods. These higher returns in the landed, as opposed to the nonagricultural, sector are what Marx labeled absolute rent, a "surplus-profit" that also constitutes a potential basis of conflict between landowning and capitalist classes.

De Janvry, despite his flawed conceptions of latifundista mentality and hacienda labor relations, provided a valuable analysis of how absolute rent contributes to a lowering of the average rate of profit and to a slower pace of accumulation in the economy as a whole (1981: 152–57). His insights, derived from the classical economics of David Ricardo as well as from Marx, are especially relevant for an understanding of the persistence of latifundismo in northwestern Costa Rica. Briefly, de Janvry argued that gains extracted in the form of rent—that is, without investing capital—constitute a surcharge on the costs of agricultural production, which in turn contributes to higher food and wage costs and lower returns to capital (see also Wolf 1983: 50–51). In other words, the landowner has no reason to invest in any kind of intensified land use or production as long as possibilities exist of earning high returns from the natural products of the soil or from rent paid by tenants. Because of this inherent contradiction, however, between rent (returns to the factor land) and profit (returns to the factor capital), ascendant capitalist classes in underdeveloped countries usually try to impose reductions in the level of rent through cheap food policies, such as controlling prices, overvaluing exchange rates, and encouraging imports of basic foods. Politically powerful landlord classes then fight for compensatory concessions. These constitute what de Janvry (p. 155) labeled "institutional rent": various kinds of direct and indirect subsidies for the production both of exports—needed to generate foreign exchange to sustain industrialization—and of luxury goods, the price of which does not affect the cost of labor.[11] Once again, the outcome of political processes becomes an essential aspect of landlord economic rationality.

Stephen Bunker's discussion of extractive economies in *Underdeveloping the Amazon* (1985) parallels de Janvry's treatment of ground rent in several respects, though with greater emphasis on ecological implications and without relying on Marxist theoretical categories. Extractive economies differ from productive ones, Bunker maintains, because "the exploitation of natural resources uses and destroys values in energy and material which cannot be calculated in terms of [returns to] labor or capital" (p. 22). Typically, such economies are based on extremely low ratios of both labor and capital to value, creating the potential for rapid increases in regional incomes and for sudden financial and environmental collapse. According to Bunker (p. 89), tropical ranching, particularly in its initial stages, is largely an extractive activity, since it relies heavily on natural values, such as native forage plants and nutrients from burned or decaying vegetation. I would add that tropical ranching's rudimentary methods of livestock management, which in earlier decades frequently resembled hunting rather than production, are another indication of its fundamentally extractive character.

Whether latifundio economics are conceived of as "rent" or as "extraction," the important point is that the dynamics of accumulation are radically different than those of classical capitalist development. Rather than investing heavily in improved technologies, employing productive human labor, attempting to capture increased market shares, or developing linkages with other production processes, latifundistas could become wealthy from harvesting natural and quasi-natural products of the land. As Juan Corradi remarked about Argentina (1985: 16), a region some Guanacastecan hacendados hoped to emulate (see Chapter 2), "land rent became the historical substitute for primitive accumulation on the *pampas*: It was capital accumulation on the cheap."[12]

The Guanacastecan Hacienda and the "Classical" Hacienda

The smattering of studies of rural northwestern Costa Rica may be classified into two distinct groups on either side of a universally recognized watershed in about 1950. The mid-twentieth century as the end or beginning of investigations on this region makes sense because of the major changes ushered in by the Costa Rican civil war in 1948, the country's attainment of self-sufficiency in beef production circa 1950, and its emergence as a major beef exporter in the early 1950s (see Chapter 6). However, electing this end or beginning point has meant not only a tendency to give short shrift to questions of transition (see Chapter 5), but also that scholars working on both sides of the great mid-twentieth-century divide have exaggerated—generally unintentionally—the gap between the "precapitalist" past and the "modern" present and future. This choice about periodization, then, is understandable, though not necessarily always fruitful.

This problem is discussed in more detail in the chapters that follow, but some of the issues involved are worth noting here. Lowell Gudmundson's (1983b) ground-breaking work on the pre-1950 history of the cattle industry and latifundismo in Guanacaste constituted a major step forward in the study of a region that Costa Rican historians had heretofore largely ignored.[13] Employing previously unexamined documentary sources, Gudmundson brought to light forgotten agrarian struggles and state reforms, identified key groups within the landowning class, and described in broad strokes the development of the regional livestock sector up to the mid-twentieth-century watershed. Nevertheless, perhaps in part as a result of his choices about periodization, Gudmundson downplayed or neglected processes crucial to an understanding of subsequent developments, such as the reconcentration in a few hands of land distributed during pre-1935 agrarian reforms and the causes of the rapid growth of herds in 1932–50 that permitted Costa Rica to switch from importing to exporting beef (see Chapter 5). More significant, his description of early-twentieth-century "hacienda peasants" as atavistic subsistence cultivators requires substantial modification. As I discuss in Chapters 4 and 5, many "hacienda," or lowland, peasants were commodity producers, and, especially after the early 1930s, they became important suppliers of feeder calves for the large estates.

Wilder Sequiera's (1985) study of the cattle elite during 1850–1900 provided an encyclopedic catalog that listed hacendados' provenance, net worth, and participation in government, as well as the size of many major properties. If his work at times employed an overly literal conception of property, assuming that hacendados actually controlled the vast expanses they claimed or owned, it nonetheless contributed significantly to an understanding of the importance of elite endogamy and inheritance as means of ensuring the continuity of latifundista power. Sequiera was not concerned with the persistence of latifundismo into the late twentieth century. But, as I argue later (in Chapters 6–9), ancestors' acquisition of low-cost land during the late nineteenth or early twentieth centuries and its later reconcentration through elite endogamy are critical elements of the seemingly "irrational" economics of today's hacendados.

Researchers on the post-1950 decades have been especially inclined to wear blinders about the "pre-capitalist" past. Rodolfo Fernández Carballo, for instance, considered "the 1950s when capitalist penetration began" (1980: 30), as if mercantile relations, wage labor, and development of the forces of production suddenly sprang full-blown from the *tabula rasa* of early-twentieth-century latifundismo. Reinaldo Carcanholo argued similarly and erroneously (see Chapter 2 below) that international market forces were the only stimulus capable of transforming the region's traditional livestock economy and that until the early 1950s there was "no concern with improving the quality of the cattle" (1977: 6). Carcanholo's thesis that most or all Guanacastecan latifundios have fragmented and given rise to modern capitalist enterprises, while phrased in terms critical of capitalist exploitation, not only was inaccurate (see Chapters 7 and 9 below), but ironically denied the need for any fundamental transformation of rural social relations that would permit greater development of the productive forces (see also Ducoudry and Lungo 1976).

Irene Aguilar and Manuel Solís (Aguilar 1985; Aguilar and Solís 1988; Solís 1981a), in investigations of the post-1950 cattle elite that represent one of the more successful efforts—in Costa Rica or elsewhere—to understand contemporary latifundismo, provided a detailed analysis of subsidized credit flows to the "modern" export-beef sector (what de Janvry—see above—terms "institutional rent").

Aguilar and Solís's discussion was noteworthy in several respects. First, in acknowledging the continued existence of underutilized latifundios and attempting to explain their rationality in terms of contemporary economic conditions, their work broke with the widespread tendency either to assume the latifundio's disappearance or to explain its presence as the result of lags or stasis. Second, in pointing to credit flows as a key prop of the extensive grazing economy, they provided a much-needed corrective to the "hamburger connection" literature, which attributes the Central American cattle boom almost entirely to world market demand and ignores political processes in producing countries. Finally, Aguilar and Solís's use of public records to penetrate the facade of corporate landownership was a major advance in the task—increasingly difficult after the 1960s—of identifying the real owners of properties.

Despite these significant steps forward, however, a number of basic elements of the problem of contemporary latifundismo are conspicuously absent from Aguilar and Solís's work. Though their treatment of credit flows is exhaustive, they completely ignore tax policies that inhibit investment and foster extensive land uses (see Chapter 7). Similarly, while analyzing the growth of livestock credit from Costa Rica's nationalized banks, they fail to even mention the deep involvement of international lending agencies in supplying the original loans for this type of "development." Most important, Aguilar and Solís, by focusing almost exclusively on the post-1950 period, underestimate both the extent to which today's cattle elite is descended from yesterday's large hacendados and the importance of foreign landlords within the regional elite.[14] This leads them to define the rationality of extensive livestock enterprises largely in terms of present-day economic conditions and to downplay the extent to which historical continuities with the "old families" of Guanacaste account for contemporary latifundismo.[15]

Land Tenure in Costa Rica: Ideology and Reality

After traversing the hot, lowland prairies of Guanacaste and northern Puntarenas, the traveler who entered Costa Rica at the Nicaraguan frontier and proceeded south some 220 kilometers along the highway would begin a sharp ascent at the Cerro de Cambronero. Here the route traverses a series of treacherous, serpentine switchbacks that in little more than a dozen kilometers lifts traffic from the

Pacific coastal plain to the temperate climate of the central plateau. The change in landscapes could hardly be more dramatic, from the scattered settlements and flat expanses of pasture in the lowlands to the neatly tended coffee farms, dense population, and industrial enterprises of the highlands. It is this Costa Rica, where the capital is located and most of the population lives, that dominates both popular and scholarly thinking. For that reason, a cautionary word is in order about images of land tenure and the large estate in the country's center and in its peripheral regions.

Costa Rica's reputation as a peaceful "agrarian democracy" of yeomen farmers is sometimes termed the "white legend" (Creedman 1977: x; Heath 1970: 96–97; see also Seligson 1980: 3–13). The main elements of this ideology include Costa Rica's supposed poverty and isolation in the colonial period; the individualistic, peaceful, egalitarian, and democratic culture this allegedly engendered; and the belief that the contemporary democratic political system is a direct outcome of these apparently auspicious antecedents (Monge 1962; Rodríguez Vega 1979). Some analysts have also asserted that Costa Rica's exceptional development within Central America was the result of the ethnic homogeneity and European descent of its population, a theme that—phrased in racist terms—figures prominently in nineteenth-century travelers' accounts (e.g., Dunlop 1970 [1847]: 113).[16] Like many stereotypes, the "white legend" has in it a grain of truth in that Costa Rica's "colonial heritage" (Stein and Stein 1970) *was* weak compared with that of other countries in the hemisphere and that this clearly had cultural and political consequences that set Costa Ricans apart from other Central Americans. Recent research, however, increasingly calls into question the "white legend's" view of colonial poverty and egalitarianism (Fonseca Corrales 1983; Gudmundson 1978b, 1986). Historians of contemporary Costa Rica also note that authoritarian episodes, while less common here than elsewhere, were not unknown and indeed have been ignored because historians' "'democratizing' compulsiveness" led them to choose other subjects of study (Schifter 1978: 194).

Since the late 1960s a heated and at times acrimonious debate has taken place over the extent of concentration or fragmentation of rural property in the nineteenth and twentieth centuries. But this discussion has been limited almost exclusively to the coffee regions of the *meseta central* (central plateau) (Baires 1975; Cardoso 1975a, 1975b; Churnside 1979; de Andrade 1967; Gudmundson 1978b, 1986; Hall

1976; Ramírez 1978; S. Stone 1975). In part because of the "white legend," which also focused largely on the *meseta*, less attention has been given to the existence of massive landholdings in peripheral regions of the country, such as the cattle estates of Guanacaste, the sugar plantations of Juan Viñas, or the banana plantations of the southern Atlantic and Pacific coasts.[17]

At the same time, it is important to keep the question of land concentration at the national level in a realistic comparative perspective. Mitchell Seligson, in a series of works that sought to deflate some of the myths surrounding Costa Rica's "agrarian democracy," reported that the country's Gini index of land concentration was the sixth highest of 54 countries worldwide, comparable in Latin America only to Colombia and Ecuador and exceeded only by Argentina and pre-1968 Peru (1977: 213; 1978: 1). Yet the economic comparison implicit in this shocking finding may be less valid than it appears at first glance. In Costa Rica, the largest properties are primarily cattle ranches and a smaller number of sugar plantations, neither the most lucrative of tropical enterprises. Most of the banana plantations in the coastal enclaves belonged to foreign transnationals and therefore had less effect on the composition and wealth of the country's upper class than if they were owned by nationals (Pérez Brignoli 1984). These considerations obviously shaped the capital accumulation possibilities of Costa Rica's landowning class. Moreover, as various studies of the coffee sector indicate, much of the capital accumulation of the Costa Rican coffee bourgeoisie was based on control of processing and marketing rather than on direct control of land and production (Cardoso 1975a, 1975b; Hall 1976; S. Stone 1975). In El Salvador, in contrast, the largest properties included many coffee plantations, which generated enormous wealth for the small landowning class (Colindres 1977).

Nevertheless, it remains true and has been too often overlooked that in Costa Rica the large estate became indisputably dominant in regions such as the northwest. Guanacaste lay within the borders of what some—in all earnestness or with caustic irony—termed the "Switzerland of Central America" (Sancho 1982 [1935]). But this province of 10,000 square kilometers appeared almost another country, with a land tenure pattern resembling that of the rest of Central America's Pacific lowlands. As two Spanish observers put it in 1906—after traveling, not on highways, but on "trails designed for deer and forest predators"—Guanacaste was a "Costa Rican Andalucía . . . [with] the rural property monopolized by a dozen large hacendados" (Segarra and Julia 1974: 351, 353–54).

Some Comparative and Methodological Implications

This "Costa Rican Andalucía," for all its similarities with the lowland latifundio regions that stretched north through Nicaragua and up to southern Mexico, was inserted in a state with a national history very different from that of its neighbors. On the one hand, an examination of Guanacastecan agrarian history can contribute to a more precise picture of rural Costa Rica, since the yeomen of the "white legend" were conspicuously absent and the land tenure pattern was (and is) anything but democratic. On the other hand, the dominance of extensive cattle grazing like that in the rest of the Central American Pacific coastal plain makes the Guanacastecan case useful for sorting out some of the interrelationships between geography, production systems, class relations, political culture, and the state. As I discuss in Chapters 3 and 4, the weakness of the Costa Rican state until well into the twentieth century, and its liberal democratic character, colored local class relations, "cultures of work," and political assumptions. This in turn complicated the imposition of unfettered landlord hegemony in ways basically unknown to hacendados elsewhere in Central America.

If the appropriation of land and labor, dominant and subordinate groups' efforts to shape state policy, and integration into international markets are central to an explanation of the problem of latifundismo, an analysis must be political-historical and operate simultaneously on several levels. In this study of Guanacaste, Costa Rica, these include:

- World markets and the political-economic forces that condition less developed countries' participation in them.
- Nation states as social formations—obviously Costa Rica, but also nearby Nicaragua—with contending classes, class fractions, and interest groups, each with particular expectations about politics, enterprise organization, and work.
- The state apparatus and the social forces in control of its key institutions.
- The province, a political category, a geographical region with spe-

cific ecological characteristics, and an economic or functional entity with a distinctive series of activities linking it to larger surrounding spaces.

- The local level—villages, settlements, and particular units of production—where individuals, family groups, informal alliances, and formal corporations encounter, with varying degrees of awareness, the larger forces impinging on their reality. Here, the categories of social class, class fraction, and interest group take on concrete historical and political meaning as individuals and groups go about their daily lives responding both to the perceived and the unperceived intrusion of larger forces and to the accumulated experience that has shaped their hopes, their assumptions about their rights, needs, and possibilities, their visions of how society should be and their place in it, and their conceptions about justice.

The uneasy tension between these levels of analysis is not easily resolved, but neither can it be avoided. To some extent it reflects the difficulty of presenting in linear form a complex series of interactions taking place over time in a number of overlapping and linked spaces. It is also partly an artifact of available sources, which are geared to juridical, social, and economic categories that often only approximate those of the researcher and which themselves change over time. More important, tension and shifting between levels of analysis grow out of what is inevitably an only partially attainable goal: the examination of a set of problems affecting a particular region, the analysis of which requires data from extra- and intraregional levels. Rather than selecting—in traditional anthropological fashion—a single, bounded object of study, I have chosen instead to view changes in the region (or in places within the region) as in part the outcome of processes centered elsewhere, changes that can best be studied with data generated elsewhere that refer to other levels of analysis. At the same time, I try to remain aware of which social groups within Guanacaste have sought participation in wider economic circuits and the ways in which local structures, histories, and traditions limit or expedite the penetration of outside forces.

A discussion of this scope inevitably contains a variety of subarguments, some of which are relevant principally to the specific case study and others of which have broader implications. The details await the reader in the chapters that follow, but I note here a few of the issues raised and their relation to larger debates. Numerous studies of *latifundio-minifundio* relations emphasize the importance of infrasubsistence smallholdings in the reproduction of rural labor, but few examine the role of peasant farms as suppliers of inputs to large haciendas in vertically integrated production sectors, such as the Guanacaste cattle industry. Fencing, similarly, is usually viewed exclusively as a tool of landlord enclosures, and indeed it often was so viewed in Guanacaste. But it was also frequently a mechanism of peasant self-defense against the encroachment of landlord cattle. Most scholars have largely abandoned the dependency school's conviction that export economies arise full-blown as a result of external demand for primary products. But few studies (with the exception perhaps of those concerned with coffee and nineteenth-century Liberalism) have explored local elite initiatives that actively sought integration into world markets or the myriad activities of lesser producers that contributed to achieving and maintaining the same end. Finally, in Central America, long racked by conflict, latifundismo sometimes had a geopolitical or a strategic logic, even in relatively tranquil Costa Rica. Especially in a border region like Guanacaste, politics at the international and national levels became closely intertwined with politics on the ground, with armed groups operating from particular haciendas, and with landlords and foreign powers acquiring properties solely because of their location rather than because of what they might produce.

PART ONE

→ The Period Before 1950

I ⟶ Formation and Consolidation of the Haciendas

They ask that Congress assure that the plaintiff demanding
measurement of property not be allowed to inscribe in a
title to *demasías* (excess lands) any extension of land beyond 2,000 percent of that specified in his property titles.
—Congressional deputy, citing a petition from
170 residents of Cañas Dulces de Liberia, 1921

The Geographical Setting

Guanacaste province takes its name from the guanacaste tree, a
squat but spectacular giant with a dome-shaped canopy of foliage so
thick that in the dry season the ground below remains cool in the
hundred-degree heat, and in the rainy season torrential downpours
slow to a mere trickle.[1] Scattered over the torrid lowland plains that
occupy most of the province, these natural umbrellas came to be
places where travelers and cowboys on long-distance cattle drives
would stop to rest. Sometimes a large, well-located guanacaste tree
attracted a few settlers, who built rude houses nearby and cooked for,
sheltered, or otherwise provided for the occasional passerby. Many of
the province's villages and towns are also named for various kinds of
vegetation, suggesting something of the exuberance of the dry tropical forest that once covered the region and the importance of trees
as landmarks for human settlement. Today, though the once dense
forest has given way to pastures and sugarcane, rice and cotton fields,
vestiges of the old wooded landscape remain along the many watercourses and on the higher slopes that form part of the volcanic chain
that runs the length of the Central American isthmus.

Contemporary Guanacaste covers 10,141 square kilometers bordered on the west by the Pacific Ocean and the Gulf of Nicoya; on the
east by Alajuela province, which it meets at the continental divide
high in the volcanic cordillera; on the south by Puntarenas province;

and on the north by the Nicaraguan border, which runs parallel to the southern shore of Lake Nicaragua and then cuts perpendicularly across the narrow Rivas isthmus that separates the giant lake from the Pacific (see Maps 1.1 and 1.2). Together with the two northernmost cantons of Puntarenas province—the Central Canton (1,842 square kilometers) and Esparza (222 square kilometers)—Guanacaste forms a distinct geographical region known in Costa Rica as the *Pacífico seco*, or "dry Pacific," because of the intense drought that occurs for five or six months each year between November and May.

A large area of rich alluvial soils is found along the west bank of the Tempisque River, the region's main watercourse, from its mouth in the Gulf of Nicoya as far north as Guardia, and—in a thinner strip— along the east bank of the Tempisque and the lower courses of the Cañas, Bebedero, and Salto rivers. These areas have historically demonstrated the greatest agricultural potential in the province.[2] Although many of the volcanic soils of the upper cordillera are quite rich, the abrupt topography contributes to rapid erosion in cleared lands, and the high winds present during much of the year have discouraged agriculturalists. Elsewhere, in the lowlands of the province, the interspersed laterite, lithosol, and planosol soils range from moderately fertile in some places to extremely poor in others (Dóndoli 1950: 68; Fournier 1974: 13–14). Average ambient temperatures of well over 27° centigrade (81° Fahrenheit) bring about a rapid and continuous breakdown of organic matter in the soil; this, in combination with leaching caused by seasonally heavy rains, has created large areas of highly mineralized soils with poor texture and low humus content.

In the lowlands each May, after a period of almost half a year in which little or no rain has fallen and in which the grass turns brittle and the deciduous trees stand bare of leaves, monsoon winds begin to blow from the west and southwest, bringing rain clouds from the Pacific. Much of this moisture is retained by the small mountains of the Nicoya Peninsula, an area that consequently tends to have somewhat higher precipitation than the Tempisque plains. The rains continue for some six months, occasionally pausing during July's *veranillo*, or "little dry season," and generally growing in intensity in September and October. Then, usually in November, the southward shift of the thermal equator that is associated with winter in the Northern Hemisphere causes a change in the direction of the trade winds from south-southwest to northeast. Hot winds from the Carib-

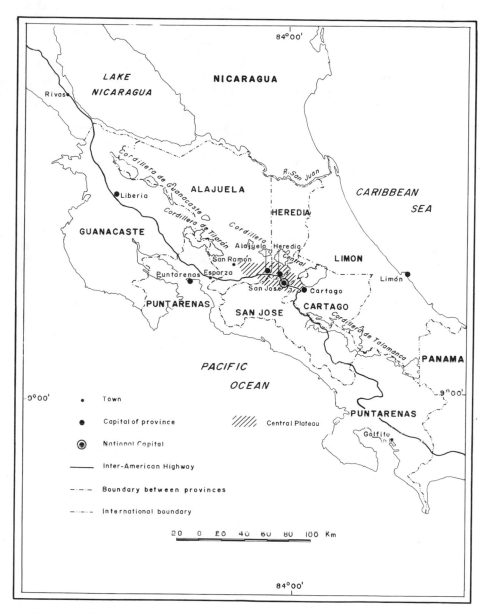

Map 1.1. Costa Rica (main geographical features and location of study area and central plateau).

Map 1.2. Guanacaste Province (towns and geographical features).

bean last until February or March, but the vast quantities of moist air and precipitation they carry are blocked from reaching the Pacific Ocean by the peaks of the volcanic cordillera, which range in elevation from 1,400 to 2,000 meters. Part of this intense moisture from the Caribbean does manage, however, to pass between the peaks and over the continental divide, where it falls in the form of a nearly permanent fog and drizzle on the upper reaches of the western slopes of the volcanoes. Climatically, therefore, the Cordillera de Guanacaste and the Sierra de Tilarán form a zone distinct from the lowland plains, inasmuch as the effect of the annual drought is absent or severely attenuated. Finally, following a period of transition in April and early May, the winds once again begin to blow from the west and southwest, bringing rain clouds from the Pacific.

The Destruction of the Indians and the Creation of Open Spaces

The Chorotegas, the most numerous of the pre-Columbian peoples of what is now northwestern Costa Rica, were among the southernmost populations of the Mesoamerican culture area. This classification is based primarily on the importance of maize-bean and cacao cultivation, the existence of Mexican-influenced religious practices and political structures, and the use of languages of the main Mesoamerican stocks, Oto-Mangué (the Chorotegas) and Uto-Aztecan (several smaller groups) (Chapman 1960; Creamer 1987; Ferrero 1975; Kirchoff 1943; Newson 1987). Indigenous groups to the south and east generally had tuber-based productive systems that supported only scattered populations with less complex forms of societal organization strongly influenced by those of the South American tropical forests. Pacific Central America, with its pronounced dry season and its often rich volcanic earth, was better suited to human settlement than the humid Atlantic regions with their year-round rains and more intensively weathered soils (MacLeod 1973. 26). By the time of the Spanish conquest, the chiefdoms of the Greater Nicoya region—defined in the archeological literature as northern Puntarenas, Nicoya-Guanacaste, and Pacific Nicaragua (Abel-Vidor 1980)—included some areas of extremely dense population linked by complex commercial and political ties both to each other and to more distant centers farther north.

The Indian populations of Nicoya-Guanacaste and Nicaragua suffered a demographic catastrophe of massive proportions in the three decades after contact (Cabrera Padilla 1989; Newson 1982, 1987; Radell 1976; Sibaja 1982). One of the most important factors in this process was the large-scale shipment of Indian slaves to aid in the conquest of Peru and in the portage of Peru-bound cargo across the Isthmus of Panama. Although this trade in slaves affected virtually all of Spanish Central America, Nicoya-Nicaragua was the most devastated region. Estimates of the numbers of Indian slaves exported from this area between the 1520s and the abolition of Indian slavery in 1549 range from Sherman's (1979: 82) low of 50,000 and MacLeod's (1973: 52) "conservative" 200,000 to Bartolomé De Las Casas's (1977 [1552]: 49) figure of 500,000, which Newson accepts as an upper limit (1987: 105). De Las Casas pointed in addition to 500,000 to 600,000 Indian deaths caused by "the infernal wars waged on them by the Spaniards and the horrible captivity in which they were kept" (p. 49).

Epidemics, cultural shock, exploitation, the uprooting of populations fleeing Spanish raiding parties, and the disruption of agricultural production also hastened the demise of the Indian inhabitants of Nicoya-Nicaragua. An additional factor, related to both disease and the destruction of indigenous social relations, was the frequent failure of Indian marriages to produce children (Cabrera 1924: 232; Matarrita Ruiz 1980a: 326; Newson 1982: 283).[3] It is estimated that the Indian population of Nicoya-Guanacaste declined 97.1 percent from 62,692 at contact in 1522 to a mere 1,800 60 years later (Newson 1982: 269).[4]

Very early in the postconquest period, then, Nicoya-Guanacaste became essentially a zone of empty spaces with minuscule scattered settlements and a single *pueblo de indios*. For the conquistadors, opportunities to acquire wealth still existed to the north, where larger numbers of Indians survived and where towns such as Granada played a key role in transisthmian transport and commerce (via the San Juan River and Lake Nicaragua). But, with little labor to exploit, many of the Spaniards in Nicoya and Nicaragua left for the boom areas of Panama and Peru. The demise of the Nicoya and Nicaragua Indian populations also encouraged the Spanish expeditions of the 1560s into the still unconquered mountainous area that became Costa Rica (MacLeod 1973: 205). Early reports of large Indian populations in Costa Rica raised hopes that fortunes might be made from the exploitation of *encomienda* Indians. But the epidemics that swept the area in 1576–81 dramatically reduced the Costa Rican indigenous population as well. This destruction of the Indian population and the failure to discover significant mineral resources meant that central Costa Rica, although increasingly settled in the seventeenth century, was destined to remain "a marginal zone of a secondary region of the colonial system" (Fernández Arias 1980: 3). In relation to this marginal zone, the nearly empty region of Nicoya-Guanacaste became itself an economic backwater.

Agrarian Structure and Subregional Differentiation

Sixteenth-century accounts contrast the fertile, well-watered Nicaraguan lakes region with the area that is now northern Guanacaste, which was said to be almost unpopulated, since it was "a land without water" (Abel-Vidor 1980; Ferrero 1975). Yet the Spaniards' lack of interest in Nicoya-Guanacaste was not only the result of the harsh environment and the destruction of the potential labor force. During the colonial period the region was also a political frontier, distant from the centers of power. The Nicoya Peninsula and the zone north of the Salto River (just south of present-day Liberia) was administered for most of the colonial period as an Alcaldía Mayor, or Corregimiento, independent from both Nicaragua and Costa Rica, but part of the Audiencia, or Capitanía General de Guatemala, that included all of Central America.[5] The area south of the Salto River, called the Valleys of Bagaces and Landecho, was administered from central Costa Rica, also part of the Capitanía General de Guatemala.

The encomienda system, under which the Crown made grants of Indians for labor service, had a brief life in the Alcaldía Mayor de Nicoya. The Nicoya Indians were first granted to Pedrarias Dávila, a conquistador and colonial governor. At his death in 1532 they passed to his widow (and, briefly, in 1544 to his daughter), illustrating that the inheritance of encomienda rights, although prohibited by the Crown until 1536 (Ots 1959: 98), occurred nonetheless (DHN, 3: 133–34; DHN, 9: 4). In 1544 Rodrigo de Contreras, also a conquistador and governor, was listed as "possessing" a large number of Indian pueblos, including León, Granada, Nicoya, and Chira (DHN, 11: 152–53), many of which he confiscated from less-powerful encomenderos, averring that they had been improperly allocated by other officials (Newson 1987: 95–96). Nicaragua was apparently devastated sooner than Nicoya by the slave trade, since a 1555 report explained that there were 27 *pueblos de indios* in Nicoya-Nicaragua and "the largest one is Nicoya, with 500 *vecinos*. Of the others, none has more than 100 *vecinos* and many have 10, 15, 20, or 24. They pay tribute in corn, cloth, beeswax, honey, and hens, which would be worth some 3,000 pesos" (quoted in Zavala 1973: 790).

In 1544 the Nicoya encomienda alone was listed as producing annual tribute worth 2,000 pesos (*DHN*, 9: 4). But even with such sizable collections, by the mid-sixteenth century it had become difficult to accumulate fortunes based on Indian labor, both because of the New Laws, which attempted with some success to limit the exploitation of encomienda Indians, and because of the small size of the surviving indigenous population, now settled in and around the single *pueblo de indios*.[6] At least as early as 1620, according to Meléndez (1975: 108–9), the labor encomienda was superseded by various types of in-kind tribute obligations and a new conception of ownership of "land without Indians" (also see *DHCR*, 3: 385).[7]

The existence of royal land grants that date from the 1560s in Bagaces and Landecho, the part of the Costa Rican jurisdiction bordering on Nicoya, suggests that private appropriation of land was under way there decades before 1620 (see *DHCR*, 3: 13–20, 71–77). These royal land grants employed a terminology that merits more detailed consideration because of its later importance in structuring land tenure and in agrarian disputes, both within the landowning class and between landowners and peasants. Specifically, the authorities gave concessions to "caballerías," "sitios," and "estancias para ganado," with the rights implied in each kind of grant undergoing a process of refinement and redefinition that, in Guanacaste, lasted well into the twentieth century.

The Crown made concessions of *caballerías* at first for crop agriculture rather than livestock, though early in the colonial period the obligation of recipients to cultivate the soil was largely forgotten. Soldiers who participated in the conquest were entitled to two or three caballerías of land for cultivation on condition that they not sell or otherwise alienate the property for a specified period, usually at least a year, and that the grant would not infringe on Indian lands.[8] In theory, caballerías were granted to those who had served on horseback, with *peonías*, a more modest measure, reserved for foot soldiers. In practice, few if any *peonías* were ever awarded, since Spanish conquerors were usually able to lay claim to having served as cavalry and eschewed the disparaging term *peón*, or foot soldier, which in the

New World had come to be associated with Indian laborers (Chevalier 1963: 53; Florescano 1976: 29; Pérez Estrada 1964: 17).

A caballería was a unit of land, but as Martínez Peláez remarks about Guatemala, "as a colonial measure of surface area it presents serious problems, because it appears defined in very different ways in the documents" (1972: 678). Ots Capdequí, in a detailed discussion of changes in the caballería over time (1959: 21–23), indicates that in the sixteenth century the Crown defined it according to the amount of seed used for sowing and the number of livestock that could graze once pastures were planted. More precise criteria emerged later, but well into the eighteenth century, in much of Spanish America, property titles frequently specified particular, local "styles" of caballería. In Guanacaste frequent disputes occurred in the nineteenth and early twentieth centuries over whether titles referred to large "old" caballerías or smaller "new" caballerías.[9] In any case, Barrett's assertion that the dimensions of the caballería "never changed [and] were set in the sixteenth century" (1979: 423–24) does not hold for Central America, though it may well have been true for central Mexico.[10]

The estancia was a royal grant of land for cattle raising that was administered by municipalities and initially did not imply full property rights; *estancia* areas were rarely specified, although boundaries were usually designated in vague terms (e.g., *DHCR*, 3: 13). The term was seldom used in Costa Rica or Nicoya after the seventeenth century. In keeping with Castilian tradition, the pastures and watering holes were to be held in common.[11] The *sitio*, or "place," was a similar colonial-tenure institution of which vestiges still existed in Guanacaste in the early twentieth century. Like estancias, sitios were grants of grazing rights made by town councils (*cabildos*) that allocated sections of municipal lands for the herds. Less frequently, grants of grazing rights were referred to *hatos* (herds), a term preserved in several Guanacastecan place names (such as Asiento Arado, formerly Hato Viejo de Arado, Santa Cruz).[12] After independence, in 1828 and again in 1874, the area of a sitio was fixed at seven caballerías (about 317 hectares) in an effort to facilitate the titling of lands (ANCR Cong. 8184—1874 and 9749—1874).[13] But initially rights to a sitio, as Florescano (1976: 30) and Chevalier (1963: 90) suggest for Mexico, did not give beneficiaries more than a negative right over pastures: that of impeding others from building corrals and shelters.

Gradually, however, a slow transformation began of sitio rights into more permanent rights to land. It was here that the term *hacienda* made its appearance, at first referring—in Guanacaste-Nicoya at least—to virtually any large livestock enterprise, and later, in the last century of the colonial period, coming to suggest a large operation with specific rights to land.[14] This transmutation of sitio grazing rights into hacienda tenure rights was facilitated by Crown provisions in the late sixteenth century for *composición de tierras,* or the legalization of de facto land occupations through the payment of fees. In the Costa Rican jurisdiction of Esparza (which included Bagaces and Landecho), where most original land titles were destroyed in English pirate attacks in the 1680s, the concept of private tenure guaranteed through composición appears to have been well established by the late seventeenth century.[15]

By 1709 herd owners in the area were applying to the judge in charge of composición to have their lands measured and delineated with *mojones,* or markers, the locations of which were clearly specified in new deeds. Although these new titles did not always indicate the area enclosed within the mojones, by 1711 at least some of the "composed" properties were being measured with a cord of 50 "*varas castellanas,*" or "Castilian yards" (41.9 meters) so that their area in caballerías could be recorded (*DHCR,* 3: 16–20).

In the Nicoya jurisdiction the process of appropriation of the soil took a somewhat different form in the uninhabited area north of the peninsula than in the peninsular zone around the pueblo de indios. In the north residents of Nicaragua began to establish herds in the early eighteenth century (Meléndez 1967), and it is only then that composición de tierras appears to have had much importance in the creation of formal tenure patterns.[16] The 1754 promulgation of a royal edict providing that local officials would receive 2 percent of the value of all titles and composiciones registered in their jurisdictions created an incentive for colonial bureaucrats to title lands (Martínez Peláez 1972: 155). The existence in the Alcaldía Mayor de Nicoya of a number of major private titles dating to 1754 and immediately thereafter suggests that local administrators applied this provision with a certain zeal.[17] Nevertheless, the detailed specification of property boundaries and the placing of stone mojones by composición officials—standard procedure in the Costa Rican Valley of Bagaces by the eighteenth century—do not appear to have been carried out as effectively in the Alcaldía Mayor de Nicoya. Natural features, such as the confluence of two creeks or a small hill, were frequently used instead of stone cairns to mark boundaries and, although they were referred to as mojones, their names and locations at times became later subjects of contention.[18] Part of the legacy of these differences was that in the late nineteenth and early twentieth centuries disputes over property boundaries were much more common in the former Nicoya jurisdiction than in the former Costa Rican zone.[19]

Early in the colonial period, in the peninsular zone around the pueblo de indios, the system of religious *cofradías*, or saints' cults, became deeply rooted under the tutelage of the Franciscans (Blanco Segura 1967: 233). These religious sodalities, a key instrument of Spanish domination in regions of the Americas with large indigenous populations, acquired properties in order to use the profits to maintain churches and to provision festivals honoring their patrons. Many cofradía holdings were cattle herds. But the grazing of cattle by private owners in unfenced sitios also accrued to the cofradías' benefit. According to regional tradition, unbranded animals found on cofradía lands or those whose ownership was disputed by private individuals became the property of San Blas or other patron saints. Precise information is not available about the amount of land in the Nicoya Peninsula controlled by these institutions in the colonial period, but cofradía properties were undoubtedly quite large. One hacienda dedicated to Jesus of Nazareth, which survived the early-nineteenth-century liberal reforms intact before passing into private hands in the 1890s, was measured in 1928 at 3,204 hectares (CN uncat. 27 and uncataloged plans).[20] Other cofradía properties were said to total over 300 caballerías at the time they were auctioned off in the 1830s and 1840s, though whether these were "old" or "new" caballerías was a subject of dispute.[21]

The presence of cofradías around the pueblo de indios made the peninsular subregion a de facto zone of smallholders, since cofradía properties were used for the cultivation of cotton, cacao, plantains, and maize by local residents (León 1942: 289–90). Communal lands granted by the Crown were also used in this way. Much of the area south of Bahía de la Culebra and Sardinal, north of Tempate and Belén, and west of the Tempisque appears to have belonged to an entity termed "the Community of the Indians of Nicoya" and to the Cofradía of San Blas and was essentially open, unappropriated land available to local peasants.[22]

These contrasting patterns of appropriation of land in the Nicoya Peninsula and in the plains to the north and east had resulted, by the

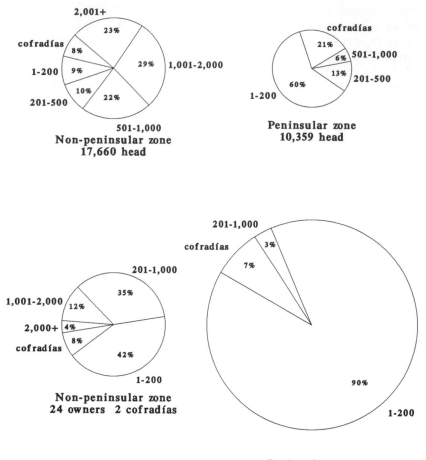

Fig. 1.1. Alcaldía Mayor de Nicoya, 1751: Cattle Ownership by Herd Size Groups and Cofradías, Non-peninsular and Peninsular Zones. Source: "Estadística de las haciendas y ganados de la Provincia de Nicoya, formada por el Vicario d. Tomás Gómez Tenorio para el cobro de los diezmos, año de 1751," in *DHCR*, 3: 112–24.

eighteenth century, in the division of the region into one subregion with a significant smallholding sector and another dominated by latifundios. The 1751 cattle census of the Alcaldía Mayor de Nicoya, taken to assess the *diezmo*, or 10 percent ecclesiastical tax, provides a revealing view of the contrast between the peninsular zone and the part of the Tempisque Valley between Costa Rica and Nicaragua (*DHCR*, 3: 112–24).[23] Figure 1.1, which summarizes the 1751 census data, highlights the contrast between the large herd sizes and the extreme concentration of cattle ownership in the northern Tempisque Valley and the more equitable situation on the Nicoya Peninsula; in the former zone 84 percent of the cattle were owned by fifteen individuals with herds of over 200 head, whereas only 19 percent of the animals in the latter zone were part of such large herds. Moreover, three members of one family—Melchor, Juan, and Manuel de la Cerda—alone held some 3,900 head (22 percent of the latifundist zone cattle) at their contiguous properties of Santísima Trinidad, San Roque, El Tempisquito, Rincón de la Vieja, and San Antonio. The average herd size in the nonpeninsular zone, 679 head, greatly exceeds that in the peninsular zone, 95 head. The geographical concentration in the nonpeninsular zone of the total herd is also evident: 17,660 head—63 percent of the total herd—were located there.

Finally, the importance of the eight cofradía properties in the peninsular zone is suggested by the relatively large size of their herds, in comparison with those of individual owners, and by the fact that they owned 2,166 head—over 21 percent—of the total herd in the zone. In the nonpeninsular zone, two cofradías from Rivas owned 1,350 head, or less than 8 percent of the total in the area. In Bagaces, in the adjacent Costa Rican jurisdiction, the agrarian structure was similar to that in the nonpeninsular latifundist zone of the Alcaldía Mayor de Nicoya. Of all areas in present-day Guanacaste province, Bagaces in the late eighteenth century had the highest level of absentee ownership—17 out of 26 owners who possessed some 18,000 of the 20,800 head (Gudmundson 1978b: 88). The cofradías in this area were also of relatively minor importance, with only 1,480 head of cattle, or 7.1 percent of the total.

Labor in the Latifundist and Smallholding Zones

There was an ethnic dimension as well to the differences between the smallholding peninsular zone and the latifundist zone east of the

Tempisque and south of the Nicaraguan border. The Crown policy of settling Indians in *reducciones*, such as the pueblo de indios at Nicoya, limited possibilities for exploiting indigenous labor in the vast, virtually unpopulated plains to the north and east. In Nicoya, however, for much of the colonial period, Crown officials brutally mistreated the Indians, employing them to weave thread and to extract natural products, such as oyster pearls, indigo, and the murex snails and brazilwood used for dyes. In 1636 the Irish monk Thomas Gage, passing through Nicoya toward the end of a twelve-year journey through the Americas, described how "the Alcalde Mayor employs all [the Indians] as slaves" in spinning and dyeing thread. Differences of opinion about the morality of this practice led to a dispute in which the alcalde attacked the local priest with a sword and severed two of his fingers, an offense for which he was immediately excommunicated (Gage 1974: 58).

That this intense exploitation changed little over the next hundred years is suggested by descriptions of the Indian revolts of the 1700s (Fernández Guardia 1938; Jinesta 1940).[24] Between 1721 and 1753 the Nicoya Indians staged several rebellions against the tribute demands of Spanish officials, expelling one governor (*corregidor*) from the province, forcing another to seek refuge in the church, and threatening the life of a third, who was only saved by the intervention of a company of mestizo militiamen. By the mid-1750s the snails used to produce the coveted purple dye were becoming scarce, but demands for deliveries of dyed thread increased with the 1758 appointment of Gabriel de Santiago y Alfeirán, a particularly exigent corregidor. Santiago y Alfeirán required cash payments, in addition to maize and dyed thread, and reneged on promises to pay laborers who built his indigo workshop, actions that ignited another uprising in 1760. On that occasion the Indians, led by the community's indigenous officials (*principales*), beat and shackled Santiago y Alfeirán and locked him up for a week. Hoping for justice from the Audiencia, they then set off to Guatemala with their prisoner, who was taken from them and freed by government troops in southern Nicaragua. Nine months later the Audiencia in Guatemala reinstated Santiago y Alfeirán and ordered the arrest of the principales who had directed the revolt, measures that sparked riots by Indian women, which allowed the leaders to escape from jail.

Santiago y Alfeirán, however, humbled by his experiences, moderated his demands during the seven years he spent as corregidor following his reinstatement. A 1765 report, for example, suggested some improvement in conditions, noting that the Nicoya Indians were now paid "in silver, clothing, or cacao" for each pound of dyed thread (*DHCR*, 3: 125–26). By 1781, however, the Indians again complained of floggings and mistreatment by local officials (Newson 1987: 279–80). One factor that may have fed revolt (and that certainly contributed to the preservation of Indian phenotypes) was the Spanish practice of settling near Nicoya tropical forest Indians captured in Talamanca, in southeastern Costa Rica, an area never conquered or settled during the colonial period. A bishop reporting on a 1751 *visita* noted that 110 of these "Indians extracted from Talamanca" resided in Cangel (near Nicoya) (*DHCR*, 2: 444). Unlike their counterparts from Nicoya, Talamancans had little experience of state society or tributary relations; they constituted a sizable group in the local indigenous population and certainly would have experienced Spanish officials' demands as especially onerous.

The small size of the Indian population was both a cause and an effect of the introduction and spread of livestock after the conquest. Faced with a labor scarcity and few economic possibilities, the logic of an enterprise based on the simple extraction of semiferal animals was attractive to Spanish colonists and their descendants. At the same time, the cattle feasted on the Indians' crops, contributing to starvation and exacerbating the initial population decline.

A similar process in which livestock expelled human population was, ironically, indirectly responsible for much of the Spanish immigration to the New World. The destruction wrought by sheep herds on the arid brushlands of west-central Spain in the late Middle Ages caused such areas to be the source of many early Spanish migrants (Butzer 1988; Hennessy 1978: 29). Further south, in Andalucía, another region from which many New World settlers were drawn, a type of extensive cattle raising developed that was unique in Europe and became a rough model for ranching in the newly conquered Americas. The peculiar feature of Andalusian cattle raising, which distinguished it from the stock-raising practices of the rest of Europe, was the economic importance of beef and hide production and the lack of integration of dairy or crop agriculture with herding (Bishko 1952). Elsewhere in Europe, particularly after the widespread introduction of forage crops, cattle were raised primarily as draft or dairy animals and played an important role as a source of fertilizer for a fundamentally agricultural economy (Bishko 1952; Grigg 1974). In

Andalucía in contrast, located south of the rainy, fertile "Iberian Humid Crescent" (Bishko 1952: 493), pastoral life predominated. The rise of ranching in this region was also a product of the social context of the *reconquista*. In frontier areas between Christian and Moorish settlements, separated by *despoblados*, or no-man's-lands, where both sides raided and fought, labor was scarce, crop agriculture was hazardous, and livestock, which could be transported under their own power and required little care, were a logical choice for specialization. Though ultimately less destructive of the environment than sheep grazing, Andalusian cattle ranching—and its New World counterparts—was similar inasmuch as it absorbed only limited amounts of labor.

Even though ranching required little human intervention, the lack of workers was a problem in the virtually empty Guanacaste plains. The geographic concentration on the peninsula of the small Nicoya Indian population, as well as Crown prohibitions on exploiting indigenous subjects outside of officially recognized pueblos, prompted a search for alternative sources of labor. By the late sixteenth century small numbers of African slaves were imported to Rivas, Nicoya, and Esparza to work on cattle ranches and on the indigo plantations, which were experiencing a minor boom that lasted until the early seventeenth century. In 1611, according to a Spanish census (cited by Thiel [1902] 1977: 24, 64), the population of the Alcaldía Mayor de Nicoya consisted of 50 Spaniards, 2,000 Indians, and 200 "Negroes, mulattoes and mestizos."[25] By the eighteenth century the *casta* element was predominant; Thiel estimates that in Nicoya out of a total population of 1,499 in 1700, 833 (55.6 percent) were "mulattoes" or "zambos," 647 (43.2 percent) were Indians, a mere 10 were classified as mestizos, and only 9 were Spaniards (p. 67). The low number of Spaniards in Nicoya is corroborated by other sources, such as one 1744 report that states that "Nicoya . . . is of Indians and Mulattoes and there are no Spaniards at all" (*DHCR*, 3: 398). In the Costa Rican jurisdiction of Esparza, which included the Valley of Bagaces, a total population of 445 was composed of 279 "mulattoes" and "zambos" (63 percent), 33 Negroes (7 percent), 39 mestizos (9 percent), 28 Indians (6 percent), and 66 Spaniards (15 percent). The small number of blacks, as opposed to mulattoes, probably reflected both miscegenation and the fact that slave shipments came from Panama rather than Africa and were thus more likely to include persons of mixed ancestry.

"In this territory," a visitor to Bagaces wrote in 1744, "there are various rude houses of straw called *hatos* [herds], where cattle, horses, and mules are bred; all the inhabitants are mulattoes, very little given to work and quite libertine" (*DHCR*, 1: 399). In spite of such widely voiced prejudices, a reflection of the dominant groups' limited control if not their envy of lower-class "immorality," the *casta*, or mulatto, came to constitute the backbone of the hacienda labor force in colonial Guanacaste-Nicoya. Castas, while free of the tribute obligations that maintained Indians in a state of legal servitude, were denied access to public office and to the more remunerative occupations, suffered more severe penalties for legal transgressions, and were prohibited from residing in the pueblo de indios or from acquiring Indian communal lands (see Martínez Peláez 1972: 268–69). Some mulattoes and mestizos held jobs in the tiny colonial militia and police forces, and a small number of mulattoes were slaves. But the limited extent of colonial Guanacastecan slavery is suggested by a 1688 census of the Valley of Bagaces, which listed 17 slaves in a total population of 297, in which the free mulatto element was predominant (*DHCR*, 3: 97–103). Nevertheless, it is unlikely, in the sparsely populated ranching zones where opportunities to flee abounded and the rhythm of work was in any case intermittent, that slave status involved such intense exploitation as in more developed plantation regions.[26]

The anomalous legal status of the castas, the discrimination they experienced, and the relative independence of cowboys on absentee-owned haciendas contributed to the formation of a distinct, cattle frontier culture. Highly mobile, often contemptuous of authority, and sometimes given to the "libertine," violent, or even criminal behavior that excited elite comment and fear, rural mulattoes and mestizos gravitated to unpoliced frontier areas, such as Guanacaste-Nicoya, where state control was weak and landlord hegemony was tenuous. There survival was possible through occasional wage labor, as well as hunting, rustling, or subsistence agriculture. From the late seventeenth century on, travelers and civil and ecclesiastical officials reflected on the difficulties of enforcing a more disciplined labor regime and of compelling the dispersed rural castas to fulfill their spiritual obligations (e.g., *DHCR*, 1: 443–44; *DHCR*, 3: 108, 339, 412; Blanco Segura 1974: 122). As was true elsewhere in colonial Latin America (Baretta and Markhoff 1978; Chevalier 1963: 112–14; Góngora 1966; MacLeod 1973: 191; Martínez Peláez 1972: 366–69;

Salazar Vergara 1985: 27–29), often only a thin line existed between the settled *casta* hacienda worker and the "vagabond" (*vago*), an appellation that originally referred to individuals who had no clear residence and who wandered from place to place (see Brading 1975: 106). In a typical comment, a Spanish governor in 1688 lamented his lack of control over the movements of the Indians and mulattoes in the Valley of Bagaces: "They live apart [from the Spaniards] and do not have fixed residences . . . ; those that belong to this province and those that belong to Nicoya and Nicaragua come and go according to their private interests" (*DHCR*, 3: 108).

The efforts of authorities to "reduce" or concentrate this scattered and mobile population for the purposes of taxation, control, and the administering of sacraments were never more than partially successful, as the laments of churchmen and the continued existence of a significant "vagabond" or "vagrant" element even in the early twentieth century suggest.

Economic Cycles and New Opportunities

Three major economic cycles affected the cattle economy of northwestern Costa Rica prior to the hacienda enclosures of the 1880s. In the early colonial period, from approximately 1560 to 1730 (Fonseca Corrales 1983: 256–59), mules, horses, and then tallow were shipped to Panama. Flour, biscuits, sugar, cacao, garlic, and tobacco were also sent from Bagaces to Panama (*DHCR*, 3: 107), but by the 1680s Peru had replaced Nicoya–Costa Rica as Panama's chief source of foodstuffs (MacLeod 1973: 275). Other factors that contributed to the decline of this early southward trade were the reorganization of the Spanish fleets that called at Panama, the massive fire that destroyed that city in 1737 (Fonseca Corrales 1983: 258), and the near extinction of the herds through excessive slaughtering of cattle for tallow. This rendered fat—used for candles and soap—was virtually the only part of the animals for which there was a market. In 1719 the governor of Costa Rica reported that in Landecho and Bagaces there were "large slaughters" of cattle for tallow and that the meat was left to rot, "since there is nobody who buys or consumes it."

The governor's limited understanding of supply and demand, as well as the fact that live animals were not truly a commodity at the time, is suggested in the same report:

From a steer they get two or three *arrobas* [of tallow—about 50 to 75 pounds], each of which they sell at eight *reales* in exchange for goods, with which they scarcely enjoy three pesos, being worth móre on-hoof the said head of cattle; *and because there is nobody who might buy it,* the different owners slaughter only in order to take advantage of the little bit of tallow they provide. (*DHCR*, 1: 384–85, emphasis added)

A British traveler to Bagaces in 1731 saw "large herds of wild cattle, which the Indians kill only to use the leather and the tallow." Killing the vultures that disposed of carrion and thus prevented epidemics was, he claimed, an offense punishable by death (Cockburn 1974: 76–77). But a mere five years later, two reports suggested that the Panama trade was over, that ships no longer called at ports on the Gulf of Nicoya, and that the cattle, in Bagaces and Landecho at least, were virtually "extinguished" (*DHCR*, 3: 340, 343). The 1751 bishop's *visita* quoted above also noted:

There was such a hurry to slaughter the cattle that the haciendas were ruined, the Indians too diminished and the towns were wiped out. In effect, the province has been reduced to a miserable state, the Indians to 300 who practice confession and communion, and the towns to one, which is that which bears the name of the same province [Nicoya]. (*DHCR*, 1: 442)

The beginning of the second economic cycle—based on sale of live cattle to Nicaragua, El Salvador, and Guatemala—coincided with the end of the tallow commerce in the 1730s and lasted until the mid-nineteenth century, several decades after independence. The mid-eighteenth-century indigo boom, spurred by the European textile industry's growing demand for dyestuffs, was centered in the more densely populated areas of Central America, such as El Salvador, where it brought about major transformations of the countryside. The direct effects of the indigo boom in northwestern Costa Rica and Nicoya were minimal, although the pueblo de indios at Nicoya and a few haciendas, such as Las Trancas west of Liberia, contained small *obrajes*, or workshops, where the dye was steeped and boiled down in huge vats.[27] For most landowners the small labor supply constituted a limit to the growth of production. A 1756 report on Nicoya, for example, noted that massive quantities of indigo grew wild, but that colonial officials had been unable to take advantage of it "because of the lack of people" (*DHCR*, 3: 127).

To the north, in contrast, in densely populated El Salvador, indigo displaced livestock production, leading to a twofold increase in the price of cattle and a threefold increase in the price of mules in 1750–80 (Floyd 1966: 476). This rapid hike in livestock prices in El Salvador provided a strong incentive in Nicaragua and Nicoya to rebuild herds devastated by the tallow trade and gave rise to a large-scale commerce in live animals. This trade was also the principal impetus for the settlement of the area around Liberia in the northern part of the Alcaldía Mayor de Nicoya. There, where the roads to Nicoya, Costa Rica, and Nicaragua converged, "in a place that served as a rodeo for the shipments of cattle that passed from Costa Rica to Nicaragua" (ANCR Cong. 7189—1870: 12v.), members of the elite from Rivas, Nicaragua, founded a village—known initially as Guanacaste—to service their haciendas.

In Rivas, which by the late eighteenth century was one of Nicaragua's major towns (Salvatierra 1939, 2: 33–37), the narrow fertile isthmus was used for labor-intensive crops, such as indigo, cacao, and tobacco, which were often produced with slave labor. Northern Nicoya, the hinterland of Rivas, was used for cattle.[28] The geographical-functional division of the Rivas economy is also suggested by an 1817 census that listed the "principal agricultural production" as 700 cacao plantations, 20 large indigo zones and "many cattle haciendas *in Nicoya*" (ibid.: 36, emphasis added; see also Cabrera Padilla 1989: 30–31). Finally, the northward direction of the cattle trade was, until 1800, enforced by Spanish regulations dictating that cattle be sold at controlled prices exclusively in special markets (*ferias*) in Nicaragua and Guatemala (Quirós Vargas 1976: 174–75; Salvatierra 1939, 3: 210–11). The Crown also required Guanacastecan hacendados to supply *ferias* in Nicoya and the Costa Rican capital of Cartago (Gudmundson 1978b: 111–12; Fonseca Corrales 1983: 279), but these were small in comparison with Central American markets to the north.

With the decline of indigo over the first half of the nineteenth century, many of El Salvador's indigo plantations were gradually converted to cattle haciendas, which then competed with Nicaragua and Nicoya for the Guatemalan market (Wortman 1975: 262). The abolition of cattle price controls in 1791 and of the cattle *ferias* in 1800 (Fonseca Corrales 1983: 277), while in a broad sense the results of economic liberalization in the last decades of Spanish rule, were also related to this switch in El Salvador from indigo to cattle. As livestock output grew near Guatemala, the major center of demand, forced commercialization was no longer needed to assure supplies.

The third economic cycle—based on sales of livestock in markets to the south, in central Costa Rica—coincided with a series of other developments, which, by the late nineteenth century, encouraged hacendados to enclose and expand their estates. These included (1) the lifting of colonial trade restrictions; (2) an increasing demand for livestock products in central Costa Rica as a result of prosperity brought on by the coffee export economy; (3) displacement by coffee of beef-cattle and food-grain production in central Costa Rica to peripheral areas of the country, such as Guanacaste; (4) the expansion, in the 1880s, of wood exports; (5) the discovery of gold in Abangares in 1884; (6) speculation about construction of an interoceanic canal utilizing the San Juan River and Lake Nicaragua, which raised expectations of new commercial opportunities and rising land values; (7) the introduction of transport and technological innovations (discussed in Chapter 2) that permitted well-run ranches to achieve higher profit levels; and (8) the ability of the Costa Rican state to extend police power to remote areas of Guanacaste and thus better control the peasantry (discussed in Chapter 3).

With independence in 1821, the revocation of the remaining provisions for forced commercialization removed an important obstacle to economic growth in the Nicoya-Guanacaste region. Some liberalization of trade occurred in the late eighteenth century as a result of the Bourbon reforms and measures taken by the Cortes, or parliament, of Cádiz to eliminate certain taxes on agricultural production and to permit trade between colonies (Cardoso and Pérez 1977: 115; Stein and Stein 1970: 89; Vega Carballo 1981: 19–21). But in Costa Rica these steps were not sufficient to generate the growth that occurred in other secondary areas of the colonial system, such as the Río de la Plata region of South America. In part as a result of the disruption in colonial trade caused by the Napoleonic Wars and the South American wars of independence, in the last decades of Spanish rule Central America entered a depression, which in Costa Rica lasted until the expansion of coffee exports in the 1830s (Cardoso and Pérez 1977: 144–45; Wortman 1975: 274–77).

The efforts of the Costa Rican government to tax steers exported to Nicaragua also played a role in the cattle trade's southward shift. In 1827 the government established a one-half *real* (one-sixteenth of a peso) tax on each steer sent from Nicoya and Santa Cruz to Nicaragua; in 1832 a similar tax of one *real* per head was applied to the export of steers from Bagaces and Cañas (Vicarioli 1952: 11, 17).

Certainly more important, however, was the growth of demand in central Costa Rica and the increase in cattle prices there. The price of a steer in Cartago went from 2 to 3 pesos in 1750, to 3 to 6 pesos in 1800, to 5 to 10 pesos in 1825, and to 15 to 35 pesos in 1850–60. In 1857 the price of a steer in Liberia was only 10 to 20 pesos (Gudmundson 1978b: 112). A French observer in 1858 noted that the 100 to 200 francs paid for a steer in Cartago was "much more expensive than in Nicaragua" (ibid.). As a result of this changed situation, more and more Nicaraguan steers began to be directed south through Guanacaste to the Costa Rican market.

The basic reason for the growth of demand for livestock products in central Costa Rica was the expansion of the coffee export economy, beginning in the 1830s and 1840s, which brought about both unprecedented prosperity and a physical displacement of cattle and food production from the *meseta central* to peripheral areas of the country, such as Guanacaste. At the beginning of the nineteenth century most agricultural land in the *meseta central*, the country's main population concentration, was in pasture. The spread of coffee cultivation occurred on lands that previously had been used for pastures, sugarcane, and food grains. By the late nineteenth century pastures in *meseta* farms had generally been reduced to the minimum required for draft animals (Hall 1976: 28, 72–83). Coffee exports also fueled a demand for livestock products and oxen for transport (Real and Lungo 1979: 14). A number of recent works call into question the traditional vision of an egalitarian, "rural democracy" in central Costa Rica in the early nineteenth century (Fonseca Corrales 1983; Gudmundson 1986). But the expansion of coffee in a society with many smallholders meant that income from the "grano de oro" was more equitably distributed than elsewhere in Central America and that its multiplier effects on other economic sectors, particularly commerce, were considerably more profound (Cardoso 1975b: 10; Pérez Brignoli 1984).

Wood, Precious Metals, and Canal-related Speculation

The expansion of timber and dyewood exports from Guanacaste in the late nineteenth and early twentieth centuries also played an important role in capital accumulation and the definition of property lines. Europe, North America, and even Peru imported large quantities of cedar, hardwoods, and dyewoods (such as brazil and mora) from Central America throughout the nineteenth and early twentieth centuries; prior to the rise of coffee in the 1830s, brazilwood constituted one of Costa Rica's principal exports (Vega Carballo 1980: 37). The decimation of the more accessible forests in Guanacaste appears to have occurred later than in Puntarenas, just to the south. As early as 1861 a group of German merchants petitioned the Costa Rican government for a reduction in taxes on cedar cut on the Nicoya Peninsula. They noted that elsewhere on the Pacific coast, where taxes were lower, even small trees were being cut, but that mature cedar still abounded along Nicoya's coast (ANCR Hac. 7019—1861: 9–11). Twenty-one years later, C. C. Nutting, a North American naturalist who spent a month collecting bird specimens at Hacienda La Palma in southern Abangares, noted that "rubber, red-wood, and mahogany trees are . . . abundant, although a market for them has not been opened in that region" (Nutting 1882: 383).

In 1882, the same year that Nutting remarked on the lack of markets for Guanacaste's timber, wood exports were declared tax free for a period of six years (ANCR Cong. 9155—1885: 2). Logging interests responded by building new roads to coastal and riverine ports, purchasing wood rights from other landowners, and doggedly defending themselves against perceived competitors. Víctor Guardia—minister of government, brother of former dictator Tomás Guardia, and a prominent Guanacaste landowner—complained of this in an 1895 letter that implicitly reflected his own increased business zeal and aspirations as a logger. According to Guardia, David Hurtado Bustos, a resident of Rivas and owner of Hacienda La Culebra, was denying loggers access to Puerto Culebra, which could only be reached by passing through his property. Guardia noted that in 1884 one Francisco Morazán purchased a large quantity of wood from Hacienda El Jobo, controlled by Hurtado's family, and then built at his own expense a road to Puerto Culebra, from where he shipped the wood to Puntarenas for export. Other hacendados, including Alejandro and Alfonso Salazar and José Cabezas, who purchased timber from the Hurtados, also used the road to export wood. But in 1894, according to Guardia, Hurtado sought to gain direct control over his forest resources and "capriciously closed the gates with wire and ordered that a difficult part of the road be obstructed so that the [logging] carts cannot pass" (ANCR Gob. 2260—1895: 4v).

Although reliable data on wood exports date only from 1883, they

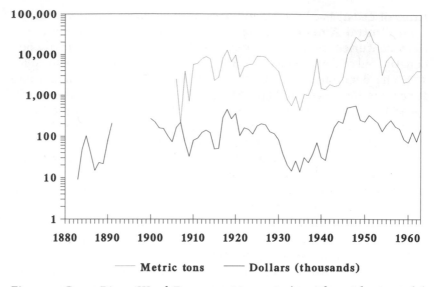

Fig. 1.2. Costa Rican Wood Exports, 1883–1963 (semi-logarithmic scale).
Source: *AE* various years.

suggest a major increase in logging during the 1880s, which lasted
until the depression of the 1930s (see Figure 1.2). The bulk of this
activity was centered in the north Pacific region, as contemporary
descriptive accounts and the brief set of available data on wood
exports by port attest.[29] The list of hacendados who accumulated
small fortunes in the wood trade in the period 1880–1930 reads like a
Who's Who of the Guanacastecan elite.[30] Legal records of the time
indicate that numerous disputes over property lines occurred as a
result of logging activities, that it was common to cut timber without permission on state and private lands, and that considerable
quantities of contraband wood were exported to Nicaragua. Even
when loggers did bother to secure permission to cut wood on state or
private lands, costs were remarkably low, and concessionaires had
ample opportunities for avoiding payment of the nominal charges
they were expected to pay for each ton of wood.[31]

　　After 1907 new state policies permitted the purchase of national
lands on credit and the payment of obligations with products of the
same lands for which credit had been extended. This encouraged a
fresh wave of deforestation. Speculators who purchased state land

sometimes simply returned it to the state once they had stripped off the timber, which constituted the major portion of its value (Soley 1949, 2: 66).

The Guanacaste wood boom occurred at a time when cattle of different owners were still generally left to graze, mingling in un-fenced pastures and woods. This semiferal cattle, unlike standing timber, could be gathered and herded when the moment came to realize its value on the market. Cattle consequently did not figure as importantly at first as did timber in encouraging hacendados to assert claims to land and define property boundaries. By the turn of the century, easily accessible timber was becoming scarce, leading both to increased poaching of wood and to intensified efforts to protect properties. In 1904, for example, the lawyer of Federico Sobrado, a Spanish immigrant and one of the principal hacendados of the early twentieth century, noted in an application for logging rights in San Juanillo de Nicoya "that the little timber which still exists is found in places where it is difficult to cut and bring to the ports and the costs are so high that they do not permit the investor an encouraging profit level" (ANCR Hac. 4627: 1).

Two years earlier, the governor rejected a similar application from a less influential citizen, remarking that "it is well known that wood has become scarce and this would lead the applicant, because of ignorance of property lines or other causes, to commit abuses by entering private lands and thus giving rise to litigation with the injured parties" (ANCR Hac. 4080—1902: 2–2v).

Sobrado's application was approved, however, and even during the decline in wood exports occasioned by the 1930s depression, his San Juanillo properties, which had the advantage of being on the coast, were producing and exporting 5,000 *trozas cúbicas* (of 27 cubic feet each) of wood per year (*El Guanacaste*, 20 Sept. 1935, 3).

Although the felling of trees generated income for rich and poor alike, the benefits of the export trade accrued to a small handful of individuals. A 1911 petition to the Congress from six major Guana-caste loggers argued against reestablishing a tax on wood exports in order to finance hospitals in Guanacaste. They justified their appeal in part because there were only "a half dozen wood exporters in the country" (ANCR Cong. 10785—1911: 1v.), in all likelihood not a greatly exaggerated estimate. The deforestation that accompanied the Guanacaste wood boom of 1880–1930 pales in comparison with that which resulted in the post-1950 period from the expansion of pastures for the beef export trade. Nevertheless, this earlier wave of forest destruction was a necessary condition for the spread of grazing lands and an important factor in the consolidation of the hacienda enterprise.

The discovery of gold in the mountains of Tilarán and Abangares in 1884, in an uninhabited region that consisted almost entirely of *baldíos*, or state lands, also provided a major impetus to the formation of latifundios, as claimants sought to title properties with promising mineral deposits. The gold find occurred in the same year that Minor Keith, the U.S. contractor who built the railroad between the *meseta central* and Costa Rica's Caribbean coast, received 800,000 acres (323,756 hectares) of land from the Costa Rican government for his services. The land grant to Keith, nearly 7 percent of the total area of Costa Rica, was significant primarily in the Atlantic region of Limón, where it provided the base for the banana enclave economy.[32] Nevertheless, in Guanacaste Keith acquired a 30,000-hectare expanse in the Tilarán cordillera and 8,172 hectares in nearby Tenorio, both areas with potential ore deposits, as well as 55,600 forested hectares on the coast of Nicoya (*CLD* 1893, 1: 409–13).[33] In addition to the land from the grant, Keith purchased four haciendas in Guanacaste and five in neighboring Puntarenas. The Tilarán property passed rapidly into the hands of British mining companies, which, by 1923, were reported to be occupying and exploiting, probably for timber as much as for mineral wealth, an additional 50,000 hectares without any legal right whatsoever (*La Gaceta Oficial*, 4 Mar. 1923, 240).

The interoceanic transport route formed by the San Juan River and Lake Nicaragua had, since the mid-nineteenth century, been the object of strategic contention between England, France, and the United States (Millett 1979, chap. 1). In the half century between the Clayton-Bulwar Treaty of 1850, which guaranteed joint U.S. and British control over any canal that might be built through Nicaragua, and the 1902 decision by the United States to build the transisthmian canal in Panama, it was widely believed in Central America that construction of a canal using the San Juan route was imminent. In 1888 a U.S. canal company signed a contract with the Costa Rican government that allowed it—if necessary—to trace a route through Costa Rican territory. In the same year the Costa Rican government, in an effort to impede canal-related speculation, prohibited all claims of state lands in the area north of a line between Tortuguero, on the Atlantic coast, and Murciélago, on the Pacific (ANCR Cong. 9498—

1888). The 1888 prohibition on land claims, however, like a similar measure passed in 1896, was not strictly enforced, and influential hacendados, such as Rivas physician Manuel Joaquín Barrios Guerra, were able to title lands in the prohibited areas without major problems.[34] Between 1889 and 1893 the American company actually began preliminary work on the canal, ceasing operations only when funds ran low (Sibaja 1974: 210). But even after the U.S. decision to build in Panama, the possibility that another canal would be built along the Costa Rican–Nicaraguan border continued to be an important cause of land speculation (Sibaja 1974: 146–48).

Consolidating the Haciendas: The Titling Process

These new opportunities for profitable use of the land required at least some change in the traditional pattern of free access to open *sitios*, or rangeland. But how did this consolidation of the hacienda occur? The question must be considered both on a juridical level and in regard to the actual assertion of control over the land with the concomitant enclosures and expulsions of peasant occupants. The juridical aspect of the problem, which will be considered here, involved monopolizing titles to lands, a process that left a fairly clear set of evidence; the actual process of appropriation and the peasant resistance this provoked are considered in Chapter 4.

In the colonial period, the lowland plain along the eastern bank of the Tempisque, between the towns of Cañas and Liberia, was the principal area of cattle production in the Costa Rican jurisdiction. In the second half of the nineteenth century, large tracts of untitled state lands interspersed with occasional absentee-owned haciendas were still found to the north and west of Liberia (in what had been the Alcaldía Mayor de Nicoya), to the south of Cañas and along the entire length of the largely uninhabited volcanic cordillera that marked the eastern border of Guanacaste province. On the peninsula, from the town of Nicoya north to Filadelfia, the traditional access of the peasantry to cofradía lands, as well as the greater agricultural potential of the alluvial soils, had brought about a denser settlement pattern and a somewhat less concentrated landholding pattern.

In each of these areas the titling of lands and the consolidation of latifundios followed a somewhat different course. Throughout the nineteenth and early twentieth centuries the Costa Rican state viewed the granting or sale of national lands as a key means of amortizing debts and raising revenue. The most notorious example was the 800,000-acre land grant to Minor Keith who, in addition to building the railroad to Limón, agreed to pay off the country's entire foreign debt. Titles to national lands were also acquired in many cases under various concession laws (*leyes de gracias*), which, rather than granting land as a means of raising revenue, did so with a view to stimulating agriculture and ranching. In Guanacaste this type of claim occurred with increasing frequency after 1870, especially in the area north and west of Liberia and along the cordillera north of the mining areas. In some cases, claimants merely paid a nominal inscription fee, as in 1878 when Baltasar Baldioceda Estrada, an hacendado from Liberia, titled three caballerías (some 136 hectares) near Puerto Culebra for a mere 8.75 pesos (ANCR JCA 5453—1878). An 1878 law, which provided free concessions of 10 caballerías (452 hectares) to individuals who formed herds of cattle of at least 300 head, encouraged hacendados to turn their animals loose in state lands adjacent to their farms as a means of expanding their properties.[35]

A similar law in 1892, intended to benefit small agriculturalists, provided concessions of unspecified size to anyone cultivating state lands. This also led to the creation of some sizable estates. The Sobrados' Hacienda Santa María, which came to include over 6,000 hectares, grew through claims of this kind, such as one of 1,044 hectares that cost the claimants two pesos per hectare (ANCR JCA 5649—1891–1893). Municipalities also auctioned *gracias*, or scrip, that could be used to claim state lands. At first these rights only permitted successful bidders to acquire lots of up to 100 hectares within the municipality. But after 1907 gracias could be used for claims outside the territory of the issuing municipality, without ever subjecting the sale to competitive bidding.[36] At various times huge grants were made on an ad hoc basis; as late as 1920, for example, the state conceded the right to 10,000 hectares in Guanacaste to one Marcial Peralta for the cultivation of henequen fiber, also giving him the option of purchasing an additional 10,000 hectares for two dollars per hectare (Soley 1949, 2: 194).

On the Nicoya peninsula the process of land monopolization, which did not reach the extremes that it did elsewhere in Guanacaste, was closely tied to the nineteenth-century liberal reforms that led to the sale of church and cofradía properties. In central Costa Rica the expropriation of ecclesiastical holdings began in the late colonial period, with Bourbon decrees in 1804–9 (Gudmundson 1983a). The alienation of church and communal lands in Costa Rica did not, however, have far-reaching effects on the country's political and agrarian structures, such as those that characterized later reforms in some other Central American countries—Guatemala and El Salvador, for example. This was due both to Costa Rica's sparse population and abundant land, which meant that fewer conflicts developed over dissolving traditional forms of property, and to Costa Rica's weak "colonial heritage," specifically the absence of a genuine "conservative reaction" originating with sectors rooted in the colonial export economy and power structure (Cardoso 1975b: 15).

Measures passed with a view to privatizing remaining communal lands in the central part of the country had an impact, nevertheless, in peripheral areas, such as Guanacaste. In the 1830s and 1840s, auctions of large properties belonging to the cofradías of the Nicoya church (and totaling hundreds of caballerías) were carried out over the objections of local residents who had long had access to these lands (Gudmundson 1983a). Legal battles and the actual physical occupation of the properties prevented the successful bidders and their heirs from taking possession of most of the lands until the late 1860s. The early nineteenth-century liberal reforms in the Nicoya Peninsula, however, were anything but thorough.[37] Some ecclesiastical lands, such as the 3,204-hectare hacienda of Jesus of Nazareth, only passed into private hands in the 1890s (CN uncat. 27 and uncataloged plans), while at least one cofradía property, the Hacienda de Nuestro Amo, which had been donated as common land to the residents of Filadelfia, remained in dispute until after 1920.

Elsewhere on the peninsula, in the late nineteenth and early twentieth centuries, many peasants gained rights to pieces of what had been ecclesiastical properties through the squatters' rights established in the 1885 Fiscal Code and the 1888 Civil Code. These measures provided that those who occupied lands "in good faith," believing them to be state lands, and who went unchallenged by the owners for three months, could obtain title after a year (Sáenz P. and Knight 1972). Even in the mid-twentieth century, however, the notion of communal property remained strong enough in some areas to inspire verbal attacks on alleged *acaparadores*, or land grabbers. In Sardinal, for example, in 1947, residents accused a Liberia politician who owned a 275-hectare farm of usurping communal or state lands that they had long freely used. The summation of his successful defense, though, indicated clearly that the era of common property and the open range had passed: "On no side does this property border on national lands and much less on the 'lands of Sardinal and Belén,' which exist only in the imagination of the *sardinaleños*" (*El Guanacaste*, 15 July 1947, 4).

Almost all colonial-era titles to haciendas, which ranged from 5 or 10 up to 100 caballerías, were smaller than their late-nineteenth- and early-twentieth-century counterparts. Occasionally Crown authorities issued deeds to much larger extensions (Fonseca Corrales 1983: 339–49; Sequiera 1985: 72–73), and the size of the caballería itself was subject to varying interpretations. But in general colonial and early-nineteenth-century haciendas were considerably smaller than the latifundios that emerged in the late nineteenth and early twentieth centuries. The most dramatic process of land monopolization by the Guanacastecan hacendados took place in the first decades of the twentieth century with the "rectification of measurements" in old deeds and the titling of "demasías," or "excess lands." These two procedures were slightly different means of arriving at the same end: the first, *rectificación de medidas*, allowed landowners to adjust the total area of a title upward to the real area enclosed within the boundaries specified in the title; the second, *inscripción de demasías*, permitted the titling of unclaimed public lands that had been occupied de facto by owners of adjacent properties. An idea of the possibilities for expansion these procedures afforded the hacienda enterprise is suggested by a 1921 petition to the Congress from 170 peasants of Cañas Dulces de Liberia, which asked "that Congress assure that the plaintiff demanding measurement of property not be allowed to inscribe in a title to demasías any extension of land beyond 2,000 *percent* of that specified in his property titles" (ANCR Cong. 12473—1921: IV, emphasis added).

The concrete reality of titling "rectifications" and "demasías" was not far removed from the petitioners' fears. Hacienda El Viejo, one of the former Nicoya cofradía properties, which measured ten caballerías (452 hectares) when it was acquired for 4,000 pesos by Alfonso Salazar Selva from Rosa Guzmán in 1881, was registered by one of Salazar's sons in 1911 with an area of 23,347 hectares (ANCR LCP r. 1264, no. 110—1895; *La Gaceta Oficial*, 9 Aug. 1928, 1028; Gudmundson 1982: 79); Hacienda El Jobo, near Liberia, a royal grant of 35.5 caballerías (1,605 hectares) dating from 1754, was expanded by Francisco Hurtado Guerra to 18,618 hectares by the 1920s (ANCR

GJC r. 1517, no. 11—1940); Hacienda Tempisque, property of the Spaniard Federico Sobrado, whose four titles totaled 7,342 hectares at the turn of the century when he purchased the land, grew to 19,221 hectares as a result of "rectifications" in 1920 (ANCR LJC r. 1264, no. 771—1920);[38] Hacienda Las Ciruelas, acquired by the North American George Wilson in 1922 as a 6,244-hectare property, expanded to 22,249 hectares in 1934 when it was remeasured and the "excess" demasías were inscribed in the property registry (ANCR LJC r. 1418, no. 177—1934).

It is important to remember that in all these cases the haciendas mentioned constituted only part of their respective owners' holdings. The largest landowners of the early twentieth century, such as those mentioned here, usually carried out "rectifications" of several properties at a time, resulting in the consolidation of titles to tens of thousands of hectares. By the 1920s there were over a dozen latifundistas who owned at least 10,000 hectares each (see Appendix A). A similar number of others owned properties of several thousand hectares each, though some who were major forces in the cattle market do not appear to have been landowners on a scale proportionate to their share of the herd.[39]

Some of the largest latifundistas listed in Appendix A, like Francisco Hurtado Guerra—who married his first cousin and thus inherited land from two branches of the Hurtado family—were descendants of the colonial elite from Rivas, Nicaragua.[40] Other hacendados with less than 10,000 hectares whose properties were often inherited from colonial forbears included members of the Alvarado, Muñoz, Santos, Rivas, and Rivera families, members of the Liberia elite with ties to Rivas (Sequiera 1985: 89–101). Other Nicaraguan landlords, like Luis Morice Belmonte and Manuel Barrios Guerra, also belonged to the Rivas elite but were more recent arrivals in Guanacaste. Like Hurtado, Barrios acquired some holdings through an advantageous marriage, in his case to Carmen Sacasa Hurtado, a daughter of two powerful Nicaraguan landholding families. Alfonso Salazar and Elías Baldioceda were Nicaraguan-descended members of the elite from Liberia, while Pánfilo Valverde, Julio Sánchez, and Maximiliano Soto Fernández were all prominent members of the central Costa Rican upper class. Non-Nicaraguan foreign landlords were relatively recent arrivals in Costa Rica, such as Minor Keith, the River Plate Trust (a mining company which acquired rights to lands in Guanacaste granted Keith as part of the Atlantic railway deal), or the French

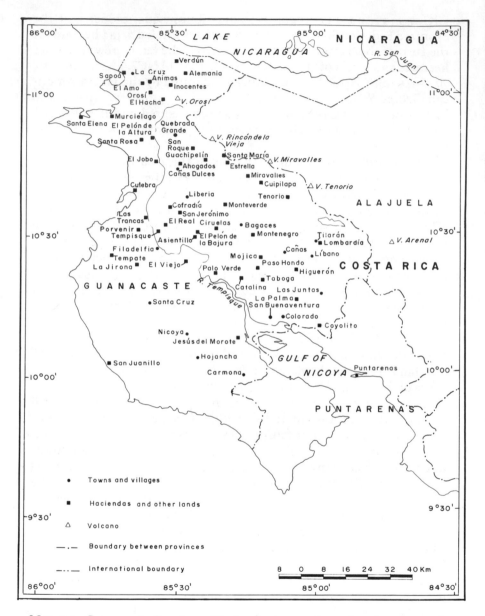

Map 1.3. Guanacaste Province: Haciendas (properties referred to in text).

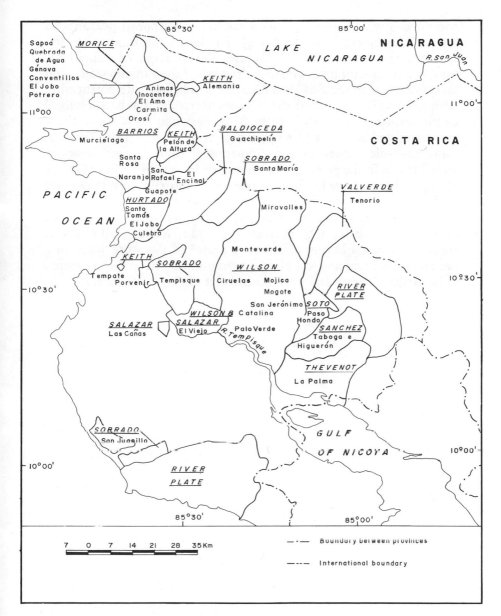

Map 1.4. Guanacaste: Principal Landowners' Holdings c.1920–c.1935 (property boundaries of those listed in Appendix A).

hacendados who hoped to start a colony of European peasants in lowland Abangares (see Chapter 4). The largest latifundista in the province, the North American George Wilson, acquired a small fortune as a contractor for Bolivian railroads and the Panama Canal and then as a logger in Pacific Costa Rica. In 1922 he formed a partnership with Alfonso Salazar to buy the Bagaces haciendas that had belonged to the former president of Costa Rica, Bernardo Soto. Once these properties and Salazar's El Viejo were "rectified," Wilson, who became the sole owner in 1925, controlled over 133,000 hectares stretching from the peaks of the volcanoes to the coast of the Gulf of Nicoya. This massive holding represented approximately 13 percent of the entire province of Guanacaste (see maps 1.3 and 1.4).

Part of the rationale for this expanding latifundismo involved changes in the technology of livestock production, as well as in the transport and marketing of cattle. Control of the work force in a period of labor scarcity was also a powerful impetus to the enclosure of haciendas. These issues are the subject of the next chapter.

2 → Technology, Transport, and Markets

> This grass is certainly most welcome and does not offer the least difficulty of having to fell trees or to weed, because it alone opens space for itself and with time augments itself prodigiously.
> —Hacendado praising African pasture grass, 1907

Even when Guanacastecan haciendas encompassed thousands of hectares, they were generally rustic enterprises, carved out of the woods or savannas, and had little in common with the opulent great estates of Mexico or El Salvador. Landowners often had large though not luxurious residences in Liberia, Rivas, or other towns, and occasionally in San José. But their country hacienda houses were usually basic affairs of unpainted wood, with roofs of clay tile—or somewhat later, sheet metal—and with living areas mounted high up on thick piles or built over dusty storerooms. A few hacendados permitted themselves the luxury of a stone and concrete foundation or masonry walls, but in most cases the few signs of ostentation reflected the rural setting rather than a preoccupation with more cosmopolitan standards of consumption. The Swedish archeologist and biologist Carl Bovallius, for example, who visited Hacienda Ciruelas in 1882, was most impressed with the owner's chairs, which had "high backs covered with jaguar [*tigre*] skins" (1977: 106). Pennsylvania zoologists Amelia and Philip Calvert, who sojourned in 1910 at Hacienda Guachipelín, north of Liberia on the slopes of the volcanic cordillera, described the simple and somewhat dilapidated hacienda building:

[It] stood on the top of a small hill, [and] was L-shaped, the inner angle of the L with a southerly exposure. Its walls were built of wide boards and the roof was partly of tiles, partly of corrugated galvanized iron. The front or south side had a veranda to which one ascended by some tumble-down tile steps; the floor of the veranda was likewise tiled while the house within had wooden floors. There were three rooms in the main part of the house and a kitchen in the shorter arm of the L. The main room opened both at the front (south) and back (north) with rather heavy wooden doors; here we ate and here our host . . . slept. . . . The windows had wooden shutters but no sashes and of course no glass—only the better and more recently built houses in the towns have glass windows. Every now and then a pig ran in at one door of our dining-room and out of the other; two cats regularly came to beg at our table at mealtime, but the three or four dogs were less frequent visitors. (Calvert and Calvert 1917: 434)

Criollo Cattle

The absence of affectation at Hacienda Guachipelín, as at the other large estates in the province, was an inevitable consequence of the low level of economic activity. As late as the eighteenth century, cattle were not truly a commodity produced for exchange, but were virtually a natural resource that reproduced itself with minimal human intervention and from which different products, such as tallow and hides, were extracted for small and ephemeral markets. Even after the growth of markets for live cattle, first in Nicaragua and El Salvador and later in central Costa Rica, this extraction of feral and semiferal animals remained the basic activity on the haciendas. The cattle, as the mid-nineteenth-century traveler John L. Stephens observed (1969, 1: 385), multiplied "almost as wild as the deer."[1] Even in 1910 the Calverts observed that "the cattle of Guanacaste are only half-tame and have a reputation for fierceness—they are 'bravos' " (1917: 419). Given the nature of the livestock, as on other Latin American frontiers, "raising cattle was at first far less important than hunting them" (Baretta and Markhoff 1978: 588).

Notions of land and livestock property were imprecise in a grazing system based on open, unfenced rangeland. Hacendados generally had rights to a number of livestock thought to be grazing in a particular *sitio* and to a proportion of the annual increase in the livestock population, which was counted and branded during an annual rodeo, or roundup. The sitios—usually natural savannas, brushland, or dry tropical forest—were often jointly owned by more than one hacendado. Until the late nineteenth century hacendados made little effort to plant pasture grass. The only fences were small, rudimentary stone or wood corrals, for branding, milking, and counting the animals, or hedgerows of *piñuela* cactus (*Bromelia pinguin*) that surrounded tiny plots of maize, beans, and rice.

Until the early twentieth century the livestock of northwestern Costa Rica were almost exclusively "creole" cattle (*ganado criollo*), feral and semiferal descendants of animals imported by the Spanish shortly after the conquest.[2] The prevalence of open sitio grazing inevitably led to the inbreeding of stock, since calves were only rarely separated from their mothers, and bulls and cows mingled without any effort to direct the selection process. *Criollo* cattle are almost universally disparaged in existing sources.[3] The governor of Puntarenas, commenting on the cattle in the Lepanto district of the Nicoya Peninsula, remarked "that they supply daily the milk necessary for [only] a dozen curds" (ANCR Cong. 18734—1938: 4–4v.). An agronomist writing in 1937 noted that criollo cattle were in general small, "very wild and lively," and difficult to handle, that cows gave birth in the woods and underbrush and tended to hide the calves, and that a growing percentage of cows were born sterile, which was probably an indication of a high level of inbreeding (Matamoros 1937: 11–15). Cattle often passed as much as a year without being checked for parasites and diseases, although on smaller haciendas such examinations were likely to occur more frequently. One report on an hacienda in Cañas noted that the cattle were only checked every two months and recommended that this be done every fifteen days and that sick animals be isolated, thus implying that this was not a general practice in the late 1930s (Castro Esquivel 1938: 15).[4] The custom of leaving bulls and heifers in the same grazing areas meant that young heifers frequently became pregnant before developing the strength for normal gestation, that cows often died giving birth, and that the young were weak. This problem was exacerbated by the failure to provide supplementary fodder to lactating cows (Biolley 1889: 64–65). The only positive qualities described in the sources on criollo cattle were that the animals searched out green plants during droughts without the intervention of their owners and that they made excellent oxen (Matamoros 1937: 15).

Mortality estimates for criollo calves ranged from 16 to 60 percent, with most of the animals succumbing to wild dogs or coyotes, tick or screwworm infections, or hunger from being abandoned in the underbrush by their mothers.[5] On the larger haciendas one of the principal tasks of the *sabaneros* (literally "savanna men")—as cowboys were called in Guanacaste—was the search for newborn calves in the open sitios.[6] Since bulls and cows mingled in the same areas, calves were born throughout the year; a more scientific system of herd management would have programmed births for the least risky, dry-season months. It was estimated in the 1930s that the search for newborn calves and the subsequent efforts to disinfect them required two to three days of a sabanero's time per calf (Matamoros 1937: 15).

Calves rescued from the hazards of the sitios, lactating cows, and those that were found in the grazing areas in an advanced state of pregnancy were confined in corrals near the center of the hacienda.[7] Here they underwent rudimentary treatment with disinfectant to heal the umbilical cord, to remove horns, and—for the male animals of seven to twelve months—castration, a procedure intended to improve the quality of the meat and decrease aggressiveness. This operation involved binding the animals' legs or tying them to a large post in the center of the corral that was also used for branding and was appropriately termed a *bramadero*, or "bellowing place." In most haciendas the castration of young steers was carried out in the early months of the rainy season, usually in June or July, so that the animals could recuperate on the more nutritious and abundant grass of that period.

Even though lactating cows frequently did not provide sufficient milk for the maintenance of their young, high calf mortality contributed to a significant surplus of milk, particularly during the rainy months of May to November. The marketing of this milk was beset by numerous obstacles. Roads and transport were inadequate, especially during the wet season, milk prices tended to drop drastically in the rainy months, and it was difficult to store dairy products in an extremely hot climate. In the face of these difficulties many hacendados opted to give the fresh milk to the peons and their families rather than face the risks of a small and uncertain market. This situation provided ammunition for those hacendados who argued for the crossing of criollo cattle with improved breeds and for increased attention to dairying. In 1907, for example, Manuel Santos, a landowner from Liberia, commented on the hacendados' failure to "squeeze the juice out of their haciendas with the milk of their cows" and noted the irony that "in no town in the Republic are milk and cheese more expensive than in Liberia, and neither does any canton in the Department [of Guanacaste] have more cattle" (in Valverde 1907: 34).[8]

Cheese and milk production was most common in the peninsular zone, where smallholders tended to have largely female herds, rather than on the large properties of Liberia, Bagaces, and Cañas, where steers predominated. In 1909, for example, Guanacaste was reported to have 1 butter manufacturer, 19 cheese manufacturers, and 192 dairies; 154 of the dairies and 9 cheese manufacturers were in the peninsular cantons of Nicoya and Santa Cruz (*AE* 1909).[9] Nevertheless, the *quesera*, or cheese plant, and the *chimbo*, a closed shed for smoking cheeses, were standard fixtures on many haciendas. Here the curd was pressed in large molds (*cinchos*), dried and preserved in the smokehouse, wrapped in cowhide containers, and sent overland or by river launch through Puntarenas to markets in central Costa Rica. For those haciendas located on the major transport routes, such as the 23,000-hectare El Viejo located near the Tempisque River ports of Ballena and Bolsón, cheese was of considerable economic importance, second in most cases only to timber and cattle as a source of revenue. In El Viejo, in the second decade of this century, each of the four *queseras* on the hacienda milked an average of 100 cows a day and produced a *quintal* (100 pounds) of the dry white product known in the entire region as "Bagaces cheese" (*queso Bagaces*).[10]

Transhumance and Latifundismo

The severity of the annual drought meant that grazing involved a seasonal migration of the herds to areas where there was surviving green vegetation.[11] Successful haciendas had to have access to dry-season *sitios* either in the moist zones of the cordillera or along the rivers or coast. Aristides Baltodano Guillén, a young Liberia agronomist and son of a prominent landholding family, described this transhumant grazing as follows:

In the dry season each hacendado takes advantage of the resources that nature provides him, some placing their cattle in the woods where the cattle stay taking advantage of the fruits of the forest: fruits of the tempisque tree, fruits and leaves of the ojoche tree, and grasses that the humid forest conserves fresh; others drive them to the banks of the rivers where the water and the vegetation along the banks maintain them; those that are able use the coasts, where the estuaries and the vegetation near the sea permit them to stay until the rains return. (Baltodano 1937: 4)

Access to the coast or to the brackish lower reaches of the Tempisque River and its tributaries was also important because it allowed animals to ingest the necessary salt and to bathe in seawater, which in the period before the introduction of antiparasite baths in the

1930s was one of the few means of controlling ectoparasite infesta-
tion. This need to control different ecological zones for transhumant
grazing was a raison d'être for latifundismo.[12] But its importance was
often overstated by apologists who confused, intentionally or not,
latifundismo as a system of control over land and transhumance as
an adaptation to seasonal aridity. The largest properties, such as
those of Wilson, Barrios, and Hurtado, comprised both "highland"
(de altura) and "lowland" (de bajura) haciendas and stretched from
the upper reaches of the volcanoes to the coasts of the Gulf of Nicoya
or the Pacific, including as well numerous large and small river
courses. Against accusations that this massive appropriation of lands
might be motivated by avarice rather than the simple requirements
of transhumant grazing, the landowners and their defenders were
always quick to raise the issue of the harsh Guanacaste dry season.
Typical of this style of argument was the response of Francisco Faerrón Suárez—who, like his father before him, was the principal lawyer for the province's hacendados—to a 1943 newspaper article titled
"More than One Hundred Kilometers of Latifundios." Writing for
readers who were mostly from smallholding, coffee-growing central
Costa Rica, Faerrón explained with patronizing self-righteousness
the difference between Guanacaste's "highland" and "lowland" haciendas:

It is not a question of "monopolized lands, without any utilization, taken
away from the labor of man through ambition or selfishness," as the author
of the article seems to understand it, but rather of sitios populated with
young cattle that include good lands and bad lands, the latter more than the
former. The good lands with forests and natural pastures are found in the
lowlands by the rivers and in the slopes of the cordilleras, where the cattle
graze in the dry season in the so-called highland haciendas. The bad lands are
the plains, covered with sparse vegetation and also with natural grass, but of
very poor quality and utilizable only in the rainy season; because in the dry
season they dry out and fire leaves the ground like a paved street. . . . In the
lowland haciendas, it is the opposite of in the highland ones. During the dry
season the cattle graze in the low regions, which in the rainy season are
inundated by the waters of the Tempisque River that form huge lakes. When
these drain off or evaporate they leave grasses where the cattle feed in the dry
season. (La Tribuna, 15 Aug. 1943, 9–10)

In the polemics over the cattle ranchers' land needs, this use of
transhumance to justify latifundismo was one of the principal recur-
ring themes.[13] Given the prevailing technology and the abundance of

land for grazing, an annual migration of the herds was a reasonable solution to difficult ecological problems. Indeed, this practice had been virtually essential to the cattle ranchers in the region since the colonial period. Transhumance, however, has very different implications when the land tenure system is based on free access to open sitios, as was the case in most of Guanacaste until the early twentieth century, than when a small number of owners actually take control of the different grazing zones and prevent others from gaining access. The impetus for this latter course of action was in part the advent of technological innovations that greatly increased the potential profitability of cattle ranching.

Artificial Pastures

The introduction of improved pasture grasses in the late nineteenth and early twentieth centuries was the first significant modification in this rudimentary system of livestock production, which, as late as 1937, was said to be maintaining "nearly the same norms and routines as a century ago" (Baltodano 1937: 7). Even in 1948 one observer, a cattleman from more-developed central Costa Rica, exaggerated only slightly when he lamented that "now the same methods and primitive systems are used that the original colonists implanted various centuries ago and in spite of there having been governments that expressed the desire to stimulate this retrograde industry" (Rossi 1948: 118).

Large areas of natural grasslands existed in the province at the time of conquest, but repeated burning, trampling by cattle, and the spread of secondary-succession brush species—*charral* or *tacotal* in local parlance—probably resulted in a long-term reduction in the carrying capacity of many sitios. People set fires in the sitios for a number of reasons: ranchers burned grazing areas each year to eliminate ticks, parasites, snakes, and other animals that could harm the cattle and to stimulate the growth of new grass, swidden cultivators, who employed fire to clear land for planting, at times lost control of their blazes and ended up incinerating large areas; hunters set blazes, hoping to attract deer to the green shoots that emerged after burning; other fires produced by simple carelessness spread rapidly during the dry season in the high winds and tinderlike vegetation of the lowlands; and finally, arson, and the burning of sitios, was one of the principal expressions of peasant resistance to landlord encroachments.

Whatever the ultimate cause of the frequent fires, and in spite of the fact that they returned minerals to the soil in the form of ash, repeated burning brought about lowered soil fertility. Fire destroyed both nitrogen-fixing legumes, which were also nutritious fodder for cattle, and microorganisms that broke down organic matter and contributed to humus formation (Daubenmire 1972a: 398, and 1972b: 51–52; Boulière and Hadley 1970: 134–37). Native grasses, referred to by the generic terms "natural pasture" or *grama*, were, in any case, of limited nutritive value and, especially in the dry season, could support only an extremely extensive grazing pattern.

Various species of foreign pasture grasses, which had evolved in association with dense populations of wild ruminants in East African savannas and which consequently were more productive and more palatable to livestock, began to be imported to the New World in the eighteenth century (Parsons 1972: 12, 17).[14] All these species of grass are aggressive invaders, able to establish themselves rapidly over wide areas and to suppress competing kinds of growth. While they respond to higher levels of soil nutrients than those in their areas of origin, they are usually well suited to the humus-poor, relatively infertile soils typical of derived savannas.

Although several varieties of African grasses were imported to Costa Rica in the 1860s (León et al. 1981: II-12), they were planted almost exclusively in highland areas of the *meseta central*. The first African forage plant to be introduced in Guanacaste was almost certainly one of the species of *Panicum* commonly referred to as *pará*, a grass already present in Nicaragua in the early 1870s (Levy 1965: 90–91).[15] It was apparently well known in Guanacaste by the 1890s, when several mentions of pará pastures appeared in descriptions of Guanacaste properties and land claims, all apparently assuming that pará was familiar to those for whom the documents were written (e.g., ANCR GJC 96—1897; Villafranca 1895: 125). Although pará is especially suited for planting in poorly drained bottom lands, where it propagates by runners, its wide adaptability and its superiority over local varieties of grama meant that it was at first planted even in haciendas on the upper slopes of the cordillera.[16]

Guinea grass (*Panicum maximum* or *Panicum jumentorum*), which grows in large clumps and reaches a height of two meters, was introduced to Costa Rica in 1885 and rapidly became the preferred grass for artificial pastures, since it was considered more nutritious than pará, grew better at higher altitudes, and remained green longer into the dry season.[17] The aggressive colonizing characteristics of this species and the consequent ease with which it could be established are suggested in the 1907 remarks of Manuel Santos, a modernizing hacendado from Liberia:

Few are the haciendas which have, outside of their [natural] fields, pastures for the care of their cattle, but forage for a finca of this kind is indispensable. The highland haciendas can be improved by spreading guinea seed in the underbrush. This grass is certainly most welcome and does not offer the least difficulty of having to fell trees or weed, because it alone opens space for itself and with time augments itself prodigiously. . . . In our finca . . . in the parts that have infertile land and where the development of the woods is poor, we have tried spreading guinea in the brush, and one year later we have seen it become pasture without the necessity of felling the thick and medium-size trees. (in Valverde 1907: 33)

Other exotic species that had an especially significant impact on the cattle industry in Guanacaste were the Australian *ajengibrillo* (*Paspalum notatum*) and the African jaragua (*Hyparrhenia rufa*).[18] *Ajengibrillo*, also called *jengibrillo*, spread so rapidly in Costa Rica that many believed it to be a native species (e.g., Feo 1911; Pittier 1978: 179; Sáenz 1955: 28; León et al. 1981: II-12). *Ajengibrillo* probably arrived in Costa Rica at about the turn of the century and jaragua in about 1910. Jaragua, because its long roots are capable of reaching subsurface water, is remarkably drought resistant. During the prolonged drought of the 1920s, jaragua was termed "the salvation of Guanacaste," and it soon became the most widespread of the foreign grasses (Acuña Acevedo 1936: 14; Parsons 1976: 130).[19] The invasive qualities of jaragua, however, are most pronounced only if it is subject to annual burning. If it is not grazed closely or burned and is allowed to reach its full height of over two meters, the stalks become increasingly fibrous and lose nutritive value (Parsons 1972: 16). The popularity of jaragua and the necessity of an annual burning, with its concomitant destruction of humus and carrying capacity, meant that the very characteristics of the grass itself locked hacendados into a system of pasture monoculture that could only be reversed with great difficulty and at great cost.

The intensification of production that these exotic grasses made possible may be appreciated if we consider that while ten *manzanas* (6.99 hectares) of natural pasture, or sitio, were required per head of cattle, pastures of pará, guinea, or jaragua could support one head per manzana in the dry season and up to three head per manzana in the rainy season (Baltodano 1937: 14; Maduro 1935: 2). In the four decades after 1909, the area in planted or "artificial" pastures in Guanacaste nearly quadrupled, from 26,000 to over 100,000 hectares, growing much faster than the total area in pastures that included less-dynamic native grasses (AE 1909; CAP 1950). In spite of the hacendados' enthusiasm for artificial pastures, however, the government was slow to recognize the foreign species' potential (León et al. 1981: II-12) and discouraged their adoption, probably inadvertently, in at least one section of the province. When protectionist legislation intended to limit the importation of Nicaraguan steers was passed in 1932, it restricted the number of cattle that could be held in each type of pasture in the frontier district of La Cruz. Ranchers who were found to have more than one steer for every 2 hectares of guinea or pará, for every 3 hectares of ajengibrillo or grama, or for every 30 hectares of unimproved sitio were considered to have exceeded the capacity of their grazing lands. This in turn was said to be prima facie evidence of possession of contraband cattle and meant that import taxes had to be paid on the excess animals, whether or not it could be proven that they had actually been smuggled from Nicaragua (ANCR Cong. 20933—1932: 8).

The spread of artificial pastures became one aspect of the conflict that arises in arid (or seasonally arid) zones where small agriculturalists coexist with large cattle ranchers and where livestock raising, rather than being part of a complementary complex of crop culture and animal husbandry as in humid temperate regions, competes with agriculture for land and water. In Guanacaste, investment in the soil required a more effective possession of that soil, and enclosures of haciendas were the logical consequence. But the expansion of pastures, hardly a major investment in most cases, was in effect a kind of enclosure, even in the absence of barbed wire fences. Guanacastecan peasants are, to this day, extremely reluctant to undertake the expensive process of clearing lands planted with grass (terrenos empastados) for cultivation, preferring instead tacotales, or areas with secondary-succession brush species. Removing jaragua or other pasture grasses from fields was a costly undertaking that even large landowners rarely considered until lucrative alternatives to cattle, as well as agricultural machinery and chemical herbicides, became widely available after 1950.

Recognizing the potential for conflict between agriculturalists and cattle ranchers, the Costa Rican government had set aside, as early as 1840, one mile of land along the coasts and the banks of navigable rivers for the free use of agriculturalists, fishermen, salt producers, and sailors. Ranchers were required to keep their cattle at least five leagues (fifteen miles) from the coast of the Gulf in order to protect the small agriculturalists, though it is extremely unlikely that this rule could ever have been strictly enforced. Subsequently the width of this maritime reserve was reduced to 2,000 yards (*varas*) in 1868 and to 200 meters in 1936 (Salas Marrero and Barahona 1980: 244–48; Vicarioli 1952: 19).[20] By 1902, however, congressional deputy Agustín Guido charged that along the Gulf of Nicoya,

The exuberance of that zone attracted the attention of the cattlemen, who, abusing the concession given in favor of the agriculturalists, have converted most of the area into enormous pastures for fattening and breeding cattle. The destruction of the forest near the estuaries and the loose cattle in the [maritime] mile have caused few people to undertake the extraction of salt, because of the lack of nearby firewood, or the cultivation of cereals, because of the damage from all those cattle. . . . The best lands have been converted into large artificial prairies for rich entrepreneurs, and an immense quantity of woods has been closed with the object of forcing out the poor agriculturalists or making them pay for the right of possession. (ANCR Cong. 4557—1902: 1–IV)

Less than two decades later, in 1920, two congressional deputies from northwestern Costa Rica, addressing their colleagues about the agrarian situation in Guanacaste, summed up more succinctly the social consequences of pasture expansion. "Up there in Guanacaste," they declared, "in many places where there used to exist settlements of small agriculturalists, there exist today only artificial pastures [*repastos*] for steers" (ANCR Cong. 15414—1920–1929: 2; also *La Gaceta Oficial*, 9 Aug. 1928, 1098).

Brahman Cattle

The second key technological innovation in livestock production, in addition to the planting of exotic species of grass for artificial pastures, was the introduction of improved breeds of cattle. In central Costa Rica, where cattle were held primarily for dairy purposes or as draft animals, European breeds such as Durham, Jersey, and Holstein had been imported as early as the mid-nineteenth century and rapidly became the dominant element in the bovine population (Vargas 1950: 15–32; Volio 1956–57). In the hot lowlands of Guanacaste, however, where ecological conditions were less favorable to European breeds and where cattle ranching was seldom sufficiently profitable even to warrant the construction of the fences necessary for stock improvement programs, hacendados made only minor efforts to cross local criollos with foreign animals prior to the 1920s.

Since 1849 the Costa Rican government had permitted tax-free imports of cattle, and in 1885 it agreed to subsidize the bringing of animals of "improved races" to Costa Rica by paying all transport costs (Salas and Barahona 1980: 673; Vicarioli 1952: 48). The latter measure had its principal impact in the dairy zones of the *meseta central*. In Guanacaste, some early-twentieth-century hacendados, such as Aníbal Santos and José Cabezas, believed that significant improvements in the herd could be obtained with the genetic material in the criollo cattle population. They argued against advocates of imported varieties that selective breeding of existing stock should be tried before expending resources to bring costly foreign bulls to Guanacaste (Jiménez 1930: 81, 86). Nevertheless, in spite of this apparent resistance to change and to investment, by 1907 a government poll of ranchers found that "the proprietors of large haciendas in Guanacaste . . . in general have cattle of good foreign races" (ANCR Gob. 699—1907: 5). Among the owners of these cattle—generally Guernsey, Red Poll, and Durham stud bulls and their offspring—were the Nicaraguan Alejandro Salazar of Hacienda El Viejo and the Spaniard Federico Sobrado of Hacienda Tempisque, both of whom had artificial pastures fenced with closely planted stalks of *piñuela* cactus. Somewhat later, in 1927, George Wilson imported eighteen Hereford bulls to his estate in Bagaces (*Escuela de Agricultura* 1934: 405). Nevertheless, in Guanacaste the long historical experience of rudimentary practices of herd management weighed heavily against rapid improvement of the stock because, as the same 1907 poll found, "many hacendados endeavor to cross [breeds], but with very little care and with less perfection, as they acquire bulls with some [foreign] blood and then turn them loose in the sitio" (ANCR Gob. 699—1907: 2).

Just as the renovation of Guanacaste's grasslands could only occur on the basis of species adapted to tropical conditions, the large-scale transformation of the cattle herd had to await the introduction of animals that had evolved in similar ecological circumstances. At the turn of the century the United Fruit Company and the massive sugar plantation at Juan Viñas, Cartago, imported Indian (*cebú* or brahman) cattle of the Mysore subrace to the Atlantic side of Costa Rica. Mysore animals, however, were best suited for draft animals, rather than for beef, and did not gain widespread acceptance (Vargas 1950: 37; Sáenz Maroto 1955: 28). The English as well had long recognized the adaptability of brahman cattle to tropical environments, and it is likely that the first brahman imports to Costa Rica, carried out in 1920 by Fernando Castro Cervantes, originated in the British West Indies. Castro Cervantes—a politician and the owner of properties in La Cruz, Guanacaste, and of the huge Hacienda Coyolar, which included parts of four cantons in northern Puntarenas province and two in northern San José—began to import cebú bulls of the Nelore subrace and to sell both pure cebú and cebú-criollo crosses to ranchers throughout Guanacaste and northern Puntarenas (Vargas 1950: 39–46; Gudmundson 1979: 70).[21]

The successful diffusion of Indian, or brahman, breeds such as the Nelore was due fundamentally to their superior adaptation to conditions in Guanacaste and to their rapid maturation and greater finished weight compared with criollo cattle. In addition, Castro's Hacienda Coyolar, part of which lay along the Puntarenas–San José railway, a line much traveled both by steers bound for market and by cattlemen with business in the central part of the country, launched a major publicity drive for Nelore bulls. It placed its finest specimens within view of passing trains and took out advertisements in national and regional newspapers that emphasized that Costa Rica could now follow Argentina's path to cattle-based prosperity (e.g., *El Guanacaste*, 15 Jan. 1939, 6).[22] Possibly as a consequence of this advertising campaign, the example of Argentina (and at times that of Texas) was frequently raised in discussions of the livestock industry—especially after 1930—often in order to argue for greater government intervention in favor of ranchers, such as that which characterized the oligarchical regimes in that country during the depression (Jiménez 1903: 15, and 1930: 82; Baltodano 1937: 11; Vargas 1950: 48–49; *El Guanacaste*, 23 Dec. 1943, 1).

Although the ranchers' hopes of becoming another Argentina did not materialize, brahman and brahman-criollo cattle contributed significantly to the profitability of the hacienda enterprise. Brahman animals thrived even in extremely arid areas with poor pasture. The mortality rate for brahman calves in the first year of life was a mere 2 percent, in large part because of their resistance to ticks and para-sites. The weight of a one-year-old Nelore calf averaged 224 kilos, whereas a one-year-old criollo calf reached only 80 kilos. At two years brahman-criollo steers often reached over 300 kilos, which was close to an acceptable finished weight and nearly three times the weight of the average criollo steer of comparable age. Criollo steers were mar-keted after six or seven years when they had reached a weight of some 400 kilos; in comparison, a brahman steer would often reach over 550 kilos after three or four years (Gudmundson 1979: 70–72).[23] Nev-ertheless, the weight advantage of brahman animals consisted in part of greater skeletal development and a relative excess of useless parts, such as the distinctive cartilaginous hump and large feet and ears. As a result, the meat yield of brahman steers in the 1940s, when both brahman and criollo animals were still being slaughtered, compared unfavorably with criollo steers (Murillo and Barquero 1943: 16; Solís 1981a: 34). But the advantages of a more rapid cycling of capital, of the brahman's superior adaptability to the difficult ecological condi-tions of the tropics, and of the saving involved in managing animals with a greater finished weight assured increasing efforts to inject Indian blood into the criollo herd.

The gradual switch to brahman cattle brought with it significant changes in the organization of production. The Indian breeds were expensive; in 1927, for example, foreign bulls in Guanacaste cost an average of 222 colones, $55.50 at the then current exchange rate, while mixed-blood, or "crossed," bulls cost 107 colones ($26.75) and criollo bulls a mere 68 colones ($17.00) (AE 1927: 45).[24] For the hacendado accustomed to "harvesting" wild animals that multiplied in wooded sitios, investment in improved cattle marked a radical departure from the past and was an early step in the development of a more typically capitalist outlook and a more scientific approach to increasing output. Even if turn-of-the-century ranchers had some-times acquired foreign bulls and then "turned them loose in the sitio," it rapidly became apparent to virtually all that expensive bulls and their offspring must be protected in fenced areas from the depre-dations of rustlers and subject to a systematic selection program.

Wire Fencing

Literature on agrarian change—in Latin America and elsewhere—has often pointed to the introduction of barbed wire fences as a potent symbol of growing landlord domination, comparable to the English enclosures and detested by rural laborers and peasants (e.g., Baretta and Markhoff 1978: 611–12; Dary 1981: 308–31; Taussig 1980: 72–73).[25] In the Guanacastecan case, this perception defines one side of a more complex reality in which both landlords and smallholders had reasons for building or for opposing fences, depending on local circumstances and balances of power. Invented in the United States in the 1870s, barbed wire diffused rapidly to other cattle-raising regions of Latin America (McCallum and McCallum 1965; Reyes 1978: 61–62). But its adoption in northwestern Costa Rica had to await returns that would justify its cost and a level of respect for property that would assure its protection.

During the first four decades of the twentieth century, the fencing of large haciendas followed an uneven, albeit quickening rhythm, largely because of low profit levels, peasant resistance, and landlord reluctance to invest. By the late 1890s Alejandro and Alfonso Salazar, owners of El Viejo, had fenced sections of the hacienda and converted into pasture a road that crossed the property, blocking public access to the Tempisque River port of Ballena (ANCR Gob. 87—1898: 4–7). A few years later, on the opposite side of the river, the United Fruit Company refused to grant local residents the traditional right-of-way across Hacienda Paso Hondo so they could travel between Cañas and the port of Bebedero (ANCR Gob. 1367—1907: 1–3v). Enclosing properties near the provincial capital of Liberia was apparently sufficiently common by 1910 that two foreign biologists, hoping to collect specimens in a brushy area, could remark that "as usual, this *charral* was enclosed by a barbed wire fence" (Calvert and Calvert 1917: 424). By the 1920s the ranks of modernizing hacendados and the lengths of barbed wire fences grew as Minor Keith and Federico Sobrado enclosed most of their holdings. Smallholders too fenced farms that contained not only pasture but sugarcane, plantains, maize, beans, and rice, though this sometimes aroused their neighbors' ire (ANCR Gob. 2025—1907). In some highland areas, such as Quebrada Grande de Liberia, peasants who cultivated coffee and other cash crops had barbed wire fences by the early 1920s (ANCR Gob. 8094—1924: 54).

But elsewhere, both landlords and peasants frequently complained about the high cost of fences in relation to the low returns from agriculture and livestock raising. Some recollections are perhaps apocryphal, such as the story about an owner of La Lupita, a small hacienda in Tempate, Santa Cruz, who on his deathbed is said to have told his wife to collect the wire from the property, because it was worth more than the land.[26] But reluctance or inability to build fences was clearly widespread and was characteristic of both large landowners and smallholders.[27]

Nor did state policies in the early twentieth century provide much incentive for constructing fences. Though the government permitted tax-free importation of barbed wire after 1904 (Sáenz Maroto 1970: 310), a 1909 law declared Guanacaste and several other areas of the country "livestock zones," where it was the responsibility of agriculturalists, rather than cattle ranchers, to construct fences to protect their crops (Vicarioli 1952: 64). Where agricultural zones abutted cattle haciendas, the lack of fences was a constant source of conflict and of anxiety for smallholding peasants. When Tilarán residents petitioned the Congress in 1918 asking to be declared an agricultural zone where ranchers would have to fence their animals, Amadeo Johanning, the interior minister, who happened to be one of Liberia's more important ranchers, argued against the request, averring that "the region of Guanacaste is principally suitable for the cattle industry, to which are dedicated large portions of land that could not be closed with fences without making enormous expenditures" (ANCR Cong. 11122—1918: 11).

Numerous other communities submitted similar petitions during the next three decades. In 1937 residents of Higuerón, in Cañas, complained that "because we are not rich (pudientes), it is natural that we do not have the capacity to fence our crops with competent fences of three or more strands of barbed wire, so as to prevent the cattle that ambulate through the cattle zone, which includes Higuerón and the entire canton of Cañas, from penetrating our fields and destroying our labors and the sustenance of our families" (ANCR Cong. 18414: 5). Four years later peasants in Río Chiquito de Bagaces echoed these concerns, noting that cattle from the Hacienda Tenorio were entering their fields and destroying their rice and maize "without compassion" (ANCR Cong. 19880—1941: iv).

Wire fencing was desired by smallholders and opposed by large ranchers as long as traditional technology prevailed in the cattle sector and livestock invaded peasant crops. Only in the 1920s and 1930s, as growing numbers of landlords attempted to improve their stock and as protectionist legislation brought rising prices, did wire fences truly begin to be a common feature of the Guanacastecan landscape.

In part because of their high price and in part because they symbolized growing landlord hegemony, the theft and destruction of wire fences became a key element of peasant resistance. Complaints were rife of "thefts of wire [and] ignoble acts of vengeance" (ANCR Cong. 13416—1924: iv.) and "disappearing" and "evaporating" fences (*El Guanacaste*, 20 Apr. 1936; Baltodano 1937: 16). Damage to fences, even more than rustling or theft of wood, became one of the main hacendado pretexts for seeking to limit traditional rights-of-way across properties.

For the hacendados, wire fencing facilitated the handling of herds and reduced labor needs, since cattle were less likely to stray. It also made it easier to deny peasants access to subsistence resources and land for cultivation. The crossing of brahman with criollo cattle and the gradual replacement of semiferal animals also implied certain changes in the labor regime. Traditionally, the easily frightened criollo cattle on the large estates often passed months at a time without seeing a human being and, consequently, had to be herded with frequent use of the lasso. The development of a brahman-criollo cross in fenced pastures permitted milder herding techniques that required fewer sabaneros, or cowboys, and resulted in a smaller weight loss for fattened steers during herding.

Increased investment in animals, including barbed wire, generally had to be accompanied by increased expenditures on veterinary medicine and antiparasite baths, which by the 1930s were a common fixture on many large haciendas. The state of animal sanitation remained poor, however, with periodic outbreaks of brucellosis and anthrax (referred to colloquially as "carbón" or "morriña") and widespread tick and screwworm infestations.[28] Beginning in 1919 the government appropriated funds for establishing antiparasite baths in "infested zones." Four years later, owners of more than 500 head were required to build arsenic baths and to vaccinate their animals against anthrax (Vicarioli 1952; Robert 1989), though it is doubtful that many complied fully with such measures. As late as 1945 there was still only one antiparasite bath in Guanacaste for every 14,000 head of cattle (León et al. 1981: II-14).

On the largest estates in the province, such as the seven contiguous Bagaces haciendas that belonged to George Wilson, the hacendados were sometimes slower in adopting the brahman-based system than were the owners of other large but more modest properties. This had implications for their willingness to invest in wire fences, especially if these were for small, rotating grazing areas rather than the outer boundaries of properties. Wilson, for example, though his estate contained some 150 kilometers of fences by the mid-1930s (Escuela de Agricultura 1934: 407), argued with Castro Cervantes, the importer and promoter of cebú bulls, that on such a massive ranch, where cattle were left unattended for six or more months, brahman animals would become uncontrollable and would tear down whatever fences were put up to contain them.[29] Wilson and most of the large hacendados to the north continued to work basically with criollo cattle, though they occasionally experimented with nonbrahman foreign breeds. Even in 1935 an agronomist writing on the Clachar family's Hacienda El Porvenir in Carrillo, while noting that it possessed the best cattle he had seen in Guanacaste, declared that non-criollo cattle had not yet been tried in that region (Maduro 1935: 1–2).[30] To the south and east in Cañas and Tilarán—nearer both to central Costa Rican markets and to Castro's El Coyolar—more cattle ranchers took steps to modernize their herds. By the mid-1930s hacendados with improved cattle included Julio Sánchez, owner of Haciendas Taboga e Higuerón and Palmar, in Cañas and Puntarenas, respectively; Maximiliano Soto of Paso Hondo in Cañas; Luis Demetrio Tinoco of Lombardía in Tilarán; and Matías and Casimiro Sobrado of El Tempisque in Liberia (Cruz 1934: 514; Vargas 1950: 46, 50). In 1935 it was reported that nearly all of the bulls in Tilarán were from Castro's El Coyolar (La Tribuna, 24 Mar. 1935, 12).

Transport and Marketing

The lack of an adequate transport network was one of the principal barriers to economic expansion in Guanacaste until the completion of the Pan-American Highway in the early 1950s. At the turn of the century the situation was still only slightly better than in the colonial era. The products of the region had three ways of reaching markets: an oxcart road to central Costa Rica, passable with certainty only in the dry season because of the lack of bridges; a similar road to Rivas, Nicaragua, generally considered to be in somewhat better condition but also without bridges; and the small launches that plied up and down the coasts of the Pacific Ocean and the Gulf of Nicoya and which, until 1865, had been nothing more than rowboats engaged in local commerce or an occasional sailboat bound for Puntarenas or Nicaragua (Calvo 1887: 132; Sáenz Maroto 1970: 475). The trip from Rivas to San José took eight to ten days on horseback and could take two to three weeks in a cart pulled by oxen. Within the province communications were also quite primitive; as late as 1924, there were only 1,250 kilometers of oxcart roads in Guanacaste, including the old "Camino Real" between Nicaragua and central Costa Rica and the branch that connected it with the towns of the Nicoya Peninsula (Cabrera 1924: 172). The government built a few bridges in the 1920s and 1930s, but this was virtually the only state effort to improve Guanacaste's transport infrastructure prior to the 1940s, when construction began on the Pan-American Highway.

The initiation of regular launch service between Puntarenas and Guanacaste river ports, such as Bebedero, Ballena-Bolsón, and Humo, was a major step toward integrating the region into the national economy. The severe shortage of basic grains that affected central Costa Rica in 1864–65, the result in part of the displacement of food crops by more lucrative plantings of coffee, led the state to purchase steam launches to facilitate the commercialization of comestibles produced in Guanacaste (Sandner 1962, 1: 125). Launch concessions were granted at first to private individuals, who received subsidies for transporting mail and who were allowed to carry passengers and freight for their own benefit at rates set by the government. In the 1890s, with the logging and mining booms, launch service took on new importance, and many new piers were constructed along the coast and on navigable rivers.

Concessionaires received large government subventions. In 1902, when ownership of the boats passed into private hands, each vessel was subsidized at the rate of 1,000 pesos per month (*Memoria de Gobernación, Policía y Fomento 1902–1903*: xx–xxi); a decade later, the monthly subsidy had risen to 1,500 pesos (Périgny 1918: 169). This state support attracted a new wave of investors to run the launches. The hacendado Federico Sobrado, for example, first came to Costa Rica at the end of the nineteenth century to operate a launch business in the Gulf of Nicoya (Lorz 1934: 380). Without exception, launch concession owners were among the largest loggers in the region or had close connections with the mining companies; they included Alberto Fait (with concessions in 1892–99 and 1920–33), José Cabezas Bonilla (1900–2), and Manuel Barahona (1902–12)—all major loggers; and H. T. Perdy (1913–18) and the Manganese Mining Company (1918–20), of which Perdy was a director. Ironically, given the loggers' interest in launch operations, one of the main difficulties of coastal transport by the early twentieth century was the large-scale silting of watercourses brought about by deforestation of the riverbanks (Cabrera 1924: 177).

Launch service, particularly after the introduction of gasoline-powered tugboats and of cattle barges capable of holding up to 100 head, assumed major commercial importance. With the completion of the San José–Puntarenas railroad in 1910, riverine and maritime shipping grew rapidly, since livestock, grain, and other cargo could be sent by boat to Puntarenas and then by rail to central Costa Rica in a total of only two or three days.[31] Expanded river traffic provided a stimulus to both hacienda and smallholder enterprises. One resident of Bolsón described the frenetic harvest-time commerce around the nearby Tempisque River port of Ballena in the 1920s:

The launches left Puntarenas seven or eight hours before and came to Ballena with the high tide. They unloaded rapidly. When they had a lot of merchandise to send from here to there and if the tide was a small one—because not all tides were the same, some days they're smaller than others—then they couldn't load and the launches stayed. One said the launch "lost the tide," or "it arrived with the tide already very old, barely unloaded and didn't have time to load." They carried away the rice, the maize of this entire zone. Some launches left with 100 sacks of maize, 300, it was an exaggeration of maize that they carried. All produced by small producers. Everyone looked for [ox] carts to go to Ballena Port and one carried rice, another maize and so on. And in the launch people went commissioned to sell ten sacks for a friend, other sacks for another friend. . . . We sent 100 sacks in good times. The agriculturalist planted to sell maize and rice. Then people brought pigs, eggs, hens, and cheese and sold it there. Hens brought a very good price in Puntarenas.[32]

Prior to the completion of the launch-rail transport link, the commercialization of livestock in central Costa Rican markets involved overland cattle drives that took from ten to fifteen days, depending on distances and weather conditions. In the 1850s semiannual "on-hoof" shipments from one major hacienda were as large as 300 head (Belly 1974: 204), though in the first decades of the twentieth century the largest hacendados usually sent more frequent but smaller shipments (Périgny 1974: 447). Wilson, for example, in the 1920s and 1930s, sent 40 to 50 head once a week if by barge or biweekly if overland, a schedule that allowed time for his employees to complete the round-trip between Bagaces and central Costa Rica. Often hundreds of steers belonging to different owners would collect in and around the small ports on the Tempisque River, waiting for barges to arrive to take them to Puntarenas.

To minimize weight loss during herding, ranchers and livestock dealers either rented pasture along the route to central Costa Rica or acquired properties that could be used for grazing animals at different points during the journey. Two major nineteenth-century hacendados, Rafael Barroeta and Francisco Giralt, controlled properties at various points from southern Guanacaste to the vicinity of the Cartago and Alajuela cattle markets (Gudmundson 1979: 73). Minor Keith's northwestern empire is also an illustrative, if perhaps extreme, example of the same phenomenon. In the 1920s and 1930s the railroad baron and his heirs had interests in Hacienda Alemania, on the Nicaraguan frontier, which—like many frontier properties— may have been used for contraband cattle imports after tariffs were imposed in 1932; Hacienda El Pelón de la Altura, 6,600 hectares of fenced sitios on the road between the border and Liberia; El Porvenir and La Lupita, in Carrillo and Santa Cruz cantons near the Tempisque River; a share in a lot in Cañas Dulces de Liberia; two large lots in Cañas and Abangares; six major properties in the Chomes-Aranjuez area of northern Puntarenas in close proximity to the rail line; and additional holdings near the Alajuela market (ANCR MP 285—1926; CN uncat.; *La Nueva Prensa*, 3 July 1926, 2; RPPG T1066, F334, N6636).

Steers herded overland to market, if grazed along the way, sustained an average weight loss of only 6 or 7 percent, whereas the figure was nearly 15 percent for those sent by barge and rail, which often did not receive any fodder during the entire trip.[33] Nevertheless, "on-hoof" shipments were more inconvenient and costly than barge-rail transport in several respects. They were generally impossible at the height of the rainy season, when rivers overflowed their banks, greater numbers of steers were lost, more employees' wages had to be paid, and, for most, pasture had to be rented not just in the vicinity of the market but at other locations on the route. By the 1940s cattle drives took place almost exclusively within the region, from Nicaragua across the border, or from distant haciendas to ports along the Tempisque River.

The mid-nineteenth-century increase in cattle prices in central Costa Rica encouraged the government to tax cattle exports and in 1849 to permit tax-free imports of cattle (see Chapter 1). These efforts to build up the national herd were not more than partially successful, especially since they encouraged Guanacastecan ranchers to specialize in fattening cattle while leaving the riskier and less lucrative business of breeding to the Nicaraguans. Until the imposition of protectionist legislation in 1932, much of Guanacaste was essentially a transit area, in which Nicaraguan steers were fattened for consumption in central Costa Rica.

The reasons for the Guanacastecans' specialization in the fattening of imported steers went beyond the incentives created by government fiscal policies. The problem of high calf mortality resulting from the low technological level of most haciendas was clearly a factor, as was the constant rustling of animals from the sitios. Many ranchers believed theft to be the major cause of the decline of cattle breeding. The 1907 comments of Pablo Rodríguez, a rancher from Liberia, detailed the severity of the situation and typified the hacendados' frustration: "There is a great outcry against this evil [rustling], to the extreme that already many people have abandoned cattle breeding and the significant fact may be noted that several old breeding haciendas have disappeared nearly completely, for example, El Naranjo, La Hedionda, Las Trancas, La Trinidad, La Esperanza, Guapote, etc." (in Valverde 1907: 27).

Steers in the final stages of being fattened for market were, by the early twentieth century, often kept in fenced artificial pastures where they could be closely guarded. This was not the case, however, with the large numbers of young animals that roamed the sitios and constituted the bulk of most haciendas' herds.

Nicaragua had a more developed cattle sector and greater hacendado hegemony at the local level. It was consequently able to provide feeder calves bred on natural savanna lands, such as those in Chontales Department, east of Lake Nicaragua, at far below Costa Rican costs (Acuña Acevedo 1936: 1; Villafranca 1895: 130). Figure 2.1, which describes cattle imports from Nicaragua and the slaughter in Costa Rica and in Guanacaste, illustrates the rapid growth of demand after 1890 and the significant contribution of imports to total consumption (until the 1930s). It is also suggestive of Costa Rica's division into two zones, one that consumed beef—basically the central plateau—and another, Guanacaste, that consumed little but produced cattle and fattened imported steers.[34]

Fattening steers for market on artificial pastures, which followed years of feeding on sitio vegetation, was a brief stage in a production process that involved very extensive use of pastures and thus required large amounts of land for it to be economical. Smallholders could breed a larger number of animals on a comparable area of grassland, but were usually unable to fatten them without severely overgrazing their pastures. In addition, since small cattle ranchers

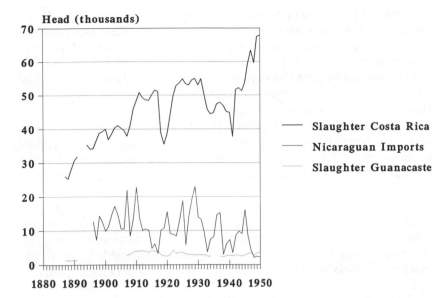

Head (thousands)

——— Slaughter Costa Rica

——— Nicaraguan Imports

——— Slaughter Guanacaste

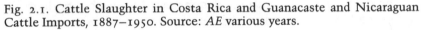

Fig. 2.1. Cattle Slaughter in Costa Rica and Guanacaste and Nicaraguan Cattle Imports, 1887–1950. Source: *AE* various years.

generally did not have access to both dry- and wet-season grazing areas, they were unable to maintain a constant herd size throughout the year and were compelled to sell their animals to avoid losing them to drought or floods. Hacendados took advantage of this, usually acquiring smallholders' feeder calves at low prices at the beginning of the dry season when the carrying capacity of pastures declined and peasants were forced to divest themselves of excess animals. The chronic shortfall in feeder-calf production, however, could only be met by importing steers from Nicaragua.

The trade in "on-hoof" cattle with Nicaragua gave rise to a significant group of intermediaries who purchased animals across or near the border and then resold them further south. Some intermediaries also participated in subsequent stages of the production process, renting pastures and "finishing" steers for market. In general, however, a few of the largest hacendados controlled the final commercialization of fattened steers in Alajuela, the principal market; in 1925–42, sales by the three largest suppliers of the Alajuela market accounted each year for between 28 and 33 percent of the total steers sold; the top nine suppliers provided between 42 and 54 percent of the steers in the same period (Gudmundson 1979: 74). When stiff tariffs were placed on foreign steers in 1932, livestock imports from Nicaragua gradually declined. At the same time, the stimulus this protectionism provided led to the rapid expansion of cattle breeding by smallholders, primarily on the Nicoya Peninsula (see Chapter 5).

The absence of road links with central Costa Rica was a perennial complaint before the completion of the Pan-American Highway in the early 1950s. For months on end in 1937, the local newspaper ran a banner headline that exemplified the prevailing sense that Guanacaste had been the victim of regionalist discrimination by national governments: "The only province of Costa Rica that does not have an inch of railroad is Guanacaste! The only province of Costa Rica in which not a single road has been constructed is Guanacaste!" (e.g., *El Guanacaste*, 8 May 1937, 1). The effect of this situation was to reinforce ties to Nicaragua, especially in the cantons of Bagaces, Liberia, and Carrillo, where in 1924 an observer commented that "for the majority of these residents it is more comfortable to go to the markets of Rivas than to those of the interior of Costa Rica" (Cabrera 1924: 116).

The first trucks and automobiles managed to reach Liberia in the 1920s, and by the early 1930s there were two small companies running trucks on a triangular route between Liberia, Cañas, and Bebedero. The Cañas–Bebedero–Liberia trip, a distance of 75 kilometers, took four and one-half hours and was feasible only in the dry season. The 1935 fare of six colones was roughly equivalent to one week's wages for a peon (*La Tribuna*, 10 Mar. 1935, 9). Although increasing numbers of vehicles attempted the difficult drive from central Costa Rica to Guanacaste during the dry season, this traffic was of little economic importance. Even in the late 1940s, when work on the Pan-American Highway was far advanced and dry-season vehicle traffic was becoming more routine, it was still reported that smallholders in the northern cantons of the peninsula preferred to market in Nicaragua the large quantities of rice, maize, and beans they produced, to avoid reliance on intermediaries (*El Guanacaste*, 30 Mar. 1946, 1).

Technological Stagnation and the Logic of Underinvestment

During this period the failure to innovate involved few economic penalties. In this sense, the dynamics of the hacienda economy differed from those characteristic of classical capitalist development, where the failure to modernize technologically carries with it the threat of eventual economic ruin as more advanced and productive enterprises achieve higher profit levels and greater market shares. The difference lies in the types of profits and production units involved in each case. In capitalist development, accelerating labor productivity resulting from technological progress in industry or agriculture is based on the capitalization of profits that are essentially derived from the surplus labor of a work force operating expensive equipment.

In the traditional Guanacastecan hacienda, in contrast, profits were usually based on the commercialization of natural or quasi-natural products, such as timber or semiferal cattle, which were extracted with only minimal investments of capital. As long as the natural resources of the huge latifundios were not exhausted, as long as the opportunity costs of using land in this extremely extensive manner were favorable, and as long as markets for the extracted goods existed, the hacendado was perfectly capable of surviving on "rent" income. Moreover, in this scheme of accumulation based principally on extraction rather than production, the possession of vast tracts of land and the resources they contained conferred additional immunity from the economic pressures of modernizing neighbors.

The existence of other economic sectors with higher rates of profit constituted an important limit to investment in livestock raising. Coffee farms in central Costa Rica, for example, had annual profit rates of about 15 to 25 percent in the 1850s (Wagner and Scherzer 1944: 196) and of as much as 33 to 56 percent some 50 years later (Hall 1978: 41–43). "The fabulous profits that were made in the coffee business attracted the greater part of the country's capital," wrote Ricardo Jiménez Oreamuno, then a congressional deputy with investments in ranching, in 1903. "Nobody thought of anything but planting coffee. The livestock industry consequently had to be neglected" (p. 7).

A French investor, commenting on the Guanacaste lowlands in 1919, also drew attention to this disparity in rates of return:

There are productive lands being exploited and there are lands that are purchased for speculation; the cattle ranches and the agricultural lands should produce annually 20 percent of the money invested in the purchase. The speculation lands should double in value in a period of five or six years. These rules serve as the base for evaluating properties in the region of Guanacaste; and business done under inferior conditions is not considered good. *It is more worthwhile then to place one's money in many other businesses offered in the country.* (Péyroutet 1919: 3, emphasis added)

A study of a small Guanacaste hacienda in 1895 painted an even more dismal picture. In addition to beef cattle, the farm also sold milk and small quantities of corn, beans, hogs, goats, and poultry, generating an annual return on invested capital of just 3 percent. If only operating capital and not the value of the property was included, the profit rate reached 8 percent, "not at all satisfactory in a country where you receive 10 percent yearly interest backed with first-class security with no effort" (Villafranca 1895: 132). Since properties could often be paid for in full simply by cutting down the trees they contained (ANCR LJC r. 1264, no. 771—1920: 25; Péyroutet 1919: 3; Soley 1949, 2: 46), cattle were not—until the 1930s at least—always the most important factor in many hacendados' rationale for owning or acquiring property.

With interest rates higher than the rate of return for livestock enterprises, yet lower than profit rates in coffee, mining, and commerce, unproductive latifundios were frequently used primarily as collateral for obtaining liquid capital. Many, if not most, of the haciendas were mortgaged to banks or private individuals, usually for about half their market value, at annual rates of interest that remained quite constant at 10 to 12 percent from the mid-nineteenth century to the 1930s.[35] Many hacendados also provided mortgages to other hacendados, hoping perhaps for defaults that would allow them to expand their holdings. For those involved in high-risk undertakings in other areas of the economy, land served not only as a source of funds and speculative rent, but as a kind of insurance as well.

Even with the technological innovations of the late nineteenth and early twentieth centuries, the hacienda economy conserved many of its traditional features. Investing in brahman cattle, improved pastures, wire fences, and veterinary medicine proved attractive to modernizing landowners alert for opportunities to make higher profits. Yet even these new elements were initially incorporated into the established system of grazing animals for most of their lives at extremely low densities in wooded sitios. More important, for the majority of hacendados who acquired properties at little or no cost through inheritance or government grants, the value of land did not have to figure in their accounting of profitability. Any increase in property values signified a potential profit, but meanwhile the resources of the hacienda provided a constant flow of income, obtainable with only minor expenditures on labor and materials and minimal management effort.

3 → Relations of Production and Domination

It is a common saying that "there is an excess of bosses and a scarcity of peons" ("que sobran patrones y faltan peones").
—Landlords' lawyer, 1921

The relations of production and domination on the Guanacastecan haciendas of the first half of the twentieth century can only be understood by examining the rural population, which often had free access to hacienda resources, with or without landlords' permission, and which supplied the haciendas with labor and goods. Rural people included agriculturalists, cattlemen, loggers, hunters, proprietors, squatters, employers, wageworkers, rustlers, migrants, miners, artisans, clandestine distillery operators, and petty merchants. Reducing such occupational and economic heterogeneity to the single category of "peasants" or "peasantry" sheds little light on either specific situations or rural people in general. Nevertheless, rather than jettisoning the "peasant" concept entirely, as some have argued ought to be done (Leeds 1977), the challenge is to find heuristic distinctions that reveal diversity and illuminate its sources.[1]

One such finer distinction, useful in analyzing haciendas, was developed by Rafael Baraona (1965) in a study of large estates in highland Ecuador and employed more recently by Cristóbal Kay (1974, 1977, 1980) in work on central Chile. Baraona and Kay distinguished "external" peasants, or independent small producers ensconced in areas surrounding the landlord enterprise, from "internal" peasants, who were laborers or tenants on the estates. In one respect Baraona's and Kay's terminology is unfortunate, because "external" and "internal" imply at first glance location in space, rather than in a web of relations. As both noted, in incompletely consolidated hacienda systems (such as that in Guanacaste) the landlord enterprise may occupy only a portion of the property, and "external" peasant squatters may have enterprises within the estate's boundaries. But if

conceived in terms of insertion in, and relation to, functioning enterprises—whether of peasants or landlord, and whatever their where-
abouts or degree of permanence—the separation between "external"
independent producers and "internal" estate employees provides a
practical starting point for categorizing two different forms of exploitation and two corresponding kinds of struggle.

The discussion in this chapter will be limited primarily to the hacienda enterprise's "internal" production relations, especially those
involving the *sabaneros* and peons who were the majority of the work
force. Other, more complex sets of relations and conflicts, if often
situated physically within the haciendas' territorial boundaries,
mostly concerned "external" peasants. The rustling, land occupations, "vagrancy," and antilandlord violence of these "external" peasants constituted limits to the development of the hacienda enterprise
and are the subject of Chapter 4.

Wage Labor on the Haciendas

Travelers in late-colonial and early-independence Guanacaste (see,
e.g., Belly 1974: 206), as well as historians of rural Costa Rica (Gudmundson 1978b: 114–16; Fonseca Corrales 1983: 268), have remarked upon the early existence of wage labor in the haciendas.
Among the cases Gudmundson cites was that of a group of Bagaces
mule drivers who in 1794 refused to accept compensation in clothing
and demanded instead their normal salary of twenty silver pesos. The
example is perhaps more remarkable than Gudmundson indicated,
because in this period coinage was extremely scarce and cacao beans
were legal tender (MacLeod 1973: 340; Creedman 1977: 24). Clearly
the Bagaces muleteers felt confident, not only of their right to payment in currency, but of their ability to enforce such prerogatives in
the face of employer efforts to renege on contractual promises.

By the mid- to late nineteenth century, census data indicate that
day laborers (*jornaleros*) were by far the largest occupational category
in the Guanacastecan population (see Table 3.1). Agriculturalists
and—in 1864—maize farmers (*maiceros*), or peasants, the two categories that would include cultivators of any significance, were clearly
of secondary importance. It would not be accurate, however, to view
these nineteenth-century day laborers as a thoroughly subordinated
labor force of fully proletarianized workers. Notwithstanding the
case of the late-colonial Bagaces mule drivers, laborers did not re-

TABLE 3.1

Guanacaste: Principal Occupations, Agricultural Sector, 1864, 1883, 1892

Occupation	Liberia		Bagaces		Cañas		Santa Cruz		Nicoya		Total	
	N	Percent	N	Percent	N	Percent	N	Percent	N	Percent	N	Percent
1864												
Agriculturalists	50	6.3%	57	15.6%			84	11.9%	13	1.7%	204	7.8%
Cattle ranchers	81	10.2	14	3.8			101	14.3	47	6.3	243	9.3
Day laborers	540	67.8	234	64.1			512	72.5	455	60.7	1,741	66.6
Loggers	2	0.3	1	0.3							3	0.1
Maize farmers	85	10.7	1	0.3			8	1.1	210	28.0	304	11.6
Cowboys	38	4.8	58	15.9			1	0.1	24	3.2	121	4.6
1883												
Agriculturalists	75	11.0	79	38.5	22	23.7	118	21.5	47	10.9	341	17.4
Hacendados	19	2.8	3	1.5	2	2.1	5	0.9	2	0.5	31	1.6
Day laborers	589	86.2	123	60.0	69	71.1	425	77.6	384	88.7	1,590	81.0
1892												
Agriculturalists	82	11.5	87	38.2	31	23.7	126	21.9	52	11.6	378	18.0
Hacendados	25	3.5	3	1.3	3	2.3	7	1.2	6	1.3	44	2.1
Day laborers	608	85.0	138	60.5	97	74.0	442	76.9	392	87.1	1,677	79.9

SOURCE: CPO, 1864, 1883, 1892.
NOTE: "Agriculturalist" in 1883 and 1892 appears to include individuals who in 1864 were classified as "maize farmers" and probably also includes small cattle ranchers. "Hacendados" in the two later censuses includes larger cattle ranchers and probably most loggers. "Day laborers" in 1883 and 1892 probably includes individuals classified as "cowboys" in 1864.

ceive all their remuneration in the form of a cash wage; employers frequently provided simple meals and temporary lodging in crude hacienda barracks. Most *jornaleros* also undoubtedly had access to land, either a plot on the landlord's property or one elsewhere in the area, that was cultivated part-time, by family members or at a point in the laborer's life cycle when he was no longer employed or considered employable.

This widespread access to land was the key element in the hacendados' constant laments about what they called the "shortage of hands" (or literally of "arms"—*escasez de brazos*).[2] As one hacendado complained in 1907:

To this province come many unknown people from various places who, without having a square foot of land, take possession of any state or private land they find, grow a few banana trees, maize, cassava, etc., and then dedicate themselves to living at the expense of the cattle ranchers, shooting the steers within their reach and hunting and fishing on other people's lands. Their garden plots are really a harmful trick, since they do not produce anything for them, being nothing more than a pretext to cover up and facilitate theft. . . . The poor service of the peons, their lack of honesty and morality, make it very difficult for businesses to develop, and discourage even the most active men, because it is well known that in this region in order to do any kind of work, it is necessary to advance funds to the peons, and these, after receiving the advances, go to other employers to offer their services, where they then receive in the same way more advances of money. (in Valverde 1907: 20–21)[3]

In 1921 the lawyer for the province's largest landowners commented in a similar vein on this inversion of classical debt peonage in which hacendados had little choice but to become creditors to their laborers:

Here it is well known—indeed notorious—that there is a shortage of workers for service in the countryside and that the hacendados have to submit to the demands of their cowboys in order to have regular service. By now it is traditional for the peons to demand advances and it is a common saying that "there is an excess of bosses and a scarcity of peons" ("que sobran patrones y faltan peones"). (ANCR GJC r. 1264, no. 5—1921: 49–50)

Some turn-of-the-century hacendados cloaked these advances with a veneer of celebratory beneficence, providing their peons money so they could gamble and drink at fiesta time (Gutiérrez 1956: 7). But rural workers' expectation of cash advances was a clear indication of their strength in a seller's labor market. As late as the mid-1930s, employers had difficulty finding workers for lumbering or other jobs without offering at least one week's wages in advance. The workers, it was said, came "already pawned," or in debt (*ya empeñados*), and even if they stayed they sometimes managed to have the advance pay counted as an extra bonus rather than as wages for their first week or more of employment.[4]

Haciendas employed several categories of labor: (1) peons, or day laborers, by far the largest group, generally contracted by the day and used for clearing pastures, and felling timber; (2) cowboys, or *sabaneros*, paid by the month and responsible for herding, treating animals' wounds or infections, retrieving newborn calves from the *sitios*, and, at times, for patrolling the property; (3) specialized workers, such as carpenters, ox cart drivers, and those who labored in the cheese works, usually paid by the month; (4) female cooks who prepared food for the other employees and sometimes had other duties, such as the care of pigs and poultry; (5) a housekeeper, or "key keeper," male or female (*llavero* or *ama de llaves*), always a trusted employee of long standing, in charge of caring for the goods of the hacienda and of minor administrative responsibilities, such as taking inventories or receiving deliveries; and (6) supervisory employees, specifically foremen (*mandadores*) and administrators, in charge, respectively, of directing peons and sabaneros and of keeping records, planning work schedules, and managing the overall functioning of the hacienda.

It is the working conditions of pre-1930s peons and sabaneros that will be examined here, both because they constituted the great majority of hacienda workers and because the sources—documentary and oral—on these categories of laborer are rich and abundant. During the first three decades of this century, working hours for hacienda peons were generally from 6:00 A.M. to 11:00 A.M. or 12:00 M. with an additional afternoon shift, usually termed the "extra job," or *faena*, from 1:00 P.M. to 3:00 P.M. or from 2:00 P.M. to 4:00 P.M. On some haciendas the faena was optional, and the wage consisted of two parts, one for the morning workday (*el día de trabajo*) and the other for the faena. Usually, the workweek consisted of six days, although the afternoon *faena* was less common on Saturday. Since laborers were in demand and were generally paid by the day, they were often able to work shorter weeks or irregular schedules that permitted them greater leisure and time for subsistence activities. Their basic implement was the machete, and they usually had to supply their own tools, but the hacendados provided food and primitive sleeping quarters.[5]

The length of the rural workday and its conceptual separation into two parts, only one of which was subjectively viewed as "the work-day," appeared to Guanacastecans of all social classes (and appears to some even today) as something natural and eternal, rather than as an outcome of contending groups' efforts to control peons' labor time. Both employers and laborers explained the division between *el día de trabajo* and *la faena* as something rooted in the physical environment, specifically the scorching midday sun of the Guanacaste lowlands, which precluded any significant effort and compelled rest. Employers in Guanacaste were no doubt familiar with the eight-hour days that after 1920 were typical of central Costa Rica, and with the longer, grueling workdays of the distant banana plantations—where the laborers were largely Guanacastecans and the noon sun was just as hot. Yet before the mid-1930s they took a dim view of the possibility of increasing the rate of exploitation through lengthening the peons' workday.

Even before the depression of the 1930s, however, and in spite of the "shortage of hands" and the relatively short workdays, the actual labor of clearing pastures was often quite arduous, especially on the large Nicaraguan-owned haciendas north of Liberia. The severity of conditions on these haciendas as compared with those in the rest of the province, even in the labor-scarce years before the 1930s, is a theme mentioned frequently in interviews with older residents of the area north of Liberia and was noted as well in the mid-nineteenth century (Belly 1974: 199–200).[6] Here it was common practice to head each group of peons with a leader, or point man (*puntero*), a trusted employee who set the pace of work. Peons cleared pastures in strips roughly two yards wide called *rondas* or *cortes*, and those whose *ronda* was not the same length as the point man's when the latter stopped at midday often received only the food ration and not their wage. Labor turnover under such conditions was high. But the proximity of Nicaragua and the presence of a continual flow of Nicaraguan migrants accustomed to working under such terms made this labor regime feasible in the border area. In addition, the monopsonistic nature of the labor market and the absence of a significant *minifundio* sector in the border zone, a result of the extreme concentration of landholding, meant that labor discipline remained more severe here than on most haciendas further south.

Skilled sabaneros were, according to all complaints about the "shortage of hands," in shorter supply than common peons (e.g., *El Guanacaste*, 8 July 1936, 6). The practice of calculating sabaneros' wages by the month grew out of the landowners' need to develop closer, long-term ties with this category of worker, as well as out of the irregular schedule of cowboys' duties. Sabaneros' responsibilities implied that they enjoyed sufficient trust to function without close supervision, and they also possessed skills critical to the hacienda's success. They might, for example, be expected to spend several days away pursuing stray steers in distant wooded sitios, or as much as two or three weeks driving cattle to market in central Costa Rica and returning on horseback to Guanacaste. In addition to their abilities with horses, lassos, and herding, sabaneros were in effect the haciendas' veterinarians, treating injuries and infections, castrating steers, and tending newborn calves.

The sabaneros' less-frequent wage payments were a mark of status, since—as in other societies—they implied greater solvency and control over household finances. Nevertheless, members of this hacienda labor aristocracy, in spite of their monthly salaries, were hardly immune from the intemperate impulses for which day laborers were (and are) notorious. Paydays were marked by heavy drinking and violence. As Bagaces resident Valeriano Pasos complained about Wilson's cowboys in 1938, police reinforcements were regularly required on the first Saturday of each month to control the knife and machete fights that "cause[d] real panic . . . in this town" (*El Guanacaste*, 4 Sept. 1938, 2).

The sabaneros' attachment to the "freedom" they believed inherent in the organization of their work and their highly variable work schedule would have made the calculation of an hourly wage quite complex. But monthly contracts were also in the employers' interest and eventually contributed to the erosion of the cowboys' cherished independence. The monthly wage, as opposed to the peons' daily or weekly wages, helped to assure, if not loyalty, at least some continuity in the sabanero work force. In contrast to the laborers' daily arrangement, however, it did not imply anything about the hours to be worked. When the position of rural labor deteriorated suddenly in the mid-1930s, this tradition of long-term employer-sabanero contracts—unquestioned by either side—facilitated the imposition of longer workdays in spite of continuing sporadic shortages for this category of laborer. Peons, less "scarce" than cowboys after the mid-1930s, abided a more intense work rhythm but rarely tolerated major increases in the hours they were required to toil. The "invisibility" of the workday in the sabaneros' monthly contract, however, made it a more difficult arena to contest with arguments or resistance founded on notions of custom or fair treatment.

Working conditions for sabaneros varied greatly, both over the course of the year and from one hacienda to another. Prior to the mid-1930s the hacendado always supplied the sabanero with the main tools of the trade: saddle, halter, boots, leggings (cueras), and lasso, as well as with a horse. The workday did not conform to a fixed schedule, but generally varied from just a few hours to ten or more hours during certain periods of the year. In the dry season, in particular, when cattle were more widely dispersed in "summer" sitios, controlling the herds required greater attention. The work itself, which often involved high-speed pursuit on horseback of runaway steers in forested sitios, was hazardous, and injuries were frequent. Usually, however, injured sabaneros could count on some assistance from their employers for medical care and support during convalescence.

Administrators, foremen, and at times sabaneros were frequently granted the right to graze their own livestock on hacienda lands. In the period of open sitios, this concession was to pasturage rights in whatever areas of planted grass the hacienda had, since in practice the use of sitio lands was not restricted. From the hacendados' point of view, conferring pasturage rights had several purposes: it was one of a series of paternalistic mechanisms to assure employee loyalty to the seemingly beneficent patrón; as a source of income for employees, it was in effect a subsidy that permitted cash wages to be maintained at a lower level; and, perhaps most important, the mixing of the hacendado's and employees' livestock in the same pastures encouraged greater employee vigilance against rustlers.[7] In the 1920s and 1930s, however, as hacendados increasingly attempted to improve their herds with selective breeding and brahman blood, the practice of conceding pasturage rights became less widespread. With the saturation of the labor market in the 1930s, granting pasturage rights as a way of attracting employees and subsidizing their salaries also became less compelling.

Hacendado concessions of land to sharecroppers or rent-paying peasant tenants were never widespread enough to constitute anything more than a tiny fraction of hacienda income. Rather, plots

were sometimes granted under various terms both to longtime hacienda peons and to "external" peasants for four basic reasons: to
reinforce peasant or peon loyalty and dependence; to subsidize peons'
wages; as a way of gaining peasant acknowledgment of hacendado
rights to particular lands; and, probably most important, as a means
of clearing land at peasant expense for eventual conversion to pasture
for hacienda cattle. Nevertheless, most sabaneros and peons received
only wages, food, and at times board as remuneration. Much more
common than actual tenantry or sharecropping was the loan of plots
under a temporary arrangement in which peasants were given access
to a piece of land for a specified period, usually from one to three
years, in return for planting it in pasture at the end of the contract.
The practice of loaning lands in return for their conversion into
pasture, however, tended to decline as the larger haciendas were
planted in grass. Even more than tenantry or sharecropping, it discouraged peasant investment in the soil and condemned its "beneficiaries" to a marginal existence.

Most hacienda peons also had access to land somewhere in the
region, either directly or indirectly through family members. Many
large haciendas bordered minifundio areas, and, except in the province's virtually unpopulated northern section, such areas were always relatively close to large properties. One 1937 report on Abangares, for example, noted that "each individual has a shack and a
small plot by the side of the road that he works two days of each week
and he spends four days as a salaried worker in private fincas" (Matamoros 1937: 4). In addition, the Nicoya Peninsula, where smallholding land tenure predominated, served as a reserve of labor for regions
of the province controlled by latifundios.

With the exception of a small number of cooks and housekeepers,
the haciendas' demand for labor was essentially for *male* labor. As
early as 1864, the year of the first population census, the smallholding
peninsular cantons of Nicoya and Santa Cruz had female-biased sex
ratios, while the cantons of Liberia and Bagaces (which included the
area that later became Cañas), dominated by latifundios, were dispro-
portionately male (see Table 3.2).[8] The out-migration of male labor
from the peninsula was also reflected in the female-weighted populations of the province's nascent urban areas. But the fact that these
male workers retained ties to the land in the region meant that the
supply of labor for the haciendas was quite rigid and constituted a
brake on economic growth and the expansion of production.

TABLE 3.2

Guanacaste: Population by Sex, by Canton, 1864, 1883, 1892

Area	1864			1883			1892		
	Males	Females	Percent males	Males	Females	Percent males	Males	Females	Percent males
Distribution of population by sex, by canton									
Liberia	1,585	1,584	50.0%	2,448	2,296	51.6%	3,063	2,820	52.1%
Nicoya	1,161	1,246	48.2	1,903	1,921	49.8	2,285	2,292	49.9
Santa Cruz	1,558	1,659	48.4	2,362	2,386	49.8	2,903	3,045	48.8
Bagaces	858	780	52.4	515	476	52.0	775	701	52.5
Cañas	—	—	—	310	285	52.1	1,217	948	56.2
Guanacaste	5,162	5,269	49.5	7,538	7,364	50.6	10,243	9,806	51.1
Sex ratios in the "urban" areas									
Liberia town	511	656	43.8	819	891	47.9	1,095	1,131	49.2
Nicoya town				359	410	46.7	376	386	49.3
Santa Cruz town				307	353	46.5	346	386	47.3
Bagaces town				254	263	49.1	180	239	43.0
Cañas town				173	172	50.1	179	222	44.6

SOURCES: *CPO* 1864, 1883, 1892.

Controlling the Work Force in a Period of Labor Scarcity

Until the mid-1930s, hacendados remarked incessantly on the labor shortages that prevented them from undertaking certain tasks, especially clearing land for artificial pastures (e.g., *El Guanacaste*, 15 Nov. 1936, 1; Lorz 1934: 386). Because of the rigidity in the labor supply, they used four basic and complementary stratagems to attract, hold, and discipline workers: (1) paternalistic favors; (2) importation of foreign laborers; (3) encouragement of a competitive and self-disciplining outlook among the workers; and (4) use of monetary incentives. The significance of hacendado paternalism, like that of peon indebtedness to the hacendado, obviously takes on different meanings depending on the balance of forces between these two social classes. In the case of late-nineteenth- and early-twentieth-century Guanacaste, "paternalistic" landlords often represented as generosity or goodwill the "gift" of hacienda resources to which peasants actually helped themselves.

Despite the hacendados' weak position vis-à-vis peasant "vagrants" and rustlers, they did their best to cultivate relationships with employees and smallholding neighbors that were imbued with the seignorial symbolism of hierarchy and domination. Much of this conventional decorum was honored in the breach, but peons asking a favor of the hacendado were supposed to speak only when addressed, to remove their hats and bow their heads (or at least avert their gaze), and to employ the honorific "patrón" (boss) as the preferred form of address.[9] Usually hacendados had little real ability to sanction violations of these informal codes, since dismissal was hardly a severe threat, at least in the era of the "shortage of hands." The patrones had, however, a genuine capacity for conceding favors to loyal hands: small cash loans, sponsorship of a baptism, medicine for an ill family member, or protection in the event of untoward problems with the authorities. Given the sometimes precarious nature of semiproletarian existence, this added measure of security clearly endowed the relationship with a potential meaning and economic importance for peons and peasants out of proportion to either their actual level of dependency or the hacendados' real strength.

Landowners were not averse to employing armed guards to evict squatters or patrol properties, particularly in the 1920s and after, but their seignorial mentality rarely translated into a use of force or

threats of violence to maintain labor discipline. Mystifying the em-
ployer-employee relationship by fostering identification with the hacienda or the patrón was usually sufficient, even if it was likely not to
be entirely successful. In a few cases, hacendados instilled respect by
playing on the fears and superstitions of their employees. Fernando
Castro Cervantes, for example, owned a large fer-de-lance (*Bothrops
atrox*) whose venom glands had been removed, unbeknownst to the
peons who watched in awe as their patrón casually draped the presumably deadly viper around his neck and shoulders.[10] This bizarre affectation, which earned Castro local celebrity as "el terciopelo" (literally
"velvet," the Costa Rican term for fer-de-lance), reportedly left many
peons terrified of their employer's supernatural powers.[11]

The goods paternalistic hacendados provided to their employees
and local peasants usually either had virtually zero opportunity cost
or were directly related to the retention of scarce labor. Grants of
small plots of land, milk or other food, and medicine, as well as the
creation of fictive kinship, or *compadrazgo*, ties, were intended not
only to retain a labor force, but to create goodwill so that the beneficiaries would be less likely to cooperate with or join that large element of the peasantry that consisted of "vagrants" and rustlers that
preyed on the haciendas.

The distribution of quinine, a malaria medicine, to hacienda peons
appears to have been particularly welcomed, even though repeated
use often caused deafness, and some hacendados complained of having to stand over their employees every morning for fifteen days in a
row to make sure they had swallowed the pills and completed the
course of treatment. Malaria, endemic in the region until the 1950s,
not only caused considerable suffering, but was a major factor both in
the periodic scarcity of labor and in the region's short workdays. As
one Liberia hacendado remembered, "You used to arrive at fincas
where there wouldn't be a single soul on his feet. Everyone was
stricken with fever. The workers could only work until ten or eleven
in the morning because they would get the chills and they weren't in
shape to go on."

Landowner generosity—whether free medicine and milk or "concessions" of grazing rights—was frequently instrumental rather than
sincere, even though observers often waxed nostalgic about the
golden age before enclosures, when class conflicts were seemingly
absent and there existed a genuine, mutual respect between employer
and employee. The issue is perhaps most clearly seen in the case of

the Bagaces haciendas—Catalina, Ciruelas, Mojica, Miravalles, Palo Verde, Monte Verde, and San Jerónimo—that had been owned by Bernardo Soto, president of Costa Rica from 1884 to 1889, and that became the property of the North American George Wilson in the early 1920s. Soto was wistfully remembered in journalistic reports:

The residents tell the chronicler: The properties of don Bernardo were common goods and the residences he had on the different fincas were hospitable refuges for those who visited, be they local people or outsiders. On these fincas there was always medicine for the sick peon or traveler, a tortilla with meat for the needy, a saddled horse for the friend, attention for all. The land was open for the people's cattle, and the very poor were given cows that had recently given birth so that they could use the milk, on the sole condition that they return the calf. (*La Tribuna*, 13 Mar. 1935, 15)

Wilson, however, who succeeded in expelling occupants of hacienda lands with the help of armed guards, was portrayed less affectionately. A local journalist, appealing to both republican sympathies and natural law, wrote that in Soto's time:

The town of Bagaces had its own life, and its inhabitants, today wounded by antidemocratic injustice, had lands to cultivate, pastures to graze their cattle, freedom to cut firewood and to fish and hunt as much as they needed. But now latifundismo acts as the owner and lord and prohibits and punishes all this that mother Nature has donated to man for his "Modus Vivendi." (*El Guanacaste*, 1 Dec. 1942, 1, 4)

In spite of this black-and-white view of hacendado paternalism, however, Soto—the supposed exemplar of landlord generosity—was hardly pleased about public use of his properties' resources. Indeed, the general administrator of his haciendas complained in 1912 in a letter to the governor of "extremely serious damages" due to "furtive hunters that penetrate in the fincas without anyone's permission," where they hunted, stole fence posts and wire, and burned the pastures. The governor responded by ordering that two justices of the peace and two policemen be placed in each of Soto's haciendas,

so that whomever the peons of his fincas discover setting fires, hunting without permission, or stealing can be apprehended without delay by the authorities who will always be there. Moreover, I have given orders to the police chiefs that any healthy person who has no property and who passes a week without working is to be judged as a vagrant. I cannot find other means to combat theft, vagrancy, and arson. (ANCR Gob. 3368—1912)

Clearly, what the landowners depicted as altruism was as much a strategy to draw peasants with a "vagrant" mentality into the work force as it was evidence of their inability to control such peasants' mobility. Moreover, as the above quotation from the governor suggests, the long history of peasant access to hacienda lands also shaped landlord perceptions of the repressive possibilities open to them. It is perhaps not surprising that the most effective enclosures of Guanacastecan haciendas in the early twentieth century were carried out by foreign hacendados who had not learned or did not respect the local rules of the game, which had evolved in the context of a weak state and dominant class, uncertain property lines, and a frontier culture that limited the quantity and quality of available labor.

Foreign workers were also less likely to be aware of the traditional order of things in Guanacaste, at least at first. Hacendados frequently voiced preferences for laborers from Nicaragua (Cruz 1934: 516; *El Guanacaste*, 15 Nov. 1936, 1; Péyroutet 1919: 6), where workers had historically been subjected to more rigorous systems of labor control and were consequently more pliable than native Guanacastecans. Nicaraguan observers too recognized these national differences in "plebeian cultures" (Thompson 1966) and work ethics. In 1948, for example, Francisco Ibarra, in *The Tragedy of the Nicaraguan in Costa Rica*, praised the heroic Nicaraguan axe men who cleared jungles for the banana companies in the south and the Nicaraguan laborers in northern Costa Rica who were responsible, "in large measure," for the country's basic food production.[12] Citing his compatriots' "tribulations and martyrdom" in Costa Rica, he reminded his southern neighbors that "the Nicaraguan has contributed with nearly Franciscan abnegation to Costa Rican progress and to the national budget from which live thousands of families in the central part of the country" (Ibarra 1948: 6, 11).

In addition to Nicaraguans, Nicoyans were sometimes mentioned as being better workers than other Guanacastecans (e.g., Péyroutet 1919: 6). It is probable that, in spite of the Nicoyans' eighteenth-century rebellions, the colonial labor system left its mark on the "Indians" there and brought about some persistent cultural differences with other Guanacastecans, who were descended from the rural *castas* of the colonial period (see Chapter 1). That "Indian" identity was still at times considered a salient ethnic category in the mid-twentieth century, especially in regard to *cofradía* participation (León 1942; D. Stone 1954), may indicate that the hacendados' preference for Nicoyan workers had some concrete basis in the value system inculcated in this group. An additional factor in the hacendados' preference for Nicaraguans and Nicoyans—or more recently, Salvadorans—over local laborers was that outsiders would be less likely to have knowledge of surrounding terrain or to have ties to local peasants, which would lead them to leave or to become involved in stealing cattle, timber, or other hacienda property. Moreover, beyond the historical conditions in the Nicaraguans' or Nicoyans' areas of origin that might have contributed to producing a "stronger" work ethic, the specific personal experiences of those who found themselves in the latifundist zone of Guanacaste produced a willingness to tolerate exploitative conditions. Having abandoned (albeit sometimes only temporarily) or been forced out of their home regions, these individuals had already suffered falling living standards, which lowered their expectations and at times their capacity to resist.

At least some hacendados took the reputation of Nicaraguan workers seriously enough to sponsor large-scale importations of labor. Alfonso Salazar Aguilar, for example, who like his father before him owned Hacienda El Viejo in the cantons of Carrillo and Santa Cruz, brought virtually all his skilled workers, such as sabaneros and cheese makers, overland from Rivas during the first two decades of this century. Many of these workers came from families that had worked for the Salazars for two generations, either on El Viejo or on the family's properties in southern Nicaragua. The trip, which took ten days by oxcart, was paid for in full by Salazar.[13] Many of the guards on Hacienda Tempisque and on the Nicaraguan-owned haciendas in the north, such as El Jobo and Santa Rosa, were also hired from Nicaragua. The preference for Nicaraguan guards no doubt reflected Nicaraguans' reputation for violence and their willingness to use weapons. This notoriety, which unquestionably had some basis in fact, grew out of Nicaragua's long history of civil conflict and despotic rule and the interpersonal relations that this engendered at the local level (see below, Chapter 4).[14] This experience of civil and interpersonal violence is important in that it contrasts sharply with the relatively pacific history and political culture of Costa Rica.

"The exploitative relationship," as E. P. Thompson remarked, "takes distinct forms in different historical contexts, forms which are related to corresponding forms of ownership and State power" (1966: 203). Descriptions of conditions in Nicaragua in the late nineteenth century leave little doubt that the average hacienda laborer there endured a more severe work regime and that a well-socialized Nicaraguan worker was less likely than the average Guanacastecan to be presumptuous about his traditional rights. In the late nineteenth and early twentieth centuries, Nicaraguan governments passed a series of laws against "vagrancy" and for the privatization of church and community lands (Morales Fonseca 1984: 102–15). The latter measures, similar to the Liberal reforms already implemented in Guatemala and El Salvador, aimed to create broader land and labor markets that could serve as a base for a coffee export economy. But even before the advent of José Santos Zelaya's Liberal regime in 1893, Conservative governments passed labor control laws simply to control an otherwise unreliable rural population.

By the early 1870s, when French traveler Paul Levy wrote a lengthy account of his experiences in Nicaragua, coercive mechanisms were already firmly established, such as agricultural judges (jueces de mesta and jueces de agricultura) who obliged peons to pay off debts with labor. Levy noted that Nicaragua was "very close to peonage," though he was somewhat ambiguous about the actual content and causes of peon indebtedness. As in Guanacaste until the 1920s, Nicaraguan peons in the 1870s often fled after receiving wage advances, a practice made possible by a labor scarcity and the availability of land on a nearby agricultural frontier. But this inverted peonage ended sooner in Nicaragua, when the government prohibited such loans in 1898. And when loans against future labor were again permitted in 1919, they were a means of enforcing what appears to have been a system close to classical debt peonage (Morales Fonseca 1984: 111).

Other indicators of the balance of forces between peon and hacendado, described by Levy, imply that Nicaraguan landowners were in a much stronger position vis-à-vis the work force than their Guanacastecan counterparts. Even though daily wages on both sides of the border were roughly equal in the 1870s, hours were longer in Nicaragua, and hacendados often provided a considerable portion of wages in goods rather than in cash, a practice that would have been unacceptable to the Guanacastecan peons of the pre-1930 period (Levy 1965, 62: 214–16).

In Nicaragua, beginning in 1880, day laborers were obliged to register with agricultural judges in their place of residence and to carry a certificate provided by their employer testifying to the nature of their work.[15] Those lacking proper documents were considered "vagrants" and could be forced to labor on public works for between 8 and 30 days. Enforcement of this legislation was probably uneven until the "iron-fisted" Liberal Zelaya regime of 1893–1909 (Bulmer-Thomas 1987: 18). Then, however, the Liberals created a pervasive apparatus of repression that included naming authorities with police powers in every canton (*jefaturas políticas*), replacing indigenous community governance with municipal structures responsible to the national state, and—equally important—changing the manner in which agricultural judges and *jueces de mesta* were appointed. Initially, under the Conservatives, the *jueces de mesta* were designated and paid by local residents, but after 1893 they rapidly became economically and politically dependent on the cantonal authorities. Receiving their positions through an increasingly developed system of clientelism, they formed the center of a growing system of informers and enforcers, which reached its height under the Somoza regimes of 1937–79.[16] Citizens were legally required to provide support to the judges or other authorities upon request (Morales Fonseca 1984: 108–15).

The 1898 account of Gustav Niederlein, a Swedish immigrant to the United States who went to Central America in search of collections for the Philadelphia Commercial Museum, reflected this consolidation of harsh authority during the 1890s (pp. 87–88). Pointing to the use of "labor books" like those imposed only a few decades before on rural Mexicans and Guatemalans, Niederlein indicated:

In Nicaragua the people have had complete liberty, but there is now some restriction on it. There is an agricultural law that practically establishes the [labor service] peonage system just described [for Guatemala and Mexico]. The laborer is free to go where he likes and to work when he likes, provided he is out of debt. But as soon as he contracts a debt, it may be in receiving only a few pesos of his wages in advance, he immediately loses his liberty. He is now bound to work out this debt in labor, as also every other debt he may contract subsequently for money or goods furnished to him. . . . As this labor is substantially the only kind to be obtained, the landowner uses every means to keep his laborers in constant debt. Every workman must be in possession of a special document showing where he works, but his landlord can transfer his claims to any one else who will pay the man's debts.

Additional repressive measures in Nicaragua exacerbated the already precarious situation of the rural poor. New legislation in 1894 provided that labor law violators could, with their employers' permission, be required to enlist in the armed forces for an unspecified tour of duty (Morales Fonseca 1984). Other laws included prohibitions on the cultivation of basic food crops, such as plantains, and work taxes that peasants were obliged to pay to large landowners (Barahona Portocarrero and Salazar 1981: 379; Booth 1982: 21).[17]

Given these conditions, and the frequent civil conflicts that racked Nicaragua, it is hardly surprising that substantial numbers of Nicaraguans migrated to Guanacaste—to work, colonize unused land, or escape violence and persecution—or that once in Costa Rica they had fewer misgivings about adjusting to the existing labor conditions. At the turn of the century, Nicaraguan rural laborers were likely to have been peasants displaced by the Liberal creation of markets in land and labor. They were also likely to have knowledge and often direct experience of an extremely repressive labor regime in which slackers and malcontents were subject to harsh penalties. This lived history clearly affected the formation of the Nicaraguans' assumptions about work and their notions about available means of recourse for grievances. It also exposed them to more intense exploitation by landlords on both sides of the border.

The pride of the sabanero in his endurance and his skill with lassos, horses, and cattle was part of a competitive ethos that the hacendados encouraged in order to discipline the work force without overt coercion. The regional literature makes frequent references to the machismo of the sabaneros (e.g., Elizondo 1978; Gamboa 1975; González 1977), a perception echoed in hacendados' recollections, as well as in contemporary commentaries on rural violence. Ramón Zelaya (1933: 5–6), for example, whose father administered some of the largest properties in the province, boasted that toughness extended up and down the social scale (and betrayed not a hint that some of it might have been mere posturing).

[Leading lawyer] *licenciado* don Víctor Guardia Quirós says that "I'll hit whoever says I'm not Guanacastecan." [And hacendado] don Maximiliano Soto Fernández opines that Guanacaste is the only school of energy that Costa Rica has and attributes the machismo of his ancestors—Generals don Tomás Guardia [an hacendado and president 1870–82] and don Próspero Fernández [an hacendado and president 1882–85]—to their Guanacastecan origin and their having lived among the vigorous trees of its forests and its resolute inhabitants. . . . In that region, a child of ten breaks wild horses, fights bulls—and goes to school. That is the secret of why Guanacaste with frequency produces men of firm and indomitable character. Accustomed to subduing horses [*bestias*], they easily acquire the desire to subdue men.

These observations, however bombastic, reflected a very real internalization by the sabaneros of values of toughness, strength, and agility, qualities essential to successful cowboys. In addition, the sabaneros themselves at times structured the labor process in order to reinforce these values, apparently with the acquiescence or active encouragement of their employers. The clearest and most dramatic example of this was the enforcement of work discipline through an unusual ritual—known as the "vulture punishment" (*el castigo del zopilote*)—that accompanied the annual rodeo on many haciendas in various parts of the province until the 1930s or 1940s.[18] The French traveler Count Maurice de Périgny, who witnessed the "vulture punishment" during a 1913 visit to Hacienda Miravalles in highland Bagaces, offered a concise account of the practice in his memoirs. The fifteen-day rodeo and branding (*fiera*) period, de Périgny noted, was characterized by a fiestalike atmosphere, with bull-riding competitions, marimba bands, and the presence of invited guests.

During the entire time the branding lasts, the sabaneros are the masters. They choose from among themselves a judge and a prosecutor, who are charged with noting each day the infractions committed by one and all, such as letting an animal escape during herding, crossing a leg over the pommel of the saddle in order to rest, or not obeying a command given by the judge. By way of sanction, they have to submit to the punishment of the vulture. [First] a vulture in an advanced state of putrefaction is tied to a very high branch; then by means of some ropes the delinquents are raised up, seated on a stick, to a greater or lesser height according to the seriousness of the infraction. During the ascent, the prosecutor pronounces the sentence and, if the person has committed the same infraction several times, he must suffer the punishment the same number of times. For serious infractions the stay under the evil-smelling bird is prolonged, and at times the guilty party is made to ascend rapidly and is then allowed to fall again with a brusque blow nearly to the level of the ground. Everybody is obliged [if they have committed an infraction] . . . to ascend to the vulture; nobody is exempt, not the administrator, nor the foreman, nor the musicians if their enthusiasm diminishes even for an instant, nor the foreigners who have come to attend the branding, unless they free themselves with a gift. The carrying out [of the punishment] is always done . . . with much merriment, always to the sound of the marimba, and everyone does it with such good humor that it is quite rare that it produces incidents. (Périgny 1974: 452–53)

Obviously the "punishment of the vulture" contained elements of the status-inversion rituals that have been observed in other cultures. And although both hacendados and former peons recalled that putrefied animals other than vultures were sometimes used in this "game," the vulture no doubt inspired particularly powerful emotions, which would have exceeded those attached to any other large rotting bird, not the least of which was disgust associated with eating carrion. The prospect of exposure to the ridicule of one's peers, perhaps more than the decaying buzzard's odor, encouraged labor discipline and a competitive ethos among sabaneros in a context where hacendados had few effective tools for sanctioning worker transgressions.

At the risk of relying on functionalist explanations (the origins of the practice are, after all, unknown and probably unknowable), the "vulture punishment," or something like it, was a "necessity" in Guanacaste. This would not have been the case, though, in Nicaragua, where it was apparently absent and where the production process on cattle haciendas was in many ways similar, but where hacendados had earlier gained the upper hand over their employees.[19] The possibility that supervisory employees could be "punished," and the reversal of dominant and subordinate social positions implied by the sabaneros' election of a "judge" and "prosecutor," also made the vulture ritual a harmless, institutionalized means of discharging hostility toward foremen, administrators, and employers. The ritual's decline in the 1930s and 1940s probably reflected greater hacendado control over the work force and, concomitantly, lessened employer tolerance for unproductive and time-consuming sabanero traditions in an economy where land and livestock prices were rising at unprecedented rates.

Increasingly, hacendados successfully confined boisterous sabanero behavior to the formal cattle expositions that began in Guanacaste in the mid-1940s (Robert 1945) and combined exhibitions and auctions of stud animals with bull-riding competitions and amateur bullfighting (without, as in the rest of Costa Rica, killing or wounding the bulls). The big cattlemen found these region-wide events to be valuable forums for exchanging information and markets for acquiring better animals, essential steps toward what was, for many, an increasingly self-conscious goal of eventually exporting beef. But the expositions also reinforced cowboys' identification with their employers in new ways, since both the bulls and those mounting them represented particular haciendas and competed, not against their own coworkers at an isolated sitio or a corral in the countryside, as was formerly the case, but against representatives of other haciendas before large audiences in the major towns.

TABLE 3.3
Costa Rica: Daily Wages in Different Regions, 1880–1955

Year	Guanacaste haciendas	Guanacaste mining zone	Limón (Atlantic)	Central Costa Rica
1880–90	0.60–0.80 pesos		1.33–1.90	1.00
1910		2–3 colones		
1916–20	0.75–2.00	2.67 miner 1.29 peon	3.00	1.00–1.50
1924–25	1.00–2.00	4.50 miner 6.00–8.00 artisan 3.50 peon		0.50–1.28
1933	1.62–2.00		2.75	1.00–1.60
1935–37	0.75–1.50 peon 2.25–2.50 rice		8.00–10.00 bananas 5.00–6.00 railroad	
1940	1.50–2.00		1.75–2.00	
1942	1.00–1.50		2.00–3.20	
1955	3.00–5.00		12.00	7.50–9.50

SOURCES: 1880–90, Churnside (1980: 31); *El Guanacaste*, 15 June 1937, 2. 1910, García (1984: 29). 1916–20, Araya (1979: 45); Churnside (1980: 31); *Diario de Costa Rica*, 4 October 1919, 6; interviews. 1924–25, Cabrera (1924: 150); Churnside (1980: 31); interviews. 1933, ANCR Gob. 14024. 1935–37, Casey (1979: 114); *El Guanacaste*, various issues. 1940, Gudmundson (1979: 69). 1942, Churnside (1980: 31); *El Guanacaste*, 8 June 1942, 1, and 22 June 1942, 1, 4. 1955, Churnside (1980: 31); interviews.

NOTE: 1880–90 amounts in pesos; all other amounts in colones. One peso was equivalent to approximately 2.50 colones. All wages are for peons unless specified.

The fourth response of the hacendados to the "shortage of hands" in the period before the mid-1930s was the use of monetary incentives to attract workers. Witold Kula, in his study of eastern European large estates, remarked that "the dominant class complains at all times and in all places of the high price of manpower" (1976: 177). While Guanacastecan landowners were not exceptional in this regard, reports of relatively high wages before the mid-1930s were more than just an artifact of the landowner complaints that abound in the sources.[20] Certainly the best indication of a seller's labor market was the widespread practice, described above, of extending salary advances and the peons' propensity for "abusing" this supposed landowner generosity by leaving with the money and then securing similar advances elsewhere. More direct evidence is provided by the government commission charged with drafting minimum-wage legislation, which found in 1933 that "the province of Guanacaste has the most acceptable salary [level for rural workers and it is] applied most uniformly and constantly sustained" (ANCR Gob. 14024—1933: 5). This observation probably reflected in part the collapse of wage levels earlier in the 1930s in coffee-growing central Costa Rica than in Guanacaste, though the commissioners did not mention that this regional difference in wages was a recent phenomenon. Rather, they simply proposed raising peons' salaries in the central provinces of Cartago, Heredia, San José, and Alajuela to the level prevailing in the north Pacific regions of Puntarenas and Guanacaste. Nevertheless, while wages on northwestern haciendas were relatively high, they did not compare with those in the Guanacaste mines or in the Atlantic coast banana plantations and railroads (see Table 3.3). All these sectors, as well as nearby smallholding zones, competed with the haciendas for labor and no doubt contributed to the "shortage of hands."

A World Turned Upside Down: Changing Conditions in the 1930s

In little more than a decade, the reality that in 1921 had caused a landlords' lawyer to despair of "an excess of patrones and a scarcity of peones" was suddenly and unmercifully inverted. The world economic crisis helped to tip the scales in favor of the hacendados, bringing drastic, fundamental changes to Guanacaste, which included significantly worsened working conditions, a general erosion of the strength of rural labor, and a transformation of previous customs and social relations. What the hacendados had been trying to accomplish with varying success since at least the turn of the century—the disciplining of an often recalcitrant labor force and the protection of properties—was achieved with a rapidity and thoroughness beyond their dreams by forces outside their control. Enclosures of haciendas had, in some areas of the province, already helped consolidate landowner power, but the depression-era collapse of export-oriented sectors of the economy and the consequent excess supply of labor shifted the overall positions of the peasantry and the hacendados faster than any barbed wire fence or private police force could have done. Yet even while new rules of the game were being established in the labor market, hacendados rededicated themselves to the task of assuring "respect for property" with enclosures and patrols. Increasingly, the rural poor felt resigned to choosing between the landlords' "offer" of employment and emigration from the latifundist zone of Guanacaste.

The depression of the 1930s led to a severe contraction in the two sectors that were most important to Costa Rica in terms of earnings and employment, coffee and bananas, as well as in the only two export-oriented, labor-intensive sectors centered in Guanacaste, wood and mining. Total exports plummeted from $18.2 million in 1929 to $8.5 million in 1932 (Albarracín and Pérez 1977: 30). The drop in coffee and banana exports, as well as the associated decline in port activity, generated considerable unemployment in the coffee-growing provinces of Heredia, San José, Cartago, and Alajuela, in the banana plantations and port of Limón, and in the port of Puntarenas. In 1932 the unemployment rate in Guanacaste was less than one-half that in the country as a whole or in any province except for Alajuela, where it was slightly more than one-half.[21] The major labor-intensive activity on the haciendas, the cutting and transporting of wood, had at this point already undergone a precipitous collapse. Gold exports (since 1924 no silver had been exported) underwent a sharp downturn and then recovered by the mid-1930s. Nevertheless, the mining zones of Abangares and, particularly, of Tilarán were entering a period of decadence even before the 1929 depression because of the gradual exhaustion of ore deposits. In 1934 the largest of the mining companies, the Abangares Gold Fields Company, which at its height employed some 3,000 workers, generally Guanacastecans, ceased operations because of declining yields of ore. Subsequently, although exports returned briefly to their predepression levels, most of the mines were abandoned to scavengers or rented to small concessionaires, who did not undertake the large investments in maintenance and construction that had previously employed hundreds of workers (Araya 1979: 45, 48).

For the large landowners, the depression was fortuitous not only from their narrow vantage point as employers in what was suddenly a buyer's labor market. Even as the rest of the country was beset by the worst crisis in its history, the Guanacaste cattle sector experienced rapid growth as a result of import substitution. State measures to protect the cattle industry, taken in 1932 initially to limit outflows of foreign exchange, contributed to an increase in land and livestock prices and encouraged both the limited introduction of labor-saving technology, particularly fences, and a more complete appropriation of the soil by the landlords. The protectionist measures also encouraged changes in the production process on the haciendas, which displaced workers and contributed to the excess supply of labor (see Chapter 5). Hacendados used the introduction of wire fencing and the gradual replacement of feral livestock, as well as their unexpected power over the suddenly abundant and increasingly dispensable laborers, as opportunities to impose new levels of labor discipline and to eradicate aspects of sabanero behavior they considered detrimental to the smooth functioning of business. As one hacendado explained:

The feral (cimarrón) cattle were quite wild when the time came to herd them from the sitios to the corrals. We used to tie a board to the head of the wildest ones to keep them from running into the woods, or we would herd them with other animals. The cowboys of that time liked to yell and carry on and run the cattle. Even in the pastures when the cattle heard footsteps they would jump and run. The criollo cattle were quite tame, but the way they were handled made them very bad. Many people worked the cattle with dogs, sicking the dogs on animals that went astray. The cattle knew from experience that at one's side came the dogs and that's why they fled. . . . When the time came to herd, everybody on the different fincas was advised, and instead of 6 or 8 sabaneros from one finca, 20 or 30 would come from various fincas. It didn't matter if herding took the entire day. . . . The new system is different. The Indian (cebú) cattle is a very nervous animal. If you run it or irritate it, it loses control and gets very wild, which forced us to work it differently. So now we don't irritate the cattle, we work it with the least lasso possible and we try to save time. Yesterday's sabanero said that the new system was for homosexuals (una mariconada) and that it was going to make the sabaneros into pansies (playos). And there were many times when we had to fire one of those sabaneros who couldn't adjust to the new system.

The clearest indication that the old order of things was giving way in the mid-1930s was the increased level of exploitation that the hacendados successfully imposed. Wages paid to hacienda peons began to fall in relation to those paid to peons in coffee-growing central Costa Rica. For virtually the first time, many Guanacastecans complained of brutally long working days, of peons laboring ten or more hours a day at obligatory and unprecedentedly long afternoon faenas, and of sabaneros beginning work at two in the morning and finishing anywhere from six in the evening to ten at night (El Guanacaste, 10 Oct. 1936, 1; 8 Nov. 1936, 1; 15 Dec. 1936, 5; 23 June 1940, 1). Hacendados ignored new minimum-wage laws, often required sabaneros to supply work implements, which customarily had been provided by employers, and frequently failed to include the previously traditional meals in laborers' remuneration (El Guanacaste, 23 Apr. 1937, 1; 22 June 1942, 1). In addition, the hacendados' earlier preoccupation with their employees' health appears to have diminished now that there was no longer "a scarcity of peones," and this in turn provoked the outrage of workers accustomed to more solicitous treatment (*El Guanacaste*, 26 Mar. 1939, 1; 10 Apr. 1946, 1). Finally, while the hacendados still complained of periodic "shortages of hands," particularly at the time of the rice harvest, they no longer reported that it was necessary to advance peons money in order to secure their services (*El Guanacaste*, 8 July 1936, 6; 8 Jan. 1937, 2; 23 Apr. 1937, 1; 12 Feb. 1939, 4).

Labor continued to be scarce during the December rice harvest, leading employers to pay high wages to harvesters and, occasionally, to import Nicaraguan peons specifically to work in the harvest (*El Guanacaste*, 12 Feb. 1939; Maduro 1935: 6). Both smallholders and some large haciendas grew rice, and, in a few cases, hacendados installed rice-husking machinery and encouraged neighboring small-holders to undertake cultivation. The Sobrados' Hacienda Tempisque in Carrillo canton was the largest rice processor in the province (Lorz 1934: 385; Maduro 1935: 6).[22] The harvest-time scarcity of workers was indicative of less-than-total labor market saturation and of the increasing out-migration of unemployed Guanacastecans during the mid- and late 1930s. That periodic labor scarcities continued throughout the 1930s and worsened for a time during the 1940s when work began on the Pan-American Highway indicates that the successful imposition of more intense levels of exploitation was probably not merely the result of the presence of larger numbers of unemployed workers. Options that small agriculturalists previously substituted for wage labor were also being reduced or disappearing. The enclosure of latifundios, backed by more effective coercion, left peasants in many areas of the province with no alternative but to leave or to become peons, often on the very properties they had previously occupied for subsistence cultivation.

After the collapse of lumber exports, the haciendas hired only small numbers of workers. In 1935, for example, George Wilson, who owned over 100,000 hectares, employed only about 200 full-time workers—an average of less than 1 permanent worker for each 500 hectares. The Hacienda Tempisque, smaller at 20,000 hectares, but more heavily capitalized with a sugar mill, a distillery, a sawmill, a soap factory, and a rice mill, employed about 300 men. The 11,000-hectare Hacienda Paso Hondo, which, like the other large estates, contained much unused land, provided jobs for only 75 full-time peons, although other laborers were employed as sabaneros and in specialized tasks (Lorz 1934: 382; *La Tribuna*, 31 Mar. 1935, 15; 17 Feb. 1935, 16; 3 Mar. 1935, 16).[23]

Obviously the sudden advent of several thousand unemployed mine and lumber workers in such a context could seriously erode the traditionally strong bargaining position of rural labor, particularly when added to the additional thousands no longer able to work elsewhere in the country or in Nicaragua, where the economic crisis was even worse.[24] But for the region's peasants, the large landowners' increasingly effective control over their land and livestock resources began to limit previously available alternatives to wage labor. Even when fresh "shortages of hands" occurred as a result of high levels of emigration or new jobs in road construction, monetary incentives played only a minor, seasonal role in securing peons.

The changing situation of the hacienda laborers in this period constituted a deterioration in the conditions of a work force that had—until the depression—sought and successfully struggled in the everyday arena of workplace negotiation for the institution of a particular variety of wage relations in preference to other, "nonproletarian" forms of remuneration. They did not do so as fully dispossessed laborers, however, but as "part-lifetime proletarians" (Wallerstein 1979) who had access to land somewhere in the region or who had depended for their reproduction (and would depend during their old age) on family members with land. To put it another way, the links between peasants "external" and "internal" to the hacienda were always close, with the same individuals or families often involved sequentially or simultaneously in both roles. This blurring of peasant and peon identities marked resistance to the hacendados' plans with a strongly "agrarian" cast.

4 ⇢ Agrarian Conflict and the External Peasantry

> The people are so accustomed to trespassing that if you find a hunter in your sitios, pastures, or yard, if you do not want to make an enemy, you had better not press charges. Moreover, we do not do so because we can be sure that it will cost us dearly. If he does not kill animals, he'll set fire to the sitios. And if you have pastures they are at the mercy of a single match, and of these there are so many that I do not know how they could be destroyed.
> —Liberia hacendado, 1907

> The avaricious, fierce, dark capitalist does not permit hunting or fishing in his properties, as if the wild animals and the fish in the water were the product of his labor. Latifundistas have closed the best roads, where they place guards who, like Cerberus, exact tolls from the unfortunates who have the ill luck to travel them.
> —Newspaper report, *El Guanacaste*, 15 August 1937

The distinction between peasants "internal" and "external" to the hacienda is analytically useful even though the same persons often occupied both positions in the region's class structure. The individual who worked as a peon on an estate during specific seasons, particular points in the life cycle, or certain days of the week, was also likely to engage in complementary activities. These included small-scale agricultural and livestock production, hunting and fishing, salt extraction, lumbering, petty commerce, artisan production, and—in some cases—rustling and brewing contraband liquor. The relationship of an external small producer, squatter, or rustler to the hacienda enterprise was considerably different than that of the peon or *sabanero* employed on the estate. Moreover, the existence of a strong external peasantry in some zones constituted an obstacle to the development of the hacienda enterprise and thus indirectly to that of the work force, or "internal" peasantry, as well. Nevertheless, as this chapter suggests, the sources of this strength derived not only from the subsistence orientation of external peasants but from their role as petty-commodity producers with relatively "modern" notions of real property.

"Vagrants," Rustlers, Drunks, and Squatters

As on cattle frontiers elsewhere in Latin America (Góngora 1966; Hennessy 1978), large landowners frequently feared nearby peasants as "thieves" and "arsonists" or despised them as "vagrants" and "usurpers" of property. Baretta and Markhoff's observation (1978: 590) that cattle frontiers were largely the result of economic choices made by governments and that they were places where nobody had an enduring monopoly of violence provides a useful starting point for an examination of rustling and what the hacendados termed "vagrancy." Guanacaste's geographic isolation, harsh environment, and low population meant that successive governments saw little reason to establish a major presence there, particularly before the depression of the 1930s. As late as 1923, in an area of over 10,000 square kilometers with a population of more than 50,000 (AE 1927), there were only 61 police, most of them stationed in Liberia, the provincial capital (Acosta 1923: 193).

This decision by the state to maintain only a weak presence carried with it a series of consequences for the social composition and behavior of the province's population. Rustling was widespread, and fugitives from other parts of Costa Rica and nearby Nicaragua came and went with impunity (ANCR GJC 703—1895). Some police were stationed in cantonal and district seats outside Liberia, but the vast rural areas saw only infrequent patrols. The negligible effect of these sporadic efforts was suggested by an 1889 letter from the governor of the province to officials in San José, complaining about cattle thieves in the Tempisque Valley: "Even though frequent expeditions are sent, like the one that just went, those people know that the convoy will not stay there and they spy on it until it retreats; and they also have the river on which to flee and the assurance that those that do not have boats will never catch them" (Bustos 1889: 113).

The term "vagrancy," as Góngora (1966) has shown, was associated throughout Latin America with cattle frontiers where feral livestock was herded by occasional day laborers, who were also periodically involved in *cuatrerismo*, the theft of four-legged animals. Originally the appellation *vago*, or "vagrant," was applied to those who had no clear residence and who wandered from place to place (Brading 1975: 106). Soon, however, it came to be almost synonymous with "rustler" and to imply what seemed to be, from the hacendados' point of view, an obstinate disdain for authority and a refusal to work on the estates. A succinct, if jaundiced, statement of this outlook was provided in a 1907 letter from José Feo, one of Guanacaste's principal hacendados, to the interior minister (Ministro de Gobernación) in San José:

The worst of evils suffered by the cattle industry in the Province of Guanacaste are the fires that are set in the fields without the hacendados being able to avoid it, because of the lack of respect which exists for property. It is well known that the majority of the fincas have been occupied by certain people whose entire patrimony is a shotgun, so that they can live from hunting and not have to work. This class of people, which does not possess any property, is that which sets fire to the fields at the wrong time, thus being the ruin of the hacendados. . . . These people do not lend themselves to working for the hacendados, since with the excuse of hunting and fishing, they refuse completely to earn a wage on the haciendas, and it is this that is the cause of rustling. When they do not find deer or other wild animals, they shoot other people's cattle. (Valverde 1907: 4)

Feo's comments, representative of hacendado opinion in the period (ANCR Cong. 11275—1917: 3; ANCR Cong. 12803—1923: 16; Bustos 1889: 113; Castro 1911: 480; Valverde 1907), reflected the desperation of ranchers who realized the futility of investing in livestock production as long as the local balance of forces remained favorable to peasant "vagrants." Even though most information on rustling inevitably derives from hacendado sources, there is little doubt that cattle theft was a serious problem. Hacienda peons were frequently charged with rustling, though they usually managed to escape prosecution by fleeing to Nicaragua or to other parts of Guanacaste (ANCR GJC 331—1898; ANCR LJC 1061—1905). Often, however, hacendados expressed fears that bringing legal charges against rustlers or trespassers would expose them to arson or violent revenge (Valverde 1907: 8, 10, 18). Some complained of losing as many as 100 steers a year to thieves (p. 36), and even in the 1940s the largest hacienda in the Tempisque Valley often lost as many as 500 steers a year to rustlers operating small launches along the rivers.[1] In various cases, rustling and violence led landowners to abandon their properties (*La Gaceta Oficial*, 18 Mar. 1923, 296; Gudmundson 1982; Valverde 1907: 20, 27).

Cattle theft took a variety of forms and involved a considerable range of actors. "Little pirates" who lived in the maritime mile came in small launches to raid large haciendas along the east bank of the Tempisque and slaughtered the animals once they had safely returned to their bases on the west side of the river (Valverde 1907: 23). There they dressed the steers right on the riverbank so that the outgoing tide would carry off the evidence, dried the meat on racks, and then sold it to logging boats or to retailers in Puntarenas. In the north of the province, where river and maritime transport was less significant, thieves either slaughtered cattle in the woods and then carried off the meat or else herded the animals to neighboring haciendas that were known to disregard brands and to overlook the questionable origin of the stock.

The occasional complicity of some large landowners in rustling is clear from legal records; many prominent hacendados were charged with cattle theft by other hacendados or by small producers, though few were ever convicted.[2] At the turn of the century, some aggrieved ranchers maintained that large companies dedicated to selling stolen livestock operated in remote border areas (Valverde 1907: 31) controlled by the Morice family, Nicaraguan hacendados from Rivas. Local butchers also purchased contraband cattle (ANCR Gob. 8094—1924: 42), a practice that allowed them to acquire cut-rate meat and avoid municipal slaughterhouse taxes. Most hacendado involvement in rustling, however, was probably limited to occasional acquisitions of a few stolen animals or the appropriation of unbranded feral cattle from open grazing areas to which they did not have title.

Drinking was another aspect of "vagrancy" that concerned hacendados, and not only because of the moral qualms about lower-class alcoholism cited in their complaints. Peasants frequently destroyed the *coyol* palms (*Acrocomia vinifera*) that dotted the *sitios* and pastures in order to produce a fermented beverage they called coyol wine. But to the hacendados' consternation, demolishing coyol palms deprived cattle of a fruit that was a key food during the worst dry-season months. Tipsy employees worked poorly, were rowdy and difficult to control, and were likely to challenge seignorial expectations about appropriate submissive comportment, undermining hacendado authority and serving as poor examples to their fellows. Some landowners even went so far as to urge the prohibition of coyol wine, since "in nearby villages there are drunken coyol sprees, and they pass weeks inebriated in the woods. . . . The same happens in the haciendas, since one constantly sees sabaneros drunk for up to a week in the streets, harming the hacendados and ruining the horses" (Valverde 1907: 16).

Prohibition of alcohol, however, like most other measures to control "vagrancy," never amounted to more than the dream of a landed class with a tenuous grip on local-level power. Only when the economic conditions of depression, the enclosures of properties, and a greater state presence strengthened the hacendados' hand would the "threat" posed by inebriated peasants and poaching "vagrants" gradually recede.

Who were the "vagrants" and rustlers? In addition to hacienda peons (and at times foremen and administrators) who were charged with cattle theft, most rustlers appear to have been residents of small villages bordering the haciendas or in the maritime mile. Some were charged with rustling several times within a few years and may have been semiprofessional cattle thieves. One such individual—Antonio Ramírez (alias "El Moreno," "the Dark One"), a resident of Cañas Dulces—had, according to latifundista Alejandro Hurtado, "lived all his life causing damage to the plaintiff's properties: hunting, burning the sitios, [and] destroying the coyol trees" (ANCR GJC 703—1895: 2v). Other "vagrants," as one government official conceded, probably stole only infrequently "to kill their hunger, slaughtering others' cattle in the woods" (Castro 1911: 480).

The view of feral cattle as a natural resource and the traditional land tenure pattern based on free access to grazing lands were important elements in the rustlers' worldview. Killing steers, particularly unbranded ones, was in their eyes little different than shooting deer; it constituted merely one of a number of manifestly legitimate activities, such as gathering firewood in forests or fishing in rivers, that happened to be against the law. Even today, in the few areas where feral cattle remain, peasants—and at times even large ranchers—condone the slaughter of wild livestock or see it as a minor infraction compared with the theft of expensive domesticated animals.[3]

State measures to control rustling were frequent but ineffective. The Congress passed a law against vagrancy in 1887, and at other times local officials made ad hoc rulings against those who had no property and did not work. The 1909 law that established Guanacaste as a "cattle zone," in which ranchers did not have to enclose their grazing areas, also prohibited transit across private properties, whether or not they were fenced, without written permission from owners. Stiff fines were provided for violators, and fines were considerably more for those caught setting fires or trespassing with firearms (Vicarioli 1952: 64).

In 1907 a mounted police force was created in Guanacaste and charged with patrolling the province, stopping rustling, and guarding against arsonists (Sáenz Maroto 1970: 311). It had little impact, though, since in 1917 and again in 1923 attempts were made to establish a civil guard, modeled on that of Spain, whose principal purpose was to be the suppression of livestock theft (ANCR Cong. 11275—1917; ANCR Cong. 12803—1923). Even the creation of the Treasury Police (Resguardos Fiscales) in 1923, a relatively well armed force responsible for enforcing tax laws and eradicating rustling and bootleg liquor operations, did not yield major results. The Treasury Police, however, eventually did become increasingly effective in repressing land invasions (see Chapter 8).[4]

The gradual increase in the size and capabilities of the law enforcement apparatus was coupled with efforts to promulgate legislation against rustling. In 1889, the provincial governor, remarking that "true liberty is order," complained that "republican habits" and "constitutional guarantees" constituted major obstacles to more effective control of rustlers (Bustos 1889: 113). By 1937, however, police and cantonal officials were authorized to keep a "Registry of Suspects" in which persons believed to be rustlers were inscribed, a measure considered partial proof (prueba semiplena) of any subsequent accusations of cattle theft (ANCR Cong. 18322—1937: 46). In 1942 another law, which even mainstream authorities on jurisprudence termed "classist" and "extremely repressive" (Salas Marrero and Barahona 1980: 768), increased penalties for rustling from the earlier six months to two years, to two to six years.

Rustling persists in Guanacaste to this day (see Chapter 8), but it clearly became less significant after the 1940s, when increased livestock prices and widespread introduction of fencing encouraged and facilitated greater hacendado vigilance. Although ranchers were unhappy about the extent of rustling, they had little incentive to invest heavily in protection as long as prices were low and cattle multiplied in semiferal herds with minimal human intervention. In the 1940s and 1950s the state increasingly assumed the costs of protection, and more efficient law enforcement contributed to the demise of the traditional *cuatrero.*

"Vagrancy," drinking, and rustling were by no means the only hacendado complaints about the rural population. By the late nineteenth century numerous communities, some quite large, existed on lands that nominally belonged to absentee latifundistas. The massive size of the latifundios, the lack of incentives to invest, the traditional free access to sitios, and the prevalence of absentee ownership combined to assure that these communities suffered relatively little hacendado pressure until the early twentieth century. Some villages, such as Colorado and San Buenaventura de Abangares, the largest settlements (other than the cantonal seat) in what was at the turn of the century Cañas canton, did a thriving commerce in grains, salt, and cattle with Puntarenas (ANCR Gob. 943—1894 and 1950—1894). Other hamlets along the Tempisque River, such as Guardia and Belén, had long produced grains for the Liberia market (ANCR Gob. 4231—1861; ANCR Cong. 17150—1934). Often these villages, called *barrios* or *caseríos*, contained schools, churches, and (after 1890) telegraph offices. They were in every sense permanent settlements, and some had, by the early twentieth century, been in possession of their lands for over 100 years (ANCR Cong. 17150—1934).

The extent of peasant occupation of private lands in the early twentieth century was indicated by a 1907 census of eleven large properties, which found 10,262 people in villages and isolated settlements within latifundio boundaries (ANCR Cong. 12473—1921: 2).[5] The population of Guanacaste at the time was estimated at 29,093 (*AE* 1907: 9), so that a minimum of 35 percent of the provincial population lived in such insecure conditions of tenancy in the censused areas alone. Because this enumeration did not include several developing centers of squatting and colonization, it can be stated without exaggeration that in the early twentieth century at least half of Guanacaste's population occupied lands to which someone else had legal title.

The ultimate outcome of these occupations varied considerably in different parts of the province and often even within the same area. The two basic results, however, may be summed up in Baraona's (1965) and Kay's (1980) terms as "external siege," where peasant enterprises developed at the expense of the landlord enterprise as a result of enduring occupations; and "internal proletarianization,"

where the growth of the landlord enterprise brought about expropriation of peasant tenures within the estate. The losing parties often
graphically described the effects of these two outcomes. In 1934, for
example, two landlords from lowland La Cruz complained of the
successful external siege of their property:

In Guanacaste there are some lands appropriate for crops and other lands that
are plains covered with natural pastures used exclusively for breeding cattle;
ours are occupied totally by the residents (vecinos), the ones appropriate for
crops, cultivated and fenced; they make us respect the unfenced portions as
if they were their own, and in the plains and natural pastures they have so
many of their cattle grazing that we are not able to put in even one animal.
(ANCR Cong. 17188—1934: 22)

Six years later, in contrast, Bagaces peasants directed a letter to the
president of the Republic, describing a landlord victory and decrying
their lack of access to municipal lands in the cordillera that could
only be reached by passing through properties enclosed by George
Wilson:

Two years ago we had to abandon our town Bagaces to come and work along
the Tempisque cultivating rice and maize, because in our town we do not
have an inch (un palmo) of land to cultivate. In order to aid our families we
have to walk 70 kilometers on foot, those of us who do not possess horses to
go on. Our entire town has deserted to other places in search of work, and
they never come back, or else they return by airplane to be buried. How
different all this would be if we possessed lands to work and roads to reach
them. Our always well-remembered [former president] don Rafael Iglesias
donated two leagues of magnificent lands to us, but what good does it do us?
We have no roads to reach them and no other way to go, since everything
belongs to the landlord Mister Wilson. (El Guanacaste, 20 Nov. 1942, 3)

What, though, motivated "external" peasants to "lay siege to"
landlords' land? Were squatters and "vagrants" or longtime latifundio
residents attempting to reproduce themselves as subsistence horticulturalists who aspired to "live from hunting and not have to
work?" Or were they petty-commodity producers with complex insertion in markets and relatively "modern" notions of real property?
The "external" peasantry as an analytical category bears further scrutiny, not only because its heterogeneity has not always been sufficiently appreciated, but also because in this period it was in constant flux.

During the late nineteenth and early twentieth centuries thousands of migrants came to Guanacaste, some to work as miners in Abangares and Tilarán and most to settle on unused lands, where they hoped to establish possession rights.[6] In 1883–92 immigration accounted for approximately one-half the province's population growth.[7] Most of this flow was from central Costa Rica and from Rivas, in southern Nicaragua, where in the second half of the nineteenth century there was "an almost massive emigration towards Costa Rica of inhabitants fleeing the frequent . . . fratricidal wars" (Guerrero and Soriano 1966: 176).[8]

As in other peripheral areas of Costa Rica, migrants from the *meseta central* were referred to as "Cartagos," though in Guanacaste most were from western Alajuela province rather than more distant Cartago. These newcomers, displaced by population growth and land concentration in the central plateau, gravitated to the cool slopes of the cordillera, which they eventually colonized as far north as Bagaces canton, and to the southern coasts and highlands of the Nicoya Peninsula. The Nicaraguans—who in appearance, culture, and speech generally resembled the "legitimate" Guanacastecans more than did the "Cartagos"—usually colonized unoccupied sections of the northern cordillera or assimilated into settled lowland areas. Increasingly, then, distinctions based on provenance arose within the Guanacastecan peasantry, with "Cartago" versus *guanacasteco* being the most salient difference.

Although the two groups tended to occupy different zones, where they came into contact relations were not always warm. Guanacastecans applied the terms "Cartago" or "*compañero* Cartago" to individuals believed unreliable, selfish, or dishonest.[9] "Cartagos," in turn, stereotyped Guanacastecans much as they did Nicaraguans, as impulsive, spendthrift, violent, and unrefined. Unlike Guanacastecans, "Cartago" migrants had little experience with beef cattle and had no recent tradition of common grazing areas. It is not surprising that at times conflicts between the two groups developed over enclosures of grazing lands. In 1938, for example, in the southern Nicoya Peninsula, longtime residents of Lepanto district complained that recent migrants from the interior were fencing sitios that they had used for cattle and logging (ANCR Cong. 18734—1936–38).[10] The "Cartagos," said the governor of Puntarenas, had created a "flourishing agriculture," which was endangered by the loose cattle of the original residents. Nevertheless, the latter, rather than expressing aversion to fencing as such, commented that traditionally they had not constructed fences except "when it is a question of crops that can pay the cost" (ibid., 1).

These contrasts between the Guanacastecans' custom of open sitio grazing and the "Cartagos'" history of coffee culture have given rise, however, to overstated claims about the two groups' contrasting outlooks regarding production for the market and possession of land. Lowell Gudmundson, while shedding much new light on early-twentieth-century agrarian conflicts (1982, 1983c), has argued in this vein, maintaining that Guanacaste had two distinct peasantries: the lowland hacienda peasants and the freeholding *campesinos parcelarios* from central Costa Rica who settled the southern part of the cordillera.[11] According to Gudmundson, the lowland hacienda peasants were part of "an almost exclusively subsistence economy, in which the land was considered 'free' ('libre y gratuita') . . . available for all without permanent appropriation [and was] converted into something like a 'fetish,' hiding its true 'legal' ownership by absentee hacendados" (1982: 76).

In contrast, "the economy of the migrant *campesino parcelario* of Tilarán, the product of more than half a century of commercial coffee cultivation in the Central Valley, was based on subsistence crops plus a surplus that could be sold in markets outside the region" (1982: 76). Gudmundson concludes that "while the *campesinos parcelarios* of the highlands demanded the distribution of parcels, their counterparts of the lowlands rejected any attempt to permanently fence or parcel the land, whether on the part of absentee proprietors or other peasants" (1982: 76–77).

The "freeholding" *campesinos parcelarios* were allegedly in a better position to benefit from government agrarian reform measures because, unlike their lowland hacienda-peasant neighbors, who Gudmundson suggests had only rudimentary notions of private property in land, the "Cartagos" were bearers of a smallholding tradition and *mentalité*.

Lowland peasants did extract subsistence resources from haciendas, either in furtive incursions or long-term occupations. But a substantial sector of the lowland "hacienda" peasantry also had a strong commercial orientation.[12] This is evident from the volume of coastal shipping from the Tempisque Valley to Puntarenas, the frequent references in a variety of sources (including many cited here) to fencing and commercial production by smallholders, the widespread cultivation of coffee in mid-altitude areas settled by Guanacastecans and Nicaraguans, the considerable size and relative permanence of some lowland squatters' holdings, and the large number of lowland agriculturalists who employed permanent wage labor (ANCR Gob. 2938—1911: 59–63). This sector of "middle" peasants or small commercial producers was far from negligible. In 1911 in Carrillo, for example, an exclusively lowland canton with few "Cartago" settlers, 53 persons employed 3 or more permanent peons; only 5 of these were among the latifundistas who controlled most of the canton's land. Similarly, two other lowland villages—Bolsón de Santa Cruz, bordering Hacienda El Viejo, and Colorado de Abangares, within the limits of La Palma—each had 17 such employers.

Many lowland smallholders remember fencing, planting hedgerows, or marking the borders of their farms with clearings (*rondas*). Cadastral plans of land claims and hacienda occupations by peasants of Guanacastecan origin also suggest a pattern of clearly partitioned parcels, often divided by fences.[13] This alone would suggest a need to qualify the notion that the lowland peasantry viewed land as a "fetish," a natural good that could not or should not be permanently demarcated or appropriated. These plans also permit an analysis of land distribution in occupied areas. As Tables 4.1–4.4 demonstrate, many lowland peasants controlled areas of over 100 hectares and were almost certainly involved in more than mere subsistence production. In fact, the plots controlled by "Cartago" peasants in highland El Líbano were on average smaller than those of lowland peasants in the occupied areas for which data are available.

It is also far from clear that the central Costa Rican migrants who occupied mining company lands had as strong a commercial orientation as Gudmundson suggests. Pedro Pérez Zeledón, an official who visited the mining areas in 1922 and prepared a report for the Supreme Court, suggested that the failure of the so-called *campesinos parcelarios* to establish permanent fields or clearly bounded farms was, in fact, an obstacle to the realization of government-sponsored parcelization schemes (see below).[14] In the absence of adequate roads, nearby markets, and processing infrastructure, these subsistence-oriented "Cartagos" grew only maize and beans. The dreams embodied in their history of smallholding coffee culture had to await both improved material conditions and more secure tenure status.[15]

The response of the "two peasantries" to government reform efforts also appears on closer examination to be less divergent than Gudmundson suggests. In general, land expropriations by the govern-

TABLE 4.1
Occupation of El Líbano Mining Zone, Highland Tilarán, 1924

Size of holding (hectares)	Occupants			Farm Area			
	N	Percent	Cumulative percent	Total hectares	Average hectares	Percent	Cumulative percent
<50	25	56%	56%	618	25	30.2%	30.2%
50>100	14	31	87	705	50	34.4	64.6
100>150	4	9	96	425	106	20.8	85.4
150>200	2	4	100	300	150	14.6	100.00
TOTAL	45			2,048	46		

SOURCES: Cabrera 1924: 159–60.

TABLE 4.2
Occupation of Sitio El Espíritu Santo, Lowland Santa Cruz and Carrillo, 1926

Size of holding (hectares)	Occupants			Farm Area			
	N	Percent	Cumulative percent	Total hectares	Average hectares	Percent	Cumulative percent
<50	37	61%	61%	551.4	14.9	11.3%	11.3%
50>100	7	11	72	582.9	83.3	11.9	23.2
100>150	7	11	84	838.9	119.8	17.1	40.4
150>200	3	5	89	499.2	166.4	10.2	50.6
200>250	4	7	96	884.0	221.0	18.1	63.8
250>300	0	0	96	0	0	0	68.6
300>350	2	3	99	631.8	315.9	12.9	81.5
350>400	0	0	99	0	0	0	81.5
400>450	0	0	99	0	0	0	81.5
450>500	0	0	99	0	0	0	81.5
550>600	0	0	99	0	0	0	81.5
600+	1	2	100	904.6	904.6	18.5	100.0
TOTAL	61			4,892.8	80.2		

SOURCE: CN 53—1926.

TABLE 4.3
Occupation of the Property of Fernando Lorenzo Brenes, Quebrada Grande de Liberia, 1946

Size of holding (hectares)	Occupants			Farm Area			
	N	Percent	Cumulative percent	Total hectares	Average hectares	Percent	Cumulative percent
<50	21	62%	62%	289.7	13.8	14.2%	14.2%
50>100	6	18	80	366.0	61.0	17.9	32.1
100>150	2	6	86	289.0	144.5	14.1	46.2
150>200	3	9	94	584.3	194.8	28.5	74.7
200>250	1	3	97	200.0	200.0	9.8	84.5
250>300	0	0	97	0	0	0	84.5
300>350	1	3	100	318.0	318.0	15.5	100.0
TOTAL	34			2,047.0	60.2		

SOURCE: CN 9269—1946.

TABLE 4.4
Occupation of Hacienda Santa Rosa, Cuajiniquil, Lowland La Cruz, 1947

Size of holding (hectares)	Occupants			Farm Area			
	N	Percent	Cumulative percent	Total hectares	Average hectares	Percent	Cumulative percent
<50	21	40%	40%	378.0	18.0	8.7%	8.7%
50>100	14	27	67	1,064.0	76.0	24.5	33.2
100>150	10	19	86	1,162.0	116.2	26.8	60.0
150>200	4	8	94	701.0	175.3	16.1	76.1
200>250	2	4	98	469.0	234.5	10.8	86.9
250>300	0	0	98	0	0	0	86.9
300>350	0	0	98	0	0	0	86.9
350>400	0	0	98	0	0	0	86.9
400>450	0	0	98	0	0	0	86.9
450>500	0	0	98	0	0	0	86.9
550>600	1	2	100	567.0	567.0	13.1	100.0
TOTAL				4,341.0	83.5		

SOURCE: CN 9565—1947.

ment in this period did little more than leave occupants in de facto possession of expropriated properties. In a few cases, such as that of La Palma (discussed below), much of the land was declared *baldíos*, open to claims under the relevant laws. In no case did these early government reforms involve any large-scale titling of plots by occupants of expropriated lands. Nevertheless, to suggest that the holdings of the lowland peasants were nothing more than "phantasmal parcels" (Gudmundson 1982: 89) obscures the frequency with which Guanacastecans, including those who occupied lowland latifundios, established permanent holdings. Moreover, when areas such as La Palma were declared open to claims, lowland Guanacastecans had few reservations about registering their plots with the cadastral survey office (e.g., CN 8049, 8050—1931).[16]

If the Guanacastecans did at times oppose the fencing of sitios by "Cartago" newcomers, this was not because they were against fencing per se or because they themselves did not also have small fenced plots, necessary to protect their crops from livestock. Rather, it was because such fencing, like that carried out by latifundistas, threatened *one aspect* of their livelihood, the breeding of cattle. But cattle breeding was never more than one element in a multifaceted strategy for survival, which also included agricultural production for subsistence and the market, hunting, fishing, and—for many—rustling. Lowland Guanacastecan peasants often sought to survive—and perhaps even prosper—as petty-commodity producers rather than as subsistence horticulturalists with a fetishized view of landed property. This "modern" aspiration, while less mystical or romantic than the image of a "preeconomic" past, was no less powerful in firing resistance to hacendado threats to peasant livelihood.

By the early 1920s landlord-peasant conflicts that had been building for decades brought what were for Costa Rica major outbreaks of antilandlord violence, some of which continued sporadically into the following decade. State intervention and ad hoc agrarian reforms defused the most serious of these confrontations, but the region's peasants— Guanacastecan and "Cartago" alike—were not always the ultimate beneficiaries of well-intentioned antilatifundista measures by distant San José governments. The most dramatic agrarian struggles of this period occurred in lowland Abangares, where villagers resisted efforts by French and later Arab latifundistas to seize lands they had always used as their own; in highland Liberia, where Nicaraguan hacendados attempted to expand into areas populated by both longtime residents and new settlers; and in the Tilarán-Abangares mining zone, where foreign mining and colonization companies confronted widespread squatting by recent arrivals from central Costa Rica.[17] Nevertheless, it should be remembered that land occupations in Guanacaste were not the elaborate, carefully planned affairs known elsewhere in Latin America (Gould 1990; Hobsbawm 1974) or indeed in contemporary Costa Rica, but were generally the cumulative effect of individual families settling unused lands. Thus, except when peasants fought for their rights to land, the occupations had more in common with frontier colonization than with organized agrarian movements.

Lowland Abangares

On the northern coast of the Gulf of Nicoya, near the mouth of the Tempisque, natural salt deposits led to the formation in the nineteenth century of two sizable communities, Colorado and San Buenaventura. Together they produced much of the salt sold in central Costa Rica, as well as that used by the region's expanding cattle industry. The land used by village residents lay inside properties with colonial-era deeds: Haciendas Abangares, La Culebra, and La Palma. Founded in the eighteenth century, La Palma was the largest estate in the region, with an estimated 40,000 to 60,000 hectares. Described by the nineteenth-century traveler John L. Stephens (1969 [1854]) as being the size of a German principality, La Palma was acquired in 1894 by a French firm, J. A. Gluck and Company, which initially did little more than exploit the hacienda's cedar and mahogany while completely neglecting the livestock and pastures (Gudmundson 1982).

Residents of the area apparently considered their isolation an advantage, but at about this time they began to receive sustained and unwelcome state attention for the first time. Not long after the French acquired the hacienda, the executive (*jefe político*) of Cañas canton, to which Colorado and San Buenaventura then belonged, referred to them as "rebellious villages" (*barrios revoltosos*) and noted that he had been obliged to punish 22 individuals there who had refused to report for military service. The provincial governor, remarking on the residents' petition to join Puntarenas province, across the gulf, declared that "what the petitioners seek is to elude the immediate action of the Cañas authorities in order to become subject to another, more distant authority, which cannot watch them closely, as well as to avoid military service" (ANCR Gob. 1950—1894: 4v).

Unlike most coastal settlements, Colorado and San Buenaventura were not protected by the legislation governing the "maritime mile." The law creating the "mile" established that titles such as La Palma's, that predated the 1754 royal *cédula* on "composition" of lands, retained rights over any coastal areas they included. Nevertheless, although area residents had occasionally been expected to make token payments to the land's legal owners for salt extracted, they suffered relatively little hacendado pressure prior to the early twentieth century. By 1908, however, Colorado and San Buenaventura residents were sufficiently concerned about their security to petition the Congress in support of a measure that would have expropriated lands for, and guaranteed the tenure rights of squatters (ANCR Cong. 12020—1908: 1). The authors of the petition clearly realized that the precarious legal status of their holdings within latifundio boundaries was a potential source of conflict, though they could hardly have envisioned the ambitious plans that eventually fired the imaginations of the French investors.

In 1917 the French foreman, Santiago Hermosel Viniegra, acquired the property as his own, almost certainly with funds generated from logging, and quickly resold it to François Thévenot, a wealthy philanthropist who hoped to establish a colony of French peasants (ANCR Cong. 14431—1926: 2; Gudmundson 1982; Péyroutet 1919).[18] Thévenot appointed as his supervisor and representative in Costa Rica Emile Bousqué, a businessman who had acquired a modest fortune in Argentine banking and who, according to some reports, supplied one-quarter of the capital to purchase the estate (ANCR Cong. 14431—1926: 1; *El Diario de Costa Rica*, 6 Apr. 1920, 5, 8). The purchase price of 2.0 million francs—equivalent in 1918 to 1.6 million colones, or $369,000—included 500,000 francs contingent on the expulsion of those occupying the property, estimated at 300 to 400 families of five or six persons each (ANCR Cong. 14431—1926: 3; *El Diario de Costa Rica*, 7 Apr. 1920, 8).[19]

Thévenot and Bousqué, inspired by the examples of Hawaii and the newly opened Panama Canal, with which "it would be more rapid to transport four or five thousand tons [of cargo] from La Palma to France than from La Palma to San José," hoped to begin large-scale pineapple cultivation and to construct a cannery on Chira Island in the Gulf of Nicoya, where the government had offered port installations (ANCR Cong. 11944—1920: 1). Additional plans called for cultivating henequen and grains for export, manufacturing prefabricated houses for post–World War I reconstruction in Europe, and building a trolley from La Palma to the gulf, using 100 kilometers of government-donated rails from bankrupt banana plantations (ibid; *El Diario de Costa Rica*, 6 Apr. 1920, 5).[20]

According to a 1926 congressional report on the "question of La Palma," one of Guanacaste's most important hacendados had warned Bousqué that, given the unreliability of local labor, it would be impossible to clear even 60 hectares for planting (ANCR Cong. 14431—1926: 4). Nevertheless, because of what the report termed Bousqué's "new conceptions of work methods"—reliance on labor contractors for clearing land and dismissing almost all the hacienda's permanent employees (*El Diario de Costa Rica*, 7 Apr. 1920, 5)—he was able to prepare 600 hectares in three months. Bousqué justified the firing of local workers by arguing that the twenty French colonists who arrived in late 1919 could meet the hacienda's labor needs.

The colonists, some of whom came with their families, were each supposed to receive 50 hectares, a loan of working capital, and a share of company profits (Péyroutet 1919: 6). Older residents of La Palma and nearby San Joaquín, however, remember that the French—or "los machos"—actually undertook little cultivation.[21] Instead, they followed the time-honored Guanacastecan subsistence strategy of hunting, but with a variation that did little to endear them to area residents. The French commonly shot not only deer and wild birds but also peasants' pigs and poultry. Other hacienda activity also had more in common with contemporary Guanacastecan practices than with the vision of a modern agroindustrial complex that inspired Bousqué and Thévenot. Lila Gómez, whose backyard contained remains of the hacienda's stone corrals, remembered that her father told her how the French often had more than 100 yokes of oxen hauling wood to the coast, where they shipped away "huge trunks in rafts tied with chains."

Bousqué's plan to expel residents of Colorado and San Buenaventura, who were technically illegal occupants of Hacienda La Palma, involved having them sign rental contracts that acknowledged Thévenot's ownership and committed them to paying a modest ten *céntimos* per hectare each year (ANCR Cong. 14431—1926: 11; Gudmundson 1982). The contract obligated occupants to give preference to Thévenot in selling products, prohibited them from felling trees without permission, and required them to report anyone attempting to cut timber. For Bousqué, the nominal rents stipulated in the contracts were of little importance. Instead, the agreements would have provided a basis for eviction proceedings or out-of-court settlements based on payments to occupants for "improvements."[22] In addition to pressuring occupants to sign rental contracts, Bousqué tried to impede salt extraction (*El Diario de Costa Rica*, 7 Apr. 1920, 8), which had been protected by the 1868 law that established the maritime mile. Moreover, the few local laborers he hired were not paid money, but were given metal tokens embossed with a palm tree, which could only be exchanged at the French storehouse. Francisco López, an elderly resident of La Palma whose father had been a peon for the French, recalled that this was one of the practices that most rankled the peasants. "Those were special coins, but they weren't worth anything in Las Juntas [de Abangares] or Cañas, they could only be used in the machos' store."[23]

Although some occupants did sign rental agreements, most rejected this effort to limit their rights. In March 1920 opposition took a violent turn when peasants assaulted the hacienda, burning the 600 hectares cleared for planting, shooting at the house where Bousqué and the police sent to guard the French had taken refuge, and destroying the fences and logs stored on the hacienda (ANCR Cong. 11944—1920: 2v; Gudmundson 1982). After the attack the French colonists abandoned La Palma, declaring that "it is impossible to continue working there because of the insecurity of our lives" (*El Diario de Costa Rica*, 8 Apr. 1920).

The French held a Colorado resident, Salvador Ysaba (or Izaba), responsible for the attacks and for organizing opposition to the rental contracts (ANCR Cong. 14431—1926: 11). Ysaba, whose signature appeared on virtually all correspondence to the government from the Colorado and San Buenaventura communities between 1894 and 1926, appears to have been a respected local leader. According to the 1911 census of agriculturalists employing three or more permanent laborers, he was also an employer and one of the more prosperous peasants in the area (ANCR Gob. 2938—1911: 62). His militant leadership was almost certainly rooted in his being a commercial producer rather than a subsistence-oriented "neo-Luddite."

Elderly residents of the area remember that when the *machos* left, "everything ended." All that remained of the hacienda were good stone corrals and a large *chagüite*, or plantain grove. The hacienda's horses and cattle were taken by one Felipe Díaz, who had been a foreman for the French, but—as one resident commented—"nobody knows if the animals were left to him or if he just took them." In all probability the latter is true, since the disposition of the hacienda's animals was not mentioned in any later documentation, nor is it plausible that hacendados not otherwise known for their generosity would grant a simple foreman such a valuable herd.

Following the 1920 attacks on La Palma and the desertion of the French colonists, Thévenot suspended payments due Viniegra for the property (Gudmundson 1982). The hacienda thus remained the property of Viniegra's widow, Clara Yateman Carranza, even though Thévenot continued to assert his rights for another four years. In 1924 Thévenot's new representative in Costa Rica tried to broker an agreement with the government to cede to the state some 4,000 hectares of La Palma occupied by peasants in return for payment of legal, surveying, and fencing costs (Gudmundson 1982). This proposal for settling "the question of La Palma" never reached fruition, in large part because it would have benefited the French owners almost exclusively and offered little in return. The following year, in anticipation of a similar arrangement, Yateman sent a surveyor to map the property, which was so vast it had never been measured. The surveyor, however, telegraphed San José that he had to suspend work because of the opposition of "the principal residents of Colorado," all of whom "are in agreement about decisively impeding [the survey] of their properties, which they assert are guaranteed by the Government of the Republic. . . . The residents of San Buenaventura are of the same disposition" (ANCR Gob. 7891—1925).

In 1926 Yateman ceded La Palma to the state for an equal extension of unoccupied public lands in Golfito, in southern Puntarenas (Gudmundson 1982; Kepner 1936: 83).[24] The occupants of La Palma were then permitted to title up to 100 hectares, of which 50 hectares were free and each additional hectare cost 25 colones, payable over ten years at 6 percent annual interest (ANCR Cong. 14679—1927: 2–15). Those who had more than 150 hectares of fenced land were allowed to acquire full title under the same conditions. Costa Rican citizens who were not occupants and who did not possess more than 50 hectares elsewhere or have a net worth of more than 5,000 colones were also allowed to register lots of up to 100 hectares.

This decree on land claims in La Palma contained provisions intended to secure an equitable division of the hacienda, such as a prohibition on acquiring lots with *gracias municipales* scrip, which had accumulated in the hands of land speculators, and a requirement that claimants occupy and cultivate their parcels. Nevertheless, these restrictions proved easy to circumvent, because of government inexperience and lack of on-the-ground supervision. In 1933, only seven years after the exchange of lands between Yateman and the state, a congressional committee justified a possible government acquisition of Hacienda Tenorio in Cañas by noting that "the good lands of La Palma [have] already been monopolized (*acaparadas*) by claimants" (ANCR Cong. 16726—1933: 23). The following year, acknowledging the growing concentration of land, the Congress reduced the maximum extension of baldíos that could be claimed in La Palma from 50 to 20 hectares (ANCR Cong. 17003—1934). By 1936 the provincial newspaper echoed the congressional committee's findings, reporting that in La Palma, as well as in other expropriated lands in Nicoya, "with simple claims of fifty or twenty hectares or with false titles fixed over the original titles, extensions of hundreds of hectares have been monopolized" (*El Guanacaste*, 20 Feb. 1936, 2).

The most extreme example involved a Levantine immigrant, Vicente Bonilla Morad, who had arrived in the Abangares mining district shortly after the turn of the century and whose small fortune was said to have derived from his work as a *coligallero*, or independent miner, who surreptitiously removed ore from the mines. In addition to property near the highland mining center of Las Juntas, Bonilla acquired 1,440 hectares of Hacienda La Culebra, which bordered La Palma. According to a report by the interior minister, Ricardo Pacheco (ANCR Cong. 19493—1940: 5), Bonilla received court permission for reconstructing his dilapidated property-line markers, a procedure termed "giving life to the boundary markers" (*avivamiento de mojones*). Interpreting this legal license both literally and liberally, Bonilla moved his *mojones* into adjacent sections of La Palma and then obtained a ruling in 1927 that awarded him 4,106 additional hectares and established his right to a total of 5,411 hectares, slightly less than the sum of his original titles and the "excess," or *demasías*.

Emboldened by this decision, Bonilla began fencing his hacienda and started proceedings against squatters. The occupants, however, without waiting for a court ruling, decided to take justice into their own hands and killed Bonilla one day when he went to inspect his maize fields.[25] Police arrested three suspects, who were later released for lack of evidence. When Bonilla's heirs pressed the evictions in court and demanded government backing to enforce rulings in their favor, the executive branch refused to provide support, "in order not to provoke a grave social conflict, which already had painful repercussions with the tragic attack that produced the death of Señor Bonilla" (ANCR Cong. 19493—1940: 2–3).

During the years of court battles between Bonilla's heirs and the state, dozens of other peasants occupied the property. Both the Bonillas and the occupants appealed to the state for an exchange of lands, like that granted the owners of La Palma in 1926 (ibid., 49–50; ANCR Cong. 18413—1937: 1). By 1939, one year before the settlement of the litigation, 39 occupants controlled 3,157 hectares of La Culebra. Finally, in 1940, Bonilla's heirs were permitted to exchange 2,557 hectares of occupied lands for an equivalent extension of unoccupied state lands elsewhere in Pacific Costa Rica. They ceded an additional 600 hectares, largely within the maritime zone, to the state without compensation.

In 1941 the state declared the remaining unoccupied part of La Palma closed to claims and established it as a "cattle zone" where agriculturalists, rather than ranchers, had to fence their fields (Vicarioli 1952: 120). By this time, however, in spite of government efforts to realize an agrarian reform by permitting peasants to claim lots, lowland Abangares had one of the most unequal patterns of land distribution in Guanacaste. To this day, the largest landowners include those, such as the Bonillas, who acquired sections of the old Hacienda La Palma either through claims of doubtful legality or through simply "giving life" to the property markers.

Cañas Dulces and Quebrada Grande

As early as the mid-eighteenth century, members of the Hurtado family, residents of Rivas, Nicaragua, acquired large haciendas north of Liberia. In 1870 Pedro, Alejandro, and David Hurtado Bustos, having inherited properties from their father's and mother's families, formed a corporation in Rivas called Hurtado Hermanos. Five years later they registered the title to their largest hacienda, El Jobo, with an extension estimated at 35.5 old *caballerías*.[26] In 1881 they purchased the adjacent Hacienda La Culebra (a different property from that in Abangares), said to contain 32 old caballerías, from the president of Costa Rica, Tomás Guardia (ANCR GJC r. 1264, no. 686— 1881: 1v, and r. 1264, no. 747—1883).[27] They then began a campaign to expand their vast holdings and started a long struggle to rid their properties of peasant occupants. But in highland Liberia, in contrast to lowland Abangares, the latifundistas expanded into areas to which they had only the most tenuous of claims.

In March 1883 the Hurtados brought suit for 1,200 pesos in damages against three occupants of El Encinal and Cañas Dulces, lands just east of El Jobo (ANCR GJC r. 1264, no. 466—1884). The Hurtados likely had legitimate rights to El Encinal, the title of which specified an extension of one old caballería (though it was later found to be 421 hectares) (ibid.; CN G1-2-1-271—1922). However, the property registry entry for the 136-hectare "Lands of Cañas Dulces" contained only vague boundary descriptions and indicated that it was owned in four equal shares, only one belonging to the Hurtados (ANCR Cong. 2858—1903: 2). The defendants in the suit, all Nicaraguans who had fenced small plots for maize cultivation, were joined the following year by four other occupants. Two squatters opted to settle out of court, agreeing to pay an annual rent of one-half *fanega* (336 pounds) of maize each and, in the case of one who had 30 steers, five pesos or one calf per year (ANCR GJC r. 1264, no. 466—1884: 9—11v). The judge ordered the arrest of a third occupant, even though nine years earlier one of the co-owners of Cañas Dulces had granted him access to the land.[28]

Following this resolution of the squatting problem, the Hurtados turned their attention to titling nearby state lands and to expanding holdings through partnerships with other hacendados. In 1882 they had claimed five caballerías of baldíos that were part of the Hacienda Pitahaya (ANCR JCA 5489—1882). Eleven years later David Hurtado registered a claim to 515 hectares in Llanuras de Cerda, in Cañas Dulces district (ANCR JCA 5666—1893: 5). In 1900 he formed a corporation with six partners to exploit Haciendas San Luis de Naranjo and Orosí, just south of the border (ANCR JCA—5942—1900). These properties—surveyed in 1921 at 4,970 and 15,862 hectares, respectively (CN G10-4-2-1-1921)—had been "composed" in 1763 and inherited by Luisa Rivas Lebrón de Mayorga, a corporation partner. In a typical case of "land rich, money poor" landlordism, Rivas de Mayorga joined wealthier hacendados, such as Hurtado and Manuel Joaquín Barrios Guerra, as her only means of actually using the properties, which were strategically located for importing steers. The Hurtado-Rivas partnership was short-lived, however. By 1912 Orosí had passed into the hands of Salvadora de Urcuyo, another shareholder, and by 1920 both properties belonged entirely to Barrios, whose sister had married de Urcuyo's son.[29]

The upper cordillera, where moist Atlantic trade winds permitted green grass to grow year-round, making excellent dry-season grazing sites, was the most coveted area in the post-1880 rush to title lands north of Liberia. In the late-colonial period, apart from scattered haciendas, the only settlement in this area was Cañas Dulces, founded—according to tradition—as a *coyolera*, or hideaway, where people congregated to drink contraband liquor made from the sap of coyol palms. In the late nineteenth century, refugees fleeing violence in Nicaragua began to colonize virgin forest on the slopes of Rincón de la Vieja volcano, just north of Cañas Dulces. With the exception of a 2,000-hectare tract claimed by Spanish immigrant José Lorenzo Barreto, these lands were largely baldíos. By the turn of the century the Nicaraguan colonists had founded a settlement called Quebrada Grande.[30]

The Hurtado brothers' massive latifundio passed intact to the next generation, with the marriage between Francisco Hurtado Guerra and his first cousin, Ana María Hurtado Aguirre. Don Paco, as Francisco was called, proved especially aggressive in expanding and consolidating the family estate. In 1920 he brought suit against ten occupants of El Encinal, Cañas Dulces, and San Roque, a section of Hacienda El Jobo (ANCR GJC r. 1264, no. 5—1920, no. 27—1920, no. 28—1920). The occupants asserted that they were not in Hurtado's property, but in lands belonging either to the Cañas Dulces community or to the state. Most were day laborers from Cañas Dulces who had been in the area for as long as ten years, with small fenced plots of maize, sugar, and coffee. They admitted felling timber, but it was, they claimed, primarily for their own use. One occupant, with a clear, albeit modest commercial orientation, described his finca in 1920 as containing eight *manzanas* (5.6 hectares) of pasture and guinea grass, one manzana (0.7 hectare) of plantains, one manzana of sugarcane, 1,400 coffee bushes, and a house measuring twelve by eight yards (ANCR GJC r. 1264, no. 3—1926: 5).

In addition to bringing suit against the occupants, Hurtado obtained a judicial order for the delineation of San Roque's boundaries. The first survey in 1920—in which Hurtado attempted to include as part of San Roque several small farms that were actually in the area known as Zacatal de Cañas Dulces—was opposed both by local residents and by the Liberia prosecutor (ANCR Cong. 12473—1921:

6–7v). Hurtado then went to San José, where the attorney general granted a writ overriding the Liberia prosecutor's opposition.

In March 1921 a new government surveyor, whose zealousness hinted at inducements beyond a humble public servant's salary, arrived to mark off the boundaries of San Roque. A petition to the Congress, signed by 170 Cañas Dulces residents, described how he proceeded:

From the corner of a farm of Señor José María Palomino Jirón, from north to south, he took the measurement up to the edge of the Tizate River, leaving inside Hurtado's boundaries the road which the residents use during the dry season . . . to go to wash. Then he came to the south corner of the same farm and measured toward the south, leaving inside Hurtado's boundaries the west fence of the same farm. Then he came to another plot of the same Palomino and of Juan Aquilino Acuña, which he divided in two, leaving a plantain grove and a sugarcane field to the west within Hurtado's boundaries. He continued south until reaching a clearing made by Hurtado, leaving him the untitled woods. (Ibid., 9–9v)

At this point Cañas Dulces residents, armed with sticks and machetes, intervened and prevented the survey from continuing. Pablo Ruiz, who as a young man joined the angry crowd near the Tizate, recalled that Hurtado, the surveyor, and six or eight peons came that day, tracing a route toward the river. Hurtado, he said, "didn't want to leave us anything more than a tiny piece of land. Then 50 or 60 men went there, and he was warned, 'If you pass there, you die!' The people were furious. I and one other asked them not to kill the peons. They nearly killed them. Those that they were going to kill were the surveyor and the señor [Hurtado]. Anyway, the man stopped the job right there."

The peasants' action brought a swift response. Although the suit against the "occupants" was under appeal, and a survey was illegal without a judge's presence, Hurtado's surveyors appeared in Cañas Dulces on April 1, 1921, escorted by twelve police from Liberia armed with Mauser rifles. When residents protested that the disputed lands were baldíos and not those of San Roque, the police commander declared that they were being surveyed by government order, that nobody had the right to oppose him, and that if anyone did, he would fire at them "the last shot" (ANCR Cong. 12473– 1921: 10). Over the next several days, the police, who—as Pablo Ruiz remembered—were "at the orders of Hurtado," took seven prisoners, among them two peasants who had signed a protest telegram published in a San José newspaper.

The prisoners were released within a few days, but legal proceedings continued against occupants of lands claimed by Hurtado. At least one Cañas Dulces "occupant" agreed to settle out of court, selling "improvements," including fenced crops and a house, to Hurtado for 790 colones (ANCR GJC r. 1264, no. 27—1921: 39). Hurtado, meanwhile, turned his attention to Quebrada Grande, just north of Cañas Dulces, where peasants had occupied San Antonio, another section of Hacienda El Jobo.

In Quebrada Grande, Hurtado began acquiring numerous small lots in and around San Antonio by paying "improvements" costs. Those that refused his offers were taken to court in a large suit, which Hurtado won in March 1922 (ANCR GJC r. 1264, no. 28—1922: 58–67). Only one defendant accepted the ruling and left the land, however. During March and April, Quebrada Grande residents attacked the main house of El Jobo with gunfire, forcing Hurtado to flee to San José with his family, burned Finca La Fortuna (part of El Jobo), destroyed 2,000 of Hurtado's coffee bushes, and killed the police agent stationed in the village (Acosta 1923: 195–96; ANCR Gob. 8094—1924: 33–34, 38–39).

Local tradition holds that Hurtado escaped from the night attack on his house only because he disguised himself as a woman and fled on horseback. This may be an apocryphal reflection of the *machista* ethos in Guanacaste, serving to demean and feminize an enemy and to excuse his escape, as well as ennobling attackers who would not fire on a woman. But while the tough don Paco's cross-dressing remains legendary in Quebrada Grande, nothing that would confirm the tale—as might be expected—appears in documentary sources left behind by the latifundistas, their lawyers, or their sympathizers in government. Following his flight, Hurtado remained in the capital for several months. Tensions in Quebrada Grande abated with the government's expropriation in 1922 of 421 hectares of El Encinal, land for which Hurtado was offered an equivalent extension of state lands of his choice.[31]

Shortly after the violence of 1922, the murdered policeman was replaced by another brought in from Nicaragua, reportedly by the Hurtados. Baltazar Brizuela, who came from Nicaragua as a boy in 1915, had vivid memories of the new police agent and chuckled about how the appointment of a brutal "authority" had turned out well for the village children. The guard had a reputation for being dangerously aggressive. On one occasion he mounted a local resident with whom he had a minor dispute and, jabbing with his spurs, forced his unfortunate victim to carry him on all fours. Outraged Quebrada Grande residents succeeded in imposing a 700-colón (approximately $160) fine for this offense and had the police agent relieved of his duties in 1923.[32] Two years later, the fine was used to construct the village's first school and to buy maps and educational equipment.

The agrarian struggle in this part of Liberia, in contrast to those elsewhere in the province, was apparently influenced to some degree by political currents from outside the region, though details remain sparse. The provincial police commander referred to the struggle against Hurtado as a "unionist movement" and blamed one Julio Robles for both the 1922 violence and the murder of the Quebrada Grande police agent (Acosta 1923). In Central America in the 1920s, the term "unionist movement" usually referred to the Partido Unionista, a group favoring Central American unity (Creedman 1977: 204), but it also sometimes connoted radical egalitarian or anarcho-syndicalist ideas, such as those later associated with the Nicaraguan nationalist hero Augusto C. Sandino (Fonseca Amador 1980: 188).[33]

Older residents recall that an individual named Julio Robles did appear in Quebrada Grande shortly before the violence of March 1922, that he was armed with a Mauser rifle, and that many people believed he would resolve disputes between Hurtado and local peasants. The Liberia police commander pursued Robles unsuccessfully for four days in northern Guanacaste, but the fugitive crossed into Nicaragua, where he was lost from sight (Acosta 1923). Apart from these few details regarding an "outside agitator" in the Cañas Dulces–Quebrada Grande events, however, it is unclear what Robles' political affiliation may have been or how he conceived his mission.

Latifundistas and their supporters also blamed the Partido Agrícola and the supporters of Jorge Volio, who later coalesced in the Partido Reformista, for inspiring or directing agrarian struggles in Cañas Dulces–Quebrada Grande (e.g., ANCR 8094—1924: 41). The Partido Agrícola, a short-lived group founded in 1922, ran a close second in the 1924 presidential elections and captured a majority in the Congress (Volio 1972: 177–80). Its leaders included members of the central Costa Rican and Guanacastecan elites, and its platform, far from being radical or even reformist, emphasized new incentives for the agricultural sector. Although one of the two Guanacastecan deputies elected under the party's banner, Francisco Mayorga Rivas, was a key proponent of agrarian reform, the other, Aristides Baltodano Briceño, was a steadfast supporter of the property rights of large landowners.[34] Nevertheless, the fact that Mayorga had sponsored legislation to expropriate lands in Cañas Dulces as early as 1903 certainly encouraged residents to defend their rights to land, even if the Partido Agrícola itself never adopted an antilatifundista stance.

The Partido Reformista, founded in 1923 by the radical priest Jorge Volio, was the first significant organization in Costa Rica to propose wide-reaching labor and land-tenure reforms (De La Cruz 1980: 141; Volio 1972). Although it was created after the violence of 1921–22 and could not be blamed for those events, Hurtado's lawyer implied in 1924 that the Volistas and the Partido Agrícola were behind what he branded "the new seditious movement . . . of some residents of Quebrada Grande over the same matters of lands" (ANCR Gob. 8094—1924: 38). The lawyer's letters to San José officials, in which he attempted to secure a firearms permit and an appointment for a protégé as a policeman in Cañas Dulces, indicated that tensions remained high some two years after the main outbreak of violence:

I wish you to do me the service of extending to me an authorization to carry a weapon. You know that my profession is not for conquering sympathies and that lawyers do not lack those that bear them ill will; and if it is true that nobody can fault me because I do not give them cause, nor do I have over me threats from anybody, it is true that I handle business of such people as don Paco Hurtado, who lives struggling against a herd of Nicaraguans (*una manada de nicas*), who nobody knows why they are there, who are constantly entering the sitio of El Jobo to take land and install shacks and dedicate themselves to theft; that every action in the Tribunals provokes threats, damages, and even uprisings, such as those that were in Cañas Dulces and Quebrada Grande. . . . I also handle other businesses of Sobrado, Barrios, and Wilson & Salazar, which are no less compromising for me, and for anyone who manages them, and because of which prudence counsels me not to go unarmed, above all at night, since you know that here they might easily shoot one in front of one's house without anybody noticing the culprit. (ANCR Gob. 8094—1924: 33–34)

If outside influences and "agitators" played a role in the Cañas Dulces–Quebrada Grande conflicts, the struggle began and was sustained largely by the residents' indigenous organization. In 1921, for example, Cañas Dulces residents directed petitions to the Congress and took up a collection to send three leaders to retrieve colonial-era deeds from archives in Nicaragua where preindependence titles for the old Nicoya jurisdiction were still held.[35] They also hired a lawyer to defend their interests. However, these well-intentioned efforts were easily frustrated. Pablo Ruiz, grandson of one of those who traveled to Managua in search of the all-important papers, reflected on the power inherent in the deeds and on the perfidy of lawyers, ruefully confessing that on returning from Nicaragua, "my grandfather left the title in my hands. He told me, 'Don't give this title to anyone.' Well, Hurtado's lawyer spoke with the village's lawyer and allied with him. In an agreement, he removed the most important and interesting and best pages. So the title was lost. It marked the boundaries and everything. But now it wouldn't be of any use anyway."

This account may reflect the widespread tendency of threatened smallholders to imbue land documents with almost supernatural qualities and to rationalize unfavorable outcomes of agrarian struggles with stories of their loss or theft. But as a historical narrative or an articulation of assumptions about appropriate action, it suggests a strong commitment to the resolution of problems through the political process. Only when these possibilities appeared exhausted, because of collusion between Hurtado and the local authorities (and perhaps between Hurtado's and the community's lawyers as well), did the peasants react in a violent manner. As in the case of La Palma and other similarly conflictive situations, the partial solution represented by government expropriations of disputed lands was achieved in large part because of the attention attracted by peasant violence.

Tilarán and Highland Abangares

Pioneers had tried to settle the heavily forested Tilarán mountains in the early nineteenth century (Sandner 1962, 1: 113). But only in the late 1880s did sustained migrations begin from the western *meseta central* and particularly from San Ramón, Alajuela, scarcely 40 kilometers away. By the turn of the century some half dozen families lived in La Cabra (later called Tilarán), where they were neighbors to two major absentee-owned properties, Alberto Fait's Hacienda La Lombardía and Roberto Crespi's Hacienda Quebrada Azul (*El Guanacaste*, 8 July 1936, 4). In nearby Abangares, migrants founded settlements in forests they presumed to be baldíos, though surveys later showed their land to be inside foreign mining companies' claims. Within two decades the flow of "Cartagos" to the southern cordillera constituted a massive land occupation, which the mining companies only belatedly tried to reverse.

The first indication of conflict occurred in 1906 as the Congress debated a proposed settlement between the government and the River Plate Company, which had acquired the rights to claim state lands granted to Minor Keith (see Chapter 1 above). Two years earlier, a presidential decree had nullified the Soto-Keith contract, under which Keith received rights to 800,000 acres of state lands, because River Plate had not cultivated any of the land it acquired from Keith. After extended litigation, an agreement allowed for the "consolidation" of River Plate's claims in a 30,763-hectare "lot" in the part of Cañas canton that was to become Tilarán and Abangares (Cabrera 1924; Pérez Zeledón 1922).[36] The prospect that this would cause disputes led highland Cañas residents to petition the Congress in 1906:

We cannot permit that our canton be the only one sacrificed. That quantity of land which the company claims includes in its totality all the lands of the canton, and it will oblige the residents to emigrate, since they are entirely agriculturalists and will not have lands to plant more crops. Thus the most flourishing town of Guanacaste [will be] reduced to misery.... In those lands there are many families with farms, and it will be a seedbed of disturbances and misery. (Quoted in Pérez Zeledón 1922: 342)

When the Congress approved the contract the following year, it added a clause that committed River Plate to the return of 2,000 hectares to the state, including those areas already occupied by squatters within eight kilometers of the cantonal seat and the additional extension needed to form a 2,000-hectare lot on either side of the Cañas River. Occupants were to be allowed to acquire rights to cultivated or fenced plots by paying five colones per hectare to the municipality.

When it came time to survey the lands, however, two difficulties emerged. For one thing, it was impossible to prove who had been in possession of plots prior to the contract with River Plate. And, as a later report on the situation noted,

The occupied parts within the eight-kilometer radius are disseminated in a large area, and perhaps not one of them is closed with fences, so that measuring and situating them on the company's general plan would be a prolonged and difficult task. . . . No [occupant] has formal or stable crops nor permanent improvements. The crops are only clearings for temporary plantings of maize or beans; and the constructions are huts, which last a short time and which can easily be moved to another place. (Pérez Zeledón 1922: 343)

As a result of this situation, hardly appropriate for modern survey-ing techniques, the contract with River Plate was modified in 1908–9 so that lands returned to the government would be measured in one tract. Occupants whose plots fell outside the 2,000 hectares were thus still considered illegal "parasites." By 1920 new invasions of the company's property had brought the number of occupants to between 300 and 400 families totaling 1,500 to 2,000 persons (ibid.).

This massive occupation led the River Plate Company to attempt a landlord-sponsored agrarian reform, offering plots to occupants at 20 colones per hectare plus survey costs. The company reserved for itself mineral and timber rights, as well as the prerogative of con-structing power and communications lines, roads and railways, and aqueducts. The high asking price and restrictive conditions, how-ever, meant that only a few occupants used this opportunity to legal-ize their holdings. The company then initiated a concerted legal and extralegal eviction effort, and "little by little a threatening atmo-sphere developed between the representatives of the company and the occupants, which nobody cared to moderate" (ibid.).

In early 1922 Frederick Hopkins, administrator for the Guanacaste Development Company, which had acquired River Plate's holdings, attempted to prevent occupants of company land from clearing and burning their parcels so they could plant at the onset of the ap-proaching rainy season (ibid.; Acosta 1923; ANCR Cong. 15708— 1930 in Gudmundson 1978a). On February 11, 50 agriculturalists from near the El Líbano mine went to the local police to request permission to cultivate lands they occupied. Gunfire broke out, leav-ing two dead and two wounded peasants and two dead company employees. Some witnesses blamed police and company employees for firing first, while others blamed the peasants. A judicial investiga-tion, however, asserted that "it would not be possible to affirm which of the bands fired first on the other" (Pérez Zeledón 1922: 342). Following the shootout,

came the sacking of the company store, which lasted all night and in which people who did not belong to the group promoting the riot took part, taking advantage of the occasion; and also, the dynamite bombs went off all night, without more result than minor damages to the ducts and the water wheel, which were repaired quickly, reestablishing the pulverization of ore after a few days. The use of dynamite ceased with the arrival of the authorities from Cañas at about 1:00 P.M. on the twelfth. (Ibid.)

The peasants' organization, in the "invasions" of mining company lands and in the 1922 violence, appears to have involved little more than ad hoc, temporary coalitions intended to attain immediate goals, such as signing petitions to San José or consolidating new areas of occupation. The "rioters" were said to have "harbored for many years vindictive sentiments in their hearts, which of fatal necessity had to explode one day given a propitious occasion." But the subsequent judicial investigation failed to find any evidence of "outside instigation" in the El Líbano attack (ibid.). Indeed, most "rioters," with the exception of those considered leaders, reported to Cañas two days after the violence to testify about the events, a manifestation of considerable faith in the possibilities of a legal, nonviolent resolution of their problems. The individual viewed as the leader, one Constantino Medrano, did not appear to testify, but he was not subsequently brought to trial or otherwise made to suffer for his participation in the violence.

Despite the drama in which irate agriculturalists and their allies employed that classic miner's weapon, the dynamite bomb, against foreign investors' property, the state response was remarkably conciliatory and continued the pattern of ad hoc agrarian reforms implemented in La Palma and Liberia.[37] In 1922 the government purchased 3,375 hectares of Hacienda Quebrada Azul in nearby Tilarán, which, like the mining companies' lands, was occupied by large numbers of "parasites" (ANCR Cong. 17003 1934; ANCR Gob. 8054 1924). The Congress also appropriated funds for purchasing up to 9,000 hectares in the mining zones, which were to be sold to occupants at cost—for twenty colones per hectare. Over the next decade, during which mining properties changed hands frequently, the government purchased almost 20,000 hectares for resale to squatters.[38]

The frequent transfers of mining properties suggest that by the 1920s speculative rather than productive considerations were likely to be most important to the U.S. and British investors that came and went in the southern Guanacaste cordillera. Mining ventures required substantial and continual capital investments and could not be expected to render immediate returns, especially once ore yields began to decline in the 1920s and 1930s (García 1984: 53). Just as lowland cattle haciendas suffered "external sieges" that constrained investment and induced landlords to sell properties to the state, the growing exhaustion of ore veins (with the virtual cessation of gold production—though not of silver—in the mid-1920s) and the no less alarming "parasite" invasions often led the companies to view "expropriation" with compensation as the most profitable option available.

Speculative acquisition of mining properties did not imply the severe pressures on squatters that might have accompanied investments by genuinely production-minded owners. After the violent events of 1922 in El Líbano, the mining companies largely ceased attempts to evict occupants, placing their hopes instead on government purchase of occupied properties. Nevertheless, once the government stepped in, peasant occupants rarely paid it for the land or received full title.[39]

Years after, the El Líbano riot remained a key reference point for the region's peasants and landlords. In the mid-1930s, for example, a U.S. company that hoped to establish a colony for German Jews fleeing Hitler's Germany acquired Hacienda Tenorio, adjacent to the Tilarán mining zone (*El Guanacaste*, 3 Oct. 1937, 1, 6). The eastern part of the hacienda had long been occupied by smallholders whose parcels had been respected by previous owners. The occupants, apparently convinced of the veracity of anti-Semitic stereotypes, expressed fears that the 1,500 refugee families would "bring capital of approximately 60 million colones [$10.7 million], a sufficient sum to monopolize half of Guanacaste" (ibid., 1). In 1937, after the company constructed barbed wire fences that cut through peasants' plots, 50 occupants marched on the hacienda house "to let the director know that they would oppose any eviction attempt in an energetic and powerful way." Then, invoking fears of renewed violence, they petitioned for government intervention "in order to avoid another El Líbano." Although this warning did not elicit a government response, it did lead the colonization company to abandon its plans. Six years later, Paul Van Zeeland, a former prime minister of Belgium, unveiled a scheme to found a colony of his compatriots in Tenorio, but when he learned of the problem posed by the "parasites," he too desisted (*El Guanacaste*, 1 Apr. 1943, 1).

Foreign Landlords, State Reforms, and Peasant "Ludditism"

The most severe agrarian conflicts of this period—in La Palma, highland Liberia, and Tilarán-Abangares—involved foreign landlords, a factor of no small importance in state efforts to settle disputes through agrarian reform. That foreigners were prominent in these confrontations reflected their importance in the Guanacaste land-owning class, their familiarity with forms of estate organization other than the "invaded" hacienda, and their greater willingness to employ coercion to evict occupants. Foreign hacendados brought with them an absolutist conception of property rights, which did not conform to the reality of early-twentieth-century Guanacaste, and notions of labor discipline that were often at odds with local tradition. Even Nicaraguan hacendado families, whose presence in northern Guanacaste frequently dated to colonial times, provoked clashes with local peasants when they tried to impose a harsher, Nicaraguan-style hacienda model. It is not surprising that the most effective corps of private hacienda guards were those formed by foreign landowners, such as Sobrado, Barrios, Hurtado, Keith, and Wilson. While private patrols were intended primarily to repel land invasions, anxieties about being gunned down by anonymous and invisible enemies, much as had occurred in the case of Vicente Bonilla Morad, were also widespread. In a typical remark, the provincial newspaper commented in 1937 that "for fear of murderers no capitalist moves around here if he is not in the custody of fifteen or twenty sabaneros" (*El Guanacaste*, 15 Aug. 1937, 6).

Guanacastecan peasants viewed foreign landlords with an apprehension rarely extended to Costa Rican hacendados. In petitions to San José, they frequently appealed to nationalistic sentiments, emphasizing the foreign citizenship of hacendados with whom they were in conflict. In a characteristic appeal, residents of Guardia de Liberia, after describing how they lost a long legal battle for their land, noted that, "consequently, the Costa Rican land where our houses and farms are belongs today to the Spaniard Señor Sobrado" (ANCR Cong. 17150—1934: 3). In 1936 letter writers to the provincial newspaper repeatedly protested that "Mister Wilson," whom one termed "the Kaiser," was charging tolls of five colones per cart on a road that crossed Hacienda El Viejo, even when the passengers were sixth-grade schoolgirls from Liberia (*El Guanacaste*, 1 June 1936, 3, and 15 Dec. 1936, 1). Five years later, residents of highland Bagaces denounced "el Mister" for ordering that large trees be felled across the trail to Aguas Claras, "to the extent that it is impossible to pass even on horseback" (*El Guanacaste*, 7 July 1941, 4). The frequent references to "the *Spaniard* Sobrado," "*Mister* Wilson," "the *Turk* Bonilla Morad," or "foreign interests" were intended to evoke images of a Costa Rica in which Costa Ricans no longer had control of the land.[40]

Such nationalist entreaties, which sought to appeal to the Costa Rican dominant class and its legislative representatives, became increasingly common during and after the intense antilandlord violence of the early 1920s. In 1921, for example, one indignant Guanacastecan congressional deputy, arguing for the expropriation of 150 hectares from the United Fruit Company's Hacienda Paso Hondo in Cañas, employed the disquieting image of the enclave already familiar to his audience from the growing debate over the company's privileges elsewhere in the country.[41] The inhabitants of the river port of Bebedero were, he said, "often harassed because of the dominion which, with or without rights, the company claims. They cannot construct or rebuild. . . . They do not even have a field to bury their dead, nor a house which they can say belongs to the community, nor a school on its own land: everything lies on a foreign soil within the Fatherland" (ANCR Cong. 12474—1921: 1–2).

Landowners too, including even prominent foreign latifundistas, employed jingoist appeals to enlist government support, asserting that occupants of their properties were aliens, almost always Nicaraguans. In 1941, for example, during the dispute between Wilson and local peasants over the road to highland Bagaces, Wilson's lawyer charged that "among the persons . . . who say they are residents of Aguas Claras are unknown people (desconocidos), of Nicaraguan nationality, who according to reports do not have their immigration papers in order" (Diario de Costa Rica, 1 July 1941, 6).

Were the Guanacastecan perpetrators of antilandlord violence in the 1920s and 1930s "anachronistic, neo-Luddite[s]," as Gudmundson (1983c: 146) has proposed? Vladimir De La Cruz has argued similarly that agrarian struggles in lowland Guanacaste were "rudimentary forms of social class struggle, including forms of banditry or criminality, which because of the absence of class consciousness develop[ed] in an instinctive or emotional way" (1980: 74).

Both views are based on the notion that Guanacastecan peasants (in the lowlands at least) were politically unsophisticated and had a "fetishized" view of landed property that did not permit identification of their "true" class interests. But these early-twentieth-century agrarian struggles, while challenging landlord threats to peasant livelihood, also manifested understanding and acceptance of legitimate authority in ways that were hardly simply "instinctive": the repeated

petitions to San José from peasants throughout the province requesting expropriations of occupied lands, the journey of Cañas Dulces
residents to distant archives in Nicaragua to retrieve old titles, the
peaceful marches of Tenorio squatters to protest foreign colonization
schemes. Violence and "banditry" were virtually always a last resort,
"rudimentary" forms of struggle perhaps, and with strong emotional
components, but employed only when other kinds of recourse were
largely or completely exhausted. The targets chosen for attack—
landlords and hacienda houses—indicate that the protagonists of
these struggles, unlike the Luddites of popular imagination, had a
clear vision of the source of their troubles and a consciousness with
substantial class content, though of a smallholder rather than a
proletarian variety.[42]

Assaults on landlords, while few in number, often obtained the
desired result—retention of access to land. This was especially the
case when a history of petitions and peaceful protestations could be
adduced as evidence of frustrated just intentions. In the Costa Rican
context, where important sectors of the dominant class from the
central part of the country were hostile to latifundismo and inclined
toward reformist solutions to social problems, antilandlord violence
was an effective tactic for attracting the attention of potential political allies. However "instinctive" Guanacastecan peasants may have
been, they acted to maintain access to land, an obvious expression of
class interest for smallholding peasants. And when they were able to
achieve this goal, through state intervention or successful "external
sieges," the disintegration of their transitory and informal organizations resulted from successfully obtaining immediate objectives
rather than from a failure of will or an undeveloped consciousness.

As the next chapter suggests, the ultimate outcomes of government reforms were not markedly different in the plains and in the
cordillera. In both zones, such efforts contributed to the consolidation of a smallholding peasantry that was to play a crucial role in
an increasingly integrated regional production structure and—indirectly—in local efforts to gain access to foreign markets.

5 ✦ The Transition to the Beef Export Economy

> The best, richest, and most productive of our farms are
> worth nothing for the bankers or moneylenders of San José.
> The progress of agriculture in these conditions has to be
> very slow; as a consequence, production becomes scarce.
> With the aid of rural credit, we will multiply our production
> a hundred times.
> —Román Mayorga, Governor of Guanacaste, 1914

> Our homeland should not be an importing country, but a
> country that exports cattle.
> —Editor of *Escuela de Agricultura* magazine, 1931

While the visionary hacendado-entrepreneur Fernando Castro Cervantes advertised his dream that Guanacaste would become rich like Argentina from the cattle business, other hacendado-politicians pushed for policies aimed at realizing that ambition. No figure bulks larger in the appreciative reminiscences of older Guanacastecan cattlemen than that of Ricardo Jiménez Oreamuno, a longtime congressional deputy, three-term president of the Republic, and owner of large haciendas in Puntarenas and San José provinces. Jiménez, who campaigned for three decades to secure protection for the livestock industry, finally succeeded in 1932, during his third term as president, in having the Congress impose high tariffs on cattle imported from Nicaragua (Jiménez 1903, 1930, 1931). Almost universally credited today with having single-handedly rescued the cattle industry from technological backwardness and economic stagnation, Jiménez has assumed near-mythical proportions in the popular imagination: in Guanacaste for his sponsorship of the 1932 protectionist laws and in the country as a whole for epitomizing the "Olympian" style of "enlightened" personalist rule that characterized early-twentieth-century Costa Rican regimes and that ended in 1936 with the conclusion of his last term in office.[1]

Guanacaste's incorporation into foreign beef markets in the 1950s was not, however, any more the result of individual prescience than it was a simple reaction to international demand. Sidney Mintz, in a critique of world-system approaches to global economic history (1977), argued forcefully for including "local initiative and local response" in the study of how peripheral regions are brought into broader economic circuits. Illustrating his position with a sketch of Caribbean production relations, highly variable over time and space, Mintz gave more attention in practice to "response" than to "initiative." But his point is nonetheless important for an understanding of the role of human agency in peripheral zones in the transitions that precede their integration into international markets.

In Guanacaste the 1930s and 1940s were such a critical period, when Costa Rica gradually ceased its dependence on imported Nicaraguan cattle, attained self-sufficiency in beef production, and—in the early 1950s—began to ship substantial quantities of live cattle and beef abroad. Far from indicating that the depression "killed" the cattle trade, as Victor Bulmer-Thomas implies in his otherwise superb treatment of the Central American economies in this period (1987: 77–78), the passage from beef importer to exporter in Costa Rica was indicative of a new dynamism rooted in "local initiatives" by the state and by large and small producers. Consciously seeking eventual access to foreign markets, local and national actors contributed to bringing about fundamental transformations that were prerequisites for participation in the international beef trade. These changes included rising livestock and land prices, directly attributable to the 1932 protectionist measures, and the strengthening of a significant group of smallholding cattle producers, which came to occupy an important position in an increasingly integrated regional production structure. The growth and consolidation of the smallholding sector, particularly in the Nicoya Peninsula and the cordillera, was the result of several new economic realities: intensified demand for feeder calves to replace lean cattle previously imported from Nicaragua; higher protection levels for rice, a key peasant crop; the modernization of agricultural-sector financial institutions; and access to land in areas not controlled by latifundios, through Costa Rica's first, little-known agrarian reform.

State Intervention in the Economy: Protectionism

The world depression of 1929 confronted all Central America with severe balance-of-payments problems, growing fiscal deficits, and sharpening social crises (Bulmer-Thomas 1987: 48–86; Merz 1937: 94–95). By the early 1930s Costa Rica, a small country with a weak domestic market, had few policy instruments for confronting an externally generated crisis of huge proportions. One area of the economy in which state intervention was feasible, however, was the Guanacaste cattle industry, dedicated in large part to fattening imported Nicaraguan steers. Costa Rican governments had taken occasional steps to protect the domestic-cattle sector since the mid-nineteenth century. Nevertheless, these measures usually became casualties of the nearly evenly matched contention between advocates of free trade and those of protectionism, which dominated discussions among economic policymakers (Calderón 1986).[2]

With Costa Rica in the depths of depression, the argument of Jiménez and his advisors that protection would generate tax revenue and result in substantial savings in foreign exchange was received favorably by virtually all interest groups in the country. The only question revolved around whether to tax imports of fattened cattle alone or of both fattened and feeder animals. Hacendados who specialized in fattening steers tended to favor a tax on fattened cattle alone, arguing that tax-free importation of lean animals should continue for at least four years, since "our cow herds cannot produce from one year to the next the steers that current consumption demands" (Gómez 1931b: 210). An agronomist in the employ of Bagaces latifundista George Wilson—whose interests included cattle breeding as well as fattening—declared himself in favor of taxing *all* imported animals, contending:

From Nicaragua, except for one or another shipment fattened on the frontier, all the cattle that enter this province are lean cattle. . . . None, absolutely none, of those who sell Nica cattle here sells his own production as it might seem. . . . What the tax would do is diminish the profit of the cattle middlemen and the fatteners and increase that of the breeders and producers, and then breeding would again expand, since it would be a better business to produce than to [just] fatten or deal in lean cattle. (Oviedo 1931: 250)

As these quotations suggest, this split in the latifundista class over fiscal policies for the cattle sector mirrored the functional division between those haciendas that bred most of their own steers and those that relied on livestock intermediaries to supply them with Nicaraguan cattle for fattening. Although members of the latter group controlled large expanses of land, generally in northern Guanacaste, and were influential within the province, their political weight at the national level was limited by their small numbers, by the fact that many were foreigners (usually Nicaraguans), and by the antiforeign and antilatifundista sentiments of the central Costa Rican elite. Because of this intraclass division and the cattlemen's lack of organization along interest-group lines, the livestock industry as a whole exerted little pressure in favor of higher tariffs, relying instead on personal efforts by President Jiménez and other influential hacendados to secure approval of new duties.[3]

When protectionist legislation finally passed in May 1932, its provisions reflected the interests of the vastly greater number of cattle ranchers involved in breeding or in both breeding and fattening steers. Even in the midst of the sometimes acrimonious discussions between breeders and fatteners, however, visionaries occasionally raised the possibility that Costa Rica would emerge as a beef-exporting nation. As an editor of the National Agricultural School's magazine remarked, "both [sides of the debate] write about what they know and understand, and both are concerned that our fatherland come to be as it should be: not an importing country, but a country that exports cattle" (Escuela de Agricultura, 19 Nov. 1931, 249).

The 1932 legislation provided for a duty of 20 colones per head on unfattened cattle imported from Nicaragua; this was to rise by 10 colones each year until 1936, though in 1934 it was permanently set at 40 colones (ANCR Cong. 20933—1932–34).[4] The law also allowed duty-free importation of heifers and cows under four years old and prohibited the slaughter of cows under eight years old that were still apt for reproduction; fattened cattle, unless of an improved variety, were charged double the usual tariff. Earlier provisions that committed the state to reimburse ranchers for the cost of importing purebred stud bulls remained in effect.[5]

The Changing Role of Small Producers

In the literature on rural Latin America, analyses of latifundio-minifundio relations almost invariably stress the smallholding sector's role as a reserve of labor for the large estates. Alain de Janvry's interpretation typifies the prevailing understanding:

The salaried labor of "free semiproletarians" settled on subsistence plots outside the *latifundio*—the *minifundistas*—constitutes a source of labor power that can be still cheaper for the landlord than servile labor. In this case two advantages are secured: the possibility of exploiting family labor on subsistence plots that cost the employer nothing, and the possibility of paying the worker for his effective labor only when it is needed. (1981: 83)

This widely held view of peasant–large farmer "functional dualism" is not incorrect, but it is incomplete, at least with regard to the post-1932 Guanacastecan livestock economy. In labor-extensive activities, such as cattle ranching, wages were a relatively minor part of an hacienda's cash expenditures. More important, smallholdings increasingly were not simply a source of "use values" or "petty commodities" that served only to subsidize the cost of rural labor, but an indispensable source of inputs for the large estates' production process (and not just for their workers' consumption, as was common in Guanacaste and elsewhere as well). After the mid-1930s, small producers provided a growing proportion of the feeder cattle required by the haciendas, animals that previously had been imported from Nicaragua. Without signifying any major change in the highly inequitable distribution of land characteristic of the region, this sector of small producers, located in areas not dominated by latifundios, in effect replaced—in the period 1932–50—the Nicaraguan ranchers who had previously provided the large Guanacastecan haciendas with unfattened feeder cattle.

This variety of latifundio-minifundio symbiosis has rarely been noted in hacienda studies, probably because most social scientists have been more concerned with resource and income distribution or the reproduction of rural labor than with levels of sectorial integration. Yet greater integration of the Guanacastecan cattle sector contributed significantly to the dynamism of both landlord and peasant enterprises, as well as to a healthier national trade balance. In areas where small and large cattle producers existed in close proximity, their new and still unequal symbiosis did not diminish competition for land, particularly since protectionism generated rising livestock and land values, which increased landlord interest in effective control of properties (Merz 1934: 4). And the asymmetries of power inherent in the smallholder-hacendado relationship were increasingly epitomized in sorrowful scenes of peasants selling their animals to large producers at rock-bottom prices at the height of the dry season, when they no longer had green grass to maintain them. But in spite of the extension of this new form of exploitation, the growth of

TABLE 5.1
Guanacaste: Distribution of Cattle, by Ownership Size Groups, 1933

Herd size	Owners	Head	Owners percent	Owners cumulative percent	Cattle percent	Cattle cumulative percent
1–10	1,788	9,685	53.1%	53.1%	7.22%	7.22%
11–20	742	10,946	22.0	75.1	8.17	15.39
21–50	531	16,526	15.8	90.9	12.33	27.71
51–100	165	11,688	4.9	95.8	8.72	36.43
101–500	112	23,283	3.3	99.1	17.37	53.80
501–1,000	12	8,058	0.4	99.5	6.01	59.81
1,001–2,000	11	13,781	0.3	99.8	10.28	70.09
2,001–3,000	4	10,398	0.1	99.9	7.76	77.85
3,001–4,000	0	0	0	99.9	0	77.85
4,001–5,000	2	9,706	0.1	100.0	7.24	85.09
5,001+	2	19,978	0.1	100.0	14.90	100.00
TOTAL	3,369	134,049				

SOURCE: Merz 1934: 10.

a more integrated production structure contributed to the economic consolidation of both large landlords and peasants, albeit generally in geographically distinct subregions.

The Guanacaste cattle census of 1933, taken primarily to facilitate the detection of contraband animals after duties were imposed, provided a detailed picture of the province's livestock economy and agrarian structure (Merz 1934). The census counted 134,049 cattle over one year old and estimated that there were an additional 27,000 calves of less than one year. Ownership of the herd, as Table 5.1 demonstrates, was extremely concentrated, with about 4 percent of owners possessing 63 percent of the total animals and 53 percent of owners holding a mere 7 percent of the total; a single owner, George Wilson, had 13,813 head on his Bagaces haciendas—more than 10 percent of the cattle in Guanacaste and 83 percent of those in the canton.[6]

Ownership concentration of foreign animals was even more extreme, since just the larger hacendados were involved in importing or fattening Nicaraguan steers. Only 37 individuals possessed all of the 15,562 Nicaraguan animals; the 6 most important fatteners controlled close to three-quarters of the total (Merz 1934: 13). The Nicaraguan cattle, almost entirely steers, were concentrated in La Cruz, then the northern district of Liberia canton; all but 126 of the 11,618 foreign animals in Liberia were in the La Cruz border region (Merz 1934: 24).

In one of the first serious efforts to examine the history of the Costa Rican cattle industry, Lowell Gudmundson remarked that the rapid herd growth of the 1940s that permitted attainment of beef self-sufficiency occurred "for reasons as yet unexplained" (1983b: 109). Yet analysis of the changing geographic distribution and sex ratios of the herd during 1933–50 provides the key to these important bovine population dynamics. Demographic growth rates tend to be quite sensitive to changes in the proportion of males to females, with heavily female populations expanding more rapidly. In Guanacaste, herd sex ratios varied widely between cantons and were indicative of a functional division between haciendas, where steers were fattened, and smallholdings, which maintained a larger proportion of cows for breeding feeder calves.

With the exception of Bagaces, a strong association existed between ownership concentration and male-weighted herd sex ratios in the different cantons (see Figure 5.1).[7] In Bagaces, dominated by Wilson's massive latifundio of over 100,000 hectares, the natural increase of the semiferal herds was enough to supply steers for fattening on the small areas of planted pasture. Even in this special case, however, the greater sex ratio of Wilson's herd compared with that of the rest of the Bagaces herd—538 as opposed to 364—is suggestive of the same functional division of breeders and fatteners *within* the canton as that which existed *between* the other cantons of the province.

The fattening of steers was the most rapid and lucrative, as well as the least hazardous, part of the production process. It demanded year-round access to sizable areas of green grass for pasturing adult animals. Many large haciendas continued to specialize in the fattening of steers, primarily because it was more profitable. But hacendados still often lacked sufficient control over the labor process to operate high-yielding breeding operations, and as prices for imported animals rose they relied increasingly on purchases from nearby smallholders. Breeding, which involved caring for fragile newborn and young calves, required less land, in part because immature, lean cattle consumed less fodder. Small cattle producers also grazed animals on public roadsides, village parks, and creek banks, thus permitting greater herd densities on their modest plots.

The growth of a sector of smallholders dedicated to the breeding of feeder calves led to a geographical redistribution of the herd within

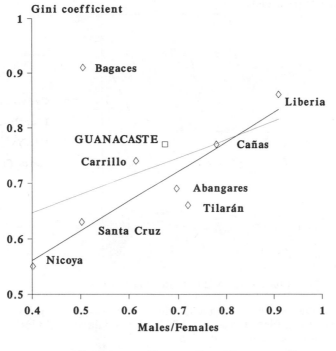

Fig. 5.1. Guanacaste: Herd Sex Ratios and Ownership Concentration, by Canton, 1933. Source: Merz 1934. The provincial total was not included in calculating correlations.

Guanacaste, apparent in a comparison of four cattle censuses taken between 1887 and 1950 (see Figure 5.2). Cow-heavy herds in traditional smallholding areas, such as Nicoya, and in recently colonized zones, such as highland Cañas, Abangares, and Tilarán, underwent rapid growth, especially after 1932, and increased their relative importance in the province's livestock economy, especially in comparison with the latifundista zones of Liberia–La Cruz and Bagaces. The change in the geographical location of the herd involved an overall tendency toward lessening inequality in ownership at the provincial level, but did not bring about any fundamental change in the differing patterns of land tenure and functional specializations of the smallholding peninsula and the latifundio zones where the steers were fattened for market.[8]

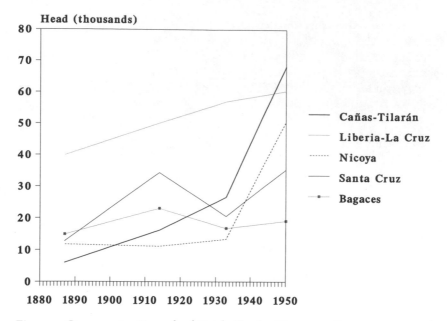

Fig. 5.2. Guanacaste: Growth of Cattle Herd, 1887–1950. Sources: 1887 and 1914, *AE*; 1933, Merz 1934; 1950, *CAP*. Cañas-Tilarán includes Abangares; Liberia–La Cruz includes Carrillo.

Strengthening the Smallholders: Protectionism

The 1932 measures to protect the cattle industry were complemented by other efforts to achieve import substitution in agriculture, most notably greater protection for domestic rice producers. The rationale for establishing higher duties on imported rice was similar to that which led Ricardo Jiménez to press for tariffs on Nicaraguan cattle. In the five years from 1926 to 1930, Costa Rica imported one-third of its rice consumption, up from 10 percent in 1920 and a mere 1 percent in 1918–19; in 1926–30 this represented an annual average of 4.21 million kilograms costing 1.49 million colones (approximately $373,000 in 1930) (Sáenz Gutiérrez and Merz 1932b: 7, 12–13). While this expenditure was somewhat less than one dollar per capita per year, it nonetheless constituted a "very strong outflow of gold" (p. 23) for a small, economically depressed country suffering from a severe shortage of hard currency. Jiménez's advisors recognized that "modern processing and cultivation methods" abroad were giving rise to "world overproduction" (p. 19). Yet they were not averse to justifying protectionist arguments with references to comparative advantage if such posturing, however contradictory it might seem, appealed to legislators' patriotism and helped assure passage of their program for import substitution in agriculture: "Costa Rica [is] so well endowed by nature that it can and must live from its own efforts, supplying itself from its own resources. [But] it has increasingly imported a greater proportion of products like maize, beans, vegetables, butter, cheese, and many others that it produces in conditions that are no better abroad" (Sáenz Gutiérrez and Merz 1932a: 6).

The campaign to protect cattle production had stressed foreign exchange savings, the demise of breeding haciendas in Guanacaste, and Costa Rica's being "at the mercy of the Nicaraguan cattlemen" (Jiménez 1903: 11; Jiménez 1931). In the case of rice, additional concerns were the generation of employment and the fact that levies on rice, though insufficient to genuinely protect local farmers, were already the second greatest source of customs revenue. To make up for lost income, those drafting the legislation recommended an increase in duties on kerosene and lard, both imported in large quantities (Sáenz Gutiérrez and Merz 1932b: 5, 12, 19). When the protectionist legislation passed in 1932, it brought higher prices for producers and contributed to a quadrupling of Costa Rica's rice production in the succeeding two decades (see Chapter 9).

Strengthening the Smallholders: Credit

Access to credit was also essential for capital-starved smallholders, whether cattle breeders or crop agriculturalists. The Chinese community was the main source of credit for smallholders in Guanacaste during the early twentieth century, as well as an important outlet for peasant production. Chinese immigrants began to arrive in the late nineteenth century, fleeing famine and economic crisis in southern China and being attracted by tales of "gold mountains" in America.[9] They rapidly attained prominence in retail trade, in spite of discrimination by local residents and the national government. The position of the Chinese as merchants, moneylenders, and intermediaries did not endear them to the rest of Costa Rican society. In 1897 the government prohibited all Chinese immigration to Costa Rica (*CLD*, 22 May 1897). In 1911 it decreed that all Chinese must be inscribed in their canton of residence in a special registry (*Registro de Chinos*) intended to control illegal aliens, which recorded data on physical appearance, immigration status, occupation, and knowledge of Spanish (*CLD*, 22 Sept. 1911; ANCR Gob. 8092—1924).

The first Chinese to settle in the towns of Guanacaste were met with bombs in Liberia and Las Juntas de Abangares, a drowning in Liberia, and a commercial boycott in Tilarán (*Costa Rica de Ayer y Hoy*, July 1956, 17, and Oct. 1956, 17). In Cañas in 1910, municipal official Abraham Acosta reported that a local policeman and "two Nicaraguan individuals" perpetrated a "treacherous assassination" against a Chinese man known as José Cantón, "the only motive that brought them to that extreme being to rob a little money they had seen another Chinese keep in the same house." The policeman, who was overheard bragging that he "would come back to repeat bloody scenes," retreated to the mountains, where he and his accomplices evaded several government patrols and staged numerous nighttime raids on nearby haciendas, stealing cattle and horses (Acosta 1911: 434).

In spite of government efforts to capture perpetrators of violent crimes, the atmosphere remained intensely anti-Chinese for several decades. In the 1930s, newspapers made frequent references to "avaricious Chinese," "Asiatic anthills" (*hormigueros asiáticos*), and so on, also insinuating that a huge Chinese conspiracy, allegedly based in Puntarenas, was trying to gain control of Costa Rican commerce (*El Guanacaste*, 1935–37; *La Tribuna*, 24 Feb. 1935, 15). By 1943, with China occupied by the Japanese and Costa Rica a vocal, if entirely symbolic, ally of the United States, the anti-Chinese climate had abated sufficiently so that restrictions on Chinese immigration were repealed (*CLD*, 21 Dec. 1943).

In many Guanacastecan communities, by the mid-1930s "chino" had become almost synonymous with "grocer." At least 200 Chinese establishments operated in the province, most of them grocery and dry goods stores (*El Guanacaste*, 23 Sept. 1936, 4). Some were quite sizable, such as the three largest stores in Cañas, all Chinese-owned, which in 1935 were reported to be worth between 25,000 and 80,000 colones, about $4,200 to $13,500 (*La Tribuna*, 10 Mar. 1935, 16). The Chinese amassed a considerable portion of this capital through money lending and intermediation, although it is far from clear that this was the major source of Chinese business profits, as the regional and national press, as well as resentful locals, frequently charged. Chinese merchants often constructed cement rice-drying platforms behind their stores and generally advanced cash to borrowers without any collateral, requiring only that the principal and interest, usually about 1 percent per month, be paid in kind at harvest time at the prices prevailing in the public markets. The borrower was usually free to dispose of any surplus as he pleased, although the problem of additional transport costs and the monopsonistic position of particular Chinese businesses in outlying areas contributed to the dependence of many individual peasants on the local Chinese.

State attempts to provide rural credit were motivated less by anti-Chinese feeling than by the permanent shortage of basic grains resulting from the physical displacement of food crops by coffee in central Costa Rica (Facio 1972: 49–50). By the first decades of the twentieth century, the country was importing large quantities of basic foodstuffs (Albarracín and Pérez Brignoli 1977). With the outbreak of World War I in 1914, Costa Rica was cut off from European coffee markets, previously its principal source of foreign exchange. The drop in export earnings made large-scale food imports untenable. It also brought a decline in tax revenues and led the country's private banks to refuse to lend funds to the government (Gil 1974: 100).

This difficult situation led the reformist administration of Alfredo González Flores to found the state-owned Banco Internacional de Costa Rica, which was financed by a government bond issue. One section of the Banco Internacional, the Agricultural Credit Boards (Juntas de Crédito Agrícola), was established to provide loans to small food producers. While anti-Chinese feeling per se rarely figured in discussions of credit policy, the peasantry's reliance on usurers—of whatever ethnicity—was a cause of worry for members of the central Costa Rican elite who viewed smallholding as the basis of the country's political stability.[10] The creation of the Juntas also generated considerable enthusiasm in Guanacaste because it marked the first time that significant amounts of credit were channeled to productive activities in outlying areas of the country. Previously, Guanacastecan hacendados often mortgaged their properties to obtain liquid capital, but they rarely invested such loans in production.

Within a short time, Juntas were established in all Guanacaste cantons. Each was supposed to have five members, three of whom were to be agriculturalists with a net worth of at least 2,000 colones.[11] Junta service was essentially a prebend, with members receiving the difference between the 12 percent interest they charged borrowers and the 6 percent the Banco Internacional assessed the Junta (Gil 1974: 105).

Large landowners and merchants were prominent members of the Juntas, which is not surprising in light of the political nature of the appointments and the net-worth criterion for membership.[12]

Juntas made loans for the production of cereals or food products other than coffee. At first individuals could borrow up to 250 colones (equivalent to slightly less than 100 dollars in 1915), a limit indicative of the government's initial concern with financing smallholders' production. In 1918, however, during the brief dictatorship of the Tinocos, the upper limit for loans was raised to 20,000 colones, where it stayed for the nearly two decades of the Juntas' existence. The early preoccupation with financing smallholders was also undermined by rules that required borrowers to mortgage their lands to the Junta, a procedure that could only be carried out with a certificate from the Public Property Registry stating that the property was duly inscribed. In a period when less than half the province's landholders had legal titles, this stipulation effectively denied many smallholders access to Junta credit. Even after provisions were made, however, for guaranteeing loans with cattle or other collateral, available credit was often concentrated in a few hands.[13]

Both the Juntas' prebendal character and the ease of obtaining "crédito chino" played a part in the demise of the Juntas de Crédito Agrícola. Junta members had to respond to the Banco Internacional for loans declared in default. During the depression of the 1930s the rise in defaulters made it difficult to find individuals willing to assume such a risk, and the credit system began to operate at a loss (Gil 1974: 115). This was especially true in the central part of the country, but the gradual demise of the Juntas at the national level could not fail to be felt in Guanacaste, in spite of the fact that many of the effects of the crisis were initially somewhat attenuated there. Even though the 1933 Law on Loans for Livestock Development greatly increased the credit available to small cattle ranchers through the Banco Internacional, the Juntas had already declined enough to require major restructuring (CLD 1933, Law 170).[14]

In 1936, with the banking system severely battered by a depression-induced fiscal crisis, the government moved to restructure the Banco Internacional, transforming it into a more streamlined entity called the Banco Nacional de Costa Rica, with clearly defined responsibilities for monetary emissions, mortgages, and commercial loans (Gil 1974: 156–58; Hernández 1942: 11–13). A reorganized agricultural credit system became part of the Banco Nacional's commercial section, with Rural Credit Boards (Juntas Rurales de Crédito) in each region responsible for administering loans. The Juntas Rurales attempted to operate in accordance with modern banking practices, though they conserved in modified form some of the prebendal principles of the earlier Juntas de Crédito Agrícola. Officers of the Juntas Rurales received daily stipends that varied between 15 and 25 colones according to the amount of interest collected in their branches. But the new Juntas also had built-in checks against corruption. Each Junta treasurer was required to post a "good faith" bond of 100 colones. In the case of the agronomists attached to each branch—who were responsible for evaluating loan requests, appraising collateral, providing technical assistance, and scrutinizing how loans were employed—the "good faith" bond was a princely 10,000 colones ($1,783 in 1937). In a further check on potential malfeasance, the agronomists had "voice but no vote" in Junta deliberations (Hernández 1942: 13, 18).

The relatively small size of loans granted reflected the Juntas Rurales' genuine concern with financing smallholder production. Junta Rural loans ranged from 50 to 1,000 colones ($9 to $178) in 1937; the upper limit was raised to 2,000 colones ($357) in 1941 (Gil 1974: 199; Hernández 1942: 17). The order in which Juntas Rurales were established in Guanacaste also indicated a preoccupation with peasant producers. The first were established in areas with significant smallholding sectors, such as Santa Cruz (1937) and Carrillo (1938); in 1939 a Junta that opened in Abangares was responsible also for Tilarán and Cañas, all areas of both large properties and smallholding peasants; and only in 1943 was a Junta opened for the Liberia-Bagaces region, the area of most extreme land concentration. In the Juntas' first six years, one-quarter of all loans—757,072 colones ($134,095)—were for livestock purchases. Some additional short-term loans of operating capital also went to smallholding cattle producers (Hernández 1942: 15–16, 31).[15] By the 1940s the beginnings of a modern credit system fueled the growth of a class of small agricultural entrepreneurs, who increasingly played an important role as suppliers of feeder calves to the haciendas and of grain to local and national markets (see De La Cruz 1986: 349–50).

Latifundismo and Costa Rica's First Agrarian Reform

Significant peasant participation in the Guanacastecan cattle economy would have been difficult without more secure access to land.

While most smallholders lived in parts of the Nicoya Peninsula or the cordillera not controlled by latifundios, many were ensconced on hacienda lands, either as long-term residents or as recent occupants. In the last years of the nineteenth century and the first half of the twentieth, the state intervened increasingly in these conflictive situations, expropriating lands for distribution to peasant occupants (see Chapter 4). The list of such measures in Appendix B suggests that these were far from isolated steps. Although government action sought primarily to maintain social peace, the stimulus given to agricultural and livestock production by this early agrarian reform also contributed to a larger participation by small cattle producers in the regional economy.

These early agrarian reforms, centered primarily in Guanacaste and adjacent areas of northern Puntarenas, were unusual if not unique in Latin America in this period.[16] Indicative of early and profound reformist impulses in Costa Rican political culture, they have only recently been the subject of research.[17] Gudmundson (1982: 76), in his work on agrarian unrest (discussed in Chapter 4), touched on the early reforms and accurately observed that previous investigators' lack of attention to the subject was part of a larger, general disregard for Guanacastecan history. But his study did not consider that new latifundios often arose in "reform" areas or that the "political elite," although frequently articulating altruistic or propeasant sentiments, often favored state intervention in agrarian conflicts for instrumental, self-interested reasons.

José Antonio Salas Víquez, who examined early programs of land distribution in the rest of the country as well as in Guanacaste, noted (1985: 100) that traditional historians of Costa Rica mistakenly viewed these and similar measures as offspring of Jorge Volio's emergence in the mid-1920s as leader of the Partido Reformista. But just as Volio could not legitimately be blamed for the agrarian strife in Quebrada Grande de Liberia, which preceded the formation of his movement by several years (see Chapter 4), he could be held responsible even less for reforms that first took place in the 1890s (when he was still a child). Salas Víquez, unlike Gudmundson, provided a detailed discussion of the mechanisms that led many early land reforms to end up with an unintended reconcentration of holdings. He also pointed out that many landlords favored expropriation, with compensation, of occupied properties as the only means of resolving intractable squatting problems, and that land distributions, particularly before 1924, were intended to generate electoral support for whatever party was in power. Like Gudmundson, however, Salas Víquez mistakenly assumed that key advocates of agrarian reform were, if not noble-minded, essentially unselfish progressives whose own holdings were not affected by the measures they shepherded through the Congress.

One reason for the lack of attention to the early land reforms is that some analysts of Costa Rican agrarian history (e.g., Camacho 1978: 91, 119; Salazar Navarrete 1979) ascribe to the agricultural frontier an exaggerated role as a "safety valve" for alleviating social tensions and suggest that the disappearance of the frontier in the 1960s was the cause of a supposedly sudden rural social crisis. A typical manifestation of such reasoning is in an article by José Manuel Salazar Navarrete, director of the modern agrarian reform agency in the late 1970s and early 1980s: "At the end of the last century and the beginning of the present century, *it was impossible* that any agrarian problem present itself inasmuch as there were hardly 200,000 inhabitants [in the country] in the last decade of the nineteenth century" (1979: 214, emphasis added).

Like many idealized dogmas about Costa Rica, this notion of the frontier's function in attenuating conflict contains its grain of truth. In sparsely settled southern and eastern Costa Rica, frontier expansion did indeed often occur without colonists coming into conflict with established and increasingly consolidated latifundios, such as those in Guanacaste. But the "safety valve" thesis also requires recognizing that the continuous migration of peasants to the agricultural frontier resulted from a *series of agrarian crises* in different regions, some of which, as in Guanacaste, were quite serious because of the existing regional systems of land tenure.

The impetus for Costa Rica's first agrarian reforms grew out of a welter of conflicting claims, tenuous and permanent occupations, and real and threatened conflicts. In Guanacaste, as early as 1900, the Congress authorized the purchase or expropriation of parts of the Haciendas Mojica, Paso Hondo, and El Viejo to provide lands for residents of the riverine port of Bebedero and to expand the region's road network (ANCR Cong. 2610—1900). In other cases the state acquired private properties to curtail actual or potential violence and to alter existing agrarian structures. Many measures passed in this period, particularly those outside Guanacaste, were essentially colonization projects that provided settlers with unclaimed, usually virgin, public lands (ANCR Cong. 17003—1934).

Yet despite the pattern of conflict and state intervention, no coherent reform program with clear goals or uniform criteria ever emerged. Provisions for the purchase, exchange, or expropriation of private lands and for their distribution to peasant occupants were always made on an ad hoc, case-by-case basis and were often not implemented. In each case, reform advocates had to argue anew for their objectives, often citing earlier violent incidents as unfortunate precedents that ought to be avoided.

In the face of peasant resistance, Guanacastecan latifundista attitudes ranged from total intransigence to professed agreement with the peasants' belief in their inherent right to land for cultivation. The persistent expansionist tactics of a Francisco Hurtado, for example, described in the preceding chapter, contrasted sharply with the conciliatory approach of Julio Sánchez Lépiz, owner of the Hacienda Taboga e Higuerón in Cañas, who exemplified what Salas Víquez (1985: 107) termed the "private enterprise" reforms of this period.[18] Cognizant of the difficulty of expelling peasant occupants from highland sections of his property, he agreed, in some cases, to pay them for "improvements" made on his lands and, in others, to sell them at low prices the plots they occupied (Gudmundson 1982: 86–87; Salas Víquez 1985: 108). Payments for "improvements" were not, in this instance, accompanied by the threats and coercion that led peasants to accept this kind of eviction elsewhere in the province (ANCR Cong. 15771—1930: 1v). Instead, Sánchez articulated a farsighted strategy of coexistence with the occupants of his property, one that nonetheless brought certain benefits to the hacienda as smallholding families who were potential sources of labor and young cattle settled on its edges. In 1930 he wrote to the administrator of Taboga, who had expressed interest in expelling the "parasites":

In reality, the land should be for him who cultivates it, not for him who has title. I cultivate the entire extension of my other farms because I do not like there to be land that does not produce. I cannot do this with "Taboga" because there I possess 25,000 manzanas [approximately 17,500 hectares] and it is beyond my possibilities to cultivate them. Neither I, in spite of the effort that you and I make, nor my children, nor my grandchildren will ever be able to cultivate that extension of land. Thus I believe we should be satisfied with what we can fence, clean, and attend. The rest must be for those who can cultivate it. That does me no harm, since I do not occupy the land; it does me good because they take up residence, produce, and improve the place. Let us do what we can without crushing those who come to plant, unless they are thieving vagrants. But the vagrants are those who here yell stupid remarks against the rich. Those who fell forest and plant maize are not vagrants. (Quoted in Marín 1972: 69–70)

Sánchez's comments contain elements of both clearly stated self-interest and purportedly selfless altruism, as well as an implicit critique of other hacendados, who failed to distinguish the criminal or "vagrant" part of the population from other semiproletarianized squatter families who were often the principal source of hacienda labor. Although Sánchez's tolerance of the occupants of his property was apparently accompanied by sincere philanthropic beliefs, other hacendados at times took similar stances simply to ward off conflicts by boosting their popularity and legitimacy with local peasants. Thus, for example, in the 1940s and 1950s, members of the Sobrado family ceded lands to the state in San Juanillo de Nicoya for distribution to peasant occupants (*Adelante*, 14 Sept. 1958, 1, 3; *El Guanacaste*, 15 July 1947, 1) and David Clachar, owner of Hacienda Tempisque, agreed in a similar case to refrain from action against residents of Guardia de Liberia who were technically illegal occupants of his property (*Pampa*, Sept. 1954, 1, 9).[19] In these instances, the Sobrados and Clachar clearly hoped to avoid both further "usurpation" of their lands and eventual government actions that could have been considerably less favorable to them.

Perhaps the most interesting case in which hacendado self-interest blended into philanthropic ideology was that of Francisco Mayorga Rivas, the principal proponent of the reform laws of 1906–32, when he served as a congressional deputy. Mayorga, longtime owner of Hacienda El Pelón de la Bajura, one of the most valuable properties in the province, was in every sense a member of the latifundista class. His mother, Luisa Rivas Lebrón, was from an elite Nicaraguan family and had inherited Haciendas Orosí and San Luis de Naranjo in Guanacaste (ANCR JCA 5942—1900). His wife, Ninfita Santos Aguirre, belonged to a leading Liberia family. Her brother, Aníbal Santos Aguirre, was a prominent local politician who served five terms in the Congress and one as governor. Her sister Lupita was a large landowner and the wife of José Cabezas, the major logger in turn-of-the-century Liberia (Valverde 1907: 29).

In spite of his thorough insertion in the landowning class, Mayorga was a staunch believer in the smallholding sector and a relentless critic of latifundistas who held vast extensions of idle land. Although sympathetic to classical Liberal philosophy—as a student in León,

Nicaragua, he won a contest with an essay entitled "God Does Not Exist" (*El Guanacaste*, 18 Aug. 1936, 16)—Mayorga was a strong advocate of state intervention when it came to solving agrarian conflicts (Gudmundson 1983b: 87–88, 194). Nevertheless, in his advocacy of agrarian reform there was an element of self-interest which never came to light and about which he was less than completely candid. At least two properties that Mayorga urged the government to acquire in the interest of peasant occupants were registered in his name (ANCR Protocolo de Raúl Ugalde Gamboa T5 F81 N150—1940). In 1908 and again on subsequent occasions, Mayorga sponsored legislation that authorized the expropriation of the *sitios* Palenque, Montañita, and Pijije (ANCR Cong. 12473—1921: 3v–4; *La Gaceta Oficial*, 13 June 1908). In the debate over the measures he never mentioned that he owned these properties (and implicitly he labeled himself a latifundista, a pejorative term). The expropriation process, as defined in one law he authored, provided that "the present possessors of small parcels in the latifundios . . . will be able to request before the Tribunals of Justice the expropriation of their farms against the proprietor of the latifundio, [provided that there is] *previous payment of the land* [by the government at a price] assessed by experts" (ANCR Cong. 12473—1921: 3v–4, emphasis added).

But after failing in many years of public life to secure government payment for his invaded holdings, Mayorga opted for a "private enterprise" reform, albeit a less successful one than that of Julio Sánchez in that it brought him no compensation. In a will he filed in 1940 at age 73, Mayorga donated 45 hectares of the sitio of Pijije to unspecified "small agriculturalists" and 53 hectares of the sitio of Montañita and Palenque "to the poor residents of Liberia for taking firewood and grazing cattle" (ANCR Protocolo de Raúl Ugalde Gamboa T5 F81 N150—1940). Pijije, like Palenque, bordered Hacienda El Pelón and was likely of special interest to Mayorga, since the occupants were undoubtedly known to him and may have worked on or stolen from his hacienda.

Far from being committed to agrarian reform "particularly when it did not directly touch their own interests," as Gudmundson (1982: 75) and Salas Víquez (1985: 106, 115) argue, at least some key members of the political elite especially favored state intervention in their own properties. Lands occupied by "parasites" often could not be placed on the market, and government purchase of such lands was frequently the only alternative available to owners of "invaded" properties. As was noted above, hacendados and peasants frequently petitioned the state for the exchange or purchase of occupied lands, citing as precedents earlier measures that had benefited their respective counterparts elsewhere in the region (e.g., ANCR Cong. 16384—1932: 2; ANCR Cong. 18413—1937: 1). The interest of both sides in state-sponsored settlements to these conflicts was described well in a 1927 letter from the interior secretary (Secretario de Gobernación) to Congress arguing against the expropriation of disputed lands in Santa Cruz:

The expropriation adopted in other cases . . . has turned out poorly and has very bad economic consequences for the Nation. Poorly, I say, because it has given occasion to unscrupulous people who find support in those antecedents. On the one hand, they occupy lands known to be private property, and on the other, with the owners, they turn a blind eye to and tacitly tolerate the parasites' continued occupation; and later, when inside their large fundo there are several small farms well attended and cultivated, [they] promote conflict so that it is resolved through purchase of the occupied lands by the state, which definitely turns out to be the one that unjustly suffers [because of] the boldness of some and the owners' lack of activity and energy in the defense of their rights before the civil tribunals. (ANCR Cong. 14791—1927: 3–5)

Some opponents of early agrarian reform measures, like the official quoted above, based their position on the potential for corruption inherent in the expropriation laws. Narrowly conceived notions of property rights and economic liberalism also figured in arguments raised against reform laws. Thus a congressional commission examining the same case of land conflicts in Santa Cruz concluded:

All state intervention in private affairs tends to diminish the private initiative so lacking in our people. The arrangement for purchasing lands . . . may be perfectly made between the interested parties, without the state having to do anything else in such deals other than guaranteeing the freedom to contract. . . . [Expropriation] would convert the state into a despoiler of lands in favor of those who have seized them, and that is in every way illegal. (ANCR Cong. 14269—1926: 4)

Defenders of the property rights of large landowners also blamed peasant occupants for carelessness if they did not present opposition in the courts to published notices that their plots were about to be claimed and registered by absentee hacendados (ANCR Cong. 10455—1909: 8). Some, such as Aristides Baltodano, a congressman and owner of Hacienda El Pelón de la Altura, maintained on occasion that latifundios did not really exist in Guanacaste except, perhaps, in the north, where foreign landlords had become established. But even such a staunch advocate of the sanctity of property at times felt compelled to temper defense of latifundista interests with propeasant rhetoric and support for reform legislation. In 1929 Baltodano sponsored a measure that authorized the state to purchase a 495-hectare occupied property in Nicoya. After citing a long list of previous agrarian reforms as precedents for his bill, he noted:

This demonstrates that the policy of the Congress has been without interruption that of subdividing latifundios in order to protect the small agriculturalist, thinking no doubt that "the most patriotic and laborious people is that where property is most distributed" and that "the peoples have prospered or declined according to whether the soil is in the power of many hands or in the power of a few hands." (ANCR Cong. 15378—1929: 1)

Almost two decades later, however, Baltodano expressed blunt opposition to the division and distribution of what he termed infertile grazing lands. Apparently forgetting his earlier claim that Guanacaste's only latifundios were in the north, he argued this time that the only latifundios were unnamed foreign-held concessions on the Pacific coast—probably the 55,600 hectares granted the River Plate Company, which were supposed to have reverted to the government, or the Sobrados's land near San Juanillo (La Gaceta Oficial, 9 Nov. 1945, 1958–59). Speaking before a Congress in which he knew there existed significant support for agrarian reform, Baltodano displayed a combination of manifest hostility toward the smallholding sector and a grudging recognition of the hard life of the peasant colonists to the north of Liberia, who, incidentally, were ensconced on lands that bordered his hacienda:

In the great reserves which Guanacaste has on the slopes of [Rincón] de la Vieja [Volcano], laborious, true agriculturalists have entered, and not only have they not been able to obtain any aid for improving roads, they have not been able to get the government to send them a surveyor . . . to measure the lots that each of these workers has. Well, if they want roads, let them build them. If the struggle for these agriculturalists is hard and difficult, let the fertility of the land compensate their effort against these hardships; [but] how can [we] think of bringing peasants to work [cattle] lands that are useless for agriculture? . . . I am not against the distribution of lands if they guarantee the effort, health, and happiness of the peasants. (La Gaceta Oficial, 9 Nov. 1945, 1959)

Baltodano's equivocal stance regarding latifundismo and the early agrarian reforms reflected not only a lack of political unity among Guanacastecan hacendados, but also a pervasive sympathy for small-holders among the central Costa Rican upper class. Although some members of the latter group, such as Julio Sánchez, had substantial investments in latifundio lands in Guanacaste, the landowners of Guanacaste and the central Costa Rican bourgeoisie—involved in coffee, sugar, commerce, and banking—were, at this time, still basically different sets of individuals and thus constituted distinct social groups. Capital accumulation in coffee-growing central Costa Rica was not, with a few exceptions, based on ownership of large amounts of land, but was based on the control of key aspects of processing and export trade. This historical peculiarity favored the development of antilatifundista ideology within the upper class and helped foster the sense that Costa Rica was indeed exceptional in Latin America and that latifundios were foreign to the national experience. The social and geographical isolation of the northwestern region from the *meseta central* accentuated these sentiments.[20]

Significant sectors of the central Costa Rican elite, and at times some upper-class Guanacastecans as well, shared the special antipathy of the Guanacastecan peasants toward foreign landlords. By the 1920s, with increased agrarian unrest and growing popular resentment of the massive land giveaways of previous governments, the mood in the Congress regarding foreign-owned latifundios had undergone a marked change. Even though the terms governing claims of state lands continued to be quite liberal, the concession of large expanses of national territory to foreign interests was no longer seen as the preferred means of amortizing debts or attracting investment, as it had been during the late nineteenth century.[21]

As class-based movements, especially the Communist Party, gained prominence in the 1930s, peasant supporters of agrarian reform took special pains to dissociate themselves from political radicalism, arguing that timely reforms could forestall the advent of communism. Farsighted landlords too frequently looked to state-sponsored reforms as means of preempting more profound changes. In 1933, for example, legislation was introduced to permit government acquisition of Hacienda Tenorio, which had been subject to bank foreclosure proceedings. Over 800 peasants from Cañas canton, many of them "parasites," petitioned the government, supporting the distribution of lands in Tenorio, but stressing that they eschewed "all subversive ideas" (ANCR Cong. 16276—1933: 5). Four years later a resident of Carrillo, writing to the provincial newspaper to urge implementation of the law that in 1900 authorized expropriation of part of Hacienda El Viejo, noted that local peasants were now forced to pay "annihilating rents" to latifundistas. Nevertheless, he felt bound to emphasize his anticommunism: "I feel it important to add . . . that the person who writes this detests communist ideas of extermination, but just because of that he cannot be in favor of the social inequality that is implied by the problem of the uncultivated latifundios of the province" (*El Guanacaste*, 23 Apr. 1937, 6).

In the 1930s many hacendados clearly believed that, as one landlord's lawyer put it, "behind those people [the 'parasites'] there are others dedicated to creating socialist conflicts" (ANCR Cong. 10609—1934: 33). Some members of the central Costa Rican upper class saw land reform as a means not only of reducing discontent, but of isolating and controlling the discontented. One such individual, Jesús Pinto, a supporter of the Tenorio project, stated:

The Government, by transforming Tenorio into a military colony, headed by an energetic and true agriculturalist, would finish off communism and the problem of those without work, since those people wish to produce just the food for their children. . . . The best advantage of Tenorio is that because of the distance, the colonists, dedicating themselves more to their crops, would not be able to be here all the time and [would] be far away from the centers of corruption into which our cities have been transformed. (*Diario de Costa Rica*, 25 July 1933, 5)

Plans to have the government acquire Tenorio never reached fruition, largely because the Congress, painfully aware of the severe fiscal crisis of the first years of the depression, refused to appropriate the 250,000 colones that would have been required to purchase the property, opting instead to permit continued colonization of available state lands.

Widespread fears in the 1930s that Communists encouraged land invasions and that advocacy of reforms might be identified with "subversion" do not appear to have arisen from any significant participation of leftists in either land occupations or reform efforts. The Communists' strategic focus at this time was not the peasantry, but rather the small proletariat concentrated in the banana plantations and urban areas. During the 1940s, however, and particularly in 1942–48 when the Communist Party entered an alliance with the reformist administrations of Rafael Angel Calderón Guardia and

Teodoro Picado Michalski, the Communists became increasingly involved with agrarian struggles. An early instance of such concern was the intervention of Communist congressman Manual Mora in negotiations surrounding the government's acquisition of Hacienda Coyolito in Abangares. After examining public property records, Mora found that the owners were attempting to defraud the government by claiming rights to 3,879 hectares occupied by "parasites" when their title specified that they only owned 916 hectares and 3,836 *square meters* of land (*El Guanacaste*, 23 June 1940, 1, 4, and 21 July 1940, 1). This revelation, the result of a simple investigation, which it appears nobody else cared to undertake, led to a proportional reduction in the state lands exchanged for the occupied parts of Coyolito.

In 1945, in Corralillos de Carrillo, part of Hacienda El Viejo, Communist participation in the agrarian reform issue took a more active turn. There, using legislation passed at the turn of the century, the government purchased some 200 hectares from the hacienda's owner in order to distribute 5-hectare lots to local peasants. Those who received lots committed themselves to paying the state 200 colones over a period of twenty years. Many began immediately to deforest their lands and the surrounding area to pay off their debt to the government.

According to longtime residents of the area, most of those who received lots in Corralillos in 1945 were supporters of the Communist Party from Filadelfia, Bolsón, and Ortega.[22] Miguel Brenes Gutiérrez, labor minister in the Picado government and owner of a large holding adjacent to Corralillos, which had been part of El Viejo, distributed barbed wire provided by the government and encouraged peasants to build fences to protect their bean patches from his cattle. In the first year of the project, beneficiaries were selected before surveyors had delineated the boundaries of the lots, and the lands of Corralillos were not planted (*Trabajo*, 27 Apr. 1946, 3). The following year, planting was carried out collectively at the urging of some of the Communist supporters who had received lands. By 1947 the process of demarcating lots was completed, but the Corralillos project did not receive continuing government attention. Following the 1948 civil war, most Communist supporters in Corralillos were evicted and replaced with backers of the new social democratic regime. As in other reform projects, the government had never provided Corralillos beneficiaries with titles, even though it had paid the previous owner of the land. This meant that victims of post-civil-war political retribution had little or no legal recourse.

This failure to provide beneficiaries of different reform measures with legal titles had a number of broader consequences. In the 1960s the government had to resurvey large parts of Guanacaste, including most of the areas that had been divided into plots under the early ad hoc reforms, in order to provide de facto occupants with secure deeds. Without such titles, smallholders had no collateral for production credit and were more vulnerable to latifundista attempts to regain control of their former lands or to expand into reform areas.

Reconcentration of lands that had been divided and distributed to occupants as a result of the reforms was a major problem. In some instances, such as that of La Palma (see Chapter 4), the process of reconcentration occurred because latifundistas took advantage of the antiquated, anarchic system of registering claims. In other cases, such as that of Luis Morice in La Cruz, part of whose holdings were exchanged for state lands in the 1940s, latifundistas sabotaged the reform process from the beginning by providing false information to surveyors about occupants' names and locations (*Adelante*, 28 Mar. 1954, 1; Fallas 1978; *Libertad*, 21 Oct. 1967, 13; Seligson 1980: 107–10).

Elsewhere in the province, the same process of reconcentration of reform plots took place because no limitations were placed on the recipients' right to mortgage or otherwise alienate their parcels. Ironically, in one of the few cases where such restrictions were imposed, the peasants themselves protested against what they saw as a "flagrant injustice"—a decree that declared the lands of Nuestro Amo in Filadelfia to be inalienable and that restricted their ability to dispose of their parcels as they pleased (ANCR Cong. 11901–1920). Even in this case, however, where well-intentioned legislators restricted the sale and mortgage of reform lands, the provisions against alienating plots proved easy to circumvent. Although many smallholders who received parcels in Nuestro Amo were able to retain their land, much of the distributed area ended up in the hands of a Nicaraguan landlord, Francisco Cubillo, who came to be known as "the owner of Filadelfia" (Hernández de Jaén, Dávila, and Jaén 1977: 56).[23]

While there are strong continuities between the basic strategy of the reforms of this period and that of the post-1961 agrarian reform, particularly in the emphasis on distributing individual parcels purchased at market prices from large landowners, the jural frameworks were quite different. Many shortcomings of the 1900–50 reform measures were attributable to the failure to legislate general guidelines for the expropriation and distribution of latifundios and the resolution of land occupations. In addition to the problem of beneficiaries losing their lands to larger owners, many approved reforms simply were never carried out, either for lack of funds or political will or because no bureaucratic structures were created that would have given an ongoing impetus to agrarian reform.

The failure, prior to 1942, to pass a law establishing general principles for the distribution of occupied lands or underutilized latifundios is one indication of the strength in the Costa Rican Congress of the advocates of the sanctity of private property. Such laws were introduced three times between 1922 and 1940 (ANCR Cong. 12636–1922: 2–5; ANCR Cong. 19204—1940: 9; ANCR Gob. 8054—1924). In all instances, opponents charged that laws of this kind would encourage land invasions, and they feared, no doubt, that this would happen in the center of the country as well as in far-off Guanacaste.[24]

The approval in 1942 of the Law on Precarious Possessors (Ley de Poseedores en Precario), which allowed owners of occupied lands to exchange them for unoccupied state lands of equal value, marked a departure from the Congress's earlier reluctance to establish general guidelines for resolving agrarian conflicts. This law, which provided the framework for large land exchanges in northern Guanacaste in the 1940s, did indeed spark a wave of land occupations throughout the country. In some cases, landlords hired "parasites" to occupy valuable lands in the central part of Costa Rica, which were then traded for more extensive properties in outlying regions (Salas Marrero and Barahona 1980: 288). Described as having "disastrous" consequences (ibid.) and as being "perhaps the biggest land give-away of all" (Seligson 1980: 32), the law was repealed in 1951 as a result of the abuses committed under its protection.

At mid-century the 1948 civil war and the repeal in 1951 of the Ley de Poseedores en Precario brought about a pause in the reform process, which lasted until the founding in 1961 of the Lands and Colonization Institute (Instituto de Tierras y Colonización, ITCO). While the strategy of distributing parcels to individual peasant families made the early agrarian reforms a precursor of the later, ITCO-sponsored effort, the inconsistent and at times chaotic way in which

the early measures were implemented also created a need for a specialized agency in charge of agrarian matters. The civil war, however,
marked the beginning of a larger, accelerated transition in which
state efforts to develop peripheral regions such as Guanacaste expanded on a variety of fronts.

Toward the Export Economy: National Beef Self-Sufficiency

In 1932–50, as a result of protectionist legislation and the new
dynamism of the hacienda and smallholding economies, Costa Rica
attained self-sufficiency in beef production. The heightened reproductive capacity of the national herd, the growing size of the annual
slaughter, and the decline in Nicaraguan steer imports were key
factors in Costa Rica's emergence as a beef-exporting nation in the
1950s. Yet in spite of the growth of the smallholding cattle-breeding
sector, national self-sufficiency in beef production occurred at the
cost of a rapid and sustained decline in per capita consumption (see

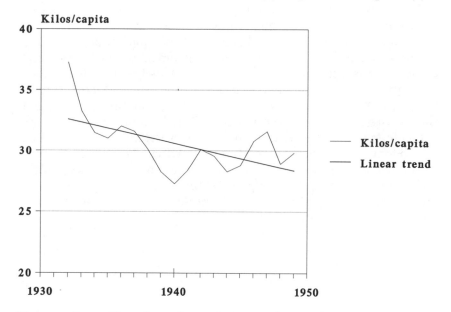

Fig. 5.3. Costa Rica: Annual per Capita Beef Consumption, 1932–1949.
Source: *AE* 1949: 189. Original data based on estimated slaughter weight of
420 and 330 kilos, respectively, for male and female animals.

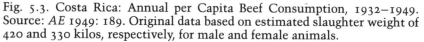

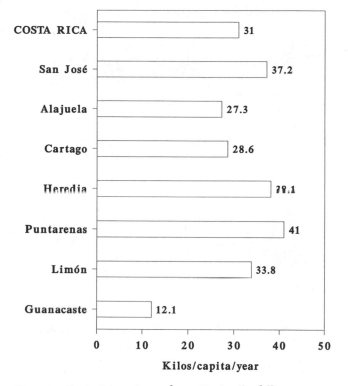

Fig. 5.4. Costa Rica: Annual per Capita Beef Consumption, by Province, 1949. Source: *AE* 1949: 189.

Figure 5.3). Inexpensive meat had long been an important component of the Costa Rican diet, but with the rise in cattle prices after 1932 and the country's entrance into the beef export economy in the mid-1950s, meat increasingly became a luxury good.

The national-level decline in beef consumption that occurred after Costa Rica became an exporter of beef (and which is discussed in Chapter 6) was presaged in Guanacaste in 1932–50. Guanacaste had long exported cattle to central Costa Rica, and as often happens in primary-product exporting areas, it sacrificed local consumption to extraregional demand. Figure 5.4, which describes beef consumption by province in 1949, shows that per capita beef consumption in Guanacaste—the major cattle-producing region—was by far the lowest of any province and less than 40 percent of the national average.[25]

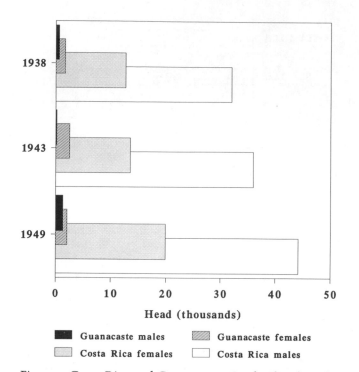

Head (thousands)

■ Guanacaste males   ▨ Guanacaste females

▨ Costa Rica females   □ Costa Rica males

Fig. 5.5. Costa Rica and Guanacaste: Cattle Slaughter, by
Sex, 1938, 1943, 1949. Source: *AE* 1945: 49–50 and 1949:
189. "Costa Rica" data do not include Guanacaste.

The quality of meat consumed in Guanacaste was also poorer than
that sent to the *meseta central*, another indication of the province's
position as an exporting region that subordinated local needs to
external markets. Unlike steers, which are fattened specifically for
consumption, cows are generally held primarily for reproductive
purposes and, after years of calving, have tough, lower-quality meat.
As Figure 5.5 shows, Costa Ricans from the central part of the country consistently consumed a much higher proportion of steer meat
than did Guanacastecans, who tended to eat low-quality cow meat.

In 1953, as Costa Rica entered the world beef market, these characteristics of beef consumption in Guanacaste became generalized to
the country as a whole. As early as 1945, leading hacendados in
Guanacaste began to lobby for permission to export fattened steers,
arguing that the market was in danger of becoming glutted (*La*

Gaceta Oficial, 9 Nov. 1945, 1959; *El Guanacaste,* 5 Jan. 1946, 4).
Although occasional exports of live cattle took place in the 1940s
(Robert 1945: 105, and 1989: 60), Costa Rica was still importing
several thousand steers each year from Nicaragua to satisfy domestic
demand. In 1947 the cattle lobby obtained passage of a law permitting the export of Nicaraguan steers that had been fattened in Costa
Rica (Robert 1989: 62–63; Rossi 1948: 125). In the same year, Congress approved a measure that allowed annual exports of up to 10,000
head of fattened cattle provided that a similar number of lean animals had been imported during the previous twelve months (*CLD*
1947: 91–92, Decree 1051).[26] Tying exports to imports in this manner
assured that any sales abroad would remain at low levels and that net
foreign exchange earnings would be minimal. In 1951, however, cattle imports from Nicaragua ceased entirely, most immediately because of a scare about the possible spread of an *aftosa* (hoof-and-
mouth disease) epidemic then ravaging Mexico (see Sanderson 1986:
134–35). But even without fears of contagion from the north, the
need for imports had largely disappeared.

Costa Rica's attainment of beef self-sufficiency in 1932–50 and its
subsequent emergence as an important beef exporter were possible,
however, not just because of the consolidation of a sector of small
cattle producers and the quantitative leap in production that this
permitted. Beef self-sufficiency involved a redefinition of the term
itself that was based on lower levels of per capita consumption. The
concepts of "exportable surplus" and "national self-sufficiency," as
well as of acceptable beef-consumption levels for the population,
proved ultimately to be political, rather than narrowly commercial
or nutritional, in nature. These new definitions were imposed on
consumers throughout Costa Rica through the operation of market
mechanisms and political forces over which they had no control.

PART TWO

✦ The Period After 1950

6 → The Beef Export Economy

> The state is the only cow the cattlemen ever really milk (El Estado es la única vaca que realmente ordeñan los ganaderos).
>
> —Liberia farm administrator, 1982

In January 1945, Enrique Robert Luján, a delegate from the Costa Rican National Cattlemen's Association (Asociación Nacional de Ganaderos), traveled to Liberia after a lapse of fifteen years to attend Guanacaste's first regional livestock exhibition. "Astonished, I asked myself how what my eyes beheld was possible," he reported, "because the last time . . . I did not see anything even resembling what I now had in front of me." Describing the "excellent condition of the most beautiful Indian cattle" at the fair, he predicted that "in the not too distant future . . . our cattlemen will have a magnificent market in Panama and the Canal Zone for their excess fattened cattle." "I enjoyed such pleasant emotions," he confessed, "that it is difficult to narrate them . . . [from] the sabaneros' happy cries to the creole beauty of the Guanacastecan women, with dark eyes and jet-black hair, mounted on spirited, stamping chargers" (Robert 1945).

This enthusiasm about new markets—though intensified in Robert's case by "indescribable emotions" aroused by the fair's "multicolored atmosphere" (p. 108)—was increasingly shared by Guanacastecan producers and key government officials. Although a few prescient ranchers had envisioned Costa Rica as a beef exporter even in the early 1930s, in the fifteen years of accelerated change between Robert's two visits to Liberia it had become almost commonplace to voice confidence in the country's impending transition from importer to exporter. The examples adduced in expressing this certainty were also closer to home; rather than pointing to distant Argentina or Texas as models of beef-exporting prosperity, optimists had to look no further than Nicaragua, which was already engaged in a flourishing commerce with "better-priced markets than our own, such as Peru, Panama [and] Cuba" (Rossi 1948: 119).

Peru and the Caribbean were to play an important role in Costa Rica's initial experience as a beef exporter, but the United States rapidly emerged as its most significant market. This entrance of Costa Rica and other Central American countries into the U.S. beef market forms part of the background necessary for an understanding of the actions and aspirations of Guanacastecan ranchers, many of whom dreamed of a regional cattle boom comparable to the nineteenth-century expansion of coffee cultivation that had enriched growers in the *meseta central*. Examining this transformation is also important because it suggests that the incorporation of previously marginal zones into international markets is not an automatic result of rising demand for primary products in metropolitan centers, as has long been implied by scholars working within the dependency and world-system paradigms. Rather, this process is better understood as a conjunction of powerful market forces with historically specific circumstances. In the case of Guanacaste, these included (1) the ongoing, concerted action of innovating hacendados, the consequences of which so excited Enrique Robert Luján, even in 1945, nearly a decade before large-scale exports began; (2) a new interest by international lending institutions in livestock development in Central America; (3) the emergence, in the aftermath of the 1948 Costa Rican civil war, of a developmentalist state, which devoted vastly greater resources to nontraditional economic sectors and peripheral areas of the country; (4) the conscious and increasingly effective political action of Guanacastecan ranchers, inspired by favorable market conditions, but not certainly predictable or entirely determined by them; and (5) changing patterns of domestic consumption, which, as was suggested at the end of the preceding chapter, resulted both from market forces and from politically inspired redefinitions of consumers' needs.

The Changing U.S. Beef Market

To begin with an analysis of changing market conditions does not necessarily mean assigning them analytic or causal priority. But even this caveat, intended to assert the importance of historical experience and human activity in the creation of an exporting zone, could be misconstrued if it were taken to imply an opposition between an abstract yet powerful "invisible hand" emanating from the metropolitan centers and concrete political and productive processes located in the periphery. The international market forces affecting the developing world, though sometimes assumed to be a natural concomitant of "capitalism," for the dependency theorist, or efficient allocators of production factors, for the neoclassical economist, are themselves likely to represent the outcome of political struggles, primarily but not exclusively in metropolitan arenas. The shaping of U.S. demand for foreign, grass-fed beef suggests the extent to which politics and power sway the supposedly free play of market forces, in the center as well as in the periphery.

In the United States, consumer groups and the fast-food industry have long attempted to counter the secular rise in beef prices and maintain levels of domestic consumption by working to increase imports from underdeveloped countries with lower production costs. The price of a Central American steer has, until quite recently, generally been about 40 percent lower than that of a U.S. steer of similar weight (Roux 1975: 363). By the 1970s the United States, with 6 percent of the world population and 9 percent of the cattle herd, accounted for 28 percent of global beef consumption (Solis 1981a: 62). The United States also accounts for almost one-third of world beef imports and, with respect to Central American beef-exporting nations, exercises near monopsony power.[1]

Steers, as was noted above, tend to have the finest meat, whereas cows sent to slaughter are usually quite tough from years of calving and are suitable primarily for hamburger or industrial-grade meat. Traditionally in the United States, this industrial-grade meat was supplied largely by milk cows past the age of reproduction. In recent decades, however, the size of the dairy herd has declined with respect to the beef herd. Moreover, beef cows are generally of greater longevity than dairy cows (Slutsky 1979: 107). With an increase in the consumption of hamburger and industrial-grade beef, wholesalers had to look abroad for new sources of supply.

In order to understand the political contention that has determined the strength of U.S. demand for foreign beef it is necessary to look briefly at the cyclical nature of cattle output in the United States. Production costs and beef prices in the United States have fluctuated in a nine- to twelve-year "cattle cycle" for approximately the last five decades. The size of the commercial cattle slaughter in the United States is closely tied to herd size, which is in turn related to the cost of cattle feed. The steer-corn ratio—the ratio of beef steer price to corn price—is the key measure of profitability in raising grain-fed cattle. In general, an inverse relationship exists between steer-corn ratio and herd size. A high steer-corn ratio is indicative of above-average profit opportunities and encourages ranchers to expand the herd by keeping more heifers for breeding purposes. Heifers usually calve at 27 to 33 months of age. These calves come to slaughter about 18 months later. It thus takes almost three years to produce a "finished" steer. The expansion phase of the cattle cycle is conditioned by this rate of increase and has usually lasted six to eight years.

At the end of the expansion phase, when the quantity of beef produced can only be marketed at lower prices, ranchers and feedlot operators are breeding and raising animals at a loss. They begin to sell cows and heifers, thus bringing about a contraction in herd size, lower prices, and a lessened capacity for herd increase. Cattle are brought into feedlots at a younger age and fed for a shorter time to a lower finished weight. The contraction phase generally lasts two to six years. When the cattle inventory is reduced enough to create high prices, those ranchers who have not gone out of business begin to rebuild their herds.

The cattle cycle in the United States has strong repercussions in other beef-producing countries. Pressures by the U.S. livestock industry to limit imports have been greatest during periods of low prices, though import quotas have—since 1979—been adjusted in order to dampen cyclical price fluctuations. When developed-country importers, especially the United States and the European Economic Community, protect domestic producers by limiting imports, they reduce international beef prices (Jarvis 1986: 108). Periods of low prices also have a direct effect on the social composition of producing groups, since financially insecure ranches and packinghouses are more vulnerable during market declines. Finally, the price paid for foreign grass-fed beef in producing countries is directly tied to the price of cow meat in the Chicago market, even if—as is almost always the case in Central America—it is really steer meat. Not surprisingly, this curious metamorphosis of steers into cows remains a sore point for many Guanacastecan ranchers (see below).

Until 1964, nations seeking to export beef to the United States had only to receive certification of their packing facilities by the U.S. Department of Agriculture (USDA). Certification was based both on the cleanliness of the particular packinghouse and on the health of the national herd. It was important for Central American countries that fresh beef from traditional South American exporters, such as Argentina and Uruguay, was banned from the United States because of the presence of *aftosa* (hoof-and-mouth disease). Separated from aftosa-endemic South America by the dense forests of Panama's Darien gap, Central American producers were strategically positioned to enter the U.S. market when it began to open in the early 1950s.[2]

The rapid rise in U.S. imports of beef in the early 1960s—principally from distant, aftosa-free Australia and New Zealand, but increasingly from Central America as well—led the U.S. cattle industry to press for protection. In 1964 the cattle cycle was nearing the end of its expansion phase, and ranchers and feedlot operators began to hold back livestock from packinghouses to protest low prices, which they charged were exacerbated by imports (*Wall Street Journal*, 24 Aug. 1964, 12). Low beef prices did not, of course, evoke any outcry from organized consumers or the fast-food lobby. Instead, low prices contributed to a shifting of the balance of forces in Congress in favor of the domestic cattle industry and against importers, consumer groups, and the fast-food industry. The latter, content with prevailing low prices, saw little reason to maintain a large lobbying presence in Washington. This provided a critical opening for U.S. cattle interests seeking to limit beef imports.

Public Law 88–482, passed in 1964 and in effect until 1979, established an import ceiling of 725 million pounds for fresh, chilled, and frozen beef, which was to be readjusted annually by the percentage of increase or decrease in domestic production in the current and the two preceding years. The quotas were ostensibly voluntary, because the State Department was concerned that mandatory quotas might violate the General Agreement on Tariffs and Trade. Nevertheless, if the secretary of agriculture determined that beef imports would exceed 110 percent of the base quotas during a given year—the so-called trigger level—the president had either to make the quotas mandatory or to suspend them altogether. If an exporting nation violated the "voluntary" agreement, the president could halt the flow of its meat by invoking powers that predated the 1964 law.

The import guidelines of P.L. 88–482 tended to increase imports at the same time production was rising and to decrease them when production was falling, thus bringing about exaggerated changes in supplies and prices. Because imports exceeded the 110 percent "trigger level" in every year between 1970 and 1979, the contention be-

tween the livestock industry, on the one hand, and the meat importers, consumer groups, and fast-food chains, on the other, focused
largely on the president's authority to enforce or suspend quotas,
with cattle ranchers pressuring for enforcement, and their opponents, for suspension.

In the mid-1970s the U.S. livestock industry was reeling from the
first years of a contraction in the cattle cycle and the additional shock
of skyrocketing grain and petroleum prices in the aftermath of the
1973 oil embargo. Lobbyists stepped up efforts to limit beef imports,
seeking to close two important loopholes in P.L. 88–482. A large
proportion of United States beef imports were passing through free
trade zones in Puerto Rico and Guam, which were not subject to the
quota law. In the years after the passage of P.L. 88–482, countries that
produced exportable beef surpluses above the level permitted under
quota regulations frequently sent large quantities to these free trade
zones. In addition, since P.L. 88–482 applied only to fresh, chilled,
and frozen meat, imports of diced beef were allowed to enter under
the "prepared" category and could not be legally limited.[3] By 1977,
in response to ranchers' demands, import quotas for some Central
American countries were lowered to reflect the existence of the
Puerto Rican loophole. Large quantities of diced beef continued to
enter the United States under the "prepared" category, however (*Wall
Street Journal*, 27 July 1972, 30).

In 1978, with the contraction phase of the cattle cycle in its fourth
year, Congress passed a bill with a "countercyclical" quota formula
strongly supported by the livestock industry. President Jimmy Carter
vetoed the bill, charging that it was inflationary, since it limited the
president's discretionary powers to permit imports above the ceiling
established in P.L. 88–482. The bill would have allowed smaller
increases in imports than those which presidents had commonly
allowed in times of tight supplies and rising prices. Significantly,
concern over the bill went beyond President Carter and U.S. consumer groups. At an October 1978 meeting of the Organization of
American States Trade Council, representatives of Guatemala, El
Salvador, Costa Rica, and the Dominican Republic, all beef-exporting
nations, lobbied U.S. officials for a veto of the proposed legislation.
This apprehension on the part of Central American and Caribbean
beef exporters also highlighted another way in which U.S. demand
was the product of political processes and not of simple market
forces. Once total beef-import quotas were determined, whether un-

der P.L. 88–482 or later laws, their allocation between different producing countries became subject to eminently political criteria, though particular increases might often be justified on purely "developmental" grounds (Williams 1986: 86–87).

In December 1979 a compromise version (P.L. 96–177) of the countercyclical bill that had so exercised the proimport lobbies was signed into law. The Meat Importers Council of America even charged that the American National Cattlemen's Association had actually authored the legislation (Shane 1980: 103, cited in Williams 1986: 86). Although providing for a minimum import quota of 567,000 tons— approximately half the previous year's import total (Jarvis 1986: 111)—the new statute curbed the president's power to allow beef imports except in cases of national emergency, disaster, or market disruption. It also established an initial increase in import quotas to counter the effects of pre-1979 contraction, to be followed by a decrease in quotas toward the end of the expansion phase of the U.S. cattle cycle, which was expected to wind up by 1986 or 1987. Then quotas would gradually increase to cushion consumers from the anticipated cyclical contraction. In the case of Costa Rica, however, it was estimated shortly after the "countercyclical" law went into effect that even if quotas were to increase in the late 1980s, after 1985 the U.S. market would no longer be able to absorb possible increases in exportable beef production (*Central American Report*, 31 Aug. 1984, 270; SEPSA 1980a: 21). In fact, as I discuss in more detail below, the expansion phase of the U.S. cattle cycle lasted longer than was anticipated, contributing in the 1980s to a worsening crisis in the Central American livestock sector.

If the strength of U.S. demand for beef from developing countries reflected the outcome of ongoing political contention more than an "invisible hand," it might be argued that market forces played a greater role within the United States itself. Even here, though, information and market structures were hardly "perfect," in the sense in which neoclassical economists might use that term. Beef prices in the United States, while influenced fundamentally by supply and demand, are set daily by the editors of the *National Provisioner Daily Market and News Service*, "a small group of men in a ramshackle old brownstone on Chicago's Near North Side" (Swanson 1979: 433). The price statistics published in this industry market report, popularly known as the Yellow Sheet, do not include highs or lows or volume traded, yet they are used to set prices for as much as

90 percent of all wholesale meat transactions and for a significant portion of futures contracts as well.

This system, which has been investigated by Congress and by Ralph Nader for possible price-fixing violations, is closely followed by packers and large ranchers in Central America, many of whom subscribe to the Yellow Sheet or receive the information it contains by telex (or more recently by fax). The price paid for steers in Central America's USDA-approved export packing plants is based directly on the Yellow Sheet's daily quotation for cow meat. The justification for this seemingly peculiar procedure is that the grass-fed beef provided by Central American exporters is industrial grade and that most U.S. domestic demand for this category of meat is satisfied by the slaughtering of dairy cows. In addition, much of the meat exported by the United States' two major foreign sources of industrial beef—Australia and New Zealand—comes from dairy and beef cows.

The irony of this arrangement, in which Central America's best steer beef is sent abroad only to be classified as "cow meat," is not lost on the ranchers or consumers in the region. In private, ranchers complain incessantly of this injustice, even though the representatives of their organizations maintain publicly that the U.S. market is by far the best. These lobbyists argue that other countries, such as Venezuela, Mexico, or Israel, have generally imported Costa Rican beef only to alleviate temporary shortages and have never absorbed volumes or paid prices comparable to those of the U.S. market. Costa Rican consumers, as I examine below in more detail, had to pay rapidly rising prices for low-quality meat on the domestic market, because of the effect that higher export prices and currency devaluations had on the availability and price of beef for national consumption.

In addition to the long-term fluctuations that accompany the cattle cycle, there was until the mid-1970s a secular increase in beef prices (see Figure 6.1) brought on by the high costs of energy-intensive grain cultivation, skyrocketing land values, rising populations, and rapidly eroding U.S. rangelands (Brown 1978a; Gardner and Nuckton 1979; Harris and Ross 1978; Ross 1980). The USDA meat classification system, which assigns higher grades to fatty, "marbled" beef, encouraged U.S. ranchers to specialize in producing steers for feedlots, and has thus contributed to the reliance on imports for meeting much of the demand for industrial-grade beef. Whereas, in 1959, 63 percent of the meat produced in the United States was classified by the Depart-

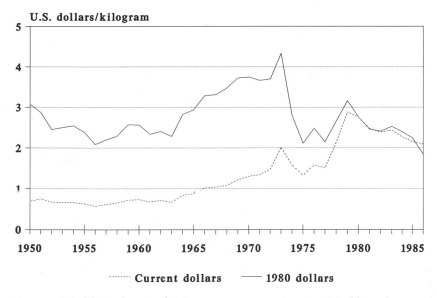

Fig. 6.1. World Market Beef Prices, 1950–1986. Source: World Bank 1988.

ment of Agriculture as "supreme," "select," or "good," by 1972, 79 percent of U.S.-produced meat was placed in those categories (Solís 1981a: 63).

In spite of their preference for grain-fed beef, U.S. consumers began to reduce the proportion of their consumption derived from steak and other choice cuts when fast-food chains began to multiply in the 1950s and 1960s. Able to provide meals at about the cost of eating at home, these restaurants have been a major force behind the shift to grass-fed beef. By 1977 nearly 40 percent of all beef used in the United States was consumed as ground beef (*Wall Street Journal*, 18 Oct. 1976, 34). And an estimated 80 percent of the steak sold in U.S. restaurants was, by 1976, actually "fake steak" or "log steak," tough grass-fed beef tenderized with recently developed meat-processing technology (*Forbes*, 15 July 1976, 47). Since 1976 consumers in the United States have reduced their beef consumption (see Figure 6.2). But this decline has had more impact on demand for premium cuts than on products made from grass-fed beef.

These changing patterns of production and consumption in the United States and the comparatively low price of foreign, grass-fed steers led to growing imports of industrial-grade beef. Australia and

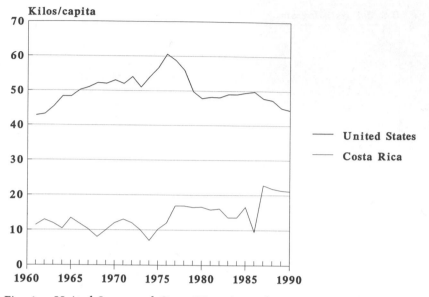

Fig. 6.2. United States and Costa Rica: Annual per Capita Beef Consumption, 1961–1990. Source: USDA.

New Zealand are by far the largest exporters of beef to the United States. In most years since the late 1970s, however, tiny, 51,000-square-kilometer Costa Rica has been, after Australia, New Zealand, and Canada, the fourth largest supplier of beef to the United States.[4] Imported beef usually accounts for less than 10 percent of domestic production in the United States. What may seem of minor significance in the United States, however, is seen differently from Central America, where pasture is often the major land use, beef is a key source of foreign exchange, and fragile national economies are vulnerable to price fluctuations and politically motivated changes in import quotas. International lending organizations and the Costa Rican state, as well as the pressures of the local cattle lobby, facilitated Costa Rica's integration into this new international market.

International Creditors Lend a Hand

International lending institutions fueled the Central American cattle boom by financing road construction and related infrastructure, funding livestock improvement programs, providing production credit, and requiring national governments and banking systems to reorganize their operations to stimulate ranching expansion (De-Witt 1977; León et al. 1981; Williams 1986). Allocations by the World Bank, the Inter-American Development Bank (IDB), and similar agencies frequently constitute direct or indirect subsidies for private capital in particular sectors of agriculture in the underdeveloped countries (Feder 1980). The World Bank's 1975 sector policy paper on agricultural credit reported that "lending for livestock operations continues to be the single most important type of credit activity" (quoted in Payer 1982: 214). Of the $3,184.0 million the Bank lent in the Latin American and Caribbean region as of mid-1979, the largest single category was livestock credit, which accounted for $903.0 million, or 28.4 percent of agricultural and rural development lending; in comparison, loans for agricultural (crop) credit amounted to $325.4 million, or only 10.2 percent (World Bank 1979: 182).

In the Costa Rican livestock sector, large ranchers initially received a disproportionate share of such loans. In the 1960s, World Bank loan contracts with Costa Rica *required* the creation by the country's Central Bank of a cattle technical extension division (León et al. 1981: V-41). In 1968, 30 percent of the Bank's first agricultural credit loan to Costa Rica was allocated to the cattle sector, with the average subloan to individual ranchers estimated at $18,000. Over the two decades of the life of the project, 90 percent of the credit went to livestock, and the average subloan soared to a handsome $57,000 (Annis 1990: 7). Nevertheless, World Bank lending to Costa Rica in the 1970s and 1980s has emphasized transportation, telecommunications, and energy projects (World Bank 1970–87).

The Inter-American Development Bank has played the key role in financing livestock programs in Costa Rica. IDB agreements with the Banco Nacional de Costa Rica specified that animal husbandry and veterinary sections had to be established in the Banco's branches in four of the country's principal cattle-raising zones (León et al. 1981: V-41). In 1961–69, the IDB's first decade of operations, fully 21 percent of loans made to Costa Rica from ordinary capital resources were for the cattle sector (IDB 1969: 51). The bank's first loan to Costa Rica—$2.6 million for livestock improvement—was channeled to 193 large ranchers through the Banco Nacional.

Subsequently, the IDB attempted to direct cattle credit to borrowers with assets of less than $60,000. But since a $60,000 ranch can still be quite large, most of the farms that benefited from the IDB program were reported to be "sizable" (DeWitt 1977: 105). As of 1977, according to an IDB report, the bank had directed $15.7 million to livestock credit, more than one-third of its total loans to the Costa Rican agricultural sector (IDB 1980: 8). Economist Peter DeWitt pointed out in an exhaustive 1977 study of IDB policy in Costa Rica that rural infrastructure projects in livestock zones benefited the cattle sector primarily. Furthermore, "of the total [IDB] contribution to the agricultural sector, *the vast majority* of funds have been channeled into livestock development projects and rural credit—with the credit provided for the cattle industry" (DeWitt 1977: 104, emphasis added).

Such lending agency decisions arose from and helped to develop the growing international beef market. They also stimulated the flow of private capital to the cattle sector and helped to assure the profitability of what has long been one of the least lucrative kinds of agricultural enterprises, the extensively operated livestock hacienda. Significantly, in the 1980s, with growing environmental consciousness and a severe crisis in the cattle sector, international lending institutions greatly reduced their livestock programs. The World Bank, for example, between mid-1979 and mid-1988, extended only $139 million in additional livestock loans to Latin America and the Caribbean, while other categories of agricultural and rural-development lending soared. This represented only 8.7 percent of cumulative agricultural credit operations (World Bank 1988: 150). Jorge Ferraris, chair of the Inter-American Development Bank's Environmental Management Committee, reflected this new awareness on the part of key international lenders when he conceded in 1987 that "in the past, neither our institution nor others considered the environmental impact [of lending] very much" (quoted in IDB 1988: 7). Nevertheless, by the time multilateral lenders tempered their earlier enthusiasm for livestock development, the landscape and social relations in many parts of rural Central America had been dramatically transformed.

The Changed Role of the State

Expansion of export-beef production occurred throughout Latin America (Buschbacher 1986; Buxedas 1977; Da Veiga 1975; DeWalt 1982; Feder 1980; Hecht et al. 1988; Myers 1981; Nations and Nigh 1978; Parsons 1976; Partridge 1984; Poelhekke 1982; Rutsch 1980;

Shane 1980; Slutsky 1979). But the particular nature of the post-1948 Costa Rican state contributed to what was probably the most dramatic and thorough process of this kind anywhere on the continent. The upheavals that rocked Costa Rica in 1940–48 and the unusual political alliances that emerged are too complex to address here. For purposes of this discussion the barest of outlines must suffice.[5] The 1948 civil war pitted an unstable coalition of anti-imperialist social democrats and conservative oligarchs against a populist but corrupt government backed by Catholic reformers and the Communist Party. When opposition forces toppled the government after a two-month conflict in which some 2,000 people died, the social democrats led by José Figueres controlled the victorious side's armed forces and the junta that held power in the wake of the war. During eighteen months of rule-by-decree following the war, they were able to lay the groundwork for an alternative model of economic development, which emphasized state support for export diversification. The junta drew much of its political support from ascendant middle sectors, whose hopes of joining the bourgeoisie had been frustrated by the virtual monopolies that dominated Costa Rica's banks, sugar mills, and coffee-processing industry. Excluded from the government for eighteen months and with the junta responsive to the interests of the middle sectors, the traditional oligarchy lost much of its political power.[6]

Even conservative upper-class Costa Ricans had long recognized that the monocrop coffee-export economy, beset by periodic crises that generated brusque variations in income and employment, was not an adequate base for sustaining a modern state apparatus. In contrast to their counterparts elsewhere in Central America, many wealthy Costa Ricans viewed social reforms as necessary for maintaining political accommodation between the dominant and subordinate classes. The social democratic forces drew on this traditional commitment to reformism as a basis for legitimizing the profound changes they hoped to effect in the country's economic structure.

The development model that Figueres and the social democratic National Liberation Party (Partido de Liberación Nacional, PLN) sought to implement was essentially a variety of import-substitution industrialization like that then advocated by the United Nations Economic Commission for Latin America (ECLA) (Furtado 1976: 242–50; Lizano 1980). The PLN model differed from ECLA's prescriptions, however, in assigning particular importance to Central

American regional integration and to the state's role as a dynamic agent in economic development. The rapid expansion of the bureaucracy in the post-1948 period occurred both because of increased state involvement in diverse aspects of economic planning and social welfare and because the social democrats sought to develop a political constituency among government functionaries that would be stronger than the fragile, impermanent coalition that had brought them to power.

The nationalization of banking was almost certainly the most significant measure of the social democratic junta during its eighteen months of rule-by-decree following the civil war.[7] The junta's creation of a new National Banking System allowed loans to be directed to areas of the country and to sectors of the economy where credit had previously been very limited or unavailable. The cattle sector, based in peripheral areas of the country not dominated by coffee and sugar and characterized by low start-up costs, was one of the few investment possibilities open to the junta's middle-class supporters (Solís 1981a). Once beef exports began in the 1950s, bank branches opened in many remote ranching areas, and the cattle sector absorbed a rapidly growing share of National Banking System credit, even surpassing—for most of the 1970s—the share allocated to crop agriculture (see Table 6.1). As was noted above, much of the credit administered through the National Banking System was originally provided by international lending institutions eager to develop the ranching sector.

In the post-1948 period the Costa Rican state, with the help of U.S. aid agencies and multilateral lending institutions, also made remarkably successful efforts to improve transport infrastructure in outlying areas.[8] The completion in the early 1950s of the Pan-American Highway and, in the 1960s, of a large system of connecting roads proved crucial in linking distant ranches in Guanacaste with export packing plants and in permitting refrigerator trailers to move rapidly from the plants to the ports, which were increasingly equipped for modern containerized shipping. In addition to providing greater access to credit and improved transport, successive Costa Rican governments also established a sizable network of institutions dedicated to livestock-related research, the extension of modern technology, and the training of technical personnel (León et al. 1981; SEPSA 1982: 27–33). Public and semipublic institutions that participate directly in activities related to the livestock sector include various

TABLE 6.1
Costa Rica: National Banking System Credit Allocations, 1956–1983
(millions of current colones, percentage of total credit, and index 1956 = 100)

							(Index 1956 = 100)		
Year	Total	Livestock	Percent	Agriculture	Percent	Total	Livestock	Agriculture
1956	374.7	51.8	13.8%	135.6	36.2%	100	100	100
1957	411.5	53.7	13.1	164.3	39.9	110	104	121
1958	464.4	59.6	12.8	201.0	43.3	124	115	148
1959	515.9	77.6	15.1	215.4	41.7	138	150	159
1960	608.0	99.8	16.4	259.5	42.7	162	193	191
1961	665.0	117.3	17.6	274.3	41.3	177	226	202
1962	673.6	126.0	18.7	250.4	37.2	180	243	185
1963	850.8	135.6	15.9	316.5	37.2	227	262	233
1964	931.4	149.2	16.0	327.0	35.1	249	288	241
1965	1,113.0	188.0	16.9	400.5	36.0	297	363	295
1966	1,148.7	211.0	18.4	407.1	35.4	307	407	300
1967	1,180.5	231.1	19.6	416.5	35.3	315	446	307
1968	1,274.8	266.2	20.9	421.3	33.0	340	514	311
1969	1,362.5	313.9	23.0	445.5	32.7	364	606	329
1970	1,509.2	355.4	23.5	492.1	32.6	403	686	363
1971	1,890.1	465.2	24.6	580.5	30.7	504	898	428
1972	2,255.8	577.1	25.6	596.8	26.5	602	1,114	440
1973	2,534.9	728.2	28.7	601.4	23.7	677	1,406	443
1974	3,153.4	931.3	29.5	690.0	21.9	842	1,798	509
1975	4,558.2	1,150.7	25.2	1,017.0	22.3	1,216	2,221	750
1976	5,618.9	1,306.9	23.3	1,280.9	22.8	1,500	2,523	945
1977	6,395.0	1,514.6	23.7	1,486.0	23.2	1,707	2,924	1,096
1978	8,100.7	1,792.4	22.1	1,733.4	21.4	2,162	3,460	1,278
1979	9,868.4	2,102.0	21.3	2,011.9	20.4	2,634	4,058	1,484
1980	11,533.3	2,508.7	21.8	2,357.6	20.4	3,078	4,843	1,739
1981	12,708.1	2,729.8	21.5	2,790.1	22.0	3,392	5,270	2,058
1982	15,473.6	2,176.0	14.1	4,233.5	27.4	4,130	4,201	3,122
1983	23,158.3	5,405.0	23.3	7,113.4	30.7	6,180	10,434	5,246

SOURCES: Banco Central data cited in Keene (1978: 19) and in Aguilar and Solís (1988: 130–31).

ministries and interministerial bodies, the country's four public universities and the Central American Cattle School located in Alajuela, the nationalized banks, the land reform agency, the National Production Council (Consejo Nacional de Producción, CNP), the state insurance company, and the National Planning Office (OFIPLAN). Programs sponsored by several international organizations and foreign aid programs, such as USAID, the Center for Tropical Agronomic Research and Teaching (CATIE), and the Inter-American Institute of Agricultural Cooperation (IICA), have also had a significant impact on the cattle sector. While the effects of this effort, unparalleled in other Central American countries, have been felt most directly on large ranches dedicated to the breeding of stud bulls and exhibition animals, the Costa Rican herd as a whole has a higher proportion of brahman blood than those of other countries in the region and compares favorably in terms of health, parturition rates, and other indices of technological advance (León et al. 1981, chap. 3).

The Pressures of the Cattle Lobby

The rise of a powerful cattle lobby in the 1950s is another element that must be considered if we are to understand the integration of Costa Rica into the international beef market. The Cámara de Ganaderos de Guanacaste was the first regional cattlemen's chamber to be formed in the country and the nucleus of what later was to become a well-organized national federation with members and supporters strategically situated in the Legislative Assembly, the ministries, the banking system, and the major political parties. While the Cámara's general goal was to promote the cattle industry and "the economic resurgence of the Province of Guanacaste" (CGG 1954: 7), its formation reflected the reaction of key hacendados to the specific conjuncture of the early 1950s. The end of cattle imports from Nicaragua and the rapid growth of the Costa Rican herd behind high tariff walls had, the ranchers argued, brought "congestion of the market" and lowered prices. Most important, as David Clachar Baldioceda, the first president of the Cámara, stressed in his first annual address in 1954, "meat is an article which [now] has worldwide demand, with very encouraging prospects" (CGG 1954: 8).

The Cámara held its founding convention in Liberia on August 30, 1953, shortly after José Figueres, leader of the social democratic forces that triumphed in the 1948 civil war, assumed his first elected term as president. This concurrence of events was hardly coincidental. Figueres had long been an advocate of state intervention in promising new sectors of the economy, of agricultural diversification, and of the use of social (rather than strict profitability) criteria in allocating credit, something now feasible through the new National Banking System. Guanacaste's leading ranchers, several of whom had been traversing the province to drum up support for a new cattlemen's organization, viewed Figueres's goals as congruent with their own hope of using public resources to facilitate expansion of the livestock sector and to gain access to international markets.

In attendance at the founding of the Cámara de Ganaderos were many of the province's leading hacendados, most of them from families that had been involved in ranching for several generations. David Clachar Baldioceda, elected president at the meeting, was a member of the family that owned the Hacienda Tempisque. The vice-president was Alberto Lorenzo Brenes, one of Figueres's closest associates during the 1948 war and a leading figure in provincial politics, who had inherited over 2,000 hectares in Quebrada Grande de Liberia from his Spanish immigrant father and traded most of it to the government in 1946 (see Chapter 5). Other officers chosen at the first convention of the Cámara were, without exception, members of the principal ranching families of Liberia, a result that reflected the dominance of the provincial capital and its upper class over the outlying regions (CGG Actas, 1: 2, 1953).[9]

The guest of honor at the founding meeting was Otilio Ulate, the conservative owner of *El Diario de Costa Rica*, who had preceded Figueres as president of the republic. Ulate offered to donate 10,000 colones—approximately $1,600—to the Cámara, and the delegates named four representatives to accept the gift (CGG Actas, 1: 18, 1953), although possibly for reasons of political propriety, this sum does not appear in the organization's published accounts for 1953–54 (CGG 1954: 9, 12). Ulate's presence at the founding of the Cámara and his offer of financial support indicate that the organization of a cattlemen's pressure group was viewed as a positive development, not only by the ascendant social democrats represented by Figueres, but also by the most conservative elements in the central Costa Rica upper class, who were generally pro-laissez-faire. These forces did not feel threatened by, and indeed appear to have welcomed, the emergence of a strengthened cattle sector in the distant northwest, where it seemed unlikely to compete for resources with the established coffee sector of the central plateau.

Cámara vice-president Alberto Lorenzo Brenes was one of the individuals key to the cattle lobby's initial success. Leading Guanacastecan ranchers involved in the early days of the Cámara repeatedly mention Lorenzo's close ties to Figueres as important in securing immediate access to the highest levels of government and rapid action on the cattlemen's demands.[10] A passage from the minutes of the Cámara's second meeting suggests something of how Lorenzo must have operated:

Don Alberto Lorenzo explained the details of his personal research in San José on the best way to use the national press as a means of publicizing the purposes and goals of the Cámara de Ganaderos, in order to gain sympathies, more members, and cooperation in everything we are pursuing. As a consequence of his negotiations and report, a plan was accepted of publishing pertinent advertisements and taking advantage of the services of newspaper writers in the dailies *La Nación, La Prensa Libre, Diario de Costa Rica,* and *La República.* (CGG Actas, 1: 23, 1953)[11]

The way Lorenzo's connections with Figueres—like him, the son of Spanish immigrants—may have been employed is suggested by the offhand way in which the Cámara confidently agreed, on the Sunday afternoon it was founded, to send a telegram to "the president of the Republic requesting a meeting for Wednesday" (CGG Actas, 1: 20, 1953). The purpose of the meeting, attended by a delegation of five, which included Lorenzo, was to request a donation of brahman bulls to improve the stock of Guanacastecan ranchers. At a second meeting with President Figueres in December 1953, hacendado-lobbyists demanded "the establishment of an annual quota for beef cattle to be exported directly by the Cámara," as well as an increase in meat prices above the level set by the government in 1952, lower bank interest rates, and financing for dairy production in Guanacaste. The second discussion with Figueres was, according to delegation member David Clachar González, "broadly satisfactory in all its aspects" (CGG Actas, 1: 35–36, 1953). Clachar González reported that Figueres had promised the Guanacaste Cámara 60 percent of the export quota when it was established.[12]

In addition to cultivating press contacts and lobbying the president for active state support, the Cámara hosted banquets and farm tours for leading ministers, deputies, bank directors, and agents of the U.S.-sponsored extension organization STICA (Inter-American Agricultural Cooperation Technical Service) then active in Guanacaste (CGG 1954: 9; CGG Actas, I: 271, 1957). With STICA, and perhaps in other cases as well, the Cámara's generosity was actually thinly disguised reciprocity. In 1955 STICA initiated an ambitious cattle-selection and range-management research program centered at El Capulín Experimental Station on the western outskirts of Liberia (Kirk 1960). But the U.S. agricultural aid establishment was clearly interested not only in technical extension but also in strengthening the cattle lobby as a political force. In addition to advising ranchers on the latest techniques in breeding, controlled grazing, and veterinary medicine, STICA provided the Cámara with a furnished locale for a provisional office, where the group's first meetings were held (CGG 1954: 13).

At times Cámara officials employed subtle forms of subterfuge to manipulate policymakers' opinions. In May 1954, for example, the Cámara received information that a legislative commission charged with studying possible increases in meat prices was planning to visit several "sample" ranches in Guanacaste in order to better evaluate the costs of beef production. The Cámara demanded and received a series of detailed changes in the commission's itinerary, including "the elimination of Santiago Ovares' farm [a relatively profitable operation in Bagaces] and its substitution by [United Fruit Company–owned] Hacienda Tenorio, because it [will be] very interesting to visit this farm in order to observe the economic disaster in the livestock business [which occurs] when efforts are made to raise the standard of living of the worker[s]" (CGG Actas, 1: 53–54, 1954).

Cámara members who were fluent in English and familiar with foreign livestock markets and technology also played an important role in the lobby's early organizing efforts. Especially important in this respect (CGG Actas, 1: 23, 1953) were the North American David Stewart Bonilla, the elder son of erstwhile Bagaces potentate George Wilson, and David Clachar Baldioceda, an English citizen descended on both sides from leading Liberia hacendados and a landowner in his own right (RP SM 2515—1941). Stewart, who retained ties in California and in his father's native Arizona, made several trips to the United States as a Cámara representative, accompanied at least once by Clachar Baldioceda, with the goal of studying modern livestock operations (CGG Actas, 1: 23, 1953).[13] These early trips involved the purchase of brahman breeding bulls from ranches in Texas and Louisiana and were part of the process of cementing a continuing relationship between leading Central American ranchers and their counterparts in the southwestern United States.[14] This relationship grew to entail not only purchases of breeding animals, but also the importing of judges for livestock exhibitions (CGG 1956: 7; Robert 1945), the education of affluent young Guanacastecans in Texas agricultural colleges, and, most important, the investment of U.S. "sun belt" capital in Central American ranchlands and packinghouses (see below, Chapter 7).

During its first year, the Guanacaste Cámara succeeded in modifying the regulations governing loans for livestock production and, more important, secured legislative approval for a bill that permitted cattle exports (CGG 1954). This law (*CLD*, Law 1754 of 1954), which established a quota system for determining the number of steers that could be exported, purportedly reconciled the conflicting interests of Costa Rican consumers, who favored an abundant supply of low-cost meat, and ranchers, who sought to divert as many cattle as possible to the more lucrative international market. The law gave the National Production Council (CNP), the state commodities agency, responsibility for determining permissible export levels by calculating the difference between total production and domestic needs. The CNP was then supposed to apportion the total export quota to different regions of the country. Estimates of total production and the allocation of each region's quota among individual ranchers were based, however, on forms filled in by members of regional Cámaras, a system that was of doubtful accuracy and that lent itself to abuses.[15]

In the early years of the export trade, many small and medium-size cattle ranchers neglected to return their declarations to the Cámara. Large ranchers, on the other hand, frequently exaggerated the size of their herds in order to obtain a larger portion of the regional export quota and to sell more of their animals at the higher international price.[16] In a comment that revealed hacendados' preoccupations regarding quotas, Manuel Jirón, then Cámara president and owner of Hacienda Las Trancas near Liberia, in 1956 criticized the "negative conduct on the part of [those] cattlemen who have proceeded fatally against their own interests and against those of the livestock industry in general" by not filling in the forms used for estimating the size of the herd. He called for "greater comprehension of [this] matter" in the future (CGG 1957: 7).

The largest hacendados in the province, who dominated the Cámara and monopolized the export of fattened steers, stood to lose if the portion of the quota allocated to Guanacaste was lowered because of the "lack of cooperation" of smaller ranchers. Although Jirón did not say so explicitly, "greater comprehension" of the cattlemen's interests implied that herd estimates were magnified at the regional and national levels. Individuals who exaggerated their declarations, however, obviously did so at the expense of their more scrupulous neighbors, who then received smaller shares of the export quota. In private, a number of the larger hacendados admit that while they initially inflated estimates of their herds to compensate for the "ignorance" of the smaller cattlemen, they later inflated their quota estimates out of simple self-interest.

In subsequent years, the provincial Cámaras and the national federation proved to be one of the most effective lobbies in Costa Rica, not only bringing strong pressures to bear around issues of credit, pricing, and export policies, but also arguing against key aspects of the agrarian reform (see Chapter 10) and for a more systematic repression of peasant squatters.[17] By the late 1970s the report of the National Federation of Cámaras de Ganaderos spoke openly of the organization's excellent relations with the then president of the Republic, Daniel Oduber, himself owner of a large hacienda in Guanacaste, with the minister of agriculture, and even with the minister of foreign relations, "who was and always will be the immediate link between the cattlemen and the U.S. Department of Agriculture" (FCG 1977, cited in Solís 1981a: 129–30). In the event that these connections in the Costa Rican government were insufficient to guarantee exporters' interests, the federation made clear that it also maintained direct relations with the U.S. embassy in San José and was continually alert for any changes in quotas, tax regulations, or other policies that could affect its members.

The Top of the Pyramid: The Export Packinghouses

Leading ranchers and Cámara spokespersons frequently liken the Costa Rican beef-cattle industry to a pyramid, the apex of which is made up of the export packing plants and below which lie the 2,000 large ranchers whose principal business is fattening steers. The base of the pyramid is made up by the approximately 40,000 small and medium-size ranchers who produce both the feeder calves for the large haciendas and the cows that end up in the municipal abattoirs and slaughterhouses serving the domestic market. This sector of smallholding ranchers, which expanded rapidly as a result of the 1932 protectionist legislation (see Chapter 5), was an indispensable part of the new export economy, even if it did not directly produce the final exported goods, the fattened steers that were sold as "cow meat" in the United States. The apex of the pyramid, however, the USDA-approved packinghouses, was something new. These modern plants were a necessary condition for the expansion of the export economy and constituted a new type of economic organization, which merged the interests of local hacendados and international capital.

At first, in 1953, live animals were shipped to Colombia, Peru, and

Curaçao. But in 1957 the Texas-based Murchison group opened Costa Rica's first export packing plant in Barranca, Puntarenas, near Guanacaste on the Pan-American Highway (Aguilar and Solís 1988: 52; CGG 1956: 9; Parsons 1965: 156). From that point on, exports were increasingly shipped already slaughtered, as chilled and boned beef, and went almost exclusively to the United States and Puerto Rico. In the following years, at times as many as seven USDA-approved export slaughterhouses were operating in different parts of the country, although since the mid-1970s the packing industry has contracted, with only four plants in operation in 1981.

Several export slaughter plants that were opened after the early 1960s, including Murchison's, have failed, victims of unanticipated losses due to cyclical price variations and fluctuations in the availability of fattened cattle, as well as of their tendency to operate well below capacity. Typically, packinghouses run at full volume for only about eight months each year, principally in the dry season, when pastures are less able to sustain large herds and when ranchers are willing to sell at low prices animals they cannot maintain on parched pastures. The slaughterhouses' seasonal calendar, like transhumant grazing in an earlier epoch, is possible only through the control—direct or indirect—of dry-season grazing sites that permit a constant flow of fattened animals to the factory. This land requirement—at once the product of local ecology, a cyclical economy, and modern packing technology—has important implications for the organization of the packinghouses and their relations with nearby hacendados, as well as for an understanding of the raison d'être of the contemporary livestock latifundio.

The survival of those packing plants that still exist depends on complex corporate structures, a diverse international capital base, and vertical integration of the production process. Ganadera Industrial, S.A. (GISA), owner of the main packinghouse in Guanacaste, is a case in point. GISA's plant, opened in 1971 just north of Liberia on the Pan-American Highway, has installed capacity for processing upwards of 300 animals per day, or approximately 72,000 during an average year, although in most years it operates far below capacity.

One-third of the shares appearing in GISA's public registry entry belong to the Adela Investment Company, a Luxembourg-based corporation founded in 1964, which aims to promote economic development in Latin America by investing in high-risk enterprises and then selling them when they mature (RP SM 15,178—1971).[18] Another third of GISA's shares are in the name of a Guatemalan who is Adela's representative, and another third belongs to various leading ranchers from Guanacaste, as well as other Costa Rican investors. GISA's board is composed of members of local landowning groups, such as the Stewart, Baltodano, Rivas, and Alvarado families, members of the central Costa Rican elite, and two residents of the United States. Since its founding in 1971 GISA's stockholders and officers have become even more international, with Argentine, Colombian, German, British, and Swiss capital also represented alongside the Costa Rican and North American investors.

GISA directors' desire to diversify the corporation's holdings has allowed some traditional landowners to exchange properties for substantial sums of money or for shares in the packinghouse or associated enterprises. Thus, for example, when GISA decided that it required land near the plant to assure a continuous flow of raw material, it entered into a partnership with the Alvarado family, owners of Hacienda San Jerónimo and adjacent properties, some of which had been in the family since colonial times (see Sequeira 1985: 199–200). The Alvarados turned over to a joint operation with GISA 5,217 hectares of grazing land, much of it watered by several rivers and thus usable year-round (RP SM 20,217).[19]

Another GISA subsidiary, Haciendas Ganaderas Costarricenses, is owned by a Panama-based company that is in turn owned by none other than GISA (RP SM 16,615—1972–79). In 1971 this subsidiary acquired various large properties in northern Guanacaste, such as Hacienda Verdún, a 3,998-hectare spread along the Nicaraguan border (CN G11516—1972). For GISA, these large properties represent one of the safest and most easily managed investments available, in addition to serving as a cushion against seasonal fluctuations in cattle prices and assuring a steady supply of fattened steers for the plant. Border properties may also at times be used in bringing contraband cattle from Nicaragua for processing in the Liberia plant. Whether this occurs with the connivance of GISA is, of course, unclear. Nevertheless, Nicaraguan cattle, stolen or purchased at lower prices across the border, have been exported in large numbers from Costa Rica to the United States.[20] In August 1976, for example, in an uncharacteristically open denunciation of the powerful GISA, the Cámara delegate from Nandayure canton demanded "firm action against a certain packinghouse that persists in introducing contraband cattle for slaughter in Liberia" (CGG Actas, 7: 376–77, 1976). A month later, a representative from the border canton of La Cruz called attention to the effect of this practice on the smaller ranchers:

TABLE 6.2

Costa Rica: Principal Exports, 1959–1985
(value in millions of dollars and as percentage of total exports)

Year	Coffee		Bananas		Sugar		Beef		Other	
	Value	Percent	Value	Percent	Value	Percent	Value	Percent	Value	Percent
1959	40.0	52.2%	19.1	24.9%	0.5	0.7%	2.9	3.8%	14.2	18.5%
1960	45.4	53.7	24.6	29.1	1.8	2.1	4.3	5.1	8.5	10.0
1961	44.9	53.3	20.7	24.6	3.1	3.7	2.7	3.2	12.9	15.3
1962	48.4	52.0	21.1	22.7	2.8	3.0	2.7	2.9	18.0	19.4
1963	45.3	47.7	22.7	23.9	5.0	5.3	5.1	5.4	16.9	17.8
1964	48.2	42.2	28.0	24.5	5.1	4.5	6.0	5.3	26.8	23.5
1965	46.8	41.8	28.4	25.4	4.5	4.0	3.1	2.8	29.1	26.0
1966	52.7	39.0	29.4	21.7	8.7	6.4	5.3	3.9	39.2	29.0
1967	54.8	38.1	30.9	21.5	8.5	5.9	8.6	6.0	41.2	28.6
1968	55.5	32.5	42.8	25.0	8.7	5.1	12.0	7.0	51.9	30.4
1969	55.7	29.4	51.4	27.1	9.2	4.8	15.2	8.0	58.2	30.7
1970	73.1	31.6	66.8	28.9	10.1	4.4	18.1	7.8	63.1	27.3
1971	59.2	26.3	64.2	28.5	12.9	5.7	20.4	9.0	68.8	30.5
1972	77.7	27.7	82.8	29.5	13.0	4.6	28.3	10.1	79.0	28.1
1973	94.0	27.3	90.6	26.3	21.5	6.2	31.4	9.1	106.8	31.0
1974	125.0	28.4	98.1	22.3	24.4	5.5	34.2	7.8	158.6	36.0
1975	96.7	19.6	144.0	29.2	48.1	9.8	32.0	6.5	172.5	35.0
1976	154.2	26.0	148.7	25.1	24.6	4.1	40.4	6.8	225.0	37.9
1977	319.1	38.5	150.3	18.1	15.7	1.9	44.2	5.3	298.9	36.1
1978	313.6	36.3	169.8	19.6	15.9	1.8	60.1	6.9	305.5	35.3
1979	315.7	33.8	190.4	20.4	17.5	1.9	81.6	8.7	329.2	35.2
1980	247.9	24.7	207.5	20.7	40.7	4.1	70.7	7.1	434.9	43.4
1981	240.1	23.8	224.8	22.3	42.0	4.2	73.9	7.3	427.3	42.4
1982	236.9	27.2	228.1	26.2	16.6	1.9	53.1	6.1	335.7	38.6
1983	230.2	26.4	240.3	27.5	23.9	2.7	31.9	3.7	346.2	39.7
1984	267.2	26.6	251.0	24.9	35.5	3.5	43.5	4.3	409.2	40.7
1985	310.1	32.2	212.2	22.0	10.4	1.1	55.7	5.8	374.6	38.9

SOURCE: BCCR 1986: 107–24.

From Hacienda Agasa 80 percent of the steers are brought from Nicaragua for the GISA plant, and through Hacienda La Libertad and [the Morices'] Quebrada de Agua [all on or near the border] there pass large quantities of said contraband. Now 325 heifers were just seized in Cabalceta, and it is believed that they were destined for export from our country. We have problems with the packing plant, because I have been requesting since June that twelve cows [be slaughtered] and have not gotten it, because Jhonny [of GISA] is a shark in the current and pays when he feels like it . . . because there are so many anomalies in the plant that we do not know how to solve them. (CGG Actas, 7: 417, 1976)

Diversification as well as vertical integration is a critical part of GISA's strategy. In the Liberia area, company directors also own one of the main rice-processing mills and one of the largest luxury hotels on the Pan-American Highway, which receives almost all the cattle and rice convention business.[21] The public property registry indicates that while these operations are technically separate companies with no official connection to GISA, the stockholders and board members are, with few exceptions, the same individuals (RP SM 23,789—1974).[22]

Beef exports grew rapidly, and by the mid-1960s they were Costa Rica's third largest source of foreign exchange after coffee and bananas (see Table 6.2). The euphoria of the early years of the cattle boom, comparable, some said, to that which accompanied the rise of coffee exports in the nineteenth century, was to be relatively short-lived, however. While exports and international prices tended to increase until the mid-1970s (aside from short-lived cyclical downturns), long-term growth slackened in the 1980s. Particularly since the U.S. anticyclical law of 1979, it has become highly unlikely that there will be any significant expansion of beef exports. Before considering the decline of the beef export economy, however, it is essential to examine briefly the politics of nutrition and the dietary changes in Costa Rica that accompanied the boom and that permitted it to take place on such a scale in the first place.

Beef Exports and Domestic Consumption

The notion that the expansion of beef exports from Central America was accompanied by declining per capita consumption has become a key tenet of a growing "hamburger-deforestation" literature that has echoes in popular thinking about the world environmental crisis.[23] It is indeed true that as growing quantities of Costa Rican

Head (thousands)

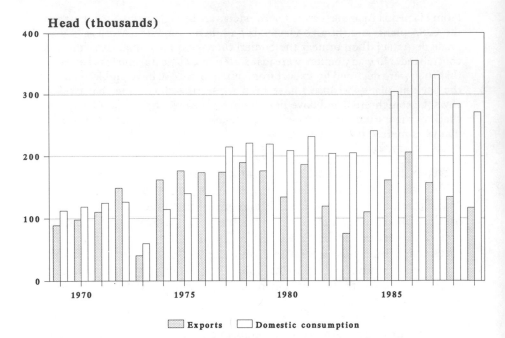

Fig. 6.3. Costa Rica: Beef Exports and Domestic Consumption, 1969–1989. Source: CNP. Data before 1974 refer to twelve-month "cattle years" from July to June of the following year. Data for 1973 are for the second half of the year. After 1973, data refer to calendar years.

beef were shipped abroad, meat, once a wage good, rapidly became a near luxury, duplicating on a national scale the classical export-zone priorities that had already given Guanacaste the lowest per capita consumption of any province (see above, Chapter 5). Until the early 1980s, Costa Rica exported nearly one-half the total head slaughtered (see Figure 6.3). The percentage of total beef weight extracted sent abroad, however, was consistently greater, since only steers—the largest animals—were processed for export.[24] While herd growth outstripped population growth for most of the boom period, and the per capita availability of beef thus theoretically increased, the export of roughly one-half the country's production brought about a trend toward lowered beef consumption that only much later began to level off (see Figure 6.2). Nonetheless, this eventual reversal of the downward tendency in per capita consumption, which began in Costa Rica in the mid-1970s, suggests that the dynamics of export-led herd expansion and associated dietary trends were actually more complex than much of the alarmist "hamburger" literature would have it.[25]

Figures on per capita beef consumption must be taken with caution, since the methods used to calculate them vary considerably from country to country and from series to series. Before Costa Rica entered the international beef market, annual per capita beef consumption, based on estimates of slaughter weight, averaged 31 kilograms (see Chapter 5). Retail weight may be conservatively estimated at 51 percent of slaughter weight, giving an annual per capita consumption figure in 1949 of 15.8 kilograms.[26]

Taking as a baseline a pre-export-boom consumption figure of 15.8 kilograms, the USDA data in Figure 6.2, which are based on retail weight, bear out the critics' claims of the sacrifice of domestic consumption to meet foreign demand (Holden 1981; Parsons 1976; Spielman 1972). Yet these data also indicate that although entrance into the export market was accompanied by drastic declines in per capita beef consumption, by the mid-1970s, when herds had expanded to meet export demand, per capita consumption began to climb, flattening off at roughly the pre-export-boom level. Lest this shift be taken as a sign of the ultimate benefits of the export boom, it should be noted that the distributive effects across income strata may not mirror overall tendencies and that the positive quantitative trend masks a negative qualitative one. Costa Ricans have increasingly consumed not only greater proportions of low-grade cow meat, but also growing amounts of offal and of contaminated or diseased steer meat unacceptable to U.S. inspectors.[27]

The immediate cause of the decline in per capita beef consumption was the steep rise in beef prices brought about by strong export demand. In Costa Rica, price ceilings for cattle and most cuts of meat for domestic consumption were (until very recently) set by the government and fluctuate within relatively narrow margins. Nevertheless, export prices—tied to the Yellow Sheet's rate for cow meat and until the mid-1980s always substantially higher than domestic prices—exerted constant upward pressure on domestic prices. The greater the disparity between the two price levels, the more the ranchers sought to elude CNP controls and divert steers to the export plants. With the appearance of domestic scarcities, a periodic occurrence during the boom years, the government's regulatory bodies came under intensified pressure from cattle lobbyists to grant the price increases ostensibly required to assure domestic supplies.

When external prices have been especially high, ranchers seeking to free steers for export often slaughtered young animals and females still able to bear young, in order to supply the domestic market (OFIPLAN 1974: 8).[28] This practice, which has also been noted in Guatemala and other beef-exporting nations, limits the potential rate of increase of the national herd (ILPES 1967: II-45). Thus, in the absence of an effective apparatus for government inspection and enforcement, the price ceiling for domestic beef not only created an incentive to evade quota rules and divert animals to the international market, but also led to shortsighted and destructive policies for herd management.

This upward pressure on domestic prices placed beef out of reach for poor consumers, particularly in rural areas. A 1978 study in Costa Rica found that annual per capita beef consumption was 32.8 kilograms in urban areas, 17.1 kilograms in rural towns, and 10.6 kilograms in rural areas of dispersed population (SEPSA 1980a: 26). Intake of animal protein varies not only with geography but also with the level of household income. In 1979 and 1981 nutritionists found significant height disparities between public and private school students six to ten years of age, disparities thought to be due to nutritional differences (Tristán et al. 1982). In overall terms, it was estimated in 1970 that the protein consumption of the lower-income half of the population was deficient by 30.1 percent, a serious enough deficit but also the lowest of any of the Central American countries (SIECA 1973: 45).[29]

In Costa Rica, the allocation of animals between the domestic and export markets is the responsibility of the National Production Council (CNP), the principal commodities agency in the public sector. The CNP is supposed to determine how much domestic demand for beef exists and how much surplus production is available for export. Each year it gathers declarations from all cattle producers about the number of animals they have and the number ready for slaughter. The CNP then calculates the "internal consumption quota" by multiplying 18.2 kilograms by the estimated population that year; what remains is placed in the "export quota."

Although an annual per capita consumption of 18.2 kilograms of beef would in most cases be adequate, providing that other proteins are also part of the diet, this amount has often not been available on the domestic market because of pressures from the cattle lobby and the artifices of individual ranchers. The export quota is allocated among different producers according to the number of steers each rancher declares. In the boom years, however, the ranchers routinely declared a larger number of steers than they actually had, so they could sell more animals at the higher price paid by the export packers. This practice in effect inflated the CNP's estimate of the total herd and thus brought about frequent domestic shortages, since the internal-consumption quota was calculated with exaggerated figures, and beef that should have been placed on local markets was shipped to the United States.

Stagnation and Decline

In 1980–83 Costa Rica suffered its most severe economic crisis since the 1930s depression (analyzed in greater detail in this book's Conclusion). The hacendados' dreams of the sustained expansion of exports—comparable, they had hoped, to central Costa Rica's success with coffee or to the Texan or Argentine cattle booms—all but collapsed after only some three decades, to be replaced with a pervasive pessimism. The change requires explanation, since the main symptoms of the crisis—especially the rapid currency devaluation—might normally be expected to benefit exporters (who would receive more Costa Rican money for each dollar from abroad) and debtors (who would repay old loans with inexpensive colones). The lack of dynamism of the Costa Rican beef-cattle sector in the 1980s also bears examination because it speaks to issues raised by the dependency or world-system perspective that, stressing metropolitan demand over historical process, has long dominated discussions of peripheral export economies in general and of tropical livestock production in particular.

The stagnation of demand for Central American beef that accompanied the expansive phase of the U.S. cattle cycle and the implementation of the 1979 anticyclical law would, at first glance, appear to support a dependency analysis. Metropolitan contraction–peripheral decline is, after all, the simple obverse of the demand-driven explanations of how new regions were incorporated into the world economy. But stagnant U.S. demand for beef coincided with an economic conjuncture in 1980–83 that should have resulted in superprofits for beef exporters from the sudden devaluation of the colón (all other things being equal, of course). The reasons why this did not occur (apart from *ceteris paribus* being at best a convenient fiction) are tied in part to the way inflation "caught up" with devaluation after mid-1982, sending a negative signal to exporters, whose costs began to rise faster than the prices paid for their final goods (BCCR 1986). But the answer is also bound up with the intricacies of regional and national policy responses to the broader crisis in the Costa Rican economy, as well as with ranchers' reactions as individual economic actors and as an organized pressure group.

Significantly, when ranchers articulated their demands about how to address the crisis, they highlighted local factors, not weak foreign markets. "In view of the progressive deterioration in beef cattle production and meat exports," the Federation of Cattle Chambers declared in a petition to the minister of agriculture in 1985, "[there is] a powerful need to declare livestock activity in a state of emergency." The Cámaras' desperation, while hyperbolic in some respects, derived both from worsened market conditions and from measures taken in the aftermath of the economic downturn, which profoundly affected their interests.[30] The petitioners continued:

The origins of the crisis through which the cattle sector is passing are the tax surcharges to which it was subject in 1982 and 1983, added to the payment of high real interest rates, both results of the transition from galloping inflation to exchange rate stability . . . , which has caused decapitalization of the producers, who with anguish accumulate losses day after day and do not receive income to meet their operating and financial obligations. (La Nación, 29 May 1985)

The rapid devaluation-inflation of 1980–83 exacerbated previously latent conflicts between exporters, whose products became more competitive in international markets, and importers, who were forced to pay seemingly astronomical colón prices for dollars or foreign wares and who were frequently unable to pass on skyrocketing costs to strapped consumers. The details of the exporter-importer confrontation need not concern us here. But the higher taxes and loan rates that irked cattlemen reflected political compromises within a state in which commercial and industrial importing interests were well represented alongside coffee, beef, and other agricultural exporters. And the range of policy instruments that could be employed in such mediation was increasingly circumscribed by demands of lending institutions for more revenue to pay foreign obligations and for the elimination of direct and indirect subsidies, such as the artificially low interest rates ranchers had long enjoyed.

Ranchers who sold fattened cattle to export packinghouses had traditionally paid few taxes: a tax of 1 percent on the value of each steer, eleven colones in various municipal levies, five colones for a stamp to finance the Rural Guard, and similarly symbolic assessments based on the weight of the "on-hoof" animal and the meat extracted.[31] In December 1981, following a rise of the dollar in little more than a year from 8.6 to 38 colones, the Legislative Assembly, responding in part to importers' calls for relief, established a tax intended to limit exporters' windfall profits. The law provided for a 10 percent tax on "the difference between the exchange rate at which hard currency from export earnings is sold and the total that the same sale would have produced had it been realized at 8.60 colones per U.S. dollar" (CLD, Laws 6707 and 6696—1981). Suddenly, cattlemen who had scarcely considered export taxes (or other taxes—see next chapter) a cost of doing business were facing payments of 500 to 1,000 colones (approximately $12.50 to $25.00 in early 1982) for each steer sold to GISA. While this represented only about 5 percent of the value of an average steer, it cut dangerously into the narrow 6.5 percent average profit margin for beef producers, which had been established in agreements with the export packers (FCG 1983: 16). By the mid-1980s some ranchers claimed that the total tax burden for each exported steer had risen to over 30 percent of the animal's value (*Realidad* 1988).

Just as ranchers had little experience with taxation, they were similarly unaccustomed to operating in genuine financial markets. Many had grown disaffected in the 1970s and 1980s with the costs of the social democrats' statist development model and were consequently infatuated with pro-laissez-faire rhetoric. But the unprecedented inflation of the early 1980s brought steep rises in interest rates, which represented a major additional burden to producers with low profit margins and few other sources of working capital. Costa Rican ranchers had long taken for granted that the National Banking System would provide credit at negative real rates of interest, allowing them a hedge against inflation or funds that could be diverted, albeit without authorization, to more lucrative activities (see next chapter). Although the high inflation of 1981–82 initially produced a sharp drop in real interest rates, by 1983–84 most loan rates had recovered to the point where ranchers, now also beset by soaring costs for veterinary and other inputs, registered a mounting number of defaults.[32] By early 1987 nearly two-thirds of Costa Rican banks' cattle loans were in arrears (Annis 1990).

This dismal situation—stagnant demand, low prices, new taxes,

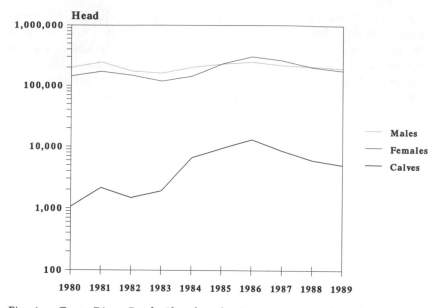

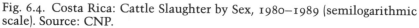

Fig. 6.4. Costa Rica: Cattle Slaughter by Sex, 1980–1989 (semilogarithmic scale). Source: CNP.

and higher operating and financial costs—jolted ranchers throughout Guanacaste and the other beef-cattle zones. Cattlemen began to slaughter cows and calves at younger ages than ever before and at rates far exceeding their reproduction (see Figure 6.4).[33] This response was distinguished from their traditional reactions to cyclical market downturns by a new indifference about maintaining breeding stock for future expansion. "The herd," one multiagency report commented in 1985, "appears to suffer from serious problems in recuperating [its earlier size]" (SEPSA et al. 1985: 18).

If this picture of rancher pessimism and dwindling herds contrasts with the uninterrupted boom portrayed in much of the "hamburger-deforestation" literature, the changes in the availability of beef that accompanied the crisis surely stand out as even more challenging to the typical assumptions of falling per capita consumption. The decline of export activity in the 1980s has permitted "record slaughters and domestic consumption" (Guardia et al. 1987: 154), with average per capita beef intake climbing above 20 kilograms by the last years of the decade (see Figure 6.2). The relative price differences between domestic and export beef, which for three decades had led ranchers to channel their steers abroad, also tended to decline after 1981, strengthening the upward consumption trend (ibid.: 156). Nonetheless, the uneven distribution of such benefits across social strata is likely still pronounced. At the end of the export boom, it seemed highly improbable that domestic demand could sustain a dynamic ranching sector. Costa Rica, having reordered its priorities to respond to political pressures and world market forces, will thus inevitably be faced with the prospect of creating alternatives in a society and a landscape transformed by the beef export economy.

7 → Changes on the Ground: The Large Properties

"I'll buy your farm, it's very beautiful."
"How much will you give me for it?"
"Two hundred thousand dollars."
"Let me think about it."
"No."

—Negotiations between the owner of Hacienda Santa
María and an alleged front man for
Lyndon B. Johnson, 1968

The persistence of large, underutilized latifundios in a dynamic modern export economy is not as paradoxical as it might seem at first. But to disentangle the connected "logics" behind this surface appearance of tradition and stasis it is important to examine the narrow social world of the Guanacastecan elite and the links between landowning families, as well as the ever-more-complex forms of corporate landholding. Distinct motivations—economic, social, speculative, and strategic—influenced those who inherited or purchased properties in Guanacaste. This novelistic cast of characters included men with suitcases of cash said to be fronting for former U.S. president Lyndon Baines Johnson, Nicaraguan dictators Luis and Anastasio Somoza Debayle, U.S. evangelist Jimmy Swaggart, Reagan White House agents who later figured prominently in the Iran-contra scandal, and a diverse roster of Costa Rican politicians and investors, Cuban and Nicaraguan exiles, and "crazy gringos" who invested huge sums in what locals considered hopelessly ambitious, misconceived schemes to transplant temperate-zone agriculture to the lowland tropics. Explaining contemporary latifundismo also means delving further into the workings of the U.S. beef market and the Costa Rican state—what one cynical ranch administrator termed "the only cow that the cattlemen ever really milk."[1]

Agrarian Structure and the Export Boom

At mid-century Guanacaste was still dominated by massive, underutilized latifundios. Twenty-two properties, averaging close to 15,000 hectares, controlled almost half of the land (see Table 7.1). The owners of these immense estates were largely members of families that, decades or even centuries before, had purchased properties at extremely low prices or acquired them through colonial titles, government grants, claims of state lands, or expansion into areas held by peasant squatters. When the beef export boom began, these landowners—many of foreign origin—were the principal beneficiaries, although a significant number of relatively new ranchers, particularly in the more recently settled canton of Tilarán, were also among the largest exporters (see Table 7.2). Just as landownership was concentrated in a few hands, steer exports were similarly distributed. As Table 7.2 indicates, in 1955–60 Guanacaste's fifteen largest exporters—roughly one-eighth of the total—accounted for over one-third of the steers sent abroad. If family groups, rather than

TABLE 7.1
Guanacaste Province: Land Distribution, 1950

Size in hectares	Farm Units			Farm Area			
	N	Percent	Cumulative percent	Hectares	Percent	Cumulative percent	Average farm size
0.7–2.8	1,297	16.6%	16.6%	2,554.4	0.4%	0.4%	2.0
3.5–6.2	947	12.1	28.7	4,376.0	0.7	1.1	4.6
6.9–9.7	691	8.9	37.6	5,505.5	0.8	1.9	8.0
10.4–13.1	387	5.0	42.6	4,422.9	0.7	2.6	11.4
13.8–20.2	857	11.0	53.6	13,980.4	2.1	4.7	16.3
20.7–33.8	1,208	15.5	69.1	30,862.3	4.7	9.4	25.5
34.5–68.3	1,376	17.6	86.7	62,558.9	9.6	19.0	45.5
69.0–120.1	532	6.8	93.5	45,357.8	6.9	25.9	85.3
120.8–171.8	199	2.5	96.0	29,054.4	4.4	30.4	146.0
172.5–344.3	168	2.2	98.2	39,552.9	6.0	36.4	235.4
345.0–689.3	74	0.9	99.1	35,762.0	5.5	41.9	483.3
690.0–1,034.3	12	0.2	99.3	9,279.8	1.4	43.3	773.3
1,035.0–2,414.3	35	0.4	99.7	48,164.8	7.4	50.7	1,376.1
2415.0+	22	0.3	100.0	322,794.4	49.3	100.0	14,672.5
TOTAL	7,805			654,226.5			83.8

SOURCE: *CAP* 1950.
  NOTE: Original data in *manzanas* (1 manzana = 0.69 hectare); original farm size intervals are continuous.

TABLE 7.2

Guanacaste: Principal Steer Exporters, 1955–1960

Exporter	Canton	Steers	Percent	Properties	Provenance
Stewart Brothers	Bagaces	2,361	6.3	Over 50,000 hectares	U.S. father acquired numerous properties in 1920s
Hacienda San Luis	Cañas	1,159	3.1		Owned by English immigrants involved in commerce (the Murrays) and central Costa Rican coffee planters (the Lindos). Acquired in 1950s
Miguel Brenes Gutiérrez	Santa Cruz, Carrillo, Liberia	1,022	2.7	Sections of El Viejo and others	Acquired part of El Viejo in 1940s. Labor minister in Picado government. Associated with Urcuyo family, hacendados in Guanacaste since nineteenth century
Sons of David Clachar	Liberia	949	2.6	Haciendas El Porvenir, Tempate, La Lupita, Asientillo	Children of leading hacendado (see below) descended from English immigrant. Properties acquired through purchase and family ties beginning in 1930s
Carlos Segnini Lupi	Abangares	897	2.4	Hacienda La Trampa	From Italian immigrant family that acquired land beginning c.1910
Julio César Pastora Molina	Liberia	813	2.2	About 4,000 hectares along border at Hacienda Verdún	Nicaraguan family with properties in Guanacaste in nineteenth century
Alejandro Hurtado Hurtado	Liberia	792	2.1	Haciendas El Jobo, La Culebra, Los Ahogados, and others north of Liberia	Nicaraguan family with properties in Guanacaste since the colonial period
David Clachar González	Liberia	744	2.0	Owned one-third of El Tempisque until 1957, when hacienda was divided, leaving him section called El Real; additional smaller properties as well	Descended from English technician who came to work on Atlantic railway and Panama Canal in late nineteenth century. Acquired numerous properties in 1930s and 1940s

Name	Location	Steers	%	Holdings	Description
Hacienda Tenorio	Cañas	722	1.9		Acquired by United Fruit Company in 1949 for breeding mules for southern Costa Rican plantations
Sociedad Ganadera La Emilia	Cañas	697	1.9	Hacienda Taboga	Owned by central Costa Rican coffee planters (the Sánchez family). Acquired in early twentieth century
Lorenzo Martínez Duarte	Tilarán	521	1.4	Numerous holdings around Tilarán	Central Costa Rican family that accumulated numerous small and medium-size properties through claims and purchases in early twentieth century
Jaime Goldemberg Pomeranic	Nicoya	509	1.4	Several holdings around Nicoya	Recent Polish Jewish immigrant
Lorenzo Brothers	Liberia	499	1.3	Property north of Liberia	Sons of Spanish immigrant who claimed state lands in nineteenth century. Political ties to José Figueres
Aristides Baltodano Briceño	Liberia	466	1.3	Hacienda El Pelón de la Altura	Family came to Liberia from Nicaragua in mid-nineteenth century. Served eleven terms in the legislature. El Pelón purchased in 1930s
Sociedad Ganadera Murciélago	Liberia	462	1.2	Hacienda El Pelón de la Bajura	Corporation with central Costa Rican, Guanacastecan, and Nicaraguan capital. Founded in early 1940s, although several partners already owned much land
Total steers exported by above		12,613	33.9%		
Total steers exported 1955–60		37,189	100.0%		

SOURCE: CGG, *Informe anual* 1955–56, 1956–57, 1957–58, 1958–59, 1959–60.

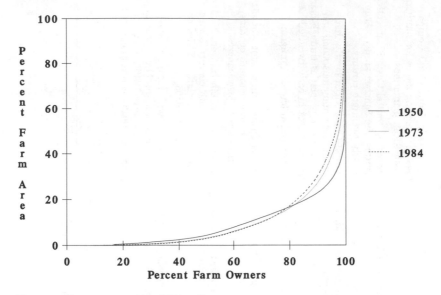

Fig. 7.1. Guanacaste: Land Distribution, 1950, 1973, 1984. Source: Tables 7.1, 7.3, and 7.4.

TABLE 7.3
Guanacaste Province: Land Distribution, 1973

Size in hectares	Farm Units			Farm Area			
	N	Percent	Cumulative percent	Hectares	Percent	Cumulative percent	Average farm size
<0.2	253	2.3%	2.3%	30.4	0.0%	0.0%	0.1
0.2–0.5	221	2.0	4.3	75.8	0.0	0.0	0.3
0.5–1.0	594	5.5	9.8	413.6	0.1	0.1	0.7
1–2	829	7.6	17.4	1,212.0	0.1	0.2	1.5
2–3	783	7.2	24.6	1,874.1	0.2	0.4	2.4
3–4	344	3.2	27.8	1,176.5	0.1	0.5	3.4
4–5	412	3.8	31.6	1,822.9	0.2	0.7	4.4
5–10	1,138	10.5	42.0	8,228.0	0.9	1.6	7.2
10–20	1,350	12.4	54.4	19,085.9	2.1	3.7	14.1
20–50	2,232	20.5	75.0	71,534.5	7.9	11.6	32.0
50–100	1,278	11.8	86.7	88,902.9	9.8	21.4	69.6
100–200	679	6.2	93.0	91,833.6	10.1	31.5	135.2
200–500	493	4.5	97.5	146,013.6	16.1	47.6	296.2
500–1,000	143	1.3	98.8	101,397.6	11.2	58.7	709.1
1,000–2,500	85	0.8	99.6	122,521.9	13.5	72.2	1,441.4
2,500+	41	0.4	100.0	252,641.0	27.8	100.0	6,162.0
TOTAL	10,875	100.0%		908,764.3			83.6

SOURCE: *CAP* 1973.

TABLE 7.4
Guanacaste Province: Land Distribution, 1984

Size in hectares	Farm Units			Farm Area			
	N	Percent	Cumulative percent	Hectares	Percent	Cumulative percent	Average farm size
<1	1,112	10.5%	10.5%	316.6	0.0%	0.0%	0.3
1–2	937	8.8	19.3	766.1	0.1	0.2	0.8
2–3	708	6.7	26.0	1,159.7	0.2	0.3	1.6
3–4	372	3.5	29.5	979.3	0.1	0.5	2.6
4–5	364	3.4	32.9	1,317.8	0.2	0.6	3.6
5–10	1,126	10.6	43.6	6,819.1	1.0	1.6	6.1
10–20	1,272	12.0	55.6	16,098.6	2.3	3.9	12.7
20–50	2,105	19.8	75.4	61,064.5	8.7	12.5	29.0
50–100	1,216	11.5	86.9	78,396.1	11.1	23.6	64.5
100–200	662	6.2	93.1	84,300.1	11.9	35.6	127.3
200–500	483	4.6	97.7	129,249.0	18.3	53.9	267.6
500–1,000	156	1.5	99.1	100,666.9	14.3	68.2	645.3
1,000+	94	0.9	100.0	224,769.6	31.8	100.0	2,391.2
TOTAL	10,607			705,903.4			66.6

SOURCE: *CAP* 1984.

individual ranchers or haciendas, are taken as the unit of analysis, the level of concentration was even greater.[2]

The dimensions of the changes in land tenure patterns that accompanied the beef export boom can be gauged by briefly examining agricultural census data from 1950 to 1984. Figure 7.1, three Lorenz curves that describe the percentage concentration of farmland in Guanacaste reported by the agricultural censuses of 1950, 1973, and 1984, indicates how the relative positions of different landowning strata changed in this period. On the one hand, the proportion of land held by the lowest eight deciles of agriculturalists deteriorated slightly during 1950–73 and remained virtually unchanged in 1984. On the other hand, the four-fifths of farm area belonging to the wealthiest fifth of landowners underwent a notable, though modest, shift toward better distribution—but only within the top fifth of landowners. This phenomenon may be interpreted on the basis of Tables 7.1 and 7.3 as a fragmentation of the largest properties (see Table 7.4).[3] Thus, for 1950–84, modifications in Guanacaste land tenure patterns have generally favored a higher intermediate stratum.

New Investors, Rising Land Values, and Fragmenting Latifundios

What processes account for the changes in land tenure captured in snapshot form by the agricultural census data? Three interrelated causes are involved in the fragmentation of the large latifundios: (1) the division of large properties between family members; (2) the sales of parts of large estates, which, taking advantage of the rapid increase in land values, raised capital for the modernization of crop production that could not be generated from the existing extensive production structure; and (3) "artificial" divisions, among family members or corporate entities, the principal purposes of which were to avoid government expropriation, to permit a more intense capitalization of sections of properties, or to allow heirs to inherit individual estates.

The characteristic titling maneuvers of the early twentieth century had been the "registration of excess lands" (inscripción de demasías) or "rectification of measurements" (rectificación de medidas) that permitted landowners to amass huge estates (see Chapter 1). From the 1940s on, however, hacendados increasingly employed a new and antithetical legal procedure—"segregation of lots"—to sell parts of properties or to divide them into sections belonging to corporations that were in turn controlled either by the original owners or by partnerships between original owners and new investors. The two Stewart brothers, for example, decided in the late 1950s that it would be "prudent" to divide their enormous holdings before their children were married and in-laws might gain a say in running the property. Many of their properties gradually passed into other hands, either because of land invasions (as in the case of the Hacienda Miravalles), expropriations (Llanos de Cortés), or purchases by investors from outside the region (El Viejo).

This fragmentation of large holdings generally appeared in property records as paper trails of frequent sales and divisions emanating from what landowners, topographers, and lawyers referred to as "mother farms" (fincas madres)—the giant latifundios assembled in the nineteenth or the early twentieth century. Sometimes the genealogical metaphor was more than a figurative allusion, as when the Clachar-Romero-Gillen partnership, which owned Hacienda Tempisque, divided the property into three separate units called Hacienda Don David, Hacienda Doña Loli, and Hacienda de Challe after the family members who took possession of the different sections.

Usually, however, the division of *fincas madres* represented the entrance of new investors onto the Guanacaste scene, even when old latifundista families divested themselves of parts of their estates. The Hurtados, for example, divided their holdings to the north of Liberia, partly in response to continued invasions by peasants in the Quebrada Grande area, and sold some of the disputed land to the family of a congressional deputy who had intervened in the squatting conflict (RP SM 8442—1964). Other "new" landlords acquired huge properties and immediately sold them off to raise capital for agroindustries or mechanized agriculture. Fernando Pinto, a San José doctor who bought Hacienda El Viejo from the Stewarts' father in the 1940s, sold much of the property to Miguel Brenes Gutiérrez, minister of labor in the pre-civil-war administration of Teodoro Picado. He then used part of this money to build a sugar mill on the bank of the Tempisque River, which was purchased by exiled Cubans in the early 1960s. In all these cases, the division of properties was partly a precautionary measure to guard against an eventual land reform and partly a means of generating investment funds.

The new investors in the Guanacaste land market were a varied lot. Some were central Costa Rican coffee planters, such as the Salazar Jiménez brothers from Heredia, who briefly owned Hacienda El Viejo in the late 1950s and early 1960s, or the Lindos and Murrays, respectively a Costa Rican coffee family and English immigrants linked by marriage, who acquired Hacienda San Luis in 1954 (RP SM 5092). After 1948, when the state began to channel vastly increased resources to outlying areas of the country and specifically to the cattle sector, ascendant middle-class investors from central Costa Rica also began to buy grazing lands. Barred from the already monopolized coffee- and sugar-processing industries and unable to meet the high start-up costs of other sectors, these aspiring ranchers turned to livestock because it offered a low-risk activity carried out on a good— land—that was certain to appreciate rapidly (Solís 1981a).

The influx of capital from outside the region and the encouraging prospect of an expanding export beef trade accelerated a long-term rise in land values that dated to the 1932 protectionist legislation and fueled further speculation (see Figure 7.2). Particularly after the passage of the agrarian reform law in 1961, it was difficult to distinguish speculators from ranchers, since those whose primary interest was speculative usually ran cattle on their land to avoid having it declared unproductive by the state, a move that would permit it to be expro-

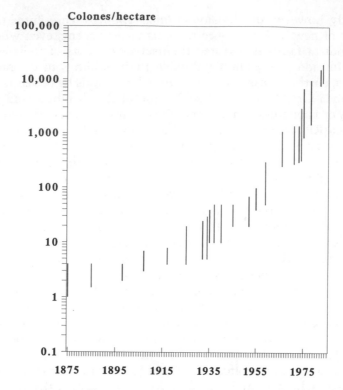

Fig. 7.2. Tempisque Valley: Range of Land Values, 1875–1983 (semilogarith-mic scale). Sources: High and low prices mentioned in various ANCR, RPPG, and CN documents; in *La Gaceta Oficial, El Diario de Costa Rica*, and *El Guanacaste*; and in field interviews. Original prices for 1875–1900 are in pesos, but are converted to colones (one peso = two colones). Prices are for properties with little or no substantial infrastructure, containing pasture, cropland, forest, or brush.

priated. Similarly, given the low profit levels of most ranching opera-tions, many individuals who would have otherwise been reluctant to invest in livestock did so only because it was also possible to reap eventual gains in real estate.

Leading landowners in Guanacaste frequently remark that nobody really knows the value of a property until a neighbor places compara-ble lands on the market and closes a sale. For the traditional land-owners of the province, the escalation in property values proved a boon in two respects. "Land rich, money poor" members of Guanacaste's upper class could sell small portions of estates and use the funds to purchase brahman cattle, build fences, improve pastures, begin mechanized production of crops, or invest in other sectors of the economy. For others, "money poor" or not, the improved situation allowed them to enter partnerships with outside investors who had capital but no land.

Examples of such alliances between Guanacastecan landowners and extraregional capital abound in the corporate registry entries of the period. In 1943, for example, Alfonso Salazar Céspedes and Fernando Alvarado Chacón, co-owners of the massive Hacienda Murciélago in La Cruz, formed a cattle corporation with several outside investors, including Alvarado's brother-in-law, Guillermo González Herrán. The 225 shares in the Sociedad Ganadera Murciélago, valued at 1,000 colones ($178) each, were paid as follows: Alvarado held a total of 88 shares, 25 of them by virtue of his rights to Murciélago, 48 for cattle on the property, and 15 paid for in cash; Salazar held 45 shares, 25 in rights to the hacienda, 11.6 in cattle, and 8.4 in cash; González paid for his 88 shares entirely in cash, as did two minor investors who purchased two shares each (RP SM 2551).[4] Nearly two decades later, in 1962, Salazar and his wife, Agüeda Ayales, created a company in which they each owned 150 1,000-colón ($151) shares. This alliance at the altar and in the corporate registry also exemplified the growing ties between landed and moneyed wealth: Salazar brought to the marriage Hacienda El Viejo, 33 hectares in Sitio Pijije, and property in the resort of Playa de Coco; his spouse-partner simply paid 150,000 colones in cash, approximately $23,000 (RP SM 9596).

The growing modernization of crop agriculture also gave rise to new types of alliances. In 1958 Dolores Clachar, owner of Hacienda Doña Loli (the section of the former Hacienda Tempisque that bore her nickname), joined with two brothers from the nearby town of Filadelfia, one of whom was an agronomist, to cultivate rice and cotton. Clachar, owner of half of the 25,000-colón shares, agreed to lend 500 *manzanas* of land and to finance the operation; Renán and Omar Agüero were to supply "technical direction" and administer the company. The agreement specified that the company's machinery could be rented to others for additional income and that any buildings constructed would become the property of Doña Loli (RP SM 6647).

A similar, if larger and more complex, alliance took place in 1973. The González Alvarado brothers, owners of Hacienda El Pelón de la

Bajura, the province's largest rice producer, appointed as officers of their company the sales, credit, and replacement-parts directors of one of the country's largest agricultural machinery companies, Maquinaria y Tractores, Limitada (RP SM T55 F72 A55).[5] El Pelón was thus assured preferential treatment in a market where equipment-supply bottlenecks during critical periods in the agricultural cycle have frequently contributed to the demise of less-influential farmers. The machinery dealer, on the other hand, captured as a customer the region's largest single purchaser of modern technology. Although it is unclear if El Pelón's owners entered this alliance in part to improve their access to low-cost loans, in other, similar cases the availability of inexpensive credit was a key consideration. A formal division between the corporate entities with title to the land and those administering the production process or supplying the machinery made it possible to obtain larger subsidized bank loans, since the "producing" company could inflate its cost estimates by including charges for land rents or machinery services provided by the "other," usually "paper" corporations (see Annis n.d.).

Growing numbers of North Americans, some of whom held grandiose ideas of introducing modern technology to "backward" Costa Rica, also purchased lands for high-risk crops such as cotton and rice, as well as for cattle. In these cases too, access to subsidized credit was frequently a significant incentive. Members of leading latifundista families (Baltodanos, Hurtados, and others) often held positions as loan officers in local bank branches, especially in Liberia, making links to the regional elite an important part of business success. Sheldon Annis has noted:

A shrewd foreign investor would take on a cash-poor but politically well-connected Costa Rican partner. Because of the small size of the country, the Costa Rican partner would almost surely have friends in the banks and in key government agencies. The partners might create a new business from scratch or, better yet, resurrect a decapitalized, marginal business. With an infusion of fresh capital . . . it could acquire physical assets. . . . With these assets for collateral, the business would then be in a strong position to apply for loans, often at negative real interest. (1990: 5)

In Guanacaste, the most prominent of these investors included a group of bankers from Coral Gables, Florida, which acquired Hacienda El Hacha in 1968 in partnership with Antonio Capella Segreda, later president of the powerful rice-growers lobby, and Gonzalo

Facio Segreda, a leading politician then associated with the National Liberation Party (PLN) (RP SM T75 F318 A204). Others included a wealthy Ohio engineer and plumbing contractor who purchased Hacienda Doña Loli in 1970 and renamed it Rancho Gesling in his own honor, and a group that also included Europeans and South Americans, which bought much of what had once been Hacienda La Culebra in order to begin cultivating jojoba beans on what they then called Rancho San Rafael. Locals often referred half jokingly to these recent arrivals as "crazy gringos," because of the misplaced certainty and the presumption with which they tried to implant temperate-zone agriculture and U.S.-style production organization in a foreign environment, and because of the offhanded way they poured huge sums into land and equipment. By the late 1970s, this tendency to overinvest in high-risk undertakings and high-priced land had left many of these foreign investors close to bankruptcy (a problem discussed in more detail in Chapter 9).

The way in which the North American newcomers sometimes operated was epitomized by the circumstances surrounding the purchase of Hacienda Santa María by John D. Cage, a Texan widely believed to be a front man for former U.S. president Lyndon B. Johnson.[6] The 5,000-hectare Hacienda Santa María was located on the slopes of the Rincón de la Vieja volcano north of Liberia. According to the previous owner, Guillermo Echeverría, the 1968 negotiations that led to the sale of the ranch took place after Cage spent two weeks visiting the property. Their discussion, as reported by Echeverría, went as follows: Cage: "I'll buy your farm, it's very beautiful." Echeverría: "How much will you give me for it?" Cage: "Two hundred thousand dollars." Echeverría: "Let me think about it." Cage: "No. Please open that suitcase."

Echeverría opened the suitcase and with great surprise found that along with Cage's clothes, it contained $500,000. Echeverría: "How is it possible that you walk around with so much money around here?" Cage: "In Costa Rica it's possible to do that, but not in another country." Echeverría then gave Cage a provisional receipt for the $200,000 (*La Nación*, 17 Jan. 1970, 6).

Obviously, most of Cage's compatriots who invested in Guanacaste real estate employed less-dramatic business practices. But the appearance in Guanacaste of large numbers of U.S. investors, whether as owners of vast properties such as Rancho Gesling and Rancho San Rafael or as minor shareholders in more modest operations, imbued the local land market with a speculative spirit that affected even economically marginal smallholders. Over the years, "Farm for Sale" signs in English, often crudely scrawled by hands not accustomed to writing, much less in a foreign language, became more and more common on roadside posts and trees.

If "crazy gringos" with abundant cash, in suitcases or not, were one factor that contributed to rapid inflation of land values in Guanacaste, the Costa Rican government's efforts to establish state-owned agroindustries were clearly another. Beginning in 1972 with the formation of the state-controlled Costa Rican Development Corporation (Corporación Costarricense de Desarrollo, CODESA), the state purchased large properties at previously unheard-of prices to provide farmland and plant sites for new publicly owned enterprises. CODESA, which was founded and grew rapidly during the eight years of social democratic administration from 1970 to 1978, was intended to invest in undertakings considered necessary for Costa Rica's development. Until the mid-1980s, when—as a result of U.S. pressure—most of its constituent companies were sold to the private sector or to cooperatives, it specialized in projects requiring massive investments that could not be raised by the private sector or that private capital viewed as highly risky.[7] In Guanacaste, CODESA subsidiaries included the Tempisque Sugar Mill (Central Azucarera del Tempisque, CATSA), Cottons of Costa Rica (Algodones de Costa Rica, ALCORSA), Pacific Cement (Cementos del Pacífico), and Agroindustrial Development (Desarrollo Agroindustrial, DAISA), which exported fruits and vegetables to the United States. CATSA in particular and, to a lesser extent, DAISA required extensive areas to assure supplies of raw material for their respective plants. The core of CATSA's operation consisted of land acquired from the section of the former Hacienda Tempisque belonging to Challe Gillen. This acreage, however, was insufficient to supply the mill's capacity, and CATSA gradually purchased various adjacent properties from other owners, who knew that they had only to hold out for as long as possible to receive what seemed like astronomical prices for their holdings.

"Artificial" Fragmentation of Latifundios

Whereas the corporate cattle exporters of the late 1950s were largely entities named after the families that controlled them or haciendas whose ownership was common knowledge, by the 1970s the real owners of the land and cattle were often unknown to almost all but themselves. Even foremen who had long served on particular haciendas and who continued to work for new owners after a property was sold were at times unaware of the identities of their employers.[8] In the 1970s it became common for investors wishing to conceal their identities or to guard against expropriation to create corporations that owned smaller sections of one property or separate parts of the production process. Thus one of these new entities might control, for example, the cattle but not the land, or the tractors but not the rice. Often these companies owned each other or were controlled by other entities domiciled in Panama or, less commonly, in the United States or Monrovia, Liberia.

Both the old, easily identified corporations and the new, obscure ones were part of an "artificial" division of estates among members of the traditional landowning class. Intermarriage within the leading families in the province often permitted large properties to be preserved or reconsolidated. It thus prevented or delayed the fragmentation of estates that might have occurred as a result of marriages to nonlandholding outsiders. Figure 7.3 describes twentieth-century marriage links among a small number of landholding families from the Liberia area and indicates how marriage was one strategy for maintaining a high degree of concentration in landownership. Rising land values and, in some cases, scale advantages in intensified crop production also encouraged siblings to leave intact estates that might otherwise have been partitioned.[9] Even when the large estates of earlier years were divided, the new owners often married members of other landowning families who already had substantial holdings.

The social world of the Liberia elite, as one member described it, "is still a question of families, although not like it once was. Even if the children wanted to move beyond that to marry, it is not probable that they would, unless they moved to San José or abroad. It is possible to say that in some cases, they would not even have the chance then."

Marriage and merger often cannot be disentangled in the lives of Guanacaste landowning families. In 1947, for example, Baltazar Baldioceda Muñoz and five of his children formed a company with a capital base of 300,000 colones ($53,476), dedicated to commerce and cattle raising on Hacienda Asientillo and three smaller nearby properties (RP SM 3587). In 1956 his daughter Angélica Baldioceda, who had

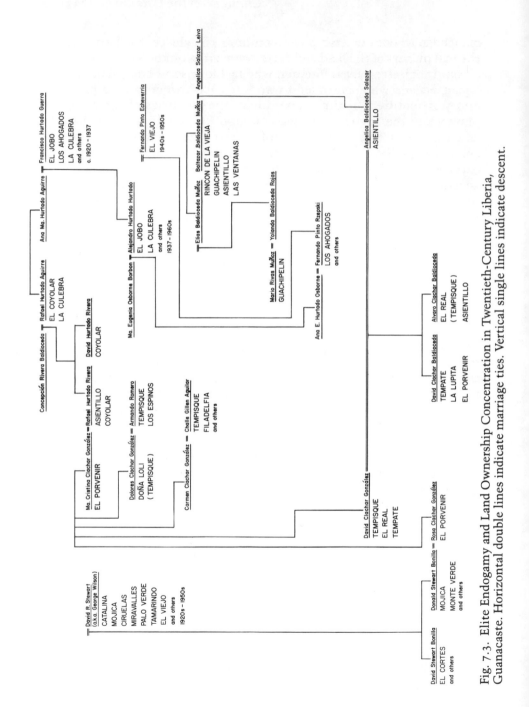

Fig. 7.3. Elite Endogamy and Land Ownership Concentration in Twentieth-Century Liberia, Guanacaste. Horizontal double lines indicate marriage ties. Vertical single lines indicate descent.

married an owner of Hacienda Tempisque, David Clachar, bought out her siblings. She and her son Alvaro became sole owners of the company. In one week in August 1971, Alvaro was named president of Hacienda El Real and also founded a new corporation called Hacienda Asientillo, which he controlled through the now-misnamed company Baltazar Baldioceda e Hijos (RP SM 16,130; RP SM 15,973).[10]

Similar marriage-mergers noted in Figure 7.3 involved other Clachar siblings contracting advantageous unions with individuals from the Hurtado and Stewart families, as well as marriages that linked an Hurtado and a Pinto, an Hurtado Aguirre with a Rivera Baldioceda, and two first-cousin Hurtados. In other Liberia families and elsewhere in the province, the pattern was similar. Even where the latifundios were divided, marriages and mergers contributed to the preservation of a more complex but only slightly changed pattern of latifundist ownership.

Geopolitics: Revolution and Counterrevolution to the North

Guanacaste's strategic location near Nicaragua contributed to other processes of geopolitically motivated land reconcentration that also contradicted the general tendency toward fragmentation of latifundios. Shortly after coming to power in the mid-1930s, Nicaraguan dictator Anastasio Somoza García began to smuggle large numbers of cattle to Costa Rica, violating a ban on exports declared in retaliation for Costa Rica's 1932 protectionist legislation.[11] As William Krehm noted in his important yet long-neglected *Democracies and Tyrannies of the Caribbean*,[12] the cattle

went to Víctor Wolf, close ally of the Costa Rican ruling house of Calderón Guardia, who fattened them on his ranch at Chomes near Puntarenas. These exports did not exist so far as Nicaraguan statistics were concerned, but turned up in Costa Rican records. The Costa Rican Statistical Report for 1943 gave cattle imports from 1942 as 8,652 head. But the Nicaraguan Year Book for 1942 placed the total exports from Nicaragua for the same year (not only to Costa Rica, but to Panama and Peru) at 1,467. The 7,185 head that entered Costa Rica from Nicaragua, but didn't leave Nicaragua for Costa Rica, were one of the many miracles of the Somoza regime. (1984: 112–13)[13]

Probably because of his involvement in this trade, Somoza began to explore the possibility of acquiring property south of the border. As early as 1940, Luis Brenes Gutiérrez and Casimiro Sobrado García, the former from a family recently established in ranching and with close ties to leading figures in the national government, the latter then an owner of the Hacienda Tempisque, traveled to Nicaragua, where they were reported to have offered to sell Somoza the Tempisque property (*El Guanacaste*, 18 Nov. 1940, 4). The reason why the sale was never finalized cannot be ascertained, but it is clear from subsequent events that the dictator's sons and successors, Luis and Anastasio Somoza Debayle, shared their father's interest in northern Costa Rican real estate.[14]

The younger Somozas' acquisition of extensive properties in northern Costa Rica was probably motivated by speculative considerations and the desire to diversify their investments outside Nicaragua, but the paramount concern was almost certainly strategic. As early as 1944, small invasions by Nicaraguan exiles based in northern Costa Rica had attempted to overthrow the Somoza dynasty (Rodríguez Vega 1980: 101). In 1959 and 1960 unprecedentedly large incursions took place under the direction of Nicaragua's Conservative Party (Blandón 1981; Millett 1979: 299–301). One key leader was Indalecio Pastora, whose family controlled Hacienda Verdún and other properties spanning both sides of the border. In addition, the dissident Nicaraguan general Carlos Pasos, treasurer of the anti-Somoza forces in this period, had acquired the Guanacastecan haciendas Paso Hondo in Cañas in 1957 and Santa Rosa in the border canton of La Cruz in 1958.[15] With several actual or potential bases for exiles near their southern border, the Somozas began to establish a presence of their own in northern Costa Rica.

Their allies in this effort were Guanacastecan landlords, some of Nicaraguan nationality or descent, who were sympathetic to the Somozas' Liberal Party, and also members of the family and administration of former Costa Rican president Teodoro Picado Michalski, who sought asylum in Nicaragua after being deposed in the 1948 Costa Rican civil war. Picado, despite his government's alliance with the Communists, had enjoyed good relations with the elder Somoza, who feared the Costa Rican social democratic opposition's ties to Nicaraguan exiles.[16] During the 1944 attack on Nicaragua by exiles, Picado's government coordinated military operations with Somoza and even permitted Nicaraguan guardsmen to operate on Costa Rican territory (Rodríguez Vega 1980: 101). Functionaries of the Picado government were also reported to be involved with Somoza's lucrative cattle-smuggling business (Diederich 1981: 28; Millett 1979: 282). Through his second wife, Etelvina Ramírez Montiel, who was from La Cruz, Picado had close ties to large landowners in the border area, including some who were later partners of both his son Teodoro Picado Lara and General Somoza's son Anastasio Somoza Debayle— who graduated from West Point together in the class of 1946.[17] Picado's labor minister, Miguel Brenes Gutiérrez, who with his brothers had acquired an extensive section of Hacienda El Viejo, had remained in Costa Rica after the war and was one of the largest Guanacaste beef exporters in the late 1950s.[18] Picado himself had also been interested in purchasing at least one hacienda in Guanacaste during 1944–48 when he was president, and he was later accused by the owner of fomenting a squatter invasion when his offer was rejected (see Chapter 8).

In 1962 Teodoro Picado Lara, a lawyer and son of the former president, brought together a group of investors that included his mother, his American wife, and his cousins René and Alvaro Picado Esquivel and formed a corporation called Compañía Agro-Pecuaria La Esperanza (RP SM 8101). Less than three months after registering the company, Teodoro, who was listed as the director, stepped down and "in substitution of the resigner and for the rest of the legal period . . . the Director appointed [was] señor Anastasio Somoza Debayle, of age, once-married, General of the Army of Nicaragua, resident of Managua" (RP SM T52 F291 A186—1962).

The same day that Somoza became a director of Agro-Pecuaria La Esperanza, he was also, with Picado's assistance, named director of Murciélago, Limitada, a company founded the year before to administer the hacienda of that name in La Cruz (RP SM T52 F290 A185). In a 1963 meeting at the hacienda, Agro-Pecuaria La Esperanza was made owner of half of Murciélago, Limitada, while Somoza retained the other half of the shares in his own name. Also in 1963, Picado founded a company with Alfonso Salazar Céspedes, who in 1943 had been part of a group that briefly owned Murciélago (see above). The purpose of this venture, however, was to exploit Hacienda El Viejo, which Salazar had recently acquired. Picado contributed 250,000 colones ($38,000) in cash, and Salazar supplied the land for the operation (RP SM T56 F137 A102). In 1964, five months after the founding of the company, new statutes adopted at a board meeting in the border town of Peñas Blancas noted that Alfonso Salazar and Anastasio Somoza Debayle were "the only partners" (RP SM T56 F541

A422). Picado once again had sold out to Somoza or had been representing him from the beginning.

With the purchase of Hacienda Santa Rosa in 1966 by a company owned by Luis Somoza Debayle, the Somozas controlled about 31,000 hectares in Guanacaste: approximately 10,500 in Santa Rosa, 16,431 in the adjacent Murciélago (CN G1-2-1-43—1952), and 4,118 in El Viejo (CN G5-1-1-557—1975).[19] The strategically located Murciélago and Santa Rosa haciendas included 70 kilometers of coastline on the Santa Elena Peninsula, and Descartes Point, which jutted out into the Pacific just a few kilometers from Nicaragua. El Viejo was on the Tempisque River, the region's major navigable inland waterway. All three properties had airstrips capable of serving large planes. In 1966 the Somozas were also reported to be seeking control of the Pastora family's holdings along the border and were said to possess an additional 30,000 hectares spanning 20 kilometers of the frontier near Los Chiles in Alajuela province (La República, 25 Apr. 1966, 1, 4; Suñol 1981: 59).

The Somozas' presence in Guanacaste aroused considerable opposition. Many Costa Ricans viewed the Nicaraguan dictators as having created "a state within a state," infringing on national sovereignty. On at least two occasions uniformed Nicaraguan National Guardsmen entered Murciélago and Santa Rosa to evict squatters (Libertad, 27 Jan. 1973, 6; La República, 25 Apr. 1966, 4). On annual visits to El Viejo in the 1960s and 1970s, according to former hacienda employees, Anastasio Somoza was always accompanied by 20 or 30 Nicaraguan National Guardsmen and by armed men in civilian dress. There he liked to recline on the hacienda house porch in a hammock embroidered with the initials A.S.—which conveniently could also be used when his partner Alfonso Salazar visited the property.

In 1968 Costa Rican fishermen in waters off Murciélago reported that they had been attacked from machine gun emplacements on shore (Libertad, 30 Mar. 1968, 3; La Prensa Libre, 26 Mar. 1968, 11). Costa Rican authorities found undocumented workers, including a Nicaraguan National Guard lieutenant, laboring on Murciélago, as well as farm machinery that had apparently been smuggled into the country (La República, 26 Apr. 1966, 11). The Association of Wood Industries accused the Somozas of smuggling huge quantities of timber into Nicaragua (La Prensa Libre, 25 Apr. 1966, 11). The press also reported in 1971 that Anastasio Somoza was providing military training at Hacienda Murciélago to Cuban exiles who intended to invade Cuba. President Figueres, while declaring that he did not believe the story, lent it credence by stating that ships that had been sighted off the coast of Murciélago "might have to do with the Cubans or contraband" (*La Nación*, 16 Jan. 1971, 25). Although nothing was ever proven regarding the reports, Somoza's ties to exiled Cubans were clearly close.[20] When "the General" was at El Viejo, area residents remember, he always received visits from the Cuban owners of the nearby Guinea sugar mill, who were partners of Costa Rican ultrarightist Hubert Federspiel (see Achío and Escalante 1985: 131). On one occasion described by residents a plane "from Cuba landed" on the hacienda runway. There it was painted and covered with branches, and the registration number was changed.

These apparent violations of national sovereignty were all the more significant because many of them were in the Santa Rosa area, a site of great historical and symbolic importance to the Costa Rican people. It was here that Costa Rican troops first clashed with U.S. proslavery filibusters led by William Walker in 1856 and where an invasion force of supporters of former presidents Calderón and Picado was defeated in 1955. In 1966 Luis Somoza, hoping to placate opponents, offered to donate 25 hectares surrounding the main hacienda house to the Costa Rican state for a museum. Conflicts with squatters in 1966 and again in 1969–70, however, sustained anti-Somoza feeling in Costa Rica at a high pitch and led to the expropriation in 1970 of over 10,000 hectares of Santa Rosa that were to be used for a national park.[21]

The anti-Somoza mood in Costa Rica intensified in 1978 as opposition to the dictatorship within Nicaragua spread. Somoza anticipated expropriation of his holdings and quietly resigned as a director of El Viejo in August 1978 (RP SM T201 F77 A68).[22] Murciélago, however, had attracted more negative attention in Costa Rica and was of much greater strategic importance because of its coastline and location near the border. Somoza was also in effect the only owner and thus found it more difficult to simply withdraw, as he had done with El Viejo. As the conflict in Nicaragua intensified, the Costa Rican state moved with uncharacteristic speed, divesting Somoza of Murciélago with an executive expropriation decree signed by President Carazo in 1978 and a legislative decree in June 1979 (*La Gaceta Oficial*, 12 June 1979, 1).[23]

Even after the decrees, however, it took some time to gain control

of the hacienda. As late as September 1979, government guards protested that Murciélago was "totally full" of cattle belonging to Luis
Gallegos, son of a former partner in Santa Rosa and owner of nearby
Hacienda Los Inocentes. The guards reported that Gallegos and his
employees had the keys to the gates of Murciélago and were using a
truck expropriated from Somoza to travel around the hacienda. They
complained that they were powerless to "impede them." Many of the
cattle in Murciélago, the guards claimed, were contraband from the
property of Manuel Centeno, which had part of its territory in Nicaragua (CGG Actas, 9: 21).

The last recorded meeting of Murciélago, Limitada, was held on
July 12, 1979, in Managua, just one week before the victory of the
Sandinista Revolution. Somoza's cousin, Alberto Bermúdez, stepped
down as director in favor of a Nicaraguan resident of Miami, Renaldy
Gutiérrez Solano, who had represented Somoza on the board since
1978.[24] Those present agreed to modify the bylaws so that "the
corporation will be able to hold ordinary and special assemblies of
shareholders outside of the territory of Costa Rica, indicating ex-
pressly for that effect the city of Asunción, Republic of Paraguay" (RP
SM T212 F507 A474).

When Somoza fled Nicaragua for Miami on July 17, 1979, it was
unclear whether he intended to remain in the United States, whose
government he considered to have "betrayed" him. The Murciélago
statutes indicate that even before leaving Managua, Somoza had
considered Alfredo Stroessner's Paraguay as a potentially more con-
genial refuge. It was there that Argentine guerrillas assassinated the
deposed dictator the following year.[25]

The Sandinistas' rise to power in 1979 and the almost immediate
beginnings of armed counterrevolution assured that northern Costa
Rica would continue to be an area of strategic contention.[26] At times,
however, purely geopolitical questions were impossible to disentangle from the economic and even religious motivations that fueled
new kinds of landownership concentration. The complexities of the
problem are illustrated by the arrival in Guanacaste in the 1980s of
two influential new investors, one an obscure millionaire from the
Virginia suburbs of Washington, D.C., the other a flamboyant, controversial fundamentalist minister.

In 1980 Cecil D. Hylton, a Virginia millionaire who had made a
fortune in construction and real estate, acquired Haciendas El Hacha,
Orosí, Agua Buena, Génova, and part of El Amo to the north of
Liberia.[27] These properties consisted for the most part of poor-quality

land primarily suitable for grazing cattle, although Hylton had ambitious plans to build holding ponds and eventually irrigate much of El Hacha with waters from the cordillera. Some Nicaraguan *contras* were based at El Hacha at about this time, and in the early and mid-1980s they occasionally may have used Hylton's other properties.[28] But this fleeting, low-level military presence—which on a large, mountainous wooded property could even have occurred without an absentee owner's knowledge—was ultimately of little or no strategic importance in the war against the Sandinista government.[29]

In addition to acquiring cattle haciendas near the border, Hylton targeted the new Guanacaste irrigation district, centered in Cañas but extending north to Liberia, where tens of thousands of hectares were soon to be irrigated at government expense (discussed in more detail in Chapter 10). Land values had risen abruptly in the district in anticipation of the high profits that would be made in crop agriculture once water became available. Many landowners, however, either were heavily indebted because of ill-fated experiences with rain-fed agriculture or lacked the capital to build the canals, pumping stations, and level fields necessary to convert extensive cattle operations to intensive cropping. Few local buyers had the capital either, and many were nervous about purchasing property in a zone the government considered a high priority for agrarian reform.

Hylton entered the irrigation district in 1981 with the acquisition of the Cuban-owned Azucarera Guanacaste, a 6,230-hectare property containing the Las Piedras sugar mill, and the Hacienda El Viejo, estimated at a minimum of 1,224 hectares.[30] The latter estate was held in a partnership with a naturalized Costa Rican citizen, Gustavo Echeverri, who also had interests in other Guanacaste properties and who became the administrator of Hylton's Liberia office. In 1981, Hylton reportedly arranged to rent for one year the U.S.-owned Rancho Gesling and to purchase it at the end of the rental contract (a sale that was never finalized).[31] By mid-1982 Hylton thus controlled more than 14,000 hectares of the best land in the irrigation district. 6,230 in the sugar plantation at Las Piedras; 6,767 at Rancho Gesling; and at least 1,224 at Hacienda El Viejo. He also owned about ten thousand hectares outside the district, most of it north of Liberia at Haciendas Orosí and El Hacha.[32] This foreign control over 20,000 hectares or more of Guanacastecan land raised the specter of a new kind of landownership concentration centered in, but not limited to, the irrigation district.[33]

The way in which Hylton's properties in Guanacaste were acquired is interesting because it illustrates how foreign investors have been able to benefit from Costa Rica's economic crisis and even from the recession that affected the United States in the early 1980s. Rather than simply purchasing Guanacaste properties, Hylton traded small but valuable pieces of Virginia real estate for large haciendas in Costa Rica.[34] The Guanacaste landlords most interested in such deals were North Americans and Cubans (a number of whom were U.S. citizens) who had first come between the mid-1960s and the early 1970s and had then suffered economic reverses in high-risk agriculture in the mid- and late 1970s. By the early 1980s, when Hylton set about building up his Guanacaste holdings, high interest rates in the United States made it difficult to buy and sell properties. One way to counteract this stagnation in the U.S. real estate market was to engage in barter with indebted foreign landlords in Guanacaste, many of whom were only too eager to take advantage of this easy way out of what they saw as an impossible situation. Since Costa Rica was in the midst of an extreme process of devaluation and inflation, properties were often undervalued in dollar terms. But the economic crisis, because it had a devastating and disruptive effect on many sectors of the Costa Rican economy, also made it temporarily more difficult even for wealthy Costa Ricans to purchase land. This in turn increased the leverage that outside purchasers, such as Hylton, could exercise over potential sellers. Hylton thus stood to benefit from inflation and devaluation in Costa Rica, from normal increases in land values, and from the massive public investment in the irrigation district.[35]

The Hylton saga took on a novel dimension in 1984 when the Virginian donated seventeen properties near the Nicaraguan border to the ministry of U.S. television evangelist Jimmy Swaggart. Most of these holdings, totaling 4,186 hectares, had been part of Hacienda El Hacha, an old wooded estate less than 20 kilometers from Nicaragua.[36] El Hacha was within the proposed boundaries of the Guanacaste National Park, a planned conservation area of 700-square kilometers linking the existing national park at Santa Rosa with forest reserves and parks in the cordillera between the Orosí and Rincón de la Vieja volcanoes (Janzen 1986). The creation of the park, intended to assure the survival and recuperation of diverse threatened species in Central America's largest remaining patch of dry tropical forest, depended for funding on foreign conservation organizations, such as the World Wildlife Fund and the Nature Conservancy (ibid., 74;

Hedström 1990: 184–86).[37] But the entrance of foreign environmentalists into the Guanacaste land market became, with the state agroindustries program and the irrigation district, yet another important factor encouraging speculation and discouraging productive investment.

Landowners in and around the proposed park area quickly became aware that conservationists' interest in their properties would contribute to faster than normal appreciation in local real estate values and that they would soon receive offers from foreign naturalists or the Costa Rican National Parks Foundation (Fundación de Parques Nacionales), which administered the park and directed negotiations for new acquisitions of land. At the same time, park administrators and Foundation negotiators discouraged productive activity on lands they hoped to acquire, in part to prevent agricultural chemical contamination and erosion and in part to begin the forest regeneration that they intended to encourage once private owners sold the land to the park. Some heavily indebted ranchers rapidly arrived at agreements with the park system; others held out for more lucrative offers, sometimes for many years, even though the threat of government expropriation loomed over unwilling owners of larger holdings.

In Swaggart's case, the El Hacha properties had been assessed for tax purposes at 3.6 million colones (equivalent in 1984 to about $80,000). The market value of the land, however, was at least ten times the assessed worth.[38] Hylton's donation thus represented approximately $1 million that could be used by Swaggart's tax-exempt Assemblies of God (Asambleas de Dios) to spread evangelical Protestantism in Central America. Hylton, in turn, could benefit from tax deductions in both Costa Rica and the United States (the formal donation took place in New Orleans and was to the Louisiana-based ministry; the Virginian also donated other properties to the Nature Conservancy). National Parks Foundation negotiators are understandably tight-lipped about the terms of land sales in the Guanacaste Park area, largely for fear of influencing deals still under discussion. Nevertheless, a "large piece" of Swaggart's land had been sold to the Park by 1990, undoubtedly for a sizable sum.[39]

Two years after Hylton donated his section of Hacienda El Hacha to Jimmy Swaggart, he "sold" him 1,416 hectares of irrigation district land in Cañas for a nominal one colón (about two U.S. cents).[40] Three months later, in March 1987, the Agrarian Development Institute (Instituto de Desarrollo Agrario) acquired the property, almost certainly at market value, as part of its land reform program in the irrigation district. Clearly Hylton knew of IDA's interest in the property and decided to pass the profits along to the minister Swaggart. In addition to whatever religious impulses may have motivated Hylton's generosity, the irrigation agency's declaration that the area in question was now officially "under irrigation," which implied an obligation to pay higher water tariffs, likely entered into his decision (see Chapter 10). Other potential tax benefits of this deal were similar to those of the El Hacha donation, though the market value of the irrigation district property was considerably higher than that of the dry cattle lands near Nicaragua. In this case, however, the funds for purchasing Swaggart's land came from Costa Rican taxpayers rather than foreign conservationists.

Why would a North American fundamentalist Protestant minister be interested in owning a massive underutilized cattle hacienda in northwestern Costa Rica? Aside from the obvious advantages of an eventual lucrative sale to the National Parks Foundation, a mixture of geopolitical and religious objectives apparently influenced Swaggart and his ministry. The Assemblies of God was one of the largest and fastest growing evangelical sects in Central America; in Nicaragua it was the third largest religious organization after the Catholic Church and the Moravians, who had long worked in the isolated Atlantic region. Religious proselytism for Swaggart and his followers was inseparable from a conservative political agenda that by the mid-1980s included fundraising for the *contras* and calls to "expel the devil" from Nicaragua.[41] Some of Swaggart's pastors linked these thinly veiled allusions to the Sandinistas to claims of divine revelations about God's "decision to bring war to Nicaragua" (Lomba 1988; Martínez 1989: 46–47).

Swaggart, though he raised funds for armed anti-Sandinista rebels, did not bring war to Nicaragua from Hacienda El Hacha. He did, however, launch a major evangelization campaign in early 1988, which included fiery, apocalyptic sermons to large crowds of followers in Panama, Costa Rica, Nicaragua, and Honduras. In Panama, General Manuel Antonio Noriega played host to Swaggart as part of his effort to court influential North Americans and deflect criticism resulting from allegations that he was involved in narcotics trafficking.[42] In Nicaragua, where his visit occurred as part of the political opening that followed the 1987 signing of the Central American Peace Plan, one Assemblies of God pastor commented days before

Swaggart's arrival that the purpose of the visit was "to show the government that we are not just four cats [insignificant], that we are a force that must be listened to and respected" (Lomba 1988: 55). A week after Swaggart's return to the United States, public revelations about his encounters with a New Orleans prostitute and his televised "confession" led the directors of his U.S. ministry to suspend him from preaching and to require him to undergo psychological treatment. Hacienda El Hacha, however, remained the property of "Jimmy Swaggart Ministries" until after the *contra* war was all but over. Central America, where the negative effects of the sex scandal were less pronounced than in the United States, continued to be a major target of Assemblies of God proselytism.[43]

Jimmy Swaggart was not the only North American to combine land speculation in Guanacaste with a geopolitical vision of the conflict in Nicaragua. Northern Guanacastecan real estate, of such strategic concern to the Somozas in the 1960s and 1970s, again became a subject of intrigue in the mid-1980s as anti-Sandinista *contras* stepped up their campaign against the Nicaraguan government and as Costa Rica sought to modernize its own paramilitary forces. In May 1985 U.S. Army Special Forces advisors began training Costa Rican Civil Guards on the Murciélago estate, which had been expropriated from Somoza. A few months later, just to the east in Hacienda Santa Elena, U.S. intelligence operatives constructed a secret airstrip, used to supply the Nicaraguan *contras*. While many of the details of these machinations are still obscure and in any case are beyond the scope of this discussion, it is important to note that these fundamentally geopolitical uses of remote rural properties contributed to the removal of considerable expanses of land from real production—in the case of the Santa Elena operation as much as 15,000 hectares.[44] No clearer articulation of the rationale for using cattle as a "cover" for nonproductive property can be found than that provided by Robert Owen who, as an emissary of the U.S. National Security Council's Lt. Col. Oliver North, organized the construction of the Santa Elena air base. In a 1985 memo to North describing his plans, he also alluded to the possibilities of using the reputation of North Americans as eccentrics as a convenient smoke screen:

The cover for the operation is a company, owned by a few "crazy" gringos, wanting to lease the land for agricultural experimentation and for running cattle. A company is in the process of being formed. It might be a good idea to have it be a Panamanian company with bearer shares, this way no names appear as owners. The gringos will own two planes, registered to the company and duly registered in the country in question. Cattle will be purchased as will some farming equipment and some land plowed. (Owen 1989: 350)

Ecology, Land Use, and the Contemporary Latifundio

If land tenure changed with the fragmentation of the main latifundios and the reconstitution of others under new auspices, land use in the livestock sector remained much the same, even though cattle occupied a larger overall space. In Guanacaste the area in pasture more than doubled from 256,633 hectares in 1950 to 594,389 hectares in 1973.[45] In 1973 pasture constituted 65.4 percent of the total 908,674 hectares in agricultural and livestock uses. Since many of the additional 74,004 hectares of brushlands counted by the census were also used for grazing cattle, as much as 73.6 percent of the province's farmland may have been used primarily for livestock.[46]

This horizontal expansion of grassland occurred at the cost of a dramatic destruction of Costa Rica's forests. In 1950, 72 percent of the country was covered with forests; 23 years later, in 1973, only 49 percent of the country remained forested; by the late 1970s estimates of the area in closed-canopy forest varied from 34 to 41 percent of Costa Rica's territory (Porras and Villarreal 1986: 20–21; Sáenz Maroto 1981: 26). A 1983 study based on satellite imagery found that only 17 percent of the country was covered with "dense forests." The northwest was—by the 1960s—the most severely affected region (see Edelman n.d.). This process of carving pasture out of the forest has been linked to a variety of ecological problems, including decreased rainfall, flooding, poor drainage, and soil erosion.

At first, pastures also spread at the expense of land in basic grains, much of which was used for subsistence rather than cash crops. In Guanacaste the area devoted to maize—the principal subsistence crop—declined from 14,711 to 12,045 hectares in 1950–73.[47] In the country as a whole the picture was not much different: the area used for crop agriculture grew from 316,175 to 490,458 hectares, but this signified a decline from 33.4 to 23.9 in the percentage of farmland under cultivation (CAP 1950, 1973). Until special incentives were offered to rice producers in the mid-1970s (see Chapter 9), the replacement of cropland by pasture meant that Costa Rica was forced

TABLE 7.5
Guanacaste: Intensity of Cattle Production, by Canton, 1950–1984

Canton	Head per hectare of pasture				
	1950	1955	1963	1973	1984
Liberia–La Cruz	0.43	0.32	1.02	0.82	0.82
Nicoya-Nandayure-Hojancha	1.48	1.12	1.43	1.30	1.15
Santa Cruz	1.27	0.92	1.23	1.19	1.09
Bagaces	1.74	1.06	1.28	0.69	1.22
Carrillo	1.11	1.09	1.17	1.23	1.07
Cañas	0.99	0.77	1.00	1.16	1.14
Abangares	0.91	0.81	0.93	1.07	1.15
Tilarán	1.10	1.06	1.18	1.38	1.23
GUANACASTE	0.91	0.71	1.17	1.06	1.07

SOURCE: *CAP* 1950, 1955, 1963, 1973, 1984.
NOTE: Liberia–La Cruz and Nicoya-Nandayure-Hojancha were each single cantons in 1950.

to import large quantities of basic foods, making it one of the fourteen countries worldwide that Lester Brown pointed to in 1978 "as rapidly approaching primary dependence on imported foodstuffs" (1978b: 137).

The rapid herd growth that followed Central America's entrance into the world beef market occurred in large part because of the expansion of pastures rather than from any significant intensification of production on existing grasslands. Although some intensification of production resulted from improved breeding practices, which permitted faster growth, higher parturition rates, and greater extraction of animals from the herd, the number of head per hectare—a key measure of production intensity—has increased only slightly in most areas of Guanacaste since 1950; in Liberia–La Cruz, where it nearly doubled, it still remained well below one head per hectare (see Table 7.5). Between 1963 and 1984 grazing density fell in five out of eight cantons (or subregions) and at the provincial level. Moreover, as Table 7.6 indicates, larger farms have the lowest grazing densities and a larger proportion of land in pasture. To some degree this reflects the biggest farms' specialization in fattening large steers, which require more fodder than small farms' feeder calves. But grazing densities declined between 1973 and 1984 on all but the smallest farms (under 50 hectares) and the largest (over 1,000 hectares) (*CAP* 1973, 1984).[48]

TABLE 7.6
Guanacaste: Land in Pasture and Cattle Production,
by Farm Size, 1973

Farm size (hectares)	Total area (hectares)	Area in pasture	Percent total in pasture	Cattle (head)	Head per hectare of pasture
<1	519.8	43.5	8.4%	1,800	41.38
1–5	6,085.5	1,784.9	29.3	6,525	3.66
5–10	8,228.0	4,492.3	54.6	10,061	2.24
10–20	19,085.9	12,359.1	64.8	20,573	1.66
20–50	71,534.5	48,598.9	67.9	64,980	1.34
50–100	88,902.9	62,997.0	70.9	79,158	1.26
100–200	91,833.6	65,275.9	71.1	75,035	1.15
200–500	146,013.6	106,480.4	72.9	116,233	1.09
500–1,000	101,397.6	72,232.9	71.2	76,580	1.06
1,000–2,500	122,521.9	82,951.4	67.7	74,151	0.89
2,500+	252,641.0	137,170.7	54.3	103,565	0.76
TOTAL	908,764.3	594,387.0	65.4%	628,661	1.06

SOURCE: *CAP* 1973.
NOTE: "Pasture" includes "artificial" (planted) and natural pastures.

The extensive land use in the cattle-ranching areas of Central America would not be predicted by traditional economic rules of optimal allocation of resources (Feder 1980: 479; Roux 1975: 373; SEPSA 1980b, 1: 45–50). According to a 1973 United Nations report on Central America, "there is no necessary correlation between actual and optimal land use, since it is common to find cattle ranches in zones where agriculture could generate greater employment and greater income" (CEPAL 1973: 29). In Costa Rica, it was estimated in the late 1970s that 428,000 hectares of pastureland were not suitable for that use, but should have remained in forest; and that 300,000 hectares of land appropriate for crop production were in other uses, primarily pasture (OPSA 1979b: 59–60). In the dry Pacific region that includes Guanacaste, only 63 percent of the 594,389 hectares in pasture in 1973 were considered apt for that use (SEPSA 1980a: 9).

The way in which Costa Rica was integrated into the U.S. beef market discouraged any significant change in the existing extensive system of cattle production. Costa Rica is only one of several countries that supply the U.S. market with grass-fed, industrial-grade beef. The price in the U.S. market constitutes a limit to the intensification of production, since any investment in improved technologies or land management may cut into narrow profit margins or reduce precarious market shares. The threat of being undercut by producers in other beef-exporting nations has thus discouraged investment in the land and the adoption of a more modern livestock production system.

U.S. quota rules had the same effect. The fear of quota reductions, long periods of low prices, or temporary market closings makes cattle producers reluctant to invest. These anxieties are not unfounded: the periodic market contractions in the United States have been felt in all exporting countries; at various times, other Central American countries have had their beef banned from the U.S. market because of contamination by pesticides; the signing of the anticyclical law in 1979 substantially reduced access to the U.S. market; and, in 1982, incidents in which Costa Rican packers shipped substandard beef intended for domestic consumption and beef contaminated with dirt to the United States brought about temporary market closings and major investigations by the Judicial Police.

Promoting Underproduction: Credit Allocation and Taxes

Considering that the cattle sector accounts for less than 10 percent of Costa Rica's export earnings and that its contribution to rural employment is minimal in comparison with crop agriculture, it is perhaps surprising that it received favored treatment in terms of National Banking System credit allocations (see Chapter 6). Essentially, it was the offer of funds by the international lending institutions and the continuous pressures exerted by the cattle lobby that accounted for this seemingly irrational phenomenon. The way in which low-cost credit and other forms of "institutional rent" (de Janvry 1981: 155) have been channeled to the cattle sector also accounts for another type of apparent irrationality—the underutilization of increasingly valuable land.

The cattle ranchers' favored access to credit has been reflected in the amount of allocations, the interest terms, the percentage of total production financed, and the low level of loan recuperation that has characterized the livestock sector (Solís 1981a). As was noted in Chapter 6 (Table 6.1), credit for livestock production grew almost twice as much in 1956–83 as that for crop agriculture (and almost three times as much in the boom period 1956–80). In both periods, cattle credit expanded considerably faster than the total amount of credit allocations. For much of the 1970s, it was not unusual for the amount of credit allotted to cattle to actually surpass that for crops. In the same period roughly three-quarters of loans to the livestock sector were long-term investment credits at low rates of interest, generally between 8 and 10 percent per year. In agriculture and industry, in contrast, only about one-quarter of total credit was granted under such terms, the other three-quarters being higher-interest, short-term operational loans (Solís 1981a: 262). With the exception of 1976–78, when inflation was about 8 percent, this cattle credit was granted at negative real rates of interest.

This transfer of public resources to private ranchers did not always result in the types of investment for which credit had been extended, however. While the magnitude of this misuse of funds is impossible to determine, considerable anecdotal evidence suggests that "easy" credit had two effects that contributed to the preservation and consolidation of undercapitalized latifundios: many ranchers invested loans in more remunerative sectors of the economy or in savings certificates at higher interest (sometimes, critics charged, "without leaving the bank"); and, principally in years when inflation was highest and actual or rumored devaluations were in the offing, they have been especially concerned with acquiring lands on credit. Since the amount of credit is limited by the value of the debtor's collateral, large ranchers have received a disproportionate share of total outlays. Their use of these funds to buy still more properties contributes to further concentration of land. It also perpetuates the low productivity of the latifundio, since the capital improvements for which credits are granted are not carried out. Moreover, the absence of effective inspections by the banks and of stricter criteria for the provision of credit has made it possible for loan recipients to divert funds with little chance of detection, such as when applications are made for loans to "purchase" animals that were actually born on the hacienda.

The privileged position of the cattle sector is also evident in the number of defaults and the percentage of total production financed by the banking system. During the 1970s, 32 percent of money loaned for livestock production was not recuperated on time, as opposed to only 16 percent of loans for agriculture and 19 percent of loans for industry (Solís 1981a: 269). In the 1980s, with the collapse of the export boom, the proportion of the banks' livestock portfolio in arrears soared still further (see Chapter 6 and the Conclusion). Despite the fact that this poor record is clearly related to the lack of criteria for granting loans (beyond those relating to collateral), little effort was made until the late 1980s to tighten controls on livestock credit. Similarly, with regard to the percentage of total production financed, the beef-cattle sector has received a higher level of support than any other agricultural subsector with the exception of coffee (Solís 1981a: 122).

The Costa Rican tax system has also encouraged extensive land use. The tax on agricultural property is established on the basis of declarations of value made by owners (León et al. 1981: VI-21-24; OPSA 1979b: 95–96; Salas Marrero and Barahona 1980: 748–52). Highly capitalized farms pay higher taxes, though many continue to pay at lower rates because assessments are only infrequently updated. Owners have often been able to avoid paying the tax on unproductive lands, which was intended to stimulate production and fragment latifundios, by claiming that unused lands are serving to protect watersheds. Lack of political will appears to be a factor as well, since in the first decade the tax on unproductive lands was in effect (1961–70), it generated only 80,000 colones in the entire country—about $12,000 (León et al. 1981: VI-24). In addition, although tax laws do contain provisions for automatically increasing assessments of properties whose value increases through public investments in roads and other infrastructure, the office charged with this responsibility was never established, supposedly because of lack of funds. Speculative rent resulting from such public investments was particularly significant in Guanacaste with the completion of the Pan-American Highway in the 1950s, the massive program to build local roads in the early 1960s, the large state investments in agroindustrial production and processing in the mid-1970s, the establishment of the Guanacaste irrigation project in the late 1970s and 1980s, and—most recently—the creation of a sizable network of parks and protected areas in the north of the province.

The Persistence of the Latifundio

It is obvious from Table 7.7 that a calculation of the opportunity cost of land based on the potential revenue generated by different land uses is not sufficient to explain the rapid expansion of the cattle sector, even during the boom years, or the perpetuation of under-

TABLE 7.7
Costa Rica: Value-added Per Hectare for Different Products, 1973

Product	Value-added (millions of 1966 colones)	Hectares	Value-added per hectare (1966 colones)
Cattle	190.3	1,558,053	122.1
Sugarcane	77.1	38,763	1,989.0
Rice	73.4	65,458	1,121.3
Maize	20.2	51,888	389.3
Beans	9.4	26,681	352.3
Sorghum	2.6	3,753	692.8
Cotton	1.2	74	16,216.2

SOURCE: *CAP* 1973 and unpublished data from Banco Central de Costa Rica.
NOTE: In 1966 colones ($1.00 = 6.65 colones).

utilized latifundios. Part of the profitability of cattle ranching in the boom years was hidden, as was suggested above, in the form of speculative rent and the diversion of low-interest credit from its intended purposes. The preference for cattle as opposed to cultivation has also been conditioned by the relative ease of managing livestock operations, by the desire to avoid labor problems, and by the risks inherent in crop production because of the highly variable rainfall in Guanacaste (see Chapter 9). To the extent that these considerations enter into landlords' decision making, they may lead to the "irrational" use of fertile land for extensive grazing.

Finally, the opportunity-cost problem and the persistence of underutilized latifundios cannot be viewed apart from the social composition and the political power of the Guanacastecan elite. Families that acquired huge estates in the early decades of the twentieth century or before have been under little pressure to modernize, both because the cost of land does not have to be considered as a factor in their calculations of profitability and because the possibilities for speculative gains are, in their cases, unsurpassable. The political power of this hacendado class has been expressed through a powerful lobby continually alert to opportunities to shape policy. Strengthened through family links and ties to leading government functionaries, this class has proven to be a serious obstacle to those forces in Costa Rican society favoring major changes in latifundist land tenure and land use patterns.

8 → The Rural Poor: Resistance, Resignation, and Retreat

The people here saw and didn't see.
—Hacendado describing how rustlers escaped
with 25 cows in 1972

In the second half of the twentieth century, antilandlord resistance in Guanacaste usually had a different tone and intensity than in the 1920s and 1930s, when indignant peasants routinely stole cattle and torched fields and even occasionally attacked hacendados with gunfire (see Chapter 4). Modernized latifundismo engendered, and indeed required, new resistance tactics—or at least the modernization of old-style rustling and squatting. The reasons for these shifts will be examined below. I want to note at the outset, however, my dissatisfaction with the notion of "resistance," which has become fashionable recently as an all-encompassing rubric for a variety of often mundane behavior. As I suggest in this chapter, "resistance" is less than fully convincing if it is not counterposed to some kind of alternative analytical category, here termed "resignation and retreat."[1] To frame the issue this way need not mean accepting at face value the surface appearances of the "calculated conformity" or "routine compliance" that, James Scott (1985) suggests, frequently mask subordinate classes' real behavior and attitudes toward powerful "superiors."[2] Instead, to raise "resignation" or "retreat" as issues is to address the problem of what happens, of what people actually do, when resistance—dramatic or "everyday"—fails.[3] It also permits a return to a primary, although not exclusive, focus on the motion of historical protagonists within particular sets of structural constraints, recognizing that accurate "transcripts" (Scott 1985: 46) that would reveal the subjective intentions behind certain actions may often be difficult or impossible to obtain.

If it is indeed true that intellectual fascination with rebellion and revolution in the 1960s and 1970s was tied to "the Vietnam war and a now fading left-wing, academic romance with wars of national liberation" (Scott 1985: xv), it is equally tempting to propose, from a similar sociology-of-knowledge perspective, that the more recent resistance literature, in elevating the prosaic to the heroic, may owe much to a mid-1980s ethos characterized by apolitical quiescence, pessimism, and worldwide reversals of movements for change. This tendency to categorize every activity of subordinate groups as resistance, however, is not a shortcoming that can be attributed to Scott, even though his innovative and elegantly wrought *Weapons of the Weak* (1985) may have inspired much of others' romanticization of foot-dragging, dissimulation, false compliance, malicious gossip, and so on. Indeed, in addition to serving as a useful corrective to versions of history that disregard the extent to which even such "everyday" resistance may limit not only local dominant classes but larger systems of domination, *Weapons* contains suggestive discussions of how levels of repression structure peasants' options and how "avoidance protest" or flight may at times be their only viable alternative (pp. 245, 299). Nevertheless, Scott, in his analysis of empirical material, did not address these largely structural aspects of the resistance problematic as systematically or with the same degree of rich detail as he did questions of agency, a fact that probably accounts for some of the more romantic readings of his work.[4]

The Smallholding Poor

The issue of "avoidance protest" or emigration, only rarely engaged in the resistance literature, is especially relevant in examining post-1950 Guanacaste. This retreat from local arenas of conflict—whether construed as defeat, accommodation, or the quest for a better life—cannot, of course, be understood apart from the context of the region's agrarian structure. While for social scientists this assertion may necessitate some empirically based scrutiny, for Guanacaste's rural poor it is understood as a self-evident truth. Juvencio Matarrita, a vigorous octogenarian agriculturalist from a dusty crossroads village in lowland Santa Cruz with the unlikely name of Paraíso ("Paradise"), articulated their prevailing understanding, albeit with unusual righteousness, eloquence, and poignancy: "Of all the criminal things that we Guanacastecans have had to suffer, the lack of land is the one that hurts the most, that has caused most pain, that [has made] the young leave for the [banana] zone, for the city. And we remain here, the old broken-down ones (*los ancianos quebrados*)."[5]

The dimensions of what the rural poor experience as "the lack of land" may be appreciated by examining key changes in regional agrarian structure during 1950–84 beyond the processes of latifundio fragmentation and reconsolidation described in the preceding chapter. In Guanacaste in this period, the number of farms under 10 hectares grew by 57 percent (from 2,935 to 4,619), though in an area that remained roughly constant (12,436 hectares in 1950, 14,833 hectares in 1973, and 11,359 hectares in 1984). As a result, average farm size for the under-ten-hectare group plummeted (from 4.2 hectares in 1950, to 3.2 in 1973, to 2.5 in 1984, a decline of over 40 percent).[6] In effect, over a period of three and one-half decades, the poorest smallholding stratum has been unable to find new land for production, and its members, whose numbers have grown significantly, have had to try to wrest a living from ever-smaller plots. It is not surprising that the number of landless has also soared.[7]

Given their meager land base, many of these peasant producers, who were especially numerous in the peninsular cantons of Santa Cruz and Nicoya, had only a sporadic and tenuous insertion in commodity markets. With few exceptions, the smallest farms participated little in the production of feeder calves for the haciendas, though they had long served the large estates as a source of partly proletarianized labor. As late as 1963, over a quarter of Guanacaste farms were involved solely in subsistence—generally rice, maize, and bean cultivation—and did not sell their production on the market. In some cantons, such as Santa Cruz, over half the farms produced for household use alone (*CAP* 1963: 244). Even in 1984, in Guanacaste, 45 percent of the bean harvest, 44 percent of yellow maize, and 55 percent of white maize were consumed in the household (*CAP* 1984: 56, 61, 63).[8]

This incomplete smallholder insertion in commodity markets, however, should not be deemed an indication of either widespread self-sufficiency or insulation from other types of powerful market forces. In the poor hamlets that dot rural Guanacaste, virtually everyone—including the landless—still aspires to be a producer, to cultivate the land, and to harvest at least "the household's expenditure" (*el gasto de la casa*), its consumption of rice, maize, and beans. But although it is not uncommon for smallholders to plant tiny plots of maize or rice with digging sticks alongside fields where steers graze or where tractors and airplanes constitute the principal tools of production, such rudimentary agriculture is increasingly a complementary activity, supplementing other kinds of income. And while some producers of use-values depend on informal, reciprocal labor exchanges with neighbors, many rely on their own scanty savings—or, as they say, on their "pulse" (*pulso*)—to purchase expensive inputs and hire wage labor. A considerable number also assume major financial obligations to the state-run banking system, hoping to have something extra left over to sell, even though fate and bad weather often permit them only the "household's expenditure" or, in the worst years, even less (Edelman 1989a, 1990).

Frequently this growing dependence on nonfarm income and the reliance of even the smallest producers on borrowed capital and hired labor reduces not only the overall importance of subsistence production for individual households, but its variety as well. When it was easier to purchase or rent land, families could use crop by-products and some of the corn and rice for poultry and perhaps pigs, thus generating extra income and making eggs and meat at least an occasional part of the diet. When pastures and cane fields increasingly constrained and at times replaced smallholders' plots, subsistence production and the diet of the rural poor became less varied.[9]

Much of the land used in this search for the "household's expenditure" is held under a variety of "informal" or "irregular" tenure arrangements—rented, sharecropped, borrowed, or occupied without permission. Almost a quarter of the farm units in Guanacaste were held under some kind of "informal" or "irregular" tenure in 1950, a proportion that remained remarkably constant over the next 23 years, but fell precipitously to about 10 percent of all farms between 1973 and 1984. A few of these "informally" or "irregularly" held properties were large tracts rented by entrepreneurs for mechanized crop production or cattle grazing. Most, however, were tiny plots used by the poorest producers. Some entered into arrangements that obliged them to clear forest or brush in return for two or three years' cultivation or usufruct rights. By the 1950s it was not uncommon to oblige holders of such lots to plant grass at the end of their contract period. After the enclosures of the 1930s and particularly in the 1950s when the beef export boom gathered steam, access to land for smallholders and squatters became more difficult. It was thus easier to secure fulfillment of such agreements than it had been in the times when "vagrant" squatters plagued the hacendados. Land-owners who now loaned land and demanded that the recipients of their generosity plant grass not only found it a virtually cost-free method of expanding pastures, but also were able to test soil fertility by observing peasants' crops. Once landlords had cleared properties of forest and brush and had planted pasture, however, they had little reason to continue lending land. The "shortage of hands" that had once led them to tolerate squatters or to provide plots as an induce-ment to attract and hold workers had also largely disappeared.

The spread of pastures (and later of mechanized crop production—see Chapter 9) had other, more deleterious consequences for the poorer smallholders. As the smallest farms became on average even smaller their proprietors were all the more likely to rely exclusively on unremunerated labor, usually from family members but at times from neighbors. Of much greater overall importance in the worsen-ing employment situation was the tremendous horizontal expansion of pastures for extensive grazing, which absorbed very little labor and often displaced more intensively operated smallholdings that had sometimes hired hands. In general, livestock farms generated ex-tremely little employment per unit of land as compared with crops (see Table 8.1), but the highly mechanized crop agriculture that be-came increasingly significant in the 1970s either absorbed approx-imately the same numbers of workers as extensive grazing (as in the case of rice) or else (as with sugar) provided primarily low-paid sea-sonal harvesting jobs.

Pasture expansion was accompanied by the growing use of tech-nological innovations that had been introduced much earlier, such as more easily managed brahman cattle and wire fences that reduced the need for mounted cowboys. More recent innovations too exacer-bated the dismal prospects of rural labor. In many cases, pastures are now cleared by herbicides sprayed from airplanes or helicopters rather than by crews of workers wielding machetes. Even where large haciendas did not employ such new technologies, they relied in-creasingly on contractors for the most labor-intensive tasks, such as clearing pastures with machetes. Labor contractors circumvent the relatively generous provisions of the Costa Rican labor laws by mov-ing constantly from farm to farm and employing large numbers of undocumented Nicaraguan workers. The hacendados, by contracting certain jobs to these roving taskmasters, saved substantial amounts in wage and fringe-benefit payments, as well as the administrative

TABLE 8.1

Costa Rica: Land Use and Employment in the Agricultural Sector, 1973

Land use	Workers employed	Percent of workers	Hectares	Percent of hectares	Hectares per worker
Crop agriculture	146,306	76.6%	424,288	13.9%	2.9
Livestock	33,363	17.5	1,558,053	51.0	46.7
Forestry	11,231	5.9	1,000,008	32.7	89.0
Other			73,933	2.4	
TOTAL	190,900	100.0%	3,056,282	100.0%	16.0

SOURCE: SEPSA 1980: 7.

NOTE: Because these data include some intensively operated dairy farms, they overstate somewhat the amount of labor employed on beef-cattle farms.

headaches involved in directing peons, usually the least motivated segment of the rural labor force.[10]

Squeezing Out the Smallholding Poor

For most of the rural poor, the lack of land and work, even if considered unjust, came to seem almost as natural a part of the Guanacaste landscape as jaragua grass, coyol palms, or the howler monkeys ("congos") whose bellowing still reverberated from the remaining patches of woods along the riverbanks. Too often spiraling land values, growing mechanization, and expanding pastures appeared to be the results of inexorable and invisible forces, though at times especially egregious actions by particular hacendados might provoke indignation or resistance. With the rise of the beef export boom, on properties where squatters had been tolerated or where laborers had been given access to small parcels as part of their remuneration, hacendados frequently canceled or refused to renew informal agreements that kept them from selling or directly exploiting valuable land. High prices for land also tempted poor peasants to sell their plots, and temporary economic crises often increased cash needs, leaving smallholders few alternatives.

The problems faced by poor rural people in their role as commodity producers also contributed to the dispossession of the smallest landowners, even if the proletarianization process did not always occur with classic thoroughness. Problems arose in securing production credit because of cumbersome bureaucratic procedures, the banks' minimum farm-size criteria for different kinds of loans, or faulty deeds that could not be used as collateral. Renting machinery and hiring labor at crucial points in the agricultural cycle were more difficult for smaller producers beset by cash-flow difficulties. Furthermore, just as peasants were at times unable to compete as producers of commodities that were also being produced on larger modern farms, they also were more reliant on intermediaries when it came time to market the fruits of their labor (Edelman 1989a).

Often little more was involved in the proletarianization of smallholders than a continuation of the enclosure process. "We had magnificent relations with the Clachars, the Viales, landlords around here," recalled a middle-aged resident of Palmira de Carrillo, in a comment that, if ingenuous in its view of landlord-peasant relations, nonetheless conveys the experience of numerous Guanacastecans. "In some ways we still do. When there is work, sometimes we have a little job on those fincas. They remember us. But then [c.1949] the lands were all closed off, you couldn't just plant anywhere anymore, except in places like Ojochal that were *montaña* (forest), too far away."[11]

Other mechanisms employed to dispossess peasant producers ranged from simple purchases to fraudulent titling schemes and evictions that sometimes involved state- and landlord-sponsored violence. Landlord pressures ran the gamut from polite offers of cash payments for peasants' titles or "improvements" to turning cattle loose on their crops. Occasionally, more sophisticated and affluent landowners, such as Luis Morice Lara of La Cruz, assembled corps of witnesses who provided false testimony in land-titling processes, effectively depriving peasants of their properties (Fallas 1978; Seligson 1980). More often, landlords were able to count on local Resguardos, or later Rural Guards, to forcibly evict occupants of lands that were in dispute. Frequently, these conflicts resulted in arrests and the burning of crops and dwellings (see below).

On two occasions land disputes led to killings: once by Morice, who assassinated peasant leader Gil Marcial Tablada in 1970, and again in 1981, when the Rural Guard shot Pedro Lara during an eviction of a squatter group occupying unused lands at Paso Bolaños, south of La Cruz. The Tablada murder attracted considerable national attention and continues to arise periodically when efforts are made to secure a pardon for the killer (see Seligson 1980: 107–10).[12] Morice, a convicted fugitive from justice, first fled to Nicaragua, but returned to Guanacaste after the 1979 Sandinista revolution. There he was rumored to enjoy the protection of local officials and was sometimes seen traveling between his haciendas and his homes in La Cruz and Liberia.[13]

Emigration and Survival

As the local balance of power increasingly shifted against the peasantry in most parts of Guanacaste, the search for alternative subsistence strategies took on new urgency. A few bolder residents of remote areas expanded their involvement in illegal activities, distilling contraband liquor ("guaro"), cultivating small patches of marijuana, or looting pre-Columbian archeological sites.[14] Others resurrected old forms of resistance and survival, such as rustling, but did so with modern twists (discussed below) that shielded them from a more consolidated landlord regime. For some, especially in outlying areas, land occupations and squatting emerged as viable tactics for realizing the dream of owning a farm (see below).

Yet at the provincial level the numbers opting to pursue these peasant survival strategies remained very small. Most chose either to stay and to "conform," at least outwardly, to changed and unfavorable conditions or to leave. Given the rural poor's bleak prospects, it is not surprising that since 1950 Guanacaste, previously a zone with positive net migration, has continually "exported" people to other areas of the country—an "avoidance protest" on a scale that dwarfs any of the more colorful or romantic forms of resistance and struggle. In 1963–73 the equivalent of 73.4 percent of the province's natural population growth—some 50,000 people—migrated elsewhere in search of employment or with family members (Fernández Arias et al. 1976: 102–3). Whereas in 1950 about 19 percent of native Guanacastecans resided outside of Guanacaste, by 1973 that figure had climbed to 34 percent and for some cantons—Bagaces, Tilarán, and Abangares—was between 40 and 50 percent (Kincaid 1987, chap. 5).[15] As Table 8.2 indicates, population growth in many areas of the province stopped or slowed dramatically in 1963–73, just when the cattle boom was gathering momentum. This effect was particularly pronounced in Bagaces, Tilarán, and Abangares, among the economically least diversified cattle zones, and in Nicoya-Nandayure-Hojancha, where medium- and large-sized ranchers were making rapid inroads on small producers. Only in Liberia and La Cruz, where significant urban

TABLE 8.2
Guanacaste: Population Growth, 1950–1984

Canton	Population				Annual Growth Rate		
	1950	1963	1973	1984	1950–63	1963–73	1973–84
Liberia	6,312	13,197	21,781	28,067	5.8	5.2	2.3
Nicoya	29,918	36,275	37,185	36,626	1.5	0.2	−0.1
Santa Cruz	13,615	23,576	29,739	31,133	4.3	2.3	0.4
Bagaces	4,079	9,836	9,828	10,103	7.0	0.0	0.2
Carrillo	7,002	11,396	14,893	18,475	3.9	2.7	2.0
Cañas	5,929	9,117	12,779	17,284	3.4	3.5	2.8
Abangares	8,344	10,189	11,633	12,575	1.6	1.4	0.7
Tilarán	9,057	12,097	12,563	14,586	2.3	0.3	1.4
Nandayure		12,038	12,058	9,604		0.0	−2.1
La Cruz	3,934	5,833	8,333	10,876	3.0	3.6	2.4
Hojancha			7,899	5,879			−2.8
GUANACASTE	88,190	143,554	170,792	189,329	3.9	1.7	0.9

SOURCE: *CPO* 1950, 1963, 1973, 1984.
NOTE: Nicoya growth rate in 1950–63 was affected by the creation of Nandayure canton and in 1963–73 by the creation of Hojancha canton. Growth rates for the Nicoya-Nandayure-Hojancha region as a whole were 3.8 percent in 1950–63, 1.7 percent in 1963–73, and −0.8 percent in 1973–84.

growth occurred in this period, and in Cañas and Carrillo, where the sugar sector absorbed a considerable number of seasonal workers, did growth rates approach or exceed the average rate of natural increase, estimated at above 4 percent (Fernández Arias et al. 1976: 102).

In the 1973–84 intercensal period, Costa Rica's annual population growth rate dropped to 2.3 percent from 3.0 percent in 1963–73. This unusually sharp decline led demographers to extol the country's experience as a model for other developing nations, a success story attributable in large measure to high levels of literacy and social welfare (Stycos 1982). In Guanacaste, where such "modernization" had considerably less impact than in the rest of the country, population growth rates fell too, but for different reasons. There, where natural rates of increase had exceeded national rates in recent decades, population growth in 1973–84 was actually negative in three cantons and below 1 percent in three others and at the provincial level as well (see Table 8.2). Only in La Cruz, where large numbers of Nicaraguan refugees settled in the early 1980s, and in Cañas, where the opening of a major irrigation district created new jobs (see Chapter 10), did population growth rates exceed the national average; in Liberia, with a small but comparatively diversified urban economy, the cantonal growth rate was the same as the national one. Assuming, conservatively, that Guanacaste's natural annual growth rate in 1973–84 was 2.3 percent (the national average), the province lost to emigration the equivalent of some 62 percent of the natural increase in its population.[16]

The stream of emigrants includes representatives of virtually all sectors of Guanacastecan society. Children of wealthy landlords leave to pursue university degrees in central Costa Rica, and, unless enticed back by sentimentality, family pressures, or the rare possibility of working locally in their profession, they frequently see little point in returning to the sleepy towns that pass for urban centers in Guanacaste. Large numbers of poor Guanacastecan women leave their villages while still in their early teens to work as domestic live-in servants in urban homes in central Costa Rica. Later in life, these female migrants frequently abandon domestic service for petty commerce or other informal-sector activities, but they generally settle in the urban areas around the capital rather than in the region of their birth. By far the largest migration from the rural areas, however, consists of adolescent and young adult men who leave to work on the banana plantations of Limón and, until the mid-1980s, southern Puntarenas.[17] So many young men make this journey that the plantations are known throughout Guanacaste simply and familiarly as "la zona" ("the zone")—short for *la zona bananera*. Accustomed to working in the extreme heat of the northwest lowlands and to living conditions that would horrify workers from more-developed central Costa Rica, Guanacastecans constitute the largest group in a heterogeneous plantation labor force that draws workers from diverse parts of the Central American isthmus.[18]

For any given migrant to "the zone," the relative strength of push-and-pull factors may vary considerably. Many young Guanacastecans relish the adventure of leaving home, becoming independent, and traveling the length of their country to obtain plantation jobs that frequently pay two or even four times what they would earn as laborers in their home province. Some, imbued with machismo and adolescent notions of their own immortality, even look forward to the extra compensation available to those willing to apply hazardous pesticides to the banana plants.[19] Others, though, view the trip south as an absolute last resort that takes them away from a treasured small-village existence to a regimented life in barracks set in a uniformly dull, flat, green landscape.

"We started at a place on the road between Nicoya and Santa Cruz and asked for work at every finca along the highway from there to Liberia," a landless eighteen-year-old from Bolsón de Santa Cruz said, describing how he and his brother decided to leave Guanacaste for the banana plantations of southern Costa Rica. "We walked a lot, for days, sometimes took trucks, and got nothing, except in Liberia where we were masons for six days. With that little money we kept going, asking for work on the road all the way to Las Juntas [Abangares] and—nothing. A truck came going to Panama and near there is Golfito, *la bananera*. We went, what else could we do? We knew there was work there, and money."

A few of the migrants view long-term work in the banana zones or as merchant seamen on fruit-company ships as a means of realizing dreams of returning home with capital for land, a small store, or a business. Most, though, whether or not they consider the trip an exciting rite of passage, are driven by less-ambitious concerns with simple survival. For them migration in search of plantation work has been a temporary seasonal or life-cycle phenomenon.

Traveling to "the zone" in the dry season and returning to Guanacaste when the rains begin in May, these young men shift in the course of a year between the rigors of proletarian plantation labor and the hardscrabble life of peasant smallholders.[20] This alternation between modes of production and their corresponding roles has some important economic and political consequences. The organization and timing of the process of peasant production result in significant wage savings for the banana companies in ways that go beyond the reproduction and maintenance of inexpensive wage labor on infra-subsistence smallholdings that has been widely noted elsewhere in the Third World. While peasant plots do constitute a subsidy to the banana companies' wage bill, the departure of seasonal banana workers just prior to the onset of the Guanacaste rainy season also facilitates company efforts to maintain high levels of turnover, since employees with more than three months' seniority are entitled to guarantees of job security and substantial benefit payments under Costa Rican labor laws.[21]

Landless migrants from Guanacaste are less likely to engage in the seasonal crisscrossing of Costa Rica characteristic of their more fortunate brethren who still have a base, however tenuous, in the small-holding sector. These individuals often view moving to "the zone" or seeking employment on banana-company ships as a relatively permanent step, precipitated by the imperatives of survival but with tremendous potential for accumulation and upward mobility. The expectations attached to this departure for extended periods at an early point in the life cycle appear to have at least some basis in reality for the more fortunate or self-disciplined migrants. Rural store owners (other than the ethnic Chinese) and older, more prosperous small agriculturalists frequently point to their early experiences as plantation employees or banana-company merchant seamen as the source of both their original capital and their business acumen.[22]

Even for seasonal migrants, however, traveling to "the zone" is something usually possible only in their youth. The physical requirements of most kinds of plantation labor are so severe that few men past their twenties are able to maintain the stamina and work rhythm demanded by the companies, where twelve-hour days of heavy exertion are not uncommon. Once unable to continue, migrants in their late twenties or early thirties either return to Guanacaste, working as ranch peons or seasonal sugarcane cutters and, if possible, engaging in other economic activities, or remain near the plantations, squatting on company or other lands and illegally felling forest to sell timber or begin cultivation.[23] The migrants' recognition that banana work is temporary, as well as the accompanying dreams of upward mobility and the reproduction of smallholding squatter households on the plantations' periphery, is important in reinforcing migrants' peasant identity and inhibiting their full identification as workers or union members while in "the zone." But at times this persistent peasant identity has, especially when imbued with the militant politics of the banana-zone labor movement, led returned migrants to turn their sights on local adversaries in Guanacaste (see Edelman 1990).

Land Invasions

Squatting, in particular, was not something that disappeared entirely from Guanacaste after 1950 only to be reestablished by Guanacastecans living in distant Limón or southern Puntarenas.[24] The consolidated latifundismo of the post-1950 period still faced considerable challenges from peasant occupants who stood their ground on land they had long held, nibbled at the edges of large properties, and—in a few cases—staged truly massive appropriations of remote, underutilized properties. The largest and most dramatic land invasion occurred in highland Bagaces, where peasants pushing north from Cañas surreptitiously entered and then took over Hacienda Miravalles, a massive, wooded latifundio on the slopes of the volcanic cordillera that belonged to the North American Stewart (Wilson) family.[25]

In the mid-1950s, when David Stewart Bonilla visited Hacienda Miravalles, he had difficulty facing the "disaster" that had befallen this part of his father's old estate. "If it wasn't for the rivers and some of the pastures, I wouldn't have known where I was. So much lumber was cut down by these people [squatters] that when I went up there to visit I didn't even recognize the place."[26]

While some of Stewart's shock and disorientation might plausibly be ascribed to an absentee landlord's lack of detailed knowledge of the geographical features of a distant holding, the squatters clearly had transformed the landscape, as well as the power relations, in Miravalles. Víctor Oviedo had loyally served the Stewarts and Wilsons for three decades as general administrator of the family's haciendas, the largest property in Guanacaste. Two years after he retired, in 1963, he laboriously recorded a legal deposition that included his recollections about the progress of the land invasion that had wrested Miravalles from his employers' control.

I stopped working with you [the Stewarts] in 1963, after 29 years. In Miravalles there was an annual average of 4,000 head of livestock—cattle and horses—8,000 manzanas [5,600 hectares] of pastures, and 10 manzanas [7 hectares] of coffee for the consumption of the haciendas. There were about 30 kilometers of telephone wire that connected [Haciendas] Miravalles, Monte Verde, Ciruelas, Tamarindo, and Mojica. In the last months of the dry season, all the cattle were taken out of Miravalles to the market. The timber [on the hacienda] was not cut. But in 1955 or '56, an occupant installed a saw mill. Then they stole the telephone and fence wire. In 1956 they took the hacienda house from us, which was the only thing that remained. More than 500 steers were eaten in the course of this time [two years] and 50 horses (*bestias*) were stolen. I remember that they slaughtered the cattle, and on the Hacienda's own horses they came to Bagaces or Liberia to sell the meat.[27] (ITCO 402—1965)

Three years later the Stewarts' lawyer stated in a court brief that beginning in 1956 "if we tried to send [to Miravalles] some old employee who knew the property, [the occupants] would run him out, threatening him with death" (Rowles 1980: 881). This humiliation of the largest landlords in the region marked the culmination of an eight-year siege that began on a modest scale in an outlying section of

what was already a remote property, albeit one that played a key role
in the transhumant grazing pattern of its owners' herds. In 1947 some
fifteen people, most of them from San Ramón in Alajuela, invaded
Miravalles and began to cut timber, especially the still abundant
pochote (Bombacopsis quinata), a valuable hardwood with large con-
ical spines on its bark. David Stewart conceded that "the invaders of
Miravalles were people who needed land," though many, he claimed,
had owned land in San Ramón, which they had sold at high prices
before invading the hacienda.[28] Whether the participants in this initial incursion were destitute peasants or cynical opportunists, their
presence did not go undetected for long. Once the Stewarts discovered
the "nesters," they immediately initiated legal action.

"Miravalles," David Stewart recalled, was "already a political foot-
ball." Teodoro Picado Michalski, president of the Republic at the
time of the first invasion of Miravalles, had, Stewart asserted, made
bids to purchase the hacienda as early as 1942, only to be rebuffed by
George Wilson, Stewart's father. The squatters who moved onto Miravalles in 1947 allegedly had support at unusually high levels of
government. According to Stewart, "one of [Picado's] cabinet ministers told the alcalde (mayor) of Bagaces to forget about any complaints we might have. But the alcalde was friendly to our position
and told us to go through another alcaldía (local government). Then
we went through the Alcaldía de Cañas and then to the courts. The
courts ruled that we were right."

This judicial recognition of the Stewarts' rights and the subsequent
expulsion of some occupants provided only temporary respite. The
social democratic administration of José Figueres, president from
1953 to 1958, was sympathetic to the plight of the Miravalles squatters and secured permission for them to remain temporarily on the
plots they occupied (Rodríguez Solera 1988: 27). This encouraged a
second invasion, which commenced in 1954 and rapidly filled Miravalles with the new mass of squatters whose presumptuous behavior
and liberal use of hacienda property had so offended the Stewarts and
their longtime administrator Oviedo. And, as if to rub salt in the
wound, the peasants' effrontery found indirect support from the
Bagaces Alcaldía that had previously been "friendly" to the landowners.

Between 1954 and 1957 several thousand peasants swarmed onto
Miravalles, founding a small town (appropriately named La Fortuna),
carving farms out of the forest, appropriating pastures for their cattle,

and, in some cases, opening businesses—grocery stores, bars, saw-mills, rice mills—which were duly licensed by the Bagaces munici-pality.[29] By 1957 all available land on the hacienda had been oc-cupied, and the flow of occupants abated. But by then the state had provided further de facto recognition to the new settlers, opening a telegraph office and a Rural Guard post and establishing a school district—all within the hacienda (Rowles 1980: 863).

The legal battle over Miravalles lasted for more than a decade after the occupation itself was a fait accompli. In 1962 the occupants and the Stewarts' representatives held two meetings in La Fortuna in an effort to reach an "amicable," out-of-court settlement. But although the occupants more than doubled the amount they were willing to pay to settle the dispute, from 20 colones (about $3.00) to 50 colones ($7.50) per manzana (0.7 hectare), the Stewarts held firm in demand-ing 250 colones ($37.75) per manzana.[30] Three years later, the re-cently founded agrarian reform agency, the Lands and Colonization Institute (Instituto de Tierras y Colonización, ITCO) completed the complex procedures needed to expropriate the hacienda and turn it over to the occupants. ITCO, under the law, could only compensate the Stewarts for Miravalles at the value they had declared for tax purposes—438,115 colones ($66,131 in 1965). This assessed value dated to 1948–49, and, as was often the case with large properties in Guanacaste, it had remained unchanged despite inflation and cur-rency devaluations in the succeeding sixteen years.

The final disposition of the case took another five years, as the Stewarts, having given up hope of recovering the hacienda, sought to extract compensation from the state that reflected the property's real value, rather than the old, artificially low tax assessment. The length of these judicial proceedings and the ultimate decision, however, are of more than passing interest because they illustrate some major obstacles faced both by peasant squatters in general and by state agencies charged with resolving agrarian conflicts. In 1969 the Costa Rican Supreme Court, after a long series of appeals, ruled in favor of the Stewarts, granting them an award substantially greater than the value assessed in 1949: 150 colones per manzana, a total of 2.8 million colones (about $415,000).[31] Even so, David Stewart com-plained in 1981, that amount "would have been all right if it had been 25 years ago."

The court ruling to award 150 colones for each expropriated man-zana was also of more than academic importance for the occupants of

Miravalles. In Costa Rica, ITCO has acted in most cases as an inter-mediary between expropriated landowners and beneficiaries of agrarian reform, requiring the latter to pay for their plots at prices that cover the compensation given the former and often administrative overhead costs as well.[32] Thus the costs of the judgment against the Stewarts would be passed on, albeit with favorable terms for payment, to the peasants who had occupied the latifundio. The long time required to win even this partial victory, and the importance of having powerful allies in the state, were but a few of the difficulties faced by the rural poor in "recuperating" land from the latifundios.

The occupation of Hacienda Miravalles was, from the peasants' point of view, an exceptional success that would be difficult to dupli-cate elsewhere in Guanacaste. The property bordered zones in high-land Cañas where squatters had successfully settled much earlier and was mountainous, forested, and far away from roads and popula-tion centers; its owners, though they had been in Costa Rica for over a generation, were still widely resented as foreigners and as latifun-distas who possessed more land than anyone else in the province; and the occupation occurred during a politically favorable conjuncture, just prior to the founding of the country's first modern agency for agrarian reform, when pressure for restructuring inequitable patterns of landownership was building in Costa Rica and throughout Latin America.

These particularities meant that what peasants sometimes termed "recuperating" land was simply not a viable option in most areas of the province. Indeed, an examination of land occupations and inva-sions during 1963–81 indicates that one or more of these conditions were present in most of the more significant attempts. Table 8.3 lists all invasions of properties in Guanacaste that occupied over 500 hectares and came to the attention of ITCO, the agrarian reform agency, between 1963 and 1981.[33] These thirteen occupations ac-counted for 92.8 percent of the total 43,080 hectares reported oc-cupied by squatters; 77.8 percent of the 1,101 occupying families were involved in these cases. The remaining instances ranged from usurpations of several hundred hectares by single occupants, cer-tainly not typical land-hungry peasants, to occupations of a few hundred square meters suitable for little more than a tiny garden or a house lot.[34]

Like Miravalles, the largest invasions, with one exception (Eva Contreras in Santa Cruz), occurred on properties owned by absentee

TABLE 8.3
Guanacaste: Principal Land Occupations, 1963–1981

Year initiated	Canton	Owner	Families involved	Area occupied	Hectares/ family
1963	Nicoya	Luz Rothe v. de Sobrado	476	9,148	19.2
1963	Nicoya	Pacific Lumber	32	1,032	32.3
1964	Nicoya	Acosta Peraza Heirs	7	606	86.6
1965	Bagaces	Stewart Brothers	79	13,450	170.3
1970	La Cruz	Finca Santa Cecilia	30	537	17.9
1971	Liberia	Hacienda Guachipelín	62	5,674	91.5
1972	Santa Cruz	Eva Contreras Pizarro	17	1,210	71.2
1974	Liberia	Andrés Sidney B.	30	980	32.7
1974	Carrillo	Heriberto Bustos C.	4	928	232.0
1975	La Cruz	Alejandro Urcuyo Barrios	11	2,000	181.8
1975	Abangares	Alberto Abdelnour	40	1,133	28.3
1978	Cañas	Hacienda Montezuma	36	2,492	69.2
1981	La Cruz	Luis Morice Lara	33	800	24.2

SOURCE: ITCO, Departamento Legal.

NOTE: "Year initiated" refers to when the occupation was brought to the attention of ITCO, not necessarily to when it actually began.

landlords, who were perceived as either foreigners or major latifundistas or both. In most cases, the invaded haciendas were wooded, remote, and underutilized, all of which made it easier for small groups of squatters to enter and build shacks undetected, and difficult for the Rural Guard to carry out rapid evictions.[35] At times, however, these initial furtive attempts had become enduring occupations. In San Juanillo, along the Pacific coast of the Nicoya Peninsula, Luz María Rothe, widow of the Spaniard Federico Sobrado, owned some 9,500 hectares, largely forested, which had been gradually occupied since the 1920s; as early as 1950, what the landowners termed "parasites" held as much as 6,125 hectares, and 264 pupils were attending eight small schools on the property (ITCO Departamento Legal 376).[36] Pacific Lumber, a company with primarily U.S. capital, also saw its holdings near Sobrado's lands invaded in the same period.[37]

A brief look at other major occupations suggests the degree to which peasants, in addition to seeking remote lands to occupy, targeted owners whom they saw as major latifundistas or foreigners or both. Hacienda Guachipelín, a large forested property in the volcanic highlands north of Liberia, belonged to members of the Baldioceda family (RP SM 3957—1949; RP SM 36,239—1978) who were among the largest latifundistas in the canton. Though they were of Nicaraguan descent, as were two of their minor partners from the Rivas and Ruiz Centeno families, the occupation of Guachipelín had more to do with the remote location of the property and resentment of its owners as latifundistas than with antiforeign feeling. This was the case as well with the mid-1970s invasion of Hacienda Montezuma in highland Cañas, which belonged to Alvaro Jenkins, a wealthy congressional deputy who used his influence to have Rural Guards evict and detain several dozen squatters and destroy their fields and huts (Pueblo, 6–13 and 13–20 Nov. 1978). In the aftermath of the expulsion and arrests, the Cañas parish priest commented, "We complain about the Nicaraguan National Guard, but here, if we are not careful, we are going to take the same road" (Pueblo, 6–13 Nov. 1978).

A few years earlier, in Finca Santa Cecilia and other nearby border properties in La Cruz, Nicaraguan landlords Alejandro and Carlos Urcuyo Barrios attempted to take that road, employing Somoza's National Guards to intimidate squatters. On several occasions in 1971, according to area peasants, Nicaraguan National Guard officers crossed the border, threatening with death the occupants of lands the Urcuyos claimed, destroying their fences, and seizing land on the Costa Rican side of the border (Libertad, 12 Feb. 1972). The following year a parliamentary commission investigating deficiencies in ITCO heard testimony from Costa Rican Rural Guards, who confessed that they too had been in the Urcuyos' pay (Libertad, 17 June 1972). At times, the guards on both sides of the frontier cooperated on the Urcuyos' behalf. When the landlords accused squatters on the Costa Rican side of rustling cattle from their Nicaraguan properties, Costa Rican Guards reportedly brought the suspects to the border, where Nicaraguan Guards urged them to forget about the supposed stolen animals and to return to Costa Rica, but to abandon " 'that little piece of [the Urcuyos'] land' so as not to have problems with the authorities" (Libertad, 14 Aug. 1971).

In 1975, in Colorado de Abangares, where decades earlier peasant squatters had assassinated hacendado Vicente Bonilla Morad (see Chapter 4), some four dozen families invaded a large ranch belonging to Alberto Abdelnour, like Bonilla a Levantine "turco." Whether anti-Arab sentiment had lingered since the conflicts of the 1930s, or whether it arose afresh in the context of new struggles over land, is difficult to tell and is ultimately unimportant. What is significant is the extent to which, for Abangares peasants, the most salient aspect of Abdelnour's identity was not that he was a landlord but that he was a "Turk." One squatter declared to the independent leftist weekly *Pueblo* that after being evicted, "we are living in the street. It will soon be a year since the Turk took our house and lot, where we had lived eighteen years. . . . The Turk has not stopped harming us, ever since he appeared here saying that from San Jorge to Las Piñuelas all the land would be his" (*Pueblo*, 19–26 Jan. 1978).

Another peasant whose property bordered Abdelnour's described an even greater injustice, again in ethnically charged terms: "When the Turk brought the guards to throw out squatters who wanted to work unused land on his farm, he took advantage of the opportunity to throw us out of our house. We were not squatters (*precaristas*). In Colorado now nobody can be tranquil with this land-grabber around" (ibid.).

The occupation of Abdelnour's Rancho Boyero was among those that ITCO considered successfully resolved by the late 1970s. But "success" in settling such conflicts was often defined largely in relation to how well tensions were defused, rather than in terms of how well agrarian structures were reformed. Evicted occupants of Abdelnour's property, after a period of "living in the street," were offered ITCO lands in distant Talamanca, in Costa Rica's Atlantic zone. Some accepted the government offer, but many, unwilling or unable to leave Colorado permanently, remained in the area, often without having gained any land to cultivate.

Even before Luis Morice Lara assassinated peasant activist Gil Tablada in 1970 (see above), he had gained notoriety as a particularly unscrupulous and brutal latifundista. A Nicaraguan, he was among the largest landowners in La Cruz, having—as he said in a 1971 newspaper advertisement—"inherited 14,000 hectares from [his] father in 1940," most of which he later traded to the state (*La Nación*, 21 July 1971; see Chapter 5). A decade earlier, writer Carlos Luis Fallas had detailed Morice's assaults on the La Cruz peasantry in an account fittingly titled *Don Bárbaro* (1978 [1960]). Fallas's conversations with La Cruz peasants, while carried out without even a pretense of scientific detachment, revealed a litany of abuses committed by this "barbarous" landlord that was unusual even by the standards of the most aggressive Guanacastecan latifundistas: providing false information to surveyors, bribing local authorities to harass and arrest squatters, naming relatives as occupants so that the state would pay him and give them land, breaking fences and loosing cattle on peasant crops, illegally seizing or logging on state lands, evicting peasants who were not on his property, and offering to pay occupants to relocate on other lands—supposedly his, but which actually belonged to others.

In the post-1960 period, as Douglas Kincaid points out, the La Cruz border region was, in terms of land occupations in Guanacaste, "in a class by itself," with more than half its rural families "precaristas" and one-eighth of its farmland in dispute (1987, chap. 5).[38] Even if these estimates of the magnitude of agrarian conflict may be high, they are indicative of important subregional particularities that would tend to support the notion that major foreign latifundistas with remote, forested holdings were the most likely targets of squatters.[39] The largest La Cruz landowners, such as the Morice and Urcuyo Barrios families, were descendants of late-nineteenth-century Nicaraguan latifundistas (see Chapter 1) who had obtained vast holdings through purchasing old hacienda titles and claiming state lands. In contrast to the situation in Liberia, just to the south, where Nicaraguan hacendado families were increasingly absorbed into Costa Rican society, many La Cruz landowners maintained Nicaraguan nationality, residence, and identity, as well as properties and connections north of the border.

La Cruz was one of the few cantons in Guanacaste where there were still, as late as the 1960s, substantial areas of state lands, either unclaimed or held illegally as the "demasías," or "excess," of large haciendas. Along the cordillera, much of this land was virgin forest, while in the lowlands peasants were attracted to the large expanses of secondary growth (tacotales) that were their preferred kind of land for swidden cultivation. The old Nicaraguan families that laid claim to much of this unused territory, especially the Urcuyos and Morices, had long attempted to impose harsh, Nicaraguan-style relations of domination in the area, although not always with great success (see Chapter 4). Among the region's peasants, this perceived barbarism fanned resentment, antilatifundista in content in the case of the numerous Nicaraguan migrants and also anti-Nicaraguan in the case of many of the Costa Ricans. For both groups of peasants, the association of these Nicaraguan millionaires with the Somoza regime was an additional source of indignation and yet another reason to retaliate against what Fallas in Don Bárbaro called "the affliction (azote) of the poor agriculturalists . . . , the immense latifundio that went along silently extinguishing all small properties" (1978: 7).

Rustling

If squatting was likely to be successful only in peripheral areas of the province, this was even more true of traditional rustling, that other perennial subject of hacendado complaint. "The people here saw and didn't see," Crisanto Alvarez Angulo recalled, describing how peasants near his hacienda in Quebrada Grande de Liberia reacted to the theft of 25 of his best animals in September 1972.

The thieves took 25 heifers (*vaquillas*) out of a herd of 404 head. We had been carrying out an inventory, and one of our peons who had a tendency toward thievery informed those people that the animals would be leaving the pasture at such and such a time. They grabbed the cattle in front—25 heifers—and herded them away. We didn't notice until the next day, and at first we thought some bull had broken a fence and they had been lost. A former peon of mine saw me in Quebrada Grande and said, "How strange, patrón, that you ordered that the cattle be herded at night." I told him I had ordered no such thing, and he insisted that the cattle had been herded at night. Something smelled peculiar.

Alvarez picked up the scent of his missing cows, but not before it was too late.

I communicated with the authorities in Liberia and La Cruz, and we followed the trail. But the people didn't give us good descriptions of the rustlers. Even one of the authorities here [in Quebrada Grande] was involved, and he helped throw the Liberia police off the trail. I offered 5,000 pesos [colones, $682] to the person who would help me find even one heifer. At that time, Nicaragua was exporting heifers to Peru. I found out that the heifers were in La Virgen [Nicaragua], on a farm that is part in Nica territory and part in Costa Rica. I went to Rivas [Nicaragua] to the slaughterhouse to tell them not to buy heifers with such and such a brand, and I spoke to the chief of the Rivas [National] Guard, who was a friend of mine. We wanted to go to La Virgen with Mauser rifles to recover the heifers, and the Nicas told us we could only enter Nica territory if the Tico [Costa Rican] guards dressed as civilians. In the end, we were never able to go.[40]

Alvarez's travails were so memorable in part because they concerned an instance of old-style rustling in an era when cattle theft had been largely transformed. Thieves on horseback seizing some two dozen cattle at dusk, colluding with corrupt employees and police, and herding their booty on hoof through the mountains to Nicaragua—these were elements of the kind of rustling that existed in Guanacaste before the widespread introduction of fencing, when there were few roads, and when state authority was at best tenuous. In highland Quebrada Grande, less than 30 kilometers from the frontier, such an operation could still be carried out in the early 1970s. In the more open, flatter terrain of the lowlands, similar attempts were generally easily foiled. "We go out a lot to the fields and our losses are few," Manuel Jirón remarked, recounting how he and his guards kept local rustlers at bay around Hacienda Las Trancas. "If some guy (un viejo) is there and starts running away, it's not that we fire a shot at him, we fire in the air. On one occasion we killed a guy's mare. The guy hid, it got dark and he fled, leaving the dead mare. If they have to run risks, they're not going to enter [the property] so much."[41]

When asked if rustling now is more serious than it was decades ago, large cattlemen virtually all affirm that the problem is worse today than ever. However, when pressed about the relative numbers of animals lost, they concede that better vigilance and a greater police presence have dramatically reduced both overall losses—measured in head or money—and the quantities seized in any one foray by rustlers.[42] Moreover, while insurance against livestock theft is sufficiently costly that ranchers only purchase policies for the finest bulls or horses, this coverage provides an added measure of security for the most expensive animals (which are also typically insured against disease, accident, and snakebite). But if livestock theft is no longer the "plague" that it was in the 1930s, when it was frequently sufficient reason not to invest in improving cattle production, the continued perception that it is worse than ever requires explanation.

Improvements in law enforcement and transport infrastructure did not lead to the disappearance of rustling itself, which some authorities have argued often occurs (e.g., Hobsbawm 1981: 151). Instead, cattle thieves were led to acquire trucks to transport contraband and elude pursuit. This modernization of rustling involved expenses that placed cattle theft largely beyond the reach of its traditional impoverished practitioners, and it also assured that motorized rustlers were almost never caught. It is this ease of escape and the failure to catch perpetrators that irk today's hacendados no end and that account more than anything else for their belief that rustling has worsened over the years. "They drive up at night with a truck and take two or three head of cattle, slaughter them, and sell the meat from the truck or in Puntarenas," one rancher commented. "You never find them."

Manuel Jirón of Las Trancas remarked in a similar vein, "Before, you would find the guts (*el mondongo*) or the skin and you would follow the trail and catch them. Now they grab the animal, they kill it, peel [skin] it, and throw it in a vehicle, and they go and sell it at the butcher's. Now with a car you don't find anything."

Hacendados' attempts to deal with this new rustling included individual efforts to better patrol properties and political pressure at the national level. In a few cases, the owners of the largest latifundios, faced with decisions about which portions of their estates to sell and which to keep, chose to retain the lands least exposed to predation. The sons of Donald Stewart Bonilla, for example, convinced that land reform beneficiaries and residents of the nearby village of Bebedero were filching cattle, retreated in the 1970s into a smaller, roughly triangular version of the old Hacienda Mojica, surrounded by a veritable moat formed by the Las Piedras, Bebedero, and Blanco rivers. Politically, rustling was an issue that agitated the provincial cattle lobby almost from the minute of its formation. In 1954, still in its first year, it urged greater government attention to the emerging problem of motorized rustling, noting:

As traffic has increased on the Interamerican Highway, thefts of cattle and the clandestine slaughtering of steers have increased in an alarming way. The Chamber of Cattlemen (Cámara de Ganaderos) urges that instructions be given to the Treasury Police of this province to redouble their vigilance and to require that trucks that drive cattle to markets in the interior of the Republic present documents specifying the origin of the cattle, the number of head, and the particular brands involved in the sale. It would be convenient to have this checkpoint before reaching Barranca [Puntarenas], hopefully in the same post where the salt used to be checked. (CGG Actas, 1: 57)

Not long after the Cámara's petition, virtually all of the suggested measures were adopted, including the creation of highway inspection posts. Lobbyists' efforts to enact stricter penalties for convicted rustlers initially bore little fruit, largely because sanctions had been increased relatively recently, in 1942 (see Chapter 4). But in 1970, as part of an overhaul of the nation's penal code, the maximum prison term for rustling was increased at the Cámara's urging from the earlier six years to ten years.[43] The minimum term, however, was set at one year, down from the previous two years. Even though courts in cattle-ranching areas have not been reluctant to impose harsh prison terms on the few livestock thieves that are caught and convicted, the reduction of the minimum penalty and the due process accorded the accused have led many cattlemen to scoff at the deterrent value of the antirustling statute. Crisanto Alvarez, whose heifers vanished into the night in Quebrada Grande in 1972, reflected widely held frustration when he remarked, "I consider the law anachronistic. When they do catch rustlers, these then post bond and go free."

Worker Resistance

In the mid-1970s, a group of Cuban investors acquired several thousand hectares of prime agricultural land near Bebedero de Cañas and installed an old sugar refinery that they had purchased in pieces in the Caribbean and elsewhere in Central America and then brought to Costa Rica. On a small knoll that separated the refinery and the owner's and administrator's houses from the flat expanse of valley land where they planned to plant sugarcane, the new owners placed a four-foot-tall figure of the Virgen del Cobre, whose gaze, they doubtless hoped, would protect them and their new enterprise from misfortune. Lest the Virgin be unable to protect herself against thieves in this alien environment, however, the Cubans took the precaution of installing around her a thick, ten-by-fifteen-foot steel-mesh cage sunk in a solid concrete foundation.

This statue of the Virgin—mounted at the most central, visible spot on a thoroughly consolidated, well-guarded enterprise, yet nonetheless imprisoned in a huge, ugly cage—epitomizes what many landowners perceive as the necessity for constant vigilance, not only of external peasants, but of their own employees. Scott (1985) fittingly observes: "Rural theft by itself is unremarkable; it is a nearly permanent feature of agrarian life whenever and wherever the state and its agents are insufficient to control it. When such theft takes on the dimensions of a struggle in which property rights are contested, however, it becomes essential to any careful analysis of class relations" (p. 265).

Most theft by employees does not fundamentally challenge property relations in the least, though it perhaps contests indirectly the division of the social product between owners and workers. Yet it nonetheless remains important in understanding a key aspect of class relations, the structuring of the labor process. Today's landowners and administrators see their relation with employees in explicitly adversarial terms, with stealing one of the principal areas of contention. At the farm with the caged Virgin, long since sold by the Cubans to a U.S. company that shifted from sugar to rice, a Costa Rican manager entrusted with day-to-day administration described this constant battle:

The worst kind of stealing is what we call "ant theft" (*robo de hormigas*), when they take small quantities of expensive spare parts to sell. So a mechanic or a [tractor] operator comes and says he needs five new rollers for a tractor. I ask him what he did with the old, worn-out ones and he says he dropped them in the mud. "Well, let's go to where you dropped them in the mud and take them out and wash them off" [I say]. "But," [he replies], "I don't remember where I dropped them." Or the mechanics who could take new 400-colón [$5.00] cans of spray lubricant whenever they wanted. Once we put a system in place to allow only one can at a time for all the mechanics, consumption was more than halved.

The control of worker pilfering has, of course, other kinds of costs. The same manager who had to control his mechanics' use of spray lubricant remarked that he had many enemies in nearby villages, mostly peons whom he had fired or accused of theft, and that they called him names behind his back, such as "snitch" or "toady" (*el sapo*). Even though he could "get 50 peons any time they're needed" just beyond the gates of the finca, he prefers to hire laborers and tractor drivers from more distant villages because "they don't come with an attitude." These employees live in barracks during the week and are trucked at company expense back to their homes, some 100 kilometers away, on Saturday afternoon, only to be picked up again before dawn on Monday.[44] Echoing hacendado concerns of an earlier era, the manager lauded these "imported" workers, all the while deploring their shortcomings:

They work hard if you watch and encourage them. Compared with people from other provinces, Guanacastecans are honest and respectful. They don't squat on others' land as much as in Limón, where the Communists influence them. Their only defects are that they like violence and gossip. But they don't kill the way Nicas do. They just drink and fight. No dance or party or festival (*tope*) or bull-riding competition (*fiesta de toros*) is complete without a good fight.

Like theft, alcoholism among employees has, for many landowners, become a convenient rationalization both for maintaining low wage levels and for introducing laborsaving technology. One Liberia hacendado, after recounting how all but his "head cowboy" had "disappointed" him, articulated the prevailing folk version of the backward-bending supply curve of labor:

A lot of the workers have a drinking problem. They work for two weeks, then don't come in for two weeks, and then come back. The worst thing is that it is usually the good men, who know how to work. I saw the writing on the wall and started to mechanize just as fast as I possibly could. Raising wages would have just made more people absent. They can't save anything. We had an incentive program years ago and told them there would be bonuses for people who never missed work outside of illness. At Christmas time that year we had about seven good men who worked for us, they had very good records, and we gave them a good bonus. We figured that they would tell everybody else what they got and that the following year—well, it didn't work. The ones we gave the bonus didn't come back. It just burns a hole in their pockets, they go on drunks. We paid in cash all the time, not in checks. The more they earn, the more they drink.

This landowner view of worker indiscipline and intemperance—typical in its deeply rooted distrust, its fear that alcohol undermines authority, and its blanket condemnation of virtually all members of the rural labor force—colors relations with even the "best" employees. In the rural villages, stories abound among current and former employees of large farms about unjustified accusations of theft, arbitrary firings, and humiliating verbal abuse from foremen and administrators. The resulting resentment is widespread and frequently gives rise to varieties of resistance that have little to do directly with appropriating a greater share of the surplus. The same farm manager who decried pervasive "ant theft" described how for five days in a row nocturnal visitors turned the ignition key in his jeep and let the battery run down, even though it was parked within view of a guard post. When one evening he finally removed the key, he found the following morning that someone had let the air out of all his tires. Only when he posted a guard every night next to the vehicle did the harassment cease.

Sometime later, the manager and his superiors were dismayed to find that information from confidential telephone conversations with the farm's Liberia office, including production and hiring plans, was apparently common knowledge among employees. The Liberia administrator (who was also a minor partner in the business), reflecting the ubiquitous suspicion governing relations with employees at all levels, even accused the manager of carelessness and disloyalty and threatened him with dismissal. After two weeks of growing desperation about the leaks and his increasingly precarious situation with the company, the manager discovered a dilapidated shed, abandoned by the former owners and overgrown with brush, that contained a telephone set hooked onto the farm's main line. There, on a dusty bench next to the telephone, was a clean imprint left by the rump of the person who had been monitoring the calls.

Assuaging the resentment and discontent behind this kind of resistance is a major preoccupation of employers and of the managers and administrators in charge of what are often called Control Departments on larger farms and haciendas.[45] While greater state participation in social welfare and the ease of "getting 50 peons any time they're needed" have diminished traditional hacendado paternalism, landowners have nonetheless had to develop, or in some cases reinvent, mechanisms for tempering dissatisfaction and for creating, when possible, worker identification with employers. Some of the larger enterprises, such as El Pelón de la Bajura, have air-conditioned buses that provide free rides to Liberia to employees on their day off. Several of the largest landowners periodically reinforce the loyalty of their upper-level employees, inviting them to vacation at company beach houses on the Pacific. One administrator of another large farm described how surprised and encouraged he was with the results of sponsoring a company soccer team, equipped with free uniforms, shoes, and balls. "It's something that keeps them out of the bars in town, so they don't get into trouble. Instead—you should have seen it—our workers went to the game in town and were cheering for *our* team, shouting *vivas!* for our finca and our team."

A number of landowners have also resurrected the old custom of lending plots of land to employees in the hope, they say, of keeping workers occupied in their free time, out of the bars and out of trouble. Especially when laborers and skilled workers reside some distance away and live in barracks during the week, employers worry about keeping them occupied during late afternoon and evening hours. While lending workers land retains all the advantages it always had of subsidizing wage costs, providing risk-free tests of soil fertility, and creating economic and psychological dependency, its fundamental instrumentality is no longer to attract scarce labor, but rather to assure the loyalty of potentially disgruntled labor that is nonetheless available in abundance. Though still not widespread, the practice of allowing employees to cultivate employers' land for their own benefit has, after almost disappearing for several decades, taken hold again on some of the larger properties, all of which contain unused areas and where the opportunity cost of using a few hectares in this way is virtually zero. In some cases, landowners provide free use of machinery and diesel fuel for these operations, although not expensive fertilizer or chemicals.

Apart from one major strike in May 1979 at CATSA (Central Azucarera del Tempisque), the state-owned sugar complex in Carrillo, class-based organization and labor actions have been notably absent among the multitudinous forms of worker resistance on large properties. The two-week action at CATSA, which involved some 1,500 refinery and field workers who struck at the end of the harvest season, generated considerable sympathy in surrounding communities, where many of the strikers lived. Area residents sprinkled plantation roads with tacks to stop company vehicles, gathered food and clothing for strikers and their families, and housed strike supporters from other parts of the country. But while the walkout initially brought some important gains in wages, housing, job safety, and health facilities, it also generated a multifaceted company response (Li Kam 1984: 43). Almost immediately, CATSA increased the number of guards from 20 to 60 and introduced harvesting equipment that could replace striking cane cutters (see next chapter). Most important, the company founded a *solidarista* association, which in a short time managed to supplant the union.[46] This worker-employer organization, like similar groups elsewhere in Costa Rica, articulated an ideology of profit sharing and mutual dependence between labor and capital, yet managed nonetheless to provide enough real benefits, especially in the area of housing, but also in health and education, that it gained support even among former union members.[47] During the 1980s other large enterprises in Guanacaste, particularly sugar mills, absorbed the lessons of CATSA and also founded *solidarista* associations.

While Guanacastecans have been the backbone of labor strikes in the banana zones, on their home turf they confront radically different and highly unfavorable conditions for organization. In contrast to the banana zones, where hundreds of workers are employed year-round on a single enterprise, few Guanacaste farms have more than a few dozen employees. The seasonality of much locally available work— and the way such jobs complement emigration to the banana plantations—further influences both the subjective identity and loyalty of the labor force and its possibilities for collective action. Stints of high-wage work in Limón or southern Puntarenas are often only months away, and the "conformist" pressures exercised by nearby families, as well as the time required to cultivate peasant plots, may detract from the willingness to take risks in potentially perilous job actions. Unions in general confront serious obstacles in Costa Rica, including high levels of factionalism and the regulation of labor conflicts by a judicial system and state organs that are typically unfriendly to worker organizations (Donato and Rojas 1985). In addition, the significant state role in social welfare and reform has contributed to the strengthening of already existing tendencies toward rural political quiescence (Kincaid 1987).

Weighing Resistance, Resignation, and Retreat

This chapter began with an exhortation, arguing that it is necessary to examine resistance in relation to its antipodes, resignation and retreat, and to shift analysis away from an exclusive focus on its romantic or even its undramatic aspects and back toward the structure side of the structure-agency relation. It concludes with a brief look at the relative magnitude of the choices, however limited, made by Guanacaste's rural poor. Obviously weighing the broad alternatives of resistance, resignation, and retreat in relation to the number of participants in each approach is fraught with conceptual and epistemological dangers. It is nonetheless sobering to consider that tens of thousands of rural poor abandon Guanacaste each decade, yet in the province's recent history the largest two land invasions involved a few thousand peasants each, and the largest rural strike lasted two weeks and involved fewer than 2,000 workers. Some 7 percent of the province's farmland may have been contested by the 9 percent of rural families that were squatters, but here too, fewer than 2,000 families were involved (Kincaid 1987, chap. 5). Clearly, the significance of one or another foot-dragging tactic or episode of resistance for the ongoing process of shaping social relations can hardly be measured or encapsulated in such terms, nor can individuals or groups be pigeonholed or often even identified as participants in one strategy alone or in combinations of strategies. In spite of the plain limitations of such gross, macrosociological generalizations, they are nonetheless important in placing the more enchanting kinds of resistance in perspective. Simply put, many more Guanacastecans opted for "avoidance protest" or for bearing, in general with stoic "conformism," what Juvencio Matarrita (quoted at the beginning of the chapter) described as the "pain" of not having enough land.

9 → Limits of the Transformation from Hacienda to Plantation

> Many will think of the benefits accruing to a small number
> of agriculturalists and even label them "privileged." This
> idea must be rejected and put aside, since if we plan to pro-
> duce with greater effectiveness we have to think of the
> means and not the persons.
> —Owners of Hacienda El Pelón de la Bajura,
> describing mechanization plans, 1950

Marxian, evolutionist, and neoclassical theorists of agrarian change
in Latin America all point to capitalism as an inexorable modernizing force. Explicitly or implicitly, those imbued with this vision of a
progressive capitalism have argued that the seemingly antiquated,
extensively operated haciendas or latifundios that long dominated
much of rural Latin America would give way to the logic of the
market and be replaced with modern, highly capitalized plantations
(see Introduction). In discussing the Guanacaste beef export economy (in Chapter 6), I argued that modern markets may, instead of
fostering constant development of the forces of production, contribute instead to the continued underutilization of increasingly valuable land and to rentier rather than genuinely capitalist strategies of
accumulation. The major intensification of land use that occurred in
Guanacaste in the post-1950 period involved crop rather than livestock production. Yet even though massive capital investments, intensified land uses, and the reorganization of production processes
transformed several large underutilized latifundios into plantation-
type farms (and other haciendas underwent less-thorough transitions), the presumption that such changes would be inevitable and
ubiquitous is hardly supported by the experiences of the last four
decades.

The limited character of the transition from hacienda to plantation
in Guanacaste can best be explained by examining the ecological and

market uncertainties affecting agriculturalists' labor and investments, the roles of the state and foreign capital in sustaining plantation production, the organization of producers groups, and the specific agronomic characteristics of the key plantation crops—sugarcane, rice, and cotton.

"La agricultura es aventurar"

"Crop agriculture is to risk, to venture." Thus commented a smallholder from the village of Ortega de Santa Cruz who, after repeated
losses from flood and drought, was considering renting his land to
others. The remark encapsulates the experience of numerous producers, large and small. Many areas of Guanacaste have large extensions of flat, exceptionally fertile alluvial and volcanic soils, but the
water available for crops varies greatly from year to year. Sometimes
the rains that are supposed to come in May appear only briefly or not
at all, and the brown and yellow pastures remain parched well into
what should have been the wet season, or "winter." In other years, the
rains come on time, fields are planted, and the landscape becomes
green. Then, after the "little summer," or *veranillo*, of late June and
July, when there is often a pause in the earlier intense rainfall, the dry
season sets in before it is due and withers the fields before they
mature. And if there is not too little water, there may be a year of
unusually heavy rains when the rivers overflow their banks, fields
are inundated, and clouds block the sun for long periods, depriving
crops of essential sunlight.

Before planting time, there is rarely any reliable indication of how
much rain will fall or how it will be distributed over the course of the
wet-season months. The rainfall statistics for 1921–79 in Figure 9.1
are from Hacienda La Pacífica, just north of Cañas, and are the
longest continuous series available for the region.[1] The climate of the
Cañas area is typical of the central Tempisque Valley, similar to
Liberia though considerably drier than the Nicoya Peninsula. The
data suggest a long-term trend toward decreased precipitation, almost certainly due to the large-scale deforestation affecting the region. It is important to note, however, that the tendency is far from
strong, as the regression line in Figure 9.1 suggests.[2] Figure 9.1 also
shows the very large variation from year to year.

The variation is even greater if individual months are analyzed
(Figure 9.2). Agricultural planning and production are greatly compli-

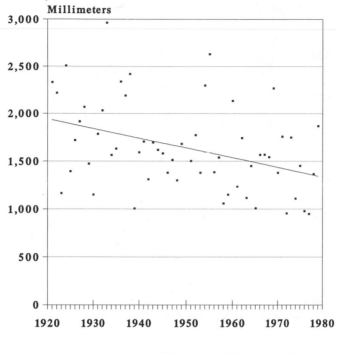

Fig. 9.1. Hacienda La Pacífica, Cañas: Annual Rainfall, 1921–1979. Sources: Hagenauer 1980; IMN, unpublished data.

cated by the wide within-month variation in wet-season precipitation. A comparison of this monthly precipitation data with Figure 9.3, which describes the agricultural calendar for the principal crops in Guanacaste, demonstrates that during the wet season the variation in precipitation—the standard deviation as a proportion of average rainfall—is greatest precisely in the months of soil preparation and planting. During these periods in the agricultural cycle, timely completion of tasks is essential to agronomic or economic success. Heavy rainfall, however, may make it impossible on many days to use machinery in the fields. In each May–November rainy season, on an average of 40 days more than 20 millimeters of rain falls within 48 hours (Hagenauer 1980). On these days it is virtually impossible to drive machinery in the fields. Faced with a high probability that on

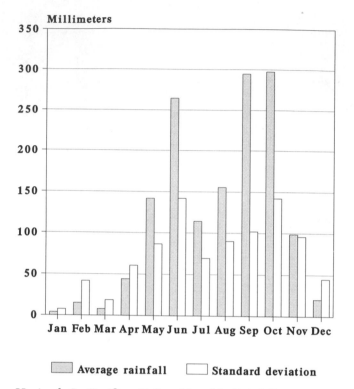

Fig. 9.2. Hacienda La Pacífica, Cañas: Monthly Rainfall, 1921–1979, Average and Standard Deviation. Sources: Hagenauer 1980; IMN, unpublished data.

many days it will not be possible to work the fields, agriculturalists often invest in extra machinery to assure that plowing, planting, and other tasks may be completed rapidly on days without heavy rain. This increases costs, and therefore the economic risks, of crop production.

It would be difficult to overstate the importance as well of the yearly variation in rainfall. Acceptable ranges of precipitation for cotton and rice do not overlap greatly. Farmers must gamble that rainfall in a given year will be suitable for the crops they plant. Cotton generally produces good yields with 800 mm to 1600 mm of rainfall (Hagenauer 1980: 48), although some agriculturalists argue that the optimum is around 750 mm and that more than 1,300 mm leads to greatly increased pest problems and severe losses.[3] Adequate water is particularly indispensable during early growth and flowering or the boll shrivels and falls to the ground. Too much water, however, reduces fiber quality. A dry period is also required in the weeks just prior to harvesting.

Dry-land rice, in contrast to cotton, needs at least 1,600 mm of rain per cycle and will produce good yields with up to 2,200 mm (Hagenauer 1980: 48), provided the rain is distributed throughout the growth period and is abundant during flowering and before the harvest when the grain is said to "thicken" (*cuajar*). Sugarcane (according to Hagenauer) does well with rainfall between 1,200 mm and 2,600 mm, though the bottom end of this range is considered unduly low by other cane growers; government extension officials consider the appropriate range for sugarcane to be 1,500–3,000 mm (SEPSA 1989: 79). In any case, for sugarcane adequate water is essential during the period of maximum growth and least important during the first months after planting and the month prior to harvesting,

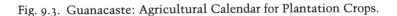

	JAN.	FEB.	MARCH	APRIL	MAY	JUNE	JULY	AUG.	SEPT.	OCT.	NOV.	DEC.
SUGARCANE soil preparation	‖‖‖‖‖‖‖‖‖‖‖‖‖‖‖‖											
planting			‖‖‖‖‖‖‖‖‖‖‖‖‖‖‖									
harvest	‖‖‖‖‖‖‖‖‖‖‖‖‖‖‖										‖‖‖	
DRY-LAND RICE soil preparation				‖‖‖‖‖								
planting					‖‖‖‖‖							
harvest										‖‖‖‖‖‖		
SORGHUM soil preparation				‖‖‖‖								
first planting					‖‖‖‖‖							
first harvest								‖‖‖‖‖				
second planting									▩▩▩▩			
second harvest		▩										▩
COTTON soil preparation			‖‖‖‖‖‖									
planting					‖‖‖‖‖							
harvest	‖‖‖‖‖											‖

Fig. 9.3. Guanacaste: Agricultural Calendar for Plantation Crops.

when the fields are usually lightly burned to eliminate the cane's sharp lower leaves and to kill snakes, thus permitting easier cutting.

In many years rainfall is outside the acceptable range for particular crops, either too high for cotton and "winter" sorghum or too low for rice. When rice is grown on poorly drained lands, even if rain is sufficient for plant metabolism there may be other, destructive effects, since the now almost universal dwarf variety is easily submerged in the event of uncontrolled flooding. Sugarcane, less likely than rice to "drown" in a flood, is also better suited to both high and low rainfall. It is often planted on the lowest portions of the flood plain, where it actually benefits from inundations, which deposit fertile silt and which leave the soil moist well into the dry-season harvest period. Except for a few irrigated areas, primarily on large farms, and some small zones with moister microclimates in Liberia and Cañas, the risk of incurring major losses in rice production in any single year is above 40 percent in most of the province (SEPSA 1980b: II, 293).[4]

Most agriculturalists do not, however, consider cotton an acceptable risk. Even though it is better suited to low-rainfall years, the probability of high rains is still considerable, the investments required are substantial, and the support infrastructure—extension, storage, and commercialization facilities—is little developed. Sugarcane, better adapted to extremes in precipitation, is rarely grown at any distance from the mills. To do so would increase transport costs, and mill personnel, who usually supervise key aspects of the production process even on independent farms, are unable or unwilling to travel. The major cropping systems in Guanacaste—indeed the possibilities of a transformation from hacienda to plantation—have been shaped by a complex interplay between these ecological and locational limits, market forces, political interests, and state planning.

Sugarcane: From Tapa de Dulce to the U.S. Market

In late-nineteenth-century Guanacaste, small-scale sugar production for local markets was of considerable significance. Some haciendas also planted cane, usually to meet their own consumption needs and occasionally to sell (Sequiera 1985: 41, 44–45). But even the largest commercial sugar operations were a far cry from the huge, highly capitalized Caribbean plantations that supplied U.S. and European markets.

Guanacaste in 1883 had 70 *trapiches*, small mills, powered by oxen, that were used to extract cane juice, which was then boiled down in large caldrons and cooled in wooden molds (Cabrera 1924: 123). This evaporation process produced *tapa de dulce*, brown-sugar loaves widely consumed in food or beverages or used to distill the almost pure alcohol called *aguardiente* (or more colloquially, *guaro*). By 1922 the number of trapiches had risen to 169, and, as a result of a piecemeal process of technological improvement that mirrored gradual changes in other sectors of the rural economy, a growing proportion of the mechanisms were made of iron rather than wood.[5]

Ingenios, industrial sugar mills, were introduced in Costa Rica in the 1880s (Solís 1981b: 55). Cuban colonists led by exiled independence fighter Antonio Maceo installed the first ingenio in Guanacaste in the early 1890s at La Mansión on the Nicoya Peninsula, in an early instance of what later became an extensive involvement by experienced Cuban entrepreneurs in the region's sugar-refining sector. After 1899, when Maceo and his compatriots returned home and the enterprise reverted to the state, the mill was acquired by Spanish immigrant Federico Apéstegui, who later sold it and acquired extensive cattle haciendas farther north in Guanacaste. Federico Sobrado, also a Spanish immigrant, opened another, larger mill on the Hacienda Tempisque at the turn of the century and received a government contract to be the exclusive producer of alcohol for the provinces of Guanacaste and Puntarenas.[6]

The growth of refining capacity and sugar production in the early twentieth century resulted from demand generated by the state-owned National Liquors Factory (founded in 1850), protectionist and pricing policies, and changing conditions in the international sugar market. Throughout the late nineteenth century, domestic production was insufficient to meet the needs of the state distilling monopoly, in spite of frequent price increases, and Costa Rica imported large quantities of sugar. In 1893, hoping to promote domestic refining, the government permitted tax-free imports of mill machinery (Sáenz Maroto 1970: 174). A decade later, it provided further encouragement by imposing a tariff of twenty céntimos per kilo on imported sugar (Barboza et al. 1981: V-1-2). Between 1909 and 1917 the duty on imported sugar fell to ten céntimos, but the rapid rise in world market prices during and after World War I provided a strong stimulus for Costa Rican producers. In 1914–27 the country actually exported small surpluses. By the mid-1920s more cane was planted in Guanacaste than at any time until the late 1970s (see Figure 9.4).[7]

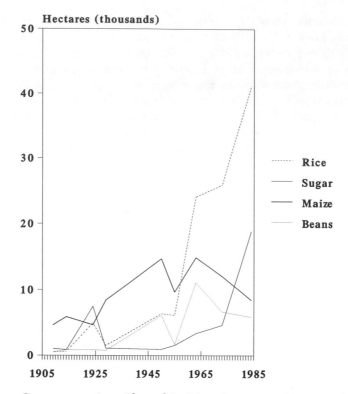

Fig. 9.4. Guanacaste: Area Planted in Rice, Sugarcane, Maize, and Beans, 1909–1984. Sources: 1909–29, *AE*; 1950–84, *CAP*.

Prices declined after 1927, and the levy on imports was lowered in 1929, which further discouraged growers and mill owners. In 1929 the government fixed a maximum price above which imports were permitted free of all duties. In 1934, when world market prices had plunged to their lowest level in decades, the maximum price was lowered again. By 1939, as a result of these disincentives, Costa Rica was once again importing sizable amounts of sugar.

Foreign exchange losses from large imports in 1939–40 led the government to intervene more actively in the sugar sector, and in 1940 it created a Cane Agriculture Protection Board (Junta de Protección de la Agricultura de la Caña) (Barboza et al. 1981: V-3). The Board's responsibilities included establishing quotas for amounts of cane to be received from independent producers by trapiches and ingenios, setting minimum prices for this cane, and fixing maximum wholesale sugar prices. At the same time, in the hope of encouraging producers, the Cane Board hiked the duty on imported sugar to 30 céntimos per kilo and guaranteed cane growers a price equivalent to 54 percent of the value of the sugar content of their cane. Nevertheless, despite several increases in prices and in the percentage of value guaranteed to growers, the country still periodically imported sugar and only occasionally exported small surpluses.

Until 1948 the cane planted in Guanacaste consisted almost entirely of low-yielding "creole" varieties. Fields received little if any fertilizer beyond the sediment deposited by floodwaters, and virtually no systematic studies had been carried out on pest and pathogen control, cultivation practices, or other aspects of increasing productivity. "Creole" cane matured unevenly, and in the late 1940s almost all those who planted it still harvested selectively, cutting ripe stalks and leaving the rest. In 1948, 90 percent of the cane produced in Guanacaste was harvested this way (*AE* 1949: 232).[8] The entire crop went to the province's 274 trapiches, since the last ingenio of the early decades of the century, battered by the depression, closed after the 1941–42 harvest.

With no industrial sugar production in Guanacaste, cane was mostly a crop of smallholders; in 1948, of the 377 cane producers in the province, only 1 had sown more than 14 hectares, and none had more than 35 hectares (*AE* 1949: 231). Smallholder domination of sugar reflected rudimentary growing and refining technology, unfavorable market conditions, and lack of state support. When this began to change over the next decade, large entrepreneurs moved in and transformed the Guanacaste sugar sector.[9]

Prior to 1948 the state had intervened in the sugar sector only to set prices and duties, devoting little attention to technological change or extension efforts that might have increased productivity. But as in the case of beef cattle, the new developmentalist post-1948 state, actively intervening in previously neglected sectors of the economy, became a major force for modernizing sugar production. State efforts on behalf of the sugar sector included expanded agronomic and technical research and extension, increased price supports and credit, reorganization of relevant institutions, and the opening of roads in outlying areas.

The Cane Bureau (Sección de Caña), created in 1948 in the newly reorganized Ministry of Agriculture, initiated large-scale testing in different zones of seed imported from Hawaii, Australia, and Barbados. Hybrids based on Barbados strains proved especially well adapted to the hot, dry lowlands of Guanacaste and often yielded 50 percent or more cane than "creole" varieties. The testing of fertilizers and other inputs permitted the development of a "package" capable of greatly increasing productivity. Unprecedented extension efforts, which unlike the agronomic research were financed largely by sugar Cámaras, or producers associations, led to continuing improvements and rapid, widespread adoption of the new technologies.

After Costa Rica imported sugar again in 1955–57, the government raised internal sugar prices from 42 to 50.50 colones ($6.85 to $8.23) per 50-kilogram bag for the 1957–58 harvest. This price hike, in combination with new state support in the form of credit, technical extension, and marketing, generated considerable entrepreneurial interest and led to the establishment of one major ingenio in Guanacaste at Hacienda Taboga and the expansion and modernization of another at El Viejo, which had been founded a few years before (see below). The United States' break with Cuba in 1960 raised even greater expectations. When Washington reassigned Cuba's sugar quota to other nations, including Costa Rica, the prospect of a lucrative, expanding export market, much like the opening of the U.S. beef market less than a decade earlier, caused eager Guanacastecan landowners to reassess the productive potential of their properties (see Figure 9.5). In an ironic twist of fate, Cuban refinery engineers and expropriated-plantation owners emigrated to Costa Rica (and elsewhere in Central America), where they applied their technical expertise, business skills, and remaining capital to the modernization of cane agriculture and the sugar industry.[10]

Even after the U.S. embargo on Cuban sugar in 1960, however, when Costa Rica received "preferential" prices for its exports to the United States, internal demand provided the major initial stimulus for cane growers and refiners. Until the late 1960s (and again in 1977–79), domestic sugar prices remained at levels well above those in international markets (with the exception of 1963; see Figure 9.6). This meant that Costa Rican consumers, as well as industries using sugar as a raw material, subsidized producers who would otherwise have had to sell much of their output at world market prices below their production costs (Achío and Escalante 1985: 66–67). U.S. preferential prices, which tend to be higher when world prices are low, also contributed to the construction of an economically rational

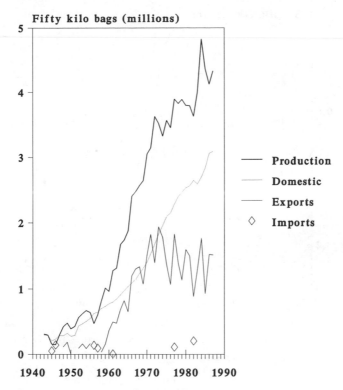

Fig. 9.5. Costa Rica: Sugar Production, Domestic Consumption, Exports and Imports, 1943–1987. Source: LAICA 1987. Note: Years refer to twelve-month period beginning in July of previous calendar year.

framework for sugar plantations and refineries. Indeed, were it not for Costa Rica's privileged access to the U.S. market, the sugar industry would have long ago been "in a grave depression" (Guardia et al. 1987: 133) or "ruined" (Achío and Escalante 1985: 66).

The institution charged with preventing such a disastrous state of affairs is the Agricultural and Industrial Sugarcane League (Liga Agrícola Industrial de la Caña de Azúcar, LAICA), founded in 1965, a hybrid association that is part regulatory agency and part advocacy group.[11] Replacing the earlier Cane Agriculture Protection Board, the new organization assumed several regulatory functions, such as setting provisional producers prices, determining internal consumption and export quotas, and the purchasing, storing, and wholesale mar-

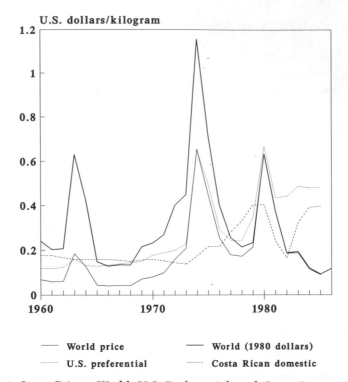

Fig. 9.6. Sugar Prices: World, U.S. Preferential, and Costa Rican Markets, 1960–1986. Sources: LAICA 1987; World Bank 1988.

keting of sugar.[12] Much of the operating credit for sugar from the National Banking System has been channeled through LAICA to the ingenios, which then provide financing to independent producers.[13] LAICA also administers warehouses in the main sugar-producing areas and sponsored the construction of modern docking facilities in northern Puntarenas, where much of the sugar from northwestern Costa Rica is exported to the United States.

Financed by new taxes on refined sugar, LAICA's board of directors has included representatives of the mill owners (Cámara de Azucareros), the regional growers organizations (Cámaras de Productores de Caña), and the Ministries of Agriculture and Industry (LAICA 1987). Although LAICA was intended to be a regulatory body, these representatives of the growers and refiners Cámaras have led it to function also as a pressure group that periodically wages lobbying and advertising campaigns for increases in consumer and producer prices (e.g., *La Nación*, 29 July 1982, 11A). A small group of mill owners with close ties to the social democratic National Liberation Party (Partido de Liberación Nacional, PLN), linked to each other through interlocking directorates and investments in the major ingenios of northwestern Costa Rica, has exercised particularly strong influence in LAICA (Achío and Escalante 1981: 80–85; also see below).

LAICA assigns portions of the internal and export quotas to every mill in the country, but refiners are permitted to exchange their allotted shares as long as total production remains on target. Such transactions have led to a regional-functional specialization in Costa Rica's sugar industry. Guanacaste and Puntarenas mills, all relatively new in comparison with those of central Costa Rica, produce virtually all raw sugar exported to the United States and only a small portion of white sugar for domestic consumption, most of which is refined in central Costa Rica.[14] The primary reason for this division is the proximity of the central Costa Rican mills to the population concentrations and food industries that are the main domestic market and the proximity of the northwestern mills to Punta Morales, Puntarenas, the modern, LAICA-administered port on the Pacific coast from which sugar is shipped to the United States. Despite this difference in the destinations of the two zones' output, the marketing system for sugar, in contrast to that for beef, establishes nearly uniform producers' prices regardless of whether the product is for the internal or the export market. While the LAICA producers' price for raw sugar is slightly lower than that for "plantation white," it does not reflect differences between domestic and international prices. Instead, LAICA, in effect the only buyer, averages price differentials so that sellers receive similar rates of return. World market fluctuations and differentials between domestic and international (or U.S. preferential) prices do not therefore lead producers to channel sugar to the higher-priced market, such as occurred with beef during the cattle boom (see Chapter 6).[15]

The post-1950 expansion of sugar production differed from that which occurred with cattle in another way as well. While the impetus to expand herds came almost entirely from abroad, and higher export prices led to declining per capita consumption of beef, the sugar boom was sustained in its early years by artificially high domestic prices and was associated with rapidly climbing per capita intake. Annual per capita consumption of sugar more than doubled from 24.8 kilograms in 1950 to 54.3 kilograms in 1975 and reached 62.4 kilograms in 1980 (Barboza et al. 1981: IV-16). Cane growers and mill officials frequently suggest that the large rise in sugar consumption since 1950, rather than representing higher intake by Costa Ricans, actually reflects sugar used by soft-drink and food manufacturers, who export much of their output.[16] Many of these industries located in Costa Rica following the creation of the Central American Common Market (CACM) in the early 1960s because wholesale sugar prices, in spite of government price supports, were still lower than in the other countries. Nevertheless, the fact that only about 13 percent of domestic sugar production since 1950 has been absorbed by industry suggests the limits of the sugar producers' reasoning, just as it raises the question of why their denials of rising real per capita consumption are so insistent (Barboza et al. 1981: IV-8).[17]

The decision to subsidize producers in order to maintain an otherwise untenable sugar sector and boost domestic sugar consumption contrasted sharply with the attitude toward the beef-cattle sector, which was also subsidized by the state, but with the goal of increasing exports, not domestic consumption. Both subsidy strategies, contradictory as they might appear at first, are consistent inasmuch as they form part of a general policy bias—seldom deliberate or explicitly articulated—that encourages consumption of wage goods, such as sugar and rice, which are inexpensive sources of calories.[18] While high-quality protein became a virtual luxury for many Costa Ricans (see Chapter 6), state policies in the same period have promoted the consumption of what nutritionists commonly term "empty calories." That these "empty calories" are produced primarily on large agroindustrial enterprises very different from the primitive trapiches of earlier years is of key importance in understanding the formulation of state policies (and, most likely, the sugar producers' obfuscationist, self-interested interpretations of soaring levels of per capita consumption).

It is around the new sugar mills that the transition from hacienda to plantation in Guanacaste has been most profound. Sugarcane, which takes fourteen to eighteen months to mature in the cool, humid central plateau, takes only twelve months in the hot northwestern lowlands. Large landowners have taken areas that only a few decades earlier were devoted almost exclusively to extensive cattle grazing and have installed modern refineries, planted cane, constructed irrigation canals, and acquired expensive machinery for all stages of the production process. The market created by the mills has also led small landowners in surrounding zones to intensify their production.

New Mills and Foreign Finance

Little, if any, of the capital used in the creation of new sugar plantations in Guanacaste has been generated from the production of the region's extensively operated livestock haciendas. Instead, foreign capital and finance have played an essential role in all the new plantations established in Guanacaste. The long-term rise in the value of properties originally acquired for ranching (or as speculative investments) has, however, facilitated the transition to capital-intensive plantation agriculture. Landlords whose holdings have appreciated have been better able to enter partnerships with new investors on favorable terms and may, with more valuable collateral, obtain larger amounts of credit.

The transformation of the Sánchez family's Hacienda Taboga in Cañas exemplifies this process. Purchased in the early twentieth century with capital produced by the family's coffee investments in central Costa Rica (see Chapters 1 and 3), the hacienda's more than 10,000 hectares remained essentially intact after it was inherited by the original owner's children, who continued to use it for cattle ranching.[19] In 1958 the family formed a new corporation with Alvaro Jenkins Morales, a prominent PLN politician who was in the process of acquiring interests in numerous properties in Guanacaste. This company built irrigation canals, planted fields that eventually covered several thousand hectares, and installed a mill capable of crushing some 250,000 metric tons of cane per year, one of the largest capacities of any ingenio in the country.

Financial support came from loans of close to $1 million from the Banco Nacional de Costa Rica, $2 million from First National City Bank of New York, and $750,000 from the Latin American Agribusiness Development Corporation, a company founded by the Bank of America, which also loaned an additional $750,000 to Sánchez Cortés Hermanos, Limitada, a family holding company (Barry et al. 1983: 256). In 1974 a reorganization of Taboga brought in new capital from other Sánchez family members, including Rodrigo Arias Sánchez (brother of Oscar, the future president), as well as from wealthy U.S. and Central American investors, such as Nicaraguan industrialist

Alfonso Robelo and Carlos Borgonovo, a member of one of the richest coffee and cotton families of El Salvador (Achío and Escalante 1981; Colindres 1977).[20]

Foreign investment and finance have also been critical to the other privately owned ingenios in Guanacaste. The El Viejo mill was, like Taboga, originally conceived in the mid-1950s as a family business by owners of a large cattle latifundio. The Pintos, however, owners of Hacienda El Viejo, were relatively new to Guanacaste and, though wealthy, did not have a coffee empire in central Costa Rica that compared with that of the Sánchez family. Some of the capital for the ingenio came from sales of the parts of the latifundio farthest from the Tempisque River and least suited to cane agriculture. By the early 1960s several new partners had entered the business, including a diverse group of Costa Ricans, Cubans, and Central Americans (RP SM T49 F426-29 A311-14). In 1975 a group headed by Alvaro Jenkins, a partner in Taboga and owner of Hacienda Montezuma (see Chapter 8), acquired El Viejo, using a loan of approximately 50 million colones ($5.8 million) from the Banco Nacional.[21] Direct loans from U.S. banks were then used to expand the mill's operations (Achío and Escalante 1981).[22]

The state-owned CATSA (Central Azucarera del Tempisque, S.A.) mill, named after Federico Sobrado, was founded during the brief 1975 sugar boom and began production three years later on land that had once been part of the Hacienda Tempisque. The decision to establish an ingenio as part of the state development corporation CODESA reflected not only the favorable market conjuncture, but also concern that sugar production was not keeping pace with domestic demand.[23] Urbanization in the sugar zones of central Costa Rica had led to soaring land prices and had taken land out of agricultural production. Influential mill owners with PLN ties, such as Alvaro Jenkins, who had interests in the Taboga and El Viejo ingenios, were also important in the formation and subsequently the administration of CATSA.[24] Using loans from Adela Investment Company (see Chapter 6) and U.S. banks, as well as money from Costa Rican government bonds, CATSA installed the most modern mill with the largest capacity in the country (purchased second-hand in Puerto Rico), with a distillery for making fuel alcohol and an agricultural experiment station. Nevertheless, by 1982, as a result of poor administration, expensive investments in equipment and land (see Chapter 7), and increased production costs in the sugar sector as a whole, CATSA's fields, equipment, and plant had deteriorated and it was virtually bankrupt.[25]

Privatization of inefficient public-sector companies was one of the main aims of the U.S. Agency for International Development (USAID), which, beginning in 1983, played an increasingly active role in economic policy-making in Costa Rica (Shallat 1989). In 1983 the government, at the urging of USAID and international lending institutions, announced its intention to open bids to divest itself of CATSA. Meanwhile, USAID included a covenant in its 1984 assistance package for Costa Rica that limited banking-system credit to CATSA and other CODESA companies and required the development of a privatization plan.

The following year the government published guidelines for selling CODESA subsidiaries, including CATSA, to private buyers. Not surprisingly, however, given CATSA's high debt and the precarious state of Costa Rican sugar production and of world markets, it did not receive any acceptable offers. The Comptroller's Office (Contraloría General de la República) estimated CATSA's assets at 3.4 billion colones (approximately $68 million). In 1987, however, a USAID holding company, the Transitory Investments Fund (Fondo de Inversiones Transitorias, FINTRA), used U.S. Economic Support Funds to acquire CATSA's shares, which it then handed over for a paltry 450 million colones (approximately $9 million) to a cooperative that included some of Guanacaste's largest sugar producers, the *solidarista* associations that had supplanted the cane workers union at CATSA (see Chapter 8), and members of the company's technical and managerial staff.[26]

The Weak Foundations of Plantation Sugar Production

The Costa Rican sugar sector rests on three shaky pillars: the U.S. preferential market, the Costa Rican government's decision to maintain artificially high domestic prices, and demand for sugar derivatives, especially fuel alcohol. While CATSA's demise indisputably stemmed in part from inefficiencies like those that frequently plague publicly owned enterprises, many of its problems were common to the sugar sector as a whole. Indeed, privately owned refineries in Guanacaste scaled back investments or closed completely in the 1980s.[27]

Even though Costa Rican sugar producers are not as immediately vulnerable to world-market price fluctuations as are beef producers, their investment patterns and long-term prospects have been strongly conditioned by market forces and shifting state policies. In 1974 the exhaustion of world supplies and the expiration of the U.S. Sugar Act, which had assigned import quotas to producing countries, caused international prices to soar. Many thought that a new order in the world sugar market was at hand, in which producing nations would receive unprecedented, high prices. But in spite of momentarily encouraging perspectives in the world market in 1974–75, the Costa Rican sugar industry has depended heavily on access to the U.S. preferential market since the early 1970s. International prices were higher than domestic prices in 1968–76, but the percentage of production exported declined, generating less hard currency and raising the implicit costs of the large increases in domestic demand; indeed, total exports have stagnated since the early 1970s, a phenomenon attributable in large measure to U.S. quotas (see below).[28]

In contrast to export-oriented cattle ranching, sugar production relies heavily on imported inputs, and growers and refiners receive prices that are not tied to international dollar prices. This means that they, like most industrialists but unlike many agro-export sectors, were hard hit by the petroleum-price shocks of the 1970s and by post-1980 currency devaluations and inflation. Increases in labor costs measured in colones have a greater impact in the sugar sector, where producers are paid in local currency, than in other labor-intensive export sectors, such as bananas, where revenues are in dollars (or equivalent colones).[29]

Sugar growers and mill owners in Guanacaste also complain of occasional shortages of cane cutters during the peak harvest period. This seasonal scarcity, however, has not been sufficient to improve workers' bargaining position vis-à-vis their employers. Large numbers of Nicaraguans enter Guanacaste each year to work in the sugar harvest. Some secure the required permission from the Labor Ministry, but many simply cross the border and make their way to the plantations. There, in keeping with their long-standing reputation as exemplary workers, the undocumented immigrants are hired, frequently at considerable savings to employers, who, although paying them the same wages as their Costa Rican counterparts, may keep them "off the books" in order to save on legally mandated benefits.[30]

Another measure that ingenio owners have taken to maintain work force discipline, albeit at a high initial cost, is the use of mechanical harvesters. Each mill owns several of these machines, built in Australia and capable of cutting 150 to 200 metric tons of cane in eight hours—40 to 60 times more than a worker. Mechanical harvesters accounted for only about 12 percent of the cane harvested in northwestern Costa Rica in 1979, but on ingenio fields they may harvest as much as one-quarter of the cane (Barboza et al. 1981: III-46).[31] The ingenios employ the mechanical harvesters primarily on weekends when, under Costa Rica's labor law, they would have to pay loaders and other workers overtime wages.[32] This underutilization of machinery constitutes a threat to any effort by harvest workers to improve their situation. In 1977 at Taboga and again two years later at CATSA, mechanical harvesters were instrumental in undermining field workers' attempts to organize for higher wages and for recognition of independent unions (see Chapter 8). Thus, this investment in capital, although expensive and probably uneconomic if viewed apart from the social context in which it is used, contributes to the maintenance of low wages for that two-thirds of the ingenio work force which labors only during the harvest months.

The high sugar prices of 1980–81, rather than constituting a bonanza for Costa Rican producers, had two effects that exposed them to even greater uncertainty. The first was the United States' introduction of import quotas for the first time since 1974. These were based on each producing country's average sales over the seven years before 1982, thus limiting any significant expansion of exports to the one foreign market that paid prices that made it worthwhile to grow and refine sugar. The second perverse effect of high sugar prices was the increasing shift by U.S. soft-drink and food industries from cane sugar to less-expensive high-fructose corn syrup. While corn syrup compared unfavorably with cane sugar in some respects—it had higher transport costs and could not yet be satisfactorily crystallized—its widespread adoption in the preferential market meant that U.S. quotas and international prices were likely to remain low. The cyclical price rises that had occurred when world stocks dwindled (and that spurred the mid-1970s ingenio investment frenzy in Guanacaste) were now a thing of the past.

If sugar consumers sought alternatives in times of high prices, it was only logical that producers would seek other options when prices fell permanently. In the early 1980s, CATSA, Hacienda Taboga, and the LAICA embarked on an ambitious program to distill sugar into fuel alcohol for U.S and Caribbean markets. CATSA had been producing anhydrous alcohol for use in Costa Rican "gasohol" since 1980, though its distillery tended to operate well below capacity. In order to facilitate alcohol exports, LAICA constructed a large alcohol-dehydrating plant, storage tanks, and loading pumps at its Punta Morales sugar port. In 1985 CATSA and LAICA produced Costa Rica's first exports of 3.9 million gallons, sold to the United States at a price of $4.8 million (LAICA 1987: 31). The following year Taboga's distillery began production of alcohol for export as well. LAICA, hoping to operate its dehydrating plant during the six months of the year when local raw material was unavailable, also began to import hydrous alcohol from Spain, Brazil, Mexico, and Italy and to process it for reexport to the United States.[33]

Exports of fuel alcohol, derived almost exclusively from sugar produced at CATSA and Hacienda Taboga, have sustained the plantations during an otherwise unpromising conjuncture. While it is too early to tell whether alcohol exports constitute an economically viable alternative in the long run, the sharp fluctuations in exports in the first three years suggest something of the program's limitations. During the 1984–85 harvest, Costa Rica exported alcohol equivalent to 361,703 50-kilogram bags, or 7.65 percent of its total sugar production (LAICA 1987: 9). The following harvest, when CATSA used its entire output to produce alcohol (LAICA 1986: 38), exports skyrocketed to the equivalent of 674,517 bags, or 14.05 percent of total production. In 1986–87, however, the country only sent abroad alcohol equal to 38,216 bags, a minuscule 0.88 percent of total sugar output (LAICA 1987: 9).

Alcohol exports were intended to safeguard producers in the face of discouraging conditions in the cane sugar market. Yet in so doing they created other kinds of vulnerabilities and development dilemmas. Cane producers who had previously wished for falling petroleum prices that would decrease production costs now hoped that prices would remain high enough to maintain alcohol prices at satisfactory levels. The 1986 decline in world oil prices was, according to LAICA, the principal cause of that year's precipitous drop in alcohol exports (LAICA 1986: 38). Although foreign interest in fuel alcohol was likely to grow as a result of newly urgent concerns about fossil-fuel carbon emissions, pressures to adopt gasoline substitutes abated in the absence of strong economic incentives. In periods of high prices, protectionist efforts by U.S. producers of alcohol fuel have intensified, provoking tremendous anxiety among Costa Rican sugar producers (LAICA 1986: 39–40). Finally, with U.S. fuel alcohol distilled from corn, Costa Rican producers were required to compete in an environment in which their comparative advantages were diminished by the large government subsidies given U.S. grain producers.[34]

Rice: State-subsidized Plantations and Cheap Wage Goods

"The cultivation of rice in Costa Rica demands very little care and no irrigation to produce two crops a year of a very superior quality," a North American observer wrote shortly before the turn of the century (Niederlein 1898a: 93). In 1924 a Guanacastecan chronicler remarked in a similar vein, "The exuberance of the land in Guanacaste is demonstrated by the fact that each year there are two harvests of those articles which are [elsewhere] planted annually and three of those planted semiannually" (Cabrera 1924: 108). Drought was clearly less of a problem then, though grain-transport costs were universally considered astronomical. Presidential advisors studying the rice sector in 1931, for example, lamented the "curious" fact that "total [transport] costs from Siam to Puntarenas—3.21 colones [$0.80] per 100 kilos or 1.80 colones [$0.45] per 46-kilo quintal—are lower than from Guanacaste to Puntarenas. The costs from Guanacaste and other places to Puntarenas [are] immensely greater than the total costs from the Far East to Costa Rica" (Sáenz Gutiérrez and Merz 1932b: 13).

Given the physical isolation of Costa Rica's rice zones, it is not surprising that over one million kilograms of rice were imported each year by the early twentieth century, in spite of efforts since 1885 to levy duties on imports (Barboza and Aguilar 1982: II-1; Sáenz Gutiérrez and Merz 1932b: 6–7). Imports of rice appear to have been of less concern to successive Costa Rican governments than were imports of cattle and sugar, probably because in the first half of the century rice did not have the major place in the diet that it has today.[35] At that time the rice produced in Guanacaste and in the country as a whole was a small fraction of the quantity of maize harvested. While protection for the livestock industry had occasioned controversy (see Chapter 5), a diverse range of merchants, hacendados, and politicians—including Fernando Castro Cervantes and the entire Guanacaste and Puntarenas parliamentary delegations—actively backed protection for rice.[36]

The social crisis of the first years of the depression of the 1930s shifted the political balance against free trade advocates and in favor of protectionism (Calderón 1986: 123). When the legislature approved new rice-import duties in 1932, it also imposed reductions in cargo fees for railroads and coastal launches in the hope of providing a further stimulus to producers. With the importation from the United States in 1936 of the first improved varieties of seed, domestic production began to increase markedly, especially in the traditional rice-growing areas of Guanacaste and Puntarenas (Barboza and Aguilar 1982: II-14; Mata 1955; also see Figure 9.4). In the forefront of this process were a small number of Liberia cattle ranchers who purchased tractors and began to experiment with semimechanized grain production on small sections of their estates, using machinery in soil preparation and planting, and occasionally in harvesting, but not in weeding or cultivation.

Few Liberia residents recall any mechanization of grain production prior to the 1940s. But a will filed in 1937 by Edgardo Baltodano Briceño, a local rancher and politician, provided for the inheritance of 44 manzanas (30.8 hectares) of "mechanized grains," which suggests that this was not unknown in the 1930s (ANCR Protocolo Manuel Rodríguez Caracas 17701: 132). In 1950 the owners of Hacienda El Pelón de la Bajura reported, probably accurately, that the 500 manzanas (350 hectares) of rice and maize they cultivated with machinery the previous year constituted the "most extensive labor of that kind in the history of Costa Rica" (Sociedad Ganadera Murciélago 1950: 10). Some small harvesters had been introduced in the region during the 1940s. But in 1949 El Pelón's owners acquired a large caterpillar-driven harvester, "the first of its kind to arrive in the country." They boasted that "the still wet and muddy ground did not constitute the least obstacle for the machine. Its capacity for collecting fallen rice was a miracle for the many people who visited us to see it working. Its yield was double that of the small harvesters with which they had been working" (Sociedad Ganadera Murciélago 1950: 22).

This "miracle," when combined with new state incentives to capitalize agricultural production, had a rapid demonstration effect. By 1955 the use of agricultural machinery on lowland rice farms was "widespread" (Mata 1955: 31). Nevertheless, the adoption of modern capital-intensive cultivation methods in the 1950s was not without problems. The owners of El Pelón, for example, noted that, depending on circumstances, investing in agricultural machinery could be economically "favorable" or "disastrous" and that skilled tractor drivers were in very short supply. Betraying a vision of modern factories in the fields that was still novel in Costa Rica, they lamented that "it [was] extremely difficult to make the operators understand Taylorist principles adapted to the machinery" (Sociedad Ganadera Murciélago 1950: 11).

The opening of the Pan-American Highway in Guanacaste in the late 1940s facilitated access to extraregional markets, undercutting "Siam" and other foreign suppliers and providing a further incentive to modernize crop production. In addition, in the early 1940s, the U.S. aid agency STICA initiated the first sustained agricultural extension program in Guanacaste. Among other projects, STICA supervised the building of simple irrigation canals from small streams into farmers' rice fields, encouraged practices such as disinfecting seeds, and experimented with soil preparation and leveling techniques. The Banco Nacional agreed to assume responsibility for 70 percent of any losses that might be suffered by rice growers receiving STICA technical supervision (STICA 1949: 19).

In 1949, as a part of the developmentalist stance of the post-civil-war Costa Rican state (see Chapter 6), public-sector institutions, together with STICA, launched a major campaign to raise maize and rice production. The Joint Emergency Program for Maize and Rice involved STICA, the Ministry of Agriculture, and the National Production Council (CNP) in an intensified effort to produce and distribute improved seeds, to introduce mechanization of harvesting as well as of soil preparation and planting, and to develop appropriate "packages" of fertilizers and other inputs.[37] One important indirect consequence of this emphasis in the 1940s on the modernization and mechanization of rice cultivation was a shift in the geographic distribution of production away from mountainous areas in central Costa Rica to the flat lowlands of Guanacaste and Puntarenas. Since these regions were characterized by extreme concentration of land-ownership, the geographic shift and the encouragement given capital-intensive production contributed to further consolidating that small group of affluent proprietors who had large areas of flat land and who had begun mechanized rice cultivation in the 1930s.[38] The owners of El Pelón, while not eschewing the extensive government and STICA support given their mechanization and irrigation efforts, clearly recognized the potential political objections to this state backing for wealthy producers:

By mentioning the term *mechanized agriculture* the concept of *small agri-culturalist* is totally lost. By trying to develop this activity, with government organizations, it is possible that many will think of the benefits accruing to a small number of agriculturalists and even label them "privileged." This idea must be rejected and put aside, since if we plan to produce with greater effectiveness we have to think of the means and not the persons. (Sociedad Ganadera Murciélago 1950: 11, emphasis in original)

In comparison with the efforts made to improve rice yields, the STICA-government Joint Emergency Program gave little attention to maize production or research. Part of the reason for this was technical in nature; most high-yield varieties of maize tested in Costa Rica were developed in northern latitudes and were poorly adapted to different photoperiods.[39] Certainly more important, however, was the fact that maize was mostly a crop of smallholders who were largely unable, and in some cases unwilling, to assume the financial burdens and risks required to shift to mechanized modern farming. This complicated extension efforts and the introduction of input "packages" that could raise yields and generate larger marketable surpluses. While smallholders employing traditional technology grew and continue to grow rice, in the case of maize no powerful social group existed that was comparable to the large, modern, rice producers that were emerging in the northwest.

In subsequent decades, considerations of comparative advantage also influenced the expansion of rice cultivation and the relative stagnation of maize. In 1965 Central American Common Market (CACM) countries agreed to establish free trade in basic grains within the region. Since at the time most of the other countries had lower production costs than Costa Rica had, the free trade protocol was a disincentive for Costa Rican growers. This led the CNP to establish an internal policy opposed to the Central American agreement that would protect one basic grain out of the four covered by the treaty—whichever had the greatest comparative advantage in terms of technological development, productivity, investment capacity of the producers, and geographic location (Piszk 1982: 4). This was plainly rice, rather than maize, sorghum, or beans (the latter not truly a grain, but covered by the agreement nonetheless).

The oil-price shock of 1972–73 brought spiraling transport and production costs and greater expenditures for imported rice. This lent growing urgency to basic-grains policy.[40] In 1973 the government announced its opposition to the free trade protocol for grain and hiked support prices to encourage domestic production. The following year it announced a National Basic Grains Program with the objective of attaining self-sufficiency in rice, maize, sorghum, and beans. The tools employed to reach this goal were to be higher support prices, guaranteed purchase of harvests by the CNP, crop insurance, increased credit allocations, and the introduction of the first locally developed, high-yield variety of rice (called CR-1113).[41] Although the program planners foresaw the need for technical assistance to improve productivity, particularly for maize and beans, in practice their efforts were directed at bringing about large, short-term increases in output. Those best equipped to do this were the large rice growers of the Guanacaste and Puntarenas lowlands.

Political pressures also gave the Basic Grains Program a decidedly "pro-rice" bent. The rice growers Cámara persuaded CNP directors to establish a support price of 142 colones ($16.57) per 160-pound sack for the 1975 harvest, 14 percent above the price recommended by the program. This capitulation to politically influential lobbyists provoked the resignation of one CNP director, who charged—presciently as it turned out—that the high price for rice was unjustified and irresponsible and could lead to huge losses for the institution.[42]

The new crop-insurance policies issued by the state-owned National Insurance Institute (INS) permitted what one rice farmer termed "risk-free agriculture." In 1973–76 about 90 percent of all insurance allocations went to rice growers, most of them in Guanacaste (SEPSA 1982: 129–31). The INS insured crops for nearly 100 percent of operating costs and made virtually no effort to apply efficiency criteria. This created a boom atmosphere. One grower, reflecting the ubiquitous cynicism of the first years of the rice program, remembered that in Liberia then:

It was like a party. New agricultural equipment agencies opened, everybody suddenly had new pick-ups and cars, and everybody planted rice. They planted it up on the sides of the volcanoes, in places where there was clay soil, and near the beach where there was only sand. Estimated minimum yields were 1,000 kilos per hectare and anything less got insurance. We [on a relatively well endowed farm] got 1,700 kilos per hectare. Sometimes insurance inspectors were bought off even if the crop was harvested. People were screwing the government through the INS.

In 1976, the third year of the program, too little rain fell, and rice growers besieged the INS with claims. In Liberia alone, 98 percent of the 8,697 hectares planted in dry-land rice were considered lost, and owners were indemnified at a cost to the INS of $2.4 million (SEPSA 1980b: III-275). Similar losses, totaling $14 million, occurred in other areas of Guanacaste and Puntarenas. In addition to the INS's losses, the CNP incurred a deficit of some $7 million from exporting excess 1975 output at prices below those it had paid growers (Piszk 1982: 16). The latter, while cushioned from the full effect of the disaster by the artificially high profits of the preceding two years and the INS policy of absorbing losses, were in many cases still heavily in debt for their fixed capital, only a small portion of which was counted by the INS as part of each year's operating budget.

The huge losses suffered by the INS and the CNP brought about a rapid reevaluation of basic-grains policy. Government specialists undertook detailed agronomic and meteorological studies, which led to the definition of "red," "yellow," and "green" zones, characterized by high, moderate, and low levels of risk. In the "red" zone the INS would not insure rice, while in the "yellow" zone it would cover 50 to 70 percent, and in the "green" zone 100 percent, of the risk. Growers in the "red" and "yellow" zones were encouraged to consider cotton as an alternative to rice. Even in the "green" zone, rice growers were urged to plant sorghum immediately following the rice harvest in order to take advantage of otherwise underutilized machinery and land. The banks also reduced credit allocations for rice and increased those for alternative crops, while the CNP cut rice-support prices, deemphasizing the production of exportable surpluses.

From 1977 to 1979, however, Costa Rica continued to export substantial quantities of rice at prices only 50 to 60 percent of domestic wholesale prices. In March 1981, at the Congress of the Basic Grains Producers Cámara in Liberia's Hotel El Sitio, several speakers, including the owner of Hacienda La Flor, former president of the Republic Daniel Oduber, expressed pride that CNP rice-support prices had "at last" fallen below world prices and that growers were no longer subsidized in this way by the state. Not mentioned in the self-congratulatory speeches, however, was that the new situation, far from being a conscious CNP policy or Cámara objective, was simply an unintended result of the sudden currency devaluation that began in late 1980. And without a hint of self-consciousness about possible logical inconsistencies, Cámara officials at the same 1981 Congress cheered the results of recent increases in the sorghum-support price, which, though in effect a subsidy, had nonetheless generated more output and permitted Costa Rica to attain self-sufficiency in hogs, poultry, eggs, and powdered milk. The advancing plans for government-sponsored irrigation of a large area of central Guanacaste (see next chapter) also caused considerable enthusiasm. Each 5,000 hectares of irrigated rice could double the country's rice exports, one speaker asserted with conviction, and if 15,000 additional hectares of irrigated rice were planted in Guanacaste, rice would actually supplant coffee as Costa Rica's most important source of foreign exchange.

The euphoria of early 1981 gave way to despair by the end of the year. Cámara leaders, swallowing their earlier pride about growing rice without subsidies, were locked in a battle with the CNP to secure support-price hikes that would keep pace with inflation. Low rainfall, shortages of fertilizer, uncertainty about support prices, and chaotic conditions in the agricultural-input market contributed to the first significant drop in rice production in Guanacaste since the 1976 drought—a decline of some 65,000 metric tons compared with 1980. Millers and large growers engaged in widespread hoarding in anticipation of price increases. The worst, however, was yet to come.

In 1982 the deepening economic crisis and an ecological disaster highlighted once more the tenuous nature of Guanacastecan rice production. With spiraling inflation and a 450 percent currency devaluation in just two years, the state could no longer maintain both low consumer prices and high support payments for growers. While the price of manufactured inputs for rice production, such as fertilizers, insecticides, and herbicides, increased about 500 percent between early 1981 and mid-1982, bank estimates of production costs increased only 247 percent (BCCR 1981, 1982). Actual total production costs, however, rose well beyond bank estimates, though growers who earlier had stockpiled inputs and replacement parts had significantly lower costs than those having to acquire these materials on the market.

The inflation and devaluation of 1982 also had unanticipated, formidable consequences for the financial system. Production costs per hectare, estimated by the banks at 20,472 colones (about $512), were, for the first time in history, higher than land prices, which ranged from 12,000 to 18,000 colones ($300 to $450) per hectare. Since land had usually been the only guarantee offered in return for production credit, many rice growers were unable to secure loans in time to begin cultivation. Because of this unprecedented situation, the INS agreed to offer a special policy, which covered nearly 100 percent of actual production costs and made it possible for growers to obtain loans without other collateral. Nevertheless, with 100 percent inflation and anticipated profit rates of only 25 to 35 percent, many growers were discouraged. Of the 53,000 hectares that the government projected would be devoted to rice in Guanacaste, only about 40,000 were actually planted.

The agriculturalists' disillusionment had another effect that threatened to undermine the grains sector. During the rapid devaluation of 1981–82, used agricultural machinery in distributors' inventories was frequently undervalued with respect to its dollar value. Indebted and sometimes ingenuous rice growers often sold their machinery to Panamanians who appeared in Guanacaste offering seemingly astronomical colón prices for tractors, combines, and earth-moving equipment. On several occasions, customs officials seized shipments of agricultural machinery that were being smuggled into Panama. With a more stable economy and the U.S. dollar as its official currency, Panama was protected against the devaluation that affected Costa Rica. Panamanians, already accustomed to operating in dollars, were more cognizant than many Costa Ricans of real replacement costs for machinery and were able to profit from the economic crisis affecting their northern neighbors.

The weather in 1982 compounded the economic difficulties facing the rice sector. In May the rains came with a fury, flooding fields and roads and isolating numerous villages in the Tempisque lowlands. Many farmers had just finished planting when the floods came and had to plant again when the waters receded. Others had to delay planting longer than usual and to rent extra machinery to complete their labors as fast as possible. Then, after the *veranillo*, or "little summer," of late June, when the rains usually lessen or stop for two or three weeks, the rains did not return. By September it was clear that most crops would be lost. All of the 40,000 hectares of rice were damaged; 12,000 hectares did not germinate, and much of the remaining area did not achieve the 75 percent germination required to collect from the INS. Nearly 6,000 hectares of maize and 1,000 hectares of cotton were lost, and farmers remarked that the sugarcane had simply stopped growing. The INS estimated that rice farmers' losses alone would reach 400 million colones, approximately $8.9 million, and declared that while it did not have funds to pay, the government would find the money somewhere (*La Nación*, 21 Sept.

1982, 4A). The state suffered additional losses through the CNP, since no foreign exchange could be earned from rice exports, and scarce dollars had to be used to import grain.

The Basic Grains Program—really the rice program—achieved some notable successes. Average yields in Guanacaste, for example, rose rapidly, approaching three metric tons per hectare by the early 1980s. But the costs of these advances were thrown into stark relief by the 1980–82 economic crisis. While in one sense the CNP was subsidizing consumers, who paid fixed retail prices below the commodities agency's costs, in reality society as a whole was subsidizing producers, since consumer prices remained well above international ones.[43] And this subvention consisted of more than the difference between artificially high support prices and artificially low consumer prices that contributed to the growing CNP deficit. Large insurance indemnifications not covered by farmers' INS premiums, inexpensive credit, and a host of direct and indirect subsidies depressing input and capital costs exacerbated public-sector and banking-system deficits.

By 1984, with Costa Rica embarked on a program of economic stabilization and structural adjustment (see the Conclusion), the CNP, under pressure from international lending institutions to reduce its immense deficit, dramatically reversed its intervention in the rice market. For the first time in recent memory, it lowered the rice-support price (SEPSA 1989: 62). It then announced that it would no longer consider itself obligated to purchase (and then to export at a loss) rice that could not be absorbed by the domestic market. In effect, the commodities agency asked farmers and private rice millers to assume many of the risks previously borne by the state, including the possibility that surpluses might have to be sold abroad at prices below the costs of production. Finally, a number of the regulatory functions previously carried out by the CNP were shifted to a newly founded Rice Office (Oficina del Arroz).

Lest these measures should cause too much economic disruption and political discontent, however, the CNP raised the rice-support price in August 1985 and also guaranteed that it would buy the entire sorghum crop, a measure intended to placate influential rice farmers, many of whom also grew—or could grow—sorghum. The boost in the producers' price for rice was not accompanied by similar increases in prices charged wholesalers, retailers, or consumers, which were set by the Ministry of Economy, Industry, and Commerce (MEIC) rather than by the CNP. This placed mill owners in a squeeze, since they were required to pay growers the higher minimum price set by the CNP but could only sell to wholesalers and retailers at the old prices set by the MEIC. The mill owners in turn decided to squeeze the farmers by refusing to pay the new minimum price. When in late 1985 it appeared that much of the harvest might be lost as a result of this deadlock, the CNP stepped in and promised to compensate the mill owners for their "losses" by selling them its own stocks at a low, subsidized price.

The CNP commitment to purchase the entire sorghum crop suggested that the agency had not entirely grasped the lessons of its dismal experiences with rice. Freshly harvested sorghum, like other grains, requires immediate drying or it rapidly deteriorates. The CNP's drying plants in Guanacaste and northern Puntarenas were equipped to process a harvest of approximately 12,000 metric tons, yet the first 1985–86 harvest was about two times greater than CNP planners expected. Farmers had obviously planted larger areas, but the use of better inputs caused average yields per hectare to jump as well. The CNP had to contract with three Liberia rice mills (and others in northern Puntarenas) to dry the sorghum it had promised to buy. And even though the plants worked around the clock, trucks had to wait several days to unload their cargo, which was often simply poured onto warehouse floors to await processing. Manufacturers of animal feed, who were expected to buy the grain from the CNP, complained that the long waits and careless processing had lowered the sorghum's quality. Then, as if to drive home to growers a warning about the ailing state of the institution with which they were dealing, the CNP paid for many sorghum deliveries with bad checks.

After 1985 the CNP and the new Rice Office left the rice support-price unchanged for three years and, together with the banks, discouraged production in Guanacaste outside of irrigated areas.[44] Although yields per hectare continued to rise, in part because of the increasing importance of irrigated farms, production did not keep up with demand, and the self-sufficiency achieved in the mid-1970s was lost within a few years. During the 1987–88 growing season, Costa Rica imported some 20,000 metric tons of rice from the United States and Thailand (*La Nación*, 11 Aug. 1988, 4A). The following year, the economy minister, Luis Diego Escalante, estimated that the country would have to import about half its total consumption (*La Nación*, 12 Aug. 1988, 8A). Remarkably, according to the new rules of the game, it again made more sense, as in the 1920s, to ship rice from "Siam" than to grow it in Costa Rica.

In Guanacaste the rice plantation as a model for replacing the extensively operated cattle hacienda had enjoyed a brief vogue, but ultimately climatic, trade, and institutional obstacles blocked its development. Virtually the only rice growers unaffected by the disasters of the 1970s and 1980s were those with irrigation works. Beginning in the 1940s, large landowners, particularly in the Liberia area, began acquiring pumps and building canals for irrigating rice fields. Since the mid-1970s, growing extensions of irrigated rice have been planted each year and account for an increasing proportion of rice area. On parts of the cattle estates, thousands of dollars per hectare have been invested in digging canals, acquiring pipes and pumps, and leveling fields with laser-guided tractors. This substantial investment has been rewarded by yields reaching five or more metric tons per hectare, nearly double those of dry-land rice. In a few cases, enterprises that once only produced livestock are now dedicated almost exclusively to irrigated rice. More typically, major rice producers, such as Hacienda El Pelón de la Bajura, Ranchos Horizonte, Hacienda Asientillo, or Hacienda El Tempisque, reap much larger profits from rice than from other production lines, but also maintain expensive breeding animals on small areas of irrigated pasture and other cattle on marginal lands.

Just as the earlier geographic shift of rice cultivation to the flat latifundio lands around Liberia had negative distributional consequences, the policy of favoring irrigated farms had significant social implications. Irrigated rice cultivation is clearly a success inasmuch as crop losses are virtually unknown. The high investments involved, however, mean that this production system is, with few exceptions, available only to the wealthiest farmers. Rice production as a whole was already highly concentrated in 1973, before the Basic Grains Program, with 66 farms of over 500 hectares (1.4 percent of total farms) accounting for over half the total harvest (CAP 1973). After the Basic Grains Program, in 1984, the number of Guanacaste farms growing rice declined from 4,620 to 3,262 (29 percent), and the concentration of output grew markedly, with the top fifth of farmers harvesting about nine-tenths of the crop (compared with about eight-tenths in 1973) (see Figure 9.7). As the next chapter points out, government plans to irrigate a vast area of Guanacaste and to "reorder" land tenure in the irrigation district

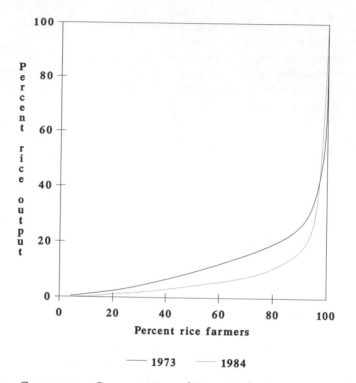

Fig. 9.7. Guanacaste: Concentration of Rice Production, 1973 and 1984. Source: *CAP* 1973, 1984.

have attempted, with a few notable but limited successes, to modify these extreme inequalities.

Cotton: "White Gold"?

Cotton was a crop of some importance in Guanacaste from the preconquest period until well into the nineteenth century, when German geologist Karl Von Seebach reported seeing it in Cañas and what is now Carrillo (1974: 220, 235).[45] In 1914–19, during World War I, and again during the late 1920s, farmers in Orotina in northern Puntarenas grew cotton, but pest infestations were a serious problem (Matarrita Acuña 1987: 11; Salas Marrero and Barahona 1980: 662). The depression-era protectionist measures that spurred production of beef and rice had no parallel in the case of cotton, although government officials, inspired by Nicaragua's early success as an exporter, began to offer farmers free seed and technical advice in the late 1930s and early 1940s.[46] Optimists predicted that cotton would come to be the "white gold" (*oro blanco*) of Costa Rica, much as coffee had earlier been the "grain of gold" (*grano de oro*) that was the basis of the country's development (*El Guanacaste*, 6 Nov. 1938, 1, 2, 6; and 20 Oct. 1941, 1).

Field trials of cotton in the Clachars' Hacienda El Porvenir in 1937 produced "extremely abundant" harvests, but no facilities existed for ginning the fiber. The experiment was an agronomic success but an economic failure (*El Guanacaste*, 23 Jan. 1937, 1). In the late 1930s a Japanese exporters association made trial plantings in northern Puntarenas and offered local agriculturalists free seed, credit, and supervision.[47] By 1941, however, when pest problems remained unsolved and with the approach of World War II, this project was abandoned as well (*El Guanacaste*, 6 Nov. 1938, 1, 2, 6; Sáenz Maroto 1970: 150). Costa Rican farmers who had entered cotton production near the Japanese project continued for another year before losing hope (Salas Marrero and Barahona 1980: 662). Two years later a Nicoya farmer briefly raised interest in cotton again when he produced yields on a trial plot more than twice those reported from northern Puntarenas (*El Guanacaste*, 20 Jan. 1943, 2). Formidable pest-control difficulties and the absence of adequate credit, extension, and marketing and processing facilities meant that cotton production, despite occasional successes, had little real promise.

Expensive, highly toxic arsenic compounds had been cotton growers' only means of chemical pest control during the experiments of the 1930s and early 1940s. After Swiss scientist Paul Müller discovered the insecticidal properties of DDT in 1939, however, it became possible not only to kill cotton pests much more effectively and inexpensively, but to control the malaria endemic in the coastal lowlands, which constituted Central America's best potential cotton zones. The widespread introduction of DDT and related compounds in the late 1940s coincided with a major surge in European and Japanese demand for cotton, based on the reconstruction of mills razed in World War II. In the early 1950s the demand fueled by the Korean War caused prices to soar again (Williams 1986: 16; see Figure 9.8).

Blessed with "the availability of cheap land and labor, and probably the highest yields received from rain-grown cotton anywhere on

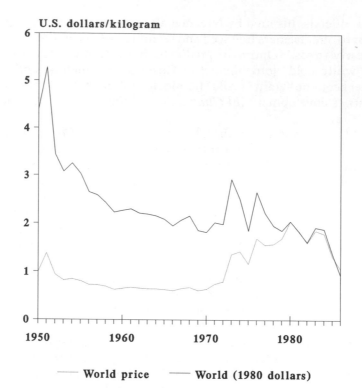

Fig. 9.8. World Market Cotton Prices, 1950–1986. Source: World Bank 1988.

earth," producers expanded fields along the length of the Pacific coastal plain between southern Mexico and Guanacaste (Parsons 1965: 151).[48] In Nicaragua, El Salvador, and Guatemala, cotton rapidly became an important export. In Costa Rica, Guanacaste was the only region with ecological conditions comparable to the rest of the Central American fertile crescent, so cotton (for this and other reasons discussed below) never assumed such importance in the country's economy. Nonetheless, during certain critical junctures, cotton has been widely viewed as a potential force for transforming Guanacaste's extensively operated cattle haciendas into highly productive plantations.

The technology behind what geographer James Parsons called "the Central American cotton revolution" (1965: 151)—new insecticides, chemical fertilizers, and machinery—was complemented by policies geared to favorable market conditions. In the 1950s the Costa Rican government employed its dual-exchange-rate policy to encourage cotton production, authorizing sales abroad at the "free" rate rather than the overvalued domestic one, thus giving exporters more colones for each dollar (Bulmer-Thomas 1987: 157, 362). In most respects, though, state measures were much the same as those that stimulated growth in beef, sugar, and rice: increased credit allocations, crop insurance, and extension, and improved transport and processing infrastructure. In several key ways, cotton policies were less contentious than those for other agricultural products. In contrast to beef and sugar, cotton was not subject to quota restraints in the major markets. And its domestic price, unlike that of rice, a staple of the Costa Rican diet, was not set by the state or of immediate concern to masses of consumers. As a result, local textile manufacturers, paying international prices for their raw material and unconcerned about whether it came from Costa Rica or abroad, did not constitute an antagonistic interest group for the politically well placed, affluent cotton entrepreneurs.

Three cotton booms hit Guanacaste: the first came during the Korean War "price bonanza"; the second peaked in 1967 and collapsed precipitously by 1971, in a period of generally stable but moderate international prices; and the third peaked in 1977, stimulated by the new popularity of denim jeans and by mounting costs for petroleum-based synthetic fabrics, and was followed by a sharp decline (see Figure 9.9). Cotton production in Guanacaste was complicated by frequent drought during the early part of the growing season and, still more common, by excess rainfall in the later part. At the end of each boom, excess rainfall and pest infestations, which tended to worsen in humid weather, brought crop losses and elevated operating costs. By the 1970s boom, INS crop insurance covered much of the risk, and cotton was, after rice and sorghum, the most widely insured crop in Costa Rica. But cotton production also required larger investments in expensive chemical pest control precisely in the worst, high-risk seasons. In those years, agriculturalists' operating costs frequently exceeded both bank cost-estimates and loans and INS coverage. Many declared bankruptcy or sold parts of properties in order to pay debts. Even more than with rice, cotton required producers to have sources of operating capital beyond what the banks provided. In "good" years, when little rain fell at the end of the cycle and few unusual pest problems appeared, cotton proved highly lucra-

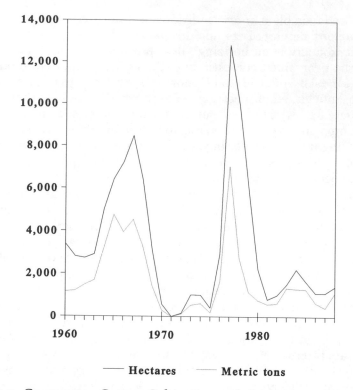

Fig. 9.9. Guanacaste: Cotton Cultivation and Production, 1960–1986.
Sources: ALCORSA, unpublished data; SEPSA, unpublished data.

tive. But yields fluctuated markedly from year to year, and the risks
were, in the opinion of many agriculturalists, unacceptably high.

The alternation of "good" and "bad" years is basically unpredictable, dictated by nature and beyond the control of producers or planners.[49] Poor weather is more likely to strike cotton fields in Guanacaste than those further north in Nicaragua and El Salvador. Though
northwestern Costa Rica is called the "dry Pacific," precipitation
patterns there are influenced to a greater degree by the almost year-
round rains of the Pacific coast of southern Costa Rica and Panama.
Monthly and yearly rainfall variations are greater and less predictable
than in the cotton zones of Nicaragua and El Salvador.

One economic consequence of this marginal ecological situation is
that Costa Rica has long had the highest production costs and the

lowest yields of any cotton-producing country in Central America. Compared with producers elsewhere, Costa Rican farmers require extra machinery to complete soil preparation and planting on days when weather permits, and they have to spray more because of the greater likelihood of excess rain. Producers with a substantial and diversified economic base are better able to risk and sustain the periodic losses bound to occur in some years because of adverse natural conditions. Even though producers of varying technological capabilities grew cotton until the second boom, which peaked in the 1960s, high costs and high risks have meant that in subsequent years only a few farmers have planted the crop and that they have done so almost exclusively with the most advanced technology.

Added to the natural obstacles facing growers are a series of government measures that were intended to stimulate cotton production but have not always had that outcome. During the 1960s boom, cotton harvested in Guanacaste was processed almost entirely in a gin on the Pan-American Highway in Cañas. Small quantities were also ginned in Nicaragua. In 1972, when the state actively began to promote direct public investment in agroindustries as a means of diversifying exports, CODESA founded a subsidiary called Cottons of Costa Rica (Algodones de Costa Rica, ALCORSA). In 1977 ALCORSA installed two gins near Liberia capable of turning out 200,000 pounds of fiber per day. It was hoped that if this did not place Costa Rica firmly on the path to becoming a cotton exporter on the scale of Nicaragua, it would at least permit the domestic textile industry's needs to be met.

ALCORSA's first year of operations inspired little confidence. Installation of the gins and warehouses was not completed on time, and harvested cotton had to be stored in the fields and insured against possible fire hazards. Outdoor storage inevitably increased the dirt content of the fiber and decreased its quality. When the cotton was finally brought to ALCORSA's storage facilities, much of it burned up in the warehouse. Following this disaster, the remaining unginned cotton was sold in Nicaragua at a fraction of the prevailing market price.

In subsequent years ALCORSA's record improved, although the failure to consolidate a strong sector of growers meant that the gins never operated at even one-half their capacity, due to a lack of raw material.[50] With most private producers retreating from cotton, ALCORSA and its directors became increasingly prominent within the small group of agriculturalists daring to plant the crop. Thus, for example, in 1980–81, by far the largest plantation in the country, at La Palma de Abangares, was on land belonging to Hacienda Solimar, of which ALCORSA's director was a board member.[51] The production process, according to one of the foremen, was supervised directly by ALCORSA, which also absorbed the entire output.

The prominence of these cotton growers and this coincidence of interests between private interests and the quasi-public ALCORSA was, at least in part, the result of a credit and insurance system that places obstacles in the way of those without large capital reserves or state backing. Bank estimates of operating costs in 1982 reached 38,463 colones (approximately $850) per hectare, an amount more than two times the prevailing price of land on which cotton is grown.[52] This raised the same difficulties in using land as collateral for production credit that were described above in the case of rice. Equally important, however, in a cultivation system with high operating costs is the timely payment of loan monies needed at key points in the production cycle. Here the banks have, according to growers, a remarkably poor record, which, added to the other risks involved, constitutes a major disincentive to those without other sources of operating capital.

Working conditions on Guanacastecan cotton farms are in several respects worse than in the rest of the agricultural sector. Payments to harvesters are lower than in other sectors of the agricultural economy, and the twice-weekly aerial sprayings of insecticide cause frequent illnesses among laborers, although the practice described in some other Central American countries of spraying while workers are in the fields has not been reported or observed. This intensive use of chemicals is also a cause of complaint by those residing in cotton-growing areas, as in La Palma de Abangares, where squatters' shacks line the roadsides just beyond the fences of the cotton fields. In addition to complaining of frequent pesticide-related symptoms (headaches, rashes, eye and skin irritation), peasants believed that chemicals used on cotton killed citrus and other crops.[53]

Because of these poor conditions and because the cotton harvest, the most labor-intensive part of the production process, coincides with the sugar harvest, only those workers who cannot find employment as cane cutters seek work in the cotton fields. In practice, the labor force used to harvest cotton is composed of three categories of particularly vulnerable workers: women, children, and migrants—frequently undocumented—from Nicaragua and El Salvador. Young

Costa Rican men in cotton-producing areas often remark that "cutting cotton is work for Nicas and Guanacos (Salvadorans)," and that they prefer traveling to cut cane at a distant sugar mill to picking cotton near their own village.[54] A cotton harvester's earnings are substantially lower than those of a good cane cutter. Women and children who pick cotton, like undocumented migrants, have few alternatives and are less likely to object to dangerous working conditions or low wages.

Following the disastrous, weather-induced rice losses of the mid-1970s, government planners limited rice cultivation to irrigated areas and "green" zones, especially in the Tempisque lowlands. Cotton, they hoped, would become the major crop in lands that were marginal for rice because of insufficient rainfall. Indeed, for several years, officials unveiled grandiose plans. In 1980, for example, they called for growing 10,000 hectares of cotton, though only about 3,000 were actually planted, and in 1982 they set a goal of 24,000 hectares, though less than 1,000 were planted. Throughout the 1980s cotton production remained at modest levels, an activity for producers with large cash reserves and state backing. Until its dissolution in 1988, the state-owned ALCORSA was by far the largest grower, cultivating at least 45 percent—and in some years over 90 percent—of the total cotton area (SEPSA 1986: 61).

ALCORSA's directors affirmed in 1984 that the company had become profitable, that prospects for cotton expansion were bright, and that it had "succeeded in encouraging Guanacastecan agriculturalists to plant cotton."

It provides them technical assistance, basic agronomy and entomology courses, and does not spare any effort in making available to them the modern technology used in its own fields and with which it has had such success. As an employer of so much labor, ALCORSA has persuaded many Guanacastecans who had emigrated to return to the plains (*pampa*), motivated by the availability of work where they have grown up. (*La República*, 9 May 1984, 23)

Despite these embellished claims, ALCORSA's demise was not long in coming. As a CODESA subsidiary, ALCORSA was put on the auction block along with CATSA and other state-owned companies targeted by USAID's privatization campaign (see above). The comptroller general had appraised ALCORSA's assets at 310 million colones (about $6 million). The first bids, in 1987, were so "exiguous" that CODESA canceled the offering. The following year, however, ALCORSA's two gins and its other assets were sold for 46 million colones (approximately $575,000) to a private corporation and a cooperative composed primarily of wealthy members of the Liberia elite and cotton growers who had been functionaries of ALCORSA (*La Nación*, 23 Dec. 1987, 4A; 1 July 1988, 4A).

As had occurred with the CATSA sugar refinery, these assets— acquired through the nation's increased indebtedness—were then transferred at bargain prices to a small number of investors, some conveniently organized as members of tax-exempt cooperatives. This latest state and USAID giveaway to private entrepreneurs, an essential plank in the government's economic liberalization program, was intended to be the subsidy to end all subsidies. But it underlined once again the very fragility of plantation production in Guanacaste. Nobody in the private sector felt sufficiently enthused by ALCORSA's offering to proffer a bid that came close to the appraised value of the company's assets. In the face of climatic obstacles, intractable insect infestations, and high risks, even the magic of the marketplace was apparently not enough to awaken entrepreneurial interest or to ensure a long-term, cotton-based transition from hacienda to plantation.

The Limits of Agricultural Intensification

The experiences with crop agriculture discussed in this chapter suggest that formidable ecological and institutional obstacles limit the intensification of crop production in Guanacaste and, consequently, the large-scale implementation of a plantation development model. The underutilized hacienda, with its ground rent or "institutional rent" potential, continues to be a rational enterprise, if rationality is understood as long-run portfolio management in a context of risk. Sugarcane and irrigated rice are partial success stories, though the former is highly vulnerable to market swings and the latter continues to benefit from state subsidies and to "externalize" costs at the expense of surrounding natural and human communities. Cotton and especially dry-land rice involved enormous losses both to the state and to private growers. The state's losses, however, particularly during the rice boom of the 1970s and the privatization campaign of the 1980s, were in effect transfers of public resources to small numbers of well-placed individuals.

This and other kinds of "institutional rent" were the sine qua non of those intensified kinds of agricultural production that emerged alongside the extensively operated livestock haciendas. Without massive public subsidies, the significant, but still often tentative, steps toward plantation agriculture would have been far fewer. Even though much capital for plantations has come from outside the region, in many cases from foreign banks, the state's capacity to continue to subsidize Guanacastecan crop production is likely to be a key determinant of future plantation expansion. Ultimately, this is a question not only of political will and the class character of the state, but also of the outcome of the economic structural adjustment process under way in Costa Rica since the mid-1980s.

The possibilities of irrigation agriculture have been proven on some of the large rice and sugar estates. The problem of cotton producers has, of course, too often been *excess* rather than insufficient rainfall and is therefore less amenable to this kind of solution. But if irrigation is indeed the only feasible means of overcoming the ecological limits imposed by highly variable and unpredictable rainfall, it raises a series of thorny social, political, and even ethical issues (discussed in the next chapter). Foremost among these is access to water, potentially as conflictive a question as control of land and one with profound implications for the future course of the region's development.

IO → The Politics of Water and Landlord Resistance

It is now the final stage of traditional struggle . . . to prevent livestock producers from being despoiled and humiliated.
—President of the cattle lobby, 1977

In the irrigation district we have carried out our nondrastic, nonviolent agrarian reform.
—Irrigation agency official, 1988

With that little story (*ese cuentico*) about water they have us working like oxen!
—Bagaces agrarian reform beneficiary, 1988

In Guanacaste the problems of inadequate and excess rainfall had long raised interest in the possibility of a large-scale water control project in fertile areas of the province that were underutilized because of drought or flooding. As early as 1946, David Clachar, one of the province's most forward-looking hacendados, wrote of the Tempisque River:

In spite of its beauty, [and] of its being in places up to 100 meters wide; in spite of its peaceful current, which in some villages one has to observe thoughtfully in order to tell which way it is flowing; in spite of the many thousands of liters of water that pass through its course each second, water and energy we are unfortunately losing every day; in spite of all this, day by day, year after year, with all [this] beauty and tranquillity, the villages and towns along its banks, from Salto de Ruiz to Bolsón, are threatened with ruin and misery and death. (Clachar 1946: 363)

Clachar went on to describe a devastating flood in 1907 when inhabitants of several villages along the Tempisque's west bank had to abandon their homes. Trees uprooted by rising waters formed a dam 500 meters long, which permanently changed the course of the river. He also noted that since 1906 "the river bed had climbed 40 inches, or 1 inch per year, this being inevitable because of . . . erosion and the accumulation of sediments" caused by logging in the cordillera (p. 364). In the face of this "bitter reality" Clachar suggested that eventually the region would have to choose one of two options: dredging some 100 kilometers of the river from its mouth in the Gulf of Nicoya to Las Trancas, near Guardia; or diverting the river to the Pacific at Bahía Panamá by building a dam 10 kilometers inland at Salto de Ruiz. The latter plan would, he argued, "easily irrigate thousands of hectares of flat lands [which are] magnificent for agriculture . . . [and] would give electricity to all of Guanacaste" (p. 365).

Clachar neglected to mention that several thousand hectares of the land that would be irrigated if the Tempisque were diverted along this route happened to belong to members of his family. The combination of self-interest and altruistic regional advocacy in his discussion of the Tempisque foreshadowed the future political significance of control over water resources in an area where latifundista and peon alike were accustomed to thinking only in terms of who possessed or owned the land. Clachar's musings about the dangers of the great river, and his inspired solutions, which must have seemed almost fantastic to many of his contemporaries, also presaged major efforts to redirect the course of the development of the province.

One of the key issues Guanacaste faced in the 1970s and 1980s was whether massive public investments in water control and irrigation would primarily reinforce the economic strength of large landowners or, alternatively, would benefit small and medium-size agriculturalists. This was a matter that went beyond the hacendados' continuing efforts to assure flows of subsidized credit and other forms of "institutional rent." It called into question not only the type of production system—extensive cattle grazing—that had long been the backbone of the region's economy, but the social relations and land tenure patterns that had permitted the reproduction of the dominant groups. For Costa Rican society as a whole, irrigation implied increased indebtedness to foreign creditors, but it also raised the possibility of new levels of productivity indeed of entirely new models of development—that could help in delivering the country from the economic crisis that loomed in the late 1970s and struck with force at the beginning of the 1980s.

Irrigation may have been one of the few solutions to the problem of drought for Guanacaste agriculturalists, but even by the early 1980s very few of the largest landowners had leveled much of their properties, acquired pumps, or built canals (see Table 10.1). Hacienda Ta-

TABLE 10.1
Guanacaste: Irrigated Farms, Early 1980s

Farm	Source of water	Irrigated hectares	Percent hectares
CATSA (CODESA)	Tempisque	1,500	18.8%
DAISA (CODESA)	Bebedero and Abangares	100	1.3
Paso Hondo and San Luis (ITCO)	Bebedero and Abangares	200	2.5
Hacienda El Real	Tempisque	200	2.5
Rancho Gesling	Tempisque	500	6.3
El Pelón de la Bajura	Tempisque	500	6.3
Hacienda Taboga	Bebedero and Cañas	3,000	37.5
Others	various	2,000	25.0
TOTAL		8,000	100.0%

SOURCE: SENARA.
NOTE: "Others" includes Ranchos Horizonte (formerly Azucarera Guanacaste) and Haciendas El Tempisque, Las Trancas, Asientillo, and San Jerónimo.

boga and the state-owned CATSA sugar plantation had the largest irrigated areas in the province. Together, these two properties controlled more than half of the 8,000 irrigated hectares in Guanacaste. After the Compañía Bananera in Limón province, they were the largest irrigated farms in the country. But in Guanacaste they were lush green exceptions in a landscape still dominated by vast expanses of pasture and brush.

The immense start-up costs for large-scale irrigated agriculture constituted a major obstacle for even the wealthiest landowners. Yet when banks or foreign partners could provide the necessary capital, few hacendados were willing to abandon entirely extensive cattle grazing and shift all their land into intensive irrigated-crop agriculture. Tax laws that penalized investment, uncertain markets, capricious weather conditions, and the heavy weight of "costumbre," or tradition, all contributed to this caution and seeming lack of entrepreneurial zeal (see Chapters 7 and 9). Irrigation required new levels of agronomic and administrative sophistication and investments in human capital, which most landowners were reluctant to undertake.

Regulations governing water use did not provide incentives for large-scale irrigation either. Agriculturalists who pumped water from the Tempisque River or its tributaries paid a fee for each cubic meter extracted, and although this fostered efficient use of water, it hardly encouraged irrigation of large areas.[1] Instead, irrigated-crop agriculture became an activity that complemented extensive cattle grazing on properties located along the major watercourses. Elsewhere, unless landowners could easily tap subsurface water or build holding ponds to capture and store water from smaller, seasonally dry rivers, irrigation possibilities were extremely limited.

In the mid-1970s, however, the Costa Rican government began to take major strides in irrigating a vast area of central Guanacaste. At first the hacendados raised ferocious opposition to the plan, when major changes in land tenure were proposed in the legislature and then defeated under pressure from the Cámara de Ganaderos. Later, their attitude changed to one of accommodation, as traditional latifundistas began to recognize, as David Clachar had done in the 1940s, that if no restrictions were placed on farm size, the irrigation plan would bring them untold advantages.

Initially the threat of state expropriations of latifundios in the project zone frightened many hacendados into fragmenting or selling their properties. By the late 1970s, when it appeared that agrarian reform efforts might be limited, a new type of latifundismo emerged based on speculative acquisition of large properties soon to be irrigated at public expense. But within a few years, during the 1980s, in part as a result of conditions attached to the multilateral credits that financed the project, the state acquired and then distributed to small agriculturalists major portions of what had been the principal latifundios of the Tempisque Valley. Latifundismo did not die entirely with the coming of the Guanacaste Irrigation District, but by the late 1980s land distribution within this one region became significantly more equitable. The large landowners that survived were not the "crazy gringos" or the ambitious newcomers who arrived in the 1960s and 1970s, but the Sánchez, Stewart, and Clachar families and others that had acquired land in Guanacaste in the early twentieth century or before.

Early Irrigation Plans

David Clachar's ambitious scheme to alter the course of the Tempisque River attracted little attention. But the argument that irrigation, drainage, and hydroelectric projects were essential for Guanacaste's development became a basic premise of post-1948 modernization plans. In the early 1950s the Ministry of Agriculture (MAG), STICA (Servicio Técnico Inter-Americano de Cooperación Agrícola), and engineers from the U.S. Department of the Interior began investigating the possibility of irrigating a 33-by-5-kilometer strip between Guardia and the Cañas River, along the west bank of the Tempisque (Bel Ingeniería 1978: 4; Mauro 1957; SNE 1981). Technicians considered much of the soil east of the big river too thin or too sandy, though their feasibility studies were no doubt influenced by the fact that the east bank was a largely unpopulated area, concentrated in a few giant latifundios, and almost entirely lacking in roads and other infrastructure. The plan called for the construction of a dam, a generator, and an artificial lake at La Cueva, just north of Liberia, another dam at Salto de Ruiz, and a pair of canals running south to Filadelfia and Belén. It also stressed the need for dredging the Las Palmas River, since it caused "practically all the flood damage" in most years (Romig 1957: 27).[2] The total cost of the project was estimated at 116 million colones, approximately twenty million dollars (Romig 1957).

The feasibility studies of the 1950s never went beyond the drawing board, although a few private landowners began to build irrigation works at their own expense on haciendas like El Pelón de la Bajura. On El Pelón and the few other haciendas that began to experiment with irrigation, leveling the soil, the most expensive initial investment, was generally carried out by constructing small ridges around the fields and then allowing the soil to settle during repeated flooding over a period of years.[3] El Pelón's experience with rice demonstrated that yields on irrigated fields were four or more times those of dryland rice. Rice could also be planted two times each year and provide excellent harvests. Other haciendas began to irrigate sugar fields and increased yields as much as three times.

In the early 1970s the MAG and the Costa Rican Electrical Institute (Instituto Costarricense de Electricidad, ICE), the state utility company, began a second series of irrigation and hydroelectric feasibility studies. In 1973, as international petroleum prices soared, ICE decided to begin work on a large-scale generation project using the Arenal River in the Cordillera de Tilarán. Since the hydroelectric plan involved increasing flows of water down the Pacific slope of the mountains, the government also founded a coordinating commission for irrigation and drainage studies, which was charged with finding effective means of utilizing the water once it had passed through the generating turbines.[4]

The Arenal-Corobicí Hydroelectric Project

In 1974, with a $50.5 million loan from the Inter-American Development Bank (IDB), which covered about one-third of the total costs, ICE began construction on the first phase of the project: a dam and an artificial lake formed from the headwaters of the Arenal River on the Atlantic slope of the cordillera (IDB 1980: 5–6). The creation of this lake—situated at 530 meters above sea level, with a capacity of 1.5 billion cubic meters of water and an area of 75 square kilometers—required the relocation of several small villages. Waters from the lake were diverted at a rate of some 80 cubic meters per second through a tunnel across the continental divide to the first generating station on the Santa Rosa River, which flows down the Pacific slope. Further downstream, at Sandillal, at an elevation of 95 meters above sea level, ICE built a second dam and generator where the Santa Rosa and Magdalena rivers meet and flow into the Corobicí.

Two IDB loans totaling $60 million financed approximately one-third of this second phase of the project (IDB 1980: 6). Waters from the Magdalena dam flow into the south and west canals, planned to be 42 and 66 kilometers long, respectively. When completed, the south and west canals will provide water to an area of 47,000 hectares. In 1981 ICE began studies for the construction of an additional dam and lake at La Cueva, northwest of Liberia, where the waters of the Tempisque would be diverted to a 40-kilometer-long north canal providing irrigation to 15,000 hectares. In addition, feasibility studies completed in the late 1970s called for the integration into the irrigation system of existing waterworks on the Tenorio and Blanco rivers and the construction of additional dams and artificial lakes along several other rivers flowing down the west slope of the cordillera, including the Enmedio, the Piedras, and the Tenorito (Bel Ingeniería 1978). Finally, when engineers detected significant groundwater reserves along the west bank of the Tempisque, ICE made plans to integrate that zone as well into the irrigation project by digging large numbers of wells.[5] In the mid-1980s project planners designed an additional canal, 15 kilometers long, in the Zapandí subdistricts on the west side of the

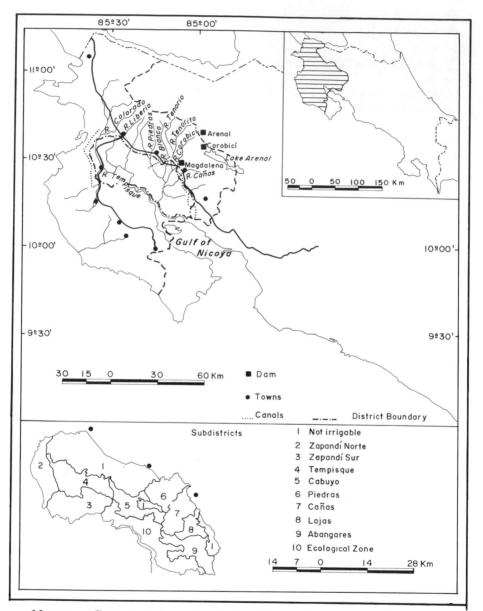

Map 10.1. Guanacaste Irrigation District (district boundaries, infrastructure [canals], rivers, subdistricts).

Tempisque with the goal of eventually providing water to an additional 20,000 hectares.

Goals of the Irrigation District

As plans advanced the borders of the district and the zones to be irrigated were modified. By the mid 1980s planners spoke of irrigating a total of 67,000 hectares, almost 8 percent of Guanacaste province, within an irrigation zone totaling approximately 187,000 hectares (about 18 percent of the province).[6] The parts of the project zone that will not be irrigated consist of hilly terrain, towns and villages, "ecological zones" and wildlife refuges totaling some 32,000 hectares, and poor soils not suitable for intensive use. The goals of the irrigation plan, as described in official proclamations, were (1) to use to maximum advantage the waters from the Arenal-Corobicí Hydroelectric Project in a region with serious problems of drought and flooding in different seasons of the year; (2) to improve living conditions in the region by generating employment, redistributing income, and changing cropping systems; (3) to increase agricultural and livestock production and productivity; (4) to promote integrated regional development with complementary agricultural and industrial sectors and an expanded service sector; and (5) to contribute to the improvement of the country's economic situation by exporting fresh and processed agricultural products (Presidencia de la República 1981: 7–8; SNE 1981: 3). Planners estimated that by incorporating large extensions of underutilized land and introducing a diversified cropping pattern that would make optimal use of available resources, it would be possible to increase the value and volume of production from the project zone four to ten times (Bel Ingeniería 1978: 21). They calculated that the project, when completed, would generate an additional 40,000 year-round jobs (SNE 1981: 4).

The achievement of these diverse objectives, however, did not depend only on appropriate technological solutions. Irrigated agriculture requires an extremely large capital investment per unit of area and careful handling of every step of the production process by trained personnel. For perishable export products, such as melons, speedy packing and transport were essential, as well as strict adherence to production schedules that would permit placing winter vegetables and fruits in the all-important U.S. market during the few months when demand peaked.[7] Irrigation also required significantly more work, often involving much longer days during the entire year, and this in turn implied altering both employers' and employees' traditional conceptions about remuneration and the labor process.

Years after irrigation had become a reality, one beneficiary of agrarian reform at Bagatzi in southern Bagaces remarked on this shift away from the old conceptions about the "workday" and the afternoon "faena," which still predominated in dry areas of Guanacaste. Trying at sunset to extract a mired tractor from an irrigated rice field with the aid of several fellow *parceleros*, some rusty chains, and a battered pickup truck, he commented bitterly that if he had a regular agricultural job he would have been home resting at 3:00 P.M. Then he expressed annoyance at how government functionaries, "preaching" about the benefits of irrigation without mentioning its drawbacks, had enticed him long ago to sign up for an agrarian reform project. "Look at us now," he declared, "we're covered with mud! With that little story (*ese cuentico*) about water they have us working like oxen!"

From the days of the first proposals for irrigation in Guanacaste it was clear that the large cattle ranchers who owned most of the land in the planned district would never "work like oxen." But it was also far from evident that they would be willing or able to work like real capitalists, investing the resources necessary to irrigate crops and completely changing their traditional reliance on extensive grazing. In addition, the plan's mention of income redistribution aroused suspicion among the usually conservative cattlemen and exacerbated their negative visceral reactions to any mention of irrigation or agrarian reform.

From the beginning, the extreme concentration of landownership in the irrigation district dominated discussion (see Table 10.2 below and Appendix C). In the early 1970s the Stewart brothers alone still owned over 40,000 hectares in the proposed district and together with five other large landowners controlled over half of the total 103,000-hectare district and the 74,000 hectares of potential irrigated area. Over three-quarters of the potential irrigable area belonged to the 22 farms possessing over 700 irrigable hectares. Critics asked whether even these wealthy latifundistas had the capital necessary to change their extensively used rangelands into irrigated fields. They also raised the more fundamental issue of whether it was fitting that massive public expenditures and increased state indebtedness should benefit only a handful of individuals who historically had shown little interest in intensifying the use of their huge holdings.

Agrarian Reform and the Irrigation District

The struggle over the kind of land tenure that would exist in the irrigation district came to the fore in early 1975 with the beginning of legislative debate over proposed regulations for the project zone. The political climate in Costa Rica at this time was marked by divisions over deepening state involvement in various sectors of the economy and, more particularly, by sharp debate in the Legislative Assembly over three different agrarian reform bills that sought major changes in the existing legislation passed in 1961.[8] The Instituto de Tierras y Colonización (ITCO), the agrarian reform agency, began in 1974 to encourage the formation of collectively run "community enterprises" (*empresas comunitarias*), a policy that aroused suspicion among conservative landholding groups.[9] In addition, in 1974–75 the number of land invasions by squatters rose in Guanacaste, reflecting in part peasant awareness of the greater political will of some sectors of the government to resolve agrarian problems in their favor.[10]

In this none-too-propitious political atmosphere, a government-sponsored bill was introduced for the Moracia Irrigation Project in Guanacaste.[11] The most controversial clause of the bill, and the one that was to arouse the greatest opposition from Guanacaste's large landowners, called for the "freezing" (*congelamiento*) of all lands in the irrigation district—a complete ban on sales, mortgages, or other potentially speculative transactions in which lands were transferred or used as collateral. The legislation also sought to establish procedures for expropriation with compensation of "excess" land in the district and for its distribution to landless peasants, including those displaced by the artificial lake behind the Arenal dam. Large landowners and their supporters in the Assembly viewed the bill as a pilot project, which, if successful, would be extended to the entire country and would threaten the sacrosanct right of private property.

The Cámara de Ganaderos de Guanacaste responded immediately to this perceived attack on its members' interests. In an assembly held on April 13, 1975, on the outskirts of Liberia in the rustic bullring of the Capulín Exhibition Field, the organization adopted a number of resolutions, some merely rhetorical and others that involved concrete action against the irrigation-project bill. Because these measures illustrate the ideological tone of the large ranchers' campaign and because they prefigured future Cámara actions, they are worth quoting at some length. Among the points resolved were these:

To combat energetically as a dangerous practice the invasions of farms encouraged by professional agitators and to demand efficient and impartial action in the application of existing laws in order to solve these problems. To oppose vigorously the proposed agrarian laws that go against existing constitutional precepts. To exert effort so that the changes that may be made in land tenure in Costa Rica are within the framework of the Agrarian Reform proposal elaborated by the Federación de Cámaras de Ganaderos de Costa Rica, which has already been given to the Executive as a contribution to the search for democratic solutions to the agrarian problem. To form a National Agrarian Policy Commission for the defense of the legitimate rights of agriculturalists and cattlemen. . . . To struggle so that political and ideological currents cease distorting the image of the entrepreneur and so public opinion comes to have a better concept of this essential element in the economic life of free societies. . . . To name three members from the Province of Guanacaste to reinforce the National Agrarian Policy Committee and that this committee gather all human and material resources in order to oppose the bill vigorously, pointing out all its defects. . . . That the problem of the so-called Arenal Irrigation District not be unlinked in its focus and treatment from the general agrarian problem of the country. . . . That the bill to freeze lands sent by the Executive to the Legislative Assembly be withdrawn. (CGG Actas, 6: 237–38)

The Cámara assembly, whose report was signed by Enrique Montiel, a congressional deputy and prominent Liberia landowner, also named a commission to meet with President Daniel Oduber. Although no record of this meeting appears in the Cámara's minutes, this was likely one of the first occasions on which Oduber, whose own Hacienda La Flor near the Liberia airport linked his interests to those of the local elite, was urged to act in accordance with his position as a major landowner rather than as a public official with broader responsibilities for the general good (see Barahona Riera 1980: 329). This first Cámara meeting on the irrigation project also sent messages of appreciation to several deputies who had supported Cámara positions on the irrigation district and named delegates to the National Agrarian Policy Commission, the proposed lobby that was to be an alliance of the Guanacaste Cámara with other sympathetic interest groups.[12]

Among the major political obstacles the Cámara confronted in its effort to discredit and defeat the irrigation district bill was the stance of the Bishop of Tilarán, Román Arrieta, whose diocese included the site of the proposed project. Arrieta, an outspoken proponent of agrarian reform, met with Cámara representatives in mid-April 1975.

According to a report of that meeting, the bishop stressed that he was against

freezing lands, establishing [maximum permissible] farm sizes, expropriations, land invasions, usurpation, all that which might be against private
property, which is against the Constitution of Costa Rica. He declared that
because of his condition as a child of God he is against communist ideology
and that he is the first anticommunist in the country. [But also] he affirmed
that land tenure, call it Agrarian Reform or no, is a problem that we have to
confront. (CGG Actas, 6: 249–50)

The National Agrarian Policy Commission created by the Guanacaste Cámara de Ganaderos mobilized widespread opposition to the
Moracia Irrigation District bill among the national cattlemen's federation, other entrepreneurial groups, and the conservative newspapers, whose editorial pages were filled with articles denouncing the
project. Considerable evidence suggests that at this time some Guanacastecan cattlemen were contemplating extralegal measures to
pressure the government, including withholding livestock from markets, blocking highways, and organizing armed groups (Barahona
Riera 1980: 320–32, 367).[13] One cattleman, quoted in the press as
demanding "independence" from Costa Rica for Guanacaste, declared:

Today they want to cause us excessive injury (*ultrajar en exceso*), to dispossess us, with a Marxist type bill, of that which we most love, our land.
That of our farms, that of our house lots. But we will know how to defend it
heroically. With reason. With words. *But also with actions, if reason does
not triumph, if words fail.* (*Excelsior* [San José], 25 Apr. 1975: 3, cited in
Rodríguez Solera 1988: 1/8, original emphasis)[14]

As a result of these pressures, Oduber agreed to withdraw the bill
for "further study" and to form a commission to draft a new agrarian
reform measure that would cover not only the irrigation district but
the rest of the country as well.[15] Among the representatives named to
the commission were spokesmen for the Cámara de Ganaderos and
other agricultural-sector Cámaras. In spite of having representatives
on the commission drafting the new bill on land tenure "reordering"
or reform, members of the Guanacaste Cámara were concerned about
"possible surprises when the Mixed Commission makes known" the
bill.

Using Abangares hacendado Carlos Segnini Lamas as an intermediary, the Cámara "respectfully demanded" that it be given access to the draft bill for agrarian reform before the president of the Republic or the Assembly in case there were any changes it deemed necessary (CGG Actas, 6: 291—13 June 1975). Remarkably, as Segnini reported back to the Cámara two weeks later, the legislative commission agreed to this demand and allotted up to three days for a meeting with the cattlemen at Liberia's Hotel Las Espuelas ("The Spurs"). Cámara leaders Gilberto Fernández and José Joaquín Muñoz Bustos argued that the Cámara should have access to a copy of the bill before meeting the commission and that if it did not, a tape should be made of the proceedings and teams of note takers organized to record the discussion on paper (CGG Actas, 6: 298–99—27 June 1975).

Throughout late 1975 and early 1976 the cattlemen and the legislative commission continued negotiations and discussions. In mid 1976 Guanacaste Cámara leader Muñoz Bustos reported that in the latest version of the agrarian reform bill it was possible to "appreciate the handling of national criteria, which he regarded as good fruits of the Cámara's campaign" (CGG Actas, 7: 333—2 July 1976). Because the bill was no longer strictly concerned with Guanacaste, Muñoz proposed that the national cattlemen's federation realize a detailed legal study of the measure's contents as soon as the commission finished its work. Although the national federation apparently agreed to have its legal consultants undertake such a study, for unknown reasons it failed to do so. This provoked a furious reaction from the Guanacaste Cámara. Muñoz charged that the national federation was blaming the Guanacastecans for not sponsoring the study, was engaging in "deceptive and frustrating action," and was "neither serious nor sincere and rather than benefiting, they hurt the national cattle producers." He called for "a process of repairing" the national federation (CGG Actas, 7: 359–60—13 Aug. 1976). Presumably this meant making the national organization a more effective advocate for the interests of the large ranchers who dominated the Guanacaste regional Cámara, the export-beef trade, and the national livestock industry.

In November 1976 Cámara leaders found out that the commission had added to the agrarian reform bill a clause establishing an upper limit of 1,000 hectares on the size of properties.[16] The president of the national federation fell into line behind the militants of the Guanacaste Cámara, writing them:

In the face of such a situation we believe that we must put all the members of the national livestock sector on a war footing (*en pie de lucha*). . . . Let all and every one of your associates know of the danger facing the livestock indus-try. . . . Our intention is that everyone be saturated with the danger to their rights and that they be ready to respond to the call of this Organization, which will possibly organize a meeting of force at the national level and will also realize campaigns through the press in which we appeal for your collab-oration. (CGG Actas, 7: 464—19 Nov. 1976)

The cattlemen grew even more alarmed when a draft version of a proposed irrigation bill was released.[17] A Cámara lawyer in San José termed this bill "very strong and dangerous" and proposed calling upon legislative "deputies of recognized fighting capacity and mak-ing them aware of the misgivings and fears of this Cámara" (CGG Actas, 7: 470—26 Nov. 1976). Other ranchers criticized the "harmful statism" behind the measure and raised questions about how the bill interpreted the "freezing" of lands and how expropriations would be compensated. Once again Cámara members agreed to initiate a cam-paign to bring their point of view to business groups, newspapers, and other communications media. Ten thousand colones (approximately $1,200) were appropriated

in order to be able to make criticisms and offer alternatives based on the positive experiences of other countries and to oppose [the bill] with concrete arguments, with possible points of unconstitutionality . . . to underwrite the expenses of technical studies in constitutional and administrative law and in agricultural economics . . . so as to support technically the eventual opposi-tion to the Project. (CGG Actas, 7: 472–73—26 Nov. 1976)

By the beginning of 1977 Cámara leaders were pessimistic about their chances of defeating the compromise agrarian reform bill and the new irrigation districts measure. Muñoz Bustos told assembled Cámara members in Liberia:

In the present year of labors it would seem possible to derive the conclusion that little can be achieved by the traditional means of struggle, such as meetings, interviews, letters, press articles, paid advertisements, and similar things. It would seem that other economic and political interests, at times acting in concert, in addition to the ineptitude of the state bureaucratic apparatus, nullify to a large degree the work of associations that, like ours, seek to defend the private entrepreneurs who produce the national wealth. It would seem then that it is necessarily time for a different struggle, notori-ous, perhaps spectacular. This will make indispensable the creation of nuclei of "cattlemen's activism" which would realize loud and effective actions through a coordinated program over a great part of the national territory, which through a sharp increase in their activities succeed in "impacting" on the power centers, so that as a result of that type of pressure measures are taken to benefit the livestock sector, which otherwise will be delayed or never taken. . . . It is [now] the final stage of traditional struggle, about to enter an urgent stage, to prevent livestock producers from being despoiled and humiliated, for which reasons it is necessary that the cattlemen rise up in twelve activist nuclei in order to make felt the defense of their rights. (CGG Actas, 8: 20–21—30 Jan. 1977)

The minutes of the Guanacaste cattle Cámara do not indicate what concrete activities, if any, the "activist nuclei" carried out. Ranchers interviewed were reticent about providing further details. Nevertheless, it appears that the Cámara's efforts achieved at least some of their intended effect. By April 1977 a Cámara official reporting on conversations with a sympathetic deputy noted that "the first [agrarian reform] project" did not have the necessary votes to win Assembly approval.[18] The irrigation districts measure, he said, would probably require an executive decree to pass because it too lacked support. The official also suggested that the February 1977 decree creating the Arenal Electrical Energy National Reserve was "unconstitutional, and for that reason should be combatted by hiring a constitutional lawyer to thus prevent the Irrigation Project." (CGG Actas, 8: 141—29 Apr. 1977)

The following year, with the inauguration of the new administration of President Rodrigo Carazo, the executive branch continued to search for an institutional framework for an irrigation district that would use waters from the Arenal hydroelectric project. It sent a bill to the Assembly proposing reforms in the law that established the National Subterranean Water Service (Servicio Nacional de Aguas Subterráneas, SENAS). In October 1978 the president of the national cattlemen's federation, a Guanacastecan landowner, cited reports that an upper limit on farm size might be included in the measure and warned "that in essence the project involves an agrarian reform" (CGG Actas, 9: 60–61—27 Oct. 1978). Mario Rivas Muñoz, another Guanacastecan hacendado who was also an Assembly deputy, reported apprehensively in early 1979 that he thought the bill would pass (CGG Actas, 9: 124—2 Feb. 1979), but in the end the cattle lobby and its supporters managed to assure its defeat.[19]

Unable to secure passage of a suitable law, the Carazo administration established the legal framework for the Guanacaste irrigation district with an executive decree in 1979. The decree made the National Irrigation Commission part of the National Electricity Service (SNE) and created a special Department of Irrigation and Drainage to administer the Guanacaste irrigation zone. While the decree provided an institutional basis for planning and building necessary infrastructure, it did not address the thorny issue of land ownership and distribution. It also suggested that the Legislative Assembly lacked the consensus and political will necessary for a sustained effort at agrarian reform, in or outside the irrigation zone.

If the minimal goals of the original irrigation project bill could only be established by executive decree, the compromise agrarian reform measure fared somewhat better. A version of this bill passed in 1982 and, among other things, assured that the agrarian reform agency, now renamed the Agrarian Development Institute (Instituto de Desarrollo Agrario, IDA), was placed on a sounder financial footing. It is not surprising, however, that the controversial upper limit on the size of properties was eliminated in the final version, just as it had been in the SENAS bill. Thus the legal machinery for administering a massive irrigation project was created without any significant changes in the regulations governing land tenure and access to resources.

The cattle lobby's intense opposition to the perceived attack on its traditional way of life, as well as its fears of agrarian reform, contributed to the weakening and dispersal of the bureaucratic structures created to direct the irrigation project. But in the late 1970s and early 1980s, as leading cattlemen increasingly came to understand the potential benefits of irrigation without reform, their hostility abated. This changed attitude permitted the PLN administration of Luis Alberto Monge to obtain legislative approval in 1983 for a new public-sector autonomous institution called the National Subterranean Waters, Irrigation, and Drainage Service (Servicio Nacional de Aguas Subterráneas, Riego y Avenamiento, SENARA). SENARA, an umbrella organization that absorbed all earlier agencies concerned with irrigation, assumed responsibility for coordinating a wide range of activities within the Guanacaste district, including most aspects of the agrarian reform.

SENARA divided the irrigation project into two districts: Arenal, with about 48,000 irrigable hectares along the east bank of the Tempisque; and Zapandí, 20,000 hectares along the west bank of the Tempisque in Carrillo and Santa Cruz.[20] The new agency, with a fresh

$20.6 million IDB loan, initiated demonstration projects in a MAG experiment station and several farms acquired by IDA, the agrarian reform agency, some 6,000 irrigable hectares in all.[21] In 1988, with additional financing of $28.7 million from the IDB and $10.5 million from the Venezuelan government, SENARA began a second stage of the project intended to irrigate an additional 14,000 hectares. An important stipulation in the IDB agreement was that half the irrigated land in each project subdistrict be in farms of under 50 hectares.[22]

The two instruments to be used in meeting this goal of greater equity were a continuation and strengthening of existing agrarian reform efforts and the application of a progressive water tariff. The push for agrarian reform involved the state in purchasing more and more land in the district, even as public-sector companies such as the Central Azucarera del Tempisque (CATSA) and Desarrollo Agroindustrial (DAISA) were sold to private (or nominally cooperative) investors. These government purchases of land, however, did not mean the creation of a permanent sector of publicly owned enterprises within the irrigation district like those that had been founded in the 1970s as part of CODESA, the Costa Rican development corporation. Rather, the state functioned in effect as an intermediary, purchasing land from private owners and distributing it in small lots to reform beneficiaries, who generally received both provisional titles and the responsibility of paying mortgages.[23]

Loans from the IDB for the irrigation project also required the establishment of water tariffs that would cover operating expenses and permit the recuperation of public-sector investments. Approved in 1985, the tariff schedule was in actuality a tax on producers in zones officially declared "under irrigation" ("puestas bajo riego"), which was intended to ensure greater efficiency and equity (La Gaceta Oficial, 27 Nov. 1985: 19–21; SENARA 1986: 88).[24] In order to encourage irrigation and greater efficiency, the tariff applied to each property was based on its irrigable hectares rather than the cubic meters of SENARA-supplied water consumed; beginning in 1986, the tariff was applied in zones declared "under irrigation" whether or not the particular farm was using the available water. The total tax of 4,400 colones (initially about $88) per irrigable hectare was estimated to be no more than one-quarter of the increase in profits obtainable with irrigation. It was to be applied in stages over a five-year period for farms over 100 hectares, while farms between 51 and 100 hectares and those under 50 hectares were only taxed at the full rate after periods of seven and ten years, respectively. Moreover, in the smallest properties, between 5 and 25 hectares, most of which were agrarian reform plots, the state committed itself to building all necessary secondary canals and other infrastructure. On the largest farms, owners were to absorb the cost of constructing secondary canals, and SENARA assumed responsibility only for connecting them to the main irrigation network. Finally, the tariff code established sanctions for producers who failed to irrigate their entire irrigable area within the periods specified by SENARA or who were otherwise inefficient in their use of water, as well as for those who did not pay their tariffs promptly.

The moment that particular zones were declared "under irrigation" became a critical concern for landowners in the district. This official declaration, with its attendant water fees, usually came only long after the largest farms were thoroughly involved in irrigated agriculture. But the imposition of the water tax became one more cost that large and small producers had to consider. While its intended—and actual—effect was to fragment and democratize property, it also contributed to a winnowing process within the group of large landlords. Those best able to face the new costs were those whose outlays for other production factors—especially land—had been particularly low. In effect, this meant that the large landowners who would endure in the irrigation district would not be the newcomers, however apparently prosperous they might be, but the old latifundista families. Cecil Hylton's Ranchos Horizonte, for example, had become one of the largest irrigated-rice producers in Guanacaste, but by the end of the 1980s it had been sold to yet one more group of wealthy outsiders (see Chapter 7). Surviving across the Río Las Piedras, the Stewarts' Hacienda Mojica remained an ironic reminder that in the irrigation district a latifundista heritage could be one element that facilitated modern production and efficiency, even long after most of the original latifundio had been divided and sold.

Changes in Land Tenure

In spite of the hacendados' campaign against both the irrigation district and the agrarian reform measures, by the late 1970s Guanacastecan landlords and prodevelopment forces in the Costa Rican state and legislature gradually reached an accommodation. As early as 1975, President Daniel Oduber articulated elements of this new understanding in a letter to a legislative commission:

We who have land in that zone are happy to know that the nation's effort to give us water, just as it has given us highways, roads, and electricity, can bring us to levels of production similar to those reached in other countries. And we are very aware that land with those [irrigation infrastructure] investments is going to be worth much more and it will be possible for us to feel that Costa Rica considers the needs of him who works the land. (*Excelsior* [San José], 4 May 1975: 1–2, cited in Rodríguez Solera 1988: 176)

The landowners had never opposed irrigation per se, only the clauses limiting farm size and "freezing" land transactions, which they viewed as an attack on property rights. Since such limits on land ownership and speculation had died in the Legislative Assembly, the hacendados eventually came to appreciate the advantages of an irrigation district in which they could maintain large properties and engage in normal real estate transactions. The irrigation at public expense of lands previously used only for extensive grazing promised extremely high returns. Similarly, since state investments greatly increased land values in the district, opportunities for profit taking grew significantly.

Another factor influencing hacendado behavior in the last half of the 1970s was the increasing activity of ITCO, the agrarian reform agency. Before 1975 ITCO had established only nine reform projects in Guanacaste.[25] Its strategy had involved founding colonization projects in remote areas, resolving land occupations—usually through state purchase of disputed lands then sold to peasant occupants—and titling farms in zones where peasants had acquired rights through long-term use of their holdings. In the mid-1970s, however, ITCO began a more aggressive effort to acquire land for distribution to landless peasants. The agency approached several hacendados whose estates it considered underutilized and urged them informally to intensify their use of the land or face expropriation; many smaller landowners received similar warnings. At times, ITCO also arranged purchases, though sometimes of poor-quality lands whose influential owners received high prices from the state.[26] In particular, ITCO's acquisition of more than 18,000 hectares of David Stewart's Hacienda El Cortés, coming only nine years after a long court battle ended with the expropriation of Hacienda Miravalles, seemed to augur ill for the Guanacastecan latifundista class.[27]

Pressures from ITCO and the possibility that an upper limit might be placed on holdings in the irrigation district or even in the entire country had a discernible effect on land distribution. In the irrigation district several landowners began to divide their properties, either selling large and medium-size parcels or creating corporations that became the legal owners of parts of their holdings. Between 1971 and 1976, for example, Donald Stewart divided the more than 20,000 hectares that remained of his share of his father's ranch into parcels of several hundred hectares each, most of which he then sold (CN G4–1-2, 160–410). He retained some 2,600 hectares of the best land in the center of the old Hacienda Mojica and some smaller sections of other properties. Other hacendados took advantage of government offers to divest themselves of lands, which were then used for agrarian reform projects or for state-owned agroindustries, such as CATSA and DAISA.

The data on irrigation district land tenure in 1973 and 1978 in Tables 10.2 and 10.3 are not strictly comparable, since the boundaries of the zone grew somewhat in that period and the 1978 figures do not include farms under 20 hectares. Table 10.3 includes only privately owned properties, not agrarian reform projects or state-owned enterprises. On the basis of this information, it is nonetheless possible to describe the principal changes in land distribution in 1973–78. The area controlled by agrarian reform projects and publicly owned companies expanded dramatically; these are listed in Table 10.4 and by 1987 totaled over 28,000 hectares, roughly 16 percent of the irrigation district area. The largest properties underwent considerable fragmentation; this was epitomized by the division of the Stewart brothers' massive latifundio, but was evident as well in several other large estates, such as Hacienda Tempisque. The area in privately owned properties over 3,500 hectares in 1978 was only slightly over half that of 1973. At the same time, the area and number of farms in medium-size properties of 35 to 70 hectares declined sharply. This can probably be attributed in part to the consolidation of production units in the category of the next largest size (between 70 and 350 hectares).

Despite the fragmentation of the largest properties, the rise of a significant public and agrarian reform sector, and the relative growth in importance of medium-size farms, land tenure in the district was still extremely concentrated in 1978. Table 10.3, which describes the 1978 distribution of privately held properties of over 20 hectares, indicates that five owners controlled 47 percent of the district area. If

TABLE 10.2
Guanacaste Irrigation District: Land Tenure, 1973

Farm size (hectares)	Farm units N	Farm units percent	Farm area (hectares)	Farm area percent	Average farm size
<0.7	53	10.7%	14.8	0.0%	0.3
0.7–2.8	97	19.6	134.9	0.1	1.4
3.5–6.3	33	6.7	156.8	0.1	4.8
7.0–13.3	56	11.3	527.5	0.5	9.4
14.0–34.3	64	13.0	1,400.8	1.2	21.9
35.0–69.3	68	13.8	3,116.4	2.8	45.8
70.0–349.3	85	17.2	13,224.4	11.7	155.6
350.0–699.3	16	3.2	7,755.3	6.8	484.7
700.0–3,499.3	16	3.2	24,668.0	21.8	1,541.8
3,500+	6	1.2	62,404.3	55.0	10,400.7
TOTAL	494		113,403.2		229.6

SOURCE: Salas F. 1974, Table 5.

NOTE: Original data in manzanas with continuous size intervals. Area includes district's 1974 boundaries, south of the Pan-American Highway on the east side of the Tempisque River. The area on the west side of the Tempisque was added to the district later.

TABLE 10.3
Guanacaste Irrigation District: Land Tenure, 1978

Farm size (hectares)	Farm units N	Farm units percent	Farm area (hectares)	Farm area percent	Average farm size
20.0–34.9	3	2.7%	74.6	0.1%	24.9
35.0–69.9	6	5.4	298.2	0.4	49.7
70.0–349.9	68	60.7	10,426.6	14.4	153.3
350.0–699.9	15	13.4	7,230.0	10.0	482.0
700.0–3,499.9	15	13.4	20,263.3	28.1	1,350.9
3,500+	5	4.5	33,897.5	47.0	6,779.5
TOTAL	112	100.0%	72,190.2	100.0%	664.6

SOURCE: Data from ITCO survey, provided by SNE, Departamento de Riego y Avenamiento.

NOTE: Does not include land reform projects or properties of state-owned corporations. Includes few properties on west bank of Tempisque. Data are only roughly comparable to those in Table 10.2 because they are based on slightly different district boundaries and do not include farms under twenty hectares.

TABLE 10.4
TABLE 10.4
Guanacaste Irrigation District: Agrarian Reform Projects and State-owned Lands

Property	Year acquired	Area (hectares)	Families
Enrique Jiménez N. Experimental Station	1963	857	
La Esperanza	1964	675	46
Corralillos	1966	411	143
San Luis	1970	1,157	60
Paso Hondo	1971	882	41
Coope Río Cañas	1972	350	45
Tamarindo	1975	958	24
Bagatzí	1975	7,900	45
Coope Llanos del Cortés	1975	5,950	18
Inmobilaria Catalina	1976	966	
Coope Belén	1976	307	22
Coope Sardinal	1979	192	21
Corobicí	1979	992	64
Hacienda Filadelfia	1980	975	120
La Guaria	1980	157	18
Bella Vita	1981	397	
Falconiana	1984	1,095	48
San Ramón	1986	330	36
Playitas	1986	400	22
Hacienda Las Lapas	1986	300	
La Soga	1986	1,350	
Ranchos Horizonte	1987	1,416	
TOTAL		28,017	773

SOURCE: IDA; SNE.

NOTE: Does not include CATSA and DAISA, both CODESA subsidiaries, which totaled 5,135 and 670 hectares, respectively, but which are no longer state-owned. Does not include Rancho Gesling (6,734), which the state is planning to acquire. Frequent minor discrepancies in size exist in data from different sources, even within the same agencies. In all cases, the most recent farm sizes are cited. Not all farms have been apportioned among agrarian reform beneficiaries.

the larger 1982 boundaries of the district, which included some 183,000 hectares, are considered, these five owners still controlled about 19 percent of the total district. Twenty owners controlled three-quarters of the area in private farms of over 20 hectares and about 30 percent of the total district. Since the irrigation zone includes urban areas, forested watersheds, and roads, as well as state-owned lands, the level of ownership concentration was actually somewhat higher than these percentages of the total district area suggest.

This continued concentration of landownership into the late 1970s

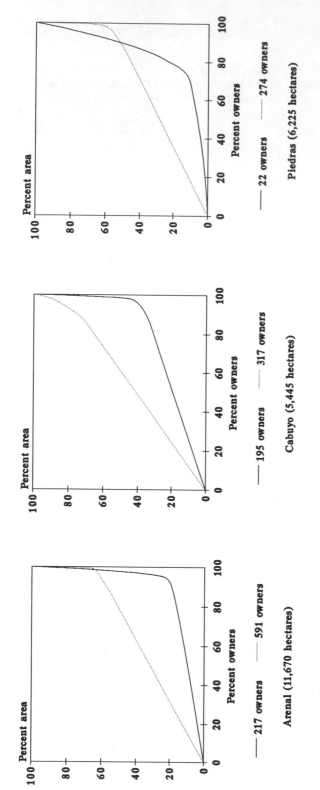

Fig. 10.1. Guanacaste Irrigation District: Land Distribution in the Arenal, Cabuyo, and Piedras Subdistricts, 1981 and 1986–87. Source: SENARA. In Arenal and Cabuyo subdistricts all but one large property (Ranchos Horizonte) were state-owned in 1981. In Piedras subdistrict, five owners held more than 500 hectares in 1981; in 1986, only one owner remained (the Stewarts, with 2,070 hectares at Mojica).

suggests that large landlords, in anticipation of the opening of the irrigation district, hoped to maintain sizable properties and either sell or exploit them intensively once water started to flow through the canals. In the first half of the 1980s, however, the highly skewed land distribution that had long characterized the region began to give way under the twin pressures of an energetic program of land redistribution and the imposition of water tariffs. Increasingly, landowners divided and sold even the medium-size holdings of between 70 and 350 hectares that had been carved out of the old latifundios during the late 1970s. Some giant estates remained in areas that had not yet been officially declared "under irrigation," such as Cecil Hylton's Ranchos Horizonte. But even this empire proved relatively ephemeral and had largely been sold off by the end of the 1980s (see Chapter 7).

A SENARA study of changes in land tenure between 1981 and 1986–87 in the Arenal, Cabuyo, and Piedras subdistricts indicated that of all the former latifundistas, only the Stewart family was able to maintain part of its former holdings (SENARA 1986 and SENARA unpublished data).[28] In five years, ownership patterns in these subdistricts shifted dramatically away from the highly skewed pattern typical of the Tempisque Valley (and of Guanacaste as a whole); significantly, in Cabuyo subdistrict, the only one declared "under irrigation" at the time of the study, the distribution approximated perfect equality (see Figure 10.1). Elsewhere, in Cañas subdistrict, the Sánchez family's Hacienda Taboga, with 1,800 irrigable hectares, was the only massive property to survive intact. By 1988, with the exception of Taboga, only four owners, two of them brother and sister, possessed more than 100 hectares in the zones officially "under irrigation."[29]

Latifundismo and Control of Water

In the first years of the irrigation project, ownership of land in the irrigation district was important primarily because it conferred control over water resources. Initially, water was a scarce resource that became a new focus of contention between large landowners and both smallholders and agrarian reform beneficiaries. Decades earlier, large landowners and their lawyers defended latifundismo in part by pointing to the need for water sources to sustain transhumant cattle herds (see Chapter 2). In the early 1980s, however, when irrigation water was still scarce, landlords sometimes attempted to extend their control over water while remaining within the boundaries of their properties. Peasants, in turn, operating under the cover of darkness, broke padlocks on sluices and pumps to irrigate their fields, hoping to avoid users fees and to divert water from the main canals before it ended up in the holding ponds of large haciendas.

These struggles over water in the early 1980s reflected a specific political and technical conjuncture. With the conflict over agrarian reform in the district temporarily resolved, large landowners believed that the executive and legislative branches of government were not interested in seriously challenging landlord power, changing existing ownership patterns, or sanctioning landlord misbehavior. Prior to the imposition of tariffs based on each farm's irrigable hectares, users paid "concession rights" based on the amount of water delivered from the main canals. The National Electrical Service (SNE), the state agency then in charge of the project, determined delivery priorities on the basis of the extent and quality of each property's secondary-canal network. This in turn depended on the amount of land that had been leveled, an extremely expensive process requiring the use of heavy earth-moving equipment. Although ITCO (and later IDA) had assisted agrarian reform beneficiaries in obtaining credit and equipment to level lands, frequent bureaucratic obstacles and long delays meant that the quality of most small farmers' secondary canals was poor compared with that of their wealthier neighbors. Large landowners thus had a de facto advantage when limited water had to be allocated among different users.

An example of a large landowner's effort to appropriate water resources occurred in 1981–82 along the south canal and the nearby Río Cañas. During the November–May dry season, Hacienda Taboga accumulated so much water from the Río Cañas in its holding ponds that the river nearly ran dry. Peasants in the adjacent San Luis agrarian reform project had counted on water from the river to irrigate rice and melon fields. The water was to be provided by the SNE, but Taboga was given priority because most of the peasants lacked the necessary pumps, suction equipment, and well-constructed secondary canals, all of which should have been provided by another agency, the IDA. No official action was taken on the arbitrary seizure of river water by the hacienda.

A similar, if less extreme, situation prevailed on the other side of Taboga along the south canal bordering the Paso Hondo agrarian reform project. Here SNE gave Taboga's sugar fields priority over the crops of agrarian reform beneficiaries, largely because the latter had what SNE considered poorly constructed canal networks and lacked the pumps necessary to distribute the water that SNE periodically channeled to Paso Hondo's primary canals. Peasants in the project expressed hope that the eventual construction of gravity-flow canals might ameliorate the situation in the future. But several were also fatalistic about both the seeming disorganization and ineptitude of the government bureaucracies on which their access to water depended and the possibilities of competing successfully for water with the powerful Sánchez Cortés family, owners of Hacienda Taboga.

The problem of "water latifundismo" and water theft largely abated by the mid-1980s as ever-larger quantities began to flow in the west and south canals and as SENARA absorbed the distinct, cumbersome bureaucracies whose contradictory regulations and actions often resulted in the near paralysis of local development and agrarian reform projects. Indeed, by the late 1980s, the problem, in some planners' eyes, had become SENARA's failure to keep pace with the growing availability of water by quickly incorporating new areas into the project. With temporarily abundant water, one SENARA engineer remarked in 1988, "We are educating the agriculturalist poorly and encouraging all kinds of inefficiencies that will become a growing burden when the rest of the district is declared 'under irrigation.' "[30]

Agrarian Reform in One Region of Guanacaste

The irrigation district in central Guanacaste has, even after little more than a decade, permitted a rapid intensification of production and the transformation of traditional hacienda enterprises into highly capitalized plantations. It has also broken the previous, near-total domination of latifundios in this one region of the province, though members of old hacendado families are prominent among the few remaining large landowners in the subdistricts declared "under irrigation"; elsewhere in the project zone they remain more powerful, but as more subdistricts are incorporated into the irrigation project they will be required to sell much of their land and to produce efficiently on whatever they retain.

A new stratum of technically sophisticated smallholders has emerged: some are agrarian reform beneficiaries, others local agriculturalists or residents of nearby towns who acquired farms simply as income-producing investments. These changes have been accompanied by major increases in employment and in the total income generated in the area. Already large sugar growers complain that at harvest time laborers are flocking to the *meloneras*, where they can pick cantaloupe for higher wages. And in the dry season the bright greens that previously were rarely seen outside of Taboga's sugar fields or El Pelón's rice fields now extend north and west of Cañas in a lush swathe of luxuriant growth.

Despite the entrepreneurial zeal unleashed by the irrigation project and by the labor force's new, if limited and seasonal, local-level bargaining power, it would be wrong to interpret the zone's economic dynamism solely as the product of free market forces. Although the state has largely divested itself of its extensive agroindustrial holdings in the area, it continues to play a critical role not only in infrastructure construction and planning and in reordering land tenure, but in extension and in the administration and financing of diverse aspects of irrigation-zone development, from housing to small-scale agroindustry. Producers in many parts of the zone are anything but free economic actors, able to choose what to produce and how to produce it. Instead, SENARA and IDA frequently mandate how much of what crops will be planted in particular areas and with what kinds of technology and finance, leaving agriculturalists with no choice but to comply.

This dictating of production options is rooted less in bureaucratic habits or arrogance than in new technological and economic imperatives. On some agrarian reform projects, such as Bagatzi, beneficiaries cultivate rice individually on adjacent irrigated ten-hectare parcels but coordinate production schedules, large-scale use of heavy machinery, and aerial fumigation. This mixture of individual and collective forms of production requires a high level of planning and coordination—much of it in state hands. If one *parcelero*'s rice matures earlier, it could rot in the field before the mechanical harvester arrives. If other smallholders wished to produce honey, citrus fruits, watermelons, or jalapeño peppers in or near the rice area, their bees and plants would be unlikely to survive the heavy doses of herbicides and pesticides applied to the rice.

The expanding band of green near the south and west canals has brought about an alteration of the natural environment, which confronts agriculturalists and the rest of Costa Rican society with novel dilemmas. Remaining patches of woods, except along watercourses and in the zone's wildlife reserves, have been felled to create fields just at the time when awareness of the deleterious effects of deforestation is becoming widespread in Costa Rica. Bird populations, attracted and nourished by the expansion of rice cultivation, have multiplied—some say a thousandfold—and on certain farms make off with half or more of the crop. Soil salinization, the bane of all irrigation systems since ancient times, has begun to appear on the more intensively operated farms in the district after less than a decade of use. The widespread application of toxic agricultural chemicals and their leaching into drainage canals, rivers, and the Gulf of Nicoya pose a long-term threat to the health of the region's human inhabitants, as well as to soils and to plant and animal life, especially in the protected "ecological zones" along the Tempisque where the runoff concentrates (Breton et al. 1990: 44; Hilje et al. 1987: 66–106; Janzen 1986: 92).[31]

The near destruction of latifundismo in the irrigation district— what one SENARA official termed "our nondrastic, nonviolent agrarian reform"[32]—had unlikely origins, which highlight its particular nature and its limited relevance to other areas of Guanacaste province or Costa Rica. Initially, the failure to establish legal limits on land-ownership concentration in the district appeared to open the door to a new wave of speculation, "neolatifundismo," and further transnationalization of Guanacastecan agriculture, with all the attendant questions this raised about social justice and sovereignty. The ranchers' early intransigence and—somewhat later—their smug, seignorial certainty about the benefits they would receive once their huge holdings were irrigated at public expense, had been, as one Liberia cattleman recognized in 1988, "a loud shot that backfired."

This "loud shot"—the mid-to-late-1970s pressures and threats intended to halt irrigation, and the early 1980s accumulation of vast expanses of land in a few foreign hands—alarmed prodevelopment forces in the Costa Rican state and, unexpectedly for many, the international agencies that financed the project. The cattlemen's campaign had been especially counterproductive inasmuch as it suggested reluctance to comply with the technical and production objectives of the proirrigation forces. The latter were not, as the Cámara de Ganaderos charged, hostile to owners' "sacred right" to do what they might with private property. Rather, they simply sought guarantees that large landowners would, if provided water, make the land produce. Unable to secure such assurances, planners increasingly viewed smallholders as one likely source of entrepreneurial energy and as logical beneficiaries of public expenditures. In the end, the mechanism to achieve both the economic-productive and the social-equity goals of the irrigation project came in the form of a clause in a loan agreement with the Inter-American Development Bank, hardly a fount of egalitarian or redistributional ideas or pro-land-reform sentiment.

The IDB requirement that half of each subdistrict be in farms of less than 50 hectares spurred the state to carry out a significant, albeit localized, agrarian reform and provided the necessary funds for land acquisitions at the same time. Together with the water tariff and SENARA's policy of assisting smallholders in the construction of canals and other infrastructure, these measures contributed to a progressive redistributional effect, though the main impetus for the effort was almost exclusively the attainment of efficiency rather than social justice. Peasant pressure, at least in the immediate area of the irrigation project, was notably absent in the period leading up to the district reforms.

These particular characteristics of agrarian reform in the irrigation district are suggestive of the difficulties similar measures face in other areas of the province, where water resources are scarce and where state and foreign development projects have had less impact. The very success of the irrigation district reform limits possibilities for a wider restructuring of land tenure patterns elsewhere. By 1987 nearly three-quarters of the land IDA had acquired for agrarian reform projects (asentamientos campesinos) in Guanacaste was in the district;[33] IDA devoted few resources to the creation of new agrarian reform projects in the other areas that constituted four-fifths of the province. While latifundismo had been dealt a serious political blow and had been effectively neutralized in one area, it remained entrenched, even in parts of the district that had not yet been declared "under irrigation."

→ Conclusion: Economic Crisis and the Persistence of Latifundismo

At the beginning of this study, I described how social scientists and historians of diverse theoretical perspectives agree that the traditional hacienda, or the underutilized latifundio with which it is virtually synonymous, will disappear (indeed, *is* disappearing). The causes of this presumed demise were supposed to be the advent of large markets and technological changes that permit intensification of production processes and conversion of haciendas into plantations. Other scholars, however, concerned principally with the deleterious environmental consequences of export-oriented cattle production rather than with large estates per se, posited a direct connection between demand for beef in the United States and the spread of extensively utilized pastures in Central America. The conclusions of the two literatures about the effects of market forces and the fate of the latifundio could hardly be more different, yet their proponents— operating in separate academic spheres—had not engaged each other.

Guanacaste, where large underutilized properties have persisted in spite of both integration into world markets and the availability of highly profitable alternative production systems, provides an apt context for evaluating these competing claims and—more broadly— for exploring the logic of the latifundio in different periods. But this "logical" analysis must, as I argue above, be rooted in a historical understanding of specific appropriation processes and real relations between agrarian social classes, as well as of the state, market forces, and ecological-demographic contexts within which such relations develop. Typologies of enterprise types and sweeping generalizations about "feudalism" or "capitalism," whether they are the goal of investigation (as was the case for many cultural anthropologists and

economists) or the implicit product of case studies (as for a generation of historians), inevitably clash with the particulars of concrete
situations and assume as well an overly determined notion of process. Much the same is true of approaches to present-day latifundismo that stress a "rationality" defined only in terms of short-run
market or credit conditions.

This lack of "fit" between abstract models and historical specifics
should not be viewed as mere "noise" in otherwise elegant analytical
systems. Rather, it is an indication that changes (or stasis) on the
ground emerge out of a many-sided interplay between forces operating at different levels and that the actions (or inaction) of actors at
each level are profoundly influenced by highly specific perceptions,
accumulated experience, and hopes. To cite but one example, foreign
and local landlords' contrasting expectations about enterprise organization or Nicaraguan and Guanacastecan laborers' distinct "cultures
of work" (discussed in Chapters 3 and 4) shaped the appropriation of
the soil and relations of production in ways that could scarcely be
predicted from a consideration of markets or geography. These elements in turn are inseparable from the actors' views of the state (in
Guanacaste and in their areas of origin) and their efforts to avoid its
reach, secure its backing, or alter its composition.

In maintaining that the latifundio has persisted in Guanacaste to
this day, it is important to remember that the picture is complicated
by what *appear* to be countervailing tendencies. Although the introduction of more productive brahman cattle and of mechanized crop
agriculture and irrigation indicates that in global terms land use has
intensified, livestock production continues to occur with highly extensive grazing densities like those of the "traditional" latifundio.
From the strictly economic point of view of the individual enterprise's costs and benefits this often seems irrational. But in seeking
to demonstrate that the modern latifundio is not a mere "cultural
lag" or "survival," I do not wish to suggest that the persistence of
large, extensively utilized estates results from some sort of hidden
logic concealing vast profits. Clearly, cattle raising continues to be an
activity with a low rate of profit, especially since the livestock-sector
crisis of the mid-1980s (see Chapter 6). Instead, a perspective of short-
run profitability obscures one essential raison d'être of today's latifundios: the long-term preservation of wealth in a context of risk.
Seemingly traditional units of production persist because the processes of appropriation of the soil and the kinds of economic develop-

ment in the region have permitted—and in some ways encouraged—both the coexistence of traditional and modern enterprises and the extensive and intensive uses of land within the same haciendas. Indeed, the economic security conferred by this complementarity of land uses within single units of production is one key factor that has allowed both the survival of the latifundio and the rise of modern plantation agriculture in recent decades.

What, then, is the logic of the latifundio and how has it changed? In the early part of the period 1880–1950, Guanacaste's remoteness and its geographical-ecological characteristics led the state to maintain only a minor presence and to encourage or at least condone the appropriation of huge properties. The extensive grazing pattern reflected difficult ecological conditions, geographical distance and poor transport infrastructure, the prevalence of rustling and related kinds of antilandlord resistance, and the availability of rent income in the form of feral cattle, timber, low-cost mortgages, and appreciation in land values. Landownership in this period did not necessarily permit hacendados to make full use of their properties, however, nor did it always allow them to realize sales on the market, since estates occupied by squatters were generally of little interest to potential buyers. The Guanacastecan peasantry's access to hacienda resources, with or without landlords' permission, must be seen as an important obstacle to more intensive processes of production and accumulation. The peasants' strength is also key to an explanation of the existence at this early stage of wage labor and of what I term (in Chapter 3) "inverted debt peonage," landlords' practice of advancing wages to mobile workers in an often futile effort to secure their services.

In the second half of the period from 1880 to 1950, new markets for wood, improved transport links, and technologies that raised the potential profitability of cattle ranching encouraged landlords to enclose haciendas. These attempts were not always successful, but when they were, latifundismo then took on an added logic—that of protecting rapidly appreciating resources from the depredations of local peasants and forcing at least some of them to labor for wages on the haciendas. The link between landownership, the accumulation of wealth, and political power became increasingly significant at the local level, where hacendados hired guards to enforce their prerogatives and suborned or otherwise influenced public officials and peasants' lawyers. This link was felt as well in the national state, as policies enacted in San José began to have a more direct impact in distant Guanacaste. By the early 1930s, with an energetic hacendado in the executive branch, protectionist policies brought new dynamism to the livestock sector, encouraging further enclosures but also giving rise to a major sector of smallholding cattle breeders in areas not under latifundista control.

State responsiveness to large landowners was not incompatible with agrarian reform and agricultural credit policies that contributed to the consolidation of this smallholding peasantry. Land reform, as practiced in this and subsequent periods, frequently allowed owners to divest themselves of properties they could not control and to receive market prices for their holdings. Both owners of occupied properties and peasant occupants often pushed for state mediation of agrarian conflicts. The presence in the state of reformists with limited but genuine developmentalist goals and a commitment to maintaining social peace facilitated the temporary resolution of many agrarian conflicts. In contrast to the rest of Central America, the sentiments of many members of the central Costa Rican elite were decidedly antilatifundista, in part because of the generally small size of coffee holdings in the country and the dominant groups' involvement in coffee processing rather than large-scale direct production. These peculiarities of Costa Rican society and politics made for some unusual alliances (see Chapter 5), as well as for credit policies that further strengthened at least some groups among the rural landholding poor. The depression of the 1930s, however, also saw a sudden saturation of the labor market, which greatly eroded rural workers' bargaining position vis-à-vis their employers.

Both the view that the underutilized latifundio was merely the outgrowth of an era of small markets and prestige-oriented landlords and the view that points to the "irrationality" of such estates inserted in a modern capitalist economy ignore important aspects of latifundista economic logic. With Guanacaste's post-1950 integration into the world beef market, various kinds of rent income—some, such as subsidized credit, institutionalized under state auspices—remain important for an understanding of the continuing underutilization and concentration of land. In addition, public-sector land purchases—for state-owned agroindustries, agrarian reform and irrigation projects, and parks and protected natural areas—often encouraged speculative rather than productive uses of properties. The region's proximity to Nicaragua also gave at least some Guanacastecan latifundios a very particular logic, with landholders, especially the Somozas and later White House Iran-contra operatives, motivated primarily by strategic concerns. As with those whose paramount motives were speculative, the acquisition of border properties as actual or potential military bases again took large areas basically out of production.

The fragmentation of the largest estates in the post-1950 period reduced the significance of transhumance as a rationale for latifundismo. The seasonal drought nonetheless continues to give rise to extensive grazing, but for a different reason: cattle and land now function as a kind of insurance for those haciendas engaged in cultivation of high-risk crops. Drought also reinforces hacendado dominance over smallholding cattle producers, who typically have to sell their animals when pastures shrivel up at the height of the dry season. The quotas and standards of quality imposed by the United States as a condition for access to the U.S. beef market further discourage intensified uses of land. Finally, pressures in favor of livestock development from international lending institutions—and, at the national level, the cattle lobby—contributed to the perpetuation of the contemporary latifundio.

It would be a mistake, however, to view the logic of the contemporary latifundio within an entirely synchronic framework, whether the emphasis is on the transformation engendered by the U.S. market or the subterfuges perpetrated by recipients of low-interest livestock loans. Contemporary latifundistas did indeed benefit from expanding international markets and from the support of a state in which they have been represented out of proportion to their numbers or their economic importance to the nation. These landowners, however, did not all have the same staying power. Particular hacendados' capacity for converting rent income into capital depended greatly on how and under what circumstances they acquired their properties. The "old families" had the incalculable advantage of "free" land—and lots of it. Their strength came not only from their earlier appropriation of the soil, but from a pronounced tendency toward endogamy that in effect re-created the historical connection between elite status and large properties.

Recent investors—Cubans, "crazy gringos," or Costa Rican outsiders—might go bankrupt after droughts, crop infestations, or failed get-rich-quick schemes. But members of the old elite hung on, perhaps selling a piece of land here, mortgaging another there, or raising exhibition stud bulls on inherited properties. Even in the few areas where agrarian reform made major inroads, such as the parts of the irrigation district declared "under irrigation," descendants of the old latifundistas were virtually the only surviving large landlords.

The logic of today's latifundio should not be seen solely in relation to contemporary conditions for another reason as well. The access to the U.S. beef market and the institutional rent streams that nurtured latifundismo have, as I indicated in Chapter 6, been significantly reduced following the economic crisis of the early 1980s. At the same time, however, the state has slashed support for the most important kinds of high-risk-crop cultivation, especially of rice and cotton, making the possibilities of a sustained transition from hacienda to plantation all the more problematical.

Latifundismo played a role, though it would be difficult to measure precisely its contribution, in the economic collapse of the early 1980s. This crisis—marked by worsened balance-of-payments difficulties, soaring foreign debt, a currency devaluation of nearly 500 percent in two years, and unprecedented inflation—resulted in large part from a stagnant productive structure, one of the most conspicuous sectors of which was constituted by extensively operated cattle haciendas. While the cattle sector occupies nearly three-quarters of the country's productive land, it creates by far the lowest amount of value-added per hectare of any agricultural activity. As I noted in Chapter 7, much of this cattle production takes place on lands that could generate greater employment and income if used for other purposes. In a context of economic crisis and structural adjustment, these negative effects of latifundismo (and others, such as ecological destruction and wealth concentration) are often exacerbated, since the state's capacity for ameliorating social problems is increasingly restricted, and competing interest groups intensify their struggles over the fast-diminishing resources of the public sector.

Following the economic collapse of 1980–1982, a modest recovery ensued, which resulted in part from orthodox stabilization and structural adjustment policies spelled out in new agreements with international lending and aid agencies. By the late 1980s, agency officials commonly touted Costa Rica as a success story for economic stabilization and for "nontraditional exports," a category that included cut flowers, ornamental plants, spices, winter vegetables, and tubers for the Latino market in the United States. Inflation fell to low double-digit levels that seemed almost insignificant by Latin American standards, growth rates remained healthy, exports did in fact diversify, and unemployment—especially in urban areas—was remarkably low. But, as I noted in Chapters 6 and 9, this new dynamism was not enough to rescue the livestock sector from crisis or to ensure conversion of haciendas into plantations. Indeed, for most Guanacastecan producers, large and small, indebtedness from the failed development schemes of the 1970s and early 1980s largely precluded participation in the new "agriculture of change" (Edelman 1990).

The crisis of the early 1980s gave a new immediacy to the question of latifundismo. The Costa Rican state's historical commitment to social welfare, unusual enough in the Central American context, has been increasingly circumscribed by forces beyond its control, such as the need to amortize the massive foreign debt. It is precisely under these circumstances, when the social welfare apparatus can no longer expand at a pace that meets people's minimal necessities, that the issues of creating rural employment, elevating production, and bringing about more equitable distributions of income and wealth take on pressing urgency. Widespread underutilization of land and policies that actively encourage this kind of stagnation are hardly compatible with these needs.

But if generous state subsidies for latifundismo have diminished in the late 1980s, the same is also true for those that previously underwrote intensified plantation production of rice, cotton, and sugar. One grim possibility, then, is a latifundismo that maintains the existing structure of land tenure but lacks even the limited dynamism of the beef export economy of the 1960s and 1970s. It is also conceivable that small, incremental changes in land distribution, carried out under state auspices, may attenuate some of the negative effects of highly skewed patterns of ownership, as has occurred in the parts of the irrigation district declared "under irrigation." It is not easy to see, however, where the resources and the political will for such an endeavor might be found, given the current process of economic retrenchment and adjustment. Tragically, it is even less likely that such a process of change would affect the vast majority of rural people in Guanacaste—those who aspire to cultivate the land but have had little or none to work and who have suffered directly and indirectly in innumerable other ways from the persistence of latifundismo.

→ Appendixes

APPENDIX A
Guanacaste: Owners of over 10,000 Hectares, c.1920–c.1935

Owner	Nationality	Hacienda or property	Canton	Hectares	Total hectares
Federico So-brado Carrera	Spanish	Tempisque	Carrillo, Liberia	19,232	35,142
		Santa María	Liberia	6,762	
		San Juanillo	Santa Cruz, Nicoya	9,148	
François Thevenot	French	La Palma	Abangares	c.40,000	40,000–60,000
Julio Sánchez Lépiz	Costa Rican	Taboga e Higuerón	Cañas	13,624	13,624
Pánfilo Val-verde (heirs of)	Costa Rican	Tenorio	Cañas	16,083	16,083
Maximiliano Soto Fernández	Costa Rican	Paso Hondo	Cañas	11,040	11,040
Elías Bal-dioceda Rojas	Costa Rican	Guachipelín (La Cueva)	Liberia	13,323	13,323
Alfonso Salazar Aguilar	Nicaraguan	El Viejo	Carrillo, Santa Cruz	23,343	28,573
		Las Cañas	Carrillo, Santa Cruz	5,230	
Manuel Joaquín Barrios Guerra	Nicaraguan	Santa Rosa	Liberia (La Cruz)	25,763	74,709
		Naranjo	Liberia (La Cruz)	4,970	
		Murciélago	Liberia (La Cruz)	10,433	
		Orosí	Liberia (La Cruz)	15,862	
		Animas	Liberia (La Cruz)	5,394	
		Carmita	Liberia (La Cruz)	2,550	
		El Amo	Liberia (La Cruz)	4,484	
		Inocentes	Liberia (La Cruz)	5,253	
Luis Morice Belmonte	Nicaraguan	Sapoá	Liberia (La Cruz)	9,398	20,488
		Conventillos	Liberia (La Cruz)	2,317	

Owner	Nationality	Hacienda or property	Canton	Hectares	Total hectares
		Potrero	Liberia (La Cruz)	3,978	
		Quebrada de Agua	Liberia (La Cruz)	1,144	
		El Jobo	Liberia (La Cruz)	1,703	
		Génova	Liberia (La Cruz)	1,948	
Francisco Hurtado Guerra	Nicaraguan	El Jobo	Liberia	18,618	39,075
		El Encinal	Liberia	779	
		Guapote	Liberia	1,192	
		San Rafael	Liberia	1,927	
		Santo Tomás	Liberia	3,561	
		Culebra	Liberia	6,062	
		maritime mile	Liberia	1,936	
		Cañas Dulces	Liberia	c.5,000	
George Wilson (a.k.a. David R. Stewart)	U.S.	Catalina	Bagaces	23,600	133,808
		Mogote	Bagaces	5,506	
		Pijije	Bagaces	3,170	
		Ciruelas	Bagaces	22,249	
		El Ensayo	Bagaces	497	
		Miravalles	Bagaces	15,476	
		Cuipilapa	Bagaces	633	
		San Bosco	Bagaces	50	
		Aguas Claras	Bagaces	100	
		Monte Verde	Bagaces	3,457	
		El Cortés, Palo Verde, Tamarindo	Bagaces	29,487	
		Mojica	Bagaces	1,375	
		San Jerónimo	Bagaces	4,763	
		state lands	Bagaces	102	
		El Viejo	Carrillo	23,343	
Minor Cooper Keith	U.S.	El Pelón de la Altura	Liberia	6,621	c.18,150
		Alemania	Liberia (La Cruz)	815	
		El Porvenir	Carrillo	c.2,000	
		Tempate	Carrillo	714	
		lot near Paso Hondo	Cañas	c.3,000	
		lot near Las Juntas	Abangares	c.3,000	
		lot near Cañas Dulces	Liberia	2,000	

Owner	Nationality	Hacienda or property	Canton	Hectares	Total hectares
River Plate Trust	British	River Plate Block	Cañas (Tilarán)	30,762	86,362
		state lands near Río Nosara	Nicoya	55,600	

SOURCES: Sobrado, ANCR LJC r. 1264, no. 771—1920; CN G1-2-1-15—1949 and uncataloged plans. Sánchez, CN 8023—1917; Marín 1972: 69. Valverde, CN G6-1-1-129—1946. Soto, *La Tribuna*, 3 Mar. 1935, 8. Baldioceda, CN G1-2-1-46—1955. Salazar, *La Gaceta Oficial*, 9 Aug. 1928, 1098; ANCR Cong. 11845—1922; CN uncataloged plans. Barrios, CN G10-4-2-2-21—1921. Morice, plans in series CN G10-1-1; G10-4-1-18—1921. Hurtado, CN G1-2-1-271—1922. Wilson, ANCR LJC r. 1418, nos. 176, 177, 179—1933; CN G4-1-1-29—1925, G4-1-1-31—1946, CN 9265—1946, 8198—1933, 8188—1933, 8187—1933, 11702—1955; ITCO, expediente sobre ocupación precaria 402. Thevenot, ANCR Cong. 11944—1920. Keith, ANCR MP 285—1922; CN uncataloged plans; *La Gaceta Oficial*, 9 Aug. 1928, 1098. River Plate, CN uncataloged plan no. 51; *La Gaceta Oficial*, 4 Mar. 1923, 240.

NOTES: Sobrado also claimed state lands in San Juanillo not listed here. Thevenot's La Palma was estimated to contain 40,000 to 60,000 hectares. In 1930 Sánchez said he owned 25,000 *manzanas* (17,520 hectares) in Taboga e Higuerón. Salazar's Sitio Las Cañas was ceded to peasant occupants in 1920. Barrios had only two-ninths rights to El Amo; he acquired most of his properties from the Urcuyos or with *gracias* from Carrillo canton. Morice acquired some properties from Barrios and the Urcuyos; in the 1930s he shared rights to Orosí with Carlos Barrios Sacasa. Hurtado's share in Cañas Dulces was about one-half; 421 hectares of El Encinal were expropriated for occupants; he was part owner of San Rafael and Santo Tomás. Keith was part owner of lots near Las Juntas and Cañas Dulces; Alemania included 4,873 hectares in Nicaragua, but it is not clear if Keith acquired that part of the hacienda. River Plate's lands were originally granted to Keith; parts of the Tilarán block were ceded to occupants; the company reportedly occupied an additional 50,000 hectares.

Guanacaste: Principal Agrarian Reform Measures, 1900–1947

Place or property	Observations	Carried out (yes or no)
	1900	
Haciendas Mojica, Paso Hondo, Cañas; El Viejo, Carrillo	Government authorized to purchase or expropriate up to 200 hectares from Mojica and Paso Hondo for the residents of Bebedero and to acquire in the same way the necessary land from El Viejo to construct a road from Bolsón to Filadelfia.	No. In the 1920s, the government bought 150 hectares of Paso Hondo (see below).
	1903	
Cañas Dulces, Liberia	Authorization for the distribution of lots of disputed lands to the occupants.	No.
	1908	
Hacienda La Palma, Abangares; El Encinal, Palenque, Sabana Grande, Cofradía, El Zacatal, La Cueva, Boquerones, Dos Ríos, Montañita, all in the cantons of Liberia and Carrillo. San Antonio Morote, Nicoya.	Authorization to purchase and distribute lands to the occupants. By 1922, 421 hectares of El Encinal had been expropriated.	In most cases, neither the purchase nor distribution were carried out. In some cases, such as La Cofradía, the purchase but not the distribution was carried out.
Lands of the River Plate Company, Cañas (present-day Tilarán)	The Company returned 2,040 occupied hectares to the state. Occupants with lots cultivated and fenced since 1907 given right to buy their land for 4 colones per hectare. The rest was to be auctioned in lots of 5 to 50 hectares.	No. Occupants remained in possession, however.
	1909	
San Antonio, Nicoya	Expropriation authorized of more than 100 hectares.	No.

Place or property	Observations	Carried out (yes or no)
	1910	
Caño Negro, El Zacatal, La Garita, Espavel, all of Cañas Dulces, Liberia	Distribution authorized of 20-hectare lots of state lands. Claimants acquire full rights if lots are cultivated for three years. Distribution of up to 6,000 hectares authorized.	Not carried out for lack of funds. President failed to execute decree. Approved again in 1924.
Colonia Carmona, Nicoya	A total of 2,017 hectares in lots of 20 hectares is donated to colonists. Beneficiaries are required to reside there and cultivate their parcels for five years.	Yes.
	1912–13	
Lands of River Plate, Tilarán	Authorization for purchase of 5,000 hectares to be divided in 50-hectare lots for current occupants.	Occupants remained in possession of lands without receiving titles.
	1914	
Sitio Las Cañas, Belén de Carrillo	Appropriation of 30,000 colones to purchase up to 17.5 caballerías.	By 1926, 5,230 hectares had been distributed.
	1920	
La Mansión, Nicoya	Right to administer and exploit the property given to the occupants.	Yes.
	1921	
Hacienda Paso Hondo, Cañas	Authorization for expropriation of 150 hectares from the United Fruit Company for the port of Bebedero.	Yes.
	1922	
Quebrada Azul, Tilarán	The state purchases 3,375 hectares for a total of 138,200 colones to sell to occupants at 40 colones per hectare.	Purchase was carried out. No clear evidence of distribution.
	1922–23	
El Líbano, Tilarán	Authorization for purchase or expropriation of up to 9,000 hectares of mining company lands. The companies refuse to sell less than 12,000 hectares. Each occupant to pay 20 colones to state for each hectare over total of 50. Government to measure and survey the occupied lands.	No.

Place or property	Observations	Carried out (yes or no)
	1924	
Jesús del Morote, Nicoya	The state spends 86,200 colones to purchase 2,151 hectares to be sold to occupants at not more than 20 colones per hectare.	Purchase was carried out, but some lands remained in dispute until 1940s.
	1925	
Copal de Nicoya and Río Seco de Santa Cruz	State is authorized to purchase these properties and to sell lots at no more than 20 colones per hectare.	No. The properties were still occupied in 1927, and in 1930 a serious agrarian crisis was reported in Copal.
Terrenos de Hoja Ancha, Nicoya (Hojancha)	Occupants of a 1,128-hectare property each given 10-hectare plots on condition they cultivate them. Occupied area over 10 hectares to be sold to the occupants at 20 colones per hectare.	?
	1926–27	
Hacienda La Palma, Abangares	The state is authorized to purchase 40,000 hectares and to donate lots of 100 hectares or more, if they are already cultivated, to the occupants. The occupants are permitted to buy up to 50 additional hectares at 25 colones each. Beneficiaries must be Costa Rican citizens with less than 5,000 colones capital and less than 50 hectares of legally registered land and must cultivate land for five years.	Yes, although it is probable that not all 40,000 hectares were distributed. During 1930s, this area was considered baldíos and open to claims.
	1928	
Lands of Sinclair and Victoria Investment Company, Tilarán	The state acquires 17,069 hectares for distribution to occupants.	Purchase was carried out, but not the distribution.
	1929	
Property of Carlos Volio Tinoco, Matina, Nicoya	State authorized to spend up to 10,000 colones to acquire 495 hectares for occupants.	Yes.
	1932	
Lands of Sacra Familia Mining Company, Tilarán	State is authorized to purchase the occupied parts of the property, which includes parts of the Aguacate mining district in Puntarenas province.	Yes.

Place or property	Observations	Carried out (yes or no)
	1937	
Hacienda Mojica, Cañas; Hacienda El Viejo, Carrillo and Santa Cruz	The Executive is urged by the Congress to carry out the expropriation decree approved in 1900. In 1940 a similar resolution is passed.	No.
	1939	
Cañas	The state donates 2,040 hectares of lands that had belonged to the River Plate Company to the Municipality of Cañas, to be sold in lots of 20 hectares to the occupants. In 1940 a price of 9 colones per hectare was established, but occupants were unable or unwilling to pay it. In 1941 legal titles still had not been distributed.	No.
	1940	
Coyolito de Abangares	An occupied area of 3,879 hectares is exchanged for state lands of similar value elsewhere in the country. It is probable that this property consisted only of 916 hectares and 3,336 square meters.	Yes.
Hacienda La Culebra, Colorado de Abangares	Exchange of 2,557 hectares of occupied land for state lands elsewhere in Pacific Costa Rica. Occupants left in possession of their parcels.	Yes.
	1941	
Aguas Claras, Bagaces	Authorization for Municipality of Bagaces to distribute lots of 10 to 50 hectares in state lands adjacent to Hacienda Miravalles.	?
	1945	
Hacienda El Viejo, Carrillo and Santa Cruz	The state expropriates part of El Viejo at Corralillos in order to distribute lots of 5 hectares to residents of Carrillo and Santa Cruz at a price of 200 colones payable over 20 years.	Yes.
	1946	
Quebrada Grande, Liberia	Exchange of 2,059 occupied hectares belonging to Fernando Lorenzo Brenes.	Yes.
Hacienda Sapoá, La Cruz	Exchange of 4,983 occupied hectares belonging to Luis Morice Lara. In 1961 this area was occupied and considered part of Hacienda Sapoá. Lands were surveyed in 1947 and again in 1957, but Morice was able to influence surveyors and maintained some of his claims to this land.	Yes. In 1947 Morice was paid 1.43 million colones.

Place or property	Observations	Carried out (yes or no)
	1947	
Hacienda Santa Rosa, La Cruz	Exchange of 4,341 occupied hectares in the northwest part of the hacienda for state lands.	Yes.

SOURCES: 1900, ANCR Cong. 2610—1900; CN 8003 n.d. 1903, ANCR Cong. 2858—1903. 1908 (La Palma and others), ANCR Cong. 12020—1908, 10455—1909, 12473—1921, 14584—1926, 15378—1929; *La Gaceta Oficial*, 4 June 1908, 1. 1908 (River Plate), ANCR Cong. 12108—1920; *La Gaceta Oficial*, 25 March 1909, 1, and 3 November 1908. 1909, ANCR Cong. 10455—1909. 1910 (Caño Negro and others), ANCR Cong. 14172—1925, 13839—1924, 17003—1934. 1910 (Carmona), ANCR Cong. 17003—1934. 1912–13, ANCR Cong. 9914—1912, 17003—1934. 1914, ANCR Cong. 11845—1914, 14269—1926; CN uncataloged. 1920, ANCR Cong. 17003—1934; *La Gaceta Oficial*, 12 September 1920, 943. 1921, ANCR Cong. 12474—1921; CN 8002 n.d. 1922, ANCR Cong. 17003—1934; ANCR Gob. 8054—1924. 1922–23, ANCR Cong. 14584—1926, ANCR Gob. 8152—1923. 1924, ANCR Cong. 17003—1934, ANCR Gob. 8054—1924, *El Guanacaste*, 26 August 1940, 2. 1925 (Copal and Río Seco), ANCR Cong. 14225–1925, 14791—1927, 15843—1930, 17003—1934. 1925 (Hoja Ancha), ANCR Cong. 17003—1934. 1926–27, ANCR Cong. 14679—1927, 17003—1934; ANCR Gob. 7883—1926, CN 8049 and 8050—1931. 1928, ANCR Cong. 17003—1934; *La Gaceta Oficial*, 14 December 1928, 1–2. 1929, ANCR Cong. 15378—1929, 17003—1934. 1932, ANCR Cong. 16384—1932. 1937, ANCR Cong. 18306—1937, 19403—1940. 1939, ANCR Cong. 18993—1939, 19878—1941; *El Guanacaste*, 14 July 1939, 1. 1940 (Coyolito), *El Guanacaste*, 23 June 1940, 1, 4, and 21 July 1940, 1. 1940 (La Culebra), ANCR Cong. 19493—1938–40. 1941, *El Guanacaste*, 17 February 1941, 2. 1945, *El Guanacaste*, 12 February 1945 and 30 November 1945; *Libertad*, 17 July 1971, 8; *Trabajo*, 27 April 1946, 3. 1946 (Quebrada Grande), CN G1-3-1-66—1946. 1946 (Sapoá), *Adelante*, 28 March 1954, 1; CN G10-1-1-149 and G10-1-1-342—1946; *Libertad*, 21 October 1967. 1947, CN G1-2-1-10—1947.

APPENDIX C
Guanacaste Irrigation District:
Landowners by Amount of Irrigable Land Owned, 1978

Owner or name of property	Potential irrigated	Unsuited for irrigation	Total hectares	Cumulative percent irrigable
Hacienda Cortés–Stewart (ITCO)	12,779.5	5,550.0	18,329.5	16.7%
Hacienda Taboga	10,360.0	0	10,360.0	30.2
CATSA	4,745.0	175.0	4,920.0	36.5
Rancho Gesling	3,562.5	3,204.0	6,766.5	41.1
Escagedo–Azucarera Guanacaste	3,195.0	3,035.0	6,230.0	45.3
El Pelón de la Bajura	2,904.0	2,975.0	5,879.0	49.1
Hacienda Mojica–Donald Stewart	2,662.5	0	2,662.5	52.6
Hacienda Tempisque	2,060.0	0	2,060.0	55.3
Carlos Aubert–Hacienda San Joaquín	1,300.0	75.0	1,375.0	57.0
Otoniel Aguilar S.A.	1,177.5	0	1,177.5	58.5
Hacienda Asientillo	1,092.5	157.5	1,250.0	59.9
Finca Zopilota	1,060.0	3,592.5	4,652.5	61.3
Hacienda Rancho Boyero	1,030.0	195.0	1,225.0	62.7
Oscar Pacheco–Hacienda Solimar	975.0	0	975.0	64.0
Finca Jiménez Núñez (MAG)	922.5	0	922.5	65.2
San Luis (ITCO)	917.5	227.5	1,145.0	66.4
Hacienda Paso Hondo (ITCO)	900.0	12.5	912.5	67.6
Bismarck Contracting Company	875.0	0	875.0	68.7
Finca Filadelfia (ITCO)	845.0	0	845.0	69.8
Lorenzo Luconi–Hda. Sta. Paula	789.8	0	789.8	70.9
Elio Espinar	757.5	0	757.5	71.9
Hermanos Retana	755.0	355.0	1,110.0	72.8
Hacienda Corobicí (DAISA)	753.0	0	753.0	73.8
Nuyiba Bonilla Ayub	742.0	0	742.0	74.8
Hacienda El Real	707.5	2,447.5	3,155.0	75.7
Agrícola–Ganadera El Viejo	612.0	612.0	1,224.0	76.5
La Boca S.A.	585.0	0	585.0	77.3
Agropecuaria El Güis S.A.	560.0	0	560.0	78.0
El Higueral	527.5	0	527.5	78.7
Raúl Solís R.	515.0	0	515.0	79.4
Juan Masís Bonilla	497.5	0	497.5	80.0
María Cecilia Bonilla Ayub	475.0	262.5	737.5	80.7
Edgar Martínez Ramírez	475.0	150.0	625.0	81.3
Federico Apéstegui Sobrado	447.5	0	447.5	81.9
Inversiones Río Orinoco	402.5	0	402.5	82.4
Humberto Gutiérrez B.	390.0	102.5	492.5	82.9
Federico Apéstegui	387.5	0	387.5	83.4
Finca Corralillo (ITCO)	382.5	0	382.5	83.9
A. Salas Arce–H. Masavi	375.0	0	375.0	84.4
Reinol González	350.0	0	350.0	84.9
Las Trancas	345.0	0	345.0	85.3
La Uvita S.A.	337.5	95.0	432.5	85.7

Owner or name of property	Potential irrigated	Unsuited for irrigation	Total hectares	Cumulative percent irrigable
Rafael Solís Rojas	337.5	22.5	360.0	86.2
Cristian Tattembach I.	327.5	0	327.5	86.6

SOURCE: ITCO survey provided by SNE.

NOTE: Total potential irrigated area, 74,472.2 hectares; total project area covered by survey, 103,241.2 hectares.

→ **Reference Matter**

→ Notes

Introduction

1. A variety of sources, including agricultural censuses, cadastral survey plans, and property and mercantile registries, serve to address this question and to develop a picture of changing regional agrarian structures and land uses. The cadastral survey (*Catastro Nacional*) is an especially rich source for the study of land tenure, land use, and squatter movements, which has rarely been employed in historical or social scientific research in Costa Rica. Indeed, some researchers (Hall 1976; Sequiera 1985) wrongly lament that few historical maps of properties are available or mistakenly claim that large properties escape cadastral survey (Aguilar and Solís 1988:160).

During fieldwork, questions about landownership were those most likely to produce undependable answers, particularly when posed to large landowners. Often, little correspondence existed between cadastral or public registry entries and hacendados' verbal claims about the modest size of their holdings. This was an important reason I opted to rely on cadastral, census, and other similar data, in spite of their evident limitations, for analyzing land tenure and land use.

2. Though Wolf and Mintz apparently developed their model without referring to Weber, it was the latter who first explicitly distinguished between "hacienda" and "plantation" types based on the jural condition of the labor force, levels of capitalization, and relations with local or distant markets (Weber 1942 [1923]: 82–109). Weber applied his model to Europe, North America, and parts of Asia, as well as to Latin America.

3. Hunt, a Peruvianist, did not refer to Martínez Alier's important work on the Sierra Central of Peru (1975, 1977a, 1977b), presented as early as 1972 at the Rome Symposium on the Economic History of Latin America. Martínez clearly demonstrated the fallacy of assuming in all cases hacendado control over the labor force (a conclusion echoed in the discussion below of early-

twentieth-century Guanacaste). Hunt recognized (1975:33) that "total control" may not exist in certain cases, but noted only that in such situations landlords were forced to offer competitive remuneration. Beyond a mention of peasant pressure for agrarian reform in Peru's La Convención valley, he did not examine in any detail the implications of this lack of control for other aspects of the behavior—and indeed for the survival—of the hacienda enterprise.

4. Hunt did not discuss here the opportunity cost of land, often an important element of hacendado decision making in situations where technology or high commodity prices permit increases in the productivity or profitability of land.

5. Incredibly, Keith says his "discussion is based on the assumption that the traditional agrarian structure of Latin America was essentially a stable one which was not altered in any fundamental way before the last years of the nineteenth century" (1977: 3).

6. Fonseca Corrales based this assertion on one rental contract. Elsewhere (1983: 270), she paints a contradictory yet more realistic picture of rural class relations, noting that Guanacastecan hacendados lacked control over the rural population and that debt peonage never took root, as it did in Mexico.

7. Some dependency thinkers have developed more fruitful ideas about landlord-peasant relations, focusing not on the presence of adjacent minifundios and latifundios at one point in time, but on the proletarianized laborer's participation in each sector over time and perhaps in different regions. Wallerstein (1979, chap. 6), for example, suggested that the apparently proletarianized rural laborers in many parts of the Third World are, in fact, "part-lifetime proletarians" whose youth and old age are not supported by the wages earned during their lives as employed laborers (or those of their families). The costs of reproducing this labor force are thus borne primarily, not by the sector that hires wage workers, but rather by the peasant or the urban "informal" sectors.

8. *Dependentistas* criticized stage theories that included Stalin's (1940) tract on the historical succession modes of production and Rostow's (1960) influential treatise on economic development (see Feder 1971: 271). Part of the impulse for assailing these theories was their manifest inability to explain Latin American reality. But considerations of political strategy were also important, at least in the case of Stalin's work, which had long influenced Latin American Communist parties. Stalin's stage theory implied that the national bourgeoisie was a progressive force that would help eliminate remaining "feudal" vestiges from Latin American societies. A key tenet of radical dependency theorists was that seemingly feudal social relations in Latin America were caused by the capitalist world market and were not really feudal.

9. Among the forces behind this transformation, Feder suggested, are the

chronic deficits in food production of many Latin American countries and the development of high-yielding (and highly profitable) crop varieties.

10. I criticize this genre at more length in Edelman (n.d.). For a different, complementary critique see Jones (n.d.). Representative works include Buschbacher (1986); Buxedas (1977); Caufield (1985); Da Veiga (1975); De-Walt (1982); Dickinson (1973); Feder (1980); Guess (1978); Nations and Nigh (1978); Parsons (1976); Partridge (1984); Roux (1975); Rutsch (1980); Shane (1980); Slutsky (1979); Spielman (1972).

11. Subsidies for luxury consumption, particularly of automobiles and household appliances, are also frequently an important aspect of government efforts to maintain legitimacy in the eyes of elites and middle classes.

12. The term "capital" originated in the word "cattle" (Vilar 1980: 205), but this etymological relation does not imply that feral animals multiplying largely on their own are functionally equivalent to productive capital in an economic sense. "Harvesting" feral livestock generates a rent that may then be "capitalized" and contribute to accumulation (see Wolf 1983: 49–50). But this is hardly the same as accumulating profits derived from investment in plant and equipment.

13. Meléndez's work (1955, 1963, 1967, 1974, 1975) constitutes an exception to the pattern of neglect. His work, however, while identifying important sources and colonial-era processes of land appropriation, emphasized formal institutions and elite politics and assumed (albeit implicitly) that rural social relations resembled those of the "classical" hacienda elsewhere in Latin America. More recent works on the colonial period include Matarrita Ruiz (1980a, 1980b) and Quirós Vargas (1976).

The reasons why scholars paid little attention to the northwest are surely complex, but reflect, among other things, what Láscaris (1975) called the *mentalidad meseteña* of Costa Rican political and academic discourse, which led social scientists to focus on the tiny *meseta central* (central plateau) and to ignore other regions.

14. For example, Aguilar and Solís assert (1988: 43)—incorrectly, as I indicate in succeeding chapters—that some formerly prominent cattle families (e.g., Wolf) have abandoned ranching or that others (Bonilla Morad, Bonilla Dib, Urcuyo) only became important in the 1940s or after. Because they consider landowners of recent foreign provenance to be Costa Rican (e.g., Clachar, Stewart, Hurtado, and others), they underestimate the long-standing importance in the region of both foreign capital and foreign models of enterprise organization (see Chapter 4 below).

15. This unintended synchronic functionalist tone is much more pronounced in Aguilar and Solís (1988) than in Solís (1981a) or Aguilar (1985).

16. Ethnic homogeneity was a major explanatory category, as well, in Seligson's analysis of why Costa Rica has been relatively free of agrarian and other social conflicts (1980:156–62).

17. In addition to the studies of Guanacaste mentioned above, the works of Bermúdez and Pochet (1981, 1986) on Juan Viñas and, especially, of Bourgois (1989) on Limón have begun to fill these gaps.

Chapter 1

1. The tree is called *conacaste* in other Central American countries. Like *guanacaste*, this derives from the Nahuatl *cuauhnacaztli*, which means ear-shaped fruit. Its botanical name is *Enterolobium cyclocarpum*.

2. "Agricultural" is used here in its original, stricter sense (retained in the Spanish *agricultura*) to mean only the cultivation of crops and not livestock production.

3. This has also been noted elsewhere in postconquest Mesoamerica (MacLeod 1973: 343; Semo 1973: 78).

4. Newson's figures conform roughly to earlier estimates. In Nicoya in 1557, according to a report by the Bishop of León cited by Thiel ([1902] 1977: 57), there were only 500 tributaries. Thiel suggests that the total population "did not surpass 3,500." Estimating total population from tribute lists, which usually included only married men, involves multiplying by a factor of 3.3, if one follows Abel-Vidor (1980: 166), or of 4.0, if one follows Newson (1987: 118). Applying both factors as lower and upper limits, the total population in 1557 would be between 1,650 and 2,000. A 1573 report notes a total of 400 tributaries in Nicoya and nearby Chira (López [1573] 1974: 45), which would indicate a population of 1,320 to 1,600. But a serious epidemic in the same year was said to have killed 300 Indians in only twenty days (Thiel [1902] 1977: 63).

5. For Costa Rican studies of the jurisdictional history of Nicoya, see Sibaja (1974), Sibaja and Zelaya (1974), and Meléndez (1963, 1967); a revanchist Nicaraguan view is provided by Alvarez (1942). At the time of conquest the Spaniards, recognizing the cultural affinities of the indigenous populations of Nicoya and Nicaragua, included much of what is now northwestern Costa Rica in the same jurisdiction as Nicaragua. From 1588 to 1786, however, with the exception of a brief period (1593–1602) in which the area was added to Costa Rica, Nicoya was a separate jurisdiction from both Costa Rica and Nicaragua and, like the rest of Central America north of Panama, was administered from Guatemala. In 1786 a reorganization of the colonial bureaucracy that created the Intendencia of Nicaragua resulted in the inclusion of Nicoya as a Partido (roughly a province) of Nicaragua. In 1812, with the promulgation of the Spanish constitution establishing the Cortes, or parliament, Costa Rica, which did not have the 60,000 inhabitants necessary to elect a representative, successfully petitioned to have residents of Nicoya (still part of Nicaragua) join it in electing a deputy to the Cortes. After independence in 1821, the towns of Nicoya joined a series of shifting al-

liances with different warring cities in Nicaragua. In 1824 local assemblies in Nicoya and Santa Cruz voted to join Costa Rica. Liberia voted to remain part of Nicaragua, but in 1825 the short-lived Congress of the Federal Republic of Central America declared the entire Partido of Nicoya to be part of Costa Rica, a position ratified by the Liberia assembly in 1828. Nicaragua did not recognize the annexation of Nicoya until 1858.

6. The degree to which the New Laws were effective in Central America remains controversial. MacLeod (1973: 108–19) is the most skeptical, while Martínez Peláez (1972), Sherman (1979), Wortman (1982), and Newson (1987) suggest at least some significant successes in replacing or reducing the burden of the encomienda system.

7. Fonseca Corrales (1983: 255) maintains that in Nicoya no evidence exists that encomenderos were able to transform encomienda rights into rights to land. In the Costa Rican jurisdiction, however, the first land grants were to former encomienda holders.

8. These conditions for *caballería* grants, described by Florescano (1976: 29–30) for Mexico and by Ots (1959: 21–22) for Spanish America as a whole, appear to have been largely the same for Costa Rica (cf. *DHCR*, 3: 71–72). Schell (1986: 60) suggests that recipients of caballería grants in Mexico were obliged to reside on and work the land for four years before it could be alienated.

9. Sequiera (1985: 74–76) suggests that the colonial-period caballería in Guanacaste was equivalent to 135 hectares, whereas in the mid-nineteenth century it was only 45 hectares. But lands with titles in "old caballerías" that were remeasured with modern surveying techniques in the twentieth century almost always turned out to be considerably larger than the 135-hectare-per-caballería figure would predict.

10. Chevalier (1963: 54–57) suggested that caballerías in sixteenth-century Mexico were irregular, measuring as little as 6 hectares or as much as 43.

11. Some authorities (Chevalier 1963: 88) state that the term *estancia* was coincd in the New World to indicate the point where nomadic herds came to rest. Bishko (1952: 511–13) has argued that the term and the institution it represented originated in municipal grants of grazing rights in late-fifteenth-century Spain, though, as Schell (1986: 41–42) indicates, this notion more likely reflected etymological continuities than genuine institutional ones (with the Castilian *estantes*, referring to a nonmigratory herd and more broadly to a fixed position for something mobile, such as a cannon emplacement). Vassberg's (1984) thorough study of sixteenth-century Castilian land tenure does not mention either estancias or sitios, which suggests that these were indeed New World institutions.

12. In 1864 a German geologist on a visit to Miravalles volcano noted that the haciendas there were referred to as "hatos" (Von Seebach 1974: 225).

13. In seventeenth-century Mexico, a sitio was equivalent to eighteen caballerías or 780 hectares (Chevalier 1963: 70).

14. Schell (1986: 57–60) provides a detailed account of the etymology of this term.

15. In 1690, for example, Capitán Juan Macoleta, having suffered "because of some dissension in the neighborhood of those valleys and damages caused by the people in his service," paid 400 pesos to the royal treasury "in order to have his hacienda secure and quiet and so that no neighbor would come near it" (*DHCR*, 3: 15).

16. References to "composed" properties and original hacienda titles generally date to this period. Examples are numerous, but include 1710 and 1711 titles to Sitio La Chocolata, Sitio El Real, and Hacienda El Tempisque (ANCR LJC r. 1263, no. 771—1920; Jiménez 1906) and the 1728 title to the Sitio del Sagrado Corazón de Jesús del Morote, in Nicoya (CN uncat. 27, n.d.; see also Fonseca Corrales 1983:339–49).

17. Among the deeds probably granted under the 1754 edict were those of the Ramos family in Santa Cruz (*Costa Rica de Ayer y Hoy* 1960: 26; *Revista de los Archivos Nacionales* 1948: 287–88) and those to six sections of Hacienda El Jobo, some 35.5 caballerías (ANCR GJC r. 1264, no. 4—1926: 31).

18. In 1906, for example, a major court case between claimants to sections of the Haciendas Tempisque and Real revolved around the question of which creek (*quebrada*) was called "the Mataperro" in the 1710 titles (Jiménez 1906).

19. Gudmundson (1979: 66) has suggested instead that more conflicts occurred in the former Nicoya jurisdiction than in what had been the Costa Rican zone because properties were registered earlier (shortly after independence) in the latter area. Colonial titles were common in both areas, however.

20. This property, donated to the cofradía in 1728 by the Spanish governor of Nicoya, contained only 200 cattle at the time of the 1751 cattle census (*DHCR*, 3: 123), an indication of the extremely extensive grazing practices at the time.

21. The estimate of the extension of auctioned cofradía lands is in a complaint by Nicoya residents that sought to halt the successful bidders' heirs from taking possession of the properties (ANCR Gob. 7349—1866: 16). The issue of "old" versus "new" caballerías was raised by Mauro Aguilar in a suit against the cofradías in which he sought to assert his rights over Hacienda El Viejo (ANCR LJC r. 1264, no. 685—1865: 9v).

22. The existence of such lands well into the twentieth century is attested to by numerous documentary sources, as well as by local oral tradition. Among the mentions of communal and cofradía lands in this area are the following: an 1878 land claim in the area of Puerto Culebra, which notes that

the claimed lot borders on the southeast with "lands of the Indians *naturales* of Nicoya" (ANCR JCA 5453); cadastral plans of Sitio Las Trancas from 1924 (CN uncat.) and Hacienda El Viejo from circa 1925 (CN G5-2-1-1) that indicate, respectively, "lands of the *vecinos* [residents] of Sardinal" and lands of El Amo, Santa Ana, El Santísimo, and La Concepción, all cofradías, as well as lands of the barrio of Belén; and several references to conflicts over such lands in the 1940s in the newspaper *El Guanacaste*.

23. Most of the northern Nicoya sitios and haciendas listed in the census may be identified in relation to place names still in use some two hundred years later: Santa Lucía de la Pitahaya, Las Trancas, Trinidad, San Roque, Santa Rosa, El Pelón, Tempisquito, Orosí, Naranjo, Rincón de la Vieja, San Antonio, Sapoá, Santo Tomás, Las Ventanas, El Jobo, Asiento Viejo (Asientillo), and Las Ciruelas. The census listed properties according to whether owners resided in Rivas (or Villa de Nicaragua, as it was sometimes called) or Nicoya; all but two of the northern Nicoya (latifundist, nonpeninsular zone) properties belonged to Rivas residents. These were two herds estimated at 1,000 head each, in sitio La Cueva, a moist upland area northeast of Liberia, and in Hacienda San Jerónimo, an area of well-watered lowlands southwest of Liberia. In Figure 1.1 data are ordered geographically, and these two herds are included in the latifundist (nonpeninsular) zone. In an interesting 1790 document reproduced by Meléndez (1967: 53–55), Haciendas La Cueva and San Jerónimo are listed as belonging to residents of Rivas, though neither belonged to the same family as in 1751. My 1751 herd estimates differ slightly from those in other sources (e.g., Fonseca 1983; Matarrita Ruiz 1980a). This is probably because of differing judgments about how to count animals referred to in the census as "head" or "livestock" not specifically identified as cattle or horses.

24. MacLeod (1983: 195, 212) describes a similar "method of siphoning off Indian cottage production," called *derrama*, in the same period in Guatemala and Chiapas. There, as in Nicoya, the practice, opposed by the clergy, provoked several minor Indian rebellions. In Nicaragua, this type of exaction was termed *repartimiento de hilados* (Newson 1987: 278–80).

25. The principal colonial racial categories may be summarized as follows: *mestizo* (European-Indian ancestry), *mulato* (European-African ancestry), and *zambo* (African-Indian ancestry). All those who were neither Indians nor whites were characterized as *castas*. In Central America, the term *ladino* was applied to all non-Indians, although *Español* was frequently applied to whites born in the New World.

26. Gudmundson (1978b: 97) notes that slaves in colonial haciendas in Guanacaste frequently occupied the post of *mandador*, or foreman, and often had the right to pasture cattle on hacienda lands (also see Martínez Peláez 1972: 276–80, 698).

27. Information from field interviews.

28. According to Ayón (1956, 2: 296–97), in mid-eighteenth-century Rivas, just before the rebuilding of herds for the on-hoof cattle trade to El Salvador, there were 400 cacao haciendas and 23 *hatos*, or herds, none with more than 100 head. Meat was reported to be extremely scarce.

29. According to the *Anuarios estadísticos*, there were no wood exports from the Atlantic coast before 1911. The data are not broken down by port after 1917. Nevertheless, in the brief period 1908–17 only 5 percent of the volume and 1 percent of the value of wood exports from Costa Rica were from the Atlantic region. The rest were from Puntarenas.

30. Among the major hacendados involved in the wood trade in this period were Alfonso and Alejandro Salazar, owners of Hacienda El Viejo; Alejandro, Pedro, Pablo, and David Hurtado Bustos, whose properties included Haciendas El Jobo, La Culebra, and La Pitahaya; Francisco and Víctor Morice, who owned much of the land in La Cruz; Juan and Alberto Fait, owners of large properties in Tilarán and of timber leases in lowland Abangares; Agustín Guido, a large landowner and deputy from Puntarenas; and Federico Sobrado, owner of Haciendas El Tempisque and Santa María. Among the important wood companies were Pacific Lumber, whose owners included the North American latifundista George Wilson; the Costa Rica Lumber Export Company, whose partners, mostly English and North American, included the principal stockholders in the River Plate Mining Company (AN GJC 230—1900); and the companies owned by Víctor Wolf and Edmundo Solís, the former with additional interests in cattle and import trade (Cruz 1934: 541), the latter with family ties to the owners of Hacienda Paso Hondo.

31. In 1906, for example, the Cañas municipal secretary charged that the Fait brothers, both large loggers, "were refusing to pay taxes and had deceived the government" (ANCR Gob. 2232—1907). In 1926 Alberto Fait became involved in what a landowner's lawyer described as "a kind of boxing match over the extraction of woods . . . [with another logger], without either of these *señores* having permission to do such a thing" on the property in question (ANCR Gob. 7891—1926). The same year a Liberia judge ruled against Juan Fait when a government minister charged "that nearly all the wood that don Juan Fait takes out of Guanacaste through Bebedero [port] has been cut without permission on lands . . . belonging to Mr. Sinclair and others" (ANCR Gob. 7886—1926).

32. In 1888 companies controlled by Keith received permission to claim an additional 280,000 hectares of state land in return for building a railroad to the north, where it was expected that an interoceanic canal would soon be constructed (Hilje 1985, 1988)

33. By 1893 Keith's rights had been reduced to a total of 400,000 acres because of his failure to cultivate the land he had claimed.

34. In 1896 Barrios, who eventually controlled almost 70,000 hectares north of Liberia, was able to claim 500 hectares in spite of the fact that the land was in the prohibited zone (ANCR JCA 5459—1896).

35. Federico Sobrado claimed state lands next to his Hacienda Santa María this way in 1897 (ANCR JCA 1096—1897). Others who claimed land under this law included the children of Salvadora Argüello de Urcuyo, widow of Vicente Urcuyo Zamora, one of the largest landowners from Rivas, who in 1912 acquired "baldíos" next to their Haciendas Orosí and San Vicente (ANCR JCA 1156—1912), and Manuel Joaquín Barrios, who on at least two occasions did the same on land adjoining his haciendas in the north of the province (RPPG T834, F132–33, F460). Barrios's daughter Amalia Barrios Sacasa was married to de Urcuyo's son, Alejandro Urcuyo Argüello, a relationship that permitted the consolidation of part of each family's inheritance.

36. These provisions were repealed in 1913, although a few years later they were reenacted just for Guanacaste (Salas Víquez 1985: 116).

37. Bolaños and Quirós (1984: 33) indicate that this was true as well of the reforms in central Costa Rica.

38. This did not include some 2,500 hectares of El Tempisque "now occupied by [Hacienda] El Viejo due to a change in the course of the [Tempisque] river" (ANCR LJC r. 1264, no. 771—1920).

39. For instance, Hacienda Verdún, the main holding of the Nicaraguan Juan de Dios Pastora, who in 1934 was reported to possess a herd of 9,000 head (Cruz 1934: 542), was probably never more than 7,000 hectares. Pastora did, however, have large holdings on the other side of the border. Similarly, the North American Milton Dunham, a major supplier of animals to the central Costa Rican market (Gudmundson 1979), appears to have owned only some 2,000 hectares in Abangares acquired from a mining company (which incidentally retained subsoil rights) (RPPG T1736 F159 A1 N15466—1923; T1066, F364–366—1935). In this case, Dunham probably rented pastures to fatten cattle for market. Another Nicaraguan cattle merchant, Francisco Cubillo Incer, may well have been among the largest landowners in Guanacaste in the 1930s and 1940s. Cubillo arrived in Carrillo canton as a poor man, but apparently he had extraordinary business acumen. Using funds derived from logging, crop agriculture, and selling livestock, he bought thousands of hectares from smallholders in Carrillo and Santa Cruz and additional lands from George Wilson. His holdings, such as Hacienda La Jirona between Filadelfia and Santa Cruz, were assembled from numerous small titles and purchases of "improvements." This complicates any estimate of his holdings.

40. Sequiera (1985: 153) details numerous other cases of marriages between cousins or other related members of the late-nineteenth-century Guanacastecan elite.

Chapter 2

1. Deer were so accustomed to livestock that even as late as the 1940s they often grazed among the cattle on remote properties (Colegial 1989).

2. Feral or semiferal cattle were also referred to colloquially as "ganado aguacatero"—"wild" or literally "avocado-eating cattle."

3. Rouse (1977), in a detailed discussion of the natural and artificial selection processes that affected *criollo* populations in the Americas, praises one supposed variety ("Rivas criollo" or "milking criollo"), which goes unmentioned in other sources on northern Costa Rican or southern Nicaraguan cattle (pp. 178–79). Rouse apparently relied on studies carried out in the 1960s at the Interamerican Institute of Agricultural Sciences (Instituto Interamericano de Ciencias Agrícolas), which mistakenly generalized about all criollos on the basis of a small sample of animals that had been artificially selected for dairy purposes (Robert 1989: 9).

4. Several hacendados interviewed mentioned that before 1950 cattle on the large estates often went without revision for six months to a year.

5. Mortality estimates are from *El Guanacaste*, 15 Jan. 1939, 6 (16 percent); S.H. Viniegra, owner of Hacienda La Palma, ANCR Gob. 699—1907: 42 (over 25 percent); Gudmundson (1979: 50) (25 to 50 percent); and *AE* 1945: 13 (60 percent on some large breeding haciendas). Causes of mortality are discussed in Matamoros (1937: 14) and *El Guanacaste*, 10 Oct. 1943, 3.

6. The term *sabanero* was also used in some other Latin American cattle-ranching regions, such as Colombia's Magdalena Valley (Deffontaines 1965: 322).

7. Sometimes these tasks were not even carried out in centrally located corrals. One Liberia hacendado recalled that in the first decades of the twentieth century, when he was a child, "the way we rounded up cattle was to sound a shell trumpet and throw some salt on the rocks so that the cattle, by associating the sound of the shell (*caracol*) with the salt, would come to certain places and there we would cure [wounds] or do what had to be done to the cattle."

8. The Calverts' account (1917: 473) corroborates Santos's observation. Commenting on the "absence of butter" in Guanacaste, they noted that hotel keepers, while serving "native cheese," had "not yet thought it necessary to supply that article."

9. Data on the number of cheese and butter factories and dairies during the early twentieth century vary widely from year to year and probably reflect changing census criteria and procedures at least as much as on-the-ground reality.

10. Interviews in Bolsón and Ortega, Santa Cruz, 1982.

11. For a detailed discussion of transhumance in Latin America, see Deffontaines (1965).

12. Even in the late 1960s, a study of the Guanacaste cattle sector reported that "the acquisition of a bajura probably ranks first in the order of ranching priorities" (V. Smith 1970: 33).

13. Perhaps the most frequent defender of the thesis that latifundismo

was nothing more than an adaptation to Guanacaste's harsh dry season was Aristides Baltodano Briceño, an eleven-term congressional deputy from Guanacaste and father of his agronomist namesake quoted above (e.g., *La Gaceta Oficial*, 9 Nov. 1945, 1958–59). It is probably not a coincidence that the Baltodanos were owners of the 6,621-hectare Hacienda El Pelón de la Altura, acquired in the 1930s from the heirs of Minor Keith and—even in the 1980s—one of the most extensively utilized haciendas in the region.

14. Parsons does not specify the dynamics of this ruminant-grass coevolution. It may be supposed that ingested seeds were propagated and fertilized by animals and that this in turn affected positively the palatableness and nutritional qualities of grass species over long evolutionary time. Crosby (1986: 288–90) suggests that a similar process occurred throughout the New World, though he mistakenly implies that virtually all significant Old World species that spread to the Western Hemisphere were of European origin.

15. *Pará* includes various closely related species of the genus *Panicum*, such as *P. purpurascens, P. altissiumin, P. barnicoide,* and *P. molle.* The latter was probably the most common in Costa Rica in the early twentieth century.

16. In 1893 Federico Sobrado already had a 100-hectare pasture of pará in Hacienda Santa María at an elevation of at least 500 meters. Smaller plantings of pará in highland areas around Cañas Dulces were made by David Hurtado Bustos and others (ANCR JCA 5649—1891; ANCR JCA 5782—1896; CN G1-2-1-15—1949).

17. Guinea grass never became as popular as jaragua, in part because cattle found it less palatable (V. Smith 1970: 58).

18. Cruz (1934: 517–18), Killinger and Mata (1955), and V. Smith (1970: 57–65) also discuss several other exotic species of grass of lesser economic importance, such as janeiro (*Eriochloa polystachya*), *gigante,* or elephant grass (*Pennistum purpureum*), pangola (*Digitaria decumbens*), and calinguero or yerba gordura (*Melinis minutiflora*). Several peasants in Santa Cruz canton showed me a pasture grass called *coyolillo,* the botanical name of which I have been unable to find. This grass is particularly difficult to eradicate once introduced; it forms small onionlike bulbs ("cebollitas") under the ground, which multiply when cut by a plough or a hoe.

19. Jaragua spread both as a result of human intervention and because it tended to replace other vegetation. Ranchers scattered jaragua seed in moist wooded sitios where cattle would graze during the dry season and trample the seed into the ground. In existing pastures, they planted jaragua late in the dry season after burning the fields (V. Smith 1970: 63).

20. Much later, in 1977, the "maritime mile" was reduced to a mere 50 meters above the high-water mark.

21. On Castro's haciendas, see ANCR Cong. 17188—1934; ANCR Cong. 19409—1939; and ANCR Gob. 10609—1936.

22. Castro's practice of placing Nelore cattle in view of train passengers has been recounted to the author in interviews.

23. Weights for finished steers are from field interviews.

24. In this book, U.S. dollar equivalents for Costa Rican currency are calculated according to the free-market exchange rates listed in Albarracín and Pérez (1977: 26), for 1907–46, and in BCCR (1986: 211–13), for 1950–85.

25. LeGrand (1986: 31), who describes landlord destruction of peasant fences in Colombia's central cordillera, is one exception.

26. La Lupita, widely considered one of the best properties in the region, measured 714 hectares when Minor Keith's heirs sold it to the Clachar family in 1935 for 52,000 colones ($8,754), a price that included 150 cows from Keith's El Pelón de la Altura. In 1981 interviews, José Joaquín Muñoz Bustos and Manuel Jirón García, cattlemen from Liberia and Carrillo, respectively, recounted versions of the story about the high cost of La Lupita's fences.

27. In 1936, for example, residents of Lepanto, on the Nicoya Peninsula, noted in a letter to the Congress that "fences are worth a lot of money and they are not constructed, except when it is a question of crops that can pay [the cost]. In cattle breeding, it is not possible to invest money in making fences, because it does not pay that cost" (ANCR Cong. 18734—1936: 1).

28. With the exception of anthrax, which was present in the colonial period, most of these diseases or vectors were believed to have arrived in Costa Rica with cattle imported from Colombia and elsewhere in the late nineteenth or early twentieth centuries (Jiménez 1903; Robert 1989: 27–32). Jiménez's (1903) contention that cattle ticks arrived in about 1890 clearly requires qualification, since Nutting (1882) described in graphic terms how these bothersome pests were well established a decade before.

29. Interview with Wilson's son, David Stewart Bonilla, 1981.

30. This specialist may not have been the most thorough observer. El Porvenir was located directly across the Tempisque River from Hacienda El Tempisque, where contemporaneous reports indicate the presence of some non-criollo animals.

31. In the decade after the opening of the railway, annual cargo traffic from the Gulf of Nicoya to Puntarenas climbed steadily from 1,000 to 3,000 metric tons. Launches carried less than 12,000 passengers to Puntarenas in 1911 and almost 23,000 in 1918. The number of cattle shipped to the Pacific port soared from less than 2,000 in 1911 to over 19,000 in 1922 (*Memorias de Fomento* 1904–10; *Memoria de Gobernación* 1898).

32. Interview, 1982.

33. Estimates from field interviews.

34. Because of the virtually open border between Nicaragua and Costa Rica, official import figures are probably greatly understated. Consumption figures, based on taxes paid to municipal slaughterhouses, were widely be-

lieved at the turn of the century to be understated and "the object of great frauds" because they did not include clandestine butchering in remote areas (Jiménez 1903: 7). But because rustling and unreported slaughtering declined in subsequent decades and because most animals were consumed in densely populated areas with greater state control, the consumption data are probably considerably more accurate than the import data.

35. Sequiera (1985: 150–51), who analyzed 27 hacienda mortgages in the period 1851–87 listed in the Costa Rican National Archives *Protocolos de Guanacaste* series, found interest rates to be somewhat lower than the 10 to 12 percent annual rates that were common in the early twentieth century (e.g., on the Urcuyo family's mortgages, see RPPG T495 F76–78 N3798–99; on the Clachars' use of a mortgage to acquire property from Minor Keith, see RPPG T1066 F334–35 N6636). Until the 1960s, when many large landowners began to "segregate lots" or form corporations (see Chapter 7), property registry entries for the largest haciendas typically contain many more mortgage inscriptions and cancellations than any other type of operation.

Sequeira also suggests that mortgages were used "exclusively for livestock activity" and that occasional large mortgages, such as one loan of 15,000 pesos in 1874 to Tomás Guardia Gutiérrez (who, though Sequeira does not mention it, was president of the Republic at the time), were indicative of the hacendados' shortage of liquid capital. Descriptions of properties and corporations in the Registro Público de la Propiedad and Registro Mercantil suggest, however, that hacendados' investments were highly diversified. It is thus unlikely that cash raised with haciendas as collateral was used only for cattle production.

Chapter 3

1. Leeds's argument that "peasantry" was a mystifying or obscurantist concept and that it be preserved, if at all, only as a heuristic device was the most extreme position within a growing consensus among North American anthropologists about the term's imprecision and the need for greater specificity (Mintz 1973; Silverman 1979; Vincent 1977). But it had at least one significant shortcoming, perhaps particularly evident to social scientists who were not products of depeasantized, advanced capitalist societies. "Peasant" (in Hispanic America, *campesino*) is a critical aspect—for many the critical aspect—of the subjective definition of self and identity for masses of rural people, something that "exists in the collective consciousness and political deed of its members" (Shanin 1982: 425). To the extent that the "peasant" category influences political behavior—whether active mobilization or "everyday" resistance—or delineates the subjectively recognized boundaries of social groups, its construction and its subcategories constitute important problems for analysis.

2. On the "shortage of hands" issue in Costa Rica as a whole, see Churnside (1980), and in Latin America, Bauer (1979).

3. The term *peón* generally referred to the poorest and least skilled rural laborers. But it was and is frequently used to include *sabaneros*, or cowboys, an occupation with higher status and remuneration.

4. Interviews with David Clachar González and Manuel Jirón García, 1981.

5. This section is based primarily on numerous interviews and on descriptions of working conditions by both peons and employers in *El Guanacaste*, the regional newspaper.

6. Interviews in Cañas Dulces and Quebrada Grande de Liberia and at Hacienda El Pelón de la Altura, 1982.

7. Martínez Alier (1975) and Orlove (1980) describe a similar custom in the livestock haciendas of highland Peru. However, the practice in Peru of replacing stolen hacienda animals with those belonging to the employees charged with herd supervision never took hold in Guanacaste, where it would likely have been difficult for hacendados to enforce.

8. The subregional differences in population sex ratios are significant at p = .006 for 1864 (χ^2 = 7.45), p = .006 for 1883 (χ^2 = 7.58), and $p <$ .001 for 1892 (χ^2 = 37.17).

9. Quirós Zúñiga (1990) provides a graphic (if somewhat exaggerated) picture of landlords' seignorial pretensions in a novel set in Hacienda El Viejo in the early twentieth century.

10. This undoubtedly fed on the rural population's rich body of superstition about snakes. Among the many fabulous beliefs encountered in fieldwork were that pregnant women can hypnotize poisonous snakes simply by staring at them; that the large, nonpoisonous boa metamorphoses into the short, venomous *bocaracá* at night; and that cutting the tail off a rattlesnake does not hurt it, since it simply becomes a *cascabel mudo* (literally a "mute rattlesnake," called a "bushmaster" in English). Though many snakes in Guanacaste are not poisonous and consume rodents that are a nuisance or a threat to humans, peasants routinely kill any that they encounter.

11. I am indebted to Carlos Camacho Nassar for sharing this information from his interviews with old employees of Castro's Hacienda Coyolar.

12. For a more detailed discussion of the use of Nicaraguan labor for the "most strenuous work" on the southern banana plantations, see Bourgois (1989: 181–83).

13. Field interviews in Bolsón and Ortega, Santa Cruz, 1982.

14. Bourgois (1989: 182–83) notes that this stereotype appears to have had some foundation as well on the banana plantations of southern Costa Rica.

15. This measure sparked a major peasant rebellion in Matagalpa in 1881, which was violently repressed by the army (Wheelock 1974: 109–18).

16. The *jueces de mesta* were rooted in the traditional Castilian Mesta, a

Crown institution that regulated livestock (and particularly sheep) herding. In the late eighteenth century, the Guatemalan colonial administration proposed establishing the *mesta* in Central America, but the Costa Rican provincial authorities determined that it was unnecessary given their region's low level of livestock development (Robert 1989: 16–17). In postindependence Liberal Nicaragua, however, these shotgun-toting "judges" had broader responsibilities for social control and law enforcement. They were only abolished once the Sandinistas took power in 1979. The 1970 U.S. government handbook for Nicaragua describes the *juez de mesta* as "a combination of justice of the peace and sheriff" (Ryan et. al. 1970: 329).

17. Gould (1990: 73) writes of Chinandega, in northern Nicaragua, that "before 1950, when a field laborer . . . encountered a landlord in the street, he often stepped into the street, joined his hands together as if praying, and said 'Santito patrón,' asking for the patrón's blessing."

18. Sources on this ritual, in addition to field interviews, include Périgny (1974: 448–53) and Delgado (1980: 74–75). González (1977: 96–104) provides a fictionalized account set in the 1940s in Abangares in what is apparently the large latifundio of the Italian Segnini family. Another variation of this practice did not have the same implications for relations of domination. Some informants recalled that in town fiestas dead vultures were formerly placed atop greased poles in climbing competitions, and successful contestants were those who ascended and descended with a feather.

19. And where it might well have attracted the attention of such meticulous observers as Bovallius (1977), Levy (1965), or Niederlein (1898b). When I queried informants who remembered the ritual in Guanacaste and who were familiar with conditions in Nicaragua, they remarked that Nicaraguan patrones were "stricter" and would not permit such "diversions."

20. Sequiera (1985: 59–62) refers to the "very low" wages on the Guanacastecan haciendas, but does not note that wages in most other zones were even lower. Although he notes the existence of a "chronic labor shortage," he does not draw the logical conclusions about what such a shortage would mean for wage levels.

21. The 1932 *Anuario Estadístico* (p. 21) listed the number of "unemployed" in each province. It did not specify the criteria used, and the numbers and rates appear low. Assuming, however, that criteria were applied relatively evenly, it is striking that Guanacaste had 6.5 unemployed per 1,000 inhabitants, while the national average was 16.7. Other provinces' rates ranged from 12.9 in Alajuela to 49.4 in Heredia.

22. Other hacendados benefited from state efforts to increase food production in non-coffee-growing areas. In 1910, in one example of such largesse, the government gave Luis Leipold, one of the principal ranchers of Cañas, an Engleberg rice-husking machine free of charge in order to stimulate production in the canton (*Memoria de Fomento 1911*: 31).

23. In 1950, shortly after United Fruit Company purchased Hacienda Tenorio, it had only "six cowhands to handle more than 2,000 head of cattle" (Unifruitco 1950).

24. As late as 1946, United Fruit Company officials estimated that "in the province of Guanacaste alone there [were] 40,000" Nicaraguans desperately seeking work as laborers (quoted in Bourgois 1989: 190). While this appraisal is doubtless exaggerated—the province's total population in 1950 was only 88,190—it does indicate employer awareness of a buyer's labor market in Guanacaste.

Chapter 4

1. Information on the Wilson latifundio from field interviews.

2. For example, court documents detail charges against the following prominent landowners: David and Alejandro Hurtado Bustos (ANCR LJC r. 581, nos. 36—1904 and 78—1906), Manuel Barahona (ANCR LJC r. 581, nos. 71—1906 and 102—1907), Luis Morice (ANCR LJC r. 718, no. 26—1915), Antonio Alvarado (ANCR LJC r. 1066, no. 1—1915), former president of the Republic Bernardo Soto (ANCR LJC r. 747, no. 227—1916), Rafael Recio (ANCR LJC r. 253, no. 118—1889), Leona Aguilar, the wife of Alfonso Salazar (ANCR LJC r. 318, no. 6—1903), Indalecio Sobrado (ANCR LJC r. 747, no. 221—1916), and Enrique Montiel (ANCR LA r. 1126, no. 26—1920).

3. In the early 1980s such areas include forested sections of Santa Rosa and Palo Verde national parks, which formerly were parts of the haciendas of the same names.

4. The manual provided to Treasury Police asked, "What conduct must the guard observe in the fulfillment of his fiscal duty? He must be active and shrewd (*malicioso*), respectful and prudent, circumspect and firm. He will avoid useless discussions and will always invoke the law in the fulfillment of his duty" (Zúñiga 1950: 5).

5. The censused areas were La Palma de Abangares, which contained the barrios of Colorado and San Buenaventura; Boquerones, containing Palmira de Carrillo; La Cueva and El Encinal, north of Liberia; Dos Ríos, Montañita, Sabana Grande, and La Cofradía, all near Liberia; San Antonio and Morote in Nicoya; and Comunidad de Carrillo. It is important to note that the highland mining areas and coastal La Cruz, both areas with many squatters, were not included in the survey.

6. According to the 1885 Fiscal Code, up to 50 hectares of state lands could be acquired simply by cultivating the plot and registering it with a court or other authority. The 1909 Heads of Families Law (Ley de Cabezas de Familia) made similar provisions. Those who occupied private lands "in good faith," believing that the lands were state-owned or that a title extended by a previous occupant was valid, could claim limited possession rights after

three months if they were not opposed by the legal owner or another claimant. Full rights could be obtained after ten years of continuous, "good faith" occupation if nobody opposed the claim (Sáenz P. and Knight 1972; Salas Víquez 1985).

7. This is based on the subtraction of an estimate of natural population increase based on birth and death data in the *Anuarios estadísticos* from the total increase indicated by comparing the 1883 and 1892 censuses. Because of probable underreporting, birth data were adjusted by a factor of 1.15 and death data by 1.25.

8. In a few cases, the government organized colonization efforts. In 1891 it granted lands in southern Nicoya to exiled Cuban independence fighter Antonio Maceo on condition that he establish a sugar mill and a colony of settlers (ANCR Cong. 2081—1891). This experiment, poignantly described by a Spanish resident of Nicoya (Apéstegui 1942: 7–28), lasted only briefly, since with Cuban independence in 1898 most of the colonists returned home (Sapper 1974: 325). In 1910 the government sponsored another settlement, called Colonia Carmona, near the abandoned Colonia Maceo (ANCR Cong. 14959—1910). This project's beneficiaries were primarily from central Costa Rica; it received sustained state support and grew rapidly in the 1930s and after.

9. With the exception of a few areas on the Nicoya Peninsula, neither group entered en masse into zones occupied by the other. Derogatory comments about "Cartagos" or Guanacastecans are unusual today, since intermarriage and small-scale population movements have blurred the boundaries and diminished the significance of this once-salient ethnic distinction.

10. Lepanto is part of Puntarenas province, but it is closely united by geography, history, and culture with the rest of the Nicoya Peninsula, which is part of Guanacaste.

11. This dichotomy has been adopted uncritically by other students of rural Costa Rica, including De La Cruz (1986) and Hilje (1985).

12. In a later work (1986), Gudmundson convincingly shows how traditional historians have erroneously constructed a vision of a pristine and "pre-economic" central Costa Rica prior to the fall from grace represented by nineteenth-century coffee expansion. It is ironic that his analysis of early-twentieth-century Guanacaste involves a comparable romanticization of the lowland peasantry's "subsistence" and antiproperty orientation.

13. For example, "Subdivisiones de el Terreno El Espíritu Santo de Las Cañas" (Santa Cruz) (CN 53—1926) and other plans cited in Tables 4.1 –4.4.

14. This is one of the few sources not cited or included by Gudmundson (1978a) in an otherwise excellent compilation of documents on the Guanacaste mining zone.

15. Interviews with descendants of "Cartago" colonists in the Nicoya highlands indicate that when coffee was introduced there, it was planted

with the most rudimentary cultivation methods, in fields that still contained underbrush and numerous fallen trees. The effective reproduction of the mental model of central Costa Rican commercial coffee gardens was, in this context at least, a long and gradual process.

16. Gudmundson cites one case in support of the "phantasmal parcel" argument, that of La Cofradía in Liberia, which several years after being expropriated " 'still [had] not been distributed [in lots] because it is occupied . . . by the residents' " (ANCR Cong. 12473—1921: 2, in Gudmundson 1982: 89). La Cofradía is in Llano Grande de Liberia, an area of extremely poor soils appropriate for extensive cattle grazing but not for agriculture. In all probability, the reason this property was not divided after expropriation had less to do with the Guanacastecan peasantry's supposed opposition to parceling land than with its tradition of leaving infertile areas open as grazing sitios.

17. These movements bear reconsideration, in spite of the fact that they were analyzed in detail by Gudmundson (1982, 1983c). As was discussed above, considerable evidence casts doubt on the neat dichotomy between subsistence hacienda peasants and market-oriented freeholders that is central to Gudmundson's interpretation. Documentary sources (some apparently not consulted by Gudmundson), as well as interviews with elderly residents, also shed new light on the course of agrarian struggles, the leadership of antilandlord movements, the peasants' aspirations and grievances, and the longer-term consequences of state efforts to settle agrarian conflicts.

18. Viniegra's plans to form a partnership with Gaston Calmette, editor of the Parisian daily *Le Figaro*, were thwarted when the influential journalist-investor was murdered by the wife of the French finance minister, whom he had accused in print of corruption.

19. Sales contracts for large properties routinely stipulated that no squatters should be on the land or that the purchase price would be reduced by the amount required to secure their departure. One of Wilson's sons remembered, for example, that "father had problems with land invasions in the lowlands, but he bought them off. He was guaranteed when he bought the property that there wouldn't be any nesters on it. This was in the contract. After he bought them out, he kept very strict control, watching any time there was an invasion."

20. These plans enjoyed support at the highest levels of government. In addition to donating steel rails and port facilities and promising tax exonerations for machinery imports, during Bousqué's first visit the government provided him with a special railway car for his trip from Limón to San José. Upon arrival he was received by the president and then sent on a special launch from Puntarenas to La Palma.

21. In Costa Rica the term *macho* (male) is commonly applied to blond or light-complected individuals, particularly if they are foreigners. Blond females are frequently referred to as *macha*.

22. This was a common strategy for dealing with occupants. That the collection of rents was often of less significance to hacendados than the eventual eviction of occupants was suggested by a letter from Fernando Castro Cervantes to the Interior (Gobernación) Ministry, in which he complained of the occupation of part of Hacienda El Coyolar in Turrubares, San José province: "The bad faith with which [the occupants] proceed stands out more when it is remembered that last year they signed IOUs to me for the amount of rent due for the occupied land. In the desire to avoid causing them difficulties and violence, they were permitted to sign these IOUs, which are now long overdue and which they have not wanted to cover. It is evident that on providing those documents, the occupants gave full recognition that they are in lands of El Coyolar; and that, by not meeting the stipulated payment and by continuing in El Coyolar, after the term [of the IOUs] has expired, they have been left in the condition of 'parasites,' as specified by article 295 of the Civil Code and Law No. 5 of October 5, 1926" (ANCR Gob. 10609—1934: 20).

23. Two other elderly residents of La Palma and San Joaquín, interviewed in 1980, also mentioned this practice. Federico Sobrado also issued tokens (*chapas*) to employees of Hacienda Tempisque in the mid-1930s, and residents of surrounding communities resented this (De La Cruz 1986: 356). One resident of Filadelfia who worked on the Tempisque in the 1920s recalled that "Sobrado made his own coins, because his money wasn't enough to pay [the employees] during the sugarcane harvest. So he would pay on Saturdays, and on Mondays and Tuesdays he would collect all the coins from the merchants in Liberia, Filadelfia, Belén, Paso Tempisque, all over. They were worth a *peseta* (25 centavos), fifty centavos and one *colón*. People used the coins in stores, they were like a guarantee [of payment]." While some haciendas had (and have) *comisariatos*, or stores, it is unusual to find mentions of these stores that view them as exploitative institutions or report overcharging, large deductions from wages, or peon indebtedness as a method of securing labor. Allegations of price-gouging, however, were often leveled against village grocers, particularly the Chinese, during the same period (see Chapter 5).

24. Shortly thereafter, the Golfo Dulce Land Company purchased the land, which became the nucleus of the United Fruit Company's Pacific coast banana plantations.

25. The setting of the attack was described in interviews in La Palma in 1980 and with Jorge Bonilla Dib (Vicente Bonilla's son) in Las Juntas in 1981.

26. El Jobo consisted of six sections: San Francisco, four old caballerías; La Mantequilla, five old caballerías; El Jobo, thirteen and one-half old caballerías; El Tempisquito, four old caballerías; San Roquito, four old caballerías; and San Roque, also called San Antonio, five old caballerías (ANCR GJC r. 1264, no. 4—1926: 18). In 1922 El Jobo was remeasured at 18,618 hectares (CN G1-2-1-271).

27. In 1922 La Culebra was remeasured at 6,062 hectares (CN G1-2-1-271).

28. Rent payments, actual or promised, were highly unusual in Guanacaste during this period. The Hurtados' success in obtaining such pledges—an unambiguous recognition of their rights that could also serve as a basis for evictions—was probably due both to the sympathies of judicial authorities and to the fact that the disputed lands were on the main road between Nicaragua and Liberia, a short distance from the main house of El Jobo and thus exposed to both state and hacendado coercion. The judicial finding was likely satisfactory from the Hurtados' point of view, since subsequent documentation mentions no appeals or further conflicts. Before 1920 the brothers' only other eviction efforts were an 1895 suit against "El Moreno" and an 1899 case against an occupant of El Encinal who was cutting timber and who turned out to be an employee of José Cabezas, to whom the Hurtados had sold wood rights. At various times, however, the Hurtados were involved in litigation with other hacendados over conflicting property claims.

29. The Urcuyo Barrios children inherited much of this property, which squatters invaded in the 1960s and 1970s (see Chapter 8).

30. This was later renamed García Flamenco after Marcelino García Flamenco, the Salvadoran schoolteacher who died in 1919 in Guanacaste while fighting to overthrow the dictatorship of the Tinocos. In January 1917 General Federico Tinoco overthrew the reformist government of Alfredo González Flores, as a result of the latter's efforts to establish an income tax and his refusal to grant concessions to foreign oil companies. Together with his brother José Joaquín, whom he appointed minister of war, Tinoco engaged in unprecedented repression and pilfering of the national treasury. Until his resignation in 1919, the disruption caused both by the Tinocos and by the frequent outbreaks of violence aimed at overthrowing them had a devastating effect on the economy, particularly in Guanacaste.

31. Hurtado did not bring any new eviction suits until 1926, when he lost one on appeal and settled another by paying the defendant's legal costs and buying "improvements" on the disputed land (ANCR GJC r. 1264, nos. 3 and 4—1926: 46).

32. Turnover was high in the thankless position of police agent in Cañas Dulces and Quebrada Grande during the early 1920s, in part because of suspicions about the loyalty of those appointed. New appointments of police agents were often preceded by flurries of telegrams between San José and Liberia inquiring about the political affiliations of candidates for the job, who in at least two cases were said to be sympathizers of the Partido Agrícola (ANCR Gob. 8122—1923), one of several organizations blamed for the unrest.

33. This kind of militancy clearly would have worried Guanacastecan latifundistas. But the particulars that prompted the police commander's allusion to "unionism," as well as his intended meaning of the phrase, remain obscure.

34. Julio Sánchez Lépiz, the wealthy owner of Haciendas Taboga e Higuerón in Cañas and a proponent of private-sector agrarian reform (see Chapter 5), was also elected to the Congress as the Partido Agrícola candidate in Heredia province, where he had the largest coffee business in Costa Rica. He refused to take part in legislative sessions, however, alleging that he was an uneducated "campesino" and that his constituents would be better served by his "substitutes" (*suplentes*), a doctor and a lawyer (Marín 1972: 93–99).

35. The three were Pastor Díaz, Jesús de la O, and Francisco Ruiz.

36. Lands elsewhere totaling 122,312 hectares were to be returned to the state.

37. Dynamite may also have been familiar to nonminers in the crowd, since informants report that it was used by loggers to split tree trunks too large to be pulled by oxen.

38. Although the Guanacaste Development Company found the price of twenty colones per hectare agreeable, it hoped to extricate itself from an intractable situation and insisted on selling a full 12,000 hectares, rather than the 9,000 initially authorized by the Congress (and it sought to retain mineral rights) (ANCR Gob. 8054—1924; ANCR Cong. 14584—1926). In 1923 it sold most of its 18,660-hectare property to the U.S.–based Sacra Familia Gold Mining Company, which then transferred it to the Sinclair and Victoria Investment Company, owned by a former president of Sacra Familia. Five years later the government acquired 17,069 hectares of this land, intending to distribute lots to occupants (ANCR Cong. 17003—1934; *La Gaceta Oficial*, 14 Dec. 1928, 1–2). In 1932 the government also purchased the remaining occupied parts of the Sacra Familia properties (ANCR Cong. 16384—1932).

39. As late as 1940, the government lowered its price, proposing that peasants pay nine colones per hectare for lands they occupied, a sum they declared was beyond their means (ANCR Cong. 19878—1941). The mining zone experienced growing land concentration after 1950, but many smaller properties were not registered until the large-scale titling programs of the 1960s.

40. In Costa Rica, as elsewhere in Latin America, Syrians, Lebanese, and their descendants are frequently referred to as "Turks" (*turcos*), probably because immigrants from the Ottoman-controlled Levant carried Turkish travel documents.

41. United Fruit's properties in Guanacaste, Hacienda Paso Hondo, which it held from about 1907 to about 1927 (ANCR Cong. 12626—1922; ANCR Gob. 1367—1907; *La Tribuna*, 3 Mar. 1935), and Hacienda Tenorio, which it acquired in 1949 and owned for five years (Colegial 1989; Unifruitco 1950), were used to fatten cattle and to breed mules for banana plantations in southern Costa Rica and elsewhere. At least as early as 1918, UFCO purchased cattle in Nicaragua and Guanacaste for its plantations in Limón and Panama. UFCO correspondence from that year indicates that, in addition to

Minor Keith's cattle, the company sought lean animals in Chontales, Nicaragua, and at Hacienda El Jobo in Liberia. It exported many head to its Panamanian plantations. UFCO canceled the Tenorio mule-breeding project in the 1950s when its engineers decided to install overhead cableways on the plantations, which replaced the animals earlier used to carry harvested fruit.

42. The image of the English Luddites as deluded atavists conforms only partially to historical reality (see Hobsbawm and Rudé 1968). Its incorporation into "proletarian" and antismallholder interpretations of Guanacastecan agrarian conflict has led some analysts to dubious conjectures about peasant consciousness. Fernández Carballo (1980: 31), for example, offers no evidence for his assertion that peasants who "destroyed their most immediate exploiter's means of production did so believing that their exploitation was due to those means and not to the entire system in which they were immersed."

Chapter 5

1. The exalted place of Jiménez in the popular imagination has impressed itself upon traditional Costa Rican historiography (e.g., Rodríguez Vega 1971).

2. Two of Jiménez's advisors pointed to this lack of coherence in comments on a draft of the 1932 law prepared for the Congress: "The most characteristic phenomenon of our livestock legislation has always been the tendency not to test the final effects of protectionist laws. A law passed today by one government is repealed tomorrow by another, without any justification. This absence of firmness, this constant oscillation of our laws, has meant that the livestock industry has not developed better, as it has in other nations where the good principles of protectionist policy have been taken to their end" (Sáenz Gutiérrez and Merz 1932a: 10).

3. Northwestern Costa Rican landowners did not organize in defense of their interests until well after 1932, probably because several of their representatives occupied important government positions, including that of president of the republic. Some short-lived regionalist organizations had been founded in Guanacaste, such as the Unión Guanacasteca, started by hacendados Antonio Alvarez Hurtado and Francisco Mayorga Rivas in the early 1900s, and the Sociedad Pro-Guanacaste of the 1920s (Alvarez Hurtado 1903; Dávila 1976). However, only the Partido Confraternidad Guanacasteca (PCG), which lasted from 1934 to 1942, ever attained any significant following or had any national impact (Dávila 1976). Because the leading faction in this group was decidedly antilatifundista, hacendados lent only conditional support. They backed PCG demands for roads and other public works, but were hostile to its call for land reform.

In 1939, when antiprotectionist forces mounted a campaign to repeal the

1932 law, the recently formed Asociación Nacional de Ganaderos (ANG) counterattacked by publishing pamphlets and advertisements in major newspapers. Two Guanacastecan hacendados, David Clachar and Miguel Brenes Gutiérrez, were officers of the association and spearheaded this effort, but in general the participation of Guanacastecans in national cattlemen's organizations in this period was limited (Robert 1989: 52–53, 116–17). The ANG was dominated by dairy farmers who were interested primarily in promoting cattle expositions in Campo Ayala, near the central Costa Rican city of Cartago.

4. Exchange rates fluctuated during the early 1930s. Twenty colones in 1932 was equivalent to $4.55; 40 colones in 1934 was worth $9.41, though by 1937 this had fallen to $7.13 as a result of devaluations.

5. Revenue from the law was supposed to fund an agricultural experiment station in Guanacaste, though as late as 1946 this still had not been started (*El Guanacaste*, 10 Dec. 1946, 1).

6. Wilson's share of the Guanacaste herd was actually larger, because he also owned cattle lands in other cantons, such as Hacienda El Viejo, which straddled Carrillo and Santa Cruz. There the presence of large properties of different owners makes it impossible on the basis of the census data to determine the size of Wilson's herds. The census may have underestimated Wilson's herd in Bagaces (and perhaps those of others as well). David Stewart, Wilson's son, recalled in an interview that when his father acquired the Bagaces haciendas in 1923, Bernardo Soto, the previous owner, guaranteed in the sales contract that the property contained 15,000 head of cattle. At the first roundup they counted "a little more" than 18,000.

7. Ownership concentration is measured by the Gini coefficient, which ranges from zero to one, with zero indicating perfect equality.

8. Between 1933 and 1950, the Gini coefficient of cattle herd ownership concentration fell from .77 to .64 (based on data in Merz 1934 and *CAP* 1950).

9. The Chinese applied the label "gold mountain" to tiny Costa Rica, as well as to other more prosperous parts of the Western Hemisphere, such as the United States. Conversations with Cañas residents, 1988.

10. Alfredo Hernández, a bank credit official, wrote about the creation in 1914 of rural lending institutions: "The need for credit was obvious in all the agricultural zones, and the small agriculturalists were financing themselves with local moneylenders who charged very high interest and who resorted to embargoing the collateral each time that some circumstance did not permit the debtor to comply punctually with his obligation. This was a true threat to the system of small property that the country is interested in conserving and developing" (Hernández 1942: 10).

11. In Guanacaste, in the initial years, no more than three members were appointed to each Junta.

12. Among the large landowners and merchants on the Guanacaste Juntas

in 1915 were Enrique Montiel, Manual Santos Estrada, and Rafael Hurtado Aguirre, in Liberia; José Chan Li, in Abangares; Benjamín Elizondo López, José Luis Apuy Li, and Salvador Fernández, in Cañas; Francisco Vargas and Miguel Jirón, in Carrillo; Eusebio Arrieta, Raimundo Brenes, and Francisco Guadamuz, in Santa Cruz; and Antonio Rosales and Carmen Noguera Campos, in Nicoya (BICR 1916).

13. In 1935, for example, the five Guanacaste Juntas made only 23 loans, averaging 2,255 colones ($380). Only the Santa Cruz Junta, which extended 16 loans, appears to have been genuinely active (BICR 1935: 41).

14. An additional problem with the Juntas was that they provided only working capital and not technical or marketing assistance. During the 1930s some extension functions were assumed by newly created government bodies, such as the veterinary service of the National Agriculture Center (Centro Nacional de Agricultura) and the National Agriculture School (Escuela Nacional de Agricultura) (León et al. 1981: II-25; Lorz 1934). The Banco Internacional also created a corps of appraisers and inspectors in 1935, since one of the Juntas' failings was their inability to assure that loans were employed for the intended purposes (Gil 1974: 121). Nevertheless, these modifications in the organization of agricultural extension and credit were not sufficient to safeguard the Juntas from the effects of the economic crisis or from their own flawed internal structure.

15. It is not possible on the basis of available national-level data to ascertain what proportion of credit went to the northwestern region or how such credit was divided between the beef and dairy sectors.

16. Outside of postrevolutionary Mexico, such efforts to alter land tenure were rare prior to the 1952 Bolivian revolution and the reforms of the 1960s inspired by the Alliance for Progress. Colonization programs, distinct from agrarian reforms in that they leave existing tenure systems essentially intact (Chonchol 1970), were more widespread in Latin America in the pre-1950 period. At times they were carried out by extremely repressive regimes, such as that of General Maximiliano Hernández Martínez in El Salvador, which distributed state lands to colonists in the mid-1930s in an attempt to reduce discontent in the aftermath of the slaughter used to put down the 1932 peasant uprising (Dalton 1972: 409; Guidos 1980: 17–18).

17. Virtually the only mention of this subject in the literature on the post-1961 Costa Rican agrarian reform is a single oblique reference by Barahona Riera (1980: 256), who writes that "from the beginning of this century, thought [on agrarian reform] grows in maturity until the thirties, when apparently the ground was prepared for initiating the task of agrarian transformations." Seligson (1980: 125) and Villarreal (1983: 83) suggest that agrarian reform began in the 1940s, but provide few details. Apart from the works of Gudmundson (1982) and Salas Víquez (1985), discussed in the text below, Hilje (1985) has analyzed early land distribution efforts in Tilarán.

18. Sánchez, however, the largest coffee grower in the *meseta central*, held views that in some respects may have been more typical of the central Costa Rican elite than of Guanacastecan latifundistas.

19. Information on Guardia is partly from field interviews.

20. In debates on reform projects, antilatifundista legislators frequently expressed concern that Costa Rica's supposed exceptionalism was threatened. One statement of this kind, typical in its preoccupation with egalitarian landownership and foreign landowners and in its misunderstanding of the history of the large estate in the northwest, was presented in 1920 by a congressional commission asked to examine one proposed reform measure: "It is an unarguable fact that the economic well-being and consequently the peace which were always the precious reward of Costa Rica have been diminished to the extent that the wise division of property cedes ground to the monopolization of lands for cultivation. It is also a troubling reality that the large latifundios that are beginning to be visible in our country have their origin in costly concessions given to foreign enterprises or in excessive claims made by state functionaries taking advantage of their high position" (*La Gaceta Oficial*, 9 Aug. 1928: 1098 [orig. 1920]).

In a similar vein, when the proposed auction of lands returned to the government by the River Plate Company raised the possibility of their acquisition by speculators, the Congress in 1923 resolved unanimously "that it be expressed to the Executive that Congress has seen with great sympathy the policy of the Executive of trying to maintain in the Republic the division of property and of avoiding the creation of latifundios" (ANCR Gob. 8152—1923). In part as a result of this resolution, the 55,600 hectares that River Plate had held in the western part of the Nicoya Peninsula were not sold to bidders but were declared *baldíos* open to claims by colonists under the relevant laws.

21. Thus in 1923 radical deputy Jorge Volio was "loudly applauded" when, arguing that the formation of a civil guard would serve only the latifundistas, he declared that Guanacaste was "a group of fiefs: Doctor Barrios, Mr. Keith, Hurtado, Urcuyo, and Cerdas, in short, at most a dozen owners. . . . Is it for the defense of these rich landlords that the Costa Rican Nation is going to spend 1.2 million colones, instead of proceeding to expropriate those lands which do not belong to them?" (*La Gaceta Oficial*, 22 Mar. 1923: 313; and Gudmundson 1983b: 89). Significantly, all the latifundistas mentioned were Nicaraguan, with the exception of Keith, a North American.

22. De La Cruz (1986: 368) lists the village of Ortega, hardly an important population center, along with Nicoya and Las Juntas de Abangares, both cantonal seats, as the important centers of Communist organizing in this period in Guanacaste.

23. "Jesús Cubillo," the protagonist of Víctor Quirós's novel *El festín de los coyotes* (1990), is a thinly disguised depiction of Francisco Cubillo.

24. In 1940 reform opponents argued that the Executive should be granted flexibility in resolving particular conflicts and that, since Congress would have to approve expropriation contracts in any case, the actual procedure proposed in the new law was not really different from how ad hoc solutions had been found up to that point (ANCR Cong. 19204—1940).

25. By 1949 rustling and clandestine slaughtering had been reduced to the point where they would not alter greatly the picture provided by official consumption figures.

26. For decades the United Fruit Company had exported large numbers of cattle of Guanacastecan or Nicaraguan origin from its Costa Rican plantations to adjacent operations in Panama. Because these movements of animals occurred within the foreign enclave, they did not appear in official statistics.

Chapter 6

1. Costa Rica's shipment of 34 percent of its beef exports to Venezuela in 1977 and of 7 percent to Israel in 1978 were among the largest sales to non–U.S. and non–Puerto Rican markets in the 1970s (SEPSA 1980a: 18). In 1985 Mexico purchased 2,400 metric tons of Costa Rican beef at a higher price than the one prevailing in the U.S. market (SEPSA 1986: 18).

2. This privileged access, however, was no more the result solely of politically neutral hygienic criteria or market forces than it was of geographical proximity. Hoof-and-mouth bacteria may be eliminated by freezing or boiling meat. Many developed countries with high sanitary standards, such as those in the European Economic Community, have long been among the main consumers of Argentine beef, which, incidentally, has always been lower priced than the Central American product (Jarvis 1986: 98). South American producers have pointed to these considerations as evidence of politically inspired protectionism promoted by U.S. lobbyists employing *aftosa* as a convenient pretext. Whether or not this is accurate, it is true that Central America, Mexico, and the Caribbean, rather than South America, have been the principal beneficiaries of U.S.-sponsored aftosa-elimination programs (Jarvis 1986: 121; Sanderson 1986: 134–35). And these have been motivated in large part by U.S. cattle interests' fears of contagion rather than selfless generosity on the part of those not otherwise sympathetic to ranchers in neighboring countries.

3. In 1976, for example, the American National Cattlemen's Association (ANCA), representing some 200,000 ranchers, threatened to sue Secretary of Agriculture Earl Butz over attempts by foreign beef producers to circumvent P.L. 88–482 by exporting to the Puerto Rican free trade zone in Mayagüez. The complaint focused on the Commonwealth Processing Corporation, an importer that chopped carcass beef into stew meat for processed-food com-

panies and fast-food chains in the United States. Commonwealth, a subsidiary of Virginia-based Bunker Hill Packing Corporation, was shipping about two million pounds per month of processed beef to the United States in 1976 (*Business Week*, 2 Aug. 1976, 20). Butz, in an effort to avoid the lawsuit, petitioned the Free Trade Zones Board to remove meat from the list of items permitted to enter the zones. Although the petition was not granted, the board did deny another packing company permission to begin operations in the Mayagüez zone.

4. USDA data indicate that during most years in the 1970s and early 1980s, Australia accounted for roughly one-half of U.S. beef imports. New Zealand supplied 20 to 30 percent; Canada, 2 to 10 percent; and Costa Rica, 4 to 6 percent.

5. The 1948 civil war continues to be the subject of considerable debate for several reasons, not the least of which is the event's importance in legitimizing or criticizing the political positions and development models of post-1948 governments, especially those controlled by the social democratic National Liberation Party. On the 1940s conflicts, see Rojas 1979 and Schifter 1979.

6. The confiscation of properties from Germans and Italians and their descendants during World War II also contributed to the weakening of the upper class, in which these groups were well represented. Expropriations also exacerbated upper-class anxiety about the populist governments of 1940–48. This was one factor in the upper classes' tactical support for the antigovernment Figueres and his social democrats, with whom they otherwise had little in common.

7. Abolition of the military was another key measure, the origins and consequences of which are beyond the scope of this discussion. Figueres probably took this step as much for instrumental as for idealistic reasons, since he viewed the army as a possible vehicle for a conservative restoration. Nevertheless, the prohibition of a standing military permitted post-1948 Costa Rican governments to devote a larger proportion of resources to social spending than would otherwise have been possible.

8. In the 1940s and 1950s, the most important U.S. agency in Guanacaste was STICA (Servicio Técnico Interamericano de Cooperación Agrícola, Inter-American Agricultural Cooperation Technical Service). Since 1961 most U.S. aid has been administered through the Agency for International Development (USAID).

9. In subsequent years, leading cattlemen from other cantons in Guanacaste became active in the Cámara. The Liberia group was most active in the initial organizing efforts, however.

10. In fairness to Lorenzo, it should be mentioned that he modestly takes exception to this view of his own importance in the early cattle lobby and claims that others have exaggerated his role.

11. In subsequent years, "taking advantage of the services of newspaper writers" was of greater significance in the Cámara's media campaign than placing paid advertisements. In its 1955–56 fiscal year, for example, the Cámara spent only 185.50 colones (about $34) on "press and radio propaganda" out of a total budget of over 146,000 colones ($24,000) (CGG 1956: 11). While funds allotted to advertising ("propaganda") were increased each year, the total amounts remained quite modest. The Cámara's success in projecting its views to the public must be attributed not to advertising per se, but rather to its contacts in the news media, who frequently wrote and gave prominence to highly laudatory articles about Cámara activities. Cámara publications often reprinted such pieces from the principal newspapers (e.g., CGG 1954: 3–4; CGG 1957: 2).

12. In these first months, other lobbying goals included ending the tax on each head of cattle in the district of La Cruz and the collection of fines for grazing on public lands in Bagaces, securing a commitment from the state insurance company to issue policies against the spread of hoof-and-mouth disease, and changing regulations governing loan collateral so that properties legally registered for less than ten years could be used to guarantee mortgages.

13. Stewart later made additional visits to Peru in order to gain access to the market and to hire a local lobbyist at Cámara expense (CGG 1957: 10–11).

14. In early 1954, for example, Cámara members purchased 30 stud bulls from the J. D. Hudquins Ranch in Texas (CGG Actas, 1: 54, 1954). In 1955, 100 brahman bulls purchased by Cámara members were flown in on a special flight from the United States (CGG 1956: 5).

15. In 1969 the law was changed to give the CNP full responsibility for carrying out an annual census of cattle available for export and setting an annual per capita internal-consumption level of 18.2 kilograms (Law 4412 of 1969), a target that was rarely reached (see Chapter 7).

16. This type of abuse did not change after 1969 when the CNP assumed full responsibility for determining quotas. Ranchers frequently declared that they had ready for export as many as two times the number of animals that were actually exported (Aguilar and Solís 1988: 21). Sometimes, when CNP inspectors were due to arrive, they "borrowed" steers from ranchers who did not have a quota (V. Smith 1970: 193–94). This, of course, affected domestic availability of beef.

17. In one of many similar instances recorded in the Cámara's minutes, Elías Baldioceda Rojas gave a detailed exposition on the "invasion" of his Hacienda Guachipelín, in the cordillera north of Liberia, and on "the necessity of defending it with rapid action by the authorities." The Cámara immediately directed a telegram to the president demanding a more energetic defense of private property (CGG Actas, 1: 160, 1956).

18. Adela's stock, which is not publicly traded, belonged in 1980 to 228 corporate owners, including Exxon, General Motors, International Telephone and Telegraph, and Nippon Steel (*Wall Street Journal*, 28 Jan. 1980, 14).

19. Aguilar and Solís (1988, chap. 5) describe similar acquisitions of large haciendas by other slaughter operations, in some cases in return for equity in the packinghouse.

20. Cattle stolen in northern Costa Rica have also ended up at the Rivas plant, where ranchers following the trail of rustlers have found hides with Costa Rican brands (see Chapter 8).

21. In Liberia, where government plans in the 1970s and 1980s to build beach resorts and an international airport never materialized, there is excess hotel capacity. While leading landowners favor the bar of one particular hotel for informal business dealings, the GISA-related hotel, at other times virtually empty, appears to survive in large part because of its privileged access to convention business.

22. This investors group is also involved in two other packing operations in Costa Rica, the Cartago Beef Packing and the GISA-owned Abangares Meat Packing companies (RP SM 13,863—1977; RP SM 8523—1970), as well as in similar operations in Honduras (Aguilar and Solís 1988: 45–50; Slutsky 1979: 148). Other Costa Rican companies linked to GISA include Hacienda Bella Vista; Carnilandia (meat for the domestic market); Agropecuaria Upala (cattle); Agroindustrial San Jerónimo (rice); Ternería GISA (cattle); and Pieles Costarricenses (leather).

23. Much of this literature mechanically attributes Latin American deforestation to North American demand for inexpensive beef. For a critical discussion of this genre, the last preserve of dependency thinking in social scientific analysis and the one instance of such theories successfully penetrating popular consciousness in the United States, see Edelman n.d.

24. A 1982 USDA Agricultural Attaché Report exaggerated only slightly when it stated that "traditionally, about 35 to 40 percent of Costa Rica's beef production is consumed domestically with the balance being exported, mainly to the U.S." Small numbers of cows were processed for export beginning in late 1985, but this never amounted to more than a tiny proportion of total exports (SEPSA 1986: 20).

25. Even much of the more recent "hamburger" literature (e.g., Caufield 1985) suggests erroneously that the beef export boom brought permanent declines in per capita consumption.

26. Yields and hence per capita consumption were probably higher. The yield figure of 51 percent is a recent average (SEPSA 1980a: 118). Yields were almost certainly greater for the "criollo" livestock that predominated before the export boom, since these animals did not have the heavy bones, hooves, and cartilaginous hump of today's brahman cattle.

27. Cattle ranchers often clear pastures with herbicides containing di-

oxin, and the excessive use of pesticides on cotton and rice in cattle zones has reached scandalous proportions (L. Hilje et al. 1987; Romero 1976). Costa Rican rice growers use the highest average applications of pesticides per hectare in Latin America (Annis 1990: 11). Export slaughterhouses throughout Central America have been temporarily closed when USDA inspectors detect dirt or chemical residues in meat. Beef that does not meet USDA standards is routinely channeled to domestic markets.

It is unlikely, however, that even the consumption of edible viscera, now available in abundance as the leavings of the export packers, has provided the poorest strata with adequate protein. For the Costa Rican population, the annual consumption requirement for all kinds of meat is estimated at 21.90 kilograms for children and 32.85 kilograms for adults, based on daily requirements of 60 grams for children and 90 grams for adults (SEPSA 1980a: 119). Nevertheless, as late as 1980, the average daily availability of *all* kinds of protein per capita was only 66 grams (Avilés and Mernies 1982: 261). In 1978 the average annual per capita consumption of viscera for the country as a whole was estimated at 3.67 kilograms (SEPSA 1980a: 118). Those rural inhabitants whose average annual beef consumption is 10.6 kilograms would therefore have to eat roughly six times as much viscera as the national average in order to meet their minimum animal protein requirements of 32.85 kilograms. While viscera consumption no doubt has contributed to the alleviation of what would otherwise be serious protein malnutrition, it has probably not been sufficient to allow many poor Costa Ricans the recommended levels of meat in their diets. Moreover, the extent to which organs and tripe may have been contaminated is rarely appreciated by poor consumers or examined by Costa Rican regulatory agencies. USAID officials, anxious to allay critics' misgivings about declining protein consumption, have sanctimoniously asserted that "edible offal and viscera [are] those parts of the animal's anatomy having the highest nutritive value" (quoted in Roux 1975: 364–65). But it is precisely fatty visceral organs that are the principal collecting points in the animal's anatomy for the carcinogenic pesticide and herbicide residues frequently detected in Central American beef and increasingly found at alarming levels in human adipose tissue and mother's milk (Barquero and Constenla 1986; Umaña and Constenla 1984).

28. Ranchers have responded in a similar way to periods of extremely low prices. But slaughtering calves and cows during periods of contraction must be viewed as a way of cutting losses rather than as an exaggerated, myopic search for short-term gains.

29. It was estimated that, in Central America as a whole in 1970, the average per capita annual beef consumption of the lower-income half of the population in Central America was 3.6 kilograms, while that of the upper 5 percent of the population was 30.9 kilograms (Roux 1975: 364). Berg (1973) has also pointed out that meat in poor homes in underdeveloped countries

tends to be eaten by adults, usually males, and is seldom included in the diets of the young. It is unclear, however, whether intrahousehold food distribution in Costa Rica follows this pattern.

30. Complaints about tax surcharges, for example, grew out of disappointment that beef exporters could not take full advantage of the exchange rate bonanza and devaluations of 1980–83. But this government effort to tax superprofits did not necessarily mean that all ranchers were forced to operate at a loss or even at lower levels of return than those to which they had historically been accustomed. "High" real interest rates had a more direct impact on profitability, although a less self-serving articulation of the Cámaras' objections might have noted that many ranchers were paying positive real interest rates for the first time. In effect, "high" loan rates represented the removal of a previously existing public subsidy (and one that was at least partially restored not long after as a result of Cámara pressure).

31. These were to finance the Livestock Department of the CNP, the Animal Health Section of the Ministry of Agriculture, the Federación de Cámaras de Ganaderos and the regional Cámaras, and the Veterinary Medicine Faculty of the National University. An additional 1 percent was withheld to guarantee payment of income tax.

32. In spite of economic liberalization in the 1980s, subsidized credit continued to expand for some time, with the cattle sector one of the largest recipients.

33. The CNP estimated in 1985 that for the herd to maintain its size, no more than 30.7 percent of males, 10.5 percent of females, and 0.7 percent of calves ought to be slaughtered. The actual figures were 36.1 percent of males, 16.9 percent of females, and 1.8 percent of calves. The female and male animals weighed on average 6.4 and 8.6 percent less, respectively, than those slaughtered the previous year (SEPSA 1986: 16).

Chapter 7

1. Interview in Liberia, 1982.

2. In the Brenes Gutiérrez, Hurtado, Baltodano, and Martínez Duarte families, for example, siblings and other close relatives of those listed in Table 7.2 exported hundreds of additional steers. Two large exporters in northern Puntarenas, if considered here, would also increase the level of concentration.

3. Between 1973 and 1984, the Gini coefficient of provincial landownership concentration declined only slightly from .82 to .81, principally as a result of this moderate fragmentation of the largest properties. Use of Gini coefficients to compare the distribution in 1950 with those in 1973 and 1984 is not likely to be very accurate, since the 1950 census employed different farm-size intervals.

4. One of the latter, Luis Gallegos Yglesias, soon became part owner of the adjacent Hacienda Santa Rosa. His son, Luis Gallegos Chacón, maintained informal control over Hacienda Murciélago even after it was expropriated from Anastasio Somoza in 1979.

5. The brothers were the sons of Maria I. Alvarado Chacón (sister of Fernando Alvarado Chacón) and Guillermo González Herrán, partners in the Sociedad Murciélago.

6. The Johnson connection was the subject of many local rumors, but is difficult to corroborate. The *Wall Street Journal* reported several times in the early 1970s that Johnson was believed to have purchased a large Costa Rican ranch (e.g., *Wall Street Journal*, 27 July 1972, 30). Similar press reports appeared in Costa Rica in the late 1960s and early 1970s.

7. Financing for CODESA was provided primarily by banks in the United States, Canada, Spain, and Brazil, as well as by the Adela Investment Corporation (Vega 1982: 171).

8. Foremen would typically describe the owner only as "a señor from Liberia" or San José, or "a North American." Usually this lack of awareness about owners' identities seemed genuine, but sometimes it was clearly feigned, very likely at the request of the owners themselves.

9. Many siblings of individuals listed in Figure 7.3 either established themselves in other economic activities or had little direct involvement in livestock beyond owning shares in cattle haciendas. This suggests that if partible inheritance norms were followed in practice, further fragmentation would have occurred. Partible inheritance was, however, often applied flexibly.

10. El Real was the former Hacienda Don David, a section of Hacienda Tempisque that had also been called El Real.

11. Somoza García became general of the National Guard in 1934 and was president during 1937–47 and 1951–56. He was assassinated in 1956. Both Krehm (1949 and 1984) and Diederich (1981: 24) note that Somoza García managed to gain considerable control over livestock marketing and exports shortly after coming to power, in part by using his National Guard to coerce competitors and in part by assuring that the ban on exports to Costa Rica was enforced only to the detriment of other ranchers. Nicaraguan National Guards celebrated their leader's business acumen in verse: "Todo lo que posee cuernos en Nicaragua, tiene cuatro patas y hace mu, es del Jefe Tacho Somoza . . . , así no lo quieras tú" "Everything that has horns, four feet and goes moo in Nicaragua belongs to Chief Tacho Somoza . . . , so don't you covet it!" Quoted in Krehm (1949: 164).

12. This work was widely read in Spanish after it was published in 1949. Only in 1984 did it appear in an English edition (and one without all the detail of the original).

13. Wolf and Calderón Guardia were both married to women from the Fournier family. The Wolfs' involvement in Nicaraguan politics and their sympathies appear to have changed little in the next generation. In 1985

Costa Rican authorities seized "large quantities of arms and other military equipment intended for Nicaraguan opposition groups in Finca Chapernal, property of the Wolf family in Puntarenas" (Morales Gamboa 1985). Víctor Wolf, Jr., Chapernal's principal owner, admitted in the mid-1980s to organizing a divinely inspired right-wing paramilitary group, commenting, "My commander isn't even on Earth" (quoted in Hopfensperger 1986: 24).

14. Following Somoza García's 1956 assassination, his son Luis Somoza Debayle served out the remainder of his six-year term and an additional term that ended in 1963. Succeeded by supporter René Schick in 1963, Luis Somoza died of a heart attack in 1967. Anastasio Somoza Debayle was president-elect at the time of his brother's death and remained in power until the 1979 Sandinista revolution.

15. In 1933, when departing U.S. Marines selected a commander of the new Nicaraguan National Guard, Pasos was one of two candidates passed over in favor of Somoza García. He joined Somoza in the 1936 coup that toppled President Juan Bautista Sacasa and also received aid from him for his textile and wood businesses. He nonetheless broke with the dictator in 1944 and left Nicaragua. Somoza briefly imprisoned him when he returned in 1947 and then forced him into exile (Diederich 1981: 26–27; Krehm 1949: 172; MacRenato 1982: 310–13; Somoza 1980: 88–89).

16. After his exile in 1948, Picado was a frequent contributor to the Somoza family newspaper, *Novedades* (Estrada 1967: 203, 252).

17. Pedro Joaquín Chamorro Cardenal, one of the most prominent Nicaraguan opposition figures, later accused Picado Lara of joining his former West Point classmate Anastasio Somoza Debayle in the 1954 torture of anti-Somoza activist Jorge Rivas Montes, who was reportedly hung by his testicles (Chamorro 1959: 51, 87). The following year, Somoza named Picado Lara commander of an exile force that staged an abortive invasion of Costa Rica seeking to "restore" Rafael Angel Calderón Guardia to the presidency (Acuña V. 1977: 71).

18. It was Miguel Brenes's brother Luis who was involved in the 1940 effort to sell the elder Somoza the Hacienda Tempisque.

19. Diederich (1981: 76) estimated that the Somozas controlled 223,000 acres (90,283 hectares) in Costa Rica in 1966.

20. When Teodoro Picado withdrew as a director of Murciélago, Limitada, in 1977 he was replaced by a Cuban, Manuel Porro, who was left in charge of running the farm (RP SM 184 F532 A652). In Nicaragua, the Somozas provided bases and training for armed Cuban exiles from before the 1961 Bay of Pigs invasion until 1975 (LeoGrande 1983: 45).

21. The peasant families that had occupied the hacienda were relocated in the San Luis agrarian reform project to the south in Cañas.

22. It is possible, however, that he maintained indirect control through a new corporation formed by his representatives.

23. Sandinista fighters were informally given access to parts of the prop-

erty in the last weeks of the battle to overthrow Somoza. They also had bases on other large haciendas in the area, in one case (El Pelón de la Altura) because a sympathetic young administrator granted access without the knowledge of more conservative, older family members who were the formal owners.

24. Gutiérrez was a key figure in the Bavaria Land Development Company, domiciled in Monrovia, which in March 1980 acquired El Viejo from Somoza partner Alfonso Salazar (RP SM T215 F335 A323; T214 F539 A481). This maneuver was probably intended to obscure continuing control of the El Viejo property by the fallen dictator.

25. On Somoza's assassination, see de la Calle (1983).

26. On early *contra* activities in northern Costa Rica, see Edelman and Kenen (1989: 269–71).

27. At his death in August 1989, Hylton was, after the local utility company, the largest landowner in Prince William County, Virginia, in suburban Washington, D.C. His land holdings there were valued at almost $97 million (*Potomac News,* 29 Aug. 1989). Most of El Hacha and Orosí belonged to Tierrica, S.A., owned by Irving Wilhite, a former Republican state senator from North Dakota, who traded some 10,000 hectares to Hylton in 1980 for about 100 acres of property scattered around the Virginia suburbs of Washington, D.C. (RP SM 21,555; *Tico Times,* 28 June 1991). Hylton's main Costa Rican company, Ranchos Horizonte, in which he held 99 percent of the shares, was founded in 1981 (RP SM T244 F35 A25). Some other properties were owned in partnership with Costa Ricans. The information in this section is based largely on interviews with individuals close to Hylton's operations (also see CN G10-1-2-388 and 389—1981; G10-1-3-25 and 26—1982). After Hylton's death in August 1989, his holdings were managed by an administrator who was a naturalized Costa Rican and a minor U.S. partner, though many were eventually sold.

28. Training camps for armed anti-Sandinistas existed on several other Guanacastecan haciendas in 1982, including El Pelón de la Bajura and the Morice family's properties in La Cruz (*Excelsior* [Mexico], 11 Aug. 1982, 1, 22–23). By 1983, however, most *contra* activity in northern Costa Rica had shifted to more heavily forested areas to the east in Alajuela, Heredia, and Limón provinces. Several informants claim that *contras* occasionally used Hylton's properties in the early and mid-1980s, although this is obviously hard to corroborate.

29. Obviously, it is difficult to establish the ultimate objective behind Hylton's operations in Costa Rica. One employee, who no longer works for Ranchos Horizonte, speculated that the Virginian might have some connection to the U.S. campaign against Nicaragua. "He came in here right after the Sandinistas took over Nicaragua. Don't tell them I said this. I could get in a lot of trouble." In May 1989, Hylton Enterprises Virginia, Inc., shifted its sights to Costa Rica's other border, acquiring 6,059 hectares of mountainous

jungle that abutted the two-kilometer-wide inalienable buffer zone along the Panamanian frontier (RP FR 25514). The U.S. invasion of Panama took place seven months later.

30. El Viejo had been divided many times since the 1940s, though not all of the "segregated" pieces always belonged to different owners. Much of Hylton's irrigation district land acquired from Azucarera Guanacaste was registered to the Pacific Land Corporation rather than to Ranchos Horizonte, which remained the public face of the operation and which presumably owned other parts of the business. A small number of properties in Liberia and La Cruz cantons were registered to Hylton Enterprises Virginia, Inc. See Indice de Propietarios, Registro Público de la Propiedad.

31. Rancho Gesling, also in the irrigation district, had suffered losses because of mismanagement. The Geslings, under pressure from ITCO to intensify crop production, were interested in divesting themselves of the property. Their administrator, a North American who was disgusted with their failure to maintain equipment and with their general lack of concern with the property, left them after ten years and went to work for Hylton.

32. The public property registry index indicates that Hylton or companies he controlled owned—as of late 1985—15,492.8 hectares (5,271.6 in Liberia, 4,783.1 in La Cruz, and 5,438.1 in Cañas). This list does not include Rancho Gesling (in Liberia and Carrillo) or El Viejo (in Santa Cruz and Carrillo). An individual close to Hylton's operations estimated his holdings in El Viejo at 7,700 hectares (11,000 manzanas), which if true would substantially increase the size of his irrigation district holdings. Although Hylton's Liberia office initially denied owning El Viejo, the acquisition was common knowledge in nearby villages, and in 1982 the property was full of cattle with the Ranchos Horizonte brand. The property registry index probably understates as well the size of his main holding at what had been the Azucarera Guanacaste (in Cañas)—which elsewhere in the property registry is listed as containing 6,230 hectares—and does not include Rancho Gesling, which Hylton briefly rented in 1982. Hylton donated 3,464 hectares of land in La Cruz and at least one property in the irrigation district to Jimmy Swaggart Ministries, and additional properties to the Nature Conservancy.

33. While Hylton's acquisition of large expanses of extensively exploited cattle land was reminiscent of earlier types of latifundismo, his irrigation district operation, dedicated primarily to wet-rice cultivation, has been highly capitalized.

34. Livestock and equipment were said to be purchased with cash. One informant close to Hylton suggested that Azucarera Guanacaste was purchased for $5 million in cash rather than bartered. Ranchos Horizonte's Virginia office refused to confirm or deny anything regarding the company's operations, with spokesman George Halfpap repeatedly remarking, "I'm not at liberty to say."

35. According to USAID personnel, Hylton also took advantage of USAID-sponsored technical studies on his properties.

36. Details of the donation are in Protocolo de Rodrigo Oreamuno Blanco, number 2979, 25 July 1984, Registro Público, Sección de Microfilm, rollo 217, imágenes 1281–85. The size of the properties is from the Indice de Propietarios, Registro Público.

37. Other donations came from the Pew Charitable Trust, the John C. and Catherine T. MacArthur Foundation, the W. Alton Jones Foundation, the Organization for Tropical Studies, and the Swedish Society for the Conservation of Nature. Some of the resources these organizations provided derived from debt-for-nature swaps in which Costa Rican dollar obligations purchased on the secondary market (usually for 20 percent or less of face value) were exchanged with the country's Central Bank for colones to be used in conservation projects.

38. Assessed values are mentioned in the donation protocol cited above. Janzen (1986: 9) suggests that typical prices for lands acquired for the park were about $200 per hectare in the mid-1980s. Much of Swaggart's land fronted on the Pan-American Highway, however, and was therefore more valuable than the average property.

39. Daniel Janzen, personal communication, May 1990. The Registro Público still showed Swaggart owning the land in mid-1991, though the data base will likely soon reflect the final transfer of titles.

40. This transaction appears in Registro Público de la Propiedad, Folio Real 5056873. The transfer was finalized on Dec. 12, 1986.

41. Assemblies of God pastors in Nicaragua also accused the Sandinistas of plotting to poison Managua's water supply and urged believers to reject the revolutionary government's vaccination campaigns, since "the only [true] health comes from God" (Martínez 1989: 46–47).

42. Interview with member of Asambleas de Dios church, Costa Rica, July 1988.

43. Hylton's properties in the irrigation district were also sold or placed in trusts at about this time.

44. Janzen (1986: 32) estimates the property held by "Odol" Corporation at about 130 square kilometers. Udall Research Corporation, registered in Panama, was the cover employed by the U.S. National Security Council's secret contra-aid network to rent Santa Elena. The National Parks Foundation later estimated that the Hacienda, owned by U.S. citizen Joseph Hamilton, contained 15,000 hectares of land and 18 kilometers of coastline.

45. The 1984 agricultural census reported 481,146.2 hectares in pasture (62.3 percent of total farmland) and 62,114.7 hectares in brush (*charrales, tacotales*) out of a total 772,030.1 hectares in farms in Guanacaste (*CAP* 1984: 38). Livestock uses—pasture and brush—accounted for 70.4 percent of the total farmland, down considerably from the 89.9 percent of eleven years

earlier. The 1984 census data, however, must be taken with great caution (González B. 1987), since some 137,000 hectares in Guanacaste that owners declared in 1973 simply disappeared in 1984, probably as a result of the increased reluctance of large landowners in 1984 to respond honestly to census takers' queries. This supposition is borne out by an examination of changes from 1973 to 1984 in total farmland at the cantonal level: 94,538.8 (69.2 percent) of the "missing" hectares—those present in 1973 but not in 1984—disappeared from Liberia and La Cruz, both cantons with predominantly large properties. These cantons also show the greatest relative declines in reported farm area over the eleven-year period.

46. In Costa Rica as a whole the area in pasture grew even faster than in Guanacaste, from 622,402 to 1,558,053 hectares in 1950–73. This 1973 figure reprosented 76.1 percent of total farmland. If 283,571 hectares of brushland are included, as much as 89.9 percent of Costa Rica's farmland may have been used for livestock (*CAP* 1950: 57; *CAP* 1973: 13). In 1984, in Costa Rica as a whole, the census counted 1,651,560.5 hectares of pasture (53.8 percent of total farm area) and 235,601.9 hectares of brush (with pasture, 61.4 percent of the total farm area of 3,070,340.1 hectares).

47. By 1984 the maize area had fallen to a mere 8,425.1 hectares (*CAP* 1984: 79,81).

48. The greatest proportional intensification occurred on farms of less than one hectare, which stocked 24 percent more animals on each hectare of grass in 1984 than in 1973.

Chapter 8

1. Rebel (1989: 117) quite appropriately criticizes the prevailing exaltation of agency over structure and the fascination with "the discovery and wielding of power even from weakness" as part of a recent tendency "to downplay the degradation and terror experienced by victims of exploitation and persecution."

2. It also need not mean positing yet another pair of reified oppositions that contribute to obscuring rather than elucidating complex and fluid realities (see Roseberry 1989: 30–33).

3. Marcus (1986), Stern (1987), G. Smith (1989), and Roseberry (1989), from rather different starting points, suggest some of the dangers in uncritically labeling as "resistance" every manifestation of subordinate groups' discontent or alienation. Limón (1989) provides a particularly candid, self-conscious, and humorous statement of the problem, admitting that he went "looking for a folklore of resistance" but ended up concerned about "lapsing into an uncritical romanticism of resistance everywhere" (p. 475).

4. Scott mentioned but did not examine in much detail the "exodus" of poorer villagers from his study site Sedaka and the importance of both urban

wage labor and the agricultural frontier as safety valves for the release of social tensions (1985: 125, 245).

5. Comment at organizing meeting of small agriculturalists, 1989.

6. These data, based on Tables 7.1, 7.3 and 7.4, actually slightly understate the decline in average farm size in the below-ten-hectares cohort and overstate the changes in the number and area of such farms. This is because the original 1950 census data are in manzanas rather than hectares, and the 1950 size interval is farms less than 9.7 hectares.

7. Kincaid (1987, chap. 5) compared the number of household heads in Guanacaste whose primary occupation was in agriculture with the total number of farms in 1950 and 1973. He estimated that of the economically active population in agriculture, 5.7 percent were completely landless in 1950, and 22.7 percent, in 1973. This method is not without problems, as Kincaid noted, since it underestimates the extent to which nonhousehold heads may have land and overestimates the effective number of farms (large owners often have more than one). But the direction of the trend is striking.

8. Later censuses did not gather comparable data on the number of farm units producing solely for household consumption. But it is likely that as average farm size in the under-ten-hectares stratum declined, the proportion of farm units producing only use values and not exchange values would have increased. It would not be accurate, of course, to regard this trend, which hardly reflected most smallholders' real aspirations, as an indication of a persistent and exclusive use-value orientation or of peasant atavism. It should be noted as well that most yellow maize is used for poultry feed and that chickens and eggs produced by the rural poor are usually sold on the market even if crops are not.

9. See, for example, Whiteford (1991), who shows that the nutritional status of children in Veintisiete de Abril, Santa Cruz, diminished in the period 1966–80, in contrast to the improvements registered at the national level.

10. In order to avoid paying benefits or complying with other aspects of labor legislation, hacendados also hire peons directly on a piece-work basis ("por contrato") to perform specific tasks (e.g., repairing fence posts or clearing firebreaks).

11. Interview, 1981.

12. Norberto Calderón, a friend of Tablada's who was also attacked by Morice but escaped unharmed, agreed four years later to provide an eyewitness account of the murder (*Pueblo*, 29 Mar.–5 Apr. 1976). Friends of Morice have tried unsuccessfully to obtain backing for a pardon from the cattle lobby. Cámara members felt that while such support for "the compañero in disgrace . . . would be a reasonable gesture of solidarity with a cattleman, a man of means, who acted in self-defense," it would be better to act on an individual basis, "without mixing in the Cámara" (CGG Actas, 9: 10–11–1978).

13. 1981 statutes of one of Morice's companies—Quebrada de Agua (RP SM T248 F265 A220)—indicate that, in spite of his fugitive status, he routinely attended meetings in Liberia, where he also owned a centrally located residence "one hundred meters south of the Banco Nacional de Costa Rica" (RP SM 30,692).

14. In some cases these looters (*huaqueros*) are semiprofessional excavators and artifact vendors who enter into sharecropping-like arrangements with other peasants (which, like sharecropping, are described as being "a medias"—"by halves"). A peasant who locates a promising archeological site may, for example, call a local *huaquero* to excavate it, and the two will then split profits from the sale of any artifacts found.

15. See Kincaid (1987, chap. 5) for a detailed analysis of recent migration patterns in Guanacaste.

16. Because rural and less-developed cantons tend to have growth rates higher than the national average (Stycos 1982), this estimate of emigration from Guanacaste is almost certainly conservative.

17. In the mid-1980s the banana companies closed the plantations in southern Puntarenas, allegedly because they were no longer sufficiently profitable. Much of their land there was converted to production of African palms, which employs very little labor, or was abandoned, in some cases to former banana-worker squatters. Kincaid's analysis of 1973 census data (1987, chap. 5) found that roughly a third of all emigrants from Guanacaste in 1968–73 went to central Costa Rica, and a quarter went to the banana zones. Most male emigrants from rural areas, however, went to the zones.

18. In the Sixaola (southern Limón province) United Brands plantation, 39.5 percent of the workers in 1983 were Guanacastecans. The next largest groups were those from Limón (14.1 percent) and Puntarenas (12.9 percent), though many of the *limonenses* were actually second-generation Guanacastecans (Bourgois 1989: 185, 236). Bourgois (pp. 185–86, 195–96) provides an interesting analysis of how the young Guanacastecans' experience in their native region facilitates their exploitation on the banana plantations.

19. Bourgois (1989: 127) suggests that Guaymí Indians were usually given these jobs on the plantations in southern Limón and northern Panama. Young Guanacastecans also express enthusiasm about earning the wage supplements given to sprayers of dangerous nematicides, such as MOCAP.

20. Banana production is generally not closely tied to seasonal fluctuations in weather, which are few in the year-round humid zones where it is centered. This alone would require the companies to rely on various sources of labor, not all of which would be linked to highly seasonal smallholder production elsewhere. As Bourgois (1989) has convincingly shown, however, recruitment of an ethnically and regionally diverse plantation labor force owes more to employer efforts to divide and control workers than to any other consideration.

21. These benefits include severance pay, the "thirteenth month" (*agui-*

naldo) Christmas bonus, and employer contributions to employee savings and retirement funds. Bourgois (1989: 185) reports that "the banana companies encourage short cycles of employment; they fire newly arrived laborers before they pass the three-month probation period so that they can not qualify for the job tenure benefits accorded to permanent workers and stipulated by Costa Rican labor law." While most migrants remain in "the zone" longer than three months at a time (the Guanacaste dry season is usually six months long), they often work for more than one company during a typical stay.

22. Only former employees who had administrative responsibilities with the banana companies pointed to a connection between skills acquired on the plantations and later nonfarm business success.

23. Harvesting sugarcane is as rigorous as much banana-plantation work, but cutters, who are paid on a piece-rate basis, tend to be older than banana workers. In a 1980 survey at one Guanacaste mill, Li Kam (1984: 39) found that more than half the cutters were over 31 years old.

24. Nor, obviously, is it the case, as Villarreal (1983: 89) claims, that "the struggles of the Costa Rican peasantry for land originated during the middle of this [twentieth] century."

25. This movement from the south into highland Bagaces involved primarily "Cartago" migrants from Alajuela, some of whom had already lived for a generation or more in Cañas or Tilarán. It coincided with similar, though smaller, land occupations to the north in highland Liberia and La Cruz carried out by "legitimate Guanacastecans" and Nicaraguans. Taken together, these land seizures constituted a major appropriation by squatters of much of the best land in the remoter sections of the cordillera.

26. Interview, 1981.

27. Actually, Oviedo worked for the Wilsons and Stewarts longer than he suggests in this document, since in a 1931 letter to the editor of an agricultural publication he was already identified as their employee (Oviedo 1931).

28. "Where else," Stewart asked in an interview, "would they have gotten the capital for sawmills and other expensive lumbering equipment?" The possibility that squatters might have acquired these accouterments of their new trade with profits from lumbering itself apparently did not occur to him, even though such conversions of natural capital into money capital were among the most typical accumulation strategies of many of the largest landowners. Indeed, Stewart reported that his father, who ceased intensive exploitation of his wood resources four years after buying his haciendas, warned him, "Son, never use up the timber, because if you ever have any trouble of the hoof-and-mouth disease in this country, you'd be ruined if you didn't have trees or logs to sell in order to keep your property."

29. Estimates of the number of occupants of Miravalles in this period vary greatly. Rowles (1980: 863) suggests that between 7,000 and 10,000 people

were involved. In 1961 the Stewarts provided the government with a list of 402 occupants, which they subsequently revised upward to 554. These figures almost certainly referred to household heads rather than to total numbers of family members; assuming, conservatively, an average family size of 4, this would suggest a total of some 2,000 occupants. Agrarian reform agency records, however, suggest that in 1965 only 79 families were occupying Miravalles ("Casos de ocupación precaria," ITCO Departamento Legal). In all likelihood, several thousand individuals (though not nearly as many as Rowles suggests) settled in Miravalles after the mid-1950s, because the population of Bagaces more than doubled in 1950–63, a phenomenon for which there is no other plausible explanation (see Table 8.2).

Most estimates of the size of Hacienda Miravalles coincide remarkably closely. Aristides Baltodano Guillén, the Stewarts' surveyor, estimated that the fincas considered part of the Hacienda totaled about 22,142 manzanas (15,499 hectares)—18,472 manzanas (12,930 hectares) inscribed in the Public Property Registry and about 3,670 manzanas (2,569 hectares) of "demasías" (Rowles 1980: 867). David Stewart's estimate of 23,000 manzanas (16,100 hectares) is nearly identical. My own investigation of cadastral and judicial records located references to 15,476 hectares (22,109 manzanas) of registered fincas that were part of Miravalles (see Chapter 1), though this would not include "demasías." ITCO Legal Department data, however, which cite a total of only 13,500 hectares, are some 2,000 hectares below these other estimates.

30. In later court proceedings they claimed that they had instructed their representative to settle claims at 150 colones ($22.64) per manzana (Rowles 1980: 864).

31. This figure was based on an estimated expropriated area of 18,472 manzanas, the registered size of Hacienda Miravalles (Rowles 1980: 876).

32. This problem is discussed in more detail in Edelman (1989a).

33. Not all land occupations or disputes came to the attention of ITCO. Many were handled in local courts and were referred to ITCO only when they were determined to be substantial conflicts in terms of either scale or merit (Kincaid 1987, chap. 5).

34. Kincaid (1987, chap. 5) employs a similar, but almost certainly more complete, ITCO data set on 94 Guanacaste land occupations in 1963–82. He suggests that "some 1,900 families, or almost 9 percent of all rural families in the province, were implicated in disputes covering almost 65,000 hectares, or 7 percent of the farmland."

35. Villarreal (1983: 97) has suggested that the rhythm of land occupations increased during the 1971–78 presidential periods, when José Figueres and Daniel Oduber, both of the social democratic Partido de Liberación Nacional, held office. Peasants presumably viewed these individuals and their party as more likely to respond positively to demands for land. Some of

the most intransigent owners of occupied properties, however, such as Alvaro Jenkins of Hacienda Montezuma, were also important figures in the
PLN.

36. By the late 1970s squatters held virtually the entire property.

37. George Wilson had been one of the initial owners of the company,
though he subsequently sold his interest to another partner, also a North
American.

38. Rodríguez Solera (1989), in an attempt to disprove the common assumption that high incidences of squatting in Guanacaste are associated at
the subregional level with high degrees of land concentration, examines all
cantons in the province except La Cruz, the one case that would clearly have
complicated his argument. Curiously, he lumps La Cruz together with Liberia in one "subregion" and, in contrast to Kincaid, completely overlooks
the high incidence of land occupations there.

39. Kincaid's estimates may be high because he relies on census data to
determine the total number of rural families. Clearly, this is the only available approach to the problem as he defines it. But in a canton with large
numbers of undocumented Nicaraguan migrants, many of whom would be
reluctant to be counted, such a procedure is fraught with potential problems.

40. Interview, 1981.

41. Interview, 1981. Virtually all of the larger properties have guards,
usually equipped with shotguns or other long arms. Some farms also have
automatic guns that fire blank rounds at random times. These are installed
primarily to frighten birds that eat rice and sorghum. But one ranch administrator, who apologized for his guards' "cheap Brazilian shotguns," remarked
that automatic guns scare "not only the *piches* (birds), but outside people
too."

42. In the first half of 1990, for example, in the cantons of Liberia, La Cruz,
Carrillo, Bagaces, Cañas, Tilarán, and Upala (Alajuela), the Judicial Police
received reports of only 69 stolen cattle (*El Guanacasteco*, July 1990: 10).

43. By way of comparison, the maximum penalty under Costa Rican law
is the 25-year prison term for murder.

44. Generally, the workday now conforms to the eight-hour maximum
permitted by law, with a schedule of 6:00 A.M. to 11:00 A.M. and 12:00 M. to
3:00 P.M. on weekdays and a half-day on Saturday. But another advantage for
employers in hiring workers from outside the immediate vicinity is that
during peak periods of labor demand, it is easier to require them to work
Saturday afternoons and Sundays. One farm administrator described how his
predecessor did this: "He used to force the workers to work on Sundays,
which is illegal, by not showing up on time Saturday with their pay. They
would stick around waiting until asked to work extra. Since they couldn't go
home without pay, they would say 'what the hell' and work Saturday afternoon. Since it was then too little time to go home, especially for those who
live around Sardinal or Santa Cruz, they would then decide to work Sunday

too. He used to threaten to fire workers who wouldn't work on Sunday. Workers then didn't know their rights. Now they do better."

45. Other varieties of public relations are directed at assuaging concerns of the broader society. At a rice farm bordering a national wildlife reserve, an administrator told me how he tried to limit criticism of pesticide runoffs by giving the poorly funded park program free fuel and mechanics' services, as well as frequent meals for its employees. He then pointed to what he saw as the danger of "ecology people": "People are always coming around to steal new technological ideas and to spread bad gossip. If we use a chemical that kills ten birds on one field and there's a guy (*carajo*) from another farm here, he'll go to Liberia and say that here they're using a chemical that killed thousands of birds and that it's an ecological disaster, and that calls the attention of the ecology people, so we have to watch it. That's one of the main reasons we limit access to the finca." Environmental concerns have by no means been limited to park employees or urban "ecology people." In 1982 residents of Santa Cruz canton rolled large logs onto airstrips used by fumigation planes, to protest the frequent spraying of populated areas with poisonous agricultural chemicals.

46. The leadership of the Sugar Workers Union (Sindicato de Trabajadores de la Caña, SITRACAÑA) had ties to a small leftist political party that also experienced major splits and loss of membership in the early 1980s, something that contributed to the union's inability to consolidate its position at CATSA. Kincaid (1987, chap. 5), while not noting these elements of the picture, cites a 1983 interview with a SITRACAÑA leader who conceded that the union was "largely defunct."

47. *Solidarista* associations, originally a uniquely Costa Rica phenomenon but increasingly found in other Central American countries, are worker-employer organizations that usually take the place of trade unions. Labor and management both give to a common employees' savings fund used to finance health, housing, and educational benefits. Based on ideas developed by Alberto Martén, José Figueres's minister of economy in the 1948–49 post-civil-war junta, *solidarismo* departs from traditional social democratic theory by positing harmony between capital and labor, and by attempting to present an alternative to unionism (Blanco and Navarro 1984). *Solidarismo*'s proponents have campaigned energetically in Costa Rica. But the spread of the movement must certainly be attributed not only to its high profile or to employer support, but to some kinds of concrete benefits, particularly in housing and education, which *solidarista* associations have been able to provide (and about which most unions were rarely concerned).

Chapter 9

1. Fleming (1986) located additional data for 1980–83 (taken just before La Pacífica was sold and the meteorological station closed down).

2. Fleming (1986) found that a regression of a slightly longer La Pacífica rainfall data series against year was significantly negative ($P<0.05$ in F-tests). The regression line in Figure 9.1 suggests that rainfall is declining at an average annual rate of 0.8 percent, but that only 14.4 percent of annual variation is explained by the downward trend.

3. Recent government recommendations call for 800–1,200 mm of rain per growing cycle (SEPSA 1989: 79).

4. The cordillera is more humid than the lowlands, but high winds and irregular terrain limit mechanized crop production there.

5. Achío and Escalante's assertion (1985) that *trapiches* appeared in Guanacaste only at the beginning of the twentieth century in association with coffee farms in Tilarán is obviously mistaken and is likely the projection of the experience of central Costa Rica onto a different regional historical reality (p. 44). The affirmation that the province was "new" to sugar production in the mid-twentieth century, yet one more instance of the treatment of the pre-1950 past as if it were static and obscure, is similarly erroneous (see Bermúdez and Pochet 1986: 12, 47).

6. Sobrado's 1903 contract with the government, which committed him to installing the mill, was an extension of an earlier agreement with Odilón Jiménez and Víctor Guardia, which apparently was never fulfilled (Sáenz Maroto 1970: 175).

7. Pre-1950 figures on crop area must be taken with caution, since they were often gathered in an unsystematic, haphazard way. The 1925 cane area was reported to be 5,200 hectares, lower than in 1924 but still remarkably high (*AE* 1925).

8. By 1963, in comparison, after the opening of two modern mills and the introduction of improved varieties of cane with uniform maturation rates, only 31.4 percent was cut selectively (Barboza et al. 1981: III-33).

9. Today the *trapiches* have largely disappeared, and the cutting of entire fields at once is virtually universal. One trapiche owner in Pinilla de Santa Cruz remarked to me in 1988 that he maintained his equipment "out of sentiment" rather than because it was profitable. He claimed that he recently made more money in one day from a group of foreigners who came to film his picturesque but antiquated operation than from producing and selling *dulce* during the rest of the year.

10. Half of the twenty foreign nationals Achío and Escalante identified as shareholders of sugar mills in Guanacaste (and northern Puntarenas) in the 1960s and 1970s were of Cuban origin (1985: 140). Since these authors failed to include the Cuban-owned Azucarera Guanacaste in their tabulation, the proportion of Cubans among foreign investors in sugar was actually higher (RP SM 26,682).

11. Technically, LAICA is a "public law" corporation (*corporación de derecho público*) chartered by the Costa Rican Legislative Assembly.

12. Consumer prices for sugar are set by the executive branch of the government.

13. This is distinct from long-term investment credit, such as that used for planting new fields, which is usually supplied directly by banks to producers, often with sacks of sugar deposited as collateral.

14. The United States imports only raw sugar in order to maintain control over the final stages of the refining process.

15. Nor does it lead export *ingenios* to be more vulnerable to changing international conditions than those producing for domestic markets.

16. Achío and Escalante (1985: 63) accept uncritically the estimate of a LAICA official who claimed that 60 percent of domestic sugar consumption was accounted for by industrial uses. Bermúdez and Pochet (1986: 79, 83) cite a figure of 65 percent.

17. Liquor production, which spurred sugar cultivation in the late nineteenth and early twentieth centuries, is now based almost entirely on residual molasses, a by-product of the refining process, rather than on sugar itself. Recent domestic-consumption figures are, however, undoubtedly inflated by contraband exports to Panama, which intensified after the currency devaluations that began in 1980.

18. "All over the world," Sidney Mintz wrote in *Sweetness and Power* (1986), "sugar has helped fill the calorie gap for the laboring poor, and has become one of the first foods of the industrial work break" (p. 149). The degree to which sugar facilitated capital accumulation in peripheral social formations and in nonindustrial sectors obviously deserves the type of analysis Mintz brilliantly carried out for England and Spain.

19. With the exception of nearly 1,000 hectares sold to the government for an agricultural experiment station.

20. During the 1986–90 presidency of Oscar Arias Sánchez, when Rodrigo was minister of the presidency, Cañas residents of all social classes frequently referred to Taboga as "la hacienda de los Arias." Robelo, who initially remained in Nicaragua as a member of the government junta following the 1979 revolution, went into exile in Costa Rica in 1982, where he headed an armed anti-Sandinista exile group. Borgonovo's brother, Mauricio, was foreign minister of El Salvador until 1977, when he was kidnapped and killed by guerrillas after the government refused to exchange him for political prisoners.

21. Such National Banking System loans often were possible only because of increased public-sector indebtedness to foreign banks or international lending institutions.

22. The mid-1970s sugar boom also saw the establishment of an *ingenio* at Las Piedras, a short distance from Taboga. Founded in 1975 by Cuban residents of Miami, the company included investors from central Costa Rica and eventually Nicaraguans and companies domiciled in Panama (RP SM

26,682). In 1981, shortly after it became operational, the ingenio and some 4,000 hectares around it were acquired by Cecil Hylton, a North American who also gained control of several other large properties in Guanacaste.

23. State intervention in the economy reached its apex during the PLN administrations of José Figueres and Daniel Oduber in 1970–78. In an effort to generate jobs and bolster flagging growth, the state (through CODESA) for the first time assumed an active role as a producer in a wide variety of economic activities. See Sojo (1984) and M. Vega (1982).

24. M. Vega (1982) has suggested that these mill owners were reluctant at this time to invest in the needed new ingenios and looked to the government to supply the required capital. The acquisition by Jenkins and other members of this group of the El Viejo mill in 1975 suggests that this was not necessarily the case. Rather, if the state would supply the capital and pay them for their administrative expertise, Jenkins and his associates saw little reason not to become involved in CATSA, especially since it did not genuinely compete (in terms of pricing or market shares) with Taboga and El Viejo.

25. In 1982 a CATSA engineer complained that the company was unable to pay a foreign firm $6,000 for repairs required on one of the boilers. As a result, the mill refused cane from numerous independent growers, and this led to huge additional losses for both CATSA and nearby farmers.

26. Economic Support Funds are USAID grants intended primarily for balance of payments support and the financing of critical imports. At times they have also been used in support of broader U.S. policy objectives (Edelman and Kenen 1989: 189; USAID 1988: 48–52).

27. The Cuban owners of Azucarera Guanacaste, for example, sold the mill and the surrounding land at Las Piedras, Cañas, in 1981, and the new U.S owner soon shifted to rice production, using the decrepit ingenio building as a warehouse for seed, fertilizer, and machinery. Average milling efficiency (sugar extracted per ton of cane), a key efficiency indicator, fell throughout Guanacaste during much of the 1970s and early 1980s.

28. This reflects relatively stagnant production during the 1970s and early 1980s. By the 1981–82 harvest, total production was almost exactly the same as in 1971–72, approximately 181,000 metric tons. But while over half the output was exported that year, in 1981–82 exports accounted for only 18 percent of sugar milled (*La Nación*, 17 May 1982, 2A).

29. For the banana companies, currency devaluations actually decreased wage costs in dollar terms and contributed initially to higher profit margins.

30. In 1982 some growers began to express concern about possible problems if "Nica communists" were hired. An administrator of the Las Piedras mill commented that while "Nicas" were better workers, some of them were probably Sandinistas and had to be watched carefully, since they might "create problems."

31. Usually from 60 to 80 percent of the cane processed by a mill comes

from its own fields. The rest is provided by nearby producers who, while nominally independent, often depend on the mill for technical assistance, credit, and transport and, at times, for providing squads of cane cutters.

32. Cutters, however, usually have to supply their own machetes and are paid according to the number of square meters they cut.

33. Hydrous alcohol was also exported to Jamaica, where it was dehydrated for reexport to the United States under the provisions of the Caribbean Basin Initiative.

34. A number of additional issues, beyond the scope of this discussion, are raised by the substitution of alcohol for fossil fuels. Given that sugarcane cultivation is energy-intensive, net savings in carbon emissions are an important indicator of the environmental impact of substitution. But with emissions occurring in producing areas, this could become one more instance where developed countries export "externalities" to environmentally stressed developing countries. The balance-of-payments implications of alcohol production for countries like Costa Rica also bear further examination, since early studies suggested that net foreign exchange earnings were likely to be negative (Achío and Escalante 1985: 111). The use of prime Third World cropland to produce fuel for First World motor vehicles raises important ethical questions, as well as concerns about food security and comparative advantages in other kinds of agricultural production.

35. Annual per capita consumption of rice, over 20 kilograms in the early 1930s, grew only slightly until the 1960s. By 1980, however, it surpassed 52 kilograms (Barboza and Aguilar 1982: I-5; Sáenz Gutiérrez and Merz 1932b: 12).

36. The advisors charged with planning protectionist measures were virtually the only ones who recognized any drawbacks. Though they were firm advocates of higher tariffs on foreign rice, they noted that while imports resulted in significant losses in foreign exchange, rice duties still constituted the government's second-largest source of customs revenues (Sáenz Gutiérrez and Merz 1932b: 5).

37. Until the mid-1970s, when the profitability of rice production increased because of higher support prices, virtually all improved rice seed used in Costa Rica was produced by the public sector, i.e., by the CNP.

38. While in 1938 some 46 percent of Costa Rica's rice area was in the north Pacific region, by 1950 the proportion had grown to 62 percent (Barboza and Aguilar 1982: I-21). In subsequent years, however, even though the Guanacaste rice sector expanded in absolute terms, its relative significance at the national level gradually declined to what it had been in the late 1930s, as a result of the opening of new lands in the central and southern Pacific regions, which had excellent soils and better rainfall.

39. Well-adapted, high-yield varieties of maize were only introduced on a significant scale in the 1970s.

40. According to the World Bank (1988), in 1972–73 world prices for rice

soared by 74 percent for U.S. grades and by 105 percent for Thai grades (measured in constant 1980 dollars).

41. Genetic material for this strain came from two important centers of green-revolution rice research, the International Tropical Agriculture Center (Centro Internacional de Agricultura Tropical, CIAT) in Colombia and the International Rice Research Institute in the Philippines. By the early 1980s some 90 percent of Costa Rica's rice area was planted with CR-1113.

42. Prices for the other three products in the program's purview were set at or slightly below recommended levels (Piszk 1982: 15). Estimates of maize costs and yields were also said by many agriculturalists to be "unrealistic" compared with those for rice and sorghum, the grains most commonly grown by larger landowners. Ruiz (1984) provides a brief description of the recent history of sorghum cultivation in Costa Rica. Like rice, this crop has been grown primarily by large farmers employing modern technology. In Guanacaste, where most sorghum production is centered, the crop is valued as a drought-resistant alternative to dry-land rice or as something to plant immediately following the rice harvest. Since large rice growers often cultivated sorghum, the Basic Grains Program also had a "prosorghum" slant. Both groups were represented by a single Cámara that purportedly included all basic grains producers, but which was actually dominated by wealthy rice and sorghum farmers. This was politically convenient, because it permitted large producers to represent themselves as advocates for small agriculturalists.

43. International prices, rather than reflecting a genuinely "free" equilibrium between supply and demand, tend to be artificially low because of the large subsidies given developed-country grain producers.

44. The large rice area of 1984 noted in Figure 9.4 contracted dramatically after 1985.

45. Von Seebach observed these fields during a temporary surge in Central American cotton production stimulated by high prices in the U.S. market during the U.S. Civil War (see Williams 1986: 14).

46. Nicaragua began exporting cotton in the 1930s. By 1937 it constituted 7.5 percent of total exports (Bulmer-Thomas 1987: 78).

47. During the early years of World War II Japan and Germany purchased Nicaraguan cotton (Williams 1986: 14). The Japanese presence in northern Puntarenas was likely part of this effort to assure a supply of cotton from Central America, though it was also rumored that the Japanese planned to launch an attack on the Panama Canal from an airfield on Hacienda Chagüite in Barranca, Puntarenas (Sáenz Maroto 1970: 150).

48. After Israel, Guatemala has long had the highest cotton yields, followed closely by El Salvador (CEPAL 1985: 24).

49. Guanacaste droughts are sometimes related to changes in Pacific Ocean currents that produce el Niño southern oscillations (Fleming 1986).

Such oscillations, in which condensation occurs over cool ocean currents instead of over land, are to some extent predictable. Agriculturalists have been especially reluctant to invest when the "Niño phenomenon" is anticipated.

50. One of the two gins was never, in fact, used at all. In 1982 the government opened bids to sell the unused gin to private investors.

51. Gilberto Fernández Solórzano has been a shareholder and board member of Hacienda Solimar since 1960 (RP SM 5994). He and several other individuals serve both in ALCORSA and in the producers group, the Costa Rican Cotton Association (Asociación Costarricense Algodonera), thus further blurring the distinction between public and private interests.

52. The bank estimate was probably well below actual costs, as cotton producers claimed. It provided, for example, for only thirteen pesticide applications, which most growers considered inadequate.

53. In 1988 Liberia school officials complained to the health minister that aerial spraying of cotton fields "within the city limits" endangered students' health and threatened to contaminate the Liberia and Santa Inés rivers, which served as sources of potable water for several communities in the canton (*La Nación*, 8 July 1988, 16A).

54. Unlike the common descriptive label "nica" for Nicaraguan, "guanaco," applied throughout Central America to Salvadorans, often has a pejorative ring to it. Salvadorans themselves sometimes use the term ironically, but in Costa Rica it also may mean "fool" or "jerk." Kincaid (1987, chap. 5) cites a remark by a Liberia cotton entrepreneur that complements these villagers' perceptions in a revealing way. Complaining about the low level of cotton development in Costa Rica compared with nearby Nicaragua, the hacendado commented that "we [Costa Ricans] have no slaves," implying that the crop could only be harvested by laborers who had absolutely no other options.

Chapter 10

1. Water fees were inevitably based on estimates of use, rather than actual volumes, which also complicated the state's revenue collections. Later, when sections of the irrigation district were declared "under irrigation," fees were collected on the basis of irrigable hectares owned by each agriculturalist. This was easier to enforce and had the added benefit of encouraging irrigation of the entire potentially irrigable area.

2. See Edelman (1989a) on how the flooding of the Las Palmas River and its tributaries has affected agricultural risk, land tenure, and the agrarian reform.

3. Later, with the widespread availability of bulldozers and other earth-moving equipment, as well as laser-guided tractors, it would become com-

mon to invest in expensive "zero leveling" without waiting years for soil to gradually settle. This permitted total mechanization of production in uniform fields and promised immediate maximum yields. Other, less-expensive methods of preparing fields for irrigation, still in use by smallholders in the district, included moving earth from knolls to fill nearby depressions in the soil and building gradients to distribute or hold water from canals.

4. This initial commission eventually became the National Irrigation Commission (Comisión Nacional de Riego, CONARIEGO).

5. In 1983 U.S. Navy Seabee engineers began digging wells in this area, though this was ostensibly intended to provide potable drinking water rather than sources of irrigation (Edelman and Hutchcroft 1984).

6. Early versions of the project called for irrigating about 74,000 hectares within a total area of 103,000 hectares (see Appendix C). This was expanded by 1980 to a planned irrigable area of 95,000 hectares out of a total project area of 115,000 hectares. Later the total project area was increased to 187,000 hectares, but the planned irrigable area was reduced to about 67,000 hectares.

7. This period coincided with the Costa Rican dry season, making irrigation indispensable for any participation in this important market.

8. Barahona Riera (1980, chap. 5) provides a detailed discussion of these proposals.

9. Members of *empresas comunitarias* generally receive a percentage of the enterprise's profits proportional to their work. Interest in this model of reform heightened after discussions at the 1972 International Meeting of Agrarian Reform Executives in Panama (Molina n.d.: 174).

10. In 1974–75 ten occupations were reported in Guanacaste involving 135 families on at least 2,248 hectares of land. Apart from the invasion of Hacienda Guachipelín, which was reported to ITCO in 1971 but actually began much earlier, this was the most intense period of squatter activity in the decade (ITCO, Departamento Legal, Guanacaste: Lista de expedientes).

11. Initially, the project was called the Irrigation District of Moracia, a name that was briefly applied to Guanacaste in the mid-nineteenth century to honor President Juan Rafael Mora for his role in defeating William Walker's invasion of Central America.

12. These deputies included Juan José Echeverría Brealey, Rodolfo Piza Escalante, Luis Cárdenas O., and the Cámara's own Enrique Montiel. The delegates named to the commission were José Joaquín Muñoz Bustos, David Clachar González, José Guillermo Brenes González, and Víctor Hugo Moreno R.

13. Barahona Riera's allegations about armed groups are obviously difficult to corroborate. Some leading ranchers I interviewed indicated that they were threatening "un alboroto" in 1975–76, but this could be interpreted as meaning anything from an uproar to a revolt.

14. This combination of demands for Guanacastecan independence and

armed groups reemerged in the late 1980s when wealthy landowners, fearful of nearby revolutionary Nicaragua and angry that "governments in San Jose take out more in taxes than they return" to the region, formed a shadowy autonomy movement widely believed to have a small paramilitary arm. Some merely sought greater economic and political autonomy within Costa Rica, while others spoke seriously of securing U.S. links for Guanacaste similar to those of Puerto Rico. One autonomy supporter summed up his sense of identity in a 1988 interview: "First, I'm Guanacastecan, then I'm Guanacastecan, and last I'm Guanacastecan. [I'm a] Costa Rican by circumstance, nothing more."

15. Actually the bill, called the Proyecto Integral de Ordenamiento Agrario Nacional, referred to "ordering" rather than "reform."

16. A lower limit of three hectares was also proposed to limit uneconomic minifundios. This, however, clearly did not concern the cattlemen.

17. This was called the Proyecto de Ley General de Distritos de Riego y Avenamiento.

18. This referred to the Proyecto Integral de Ordenamiento Agrario Nacional.

19. It was introduced again in 1981, but in 1982 the cattle lobby and its supporters again managed to block it.

20. The Arenal district contains the Cañas, Lajas, Abangares, Piedras, Cabuyo, and Tempisque subdistricts. The Zapandí district is divided into two subdistricts, Zapandí Norte and Zapandí Sur.

21. These included the Estación Experimental Enrique Jiménez Núñez, acquired from Hacienda Taboga, and the IDA projects at Bagatzi (earlier called Llanos del Cortés), Paso Hondo, and Magdalena.

22. Interview with Luis Diego Castillo, director, Departamento de Riego, SENARA, 1988. Rodríguez Solera (1988: 208) notes that the 1987 IDB contract required the government to acquire nearly half of the land to be irrigated. This, however, should not be interpreted as an uncharacteristic lapse by an institution otherwise known for its strong private-sector orientation. The purpose of this state involvement was simply to speed the fragmentation of underutilized large properties and to create a new class of efficient small agriculturalists.

23. To prevent speculation, most agrarian reform beneficiaries received provisional titles, which prohibited selling plots but permitted using them as loan collateral. After ten years, beneficiaries receive full titles to replace the provisional ones, a process they sometimes refer to as "liberation." It remains to be seen whether beneficiaries freed from the restrictions of their provisional titles retain possession of their land.

24. Some SENARA officials prefer to speak of the water tariff not as a tax but as an "input," akin to fertilizer or insecticide, which ought to produce more than the agriculturalist spends to acquire it.

25. Two of these involved the distribution to peasant squatters of long-occupied giant latifundios, the Stewarts' Hacienda Miravalles in highland Bagaces and the Sobrados' San Juanillo in coastal Nicoya and Santa Cruz (see Chapter 8). A third, Corralillos in Santa Cruz, grew out of an ITCO program to provide titles to occupants of state lands who, in this case, were ensconced on a property that the government had distributed in the 1940s (see Chapter 5). Yet another project, named Gil Tablada after the peasant leader murdered in 1970, resulted from a punitive expropriation of 537 hectares in La Cruz belonging to fugitive assassin Luis Morice (see Chapter 8). ITCO's actions in Guanacaste had been directed at resolving de facto occupations or disposing of already available state lands. Only rarely did the agency actually purchase unoccupied land for distribution to the landless.

26. One possible conflict of interest, never investigated, involved Cámara leader Muñoz, who was director of ITCO in 1978 during the first year of the Carazo administration. During or shortly after his service as head of the land reform agency, his relatives sold ITCO two properties, La Fe S.A. (RP SM 27,318) and "Eida Fonseca," said by local peasants to be low-quality land. Even in the unlikely event that these transactions did not involve conflict of interest, the naming of a longtime director of the cattle lobby as director of the agrarian reform agency surely says a great deal about the conservative biases of the Costa Rican land reform.

27. ITCO's acquisition of Llanos del Cortés, or Finca Wilson, as the property was also called, was technically a purchase. In an interview, however, Stewart insisted on referring to the transaction as an expropriation, since it took place against his wishes.

28. Sixteen hundred hectares belonging to Ranchos Horizonte (Cecil Hylton) in Cabuyo subdistrict were subsequently donated to Jimmy Swaggart Ministries and then acquired by IDA for eventual use in the agrarian reform program.

29. This is based on SENARA's 1988 "Padrón de Usuarios del Distrito de Arenal," which lists all water fees paid in the Cañas and Cabuyo (but not the Piedras and Arenal) subdistricts, the only ones officially "under irrigation" (the Stewarts' Hacienda Mojica in Piedras subdistrict had not yet been affected). After Taboga, these "large" owners (and their irrigable hectares) were Toscano Luconi Cohen (321), Carlos Ulate Barrantes (177), Elba Nidia Ulate Barrantes (222), and Agustín Vargas Barahona (111).

30. Interview with Luis Diego Castillo, director, Departamento de Riego, SENARA, 1988.

31. The problem of chemical contamination in coastal areas of the Palo Verde National Park and the adjacent Dr. Rafael Lucas Rodríguez Caballero National Wildlife Refuge is exacerbated by the Fila Catalina, a small range of hills that blocks drainage into the Tempisque except at a few points where toxic runoff from a wide area becomes concentrated.

32. Interview with Luis Diego Castillo, 1988.

33. Basic data on agrarian reform projects are remarkably inconsistent, even when provided by different offices of the same agency. This estimate compares the data on irrigation zone projects with SEPSA's (1989: 81) December 1988 figure of 38,933 hectares in *asentamientos campesinos* in the Chorotega planning region (Guanacaste and northern Puntarenas).

→ References Cited

Institutions and Archives

ALCORSA   Algodones de Costa Rica, S.A.
ANCR   Archivos Nacionales de Costa Rica
  Cong.   Congreso
  Gob.   Gobernación
  Hac.   Hacienda
  CA   Cañas Alcaldía
  GJC   Guanacaste Juzgado Civil y del Crimen
  JCA   Juzgado de lo Contencioso Administrativo
  LA   Liberia Alcaldía
  LCP   Liberia Juzgado Civil y Penal
  LJC   Liberia Juzgado Civil y del Crimen
  MP   Mapas y Planos
  Protocolos (Notarial records, Sección Jurídica)
  r.   remesa
  no.   number of case
  —1905: 3   year and page or folio
  v.   *vuelto* (back side of folio)
BCCR   Banco Central de Costa Rica
BICR   Banco Internacional de Costa Rica
CEPAL   Comisión Económica Para América Latina
CGG   Cámara de Ganaderos de Guanacaste
  Actas   Libros de Actas (meeting minutes)
CN   Catastro Nacional
  G3-2-1-23 CN archives ordered by province, canton, district, property.
  Other CN references are to registration numbers of properties or to
  uncataloged plans in Sección de Guanacaste, some of which are
  numbered and some unnumbered.

CNP   Consejo Nacional de Producción
FCG   Federación de Cámaras de Ganaderos de Costa Rica
ICE   Instituto Costarricense de Electricidad
IDA   Instituto de Desarrollo Agrario
IDB   Inter-American Development Bank
ILPES   Instituto Latinoamericano de Planificación Económica y Social
IMN   Instituto Meteorológico Nacional
INS   Instituto Nacional de Seguros
ITCO   Instituto de Tierras y Colonización
LAICA   Liga Agrícola Industrial de la Caña de Azúcar
OFIPLAN   Oficina de Planificación Nacional
OPSA   Oficina de Planificación del Sector Agropecuario
PLN   Partido de Liberación Nacional
RP   Registro Público de la Propiedad
    T   Tomo or volume
    F   Folio
    A   Asiento or entry
    N   Number of property
    RPPG   Partido de Guanacaste
    RP SM   Registro Público, Sección Mercantil.
            Citations of RP SM documents that do not refer to T, F, A, and
            N include the cédula or registration number of the entity and
            are in the Registro's microfiche files.
    RP FR   Registro Público, Folio Real. *Folios reales* are numbered
            registration documents in the computerized property registry
            data base.
SENARA   Servicio Nacional de Aguas Subterráneas, Riego y
  Avenamiento
SEPSA   Secretaría Ejecutiva de Planificación Sectorial Agropecuaria
SIECA   Secretaría Permanente del Tratado General de Integración
  Económica Centroamericana
SNE   Servicio Nacional de Electricidad
STICA   Servicio Técnico Inter-Americano de Cooperación Agrícola
UFCO   United Fruit Company
USAID   U.S. Agency for International Development
USDA   U.S. Department of Agriculture

Frequently cited works

AE   *Anuario estadístico* (annual volumes, some early volumes titled
        Informe estadístico). San José: Dirección General de Estadística y
        Censos.

CAP   *Censo agropecuario.* San José: Dirección General de Estadística y
        Censos, 1950, 1955, 1963, 1973, 1984.
CPO   *Censo de población.* San José: Dirección General de Estadística y
        Censos, 1864, 1883, 1892, 1927, 1950, 1955, 1963, 1973, 1984.
CLD   *Colección de leyes y decretos* (annual volumes, some titled *Co-
        lección de las disposiciones legislativas y administrativas*).
DHCR   *Colección de documentos para la historia de Costa Rica,* 3 vols.
        Selections by Carlos Meléndez from nineteenth-century edition
        edited by León Fernández. San José: Editorial Costa Rica, 1976.
DHN   *Colección Somoza: Documentos para la historia de Nicaragua,*
        17 vols. Madrid: Imprenta & Litografía Juan Bravo: 1954–57.

Memorias (government ministry reports)

Memoria de Fomento
Memoria de Gobernación
Memoria de Gobernación, Policía y Fomento
Memoria de Seguridad Pública

Newspapers and Periodicals

Adelante
Central American Report (Guatemala)
Costa Rica de Ayer y Hoy
Diario de Costa Rica
Escuela de Agricultura
Excelsior (Costa Rica)
Excelsior (Mexico)
Forbes
La Gaceta Oficial
El Guanacaste
El Guanacasteco
Libertad
La Nación
La Nueva Prensa
Pampa
El Pampero
La Prensa Libre
Potomac News (Woodbridge, Virginia)
Pueblo
La República
Revista de los Archivos Nacionales
Tico Times

Trabajo
La Tribuna
Wall Street Journal

Books and Articles

Abel-Vidor, Suzanne. 1980. "The Historic Sources for the Greater Nicoya Archeological Sub-Area." *Vínculos* 6, nos. 1–2: 155–86.
Achío Tacsan, Mayra, and Ana Cecila Escalante Herrera. 1981. "Los grandes empresarios azucareros: Costa Rica 1960–1978." *Cuadernos Centroamericanos de Ciencias Sociales* 9: 65–88.
——. 1985. *Azúcar y política en Costa Rica*. San José: Editorial Costa Rica.
Acosta, Marcos A. 1923. "Informe de la Comandancia de Plaza de Guanacaste." In *Memoria de la Secretaría de Seguridad Pública año 1922*, pp. 192–99. San José: Imprenta María v. de Lines.
Acosta C., Abraham. 1911. "Informe anual administrativo correspondiente al Cantón de Cañas." In Carlos M. Jiménez, ed., *Memoria de Gobernación y Policía 1911*, pp. 490–94. San José: Tipografía Nacional.
Acuña Acevedo, Moisés. 1936. "Informe sobre la industria ganadera y pastos en la zona de Guanacaste." University of Costa Rica thesis.
Acuña V., Miguel. 1977. *El 55*. San José: Librería Lehmann.
Aguilar, Irene. 1985. "Una caracterización socio-económica del grupo ganadero-exportador (los casos de San Carlos y Guanacaste) 1960–1980." *Serie Investigaciones* 5. San José: Instituto de Investigaciones Sociales, Universidad de Costa Rica.
Aguilar, Irene, and Manuel Solís. 1988. *La élite ganadera en Costa Rica*. San José: Editorial de la Universidad de Costa Rica.
Albarracín González, Priscilla, and Héctor Pérez Brignoli. 1977. "Estadísticas del comercio exterior de Costa Rica (1907–1946)." *Avances de Investigación* [Proyecto de Historia Social y Económica de Costa Rica] 5: 155.
Althusser, Louis, and Etienne Balibar. 1970. *Reading Capital*. London: New Left Books.
Alvarez, Miguel Angel. 1942. *De como perdimos las provincias de Nicoya y Guanacaste*. Granada: Escuela Tip. Salesiana.
Alvarez Hurtado, Antonio. 1903. "Para los guanacastecos." *Pandemonium* 2, no. 2 (June): 3.
Annis, Sheldon. n.d. "Dual Debt in Agriculture: The Relationship between Economic and Environmental Borrowing." Manuscript.
——. 1990. "Debt and Wrong-Way Resource Flows in Costa Rica." *Ethics and International Affairs* 4: 1–15.
Apéstegui, Federico. 1942. *Recuerdos de antaño*. San José: Imprenta La Tribuna.

Arauz Aguilar, Armando. 1987. *El Doctor Francisco Vargas Vargas: Historia, leyenda y mito de los llanos*. N.p.

Araya Pochet, Carlos. 1979. "El enclave minero en Centroamérica, 1880–1945: Un estudio de los casos de Honduras, Nicaragua y Costa Rica." *Revista de Ciencias Sociales* 17–18 (Mar.–Oct.): 13–59.

———. 1982. *Historia económica de Costa Rica 1821–1971* (4ª edición). San José: Editorial Fernández Arce.

Assadourian, Carlos Sempat. 1973. "Modos de producción, capitalismo y subdesarrollo en América Latina." *Cuadernos de Pasado y Presente* 40: 47–77.

Avilés, Raquel, and Jorge Mernies. 1982. "La disponibilidad de alimentos en Costa Rica: 1971–1980." *Revista Médica del Hospital Nacional de Niños* 17, nos. 1–2: 255–64.

Ayón, Tomás. 1956. *Historia de Nicaragua*, 2ª edición, 3 vols. Madrid: Escuela Profesional de Artes Gráficas.

Baires Martínez, Yolanda. 1975. "Las transacciones inmobiliarias en el Valle Central y la expansión cafetalera de Costa Rica (1800–1850)." University of Costa Rica thesis.

Balta, J. 1922. "Informe sobre la cuestión de Tilarán." *Diario de Costa Rica*, 8 Feb., 2.

Baltodano Guillén, Aristides. 1937. "Apuntes agropecuarios referentes a Guanacaste." University of Costa Rica thesis.

Barahona Portocarrero, Amaru, and Mario Salazar Valiente. 1981. "Breve estudio sobre la historia contemporánea de Nicaragua." In Pablo González Casanova, ed., *América Latina: historia de medio siglo*, vol. 2, pp. 377–404. Mexico: Siglo XXI.

Barahona Riera, Francisco. 1980. *Reforma agraria y poder político*. San José: Editorial Universidad de Costa Rica.

Baraona, Rafael. 1965. "Una tipología de haciendas en la sierra ecuatoriana." In Oscar Delgado, ed., *Reformas agrarias en América Latina*, pp. 688–96. Mexico: Fondo de Cultura Económica.

Barboza V., Carlos, and Justo Aguilar F. 1982. *Desarrollo tecnológico en el cultivo del arroz*. San José: Consejo Nacional de Investigaciones Científicas y Tecnológicas.

Barboza V., Carlos, et al. 1981 [Barboza V., Carlos, Justo Aguilar F., and Jorge León S.]. *Desarrollo tecnológico en el cultivo de la caña de azúcar*. San José: Consejo Nacional de Investigaciones Científicas y Tecnológicas.

Baretta, Silvio Duncan, and John Markhoff. 1978. "Civilization and Barbarism: Cattle Frontiers in Latin America." *Comparative Studies in Society and History* 20, no. 4: 587–620.

Barquero, Mercedes, and Manuel A. Constenla. 1986. "Residuos de plaguicidas organoclorados en tejido adiposo humano en Costa Rica." *Revista de Biología Tropical* 34, no. 1: 7–12.

Barrett, Ward. 1979. "Jugerum and Caballería in New Spain." *Agricultural History* 53: 423–37.

Barry, Tom, et al. 1983 [Barry, Tom, Beth Wood, and Deb Preusch]. *Dollars and Dictators: A Guide to Central America*. New York: Grove.

Bauer, Arnold J. 1979. "Rural Workers in Spanish America: Problems of Peonage and Oppression." *Hispanic American Historical Review* 59, no. 1: 34–63.

BCCR. 1981 [Banco Central de Costa Rica]. *Avíos arroz mecanizado*. San José: Departamento de Crédito de Desarrollo, BCCR.

———. 1982. *Avíos arroz mecanizado*. San José: Departamento de Crédito de Desarrollo, BCCR.

———. 1986. *Estadísticas 1950–1985*. San José: División Económica, BCCR.

Bel Ingeniería, S.A. 1978. "Proyecto de riego cuenca baja del Tempisque— Plan maestro." Mimeo.

Belly, Félix. 1974. "Guanacaste, tierra casi virgen, de inmensas vacadas, 1858." In Carlos Meléndez, ed., *Viajeros por Guanacaste*, pp. 195–208. San José: Ministerio de Cultura, Juventud y Deportes.

Berg, Alan. 1973. *The Nutrition Factor: Its Role in National Development*. Washington: Brookings Institution.

Bermúdez Méndez, Nora, and Rosa María Pochet Coronado. 1981. "La actividad agrícola e industrial de la caña de azúcar en tres distritos: Tacares, Juan Viñas y Cañas." *Cuadernos Centroamericanos de Ciencias Sociales* 9: 1–64.

———. 1986. *La agroindustria de la caña de azúcar en Costa Rica: modificaciones económicas y sociales (1950–1975)*. Buenos Aires: Consejo Latinoamericano de Ciencias Sociales.

BICR. 1916 [Banco Internacional de Costa Rica]. *Memoria anual*. San José: BICR.

———. 1935. *Memoria anual*. San José: BICR.

Biolley, Paul. 1889. *Costa Rica and Her Future*. Washington, D.C.: Judd & Detweller.

Bishko, Charles Julian. 1952. "The Peninsular Background of Latin American Cattle Ranching." *Hispanic American Historical Review* 32, no. 4: 491–515.

Blanco, Gustavo, and Orlando Navarro. 1984. *El movimiento solidarista costarricense*. San José: Editorial Costa Rica.

Blanco, José Antonio. 1974. "Con la fragata Joaquina en el Puerto de Culebra, 1807." In Carlos Meléndez Chaverri, ed., *Viajeros por Guanacaste*, pp. 115–22. San José: Ministerio de Cultura, Juventud y Deportes.

Blanco Segura, Ricardo. 1967. *Historia eclesiástica de Costa Rica*. San José: Editorial Costa Rica.

Blandón, Jesús M. 1981. *Entre Sandino y Fonseca*. Managua: Departamento de Propaganda y Educación Política, Frente Sandinista de Liberación Nacional.

Bolaños A., Margarita, and Claudia Quirós Vargas. 1984. "Las tierras comunales indígenas y la política liberal agraria. El caso de Cot: 1812–1890." *Revista de Ciencias Sociales* Edición Especial Antropología No. 1 (July): 23–36.

Booth, John A. 1982. *The End and the Beginning: The Nicaraguan Revolution.* Boulder, Colo.: Westview.

Boulière, François, and Malcolm Hadley. 1970. "The Ecology of Tropical Savannas." *Annual Review of Ecology and Systematics* 1: 125–52.

Bourgois, Philippe I. 1989. *Ethnicity at Work: Divided Labor on a Central American Plantation.* Baltimore: Johns Hopkins University Press.

Bovallius, Carl. 1977 [1887]. *Viaje por Centroamérica 1881–1883.* Managua: Fondo de Promoción Cultural, Banco de América.

Brading, David. 1975. "Estructura de la producción agrícola en el Bajío, 1700 a 1850." In Enrique Florescano, ed., *Haciendas, latifundios y plantaciones en América Latina,* pp. 105–31. Mexico: Siglo XXI.

Brenner, Robert. 1976. "Agrarian Class Structure and Economic Development in Pre-Industrial Europe." *Past and Present* 70, no.1: 30–75.

Breton, Yvan, et al. 1990 [Breton, Yvan, Eduardo López Estrada, Elizabeth Houde, and Clara Benazara]. *La diversidad de la pesca costera en Costa Rica: parámetros para una antropología marítima aplicada.* Quebec: Département d'anthropologie, Université Laval.

Brown, Lester. 1978a. "Why Meat Will Cost More and More and More." *Human Nature* 1, no. 9: 84.

———. 1978b. *The Twenty-Ninth Day.* New York: Norton.

Bulmer-Thomas, Victor. 1987. *The Political Economy of Central America Since 1920.* Cambridge: Cambridge University Press.

Bunker, Stephen G. 1985. *Underdeveloping the Amazon: Extraction, Unequal Exchange, and the Failure of the Modern State.* Urbana: University of Illinois Press.

Buschbacher, Robert J. 1986. "Tropical Deforestation and Pasture Development." *BioScience* 36, no. 1: 22–28.

Bustos, Juan V. 1889. "Carta del Gobernador de Guanacaste al Secretario de Estado en el Despacho de Gobernación." In *Memoria de la Secretaría de Gobernación, Policía y Fomento 1889,* unpaginated. San José: Tipografía Nacional.

Butzer, Karl W. 1988. "Cattle and Sheep from Old to New Spain: Historical Antecedents." *Annals of the Association of American Geographers* 78, no. 1: 29–56.

Buxedas, Martín. 1977. "El comercio internacional de carne vacuna y las exportaciones de los países atrasados." *Comercio Exterior* (Mexico) 27, no. 2: 1494–1509.

Cabrera, Víctor M. 1924. *Guanacaste: libro conmemorativo del centenario de la incorporación del Partido de Nicoya a Costa Rica.* San José: Imprenta María v. de Lines.

Cabrera Padilla, Roberto. 1989. *Santa Cruz Guanacaste: una aproximación a la historia y la cultura populares.* San José: Guayacán.

Calderón, Manuel. 1986. "Proteccionismo y librecambio: Costa Rica (1880–1950)." In Carmen Lila Gómez et al., *Las instituciones costarricenses del siglo XX,* pp. 103–30. San José: Editorial Costa Rica.

Calvert, Phillip Powell, and Amelia Smith Calvert. 1917. *A Year of Costa Rican Natural History.* New York: Macmillan.

Calvo, Joaquín B. 1887. *Apuntamientos geográficos, estadísticos e históricos.* San José: Imprenta Nacional.

Camacho, Daniel. 1978. "¿Por qué persiste el juego democrático en Costa Rica?" In Chester Zelaya, ed., *¿Democracia en Costa Rica? Cinco opiniones polémicas,* pp. 85–128. San José: Editorial Universidad Estatal a Distancia.

Carcanholo Fogaça, Reinaldo A. 1977. "El desarrollo capitalista agropecuario de Guanacaste: Una interpretación." *Revista de Ciencias Sociales* 13 (Mar.–Oct.): 1–20.

Cardoso, Ciro F. S. 1975a. "La formación de hacienda cafetalera costarricense en el siglo XIX." In Enrique Florescano, ed., *Haciendas, latifundios y plantaciones en América Latina,* pp. 635–67. Mexico: Siglo XXI.

———. 1975b. "Historia económica del café en Centroamérica (siglo XIX): estudio comparativo." *Estudios Sociales Centroamericanos* 10: 9–55.

Cardoso, Ciro F. S., and Héctor Pérez Brignoli. 1977. *Centroamérica y la economía occidental (1520–1930).* San José: Editorial de la Universidad de Costa Rica.

———. 1979. *Historia económica de América Latina,* 2 vols. Barcelona: Editorial Crítica.

Cartín, Sandra, and Ileana Piszk. 1980. "La producción de granos básicos en Costa Rica. Instituciones estatales y fuerzas sociales. Período de diversificación económica." *Revista de Ciencias Sociales* 19–20 (Mar.–Oct.): 25–35.

Casey Gaspar, Jeffrey. 1979. *Limón: 1880–1940 Un estudio de la industria bananera en Costa Rica.* San José: Editorial Costa Rica.

Castro Esquivel, Rodrigo. 1938. "Ganadería en Guanacaste." University of Costa Rica thesis.

Castro R., Zenón. 1911. "Informe del Gobernador de la Provincia de Guanacaste." In Carlos M. Jimènez, ed., *Memoria de Gobernación y Policía 1911,* pp. 478–81. San José: Tipografía Nacional.

Caufield, Catherine. 1985. *In the Rainforest.* New York: Knopf.

CEPAL. 1973 [Comisión Económica Para América Latina]. *Tenencia de la tierra y desarrollo rural en Centroamérica.* San José: Editorial Universitaria Centroamericana.

———. 1985. *América Latina y la economía mundial del algodón.* Santiago: Naciones Unidas, Estudios e Informes de la CEPAL No. 50.

CGG. 1954–60 [Cámara de Ganaderos de Guanacaste]. *Informe anual.* Liberia: CGG.

————. 1976. *Informe de labores*. Liberia: CGG.

Chamorro, Pedro Joaquín. 1959. *Estirpe sangrienta: los Somoza*. Buenos Aires: Editorial Triángulo.

Chapman, Anne M. 1960. *Los Nicarao y los Chorotega según las fuentes históricas*. San José: Publicaciones de la Universidad de Costa Rica.

Chevalier, François. 1963 [1952]. *Land and Society in Colonial Mexico: The Great Hacienda*. Berkeley: University of California Press.

Chonchol, Jacques. 1970. "Eight Fundamental Conditions of Agrarian Reform in Latin America." In Rodolfo Stavenhagen, ed., *Agrarian Problems and Peasant Movements in Latin America*, pp. 159–72. New York: Anchor.

Churnside, Roger. 1979. "La concentración de la tierra en Costa Rica (1859–1935) en torno a algunos métodos en el análisis de su estructura." *Cuadernos Centroamericanos de Ciencias Sociales* 2: 17–35.

————. 1980. "Organización de la producción, mercado de fuerza de trabajo y políticas laborales en Costa Rica 1864–1950." *Avances de Investigación* 38: 1–31.

————. 1981. "Concentración de la tierra en 1935 y 1800–1850: algunas consideraciones de tipo metodológico." *Revista de Ciencias Sociales* 21–22 (Mar.–Oct.): 7–34.

Clachar, David. 1946. "Peligros y perspectivas del río Tempisque." *Revista del Instituto de Defensa del Café* 17: 363–65.

Cockburn, John. 1974. "Peripecias e infortunios en tierras de Nicoya, 1731." In Carlos Meléndez Chaverri, ed., *Viajeros por Guanacaste*, pp. 71–92. San José: Ministerio de Cultura, Juventud y Deportes.

Colegial Martínez, Carlos. 1989. "Hacienda Tenorio." In Clyde S. Stephens, ed., *Bananeros in Central America*, pp. 205–9. Alva, Fla.: Banana Books.

Colindres, Eduardo. 1977. *Fundamentos económicos de la burguesía salvadoreña*. San Salvador: UCA Editores.

Corradi, Juan E. 1985. *The Fitful Republic: Economy, Society, and Politics in Argentina*. Boulder, Colo.: Westview.

Costa Rica de Ayer y Hoy. 1957. "Copia fiel de documentos relativos a la donación de terrenos de Bernabela Ramos al Santo Cristo de Esquipulas en Santa Cruz de Guanacaste." *Costa Rica de Ayer y Hoy* 5, no. 27: 26–30.

Creamer, Winifred. 1987. "Mesoamerica as a Concept: An Archeological View from Central America." *Latin American Research Review* 22, no. 1: 35–62.

Creedman, Theodore S. 1977. *Historical Dictionary of Costa Rica*. Metuchen, N.J.: Scarecrow Press.

Crosby, Alfred W. 1986. *Biological Imperialism: The Biological Expansion of Europe, 900–1900*. Cambridge: Cambridge University Press.

Cross, Harry E. 1979. "Debt Peonage Reconsidered: A Case Study in Nineteenth-Century Zacatecas, Mexico." *Business History Review* 53, no. 4: 473–95.

Cruz, Luis. 1934. "La ganadería en Costa Rica." In Lino Bergna and Alejandro Zen, eds., *Anuario general de Costa Rica,* pp. 514–45. San José: Borrasé Hermanos.

Dalton, Roque, ed. 1972. *Miguel Mármol: Los sucesos de 1932 en El Salvador.* San José: Editorial Universitaria Centroamericana.

Dary, David. 1981. *Cowboy Culture: A Saga of Five Centuries.* New York: Knopf.

Daubenmire, R. 1972a. "Some Ecological Consequences of Converting Forest to Savanna in Northwestern Costa Rica." *Tropical Ecology* 13, no. 1: 31–51.

———. 1972b. "Standing Crops and Primary Production in Savanna Derived from Semideciduous Forest in Northwest Costa Rica." *Botanical Gazette* 133, no. 4: 395–401.

———. 1972c. "Ecology of Hyparrhenia rufa in Derived Savanna in Northwestern Costa Rica." *Journal of Applied Ecology* 9: 11–23.

Da Veiga, José S. 1975. "A la poursuite du profit: Quand les multinationales font du 'ranching.'" *Le Monde Diplomatique,* Sept., 12–13.

Dávila Cubero, Carlos. 1976. "¡Viva Vargas! Historia del Partido Confraternidad Guanacasteca." University of Costa Rica thesis.

de Andrade, F. Moretzsohn. 1967. "Decadência do Campesinato Costarriquenho." *Revista Geográfica* 66: 135–52.

Deffontaines, Pierre. 1965. "Transhumance et mouvements de bétail en Amérique latine." *Les Cahiers d'Outre-Mer* 18, no. 71: 258–94; 18, no. 72: 321–41.

de Janvry, Alain. 1981. *The Agrarian Question and Reformism in Latin America.* Baltimore: Johns Hopkins University Press.

de la Calle, Angel Luis. 1983. "Yo maté a Somoza: entrevista con Gorriarán Merlo." *El País Semanal* (Madrid) 8, no. 331 (Aug. 14): 10–17.

De La Cruz, Vladimir. 1980. *Las luchas sociales en Costa Rica 1870–1930.* San José: Editorial Costa Rica and Editorial Universidad de Costa Rica.

———. 1986. "Notas para la historia del movimiento campesino en Costa Rica." In Carmen Lila Gómez et al., *Las instituciones costarricenses del siglo XX,* pp. 319–76. San José: Editorial Costa Rica.

De Las Casas, Bartolomé. 1977 [1552]. *Brevísima relación de la destrucción de las Indias.* Havana: Editorial de Ciencias Sociales.

Delgado, Ulises. 1980. *Libro azul de San Antonio de Nicoya.* San José: Ministerio de Educación Pública.

Dengo, G. 1962. *Estudio geológico de la región del Guanacaste, Costa Rica.* San José: Instituto Geográfico.

DeWalt, Billie R. 1982. "The Big Macro Connection: Population, Grain and Cattle in Southern Honduras." *Culture and Agriculture* 14: 1–12.

DeWitt, R. Peter. 1977. *The Inter-American Development Bank and Political Influence With Special Reference to Costa Rica.* New York: Praeger.

Dickinson, Joshua C. 1973. "Protein Flight from Latin America: Some Social and Ecological Considerations." In David Hill, ed., *Latin American Development Issues, Proceedings of the Conference of Latin Americanist Geographers* 3: 127–32.

Diederich, Bernard. 1981. *Somoza and the Legacy of U.S. Involvement in Central America*. New York: Dutton.

Donato, Elisa M., and Manuel Rojas Bolaños. 1985. "Problemas y perspectivas del sindicalismo costarricense." *Aportes* 24 (Apr.–May): 30–34.

Dóndoli, C. 1950. "Liberia y sus alrededores, nota geoagronómica." *Suelo Tico* 4, nos. 18–19: 65–69.

Ducoudry, Louis, and Mario Lungo. 1976. "La 'modernización' capitalista de Guanacaste y la problemática de la vivienda rural." *Estudios Sociales Centroamericanos* 15: 11–20.

Duncan, Kenneth, and Ian Rutledge. 1977. "Introduction: Patterns of Agrarian Capitalism in Latin America." In *Land and Labour in Latin America*, pp. 1–20. Cambridge: Cambridge University Press.

Dunlop, Robert Glasgow. 1970 [1847]. "Viajes en Centro América." In Ricardo Fernández Guardia, ed., *Costa Rica en el siglo XIX: Antología de viajeros*, pp. 103–21. San José: Editorial Universitaria Centroamericana.

Edelman, Marc. 1981. "Apuntes sobre la consolidación de las haciendas en Guanacaste." *Avances de Investigación* (Instituto de Investigaciones Sociales, Universidad de Costa Rica) 44: 1–65.

———. 1983. "Recent Literature on Costa Rica's Economic Crisis." *Latin American Research Review* 18, no. 2: 166–80.

———. 1985. "Extensive Land Use and the Logic of the Latifundio: A Case Study in Guanacaste Province, Costa Rica." *Human Ecology* 13, no. 2: 153–85.

———. 1987a. "El distrito de riego de Guanacaste (Costa Rica) y la política del agua." *Anuario de Estudios Centroamericanos* 13, no. 1: 95–111.

———. 1987b. "From Central American Pasture to North American Hamburger." In Marvin Harris and Eric B. Ross, eds., *Food and Evolution: Toward a Theory of Human Food Habits*, pp. 541–61. Philadelphia: Temple University Press.

———. 1989a. "Illegal Renting of Agrarian Reform Plots: A Costa Rican Case Study." *Human Organization* 48, no. 2: 172–80.

———. 1989b. "The Somozas' Properties in Northern Costa Rica." In Marc Edelman and Joanne Kenen, eds., *The Costa Rica Reader*, pp. 242–49. New York: Grove Weidenfeld.

———. 1990. "'When They Took the Muni': Political Culture and Anti-Austerity Protest in Rural Northwestern Costa Rica." *American Ethnologist* 17, no. 4: 126–47.

———. n.d. "Rethinking the Hamburger Thesis: Declining Beef Exports and Continuing Forest Destruction in Central America." Manuscript.

Edelman, Marc, and Jayne Hutchcroft. 1984. "Costa Rica: Modernizing the Non-Army." *Report on the Americas* 18, no. 2 (Mar.–Apr.): 9–11.

Edelman, Marc, and Joanne Kenen, eds. 1989. *The Costa Rica Reader*. New York: Grove Weidenfeld.

Elizondo Arce, Hernán. 1978. *Memorias de un pobre diablo*. San José: Editorial Costa Rica.

Escalante H., Ana Cecilia, and Mayra Achío T. 1980. "La industria azucarera en Costa Rica a partir de 1960: un sector capitalista desarrollado." *Revista de Ciencias Sociales* 19–20 (Mar.–Oct.): 37–51.

Escuela de Agricultura. 1934. "Con el gran empresario Mister Wilson de poderosa visión y asombroso dinamismo." *Escuela de Agricultura* 6, no. 11: 404–9.

Estrada Molina, Ligia. 1967. *Teodoro Picado Michalski: su aporte a la historiografía*. San José: Imprenta Nacional.

Facio, Rodrigo. 1972. *Estudio sobre economía costarricense*. San José: Editorial Costa Rica.

Fallas, Carlos Luis. 1978 [1960]. *Don Bárbaro*. Heredia: Universidad Nacional—Cuadernos Prometeo No. 6.

FCG. 1977 (Federación de Cámaras de Ganaderos de Costa Rica). *Memoria anual*. San José: FCG.

———. 1983. *Problemática de la ganadería bovina y propuestas para su reactivación en el corto plazo*. San José: FCG.

Feder, Ernest. 1971. *The Rape of the Peasantry*. Garden City, N.Y.: Anchor.

———. 1980. "The Odious Competition Between Man and Animal over Agricultural Resources in the Underdeveloped Countries." *Review* 3, no. 3: 463–500.

Feo, José. 1911. "Forrajes (una opinión)." *Boletín de Fomento* 1, no. 1: 44–45.

Fernández Arias, Mario E. 1980. "Apuntes acerca de las bases de la evolución de la estructura agraria cafetalera en Costa Rica." *Avances de Investigación* (Instituto de Investigaciones Sociales, Universidad de Costa Rica) 36: 1–21.

———. 1983. *Evolución de la estructura de la tenencia de la tierra en Costa Rica: café, caña de azúcar y ganadería (1950–1978)*. San José: Instituto de Investigaciones Sociales, Universidad de Costa Rica, Serie Investigaciones 1.

Fernández Arias, et al. 1976 [Fernández Arias, Mario E., Anabelle Schmidt, and Víctor Basauri]. *La población de Costa Rica*. San José: Editorial Universidad de Costa Rica.

Fernández Carballo, Rodolfo. 1980. "Organización y luchas campesinas en Guanacaste, 1950–1970." Paper presented at the IVº Congreso Centroamericano de Sociología, Managua, Nicaragua, July 1–5.

Fernández Guardia, Ricardo. 1938. "La sublevación de los indios de Nicoya en 1760." *Revista de los Archivos Nacionales* 2, no. 7–8: 362–66.

Ferrero, Luis. 1975. *Costa Rica precolombina*. San José: Editorial Costa Rica.

Fleming, Theodore H. 1986. "Secular Changes in Costa Rican Rainfall: Correlation with Elevation." *Journal of Tropical Ecology* 2: 87–91.

Flichman, Guillermo. 1977. *La renta del suelo y el desarrollo agrario argentino*. Mexico: Siglo XXI.

Florescano, Enrique, ed. 1975. *Haciendas, latifundios y plantaciones en América Latina*. Mexico: Siglo XXI.

———. 1976. *Origen y desarrollo de los problemas agrarios de México 1500–1821*. Mexico: Ediciones Era.

Floyd, Troy. 1966. "The Indigo Merchant: Promoter of Central American Economic Development, 1750–1808." *Business History Review* 29, no. 4: 466–87.

Fonseca Amador, Carlos, ed. 1980. *Viva Sandino obras tomo 2*. Managua: Nueva Nicaragua.

Fonseca Corrales, Elizabeth. 1983. *Costa Rica colonial: la tierra y el hombre*. San José: Editorial Universitaria Centroamericana.

Foster-Carter, Aiden. 1978. "Can We Articulate Articulation?" In John Clammer, ed., *The New Economic Anthropology*, pp. 210–49. New York: St. Martin's.

Fournier O., Luis A. 1974. "Las zonas de vida del Guanacaste." *Revista de la Universidad de Costa Rica* 38: 11–19.

Frank, André Gunder. 1969. *Capitalism and Underdevelopment in Latin America*. New York: Monthly Review Press.

Furtado, Celso. 1976. *Economic Development of Latin America*. 2d ed. Cambridge: Cambridge University Press.

Gage, Thomas. 1974. "Viaje a Nicoya y abusos que se cometían con los indios 1636." In Carlos Meléndez Chaverri, ed., *Viajeros por Guanacaste*, pp. 53–61. San José: Ministerio de Cultura, Juventud y Deportes.

Gamboa Alvarado, Gerardo. 1975. *Del folklore costarricense: relatos de la bajura y de la serranía*. San José: Editorial Fernández-Arce.

García Murillo, Guillermo. 1984. *Las minas de Abangares: Historia de una doble explotación*. San José: Editorial de la Universidad de Costa Rica.

Gardner, B. Delworth, and Carole Frank Nuckton. 1979. "Factors Affecting Agricultural Land Prices." *California Agriculture* 33, no. 1: 4–6.

Gil Pacheco, Rufino. 1974. *Ciento cinco años de vida bancaria en Costa Rica*. San José: Editorial Costa Rica.

Gómez A., Juan. 1931a. "Carta al Sr. Ministro de Fomento respecto al problema de la ganadería." *Escuela de Agricultura* 3, no. 4: 73–80.

———. 1931b. "El problema de la ganadería en Costa Rica." *Escuela de Agricultura* 3, no. 9: 209–12.

———. 1931c. "Y el señor Gómez contestó así." *Escuela de Agricultura* 3, no. 11: 251–53.

Góngora, Mario. 1966. "Vagabondage et société pastorale en Amérique latine (Specialment au Chili central)." *Annales Economies Sociétés Civilisations* 21, no. 1: 159–77.

González, Edelmira. 1977 [1946]. *Alma llanera*. San José: Editorial Costa Rica.

González B., Rodrigo. 1983. "Guanacaste: fraccionamiento del latifundio y capitalismo." *Avance de Investigación.* Heredia: Universidad Nacional, Escuela de Ciencias Agrarias.

———. 1987. "Consideraciones sobre el Censo Agropecuario de 1984." *Revista de Ciencias Sociales* 37–38 (Sept.–Dec.): 91–101.

Gould, Jeffrey L. 1990. *To Lead as Equals: Rural Protest and Political Consciousness in Chinandega, Nicaragua, 1912–1979.* Chapel Hill: University of North Carolina Press.

Grigg, David B. 1974. *The Agricultural Systems of the World: An Evolutionary Approach.* Cambridge: Cambridge University Press.

Grindle, Merilee S. 1986. *State and Countryside: Development Policy and Agrarian Politics in Latin America.* Baltimore: Johns Hopkins University Press.

Guardia Quirós, Jorge, et al. 1987 [Guardia Quirós, Jorge, Alberto Di Mare, and Thelmo Vargas]. *La política de precios en Costa Rica.* San José: Consultores Económicos y Legales.

Gudmundson, Lowell. 1978a. "Documentos para la historia del distrito minero del Guanacaste: ¿enclave minero?" *Revista de Historia* 3, no. 6: 129–62.

———. 1978b. *Estratificación socio-racial y económica de Costa Rica: 1700–1850.* San José: Editorial Universidad Estatal a Distancia.

———. 1979. "Apuntes para una historia de la ganadería en Costa Rica, 1850–1950." *Revista de Ciencias Sociales* 17–18 (Mar.–Oct.): 61–111.

———. 1982. "Las luchas agrarias de Guanacaste, 1900–1935: Campesinos parcelarios y de hacienda, respuestas al capitalismo agrario y al reformismo político." *Estudios Sociales Centroamericanos* 32: 75–95.

———. 1983a. "The Expropriation of Pious and Corporate Properties in Costa Rica, 1805–1860: Patterns in the Consolidation of a National Elite." *The Americas* 39, no. 3: 281–302.

———. 1983b. *Hacendados, políticos y precaristas: la ganadería y el latifundismo guanacasteco 1800–1950.* San José: Editorial Costa Rica.

———. 1983c. "Peasant Movements and the Transition to Agrarian Capitalism: Freeholding versus Hacienda Peasantries and Agrarian Reform in Guanacaste, Costa Rica, 1880–1935." *Peasant Studies* 10, no. 3: 145–62.

———. 1986. *Costa Rica Before Coffee: Society and Economy on the Eve of the Export Boom.* Baton Rouge: Louisiana State University Press.

Guerrero C., Julián N., and Lola Soriano de Guerrero. 1966. *Monografía de Rivas.* Rivas: IFAGAN.

Guess, George. 1978. "Narrowing the Base of Costa Rican Democracy." *Development and Change* 9, no. 4: 599–609.

Guidos Véjar, Rafael. 1980. *El ascenso del militarismo en El Salvador.* San Salvador: UCA Editores.

Gutiérrez Santana, Francisco. 1956. "La ciudad de Liberia a fines del siglo pasado." *Costa Rica de Ayer y Hoy* 7, no. 37: 14–17.

Hagenauer, Werner. 1980. "Análisis agro-metereológico en la zona de Cañas y Bagaces (Guanacaste) en los años 1921 a 1979." *Informe Semestral* (Instituto Geográfico Nacional), July–Dec., 45–59.

Hall, Carolyn. 1976. *El café y el desarrollo histórico-geográfico de Costa Rica.* San José: Editorial Costa Rica y Universidad Nacional.

————. 1978. *Cóncavas: Formación de una hacienda cafetalera 1889–1911.* San José: Editorial de la Universidad de Costa Rica.

Harris, Marvin. 1964. *Patterns of Race in the Americas.* New York: Norton.

Harris, Marvin, and Eric B. Ross. 1978. "How Beef Became King." *Psychology Today* 12, no. 5: 88–94.

Heath, Dwight B. 1970. "Costa Rica and Her Neighbors." *Current History* 58, no. 342: 95–101, 113.

Hecht, Susanna B., et al. 1988 [Hecht, Susanna B., Richard B. Norgaard, and Giorgio Possio]. "The Economics of Cattle Ranching in Eastern Amazonia." *Interciencia* 13, no. 5: 233–40.

Hedström, Ingemar. 1990. *¿Volverán las golondrinas? La reintegración de la creación desde una perspectiva latinoamericana,* 2ª edición. San José: Departamento Ecuménico de Investigaciones.

Hennessy, Alistair. 1978. *The Frontier in Latin American History.* Albuquerque: University of New Mexico Press.

Hernández, Alfredo E. 1942. *La organización agraria de Costa Rica y el desarrollo del crédito rural.* San José: Banco Nacional de Costa Rica.

Hernández de Jaén, Mireya, Carlos Dávila, and Julio C. Jaén. 1977. *Monografía del cantón Carrillo 1877–1977.* San José: Editorial de la Universidad de Costa Rica.

Hilje, Luko, et al. 1987 [Hilje, Luko, Luisa E. Castillo, Lori Ann Thrupp, and Ineke Wesseling]. *El uso de los plaguicidas en Costa Rica.* San José: Editorial Universidad Estatal a Distancia.

Hilje Quirós, Brunilda. 1985. "Apropiación y distribución de la tierra en Tilarán, 1880–1943." *Revista de Historia* Número Especial Historia Agraria: 161–75.

————. 1988. "Legislación agraria y apropiación de la tierra en Guanacaste: el caso de Cañas (1884–1907)." *Revista de Historia* 17: 69–97.

Hobsbawm, Eric J. 1969. "A Case of Neo-Feudalism: La Convención, Peru." *Journal of Latin American Studies* 1, no. 1: 31–50.

————. 1974. "Peasant Land Occupations." *Past and Present* 62: 120–52.

————. 1981. *Bandits.* Rev. ed. New York: Pantheon.

Hobsbawm, Eric J., and George Rudé. 1968. *Captain Swing.* New York: Pantheon.

Holden, Robert H. 1981. "Central America Is Growing More Beef and Eating Less, as the Hamburger Connection Widens." *Multinational Monitor* 2, no. 10: 17–18.

Hopfensperger, Jean. 1986. "Costa Rica: Seeds of Terror." *The Progressive,* Sept., 24–27.

Hunt, Shane. 1975. "La economía de las haciendas y plantaciones en América Latina." *Historia y Cultura* 9: 7–66.

Ibarra Mayorga, Francisco. 1948. *La tragedia del nicaragüense en Costa Rica.* San José: Imprenta Borrasé.

IDB. 1969 [Inter-American Development Bank / Banco Interamericano de Desarrollo]. *Informe anual.* Washington: BID.

———. 1980. *El BID en Costa Rica.* Washington: BID.

———. 1988. *The IDB and the Environment.* Washington: IDB.

ILPES. 1967 [Instituto Latinoamericano de Planificación Económica y Social]. *Centroamérica: Análisis del sector externo y de su relación con el desarrollo económico.* Santiago, Chile: ILPES.

Janzen, Daniel H. 1986. *Guanacaste National Park: Tropical Ecological and Cultural Restoration.* San José: Editorial Universidad Estatal a Distancia.

Jarvis, Lovell S. 1986. *Livestock Development in Latin America.* Washington: The World Bank.

Jiménez Oreamuno, Ricardo. 1903. *Protección a la industria pecuaria. Discurso pronunciado en el Congreso por el Diputado Ricardo Jiménez en la sesión del 28 de julio de 1903.* San José: Imprenta de Avelino Alsina.

———. 1906. *La Sala de Casación y el Sr. Santos.* San José: Imprenta de Avelino Alsina.

———. 1930. "Don Ricardo ex-Presidente de la República, desvanece la leyenda de las vacas criollas 'cajueleras.'" *Escuela de Agricultura* 2, no. 4: 81–86.

———. 1931. "Origen y evolución de nuestra ganadería." *El Maestro* 5, no. 8: 174–83.

Jincsta, Ricardo. 1938. *La garganta del Guanacaste. Estudio de geografía histórica adecuado a la economía nacional.* San José: Falco Hermanos.

———. 1940. "Las industrias del añil y caracol de púrpura." *Revista de los Archivos Nacionales de Costa Rica* 4, no. 5–6: 302–4.

Jones, Jeffrey R. n.d. "Cattle, Culture and Environment: The Social Context of Deforestation in Costa Rica." Manuscript.

Katz, Friedrich. 1974. "Labor Conditions on Haciendas in Porfirian Mexico: Some Trends and Tendencies." *Hispanic American Historical Review* 54, no. 1: 1–47.

Kay, Cristóbal. 1974. "Comparative Development of the European Manorial System and the Latin American Hacienda System." *Journal of Peasant Studies* 2, no. 1: 69–98.

———. 1977. "The Development of the Chilean Hacienda System, 1850–1973." In Kenneth Duncan and Ian Rutledge, eds., *Land and Labour in Latin America*, pp. 103–39. Cambridge: Cambridge University Press.

———. 1980. *El sistema señorial europeo y la hacienda latinoamericana.* Mexico: Ediciones Era.

Keene, Beverly. 1978. "La agroindustria de la carne en Costa Rica." San José: Confederación Universitaria Centroamericana.

Keith, Robert G., ed. 1977. *Haciendas and Plantations in Latin American History*. New York: Holmes & Meier.

Kepner, Charles. 1936. *Social Aspects of the Banana Industry*. New York: Columbia University Press.

Killinger, Gordon B., and Jorge Mata Pacheco. 1955. "Forrajes y su uso en Costa Rica." *Suelo Tico* 32 (Mar.–Dec.): 221–22.

Kincaid, A. Douglas. 1987. "Agrarian Development, Peasant Mobilization and Social Change in Central America: A Comparative Study." Ph.D. dissertation, Johns Hopkins University.

Kirchoff, Paul. 1943. "Mesoamerica: Its Geographic Limits, Ethnic Composition and Cultural Characteristics." *Acta Americana* 1, no. 1: 92–107.

Kirk, W. G. 1960. "La industria ganadera de Costa Rica. Reporte de dos visitas hechas a Costa Rica bajo el contrato de la Universidad de Florida a través de STICA." San José: STICA.

Knight, Alan. 1986. "Mexican Peonage: What Was It and Why Was It?" *Journal of Latin American Studies* 18, no. 1: 41–74.

Krehm, William. 1949. *Democracia y tiranías en el Caribe*. Mexico: Unión Democrática Centroamericana, Departamento Editorial.

———. 1984. *Democracies and Tyrannies of the Caribbean*. Westport, Conn.: Lawrence Hill.

Kula, Witold. 1976. *An Economic Theory of the Feudal System*. London: NLB.

Laclau, Ernesto. 1971. "Feudalism and Capitalism in Latin America." *New Left Review* 67: 19–38.

LAICA. 1986 [Liga Agrícola Industrial de la Caña de Azúcar]. *Informe Anual de Labores 1985–86*. San José: LAICA.

———. 1987. *Informe de Labores Período 86–87*. San José: LAICA.

Lambert, Jacques. 1967. *Latin America: Social Structure and Political Institutions*. Berkeley: University of California Press.

Lanuza Matamoros, Alberto. 1983. "La formación del Estado nacional en Nicaragua: las bases económicas, comerciales y financieras entre 1821 y 1873." In Alberto Lanuza, Juan Luis Vásquez, Amaru Barahona, and Amalia Chamorro, *Economía y sociedad en la construcción del Estado en Nicaragua*, pp. 8–138. San José: Instituto Centroamericano de Administración Pública.

Láscaris, Constantino. 1975. *El costarricense*. San José: Editorial Universitaria Centroamericana.

Leeds, Anthony. 1977. "Mythos and Pathos: Some Unpleasantries on Peasantries." In Rhoda Halperin and James Dow, eds., *Peasant Livelihood: Studies in Economic Anthropology and Cultural Ecology*, pp. 227–46. New York: St. Martin's.

LeGrand, Catherine. 1986. *Frontier Expansion and Peasant Protest in Colombia, 1850–1936*. Albuquerque: University of New Mexico Press.

LeoGrande, William M. 1983. "Cuba and Nicaragua: From the Somozas to the Sandinistas." In Barry Levine, ed., *The New Cuban Presence in the Caribbean*, pp. 43–58. Boulder, Colo.: Westview.

León, Jorge S. 1942. "Nicoya: El ambiente y la vida de un pueblo antiguo." *Revista de los Archivos Nacionales* 6, no. 5–6: 280–305.

León, Jorge S., et al. 1981 [León, Jorge S., Carlos Barboza V., and Justo Aguilar]. *Desarrollo tecnológico en la ganadería de carne*. San José: Consejo Nacional de Investigaciones Científicas y Tecnológicas.

Levy, Pablo. 1965 [1873]. "Notas geográficas y económicas sobre la República de Nicaragua." *Revista Conservadora del Pensamiento Centroamericano* 59: 1–42; 60: 43–106; 61: 107–74; and 62: 175–250.

Li Kam, Sui Moy. 1984. "Las nuevas modalidades laborales en la agroindustria del azúcar (Estudio de caso)." *Revista de Ciencias Sociales* 27–28 (Mar.–Oct.): 31–44.

Limón, José E. 1989. "Carne, Carnales, and the Carnivalesque: Bakhtinian Batos, Disorder, and Narrative Discourses." *American Ethnologist* 16, no. 3: 471–86.

Lizano Fait, Eduardo. 1980. "Los modelos económicos: sus alternativas." In Guillermo Paz, ed., *Los problemas económicos del desarrollo en Costa Rica*, pp. 119–36. San José: Editorial Universidad Estatal a Distancia.

Lomba, Mariuca. 1988. "Qué buscaba y qué encontró Jimmy Swaggart en Nicaragua." *Pensamiento Propio* 6, no. 49: 53–56.

Long, Norman. 1975. "Structural Dependency, Modes of Production and Economic Brokerage in Rural Peru." In Ivar Oxaal, Tony Barnett, and David Booth, eds., *Beyond the Sociology of Development: Economy and Society in Latin America and Africa*, pp. 253–82. London: Routledge & Kegan Paul.

López de Velasco, Juan. 1974. "Sobre el pueblo de Nicoya y la Isla de Chira, 1573." In Carlos Meléndez Chaverri, ed., *Viajeros por Guanacaste*, pp. 41–46. San José: Ministerio de Cultura, Juventud y Deportes.

Lorz, Víctor. 1934. "Visión del Guanacaste." *Escuela de Agricultura* 6, no. 12: 345–97.

McCallum, Henry D., and Frances T. McCallum. 1965. *The Wire That Fenced the West*. Norman: University of Oklahoma Press.

MacLeod, Murdo J. 1973. *Spanish Central America: A Socioeconomic History 1520–1720*. Berkeley: University of California Press.

———. 1983. "Ethnic Relations and Indian Society in the Province of Guatemala ca.1620–ca.1800." In Murdo J. MacLeod and Robert Wasserstrom, eds., *Spaniards and Indians in Southeastern Mesoamerica*, pp. 189–214. Lincoln: University of Nebraska Press.

MacRenato, Ternot. 1982. "The Rise to Power of Anastasio Somoza García." *New Scholar* 8: 300–17.

Maduro, Robert L. 1935. "Informe Hacienda 'El Porvenir' Carrillo." In Trabajos sobre ganadería. Agriculture School theses in University of Costa Rica library.

Marcus, George E. 1986. "Contemporary Problems of Ethnography in the Modern World System." In James Clifford and George E. Marcus, eds., *Writing Culture: The Poetics and Politics of Ethnography*, pp. 165–93. Berkeley: University of California Press.

Margolis, Maxine. 1977. "Historical Perspectives on Frontier Agriculture as an Adaptive Strategy." *American Ethnologist* 4, no. 1: 42–64.

Marín Cañas, José. 1972. *Julio Sánchez*. San José: Ministerio de Cultura, Juventud y Deportes.

Martínez, Abelino. 1989. *Las sectas en Nicaragua: oferta y demanda de salvación*. San José: Departamento Ecuménico de Investigaciones.

Martínez Alier, Juan. 1975. "Los huachilleros en las haciendas de la Sierra Central del Peru desde 1930." In Enrique Florescano, ed., *Haciendas, latifundios y plantaciones en América Latina*, pp. 433–44. Mexico: Siglo XXI.

———. 1977a. "Relations of Production in Andean Haciendas: Peru." In Kenneth Duncan and Ian Rutledge, eds., *Land and Labour in Latin America*, pp. 141–64. Cambridge: Cambridge University Press.

———. 1977b. *Haciendas, Plantations and Collective Farms: Agrarian Class Societies—Cuba and Peru*. London: Frank Cass.

Martínez Peláez, Severo. 1972. *La patria del criollo*. San José: Editorial Universitaria Centroamericana.

Marx, Karl. 1967. *Capital*. 3 vols. New York: International Publishers.

Mata Pacheco, Jorge. 1955. "Generalidades del cultivo del arroz en Costa Rica." *Suelo Tico* 32 (Mar.–Dec.): 30–33.

Matamoros, Yanuario. 1937. "Informe sobre suelos en la región de Abangares." In Trabajos sobre ganadería. Agriculture School theses in University of Costa Rica library.

Matarrita Acuña, Alexis. 1987. *El cultivo del algodón*. San Jose: Editorial Universidad Estatal a Distancia.

Matarrita Ruiz, Mario. 1980a. "La hacienda ganadera en el Corregimiento de Nicoya." University of Costa Rica thesis.

———. 1980b. "Elementos para una interpretación de la dominación española en Nicoya." In Congreso sobre el Mundo Centroamericano en Tiempo de Fernández de Oviedo, ed., *V° Centenario de González Fernández de Oviedo*, pp. 323–30. Nicoya, Costa Rica: Comisión Nacional Organizadora.

Matos Mar, José. 1976. *Yanaconaje y reforma agraria en el Perú*. Lima: Instituto de Estudios Peruanos.

Mauro Rodín, Fernando. 1957. "Proyecto de irrigación del valle del Tempisque." *Informe Trimestral* (Instituto Geográfico Nacional), Oct.–Dec., 22–23.

Mayorga, Román. 1915. "Informe del gobernador de la provincia de Guanacaste." In Juan Rafael Arias, ed., *Memoria de Gobernación y Policía 1914*, pp. 261–70. San José: Tipografía Nacional.

Meléndez Chaverri, Carlos. 1955. "Bagaces, un pueblo en olvido." *Boletín del Museo Nacional* 2, no. 2: 1–46.

―――. 1963. "La verdad histórica en torno a la anexión del Partido de Nicoya a Costa Rica." *La Nación*, July 25, 11–12.

―――. 1967. "Liberia en sus orígenes." *Informe Semestral* (Instituto Geográfico Nacional), July–Dec., 41–68.

―――. 1975. "Formas en la tenencia de la tierra en Costa Rica durante el régimen colonial." *Revista de Historia* 1, no. 1: 104–44.

―――, ed. 1974. *Viajeros por Guanacaste*. San José: Ministerio de Cultura, Juventud y Deportes.

―――, ed. 1978. *Documentos fundamentales del siglo XIX*. San José: Editorial Costa Rica.

Merz, Carlos. 1934. *Resultados y conclusiones del censo del ganado vacuno en la Provincia de Guanacaste*. San José: Imprenta Nacional.

―――. 1937. "Coyuntura y crisis en Costa Rica de 1934 a 1936." *Revista del Instituto de Defensa del Café* 31: 87–101.

Millett, Richard. 1979. *Guardianes de la dinastía*. San José: Editorial Universitaria Centroamericana.

Mintz, Sidney W. 1956. "Cañamelar: The Subculture of a Rural Sugar Plantation Proletariat." In Julian H. Steward, ed., *The People of Puerto Rico*, pp. 314–417. Urbana: University of Illinois Press.

―――. 1973. "A Note on the Definition of Peasantries." *Journal of Peasant Studies* 1, no. 1: 91–106.

―――. 1977. "The So-called World System: Local Initiative and Local Response." *Dialectical Anthropology* 2, no. 4: 253–70.

―――. 1978. "The Role of Puerto Rico in Modern Social Science." *Revista/Review Interamericana* 8, no. 1: 5–16.

―――. 1986. *Sweetness and Power: The Place of Sugar in Modern History*. New York: Penguin.

Molina Molina, María Lorena. n.d. "Algunos apuntes sobre reforma agraria." San José: Escuela de Trabajo Social, Universidad de Costa Rica. Mimeo.

Moncayo C., Víctor Manuel. 1976. "¿Es capitalista la renta de la tierra?" *Ideología y Sociedad*, Apr.–Sept., 36–64.

Monge Alfaro, Carlos. 1962. *Historia de Costa Rica*. San José: Trejos Hermanos.

Montero Barrantes, Francisco. 1891. *Apuntamientos sobre la Provincia de Guanacaste en la República de Costa Rica*. San José: Tipografía Nacional.

Morales Fonseca, Manuel. 1984. *Nicaragua: Y por eso defendemos la frontera. Historia agraria de las Segovias occidentales*. Managua: CIERA-MIDINRA.

Morales Gamboa, Abelardo. 1985. "El clima bélico y la alteración de la paz," *Aportes* 25: 5–6.

Mörner, Magnus. 1973. "The Spanish American Hacienda: A Survey of Recent Research and Debate." *Hispanic American Historical Review* 53: 183–216.

———. 1977. "Latin American 'Landlords' and 'Peasants' and the Outer World During the National Period." In Kenneth Duncan and Ian Rutledge, eds., *Land and Labour in Latin America*, pp. 455–82. Cambridge: Cambridge University Press.

Murillo, Napoleón, and Humberto Barquero. 1943. "Ganado de engorde en Costa Rica." University of Costa Rica thesis.

Myers, Norman. 1981. "The Hamburger Connection: How Central America's Forests Become North America's Hamburgers." *Ambio* 10, no. 1: 3–8.

Nations, James D., and Ronald B. Nigh. 1978. "Cattle, Cash, Food, and Forest: The Destruction of the American Tropics and the Lacandón Maya Alternative." *Culture and Agriculture* 6: 1–5.

Newson, Linda. 1982. "The Depopulation of Nicaragua in the Sixteenth Century." *Journal of Latin American Studies* 14, no. 2: 253–86.

———. 1987. *Indian Survival in Colonial Nicaragua.* Norman: University of Oklahoma Press.

Niederlein, Gustavo. 1898a. *The Republic of Costa Rica.* Philadelphia: Philadelphia Commercial Museum.

———. 1898b. *The State of Nicaragua of the Greater Republic of Central America.* Philadelphia: Philadelphia Commercial Museum.

Nutting, C. C. 1882. "On a Collection of Birds from the Hacienda La Palma, Gulf of Nicoya, Costa Rica." *Proceedings of the United States National Museum* 5: 382–409.

OFIPLAN (Oficina de Planificación Nacional). 1974. *Estrategia y plan global: Versión preliminar.* San José: OFIPLAN.

OPSA (Oficina de Planificación del Sector Agropecuario). 1979a. *Programa agropecuario, recursos naturales y agroindustrial. Período 1979–1982.* San José: OPSA.

———. 1979b. *Diagnóstico del sector agropecuario de Costa Rica 1962–1976.* San José: OPSA.

Orlove, Benjamin S. 1977. *Alpacas, Sheep and Men: The Wool Export Economy and Regional Society in Southern Peru.* New York: Academic Press.

———. 1980. "The Position of Rustlers in Regional Society: Social Banditry in the Andes." In Benjamin S. Orlove and Glynn Custred, eds., *Land and Power in Latin America: Agrarian Economies and Social Processes in the Andes*, pp. 179–94. New York: Holmes & Meier.

Ots Capdequí, J. M. 1959. *España en América: el régimen de tierras en la época colonial.* Mexico: Fondo de Cultura Económica.

Oviedo, Víctor. 1931. "El problema de la ganadería en Costa Rica: El impuesto al ganado de carne." *Escuela de Agricultura* 3, no. 11: 249–81.

Owen, Robert. 1989. "Building a Contra Air Base." In Marc Edelman and Joanne Kenen, eds., *The Costa Rica Reader*, pp. 349–54. New York: Grove Weidenfeld.

Palerm, Angel. 1980. *Antropología y marxismo*. Mexico: Nueva Imagen.

Parsons, James J. 1965. "Cotton and Cattle in the Pacific Lowlands of Central America." *Journal of Inter-American Studies* 7, no. 2: 149–59.

———. 1972. "Spread of African Pasture Grasses to the American Tropics." *Journal of Range Management* 25: 12–17.

———. 1976. "Forest to Pasture: Development or Destruction?" *Revista de Biología Tropical* 24, supl.1: 121–38.

Partridge, William L. 1984. "The Humid Cattle Ranching Complex: Cases from Panama Reviewed." *Human Organization* 43, no. 1: 76–80.

Payer, Cheryl. 1982. *The World Bank: A Critical Analysis*. New York: Monthly Review Press.

Pérez Brignoli, Héctor. 1984. "Reckoning with the Central American Past: Economic Growth and Political Issues." *Working Paper* 160. Washington: Latin American Program, Wilson Center.

Pérez Estrada, Francisco. 1964. "Breve historia de la tenencia de la tierra en Nicaragua." *Revista Conservadora del Pensamiento Centroamericano* 51: 15–22.

Pérez Zeledón, P. 1922. "Señor Presidente de la Corte Suprema de Justicia." *La Gaceta Diario Oficial*, Apr. 2, 341–44.

Périgny, Comte Maurice de. 1918. *La République de Costa Rica: Son Avenir économique et le Canal de Panama*. Paris: Félix Alcan.

———. 1974. "Las graciosas haciendas y poblados del Guanacaste 1913." In Carlos Meléndez, ed., *Viajeros por Guanacaste*, pp. 443–65. San José: Ministerio de Cultura, Juventud y Deportes.

Péyroutet, H. 1919. "Colonización francesa en Costa Rica." *Diario de Costa Rica*, Oct. 2, 3 and 6; Oct. 3, 3 and 6.

Piszk, Ileana. 1982. "La producción de arroz en Costa Rica: políticas estatales y fuerzas sociales." *Avances de Investigación* 46: 1–63.

Pittier, Henri. 1978 [1909]. *Plantas usuales de Costa Rica*. San José: Editorial Costa Rica.

Poelhekke, F. G. M. N. 1982. "The Struggle for Land in Brazilian Amazonia, Consequent on the Expansion of Cattle-Raising." *Boletín de Estudios Latinoamericanos y del Caribe* 33 (Dec.): 11–33.

Porras Zúñiga, Anabelle, and Beatriz Villarreal Montoya. 1986. *Deforestación en Costa Rica*. San José: Editorial Costa Rica.

Presidencia de la República. 1981. *Menos agua al mar: zona de riego Guanacaste*. Guanacaste: Presidencia de la República.

Quirós Vargas de Quesada, Claudia. 1976. "Aspectos socioeconómicos de la ciudad de Espíritu Santo de Esparza y su jurisdicción (1574–1848)." University of Costa Rica thesis.

Quirós Zúñiga, Víctor Manuel. 1990. *El festín de los coyotes*. San José: Guayacán.

Radell, David R. 1976. "The Indian Slave Trade and Population of Nicaragua During the 16th Century." In William M. Denevan, ed., *The Native Populations of the Americas in 1492*, pp. 67–76. Madison: University of Wisconsin Press.

Ramírez B., Mario A. 1978. "La polémica de la concentración de la tierra en Costa Rica: mitos e ideologías." *Cuadernos de Historia* 26: 1–55.

Real Espinales, Blas A., and Mario Lungo Ucles. 1979. "La problemática regional en Centroamérica." *Estudios Sociales Centroamericanos* 23: 9–33.

Realidad. 1988. "Piden que salve de la ruina a los agricultores." *Realidad* 4, no. 18: 7–9.

Rebel, Hermann. 1989. "Cultural Hegemony and Class Experience: A Critical Reading of Recent Ethnological-Historical Approaches (Part One)." *American Ethnologist* 16, no. 1: 117–36.

Revista de los Archivos Nacionales. 1948 [1771]. "El Ilustrísimo don Carlos de Vílchez i Cabrera, Obispo de Nicaragua y Costa Rica, concede licencia para la erección del templo en el pueblo de Santa Cruz del Diriá." *Revista de los Archivos Nacionales* 12, no. 3–4: 287–88.

Reyes Posada, Alejandro. 1978. *Latifundio y poder político*. Bogotá: Centro de Investigación y Educación Popular, Serie Colombia Agraria 2.

Rivera Urrutia, Eugenio. 1982. *El Fondo Monetario Internacional y Costa Rica 1978–1982*. San José: Departamento Ecuménico de Investigaciones.

Robert Luján, Enrique. 1945. "Resultados de la Primera Exposición Ganadera de Liberia, Guanacaste." *Revista de Agricultura* 17, no. 3: 99–108.

———. 1989. *La ganadería en Costa Rica*. San José: Cooperativa de Productores de Leche Dos Pinos.

Rodríguez Solera, Carlos Rafael. 1988. "Estructura agraria de Guanacaste y políticas estatales en el Distrito de Riego Arenal-Tempisque." University of Costa Rica thesis.

———. 1989. "Concentración de la tierra y precarismo en Guanacaste: 1950–1970." *Revista de Ciencias Sociales* 43 (Mar.): 73–80.

Rodríguez Vega, Eugenio. 1971. *Los días de don Ricardo*. San José: Editorial Costa Rica.

———. 1979 [1953]. *Apuntes para una sociología costarricense*. San José: Editorial Universidad Estatal a Distancia.

———. 1980. *De Calderón a Figueres*. San José: Editorial Universidad Estatal a Distancia.

Rojas Bolaños, Manuel. 1979. *Lucha social y guerra civil en Costa Rica*. San José: Porvenir.

Romero García, Alejandro. 1976. "Plaguicidas en los agroecosistemas tropicales: evaluación del conocimiento actual del problema." *Revista de Biología Tropical* 24, supl. 1: 69–77.

Romig, William D. 1957. "Proyecto del valle del Tempisque." *Informe Trimestral* (Instituto Geográfico Nacional), Oct.–Dec., 24–28.

Roseberry, William. 1978. "Historical Materialism and The People of Puerto Rico." *Revista/Review Interamericana* 8, no. 1: 26–36.

———. 1989. *Anthropologies and Histories: Essays in Culture, History, and Political Economy.* New Brunswick, N.J.: Rutgers University Press.

Ross, Eric B. 1980. "Patterns of Diet and Forces of Production: An Economic and Ecological History of the Ascendancy of Beef in the United States Diet." In Eric B. Ross, ed., *Beyond the Myths of Culture: Essays in Cultural Materialism,* pp. 181–225. New York: Academic Press.

Rossi Chavarría, Hernán. 1948. "Consideración del problema de abastecimiento de carne en Costa Rica y los principales factores que la afectan." *Suelo Tico* 4, no. 2: 117–37.

Rostow, W. W. 1960. *The Stages of Economic Growth.* Cambridge: Cambridge University Press.

Rouse, John E. 1977. *The Criollo: Spanish Cattle in the Americas.* Norman: University of Oklahoma Press.

Roux, Bernard. 1975. "Expansion du capitalisme et développement du sous développement: l'intégration de l'Amérique Centrale au marché mondial de la viande bovine." *Revue du Tiers Monde* 16: 355–80.

Rowles, James. 1980. "Instituto de Tierras y Colonización vs. Sociedad Stewart Hermanos Ltda." In Oscar Salas Marrero and Rodrigo Barahona Israel, eds., *Derecho agrario,* 2ª edición, pp. 861–97. San José: Oficina de Publicaciones de la Universidad de Costa Rica.

Rudé, George. 1980. *Ideology and Social Protest.* New York: Pantheon.

Ruiz, Adolfo. 1984. "La agricultura del sorgo en Costa Rica." *Revista de Ciencias Sociales* 27–28 (Mar.–Oct.): 45–53.

Rutledge, Ian. 1987. *Cambio agrario e integración: el desarrollo del capitalismo en Jujuy, 1550–1960.* Buenos Aires: Estudios Comparados Interdisciplinarios de la Realidad Andina and Centro de Investigaciones en Ciencias Sociales.

Rutsch, Matilde. 1980. *La cuestión ganadera en México.* Mexico: Centro de Investigación para la Integración Social.

Ryan, John, et al. 1970 [Ryan, John Morris, Robert N. Anderson, and Harry R. Bradley]. *Area Handbook for Nicaragua.* Washington, D.C.: U.S. Government Printing Office.

Sabato, Hilda. 1989. *Capitalismo y ganadería en Buenos Aires: la fiebre del lanar, 1850–1890.* Buenos Aires: Editorial Sudamericana.

Sáenz Gutiérrez, Gerardo, and Carlos Meza. 1932a. *Protección para la ganadería (ley especial) y protección arancelaria para los productos derivados de la industria ganadera.* San José: Imprenta Nacional.

———. 1932b. *Estudio sobre el establecimiento de un aforo proteccionista para el arroz y las posibilidades de un monopolio del Estado para la harina de trigo.* San José: Imprenta Nacional.

Sáenz Maroto, Alberto. 1955. *Los forrajes de Costa Rica.* San José: Editorial Universitaria.

———. 1970. *Historia agrícola de Costa Rica*. San José: Oficina de Publicaciones de la Universidad de Costa Rica.

———. 1981. *Erosión, deforestación y control de inundaciones en Costa Rica*. San José: Facultad de Agronomía, Universidad de Costa Rica.

Sáenz P., Carlos, and Foster Knight. 1972. "Aspectos jurídicos y económicos de la titulación de tierras en Costa Rica." *Revista de Ciencias Jurídicas* 20–21: 129–236.

Salas F., José Carlos. 1974. "Proyecto de Riego de Arenal. Informe de reconocimiento de las condiciones agroeconómicas." San José: Servicio Nacional de Electricidad. Mimeo.

Salas Marrero, Oscar, and Rodrigo Barahona Israel. 1980. *Derecho agrario*, 2ª edición. San José: Oficina de Publicaciones de la Universidad de Costa Rica.

Salas Víquez, José Antonio. 1985. "La búsqueda de soluciones al problema de la escasez de tierra en la frontera agrícola: aproximación al estudio del reformismo agrario en Costa Rica 1880–1940." *Revista de Historia* Número Especial Historia Agraria, 97–149.

———. 1987. "La privatización de los baldíos nacionales en Costa Rica durante el siglo XIX: legislación y procedimientos utilizados para su adjudicación." *Revista de Historia* 17: 63–118.

Salazar Navarrete, José Manuel. 1979. "Política agraria." In Chester Zelaya, ed., *Costa Rica contemporánea*, vol. 1, pp. 211–32. San José: Editorial Costa Rica.

Salazar Vergara, Gabriel. 1985. *Labradores, peones y proletarios: Formación y crisis de la sociedad popular chilena del siglo XIX*. Santiago: Ediciones Sur.

Salvatierra, Sonfonías. 1939. *Contribución a la historia de Centroamérica*. Managua: Tipografía Progreso.

———. 1947. *Compendio de historia de Centroamérica*. Managua: Tipografía Progreso.

Sancho, Mario. 1982 [1935]. *Costa Rica, Suiza centroamericana*. San José: Editorial Costa Rica.

Sanderson, Steven E. 1986. *The Transformation of Mexican Agriculture*. Princeton: Princeton University Press.

Sandner, Gerhard. 1962. *La colonización agrícola de Costa Rica*, 2 vols. San José: Instituto Geográfico Nacional.

Sapper, Karl. 1974. "Del norte al sur, a través del Guanacaste 1899." In Carlos Meléndez, ed., *Viajeros por Guanacaste*, pp. 315–31. San José: Ministerio de Cultura, Juventud y Deportes.

Schejtman, Alexander Z. 1975. "Elementos para una teoría de la economía campesina: pequeños propietarios y campesinos de hacienda." *El Trimestre Económico* 42, no. 2: 487–508.

Schell, William, Jr. 1986. *Medieval Iberian Tradition and the Development of the Mexican Hacienda.* Syracuse: Maxwell School Latin American Series, no. 8.

Schifter Sikora, Jacobo. 1978. "La democracia en Costa Rica como producto de la neutralización de clases." In Chester Zelaya, ed., *¿Democracia en Costa Rica? Cinco opiniones polémicas*, pp. 172–246. San José: Editorial Universidad Estatal a Distancia.

Schneider, Harold K. 1974. *Economic Man: The Anthropology of Economics.* New York: Free Press.

Schultz, Theodore. 1964. *Transforming Traditional Agriculture.* New Haven: Yale University Press.

Scott, James C. 1985. *Weapons of the Weak: Everyday Forms of Peasant Resistance.* New Haven: Yale University Press.

Segarra, José, and Joaquín Juliá. 1974 [1906]. "Por los caminos pintorescos del Guanacaste." In Carlos Meléndez, ed., *Viajeros por Guanacaste*, pp. 341–61. San José: Ministerio de Cultura, Juventud y Deportes.

Seligson, Mitchell A. 1977. "Agrarian Policies in Dependent Societies: Costa Rica." *Journal of Interamerican Studies and World Affairs* 19, no. 2: 201–32.

———. 1978. "Agrarian Reform in Costa Rica: The Evolution of a Program." *Land Tenure Center Paper No. 115*, University of Wisconsin-Madison.

———. 1980. *Peasants of Costa Rica and the Development of Agrarian Capitalism.* Madison: University of Wisconsin Press.

Selser, Gregorio. 1979. *Sandino, General de Hombres Libres.* San José: Editorial Universitaria Centroamericana.

Semo, Enrique. 1973. *Historia del capitalismo en México. Los orígenes 1521–1763.* Mexico: Era.

———, ed. 1977. *Siete ensayos sobre la hacienda mexicana 1780–1880.* Mexico: Instituto Nacional de Antropología e Historia.

SENARA. 1985. [Servicio Nacional de Aguas Subterráneas, Riego y Avenamiento]. *Propuesta para el Desarrollo Acelerado del Proyecto de Riego Arenal-Tempisque.* San José: SENARA.

———. 1986. *Proyecto de Riego Arenal-Tempisque, II etapa: informe de proyecto.* San José: SENARA.

———. 1987. *Proyecto piloto de riego del Valle del Tempisque.* Cañas: SENARA.

SEPSA. 1980a [Secretaría Ejecutiva de Planificación Sectorial Agropecuaria]. *Características de la ganadería de carne y lineamientos de política.* San José: SEPSA.

———. 1980b. *Zonificación agropecuaria con énfasis en las areas de mayor riesgo para el cultivo del arroz de las sub-regiones Cañas, Liberia y Santa Cruz*, 4 vols. San José: SEPSA.

———. 1982. *Información básica del sector agropecuario de Costa Rica 2.* San José: SEPSA.

————. 1983. *Encuesta nacional de ganado bovino 1982.* San José: SEPSA.

————. 1985. *Información básica del sector agropecuario de Costa Rica 3.* San José: SEPSA.

————. 1986. *Comportamiento de las principales actividades productivas del sector agropecuario durante 1985.* San José: SEPSA.

————. 1989. *Información básica del sector agropecuario de Costa Rica 4.* San José: SEPSA.

SEPSA et al. 1985 [Secretaría Ejecutiva de Planificación Sectorial Agropecuaria, Instituto Interamericano de Ciencias Agrícolas, Ministerio de Agricultura y Ganadería, Banco Nacional de Costa Rica, Federación de Cámaras de Ganaderos, Oficina Nacional de Semillas]. "Programa de reactivación de la ganadería bovina en Costa Rica." Mimeo.

Sequiera Ruiz, Wilder Gerardo. 1985. *La hacienda ganadera en Guanacaste: aspectos económicos y sociales 1850–1900.* San José: Editorial Universidad Estatal a Distancia.

Service, Elman R. 1955. "Indian-European Relations in Colonial Latin America." *American Anthropologist* 57, no. 3: 411–25.

Shallat, Lezak. 1989. "AID and the Secret Parallel State." In Marc Edelman and Joanne Kenen, eds., *The Costa Rica Reader,* pp. 221–27. New York: Grove Weidenfeld.

Shane, Douglas R. 1980. *Hoofprints on the Forest: An Inquiry into the Beef Cattle Industry in the Tropical Forest Areas of Latin America.* Washington, D.C.: Office of Environmental Affairs, U.S. Department of State.

Shanin, Teodor. 1982. "Defining Peasants: Conceptualisations and Deconceptualisations: Old and New in a Marxist Debate," *Sociological Review* 30, no. 3: 407–32.

Sherman, William L. 1979. *Forced Native Labor in Sixteenth Century Central America.* Lincoln: University of Nebraska Press.

Sibaja Chacón, Luis F. 1974. *Nuestro límite con Nicaragua.* San José: Instituto Tecnológico Don Bosco.

————. 1982. "Los indígenas de Nicoya bajo el dominio español (1522–1560)." *Estudios Sociales Centroamericanos* 32: 23–48.

Sibaja Chacón, Luis F., and Chester Zelaya. 1974. *La anexión de Nicoya.* San José: Imprenta Nacional.

SIECA. 1973 [Secretaría Permanente del Tratado General de Integración Económica Centroamericana]. *El desarrollo integrado de Centroamérica en la presente década.* Buenos Aires: Instituto Para La Integración de América Latina.

Silverman, Sydel. 1979. "The Peasant Concept in Anthropology." *Journal of Peasant Studies* 7, no. 1: 49–69.

Simpson, James R., and Donald E. Farris. 1982. *The World's Beef Business.* Ames: Iowa State University Press.

Slutsky, Daniel. 1979. "La agroindustria de la carne en Honduras." *Estudios Sociales Centroamericanos* 22: 101–205.

Smith, Gavin. 1989. *Livelihood and Resistance: Peasants and the Politics of Land in Peru*. Berkeley: University of California Press.

Smith, Vernon Arthur. 1970. "Beef Cattle Production and Marketing in Guanacaste, Costa Rica." Ph.D. diss., University of Florida.

SNE. 1981 [Servicio Nacional de Electricidad]. "Proyecto de riego de la cuenca baja del Río Tempisque." San José: SNE, Departamento de Riego y Avenamiento. Mimeo.

Sociedad Ganadera Murciélago. 1950. "Informe presentado por la Sociedad Ganadera Murciélago al Consejo Nacional de Producción." *Producción Nacional* 1, no. 3: 10–32.

Sojo, Ana. 1984. *Estado empresario y lucha política en Costa Rica*. San José: Editorial Universitaria Centroamericana.

Soley Güell, Tomás. 1949. *Historia económica y hacendaria de Costa Rica*, 2 vols. San José: Editorial Universitaria

Solís Avendaño, Manuel A. 1981a. "La ganadería de carne en Costa Rica." Master's thesis, University of Costa Rica.

———. 1981b. "La agroindustria capitalista en el período 1900–1930 (los ingenios azucareros)." *Revista de Ciencias Sociales* 21–22 (Mar.–Oct.): 55–71.

Somoza Debayle, Anastasio. 1980. *Nicaragua Betrayed*. Boston: Western Islands Publishers.

Spielman, Hans O. 1972. "La expansión ganadera en Costa Rica: Problemas de desarrollo agropecuario." *Informe Semestral* (Instituto Geográfico Nacional), July–Dec., 33–57.

Squibb, Robert L. 1945. "Mejoramiento ganadero en Guanacaste." *Revista de Agricultura* 17, no. 7: 343–48.

Stalin, Joseph. 1940. *Dialectical and Historical Materialism*. New York: International Publishers.

Stein, Stanley J., and Barbara H. Stein. 1970. *The Colonial Heritage of Latin America*. New York: Oxford University Press.

Stephens, John L. 1969 [1854]. *Incidents of Travel in Central America, Chiapas and Yucatan*. New York: Dover.

Stern, Steve J. 1987. "New Approaches to the Study of Peasant Rebellion and Consciousness: Implications of the Andean Experience." In Steve J. Stern, ed., *Resistance, Rebellion, and Consciousness in the Andean Peasant World 18th to 20th Centuries*, pp. 3–25. Madison: University of Wisconsin Press.

Steward, Julian H., ed. 1956. *The People of Puerto Rico*. Urbana: University of Illinois Press.

STICA (Servicio Técnico Inter-Americano de Cooperación Agrícola). 1949. *Progress in Agriculture in Costa Rica: Summary Report 1942–1948*. Washington, D.C.: Institute of Inter-American Affairs.

Stone, Doris. 1954. *Apuntes sobre la fiesta de la Virgen de Guadalupe celebrada en la ciudad de Nicoya*. San José: Museo Nacional.

Stone, Samuel. 1975. *La dinastía de los conquistadores*. San José: Editorial Universitaria Centroamericana.

Stycos, J. Mayone. 1982. "The Decline of Fertility in Costa Rica: Literacy, Modernization and Family Planning." *Population Studies* 36, no. 1: 15–30.

Suñol, Julio. 1981. *Insurrección en Nicaragua: la historia no contada*. San José: Editorial Costa Rica.

Swanson, Wayne. 1979. "Playing for High Steaks: The Meat Price Tip Sheet." *The Nation* 229, no. 14 (Nov. 3): 433–35.

Taussig, Michael. 1977. "The Evolution of Rural Wage Labour in the Cauca Valley of Colombia, 1700–1970." In Kenneth Duncan and Ian Rutledge, eds., *Land and Labour in Latin America*, pp. 397–434. Cambridge: Cambridge University Press.

———. 1980. *The Devil and Commodity Fetishism in South America*. Chapel Hill: University of North Carolina Press.

Taylor, William B. 1972. *Landlord and Peasant in Colonial Oaxaca*. Stanford: Stanford University Press.

Thiel, Bernardo A. 1977 [1902]. "Monografía de población de la República de Costa Rica." In Luis Demetrio Tinoco, ed., *Población de Costa Rica y Orígenes de los Costarricenses*, pp. 15–72. San José: Editorial Costa Rica.

Thompson, E. P. 1966. *The Making of the English Working Class*. New York: Vintage.

Tosi, Joseph A. 1976. "Transformación del bosque en pastizal: ¿desarrollo o destrucción? (comentario)." *Revista de Biología Tropical* 24, supl. 1: 139–42.

Tristán, Mario, et al. 1982 [Tristán, Mario, Sylvia Salazar, and Alberto Guerra]. "Evolución de la talla 1979–1981 Costa Rica." *Revista Médica del Hospital Nacional de Niños* 17, no. 1–2: 285–96.

Umaña, Virginia, and Manuel Constenla. 1984. "Determinación de plaguicidas organoclorados en leche materna en Costa Rica." *Revista de Biología Tropical* 32, no. 2: 233–39.

Unifruitco. 1950. "New Ranch at Tenorio—La UF compra una hacienda ganadera en las altiplanicies occidentales de Costa Rica." *Unifruitco*, Oct., 10–11.

USAID. 1988 [U.S. Agency for International Development]. *The Effectiveness and Economic Development Impact of Policy-Based Cash Transfer Programs: The Case of Costa Rica*. Washington, D.C.: USAID.

Valverde, Pánfilo J. 1907. *Industria pecuaria: la cría de ganado y el abigeato en la Provincia de Guanacaste*. San José: Tipografía Nacional.

Van Young, Eric. 1981. *Hacienda and Market in Eighteenth-Century Mexico: The Rural Economy of the Guadalajara Region, 1675–1820*. Berkeley: University of California Press.

———. 1983. "Mexican Rural History Since Chevalier: The Historiography of the Colonial Hacienda." *Latin American Research Review* 28, no. 3: 5–61.

Vargas Coto, Joaquín. 1950. *El desarrollo de la ganadería en Costa Rica*. San José: Imprenta La Nación and Ministerio de Agricultura e Industrias.

Vassberg, David E. 1984. *Land and Society in Golden Age Castile*. Cambridge: Cambridge University Press.

Vega, Mylena. 1982. *El Estado costarricense de 1974 a 1978: CODESA y la fracción industrial*. San José: Editorial Hoy.

Vega Carballo, José Luis. 1980. *Hacia una interpretación del desarrollo costarricense*. San José: Porvenir.

———. 1981. *Orden y progreso. La formación del Estado nacional en Costa Rica*. San José: Instituto Centroamericano de Administración Pública.

Vicarioli, Iride. 1952. *Arreglo cronológico de legislación ganadera*. San José: Ministerio de Agricultura e Industrias, Imprenta Nacional.

Vilar, Pierre. 1980. *Iniciación al vocabulario del análisis histórico*. Barcelona: Editorial Crítica.

Villafranca, Richard. 1895. *Costa Rica: The Gem of the American Republics*. New York: Sackett & Wilhehns.

Villarreal Montoya, Beatriz. 1983. *El precarismo rural en Costa Rica 1960–1980*. San José: Editorial Papiro.

Vincent, Joan. 1977. "Agrarian Society as Organized Flow: Processes of Development Past and Present." *Peasant Studies* 6, no. 2: 56–65.

Volio, Marina. 1972. *Jorge Volio y el Partido Reformista*. San José: Editorial Costa Rica.

Volio Mata, Alfredo. 1956–57. "La ganadería en Costa Rica." *Revista de Agricultura* 28, no. 7: 261–68; 28, no. 8: 308–18; 28, no. 9: 365–71; 28, no. 11: 451–56; 29, no. 1: 9–14; 29, no. 2: 50–52; 29, no. 4: 125–28; 29, no. 5: 157–64; 29, no. 6: 196–202; 29, no. 7: 234–40; 29, no. 8: 270–74; 29, no. 10: 306–11.

Von Seehach, Karl. 1974. "Visita a algunos de los volcanes de Guanacaste 1864." In Carlos Meléndez, ed., *Viajeros por Guanacaste*, pp. 209–40. San José: Ministerio de Cultura, Juventud y Deportes.

Wagley, Charles, and Marvin Harris. 1955. "A Typology of Latin American Subcultures." *American Anthropologist* 57: 428–51.

Wagner, Moritz, and Carl Scherzer. 1944 [1856]. *La República de Costa Rica en Centro América*. San José: Yurustí.

Wallerstein, Immanuel. 1979. *The Capitalist World Economy*. Cambridge: Cambridge University Press.

Warman, Arturo. 1976. *. . . Y venimos a contradecir. Los campesinos de Morelos y el Estado nacional*. Mexico: Casa Chata.

Wasserstrom, Robert. 1977. "Land and Labour in Central Chiapas: A Regional Analysis." *Development and Change* 8: 441–63.

Weber, Max. 1942. [1923] *Historia económica general*. Bogotá: Fondo de Cultura Económica.

Wheelock Román, Jaime. 1974. *Las raíces indígenas de la lucha anticolonial en Nicaragua*. Mexico: Siglo XXI.

Whiteford, Michael B. 1991. "From *Gallo Pinto* to "Jack's Snacks": Observations on Dietary Change in a Rural Costa Rican Village." In S. Whiteford and A. Furgeson, eds., *Harvest of Want: Food Security and Hunger in Central America and Mexico*, pp. 127–40. Boulder, Colo.: Westview.

Williams, Robert G. 1986. *Export Agriculture and the Crisis in Central America*. Chapel Hill: University of North Carolina Press.

Wolf, Eric R. 1955. "Types of Latin American Peasantry: A Preliminary Discussion." *American Anthropologist* 57, no. 3: 452–70.

———. 1956. "San José: Subcultures of a 'Traditional' Coffee Municipality." In Julian H. Steward, ed., *The People of Puerto Rico*, pp. 171–264. Urbana: University of Illinois Press.

———. 1978. "Remarks on The People of Puerto Rico." *Revista/Review Interamericana* 8, no. 1: 17–25.

———. 1982. *Europe and the People without History*. Berkeley: University of California Press.

———. 1983. "On Peasant Rent." In Joan P. Mencher, ed., *The Social Anthropology of Peasantry*, pp. 48–59. Atlantic Highlands, N.J.: Humanities Press.

Wolf, Eric R., and Sidney W. Mintz. 1957. "Haciendas and Plantations in Middle America and the Antilles." *Social and Economic Studies* 6, no. 3: 380–412.

World Bank. 1970–1987. *Annual Reports*. Washington, D.C.: World Bank.

———. 1988. *Commodity Trade and Price Trends*. Washington, D.C.: World Bank.

Wortman, Miles L. 1975. "Government Revenue and Economic Trends in Central America, 1787–1819." *Hispanic American Historical Review* 55: 251–86.

———. 1982. *Government and Society in Central America, 1680–1840*. New York: Columbia University Press.

Zavala, Silvio. 1973. *La encomienda indiana*, 2ª edición. Mexico: Fondo de Cultura Económica.

Zelaya, Ramón. 1933. *Tierra guanacasteca*. San José: Imprenta de La Tribuna.

Zúñiga Montúfar, G. 1950. *Manual de instrucción fiscal*, 2ª edición. San José: Imprenta Nacional.

→ Index

In this index an "f" after a number indicates a separate reference on the next page, and an "ff" indicates separate references on the next two pages. A continuous discussion over two or more pages is indicated by a span of page numbers, e.g., "pp. 57–58." *Passim* is used for a cluster of references in close but not consecutive sequence.

Library of Congress Cataloging-in-Publication Data

Edelman, Marc.
  The logic of the latifundio : the large estates of northwestern
Costa Rica since the late nineteenth century / Marc Edelman.
    p. cm.
  Includes bibliographical references and index.
  ISBN 0-8047-2044-4 (acid-free paper)
    1. Latifundio—Costa Rica—Guanacaste—History—20th century.
  2. Haciendas—Costa Rica—Guanacaste—History—20th century.
  3. Agriculture—Economic aspects—Costa Rica—Guanacaste—
History—20th century. I. Title.
HD1471.C82G84 1992
333.3′097286′6—dc20   91-45600
                                   CIP